W9-CBU-893

Why Do You Need This New Edition?

If you're wondering why you should buy this new edition of *Motivation: Biological, Psychological, and Emotional,* **here are 3 good reasons!**

❶ *Motivation* is now divided into five distinct sections that provide an eclectic overview of motivation and emotion, while looking at the sources of motivation from three distinct perspectives: **biological, psychological,** and **environmental.** Each part is introduced by a short preview and comprises a major theme that unites the concepts contained in these chapters.

❷ Web addresses are now included throughout the text so students can find additional information related to specific topics of motivation or emotion that interest them.

❸ Over 200 **new references** have been added.

THIRD EDITION

Motivation

Biological, Psychological, and Environmental

Lambert Deckers

Ball State University

Allyn & Bacon

Boston   New York   San Francisco
Mexico City   Montreal   Toronto   London   Madrid   Munich   Paris
Hong Kong   Singapore   Tokyo   Cape Town   Sydney

Acquistions Editor: *Michelle Limoges*
Editorial Assistant: *Christina Manfroni*
Director of Marketing: *Brandy Dawson*
Production Editor: *Pat Torelli*
Editorial Production Service: *S4Carlisle Publishing Services*
Manufacturing Buyer: *JoAnne Sweeney*
Electronic Composition: *S4Carlisle Publishing Services*
Cover Administrator: *Joel Gendron*
Cover Designer: *Jennifer Hart*

Between the time website information is gathered and then published, it is not unusual for some
sites to have closed. Also, the transcription of URLs can result in typographical errors. The
publisher would appreciate notification where these errors occur so that they may be corrected in
subsequent editions.

Photo Credits: p. 315 Esbin Anderson/Omni-Photo Communications; p. 316 (*top three images*) Getty Images;
p. 316 (*bottom*) Corbis; p. 317 (*top*) Ron Chappel/FPG International; p. 317 (*bottom*) Larry W. Smith/Getty Images

Library of Congress Cataloging-in-Publication Data

Deckers, Lambert.
    Motivation : biological, psychological, and environmental / Lambert Deckers. — 3rd ed.
      p. cm.
    Includes bibliographical references and index.
    ISBN 978-0-205-61081-5
    1. Motivation (Psychology)—Textbooks.   I. Title.
    BF503.D44 2010
    153.8—dc22   2008043246

10 9 8 7 6 5 4 3 2   HAM   13 12 11 10

Allyn & Bacon
is an imprint of

www.pearsonhighered.com

ISBN-10:   0-205-61081-1
ISBN-13: 978-0-205-61081-5

To Lisa, Erik, and Cindy

CONTENTS

PREFACE

To Instructors

In this text, motivation means "to be moved into action" or, for a more cognitive orientation, "to be moved into cognition, feeling, and action." If motivation refers to inducement of action, feelings, and thought, then what is the source of this inducement? As conveyed by the title, this book provides answers by describing biological, psychological, and environmental sources of inducement. Biological refers to the material aspects of the body, nervous system, and brain. Psychological refers to drives, psychological needs, and personality traits. Environmental sources are composed of incentives and goals. The anticipation of their occurrence motivates behavior. These domains of motivation guided the selection of the eclectic topics that are covered in this text. There are a vast number of topics that could be included in the study of motivation. After all, the task of psychology is to describe behavior or, more precisely, changes in behavior. The study of motivation in its many guises attempts to describe and explain how this happens.

Third Edition

The third edition continues with the same eclectic approach as the two prior editions but with many changes and updates. There are over 200 new references that describe new topics, findings, and theories about motivation and emotion. Older topics that are no longer current have been deleted in order to provide space for this newer material. This new edition also contains many web addresses, which have been checked for accuracy and accessibility, where students can find additional information about a topic.

To Students

Motivation refers to the "why" of behavior, not the "how." Why do we engage in certain behaviors and have certain feelings and thoughts but not others? Are we not motivated? Are we motivated by or for something else? I hope that reading this book will provide answers and contribute to your self-discovery as well as help you understand what motivates some of your behaviors and not others. By applying the principles of motivation, a person can institute self-change. Are there ways you wish to behave, or do you act in ways that you wish you didn't? In the process of change, do people change the environment or alter something about themselves in order to make these changes happen? Perhaps you will find insights and answers in the following pages.

ACKNOWLEDGMENTS

I would like to acknowledge that trying to understand the "why" of behavior is probably one of the most fascinating endeavors that a person can pursue. Thanks to Ball State University, it has been possible for me to do this. I would like to thank all former students in my motivation and emotion course who read the book and provided feedback. An appreciation also goes to my colleagues, Thomas Holtgraves and David Perkins, who were sounding boards for my ideas. I would also like to thank Professor G. W. Farthing at the University of Maine for providing helpful feedback on the second edition. An expression of gratitude goes to my wife, Cindy Ruman, for her expertise and help. I also express my appreciation to those individuals who reviewed the second edition on behalf of Allyn and Bacon for their help in shaping the third edition: Samuel L. Clay II, Brigham Young University–Idaho; Stephen Crites, University of Texas at El Paso; Eric Murphy, University of Alaska–Anchorage; Terry F. Pettijohn, Ohio State University; and Jutta Street, Campbell University.

ABOUT THE AUTHOR

Lambert Deckers is a professor of psychological science at Ball State University in Muncie, Indiana. He teaches courses mainly in motivation and emotion, psychology of learning, and history and systems of psychology. Professor Deckers is a charter member of the Association for Psychological Science and has conducted research in the psychology of humor in the United States and Germany.

PART ONE

Introduction and History

What is motivation? Chapter 1 contains a description of motivation as the process by which a person is moved into action. Motivation can originate from internal sources, described as biological and psychological variables, and from external sources, such as incentives and goals. Emotions are a special case of an internal source of motivation. Internal sources developed during our common evolutionary history, and during an individual's unique personal history, while the external sources refer to what is available in the environment. The source of motivation determines specific behavior as if the person had no choice in the matter. As the philosopher Spinoza (1677) wrote long ago, "The knowledge of an effect depends on and involves the knowledge of a cause." The effect is the behavior and the cause is the source of motivation. How do we come to know all of this? Psychologists use the scientific method in order to identify with the greatest confidence the sources of motivated behavior. This endeavor involves experimental and correlational research.

What ideas from history shed light on the process of motivation? Chapter 2 describes hedonism, Darwin's theory of evolution, and Sigmund Freud's theory of unconscious motivation. Hedonism refers to the anticipation of pleasure and pain as the motivation for approach and avoidance behavior. Philosophers state that people strive to maintain a positive hedonic balance—that is, in the long run positive feelings exceed negative ones. Individuals differ, however, in what provides pleasure and pain. The process of evolution fashioned human nature, which refers to psychological mechanisms and universal motives—that is, motives possessed by every human. Psychological mechanisms also determine what incentives we have in common.

Freud's theory of unconscious motivation made psychologists realize that people are not always aware of those events that motivate their behavior. Furthermore, the motivation of behavior is the result of a process rather than of a static event. Only the outcome of the process reaches consciousness, not the process itself. For instance, a person can feel a physical attraction for another but not be aware of the process that gave rise to that attraction.

The cumulative effects of evolutionary history and personal history reside within the individual as physiological or psychological motives and as a value system that places different weights on the importance of different incentives. The future, in contrast, is represented by our anticipation of incentives and goals. Early psychologists recognized that motives and incentives are complementary like hunger and food, the power motive and political office, fear and a dangerous situation, or the value placed on money and a paycheck. More intense motives and greater incentives combine to increase motivational strength. Historically, emotion was the outward expression along affective, physiological, and facial channels in order to prepare us for action that serves the aim of the emotion. Emotions were seen as providing the impulses for thoughts and actions.

1

1 Introduction to Motivation and Emotion

"There's no free will," says the philosopher; "to hang is most unjust."
"There is no free will," assents the officer; "we hang because we must."
—Ambrose Bierce, 1911

Either our actions are determined, in which case we are not responsible for them, or they are the result of random events, in which case we are not responsible for them.
—Hume's Fork

■ In order to prepare the groundwork regarding the concepts of motivation and emotion, consider these questions:

1. What is the definition of motivation?
2. What is the difference between motives and incentives?
3. Are there different sources of motivation?
4. How is motivation reflected in thinking and behaving?
5. What is emotion? How does it motivate behavior?
6. How is research conducted in motivation and emotion?

Meaning of Motivation

When their train engine broke down in the story *The Little Engine That Could,* the toy dolls asked various passing engines if they would pull their train the remaining distance over the mountain to the next town. Shiny New Engine came, and the dolls asked it to pull their train over the mountain. Shiny New Engine replied, "I pull the likes of you? Indeed not!" Later, Big Strong Engine came by, and the dolls asked it to pull their train over the mountain. Big Strong Engine very importantly said, "I won't pull the likes of you!" Subsequently, Rusty Old Engine chugged by, and the dolls asked it for help. Rusty Old Engine complained of being tired and answered, "I cannot." Soon Little Blue Engine passed along. Although not very strong, it was moved by the tearful pleading of the dolls and importance of getting the goods on the train to the town. While working hard going up the mountain, Little Blue Engine repeated the famous line "I think I can" over and over, and on achieving the goal, finished by saying "I thought I could" over and over (Piper, 1954/1961). The difference among the engines illustrates the differences between *could* (*can*) and *would* (*will*). Shiny New Engine and Big Strong Engine undoubtedly could but would not; they were not motivated to do the job. They were not moved by the pleading of the toy dolls or by the incentive of getting the goods over the mountain. Rusty Old Engine perhaps would but could not. It may have been motivated to do the job but lacked the capability to do so. Only Little Blue Engine both could and, more importantly, would. It was both capable and motivated to do so.

The purpose of this section is to consider the issues surrounding the definition of motivation. Is the motivation of behavior linked to internal events like wants and desires, as well as external events that pull or repel? Are nonmotivational ingredients like ability and knowledge also necessary for behavior?

To Be Moved into Action

Consider the implication for motivation of the following statements:

Hunger drives a person to raid the refrigerator for food.
Music provides the impulse to dance.
The residence hall students enjoyed playing volleyball Sunday afternoon.
If you pay your credit card bill on time, then you will avoid an interest payment.
Students attend classes at the university in order to earn a bachelor's degree.

The individuals in these examples who ate, danced, played volleyball, paid their bills on time, and attended classes were motivated to do so. Individuals who did not were not motivated to do so or were motivated to do something else. To be **motivated** is to be moved into action, or to decide on a change in action, according to the philosopher Arthur Schopenhauer (1841/1960). He was one of the first to speculate on the relationship between motivation and behavior. Action or behavior does not occur spontaneously but is induced by either internal motives or environmental incentives. According to Atkinson (1958/1983) and McClelland (1987), a **motive** is a person's internal disposition to be concerned with and approach positive incentives and avoid negative incentives. An **incentive** is the anticipated reward or aversive event available in the environment. A motive is linked to an incentive, since attaining an incentive is the goal of a person's motive (Atkinson, 1958/1983; McClelland, 1987). Hunger is a motive for eating. An interest charge is the incentive for timely bill paying, and a bachelor's degree is the incentive for attending classes. Sometimes, however, the distinction between motives and incentives is not clearly maintained. For example, in a murder mystery, detectives may ask, "What was the perpetrator's motive?" when they meant to say, "What was the incentive for committing the crime?" In other instances, it is difficult to specify the exact source that moves an individual into action: motive or incentive. To illustrate, is pleasure the motive for dancing and is music its incentive? In a volleyball game is the thrill of competition the motive and is winning the incentive? Keep in mind that in trying to understand what motivates behavior sometimes psychologists emphasize internal sources or motives, while at other times they emphasize environmental sources or incentives.

The link between incentives and motives was also anticipated by Schopenhauer (1841/1960), who maintained that it is not possible simply to be motivated. It would make no sense if an individual were to say, "I am motivated." Motivated to do what or for what?

Motives
Physiological needs
Psychological needs

External objects
Incentives
Goals

FIGURE 1.1   Motivation as a Journey. Motives push the train to its destination and external tangible objects pull the train to its destination—that is, the end-state. Similarly, motives push a person toward some end-state while external incentives pull a person toward the end-state.

People are always motivated toward something or away from something. In the opening examples individuals were motivated toward eating, dancing, enjoyment, and a bachelor's degree, and they were motivated away from making an interest payment.

Push and Pull.   This section presents a push/pull metaphor that will help clarify the distinction between motive and incentive, as well as their connection. Little Blue Engine's journey over the mountain to the next town illustrates both the push and pull aspects of motivation. Motivated behavior results from a person being pushed and pulled toward some end-state (see Figure 1.1). Internal dispositions referred to as motives (desire, want, longing) push individuals toward some end; for example, Little Blue Engine's desire pushed it toward the next town. External objects, referred to as incentives and goals, pull individuals toward an end-state; for example, the dolls' pleadings and the importance of the town pulled Little Blue Engine. For human motivation, biological and psychological motives push an individual into action while environmental prospects like incentives and goals pull an individual.

Figure 1.2 illustrates push/pull motivation with a motive for food, a motive to belong, and the goal of a university degree. The biological need for food (hunger) motivates people to eat. Hunger pushes an individual toward places where food is available. The strength of the motive to belong determines the amount of time an individual relates to others. This psychological need pushes people toward others in order to affiliate with them. The goal value of a university degree determines the degree of academic effort that students put forth. Academic behaviors are the means by which students are pulled toward a university degree.

Some refinements are necessary for the push/pull concept of motivation. Individuals are not pushed or pulled at random but instead are directed toward specific ends. A person's internal disposition specifies the nature of this end-state. Internal dispositions may consist of biological motives like hunger, psychological motives like the need to belong, or a value system that confers worth on a university degree. Figure 1.2 illustrates that hunger pushes a person toward food and a belonging-need pushes a person toward people. In addition, a person's values determine the pulling power of a particular incentive or goal, such as the value placed on a university degree. Either by push, pull, or their combination, individuals are motivated toward the appropriate end where motives and incentives become linked together. There, for example, eating satisfies hunger, relating to others fulfills the need to belong, and completing university requirements achieves the goal of graduation.

Emotions as Motives.   Emotions are a special case of push motivation. For example, fear, anger, disgust, and sadness push individuals toward end-states defined by the aim of the

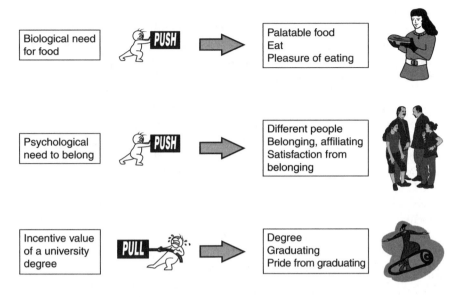

FIGURE 1.2 Push/Pull Motivation. Motives like biological needs and psychological needs act like push motivation while external incentives and goals act like pull motivation.

emotion. One definition describes **emotion** as "a universal, functional reaction to an external stimulus event, temporarily integrating physiological, cognitive, phenomenological, and behavioral channels that facilitate fitness-enhancing, environment-shaping responses to the current situation" (Keltner & Shiota, 2003, p. 89). First, notice that several channels or response variables are motivated to occur in an integrated manner in order to achieve the aim of the emotion. An emotion involves physiological changes that make behavior possible while it also guides thought processes and provides the "feel" of the emotion. Second, the integrated set of responses is designed to aid survival as individuals deal with environmental demands, such as danger, a blocked goal, or a significant loss. Finally, emotions are universal, which implies that all people experience them similarly.

What Motivates Behavior?   What pushes or pulls a person toward the end of a motivational sequence? How does hunger and the belonging motive push a person? How does a university degree pull a student? Does motivation stem from material stimuli (incentives), consummatory behavior with those stimuli, or accompanying subjective feelings? In Figure 1.2, food, people, and a university degree are the incentives that motivate people. The end of the motivation sequences is also marked by *consummatory* (to consummate = to finish) *behavior,* which signals the end of the motivational sequence. The consummatory behaviors in Figure 1.2 are eating, affiliating with others, or receiving a university degree. *Subjective feelings* that accompany consummatory behavior may also serve as the basis for motivation, such as the pleasure of eating, the happiness derived from relating to others, and the pride felt upon graduation.

Energy for Motivation.   To be motivated—that is, to be moved to behave or to think—assumes a supply of energy. Without energy to power muscles and the neurons of the brain, motivation is impossible. An event that motivates behavior or thought is one that also releases stored energy that makes behavior and thought possible. Psychological and physical energy are the two major categories of energy for motivation. **Psychological energies** or mental energies have gone by the names cathexis, self-regulation energy, adaptation energy, and processing resources. Cathexis refers to the accumulation of energy within the brain's neurons as hypothesized in 1895 by Sigmund Freud (Wolman, 1984). Behavior occurs when neurons are able to achieve a lower level of energy. This process of cathexis is accompanied by pleasure. Thus, cathexis serves as both a source of energy and as a motive for behavior. Adaptation energy was coined by Hans Selye (1976), the founder of the stress concept. He assumed the body possessed a certain amount of adaptation energy that could be used to overcome stress. Over a lifetime, humans experience a wide variety of stressors. The body's ability to adapt depends upon the amount of available adaptation energy. When a person's adaptation energy runs out, according to Selye, motivation and life cease. Self-regulation or self-control resembles energy that is presumably used for initiating or inhibiting behaviors. For example, if psychological energy is used to resist temptation, then less energy should be available to complete some other psychological task (Baumeister et al., 1998). Processing resources are those capacities that allow the mind to carry out operations that are necessary for the motivation of behavior. Information from the environment impinges on the human senses and is briefly held in sensory memory where some of it is selected and sent along for further processing. The incoming information is combined with other knowledge that is retrieved from long-term memory. The combined information provides the basis for developing preferences, making decisions, developing goals, and eventually taking action.

Physical energy, in contrast to psychological energy, has a material existence. It exists mainly in the form of glucose, which powers the brain and muscles. Without glucose, motivation would not be possible. When muscles run low on glucose an individual feels fatigued and is inclined to rest. The brain is a voracious user of energy and consumes proportionately way more glucose than the rest of the body. In order to function, the brain utilizes 25% of all glucose yet it comprises only 2% of the body's weight (Magistretti, 1999). There are instances when certain areas of the brain require more energy than others just as our legs use more energy than our arms do when bicycling. For example, part of information processing requires the formation of memories. When young and old rats learn a maze, glucose is used for energy in that part of the brain responsible for laying down memories. In the case of older rats, when their supply of glucose runs low, their memory for the maze becomes impaired (McNay et al., 2000; McNay & Gold, 2002; McNay et al., 2006).

Knowledge, Competence, and Motivation

A student may be motivated to obtain summer employment to pay tuition, to earn a university degree, and to eventually become a practicing psychologist, but being motivated is not the sole factor for these events to be realized. The student must also know how to accomplish these goals and be capable of doing so. Cognitive knowledge is important because it enables the individual to evaluate incentives, understand how to attain them, and assess the chances of success. Competence means being capable of performing the behavior necessary to achieve a desired end. Thus, a person may fail to accomplish a task because she did not know how, was not able, or was not motivated to do so. For instance, what determines whether a person makes his bed in the morning? Bed making depends on three factors: knowledge, competence, and motivation. Knowledge implies that a person knows how to perform the behavior and knows the goal of the behavior. A person must know how to do the tasks of bed making, such as straightening the covers and tucking in the sheets. Competence implies being able to execute the behavior. An individual may not be capable of making the top bed of a triple bunk even if he possesses the knowledge. Nevertheless, even if a person has the knowledge and competence, the bed will still not be made if there is no motivation to do so. Motivation is the impetus or reason for doing the behavior; it initiates the action. So, did you make your bed this morning? If not, the reason is most likely a lack of motivation and probably not a lack of knowledge or capability. In the study of motivation, we assume that an animal or a person has the knowledge and competence to perform the behavior. Whether the behavior occurs, however, depends on motivation.

Section Recap

To be *motivated* means to be induced or moved into action or thought by either the push of a motive or the pull of an incentive. A *motive* is an internal disposition that pushes an individual toward some desired end, which is the incentive. An *incentive* is a valued feature of the environment that pulls an individual toward it. *Emotions* push an individual along multiple channels (affect, physiology, behavior) in order to adapt to the environment. The physical features of the incentives, consummatory behavior with the incentive, or accompanying psychological feelings all contribute to motivation. Although motives and incentives are the causes of behavior, psychological (mental) energy or physical energy (glucose) are necessary to actually power behavior or thought. In addition to motivation, knowledge and competence are also necessary if behavior is to occur. The study of motivation concerns the relation between motives, incentives, and behavioral acts.

Sources of Motivation

Motivation stems from the sequence of events that moves from motives or anticipated incentives to end-states where motives are satisfied or incentives are attained. In order to understand how motivation works, scientists sometimes concentrate on a person's internal dispositions (motives) and sometimes on external incentives. In Figure 1.2 internal dispositions are hunger, the need to belong, and the value system about a university degree. The external incentives are palatable food, nice people, and opportunities provided by a university degree. Internal dispositions that push are classified either as *biological variables* or as *psychological variables* while external sources that pull the person are labeled *environmental variables*—that is, as incentives and goals. These variables compose the title of this book.

The purpose of this section is to explore the various sources of motivation: biological and psychological sources that stem from our common evolutionary past and each individual's own past and external sources that take the form of incentives or goals that attract or repel.

Internal Sources

A person's biological attributes (variables) and psychological dispositions (variables) determine what will be motivating.

Biological Variables.   Biological variables refer to material characteristics of the body and brain that serve to motivate behavior. Hunger in Figure 1.2 as a biological variable correlates with a particular state of the human body, such as little food in the stomach, a rapid decline in blood glucose, and the interplay among various hormones. As a general rule, as biological indicators of hunger increase, the motivation for acquiring, preparing, and eating food increases.

As an illustration of the effects of a specific biological variable on motivation, consider the influence that **ghrelin** has on hunger. Ghrelin is a hormone that is released in the stomach and promotes hunger and eating. This hormone travels in the bloodstream, is high before meals, and decreases after eating (Cummings et al., 2004). In one experiment, Wren and coresearchers (2001) injected ghrelin into the bloodstream of one group of participants. Then they injected saline (placebo) into another group. In order to determine the effects of ghrelin, participants rated their hunger and then were provided a buffet lunch during which they could eat as much as they wanted. The results indicate that participants given ghrelin reported greater hunger and ate more (measured in calories) than participants infused with saline. In addition, prior to their lunch ghrelin participants also indicated that they would eat more.

Psychological Variables.   Psychological variables refer to motives and are studied indirectly through measurable indicators. For example, anxiety and happiness are psychological variables that are indicated by perspiration and smiles. Psychological questionnaires and scales can also indicate the amount of a psychological variable, like stepping on a bathroom scale indicates a person's weight. Higher scale scores usually indicate a greater amount of a psychological variable, such as a need or motive. As a general rule, as indicators of a psychological need increase, the motivation for need-relevant incentives, consummatory behaviors, and associated feelings increase.

As an illustration of the effects of a psychological variable on motivation, consider the influence that the **need to belong** has on trying to be included in a group. The need to belong arises when a person's current level of social affiliation is persistently below a preferred level. Individuals satisfy their need to belong with behaviors that lead to group affiliation. The extent this is achieved may depend on how well people interpret the social cues that signal inclusion or exclusion from a group. Individuals with a higher need to belong are hypothesized to be more accurate at interpreting such social cues. In order to test this hypothesis, Pickett and coresearchers (2004) used the *Need to Belong Scale* to select participants, who varied in the amount of this need. Next, the participants were tested for their accuracy in identifying facial expressions of anger, fear, happiness, and sadness. The results of the research supported the hypothesis. Individuals with a higher need to belong were more accurate in their identification of emotional expressions than were individuals with a lower level of this need.

> ➤ You can measure your need to belong at http://www.duke.edu/~leary/Need2Belong.rtf

Linking Biological and Psychological Variables

The brain and mind are intertwined. According to the concept of **reductionism,** the mind's mental processes can be reduced to the activity of the neurons in the brain. Conversely, according to the concept of **emergence,** the brain's neuronal activity issues forth mental processes—that is, the mind is an emergent property of the brain. However, reductionism and emergence, although opposite, are not equivalent. To elaborate, both hunger sensations and recognizing emotions in others can be reduced to and can emerge from actions of the neurons in the brain. For example, the psychological sensation of hunger is measurable with scales that ask: How hungry are you? Estimate how much you can eat. How full do you feel? How strong is your desire to eat? The intensity of a person's responses on these scales increases with the length of time since the last meal. These scale measurements are reducible to parallel events that happen in the body and brain. There are parallel occurrences with regard to glucose in the bloodstream, food in the small intestine, circulating food-related molecules, and various brain chemicals. These events are monitored by various areas in the brain, such as the hypothalamus. Conversely, the psychological sensation of hunger emerges into consciousness as a result of the brain's monitoring activity (Geary & Schwartz, 2005). In addition, as noted in research on the need to belong, individuals differ in their ability to recognize facial expressions associated with emotion. Attempts have been made to reduce facial recognition to different mechanisms that operate in the right cortex of the brain. When a relevant mechanism becomes impaired, for example, facial recognition suffers (Adolphs et al., 2000). Conversely, mental recognition of facial expression emerges from computations made by the brain from sensory information about the face. The mind versus brain distinction is important because scientists sometimes use the mind and sometimes the brain in order to explain the motivation of behavior. For example, hunger is a feeling in the mind that determines how motivated a person is to eat. Yet, the amount of food in the stomach or the rapid decline in glucose are events that occur in the body. These bodily events also determine the motivation to eat. In the first example, the mind is used; in the second, the body is used to explain the motivation of hunger and eating.

External Sources

The environment is an obvious source of motivation. *Environmental variables* refer to those characteristics of incentives and goals that have the ability to attract or repel. Positive characteristics attract or pull us toward the incentive while unattractive ones repel us. As a general rule, incentives and goals with higher values of attraction or repulsion are more motivating than those with smaller values. Thus, if the value of an incentive can be determined, then its motivational power is known.

One example of the relationship between incentive value and motivation occurs between the value of the academic experience and student behavior, such as attending classes and studying. With a questionnaire approach, students could be asked the extent they found their coursework interesting, valuable, and important, and if they had reasons for doing it. Using such an approach with high school students, Legault and coresearchers (2006) found that declines in the value of schoolwork were associated with lower GPAs, less time spent studying, and greater intentions to drop out. Another instance of the perceived value of university courses refers to their perceived instrumentality—that is, their function in rendering future rewards (Miller & Brickman, 2004). The instrumental value of a course is measured by requiring students to rate such statements as "Good grades lead to other things that I want (e.g., money, graduation, good job, certification)" (Greene et al., 1999, p. 431). Higher endorsements of such statements reflect a greater valuation of academic courses. Researchers have found that students earned higher grades in more valued courses (Greene et al., 1999) and indicated a greater willingness to do the required academic work (Miller et al., 1999).

The Past as a Source of Motivation

Recall that internal dispositions refer to biological and psychological motives that push individuals into action. But, how did biological and psychological motives develop and what is their function? Recall, also, that environmental variables describe the value of incentives and their ability to attract or repel. How do values concerning incentives develop?

Evolutionary and Personal History.   Push motivation depends on characteristics of the body, brain, and mind—that is, on biological variables and on psychological variables. These two variables are the result of our evolutionary history and personal history. **Evolutionary history** or the remote past refers to the effects of millions of years of natural selection in shaping motives and emotions that aided survival of the individual and the species. As a consequence of natural selection, relevant motives or emotions increase in frequency in the population. For example, motives that promote eating and drinking aid the survival of the individual while motives that promote sexual behavior help perpetuate the human species. The emotion of fear, however, motivates individuals to avoid danger or dangerous animals like black widow spiders, pythons, and Komodo dragons.

The field of **evolutionary psychology** attempts to understand current human behavior by relating it to our evolutionary past (Buss, 2005; Cosmides & Tooby, 2005). Evolutionary psychology when applied to motivation is an attempt to describe and understand the origin of psychological motives through natural selection. How do biological and psychological motives aid the survival of the individual or humans in general? Fear of snakes, gender differences in what provokes jealousy, the universal appeal of music, and our preferences for sweets are all examples of behaviors that evolutionary psychologists have tried to explain in terms of natural selection. In other words, these motives presumably evolved because they aided human survival.

Personal history refers to an individual's experience from conception to the present. These experiences help shape an individual's motives and system of values about incentives. Incentive value becomes an important explanatory concept when the incentive or goal is not linked to any obvious psychological or biological motive as in the case of money and course grades. Value is the pulling quality of an incentive or goal. Individuals learn that $100 is more valuable than $10 and that an *A* grade is more valuable than a *B*. The greater value determines that individuals are motivated to labor longer for $100 than for $10 and to study harder for an *A* than for a *B*.

Individual Differences.   The study of motivation involves the search for general laws of behavior that apply to all humans. Yet when it comes to the study of preferences, for example, differences among people seem to negate the possibility of general laws. For example, people differ in their preferences for food, music, and recreation. Can general laws be formulated to account for why people differ in what motivates them? One simple answer is that people themselves are different in such characteristics as psychological needs and personality traits. In addition, individual differences in motivation become apparent from the fact that humans create different environments in which to live. According to Bandura's (2006) **agentic theory,** rather than merely reacting, humans also intentionally create the circumstances of their lives. People are not slaves to their environments and instead seek out or create environments in order to satisfy their psychological motives (John & Robins, 1993; Winter et al., 1998). For example, one could speculate that most individuals who possess a stable need to belong will seek careers that will allow them to affiliate with others (Winter et al., 1998). In the case of people who differ in the level of extraversion, those with a high level are more likely to prefer large parties compared to individuals with a low level of extraversion (Argyle & Lu, 1990).

Combined Internal and External Sources Motivate Behavior

The push/pull metaphor of motivation suggests that internal and external sources combine to motivate behavior in both animals and humans. This joint effect is illustrated by the combined effects of a thirst drive and a water reward. Kintsch (1962), for example, produced various levels of a thirst drive by limiting rats' access to water. He then conditioned rats to run to the end of an alley where different amounts of a water reward were available. How rapidly the rats responded depended on the combined effects of the thirst drive and water reward. Notice in Figure 1.3 that the rats responded fastest with a high thirst drive and a high water reward. Responding was slowest for the combination of a low thirst drive and small water reward. As a general rule, as the size of the internal motive (thirst drive) and external reward (water) increases, motivated behavior increases.

With humans, more complicated interactions between internal and external sources prevail. For instance, how motives determine the value of incentives depends on characteristics

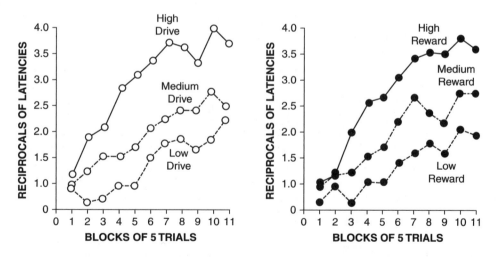

FIGURE 1.3   Drive and Reward Motivate Behavior. On the left, starting speed increases as the magnitude of the thirst drive increases. On the right, starting speed increases as the magnitude of the water reward increases. Response speed was fastest when high thirst drive was combined with high water reward, and was slowest when low drive was combined with low reward.

Source: From "Runway Performance as a Function of Drive Strength and Magnitude of Reinforcement" by W. Kintsch, 1962, *Journal of Comparative and Physiological Psychology, 55,* figures 1 and 2, p. 883. Copyright 1962 by American Psychological Association. Reprinted by permission.

of individuals. For example, the deprivation of personal resources, such as money or food, influences incentive value, but does so differently for men and women. For example, to what extent does feeling deprived affect one's preferences for how much an ideal member of the other sex should weigh? To answer this question, Nelson and Morrison (2005, study 1) asked men and women if they were carrying any money. Presumably being aware of not carrying any money made people aware of being deprived. The results in Figure 1.4 indicate that deprived men preferred heavier women than non-deprived men did while for women feeling deprived made no difference. In another study (study 4), men and women either entering or leaving the campus dining hall were asked to state the ideal weight for a member of the other sex. Entering students were assumed to be food deprived (hungry) while those leaving were considered not food deprived (sated). The results in Figure 1.4 show that hungry men preferred heavier women than sated men did while for women food deprivation made no difference. The temporary awareness of one's state of deprivation of either money or food increased men's preferences for heavier women. However, women did not exhibit this difference. Thus, individual differences prevailed, since men were affected by deprivation while women were not.

In another complication, the interacting effects of motives and incentives can also occur when the same substance serves as both. This dual effect occurs for money and food. Money deprivation can produce a motive that affects the value of food and food deprivation can produce a motive that affects the value of money. Money, obviously, can be used to buy food in order to satisfy hunger. So as a person's hunger increases, she is willing to spend more money for food. Yet, the reverse also seems to be true; hunger determines the incentive value of money. To illustrate, Briers and coresearchers (2006, Exp. 1) compared hungry and sated men for their willingness to donate money to charity. The results showed that

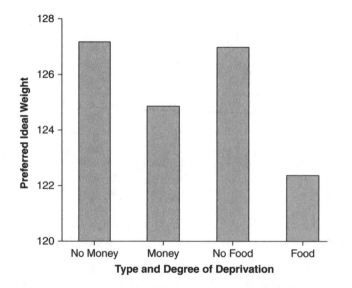

FIGURE 1.4   Deprivation Determines Preference in Men. When deprived of food or money, men preferred heavier women than did men who were not deprived. Women's preferences were not affected by their deprivation state. Data for women are not shown.

Source: Adapted from "The Symptoms of Resource Scarcity: Judgments of Food and Finances Influence Preferences for Potential Partners" by L. D. Nelson & E. L. Morrison, 2005, *Psychological Science, 16,* pp. 169, 172.

hungry men were less likely to donate to charity than non-hungry men were likely to do. In experiment 2, the researchers induced hunger in female participants with the scent of freshly baked brownies. The results showed that hungry participants were less likely to donate money as part of a computer game than non-hungry participants were willing to donate. Thus, in both experiments hunger increased the incentive value of money. Because money was now considered more valuable, participants were less willing to part with it. In experiment 3, a desire for money was manipulated by asking both male and female participants to "list all of the things they would dream of buying if they won" a lottery. The dream of winning a large lottery (25,000 Euros, about $38,000) presumably created a strong motive while the dream of winning a small lottery (25 Euros, about $38) presumably created a weak motive for money. Then as part of a taste test, participants were allowed to eat as many M&M candies as they wanted. Participants with a strong motive for money ate more M&M's than did participants with a weak motive. In this case, an increase in the motive for money was associated with an increase in the value of food (M&M's) and consequently participants ate more.

Motivation Sequence

Motivation is like a journey that consists of a sequence of events as illustrated in Figure 1.2. The sequence begins with a choice of the motive to be satisfied or the goal to be achieved.

Choice refers to the selection of the motive or incentive from those vying for satisfaction. A senior in high school has several choices to make, including whether to enter the armed forces, seek employment, or attend a vocational college or a university. Which option is chosen depends on the intensity of the motive, the attractiveness of the incentive, the likelihood of success, and the amount of effort required to succeed. Choice is only the first step. Next, an individual must be motivated to do what is required to realize her choice. **Instrumental behaviors** are those motivated activities in which a person engages to satisfy a motive. Working for money, studying to pass a test, and acting kindly toward people are all examples of instrumental or motivated behavior. Working, studying, and acting kindly are instrumental in earning money, passing exams, and being liked. Often, an individual can also choose from among several different ways of satisfying a motive. For instance, in the process of finding a job a person may choose from among reading want ads, visiting an employment agency, or consulting the university placement office. Aspects of instrumental behavior that reflect motivation include duration, frequency, and intensity. *Duration* or *persistence* refers to the amount of time a person persists to satisfy a motive. For example, how many years is a person willing to spend preparing for a chosen career? *Frequency* refers to the rate of engaging in a particular behavior. A person who exercises six days per week does so more frequently and presumably is more motivated than the person who does so three days per week or not at all. The *intensity* or effort of behavior varies directly with motivation. For example, the quicker rats start to run down the alley for a water reward (Figure 1.3), the greater the intensity of motivation. The motivation sequence ends when the motive is satisfied or the goal is achieved, which defines the end-state.

Emotions

A person's consciousness is often deluged with sensations like cold, hot, thirst, hunger, and pain. These sensations serve to motivate specific actions in order to alleviate their unpleasantness. In addition to these sensations, however, there are other distinct feelings that also motivate behaviors. These are known as emotional feelings or affect, such as happy, love, sad, anger, fear, shame, and disgust. Like the word *motivation,* which means to be moved into action, the term **emotion** from the Latin word *emovere,* means to move out. When people experience an emotion they are ready to move in a certain way (Leeper, 1948). It is as if emotional feelings ready a person for actions that are crucial for the experienced emotion (Frijda, 1986, 2007). The action is motivated in order to achieve the goal of the emotion. Thus, when experiencing anger in an unpleasant situation, for example, a person may be moved to verbally or physically aggress toward an intended target (Berkowitz & Harmon-Jones, 2004). But when experiencing an opposite emotion, say fear, a person is moved to engage in an entirely different set of behaviors, such as to withdraw in order not to incur harm. The behaviors differ because the goals of anger and fear differ.

Many emotional feelings are linked to facial expressions. Feelings without distinctive facial expressions are not considered emotions by some psychologists (Ekman, 1984, 1994a; Izard, 1971). For example, is there a facial expression that signals romantic love? However, instead of clearly identifiable facial expressions there may be other mannerisms of a person that signal emotions, such as posture or head movement. For example, head and gaze movement are in opposite directions for pride and shame. The head and gaze move upward for pride and downward for shame (Keltner & Shiota, 2003). Finally, emotion can influence an individual's thinking much like hunger makes us think of food. Positive emotional feelings seem to expand thought while negative emotional feelings restrict thought (Fredrickson & Branigan, 2005).

Section Recap

The sources of motivation are either internal in the case of push motivation or external in the case of pull motivation. For push motivation, biological variables describe a person's brain and nervous system while psychological variables describe properties of a person's mind, like psychological needs. Biological and psychological variables are conceptually linked through reductionism and emergence. *Reductionism* is the principle that concepts from psychology can be explained by reducing them to a principle based on the body's physiology or brain. *Emergence* is the reverse of reductionism and represents the view that the brain's neuronal processes generate psychological feelings, which can motivate people to act. Environmental variables describe external sources of motivation, such as incentive value and goal level. As value or level increases, motivation increases. Motivation has different origins. One is the *evolutionary history* of humans, which embraces our remote past. The purpose of *evolutionary psychology* is to describe and explain motivated behavior in terms of human evolutionary history. *Personal history* refers to a person's lifelong experiences, which help determine what motivates the individual. Motivation depends on stable individual differences, such as psychological needs and personality traits. Thus, what motivates one individual may not motivate another. Also, people do not merely react but also act by anticipating, selecting, creating, or altering their environments according to *agentic theory*. Internal sources like drives and needs interact with external sources like incentives and goals to motivate behavior. Incentive deprivation can be interpreted as affecting an internal drive or as affecting the value of the incentive. Furthermore, the same substance can serve as a drive source in one situation and an incentive in another. Motivation represents a sequence that begins with the choice of a motive or goal. Once a choice is made, a person is motivated to engage in *instrumental behavior* that will eventually satisfy the motive or achieve the goal. The end-state of the sequence occurs when the motive is satisfied or the goal is achieved. *Emotion* comes from the Latin word *emovere,* meaning to move out. Emotions also serve as motives. When a person experiences an emotional feeling she is ready to act in a manner that motivates her to accomplish the goal of the emotion. Emotions are linked to facial expressions, certain gestures, and can influence thought processes in addition to providing an impulse for behavior.

Study of Motivation and Emotion

Imagine the goal of earning a coupon from a fast-food restaurant versus earning a bachelor's degree. Both goals motivate behavior but both cannot be investigated in the same manner. A psychologist can study the extent the food coupon motivates performance on some laboratory task. For instance, how many anagrams or arithmetic problems will a participant solve in 10 minutes in order to achieve this goal? However, studying how a bachelor's degree motivates behavior over several years cannot be done in the laboratory. In this case, it is necessary to use questionnaires and survey a group of students over a number of semesters. Perhaps it will be discovered that the likelihood of earning a bachelor's degree depends on how intrinsically motivated students are to study the material in their classes. Thus, in one case an experimental method can be employed, while in the other a correlational method is necessary.

Conduct the following thought experiment: Re-create in your mind as vividly as possible a situation in which you were greatly embarrassed. Now concentrate on these memories long and hard. Do you feel embarrassed all over again? Is your face getting warm and red? Would this be an effective way to study emotions by re-creating them from memory? Maybe you are not feeling this emotion at the same intensity but only as a weak reminder of what you originally experienced. If psychologists wanted to study intense emotions, it would not be ethical to embarrass, frighten, or anger someone in a laboratory in order to study these emotions. It might be possible to study mildly felt emotions in the laboratory, but extremely intense emotions likely would have to be investigated as they occur naturally in people's lives.

The purpose of this section is to describe two different methods by which research is conducted on motivation and emotion. *Experimental* research is usually conducted in a laboratory. It involves manipulating a motivational variable to determine the effects on any behaviors; these effects are indicative of motivation. *Correlational* research, in contrast, is different, since it does not manipulate a variable. Instead, it involves measuring an existing motivational variable to determine how the measured values are associated with behavioral indicators of motivation.

Research in Motivation

Whether experimental or correlational research is employed depends on the phenomenon being investigated but also on the feasibility and the ethics of doing so.

Experimental versus Correlational Research. How long will individuals persist at a task as a function of the amount of incentive and their need to achieve? One way to answer this question might be to conduct an investigation in which participants are promised a reward of $1 or $5 for solving a series of anagrams. The anagrams that are used have no solution, but the participants do not know this. One group of participants has a relatively high need to achieve, while the other group has a relatively low need to achieve. The groups were drawn from a large set of individuals who were evaluated earlier for their need to achieve. Thus, the experiment contains two independent variables. The **experimental variable** is the one manipulated by the experimenter to create different levels or values. Participants are randomly assigned to the conditions representing the levels on this variable. In this example, participants in each group were randomly assigned to receive either $1 or $5. The **correlational variable** contains levels that are measured but not created by the experimenter. Different participants represent different levels on the correlational variable. In this example, different participants were selected to represent a low and high need to achieve. The **dependent variable** refers to behavior that depends on the experimental variable, in the case of experimental research. The dependent variable is associated with the levels on the correlational variable, in the case of correlational research. In the given example, the dependent variable is how many seconds a participant persists at trying to solve the anagrams before giving up. The result of this hypothetical investigation, as shown in Figure 1.5, reveals greater persistence for $5 than for $1, especially by low- compared to high-need-to-achieve participants. This investigation would most likely be both feasible and ethical to conduct, especially if participants received the promised reward.

Feasibility and Ethics. It is neither feasible nor ethical to study some motivational phenomena in the psychological laboratory. In experimental research, different intensities of a motive can be created to determine how this will affect behavior. However, there is a limit to how intense the motive can be. With correlational research, a greater range of motive intensities is possible. Many motives occur naturally, and their intensity is measured along with changes in behavior. One question that arises is whether the results from laboratory

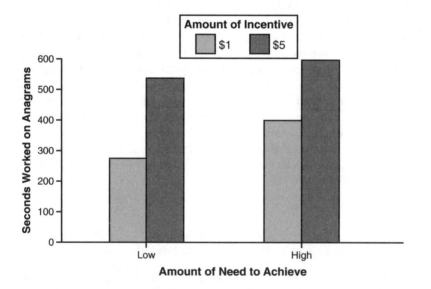

FIGURE 1.5 **Motives, Incentive, and Persistence at Task.** These hypothetical results show that both low- and high-need-to-achieve participants persisted longer in trying to solve the anagrams for a $5 reward than for a $1 reward. This difference in persistence was greater for low- than for high-need-to-achieve participants. In addition, overall high-need-to-achieve participants were slightly more persistent.

experiments are the same as those from correlational studies done in natural settings. Anderson and associates (1999) have concluded that research from laboratory studies and from natural settings provides similar results. For example, they found that depression showed similar relationships with various behaviors in both laboratory and hospital settings.

In the study of hunger, it has been found that different degrees of hunger can be created experimentally or different degrees of hunger that occur naturally can be measured and then correlated with behavior. For example, does food deprivation produce an image of food that guides the search for food (Warden, 1931)? Would the strength of the image and the motivation for food change with the degree of hunger? But how long could human participants practically and ethically be deprived of food to study the hunger–food image relationship? Because of practicality and ethics, these two questions may be answerable partly in the psychological laboratory and partly from events that happen in the world. Some motivation experiments are appropriate in the psychological laboratory because the conditions studied are not too severe for the human participants. Biner and associates (1995, 1998) manipulated hunger by asking one group of students not to eat breakfast or lunch and asking another group to eat both meals prior to reporting for a 1:00 P.M. experiment. Students complied voluntarily with the requests. Would it have been ethical to ask human participants to go for even longer periods without food? Animal research is also employed to study the relationship between hunger and food motivation. For example, Snyder (1962) deprived rats of food for 2, 6, 12, or 22 hours. He then trained the rats to run down to the end of a runway where he'd placed the reward: a saccharine solution. Would it have been ethical to deprive the rats for longer than 22 hours?

Research in a Natural Setting. Clearly, there are conditions of motivation that are neither practical nor ethical to study in a laboratory. It is neither practical nor ethical to ask people to deprive themselves of food for long periods of time, although some may do this of their own volition. For example, people with anorexia and hunger strikers go voluntarily without food for much longer periods of time than in the typical psychology experiment. Brozek and associates (1951) studied the effects of a semistarvation diet on a group of male conscientious objectors during World War II. The men were put on a very restricted diet for 24 weeks, during which time they lost an average of 37 pounds. Over the 24 weeks their motivation for food increased while that for sex and activity decreased. In addition, their thoughts and actions were preoccupied with food the entire time. Food assumed the dominant theme in conversation, was the focus of their attention at movies, was involved in daydreaming and was the subject in reading matter, such as cookbooks and recipes. By the end of the experiment, almost 59% of the participants reported being hungry most of the time. However, in O'Malley's (1990) description of hunger strikers, feelings of hunger eventually go away. Does this mean that the preoccupation with food and its images also disappears? This question is not answerable by an experiment, since it would not be practical or ethical to subject individuals for such long periods of time without food. Thus, some questions are not answerable through experimentation and instead can only be answered by investigating phenomena when they occur naturally. For example, people with anorexia and hunger strikers could be interviewed to determine the extent of their hunger symptoms and preoccupation with food.

Research in Emotion

Emotion is an assortment of experiences that include subjective feelings, facial expressions, neurophysiological changes, and emotion-linked behavior. Emotions are evoked by external events. For instance, an insult induces anger, seeing old friends creates happiness, or walking on a dark deserted street elicits anxiety. A variety of experimental procedures are employed to induce emotions in the laboratory (Gerrards-Hesse et al., 1994). To what extent can emotions be created in the laboratory and to what extent must a naturally occurring emotion be relied on for study? For example, sadness has been studied in the laboratory with a mood induction technique. In one procedure participants read a list of either positive, negative, or neutral statements that were relevant to the lives of students (Seibert & Ellis, 1991). An example of a happy mood induction sentence is "Being in college makes my dreams more possible," while an example of a sad mood induction sentence is "I feel a little down today." Showing clips from various movies can be used to produce sadness, tears, and the urge to cry. The films *The Champ* (1979), *Brian's Song* (1971) (Marston et al., 1984; Martin & Labott, 1991), and *My Life* (1995) evoked tears in some participants who viewed them in a laboratory setting (Spatny, 1997). Playing sad music is another emotion-inducing technique. Stratton and Zalanowski (1994) were able to show the emotion-inducing properties of both the melody and lyrics of the song *Why Was I Born?* which is about unrequited (i.e., unreciprocated) love. Both separately and combined, music and lyrics have an effect on emotions. Depression increases most in response to music plus lyrics, while positive affect increases most to music alone. Finally, sounds in general, like cries, screams, and shouts of joy, can also evoke emotional feelings in the laboratory (Bradley et al., 1994).

The phrase "my heart is broken" describes an intense emotional experience. Can experimentally induced emotions match the intensity of emotions felt in life, such as a broken heart? Is experimentally induced sadness from movies or music felt to the same degree as that of parents grieving the death of their child or a family grieving the death of their faithful dog? As in the case of motivation, feasibility and ethical concerns prevent the study of intense emotions in the laboratory, and thus these emotions can only be investigated as they occur naturally. A case in point were people's reactions to the news that on September 11, 2001, four hijacked airplanes were used in terrorist attacks on the United States. One airplane crashed in Pennsylvania and had not reached its intended target. A second airplane crashed into the Pentagon, and two more airplanes crashed into the World Trade Center's towers in New York City. In researching people's emotional reactions to these events, Fredrickson and coresearchers (2003) asked individuals living in Michigan to "think back to the September 11th attacks and the days that have passed since then." Next, participants were to rate how frequently they had experienced various emotions, with the scale 0 = never to 3 = most of the time. Figure 1.6 shows the three most frequently experienced negative emotions and positive emotions. Anger, sadness, and fear are understandable negative emotional reactions to the attacks. Fredrickson and coresearchers point out that positive emotions can also occur, depending on an individual's focus. For example, people could be grateful that relatives and friends living nearby were alive. Individuals could be interested and curious how the U.S. government was going to respond. Finally, reports of death and destruction that resulted from the attack were in stark contrast to their feelings of love, closeness, and trust of family and friends.

Sources and Scope of Motivation

If motivation is the inducement of an individual's actions, thoughts, and feelings, then what is the source of this inducement? As the book's title implies, psychologists can look to the *biological*—that is, the nature of the body and specifically the structure and workings of the

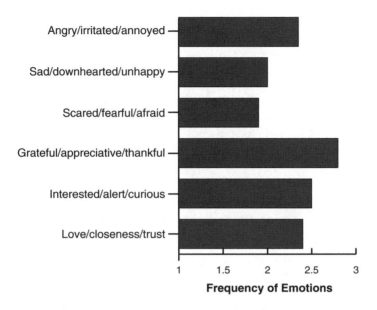

FIGURE 1.6   Emotions to Terrorist Attack. The frequency with which positive and negative emotions were experienced as a response to the aftermath of the September 11th terrorist attack on the World Trade Center in New York City and on the Pentagon.

Source: Adapted from "What Good Are Positive Emotions in Crises? A Prospective Study of Resilience and Emotions Following the Terrorist Attacks on the United States on September 11, 2001" by B. L. Fredrickson et al., 2003, *Journal of Personality and Social Psychology, 84,* table 2, p. 370.

brain. Part of the biological view is the consideration of how the brain evolved. What function did it play in our evolutionary past and how does that function affect human motivation today? The *psychological* refers to properties of the human mind, in contrast to the body and brain. The psychological is represented by motives, such as psychological needs, wants, and desires, but also by other characteristics, such as personality traits. And finally, the *environmental,* which is divisible into two categories. The first concerns the objective environment—that is, material things, such as money, grades, or prizes. The second concerns the cognitive representation of some external event, which is a case of cognitive motivation. For example, graduation is not a thing but the mental representation of some event that a student can visualize in her mind's eye. The mental representation is the goal which attracts or draws a student toward it. However, if a mental representation is viewed negatively, then it would actually repel the individual and provide motivation for behavior so that it would not happen.

Furthermore, the sources of motivation cut across various disciplines within psychology. Biological sources are a main consideration in disciplines that examine motivation and emotion in terms of an organism's autonomic and central nervous systems. These areas are covered in biological and physiological psychology and are also covered in neuroscience outside of psychology. The relationship between arousal and performance is considered in sports psychology, and the relationship between stress and well-being is covered in health psychology. Internal sources, like psychological needs, personality traits, and self-esteem, are included in the areas of social psychology, personality, and personal growth.

Psychological needs are also examined in consumer psychology and advertising. In addition, social psychology often covers emotions, since other individuals are a major source of emotional experiences. Environmental sources of motivation, such as incentives, are found in courses on learning, conditioning, and behavior analysis. Behavior modification, for instance, relies heavily on external incentives to change behavior. Incentives and goals also receive treatment as a part of industrial psychology and work motivation. Finally, clinical psychology and the study of psychopathology also include the topic of motivation. For instance, amotivation (the complete absence of any motivation) and the overpowering motivation for drugs (as in addiction) are two opposite ends of the motivation continuum studied in these fields.

Section Recap

Feasibility and research ethics determine whether a phenomenon is studied using an experimental or correlational method. Experiments involve a researcher manipulating an *experimental variable* to create different values. Participants are randomly assigned to conditions or treatments representing the different levels of the manipulated experimental variable. Naturally occurring motivational and emotional events are studied using *correlational variables,* which involve the measurement of preexisting levels or values. The *dependent variable* refers to behavior and depends on the experimental variable or is associated with the correlational variable. Moderately intense motives and emotions can be studied in the laboratory. Very intense motives and emotions, however, are less feasible and also unethical to create in the laboratory. Instead, they are studied in actual situations using correlational research methods.

The study of motivation involves the study of biological variables—that is, what do the body and brain contribute? The study of psychological variables involves examining how mental processes contribute to motivation. Environmental variables are examined to determine how material incentives and their mental representations motivate individuals. Finally, the study of motivation is applicable to many different disciplines.

ACTIVITIES

1. Suppose 100 people were offered a choice between $1 or $100. Would it be correct to assume that almost all of them would choose $100? If so, what does this suggest about the value of an incentive in determining choice? What does the choice of $100 suggest about people's value system as a motive for money? Is there another value system that causes a person to select $1 over $100? What might that alternative value system be?

2. Which of the following two options is more likely to lead to success in life? Why?

   a. Above average intelligence coupled with average motivation to achieve success
   b. Average intelligence coupled with above average motivation to achieve success

3. People's emotions can be observed in the TV news. Try to imagine what emotion someone is feeling in a particular situation, such as witnessing a terrible traffic accident; experiencing a hurricane, tornado, or earthquake; or winning the lottery. Can you detect the individual's emotions based on facial expressions, tone of voice, or behavior?

2 The History of Motivation and Emotion

He that would know what shall be, must consider what hath been.
—*H. G. Bohn, 1855*

We hold these truths to be self-evident, that all men are created equal, that they are endowed by their Creator with certain unalienable Rights, that among these are Life, Liberty and the Pursuit of Happiness.
—*Declaration of Independence, July 4, 1776*

■ As implied in the opening quote by Bohn, in order to understand motivation and emotion, we should consider what was known about them in the past. The following questions are guides for considering how psychology's past paved the way for the study of motivation and emotion in the present:

1. What is hedonism, and how is it a source of motivation?
2. What are instincts, and how do they affect motivation?
3. How does Darwin's concept of natural selection help explain what motivates people today?
4. How are internal and environmental sources of motivation described in the history of psychology?
5. How did philosophers and early psychologists describe emotion?

Brief History of Motivation

In imagination, transport yourself back 100,000 years to the banks of the local river in your area. Your tribe spent most of the day traveling up and down the river's banks hunting and fishing and gathering grubs, fruits, and other edibles. However, not everyone worked equally hard. Some individuals produced a lot of food for the tribe, while others produced none at all. You may have thought to yourself, "Some people in our tribe are not motivated" or "I wish everybody in our tribe were as motivated as me." In other words, you invented the concept of motivation to account for these differences in behavior. The point of this imaginary scene is that humans have probably been thinking about their own and others' motivation for a long time, certainly long before the beginning of psychology in 1879 (Boring, 1965).

The purpose of this section is to describe the ideas of philosophers and early psychologists regarding motivation. Their ideas include basic sources, hedonism, instincts, unconscious motivation, drives, psychological needs, and incentives.

Aristotle's Theory

If to motivate is to induce or to cause a change in behavior, then the ancient philosopher Aristotle (384–322 B.C.) was probably one of the first to advocate a theory of motivation. Writing between 347 and 335 B.C., he describes four different types of causes: efficient, final, formal, and material (Peck, 1942). These four causes are still relevant for psychology (Killeen, 2001) and provide insight into the source's motivation. Aristotle's efficient causes refer to triggers of behavior. These are a person's current motives and incentives. For example, the sight of your favorite dessert triggers eating it. His final causes refer to the aim or purpose of motivated behavior. It is the goal of the behavior. The aim of eating, for example, is to provide nourishment to the body. Formal causes refer to integrating the concept of motivation into models, hypotheses, or theories of behavior. Continuing the eating example, Darwin's theory of evolution maintains that humans evolved a preference for sweets during a time of scarcity. People were motivated to eat sweets since they provided a rich source of energy that was beneficial for survival. Finally, Aristotle's concept of material causes refers to the material of which a thing is made. The brain can be considered the material cause of motivated behavior. For instance, the material cause for eating dessert refers to the events occurring in the brain. In this case, the sight of dessert activates the brain's hypothalamus and contributes to the desire and the anticipated pleasure for sweets.

Hedonism

Two bumper stickers from times past read: "If it feels good, do it" and "If it's no fun, why do it?" Are these edicts accurate descriptions of human conduct? If so, are we merely pursuers of pleasure and avoiders of pain? Some early philosophers and pioneer psychologists agree that we are. We can see from Table 2.1 that this view has a long history.

Ancient Sources.   Nearly 2,400 years ago Greek philosophers were already discussing motivation under a principle known as **hedonism**—the pursuit of pleasure and the avoidance of pain. Although today the term *hedonism* often refers to sensory pleasures derived from food, drink, and sex, for philosophers the term meant striving for the greater good. The phrase "the Pursuit of Happiness" from the Declaration of Independence probably means a striving for the greater good. It is doubtful that the signers of the Declaration meant for people to stop working and party all the time. While it is true that sensory pleasure might be attained from spending your tuition money to pay for nightly partying, a hedonically greater benefit would result if that money were used to pay for your tuition and subsequent education. One of the first promoters of hedonism was the famous Greek philosopher Socrates (470–399 B.C.), who claimed a person should follow a course of action for which pleasure exceeds pain (see Table 2.1). Further, Socrates claimed that the only reason a person would not do so is because he lacks complete knowledge of the pleasure or pain that can result. For Democritus (460–370 B.C.), it was both natural and good for people to follow this course (see Table 2.1), although he could not identify what was pleasurable or painful independent of a person's behavior. Something was pleasurable if an individual strived for it, and something was painful if an individual avoided it. But what was pleasurable or painful could differ for each individual. No matter what these things were, pleasure was to be pursued and pain was to be avoided (Hyland, 1973).

TABLE 2.1   Quotes Illustrating the History of Hedonism as Motivation

SOCRATES (470–399 B.C.): "The right choice remains that in which the pleasures exceed the pains; this is the preferred course. The wrong choice remains that in which the pains outweigh the pleasures; this course is to be rejected" (Weiss, 1989, p. 518).

DEMOCRITUS (460–370 B.C.): "The good is the same for all men in the sense that it is good for them to pursue pleasure and avoid displeasure or pain" (Hyland, 1973, p. 291).

EPICURUS (341–271 B.C.): "We do not choose every pleasure either, but we sometimes pass over many pleasures in cases when their outcome for us is a greater quantity of discomfort" (Long & Sedley, 1987, p. 114).

THOMAS HOBBES (1640): "This motion, in which consisteth *pleasure* or *pain*, is a *solicitation* or provocation either to draw *near* the thing that pleaseth, or to *retire* from the thing that displeaseth" (Hobbes, 1640/1962, p. 31).

JOHN LOCKE (1690): "*Good*, the *greater good*, though apprehended and acknowledged to be so, does not determine the *will*, until our desire, raised proportionately to it, makes us uneasie in the want of it" (Locke, 1690, ¶ 35).

JEREMY BENTHAM (1789): "Nature has placed mankind under the governance of two sovereign masters, *pain* and *pleasure*. . . . The general tendency of an act is more or less pernicious according to the sum total of its consequences" (Bentham 1789/1970, pp. 11, 74).

HERBERT SPENCER (1899): "Those races of beings only can have survived in which . . . agreeable . . . feelings went along with activities conducive to the maintenance of life, while disagreeable . . . feelings went along with activities . . . destructive of life" (Spencer, 1899, p. 280).

EDWARD LEE THORNDIKE (1911): "The Law of Effect is that: *Of several responses made to the same situation, those of which are accompanied . . . by satisfaction to the animal . . . will be more likely to recur; those which are accompanied . . . by discomfort to the animal . . . will be less likely to occur*" (italic in original; Thorndike, 1911, p. 245).

SIGMUND FREUD (1920): "[The pleasure principle] does not abandon the intention of ultimately obtaining pleasure, but it nevertheless demands and carries into effect the postponement of satisfaction, the abandonment of a number of possibilities of gaining satisfaction and the temporary toleration of unpleasure as a step on the long indirect road to pleasure" (Freud, 1920, p. 10).

ROGER BROWN and RICHARD HERRNSTEIN (1975): "Barring the rare inborn movements, human behavior obeys the law of effect, *and nothing else*" (Brown & Herrnstein, 1975, p. 169).

One might get the impression that Socrates and Democritus meant that we should "eat, drink and be merry as if there is no tomorrow." On the contrary, they felt that our pursuits should be followed in moderation, since this leads to greater pleasure in the long run. The idea of moderation was developed further over a century later by Epicurus (341–271 B.C.), who maintained that pleasure and pain average out. Thus, we might forgo certain intense pleasures if subsequent pain of greater magnitude is a result (see Table 2.1). For instance, an individual might drink alcohol in moderation, thereby avoiding the painful aftereffects of overindulgence. Similarly, moderation may require experiencing pain prior to pleasure. An individual may endure immediate pain because longer-lasting pleasure may be a consequence (Long & Sedley, 1987). To illustrate, a university student might forgo the immediate benefit of earning money at an unskilled job in hopes that spending her time earning a university degree will provide more meaningful and fruitful employment later. Or a student may forgo a party Thursday night in order to study for Friday's exam on the assumption that good exam performance will produce longer-lasting pleasure than a good party. The party, although providing immediate pleasure, may result in a hangover and poor exam performance the next day, thus compromising long-term gain.

Later Philosophers.   Extra credit for doing additional coursework or a monetary fine for exceeding the speed limit are examples of incentives that motivate behavior. The roots of **incentive motivation** can be found in the writing of Thomas Hobbes in 1640 (see Table 2.1). Incentives are anticipated events that are approached if pleasurable and avoided if painful. Our ability to anticipate that an incentive will be pleasant or unpleasant depends on our remembrance of a similar incentive producing that feeling in the past. Thus, Hobbes (1640/1962) reasoned that a feeling of pleasure leads us to approach the situation responsible for that feeling, while an unpleasant feeling leads us to avoid the situation that produces it.

Incentives are in the future, and their power to provoke approach or avoidance behavior depends on how delayed they are. For example, does a person want an unchallenging minimum wage job immediately after high school graduation, or is she willing to wait for better-paying and challenging work after college? The often-cited conflict between a small immediate reward versus a large delayed reward is evident in the writings of John Locke in 1690 (see Table 2.1). He stated that a person may acknowledge that there may be a greater good or goal than those immediately available. These immediate rewards, however, appear to evoke a desire so strong that a person is unable to resist. Thus, in order for the delayed greater good to motivate behavior, it must evoke a desire stronger than the desire for immediate pleasure. Locke gives the example of an alcoholic who acknowledges that his health and estate are of greater value than drink. This same alcoholic, however, is unable to resist the lure of immediate drink and drinking companions (Locke, 1690).

The 18th-century philosopher Jeremy Bentham (1789/1970) put it bluntly: we are the servants of pain and pleasure (see Table 2.1). Like Hobbes before him, Bentham saw the intertwining nature of the positive and negative consequences of our actions. The anticipated consequences, both pleasant and unpleasant, determine the likelihood of our behavior. Here we see the beginning of decision theory: Of the incentives available to us, which should we choose? To illustrate, in making a decision of whether to attend a university, a person weighs both the pleasant and unpleasant aspects of attending versus doing something else. The outcome of this weighing determines the person's decision (Bentham, 1789/1970). Bentham used the phrase **principle of utility** to describe the idea that our actions are determined by whether they increase or decrease our happiness. An object has utility if it benefits us, inducing pleasure or happiness, but it also has utility if it prevents pain or unhappiness. Money, for example, has utility because it can buy goods and services, which provide an increase in pleasure and a decrease in pain.

Sigmund Freud.   Listed in *Time* (March 29, 1999) as one of the 20 most influential minds of the 20th century (Gay, 1999), Sigmund Freud wrote on hedonism, instincts, and unconscious motivation. Although his theories have been criticized for their lack of scientific rigor, his ideas are still influential today in psychology, literature, and the arts. The theme put forth by Democritus and Epicurus—that of postponing immediate pleasure or enduring immediate discomfort for subsequent greater pleasure later—is repeated by Freud (1920), who postulated two principles relevant for increasing pleasure and decreasing pain (see Table 2.1). For Freud, pleasure was in contrast to unpleasure. In his **pleasure principle,** he referred to a person's pursuit of pleasure, which is attained from a decrease in psychological tension especially when it follows from a sudden increase in tension. While pleasure results from reducing or keeping psychological tension as low as possible, unpleasure results when tension increases. Pleasure is also obtained from gratifying unconscious instinctual impulses or desires. According to Freud's **reality principle,** circumstances may force the individual to postpone immediate pleasure or endure discomfort if the result is greater pleasure later.

Edward Lee Thorndike. Pain and pleasure motivate behavior when those feelings reach our awareness. Herbert Spencer (1881/1977) claimed that humans strive to bring feelings of pleasure into consciousness while also trying to drive out feelings of pain. In addition, he contended that pleasure supports behaviors that benefit life while pain prevents behaviors that destroy life. Is it possible to empirically demonstrate that pain and pleasure motivate behavior? In an early empirical demonstration, Thorndike (1898, 1911) rewarded a cat with food for escaping from a box. Thorndike observed that over a series of attempts the cat's escapes occurred faster and faster. In applying Spencer's formulations, escape brought forth a feeling of pleasure into the cat's consciousness and the behavior that brought it about was beneficial to the cat. Based on his research, Thorndike (1898, 1911) formulated an idea, similar to Spencer's, which was the **law of effect:** the cat escaped because of the satisfaction that resulted from escaping, whereas remaining in the box was associated with less satisfaction or with dissatisfaction (see Table 2.1). In general, a satisfying effect strengthened behavior, and a dissatisfying effect weakened behavior. Thorndike, of course, was faced with the problem that the cat could not tell him whether escape and food provided pleasure. Thorndike assumed that an animal behaves in order to attain a satisfying state and to remove a dissatisfying state. Can this assumption alone explain the cat's behavior? Another way of explaining behavior began when John Watson (1913) introduced *behaviorism.* This school of psychology emphasized observable behavior and its consequences rather than the subjective experiences of pain and pleasure. Thus, whereas Thorndike emphasized the pleasure or satisfaction derived from the cat's escape, Watson would have emphasized the actual freedom as the source of motivation for the cat.

Law of Effect Today. Thorndike's law of effect is widely accepted today but with an emphasis on the observable consequences of behavior, which are referred to as reinforcers and punishers. This law avoids the subjective and unobservable nature of hedonism. Instead, *reinforcers* are defined as observable stimulus consequences that increase and maintain behavior. For example, a food pellet resulting from a lever press is a reinforcer, provided the pellet increases or maintains the rat's lever pressing. A *punisher* is a stimulus consequence of behavior that reduces the frequency of the behavior. A loss of privileges for a child as a consequence of misbehavior is a punisher, provided that the misbehavior decreases. Today, many psychologists accept the view that human behavior is determined by the law of effect (Brown & Herrnstein, 1975; see Table 2.1). This law may sound similar to hedonism as proposed by the Greek philosophers some 2,400 years ago. However, hedonism emphasizes the subjective nature of motivation: pursue pleasure and avoid pain. The law of effect, however, emphasizes the objective nature of motivation: some stimuli increase behavior and other stimuli decrease it. There is no claim in the law of effect that the stimuli we approach provide some degree of pleasure or that those we avoid produce varying degrees of discomfort or pain if we fail to do so. The two principles emphasize different sources of motivation: internal and external.

Current Trends.   Current research has expanded the study of hedonism to include the function of self-control. Already in 1690 Locke noted that the distinction between pleasure and pain is easy to make when they are compared, side by side, in the present. The distinction becomes obscure, however, when trying to compare present feelings with future feelings. For example, compare the pleasure of spending this evening with friends versus the pleasure from earning a high exam score next week because you chose to study instead. If these sources of pleasure occurred simultaneously, Locke would argue that a student would have no trouble making a decision as to which was the greater pleasure. However, the decision becomes more difficult, according to Locke, because the pleasure from a high exam score is obscure due to its distance in the future. Over 300 years later psychologists are researching what characteristics, for example, determine a person's choice between rewards that bring immediate smaller pleasure at the expense of larger delayed pleasures, such as the pleasure of friends tonight versus the pleasure of exam success next week.

Current research uses the term *impulsiveness* to describe individuals who display the tendency to choose smaller rewards while *self-control* (self-discipline) describes those who can choose larger but delayed rewards (Logue 1988, 1998). Research shows that greater self-control provides benefits, such as better academic achievement. For example, Duckworth and Seligman (2005) employed several measures of self-discipline, such as the *Brief Self-Control Scale*. This scale permits individuals to rate themselves on such abilities as being able to resist temptation, think through the alternatives of their actions, and work toward long-term goals. A higher score on the *Scale* means a person has a greater ability to exercise self-control. Duckworth and Seligman found that eighth graders with greater self-control earned higher GPAs regardless of their level of intelligence. Tangney and coresearchers (2004) also found that higher scores on the *Brief Self-Control Scale* were associated with higher grades for university students, a better degree of adjustment, less alcohol abuse, and better interpersonal relationships and skills.

Positive psychology is another new front in the study of hedonism. Recall that there are two aspects to hedonism: decrease unhappiness or pain and increase happiness or pleasure. Locke would argue that unhappiness has a greater motivational impact because when experienced an individual is motivated to reduce that feeling. Happiness, however, is a future promise based on a person's current actions. As a result of the immediacy of unhappiness, psychologists have been mostly concerned with its reduction by treating, for example, depression, grief, anxiety, and distress. There had been little concern in going beyond the alleviation of unhappiness. However, 1999 marked the formal beginning of the discipline of positive psychology with the publication of a series of articles that addressed positive experiences, positive personality, and the social context for positive feelings (Seligman & Csikszentmihalyi, 2000). **Positive psychology** is the scientific investigation of possible factors that promote people, groups, and institutions to function at their best (Gable & Haidt, 2005). These factors may provide people with a prescription for what is good for them. For example, how should students spend their discretionary income, which is what remains after paying for tuition, books, and lodging? One piece of advice is that greater happiness ensues when money is spent on experiences, such as concerts, sporting events, and movies, rather than on material possessions, such as televisions and clothes (Van Boven, 2005).

Evolution and Motivation

Recall from Chapter 1 that evolutionary psychology attempts to understand current human behavior by relating it to our evolutionary past (Buss, 2005; Cosmides & Tooby, 2005). Evolutionary psychology assumes that humans are born with existing motives or are disposed to develop motives that prompt behaviors beneficial for survival. But how did these motives and dispositions originate? The answer to these questions come from one of the most influential theories ever devised to help us understand motivation.

Charles Darwin.   Do hedonism and a sensitivity toward utility occur in all animals and humans? Is this universal? Would the bases for these psychological traits have evolved over millions of years? Charles Darwin, as one of the originators of a **theory of evolution,** introduced two concepts in his book *On the Origin of Species by Means of Natural Selection* (1859/1936) that may answer these questions. *Variation* means that different values of a particular trait vary in frequency in the population. *Selection* means that certain trait values are selected for by the environment and aid survival (Endler, 1986). The evolution of the running speed of cheetahs is an example (see Figure 2.1). Cheetahs vary in running speed: slow, medium, and fast. The ability of a cheetah to obtain food depends, in part, on how fast it runs. When all their prey are slow, all cheetahs are able to eat. Even the slowest cheetah is

Original Population		Evolved Population
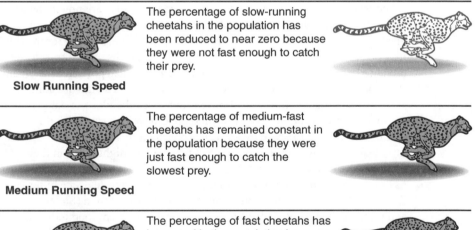		

Slow Running Speed — The percentage of slow-running cheetahs in the population has been reduced to near zero because they were not fast enough to catch their prey.

Medium Running Speed — The percentage of medium-fast cheetahs has remained constant in the population because they were just fast enough to catch the slowest prey.

Fast Running Speed — The percentage of fast cheetahs has increased in the population because they were fast enough to catch more of the prey they pursued.

FIGURE 2.1   Variation and Selection in Evolution. The percentage of slow-, medium-, and fast-running cheetahs changes over succeeding generations. Slow-running cheetahs decrease in the population because they are not fast enough to catch even the slowest prey. Medium-fast cheetahs hold their own, since they can catch the slowest prey. Fast-running cheetahs increase in the population because they can catch a greater amount of the prey they pursue.

fast enough to run after the slowest prey. However, if all the slow prey are eaten, then only faster-running cheetahs will survive, since only they are going to be able to catch the remaining faster-running prey. Thus, the faster-running prey select for faster-running cheetahs and select against slower-running cheetahs. Consequently, faster-running cheetahs have a greater chance of survival than slower-running cheetahs, since the faster-running cheetahs are more likely to capture the prey they need for food. Darwin (1859/1936) also reasoned that physical traits are inherited. Thus, the physical equipment for fast running, such as powerful muscles, strong heart, and lung capacity, is transmitted to succeeding generations.

Darwin also introduced the concept of **population thinking,** which refers to the idea that every individual in a population is different (Mayr, 2001). Thus, rather than emphasize the similarity among people, population thinking emphasizes that each individual is unique. An implication of population thinking is that any motivational element does not apply equally to all individuals much like the average size shoe does not fit everyone. In psychology, population thinking translates into the area of individual differences, such as psychological needs (Chapter 8) and personality traits (Chapter 9). For example, people vary in their need to belong and thus each person expends different amounts of effort in order to affiliate with others. People also vary in personality traits. For instance, more extraverted individuals might expend additional effort to attend parties than less extraverted individuals would.

Herbert Spencer.   As described earlier, Spencer stated that pleasurable behavior benefitted life while painful behavior did not. Spencer believed that this function of pain and pleasure resulted from evolution (see Table 2.1). Suppose there was variation in the amount of pleasure or discomfort produced by a particular behavior and that this behavior is important for the survival of the organism. Pain and pleasure become selecting agents for those behaviors, much like fast-running prey selects for fast-running cheetahs. Pleasure selected behaviors that promoted survival value while pain selected behaviors that protected the organism from harm. For example, fear may have evolved as a motive to avoid dangerous animals.

Assume that a child's level of fear increases the closer a dangerous-looking animal approaches. However, the extent to which fear develops varies. Children who become easily afraid are more likely to avoid dangerous creatures and survive. Children who develop little fear may draw closer to these creatures, which might result in their harm. For another illustration, consider the fact that spoiled food produces a bitter taste, while nutritious food has a more pleasing taste. Young infants prefer a sweet taste over a bitter taste and are therefore more likely to eat nutritious food and reject spoiled food (Steiner, 1977). If this ability and preference had not evolved, then infants would accept food indiscriminately, including that which produces potentially life-threatening diarrhea and dehydration.

Instincts.   Hedonism can motivate a variety of behaviors. Other motivational sources, however, provide the impetus for only a limited class of behaviors. **Instinct,** for instance, is an internal stimulus that induces a specific pattern of behavior in a species. It is considered to be an inherited disposition that shows itself as behavior in the presence of a limited range of stimuli. Instincts are characteristic of an entire species, are influenced little (if at all) by learning, and have survival value for the organism (Fletcher, 1966). Although instincts are evoked by external stimuli, early psychologists considered them responsible for energizing or powering the muscles into a fixed pattern of behavior. One early proponent of human instincts was William James (1890/1950), who emphasized that the impulse to action was an important component of instinct. William McDougall (1908), another popularizer of the idea of instincts, also felt they were the principal instigators of human behavior and that without instinct humans would be incapable of any type of action. James (1890/1950) postulated 38 instincts, which ranged from sucking, crying, and smiling to play, jealousy, and love. An important characteristic of instincts for James was that "instincts are implanted for the sake of giving rise to habits" (p. 402). In order for a particular behavior pattern to become habitual, it is helpful if the behavior already occurs naturally. To illustrate, walking is the most efficient way for humans (without disabilities) to get around, and it is probably much easier for a child to learn to walk if it is instinctive to do so. Even before a child is able to walk on its own, a young infant will make reflexive walking movements (not under voluntary control) when it is held upright with its feet touching the floor (Eibl-Eibesfeldt, 1989).

The idea of instincts as a source of motivation eventually lost popularity in psychology for several reasons (Fletcher, 1966). One was that the list of instincts became quite long. It could conceivably reach the point where every behavioral act would be the result of an instinct. The second reason was that some instincts appear contradictory, such as fear versus curiosity. Where does curiosity end and fear begin, for example, when entering an abandoned house in a secluded woods? Finally, it was very difficult to determine if instincts were truly innate and occurred without the benefit of any experience or whether all behavior was the result of experience no matter how little. Perhaps walking by a child is not instinctive but is learned from example, by imitating the walking of the mother or father.

Current Trends.   Some psychologists are trying to understand the instinctive nature of smiles and laughter in terms of their survival value. Laughter occurs in all humans and begins very early in a child's life. These two characteristics suggest that laughter comes from our evolutionary past (Weisfeld, 1993). One survival benefit is that laughter aids children in mastering their social environment by responding to incongruities, such as word play and social, sexual, and aggressive topics. Laughter resulting from being tickled also provides benefits. Tickling promotes adult-child interaction, and laughter is a way for the child to reward the tickler. Another survival benefit is that the act of tickling, in turn, provides the child with practice for defending vulnerable body parts. As the child becomes older and these skills are developed, she becomes less ticklish. Finally, laughter is a social lubricant that helps maintain social interaction among individuals (Weisfeld, 1993).

Unconscious Motivation

Another historical theme in the analysis of motivation is the role of awareness. A person may explain a raid on the refrigerator by saying, "I was hungry" or explain her choice of a particular movie by stating, "My favorite actor was in it." In these examples, the person is aware of the motives for her behavior. Yet there are instances when the motives and incentives for some actions are tacit or are incorrectly stated (Nisbett & Wilson, 1977). Inaccessibility to one's motives characterizes *unconscious motivation*.

Freud's Conscious-Unconscious Distinction.   Sigmund Freud (1920/1943) described a very influential theory of unconscious motivation in his book *A General Introduction to Psychoanalysis*. According to Freud, awareness results when motives have entered consciousness from either the preconscious or the unconscious. Using two rooms as a metaphor (see Figure 2.2), the **preconscious** part of a person's mental apparatus is represented by the small room, which contains thoughts, feelings, sensations, and memories. A person's "consciousness as a spectator" (p. 261) resides in this small room and serves as the focus

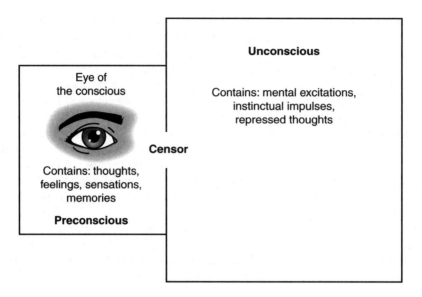

FIGURE 2.2 Freud's Concept of Motivation. Freud used two adjoining rooms separated by a doorway as a metaphor for his unconscious and preconscious motivation. Unconscious thoughts and impulses reside in the large room and try to enter the preconscious by slipping by the censor, who is standing guard between the two rooms. Thoughts and impulses in the smaller room of the preconscious compete for the attention of the conscious.

of awareness. The large room represents the **unconscious** "in which the various mental excitations are crowding upon one another, like individual beings" (p. 260). This part of the mental apparatus is unavailable to a person. It contains instinctual impulses, repressed thoughts, and other mental stimuli. For material to proceed from the large room (unconscious) to the small adjoining room (preconscious), it must pass through the doorway separating the two rooms. Here stands a door keeper or censor who determines what mental excitations are allowed entry into the room of the preconscious. If some mental events have gained entry, then they may yet be driven out if found to be unacceptable or anxiety provoking. Freud uses the term **repression** to refer to those mental excitations that have made it to the doorway and have been turned back by the door keeper. This makes them incapable of becoming conscious. Freud (1915b) conceived repression as a means of protecting us from the unpleasure that would result if we became aware of some of the impulses residing in our unconscious. The idea of unpleasure means that the instinct might produce anxiety, embarrassment, or punishment from others. Under certain circumstances, however, these instinctual needs can reach awareness in jokes, dreams, slips of the tongue, and neuroses (Freud, 1920, 1920/1943). However, if mental events cross the threshold into the small room (preconscious), it does not mean that an individual is automatically aware of them. A person only becomes aware of these mental excitations or thoughts if they attract "the eye of consciousness" (Freud, 1920/1943, p. 260).

Motivational Instincts and the Unconscious.   Motivation for Freud was based on the satisfaction of unconscious instinctual impulses (Freud, 1915a). Originating in the body, instincts reach consciousness, where they exert *pressure*, which is really their demand for satisfaction. The *aim* or goal of every instinctual need is for the reduction of this pressure.

The *object* of the instinct is the incentive that allows the instinct to meet its aim. The object can be external or can be a body part providing for the reduction of the instinctual need. The *source* of the instinct is the body part or perhaps a chemical change in the brain from which the instinct originates. However, we are only aware of the aim or goal of the instinct in our mind (Freud, 1915a). According to Freud (1924), there are three groups of instincts. Sexual or life instincts are those that operate to maintain and transfer life to successive generations. Death instincts, in contrast, manifest themselves as aggressive and destructive impulses. Sexual and death instincts mix and fuse together in living creatures but also compete for supremacy so that at times one instinct and then the other is dominant. A third type includes the ego or self-preservation instincts. Freud saw motivation as an increase and decrease of instinctual excitation invading our minds. An increase in excitation produces unpleasure (pain), and a decrease produces pleasure. The ultimate pleasure is to keep excitation as low as possible or at least keep it constant. Low excitation is the aim of the death instinct. Yet Freud (1920, 1924) recognized that people also experience pleasure from an increase in excitation, such as that occurring with heightened sexual tension and its sudden release. He theorized that there were instances when tension could be pleasurable and that the lowering of tension in some cases could be painful (Freud, 1924).

Satisfying Unconscious Impulses.   Much of Freud's writing is concerned with the satisfaction of instinctual needs that may be considered socially unacceptable or even personally unacceptable. An example of an unacceptable impulse is a "desire to see the organs peculiar to each sex exposed" (Freud, 1905, p. 98). Many of our sexual and aggressive instincts, for example, are repressed because awareness of them would produce anxiety or social punishment. Thus, much of Freud's theorizing concerned how these unacceptable instinctual needs are reduced and satisfied. In *Jokes and Their Relation to the Unconscious* (1905), Freud describes humor as one way of satisfying instinctual impulses. Consider his riddles: "What is a cannibal who has eaten his father and his mother?—An orphan.—And if he has eaten all his other relations as well?—The sole heir.—And where will a monster of that kind find sympathy?—In the dictionary under 'S'" (p. 153). Laughing at these riddles results in a partial satisfaction of the death instinct, which is preferable to actually committing a murder. The death and sex instincts can be satisfied by laughing at jokes containing aggressive and sexual themes. Since such aggressive thoughts and acts can be anxiety provoking, they are subject to repression in order to prevent their awareness. However, through the joking process, these instinctual needs can get around repression to some degree and express themselves, thus offering some satisfaction. A second source of pleasure in jokes lies in saving the energy that is expended in repression. Since the repressed impulse is manifested momentarily in the joke, there is a corresponding savings in psychic energy. The energy used for repression is now no longer needed and can thus be expended in other ways, such as laughing at the joke (Freud, 1905).

Dreams are another way instinctual impulses are satisfied. During sleep there is a relaxation of censorship, and so it is easier for unconscious impulses to enter into consciousness. Even during sleep, however, according to Freud, the unconscious impulse undergoes some censorship whereby the impulse is disguised. The reason for the censorship is that it protects our sleep from being disturbed. If the dream were too real we would be awakened. The actual dream, as reported, is known as the *manifest content*, while the unconscious impulses the dream represents are known as the *latent content*. Sticks, umbrellas, knives, and guns are manifestations of the penis, according to Freud. Ships, caves, jars, and boxes are manifestations of the vagina. "*The act of mounting* ladders, steep places, or stairs is indubitably symbolic of sexual intercourse. On closer reflection we shall notice that the rhythmic character of this climbing is the point in common between the two, and perhaps also the accompanying increase in excitation—the shortening of breath as the climber ascends" (Freud, 1920/1943, p. 141). Thus, dreams about sex, even when disguised, allow for the satisfaction of our sexual urges (Freud, 1915b, 1920/1943).

Current Trends.   Unconscious motivation in Freud's theory favors a push orientation. The aim of an instinct is to reduce the pressure that is felt much like the aim of hunger is to push a person to reduce feelings of hunger. However, because instincts reside in the unconscious, individuals are not aware of the source of these pushing effects. They are only aware of being pushed. Current research trends on unconscious motivation, however, have emphasized a pull rather than push orientation. Goals are in the unconscious or below the level of awareness. When goals are activated into consciousness they are then acted on. For example, suppose during class your professor says "check to see that your cell phone is off." You did not hear your professor because your were talking to your neighbor. Several minutes later, for no reason that you could discern, you check your cell phone. In this example, *check cell phone* reached consciousness in the form of a goal on which you acted. However, you were not aware of how it reached consciousness.

The previous example illustrates **automaticity,** or automatic processes which refer to external events controlling mental processes without a person being aware what events were responsible (Bargh & Barndollar, 1996; Bargh & Chartrand, 1999; Bargh & Williams, 2006). An *automatic process* refers to behavior that is carried out with little conscious control or awareness. For example, a person drives the same route to school or work with little conscious awareness, control, and effort—in effect, being on automatic pilot. According to these researchers, the perception of a person or situation can trigger a behavior-relevant intention. This intention, in turn, is linked to actual behavior. This whole chain occurs automatically, without the person being consciously aware of what triggered her intention and subsequent behavior.

Internal Sources of Motivation

A wheel rolls because it has the feature of being round. A rock sinks and wood floats because of the nature of their structure or composition. Could these objects respond to their environments any other way? Similarly, how animals and humans respond to their environment may depend partly on their internal structure—that is, on such internal sources of push motivation as drives and needs.

Drive Concept.   In his book *Dynamic Psychology*, Woodworth (1918) distinguishes between mechanism and drive. **Mechanism** refers to how we do something, while **drive** refers to what induced us to do it. To help explain the relationship between the two, consider the mechanism that drives a bicycle. Your bicycle is leaning against a tree, not moving, for the obvious reason that no power has been applied to make it move. If you get on your bicycle and push on the pedals, then this drives the front sprocket, the chain, the rear sprocket, and finally the rear wheel. The bicycle moves. For Woodworth (1918), drive is the power you applied to the pedals, which sets a series of mechanisms in motion from movement of the front sprocket to movement of the rear wheel. In some instances a stimulus drives behavior as long as the stimulus is present and ceases when the stimulus is removed. Woodworth uses the knee jerk reflex as an example. A tap below the knee drives the sensory neuron, which drives the motor neuron and then the thigh muscles, causing the leg to jerk. The instant this is accomplished, the behavior ceases, since the stimulus is no longer present. In other instances, however, when the external stimulus ceases, the drive tendency is still present. Woodworth uses the example of a hunting dog trailing prey. The end point for the dog is finding the prey, and this drives the dog to follow the trail with its nose. If the trail is lost, the dog is driven to search for it so as to eventually achieve its goal. Thus, even though the stimulus of the scent is momentarily broken, the behavior does not cease, as it would with a reflex. Hunger and thirst drives that result from food and water deprivation persist until the goals of eating and drinking have been accomplished. Drive is the initial inducement of behavior and remains in effect in some part of the mechanism. That is, it remains in some part of our nervous system until behavior eventually results. Research on drive focused on drive as the deprivation of some incentive. Warden (1931), for example, used rats to determine the relative strength of various drives, such as the maternal, thirst, hunger, sex, and exploratory drives. Figure 1.3 shows the effects of thirst drive on the speed by which rats begin to run toward a water incentive.

Psychological Needs. Psychological need was an early motivational concept similar to drive. Whereas drive was often viewed as the result of deprivation of some incentive, need was considered to be an inherent characteristic of humans. While different levels of drive could be experimentally manipulated within an animal, need was assumed to already exist in different amounts in individuals. Need intensity was thus measured via some scale, questionnaire, or projective test (see Chapter 8). Georges Le Roy (1764/1974) claimed the existence of the need for food, clothing, shelter, love, external stimulation, and rest. The psychologist Henry Murray (1938) formalized the study of needs and concluded that they are a major source of human motivation. According to Murray, **primary needs,** or **viscerogenic needs,** are physiological in nature and are characterized by bodily satisfaction. These would include the need for air, water, food, sex, lactation, urination, rest and sleep, defecation, and physical stimulation and the need to avoid harm, noxious stimuli, heat, and cold. **Secondary needs,** or **psychogenic needs,** are concerned with mental or emotional satisfaction and depend on or are derived from primary needs. Murray considered that all needs are hypothetical processes referring "to an organic potentiality or readiness to respond in a certain way under given conditions" (p. 61). Once instigated, a need will persist as an electrical chemical process in the brain, which corresponds to a feeling of desire. Behaviors instigated by need cease when the goal of satisfying the specific need has been achieved. Needs can be evoked by an internal physiological process but also by environmental demands, which are either to be approached or avoided. To illustrate: a person's need for affiliation is brought on by the presence of other people and causes him to seek out individuals to be with.

Murray (1938) postulated the existence of some 22 psychogenic needs. Table 2.2 defines six of his needs that are still of interest today along with sample statements from different scales he used to measure the level of each need.

Current Trends. Psychologists have not stopped with Murray's psychological needs or motives. Instead additional motives are being formulated. In a review of motives formulated in the last decade of the 20th century, Pittman (1998) describes some newer ones that are of interest to psychologists. For example, the need for closure refers to a person's preference

TABLE 2.2   Six of Murray's Needs and Sample Statements from Murray's *Psychological Insight Test*

Instructions: Read each statement carefully and make up your mind whether it is more *or* less *for you than it is for the average. Use the following rating scale:*
Below average = −3, −2, −1
Above average = +1, +2, +3

Achievement   To accomplish difficult tasks, surpass self and others
Sample statement: "I am driven to ever greater efforts by an unslaked ambition."

Affiliation   To approach others, win their affection; to remain loyal to friends
Sample statement: "I am in my element when I am with a group of people who enjoy life."

Autonomy   To be independent and free, to resist coercion
Sample statement: "I am unable to do my best work when I am in a subservient position."

Dominance   To control your environment, to influence and direct others
Sample statement: "I enjoy organizing or directing the activities of a group—team, club, or committee."

Order   To put things in order, to organize, to be neat and clean
Sample statement: "I know what I want to say without having to fumble about for the right word."

Understanding   To ask questions, seek answers, to analyze events, to enjoy using theory, logic, reason
Sample statement: "I enjoy reflection and speculation as much as anything."

Source: Adapted from *Explorations in Personality* by H. A. Murray, 1938, New York: Oxford University Press.

for a nonambiguous conclusion. The motive to survive refers to the knowledge that one's life will eventually end and that everything possible must be done to postpone death. However, whenever a new psychological need is formulated, it must be evaluated carefully to determine if it aids our understanding of behavior. Otherwise, the list of psychological needs could become quite long, thereby decreasing their explanatory power. As a consequence, the idea of needs may decline in popularity and be abandoned, as did the focus on instincts early in the 20th century. Pittman (1998) proposes that various minor psychological needs or motives are derivable from a few basic ones.

A very basic psychological need is one that should be shared by all people. An example would be **existential concerns** about life's most basic challenges (Koole et al., 2006). Existential concerns become paramount as a consequence of some tragic event, such as a death, illness, accident, natural disasters, or acts of war. They cause people to ask questions about why this happened, what it means, and make them change the course of their lives in profound ways. There are five major existential concerns that can motivate people in different ways. A concern about one's own death promotes a desire to maintain life. A concern with isolation emphasizes that we have a need to associate with others rather than be isolated and be unable to share meaningful experiences. Identity concerns deal with self-insight, a person's role in the world, and the boundaries between the self and others. A concern with freedom questions the extent a person has free will and is responsible for his or her actions versus being controlled by external factors. A final concern involves the question of whether life has meaning or if it is a series of randomly occurring events that are without meaning (Koole et al., 2006). It may be possible that many psychological needs are derivable from these five existential concerns. For example, a need for safety comes from a concern about death. Affiliation and belonging needs are derived from a concern about isolation. Concerns about freedom promote a need for autonomy.

External Sources of Motivation

Even though a person may know how to do something, this does not mean she will. A person might say, "I know how to make my bed but why do it?" A reason for doing something is provided by *incentives*, which are external stimuli that attract or repel an individual (e.g., anticipated rewards or punishers). Tolman and Honzik (1930) provided one of the first demonstrations that the presence or absence of an incentive affects the motivation of behavior. First, they had rats experience a maze for 10 trials with or without a food incentive in the goal box. Then, on the 11th trial, the incentive conditions remained the same for some rats, but for others the incentive conditions were switched.

Their results in Figure 2.3 show that the number of errors the rats made in traversing the maze depended on experience gained over trials and on the presence or absence of the food incentive or reward. The fewest number of errors per trial occurred for the continuous reward group (i.e., "food"), which benefitted from the food incentive on every trial. The most errors were made by the continuous nonreward group (i.e., "no food"), which never benefitted from the food incentive on any trial. The motivational benefits of the incentive are most apparent for the other two groups when a reward was suddenly introduced or removed. In Figure 2.3, when food became available on trial 11 for the nonreward-reward group (i.e., "food available"), there was a rapid drop in the number of errors. When food suddenly disappeared on trial 11 for the reward-nonreward group (i.e., "food removed"), there was a rapid increase in the number of errors. Thus, the number of errors changed as the incentive changed.

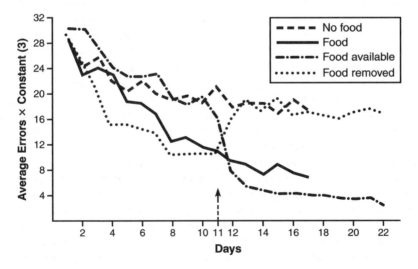

FIGURE 2.3 Incentive Change and Performance. When a food incentive becomes available on trial 11, there is a sudden decrease in the number of errors rats made in traversing a maze.

Source: From "Introduction and Removal of Reward, and Maze Performance in Rats" by E. C. Tolman and C. H. Honzik, 1930, *University of California Publications in Psychology, 4*, figure 4. Copyright 1930 The Regents of the University of California.

External and Internal Sources Induce Behavior

The motivation of behavior depends on both internal and external sources. Feelings of pleasure, instincts, drives, and psychological needs are internal sources of motivation, while positive and negative incentives are external sources. To induce behavior, however, both sources are necessary; either one alone will not do it. Two early psychologists from rather diverse fields were quite aware of this point. Carl Warden and the Columbia University group were animal psychologists who used rats to verify the necessity of combining internal and external sources for motivation. Kurt Lewin, however, was a Gestalt psychologist who relied on research in human motivation to illustrate this point.

Warden's Incentive-Drive Link.   Warden (1931) delineated the difference between internal and external sources of motivation based on his work with rats. For Warden, motivation involved both internal or drive factors and external or incentive factors. Drive was an aroused action tendency that resulted from deprivation and led the animal to seek out the appropriate incentive. An incentive was an external object that also operates to arouse some internal physiological state or tendency on the part of the organism to approach or avoid it. Warden's **incentive-drive** concept holds that drives and incentives match up, like hunger matches with food, thirst with water, and curiosity with novel stimuli. These incentive-drive matchups mean that drive is "a reaction tendency directed toward an incentive" (Warden, 1931, p. 15) and that both are necessary for motivating behavior.

Animal psychologists, using the Columbia Obstruction Box, determined how many times a rat would cross an electrified grid (obstruction) in order to reach the incentive of which the animal had been deprived. For example, following deprivation, how many electrified grid crossings will the rat make for food or water, a sex partner, or the opportunity to explore a complex maze? A greater number of grid crossings point to a stronger incentive-drive match. There were two major findings. First, as drive increases, so does the number of grid crossings. Second, as incentive delay increases, the number of grid crossings decreases. In one experiment, Warner (1928/1931) deprived rats of food from zero to eight days and then determined how many grid crossings they would make for a food incentive. The results in Figure 2.4a (for zero to four days of deprivation) show that as the hunger drive increased, the number of grid crossings increased and then leveled off. In an experiment on incentive delay, Hamilton (1929/1931) determined the number of grid crossings hungry rats made for food that was delayed zero to 180 seconds after reaching the other side. The results in Figure 2.4b show that as food incentive delay increased, the number of grid crossings decreased.

Lewin's Field Theory.   Lewin (1936, 1938) postulated **psychological force** as a way of accounting for internal and environmental sources of motivation. According to Lewin's (1936) field theory, human action takes place within a person's *life space*, which is the person's current internal and external environment. The life space contains objects and possible activities of which a person is aware and which attract or repel him. For instance, you may be aware of reading this book, that you are hungry, and that you have a date at a pizza restaurant later today. *Forces* or motivational factors within the life space cause a person to move from one object or activity to another. Objects or activities that have *positive valence* attract the individual; they are approached or wanted. Objects that have *negative valence* repel the individual; they are avoided or not wanted. Lewin (1938, p. 160) cites the Tolman and Honzik results (see Figure 2.3) as an example of the effects of incentive valence on

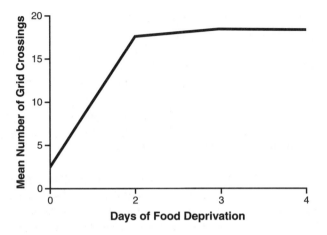

FIGURE 2.4a   Drive and Performance. As the number of days of food deprivation increases, rats make more crossings of an electrified grid in order to obtain food.

Source: From "A Study of Hunger Behavior in the White Rat by Means of the Obstruction Method" in C. J. Warden, Ed., *Animal Motivation* (table 3), 1931, New York: Columbia University Press.

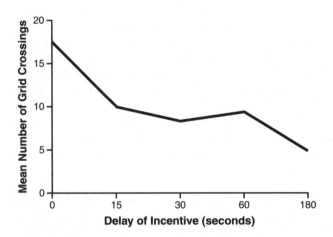

FIGURE 2.4b   Incentive Delay and Performance. As the length of the delay for a food incentive increases, the number of electrified grid crossings made by hungry rats decreases.

Source: From "The Effect of Delayed Incentive on the Hunger Drive in the White Rat" in C. J. Warden, Ed., *Animal Motivation* (table 6), 1931, New York: Columbia University Press.

performance. According to Lewin, humans are also forced from one activity or another depending on the valences of those activities. A scheduled exam forces you to keep reading, but as time for your pizza date draws near you will instead be heading for the restaurant. Psychological force depends on both the valence of the incentive and the psychological distance to the incentive. Psychological distance can refer to both time or physical space. Incentive delay illustrates psychological distance in terms of time. In Figure 2.4b, for instance, the psychological force of the food incentive to attract a rat decreases the more the incentive is delayed. The nearness of a toy to an infant illustrates psychological distance in terms of physical space. An infant may prefer a closer toy over one that is farther away, which to Lewin meant that the preferred toy had a shorter psychological distance (Lewin, 1933). Thus, the more "interesting" your date and the tastier the pizza, the stronger the forces that attract you to this outing. The farther away in time your date is, however, the weaker the force that attracts you to it.

Tension is the term Lewin (1936) used to label a deficit in the person's internal environment. Tension can result from an unfulfilled intention, a physiological need, or a psychological need. For example, being deprived of food or not knowing the course material well enough to pass an exam puts a student in a state of tension. The result of tension is to instill valence on relevant environmental objects. Tension from hunger increases the positive valence of pizza, and tension from being unprepared increases the negative valence of an exam. When the desired object or incentive is attained, then tension dissipates and the valence of the incentive approaches zero. Combining internal and environmental factors of motivation in Lewin's (1938) system results in the following formula:

$$\text{Psychological force} = \frac{\text{Valence of goal properties; tension in person}}{\text{Psychological distance between person and goal}}$$

(Lewin does not claim this formula is always correct but it is a good approximation to help in remembering the relationship among force, valence, tension, and psychological distance.) Although it is not clear whether valence and tension should be added or multiplied together, what is important is that force or inducement to action depends on both incentive valence or goal activity and tension. Force, however, decreases with psychological distance. Usually, the closer in time an individual is to attaining the incentive, the shorter the psychological distance. To illustrate the formula: how hard a student is forced to study for an exam depends on how important it is for the student to do well (valence), how unprepared he is at the moment (tension), and how many days away the exam is scheduled (psychological distance).

Current Trends.   The results in Figure 2.4 and Lewin's formula bring out two major aspects of incentive motivation: value and delay. In the case of food, its incentive value increases with deprivation (Figure 2.4a) and with amount. However, the value of any incentive decreases with delay—that is, how far in the future the incentive becomes available (Figure 2.4b). Incentive delay relates to the future orientation of motivation. People are motivated by the anticipated consequences of what their behavior will bring them either immediately or after some delay. Today the effects of delay on incentive value are organized by **temporal motivation theory** (Steel & König, 2006). In this theory as well as in Lewin's, incentive value increases with amount and decreases with delay. An added feature of temporal motivation theory, however, is that the effects of delay depend upon individual differences. For some individuals incentive value declines steeply with delay while for others it declines slowly. Consider the choice between eating one cookie now versus choosing two cookies for tomorrow. How much the value of two cookies declined when delayed one day determines whether its value is below or above the value of one cookie now. For some individuals the decline is rapid and the two-cookie value falls below the single-cookie value now. These individuals choose to eat one cookie now. For others, the decline is slower and the two-cookie value remains above the single-cookie value now. They select the choice of two cookies tomorrow. One type of difference among individuals is how substance abusers differ from non-abusers in the rate at which the value of a non-drug reward declines as it fades into the future. In general, the value of an incentive, such as money, declines faster for substance abusers than for non-abusers (Green & Myerson, 2004; Johnson et al., 2007). Thus, drug abusers are more likely to choose a smaller amount of money available imme-diately while non-abusers are more likely to choose a larger delayed amount. At present, temporal motivation theory is also used to explain procrastination (Steel, 2007). What should a student do this evening: study in anticipation of earning a high exam score tomorrow or procrastinate and watch a movie? According to temporal motivation theory, the interplay between the changes in the value of grades and movies with time explains the student's choice (see Chapter 10).

Section Recap

This section described ways that philosophers and early psychologists explained motiva-tion. First, Aristotle's four causes are analogous to four sources of motivation: efficient, final, formal, and material.

Ancient philosophers thought *hedonism* might be an explanation. Hedonism refers to the pursuit of pleasure and the avoidance of pain as averaged over the long run. According to Hobbes (1640/1962) and the concept of *incentive motivation*, positive incentives are ap-proached because they produce pleasant feelings, while negative incentives are avoided be-cause they produce unpleasant feelings. Bentham's (1789/1970) *principle of utility* describes behavior as being governed solely by the pursuit of pleasure and avoidance of pain. The util-ity of an object either increases happiness or decreases unhappiness or pain. Freud proposed his *pleasure principle*, which refers to a person's pursuit of pleasure. This pursuit was guided by his *reality principle*, which means that pleasure may have to be postponed until a later, more opportune time. Thorndike (1898) used a cat's escape from a box to provide an empirical demonstration of hedonism. From his work he formulated his *law of effect:* be-havior followed by satisfaction is stamped in while behavior followed by dissatisfaction is stamped out. Currently, the law of effect emphasizes the role of observable reinforcers to increase behavior and observable punishers to decrease behavior.

Darwin (1859/1936) was one of the originators of the *theory of evolution*, which ac-counted for the change in frequency of some physical trait. From variation among traits, the environment selected or favored some traits because they specifically aided in the organ-ism's survival. *Population thinking* emphasizes that each individual is unique, which trans-lates into individual differences in psychological needs and personality traits.

According to Spencer (1899), preferring pleasure to pain may be an attribute of liv-ing creatures that has aided their survival. *Instinct* is an inherited predisposition that has sur-vival value for the animal. It is like an internal stimulus that induces a specific pattern of behavior in a species. Freud relied on instinctual impulses residing in the unconscious to account for motivation. According to Freud, the conscious refers to awareness of thoughts and impulses that are residing in the *preconscious*, which contains thoughts, feelings, and memories. The *unconscious* is the part of one's mental apparatus that is unavailable to the individual and contains instinctual impulses, repressed thoughts, and other mental excita-tions. Anxiety- and shame-provoking impulses and thoughts are prevented from reaching the preconscious or awareness through a process known as *repression*.

Currently, *automaticity* resembles unconscious motivation in that a person is unaware of the origin of a thought, such as the origin of a goal or the associated goal-achievement behavior.

Other internal sources of motivation involve drives and primary and secondary needs. *Drive* is the internal stimulus that motivates action and remains in effect even after the instigating stimulus has been removed. *Primary needs* have a physiological basis and include the needs for air, food, water, and sex. *Secondary needs* are derived from primary needs and relate to psychological satisfaction of physiological desires but also to psychological motives, such as achievement and affiliation.

Existential concern is a very basic psychological need that centers around questioning the meaning and implications of one's life. *Incentives* are external stimuli that attract or repel (i.e., anticipated rewards or punishers). *Incentive-drive* is an important construct linking environmental and internal sources of motivation. According to this concept, incentives and drives coordinate so that the appropriate incentive satisfies the corresponding drive, like putting on a sweater alleviates feeling cold. Lewin's concept of *psychological force* ties external and internal sources of motivation together. Force becomes stronger based on the incentive valence and tension within the person but weakens as the distance of the incentive increases.

Brief History of Emotion

The word *emotion* has undergone a change in meaning regarding its reference to movement. Initially, it meant movement of a physical phenomenon. For instance, in 1692 Locke wrote of how exercise stirs the emotion of a person's blood or pulse (see the *Oxford English Dictionary*). By the 1800s *emotion* was used in reference to movement of events that were not visible but were inferred (Gillis, 1988).

The purpose of this section is to describe the views of philosophers and early psychologists on various aspects of emotion.

Emotion as Subjective Feeling

As a state of mind, the subjective "feel" of emotion has been separated from feelings produced by other bodily processes. According to the Greek philosopher Aristotle (384–322 B.C.), mixtures of pain and pleasure could arise solely from the body (such as itches and tickles) or from the body and soul (such as hunger and thirst). Emotions, however, were mixtures arising only in the soul (Fortenbaugh, 1975). For the philosopher Descartes (1649/1968), emotions were feelings but not like those resulting from environmental stimuli (such as smell, sound, or vision) or from internal stimuli (such as hunger or thirst). He also excluded feelings regarding thoughts or intentions. One of the first American psychologists to write eloquently about emotion was William James (1892), who referred to emotions' subjective part as "mind stuff" (p. 378). In fact for James, the mind stuff of emotions was our awareness of accompanying bodily symptoms. If those were somehow removed from awareness, then the only content remaining would be a cold, neutral state of intellectual perception. For example, what would grief "feel" like if tears, sobs, and "pangs in the heart" were removed? For James there would be no feeling but only a cold cognition about some terrible circumstance. As part of subjective feeling, Woodworth (1921) added the conscious awareness of the behavioral impulse that accompanies emotion. In his *The Laws of Feeling,* F. Paulhan

(1887/1930) claimed that an emotion floods consciousness, thereby directing a person's attention specifically to the experience.

Basic Emotions

The idea that there is a basic set of emotions from which all other emotions can be derived was discussed as early as 300 B.C. Greek philosophers such as Aristotle (384–322 B.C.) and Epicurus (341–271 B.C.) mentioned the basic emotions of joy, fear, envy, love, anger, and hatred, with additional emotions being combinations of these more central ones (Fortenbaugh, 1975; Long & Sedley, 1987). Much later, the 17th-century philosopher René Descartes (1649/1968) devised a similar list of six basic or primitive emotions: wonder, love, hatred, desire, joy, and sadness. In addition, he maintained that the emotion of hope stems from the desire that certain events will happen. Fear, by contrast, is the desire that certain events will not happen. Descartes also provided a possible answer as to why there are more negative than positive emotions. According to Descartes, it is more important to escape and avoid things that may destroy us than to acquire things that are beneficial but not necessary for existence. Indeed, negative emotions are signals of things that are harmful. For example, when afraid it may be wise to run away and increase the likelihood of surviving. Negative emotions can prompt beneficial action. For instance, anger may force people to stand up for their rights rather than being taken advantage of. Happiness and joy may be beneficial as well, but they are often not as important for our immediate survival. James (1892), however, disputed the value of trying to categorize emotions. He felt that it was more important to explain why events could produce physiological arousal in the individual and a variety of resulting emotions.

There was also early awareness that certain events and their cognitive interpretation triggered emotional experiences. Aristotle reasoned that the thought of imminent danger caused fear, that being unjustly insulted resulted in anger, and that the thought of disgrace brought about shame (Fortenbaugh, 1975). An example of cognitive interpretation is Aristotle's superiority theory of humor, which was also endorsed by Hobbes (1640/1962). According to this theory, laughter and amusement arise when a person perceives a prominence in him- or herself in comparison to the inferiority of other individuals (Fortenbaugh, 1975).

Emotion as Motive for Action and Thought

The impression that emotions serve as motives to push individuals into action is apparent in the writings of early Greek philosophers. Zeno (350–258 B.C.) and Chrysippus (280–206 B.C.) described emotion as providing irrational and excessive impulses (Long & Sedley, 1987). These impulses provide a push for people to act irrationally and without reason or judgments, such as when a person acts in anger and regrets it later. This idea that emotions push was continued by Descartes (1649/1968) who wrote "the principal effect of all the passions [emotions] is that they incite and dispose the mind to will the things to which they prepare the body." As Descartes illustrated, fear wills a person to flee and courage wills a person to fight. This observation by Descartes serves to tie emotions to motivation—that is, emotions are an internal source of motivation that push humans into action toward a specific aim. In one of the first psychology textbooks, Stout (1903) remarks that "the typical varieties of emotion are each connected with certain characteristic directions of conation—trends of activity" (p. 190). Later, Woodworth (1921) repeated this theme, stating that emotion is an impulse toward a specific action or certain result and not just a preparation for action in

TABLE 2.3   Stout's View of the Class of Ideas Revived by Emotions

Emotion	Idea Revived by Emotion
Joy	"success and gratification"
Grief	"loss and defeat"
Fear	"danger"
Anger	"insult and injuries"
Jealousy	"encroachment of others on . . . our own peculiar possessions"

Source: Adapted from Stout, 1903.

general. Fear is the impulse to flee from danger, while anger is the impulse to strike an of-fending person. Currently, the term **action readiness** refers to the tendency of an emotion to serve as motive for an action specific to the emotion being experienced (Arnold, 1960; Frijda, 1986, 2007). However, Margaret Washburn (1928), the first woman to receive a PhD in psychology (Scarborough, 1990), challenged this view with her concept of motor ex-plosion. This refers to nonadaptive muscular responses that occur during intense emotion. For example, "jumping for joy" is a motor explosion that seems to have no purpose. Fur-thermore, although emotion can aid thinking, it can also cause mental panic, such as hav-ing "the effect of making our brain whirl" (Washburn, 1928).

Emotion also directs thought. In *The Groundwork of Psychology*, Stout (1903) posed the consideration that emotion directs our thinking, an idea currently receiving attention from psychologists (Clore, 1994; Frijda, 1994, 2007; Niedenthal & Kitayama, 1994). According to Stout, each emotion revives a certain class of ideas that are congruent with that emotion (see Table 2.3). Thus, depression directs an individual's mind to the dark side of things, while a cheerful disposition brings forth thoughts of success and progress. When angry, one's mental meanderings encourage ideas of injury, neglect, or persecution, while fear activates thoughts of danger and insecurity.

Accompaniments of Emotion

The early view of emotion was that of a movement of events along physiological channels and facial expressions. It is as if emotions moved a person physiologically and facially, ac-cording to philosophers and early psychologists.

Physiological Arousal.   "A broken heart" is an often-used metaphor for disappointment and sadness in popular songs. The heart as the seat of emotion has had a long history. Ac-cording to Aristotle (384–322 B.C.), blood boiling around the heart causes a person to turn red with anger. "The quaking of the heart causes the whole body to quake, following the heart's motion and from this comes stammering and hesitation in speech," wrote Luis Vives in *Of the Soul and Life* (1538/1974). Descartes (1649/1968) also considered bodily mani-festations of emotion to involve changes in the heart and blood flow. The nature of the link between subjective emotions and patterns of physiological arousal began in the writings of Francis Bacon (1627/1974). For him, certain emotions produced their manifestations by arousing the body. Some examples from Descartes and Bacon of subjective emotions and accompanying physiological reactions are given in Table 2.4. For Descartes the subjective

TABLE 2.4   Ideas on the Physiological Accompaniments of Emotion of Bacon and Descartes

Emotion	Physiological Accompaniment
Fear	Paleness, trembling, hair erection, startle, screeching
Grief	Sighing, sobbing, groans, tears, distorted face, grinding of teeth
Joy	Vigor of eyes, singing, leaping, dancing, at times tears
Anger	Paleness, blushing, trembling, foaming at mouth
Lust	Flagrancy in eyes, priapism
Love	Pulse is fuller and stronger, heat in breast
Hate	Pulse is feebler and quicker; cold alternates with heat in breast
Sadness	Pulse is feeble and slow; feel constriction around heart

experience provided the body with useful information on how to act, with physiological arousal being the basis for that action. The physiologist Walter Cannon (1929/1953) later elaborated the view that arousal energizes emotional behavior (e.g., fear energizes running, and anger energizes fighting). For William James (1890/1950) bodily arousal was the source of information for the subjective experience. He maintained that an exciting event produced reflexive bodily changes. An individual's perception of these changes in consciousness is the emotion. Also writing about emotion in the same vein as James was Francis Sumner, who was the first African American in the United States to earn a PhD in psychology (Guthrie, 1998). Sumner (1924) surmised that consciousness registered an aggregate of bodily changes in order to generate an emotion. However, a person is unable to state the specific origin of these bodily changes even though they provide for a distinction among different emotions, such as love, fear, and anger. Furthermore, sometimes bodily changes are the same, such as tears of joy or of sorrow. Hence, other bodily information must be available in order for a person to feel these separate emotions.

Facial Expression.   It is difficult to conceive of emotional experiences without accompanying facial expressions. Both Bacon (1627/1974) and Descartes (1649/1968) viewed changes in facial expressions as outward signs of emotion. The social importance of these expressions was elaborated at about the same time by Marin Cureau de La Chambre (1663/1974). He felt that facial expressions of emotions were more likely to occur in the presence of others because of their effects. He reasoned that women and children are quicker to cry in order to make known their need for help when in the presence of others than when alone. Similarly, laughter is more likely to occur in a social setting and is a social instrument that acts to make our feelings known. In *The Expression of the Emotions in Man and Animals* (1873), Darwin wrote that the expression of emotion was mostly innate, although some expressions require practice on the part of the individual before they are fully developed. Darwin felt that expression serves to communicate our emotions and "reveal the thoughts and intentions of others more truly than do words" (p. 366). A current debate regarding the relationship between emotion and facial expression is described in Chapter 14. One view is that facial expressions are like indicator dials reflecting our internal subjective emotions (Buck, 1984). Another view is that facial expressions serve more as signals to others to satisfy social motives (Fridlund, 1991a, 1992). For example, a sad face means "help me," while an angry face means "don't mess with me."

Current Trends. According to William James (1884/1948), an emotion is synonymous with the subjective awareness of bodily actions. Also, each shade of emotion would have a unique bodily reverberation or its own profile of physiological responses. James's theory led to a long history of research trying to demonstrate the parallel between emotional feelings, on the one hand, and specific activity of the nervous system, on the other. In an early experiment along these lines, Ax (1953) frightened and angered his participants while simultaneously recording heart rate, respiration, face and hand temperature, and electrodermal (skin conductance) responses. The results were promising for James's theory. Ax discovered different physiological profiles for anger and fear. Nevertheless, in spite of this early promise, 50 years and many experiments later, psychologists have concluded that discrete emotions "cannot be fully differentiated by visceral activity alone" (Cacioppo et al., 2000, p. 184). Yet the search continues for the parallel between subjective emotional feelings and bodily responses.

The search, however, has shifted from the body to the brain. A current research strategy is that with the aid of brain imaging technology, attempts are made to identify brain maps that correspond to emotional feelings. The brain map of an emotion would correspond to areas in which there is greater activity, such as oxygen and glucose use. Brain imaging technology is starting to uncover sites that are relevant for processing emotion stimuli that lead to different emotional feelings and accompanying behavior (Barrett & Wager, 2006; Damasio, 2003; Murphy et al., 2003; Phan et al., 2002, 2004; Wager et al., 2003). Perhaps eventually, neuroscientists will discover that each emotional experience will have a unique brain map as James had imagined would be the case with physiological response profiles.

Section Recap

Initially, emotion meant observable movement but later it came to mean the unobserved movement of feelings. Currently an emotion consists of the integration of affective feelings, physiological arousal, behavior, and facial expressions. Early philosophers and psychologists formulated a list of basic emotions which, like today, involves more negative than positive emotions. Each emotion was thought to have an accompanying physiological profile but also a set of accompanying thoughts. The appraisal of certain situations was linked to specific emotions. Aristotle and Hobbes, for example, felt that appraising ourselves as superior to others produced amusement and laughter. There are two early interpretations of physiological arousal: providing information for the subjective feel of emotion (according to James) and serving as a readiness for action (according to Cannon). In fact, for philosophers emotion provided an impulse to action or a motive for action. The term *action readiness* means that emotions yield tendencies to act in a manner distinctive of a particular emotion in order to fulfill the aim of the emotion. Facial expressions have been interpreted as a way of making our feelings or social intentions known to others. Finally, although each emotion does not have a specific physiological profile, researchers are looking for maps of activated neurons in the brain that would correspond to emotional feelings.

A C T I V I T I E S

1. According to Socrates (470–399 B.C.), the right choice is one where pleasure exceeds pain. The reason for making the wrong choice is a lack of knowledge. Regret is an example of a wrong choice: pain exceeds pleasure. A person believes initially that her actions will result in more pleasure than pain; when she discovers that pain exceeds pleasure, she experiences regret. Discuss with a fellow student any of your actions that resulted in regret.

   a. Did regret occur because pleasure was less than expected, or because pain was greater than expected?

   b. Based on your analysis, would you behave the same way again? Explain.

   c. In order to "know" the pain and pleasure of one's actions, is it necessary to feel those sensations?

   d. Do you think some people have problems with the law because they do not know or foresee the consequences of their actions?

2. Does your unconscious play while you sleep? Try recording your dreams for several nights in a row. Train yourself to wake up after you have been dreaming for several minutes. Immediately after waking, record your dream on a tape recorder or on a notepad. After analyzing several dreams, do you think Freud was correct that your manifest dream is just a reworking of some latent dream message?

PART TWO

Biological Properties
of Motivation

Does the makeup of the human body and mind determine what is motivating? In 1748, the Frenchman La Mettrie published his book *Man a Machine*, which introduced the idea that the human body is a machine. This machine, however, is different because it has self-awareness/consciousness. Chapter 3 (Evolutionary Antecedents of Motivation) examines how the machine progressed to its current form. The human body evolved because it became the best solution for problems of survival. As a result of evolution, humans possess motives and values that are geared toward survival. Motives and values include what we prefer for the beginning and the maintenance of interpersonal relationships, for what we fear, the foods we prefer, even the music we enjoy. These preferences emerge in consciousness as likes and dislikes, which motivate behaviors.

Hedonism motivates beneficial behavior, but can it also explain behavior that is detrimental to a person? Chapter 4 (Addictions and Addictive Behaviors) assumes that pleasure is the reward provided by the natural environment for behaviors that benefit survival. However, we have learned to enhance these pleasures by artificial means with psychoactive drugs like nicotine and alcohol and activities like gambling. Addictive behaviors are examples of natural motivation gone awry. Pleasures designed to reward behaviors necessary for survival are now enjoyed for their own sake to the point of being detrimental to our health.

If the body is a machine, then what motivates a person to keep it in good condition? Chapter 5 (Homeostasis: Temperature, Thirst, Hunger, and Eating) states that sources inside and outside a person provide the motivation for the maintenance of the body. Internally, unpleasant feelings of hot or cold, thirst or hunger motivate behaviors to reduce those feelings. Externally, incentives like food, especially sweets and fats, and clothes for temperature control also prompt motivation. The incentive value of food can be so strong, however, that people eat to obesity while others shun it to the point of emaciation (anorexia).

Is behavior always performed as efficiently as possible? Or does efficiency depend on the level of body arousal? Chapter 6 (Behavior, Arousal, and Affective Valence) examines how the body's degree of arousal determines the efficiency of behavior. Physiological arousal that is too low or too high is associated with poor performance; intermediate arousal is best. Arousal is also associated with the pleasantness of affect. Arousal is most pleasant at middle intensities; too little arousal is akin to boredom and too much arousal is distressing. Arousal comes from stimulus novelty, incongruity, and complexity as found in humor, music, and suspenseful films.

Finally, can the body as machine have too many demands placed on it? Chapter 7 (Stress, Coping, and Health) shows that if the demands for motivation are too many or too intense, then the machine does not fare well. It breaks down both physically by getting sick and psychologically by worry, anxiety, tension, and unhappiness. Appraisal, social support, and personality traits, however, can intervene between a demand and its potential negative impact. Also, a person can deal directly with the stressor through problem-focused coping or with the stress through emotion-focused coping.

CHAPTER

3

Evolutionary Antecedents of Motivation

Human nature is the same all over the world, but its operations are so varied by education and habit that one must see it in all its dresses in order to be entirely acquainted with it.

—Lord Chesterfield, 1747

Human action can be modified to some extent, but human nature cannot be changed.

—Abraham Lincoln, 1809–1865

■ In reading this chapter, keep the following questions in mind. They concern universal dispositions, which are characteristic of all people and which play a role in motivating certain behaviors.

1. What is human nature, and how does it relate to motivation and emotion?
2. Are there dispositions or universal motives that apply to all humans?
3. What are the evolutionary and social characteristics for mate preferences, reproductive behavior, and jealousy?
4. What is the contribution of evolution to fear?
5. How did food preferences evolve?
6. Why do people the world over enjoy music?

Evolution of Universal Motives

Where in a person's past is the motivational origin of his or her behavior? By way of analogy, what caused the fall of the last domino pictured in Figure 3.1? Notice that some event must have toppled the first domino, which eventually led to the fall of the last one. Is the cause the domino prior to the last one or the one prior to it and so on back to the initial event? In the case of a person's current behavior, is the motivation in the recent past like the fall of an immediately preceding domino or in the remote past like the very first domino? Now imagine a man and woman of average height dancing together. First, the man most likely is taller than the woman. This height difference reflects our evolutionary history, which is analogous to the fall of the early dominos. In addition, our imaginary couple is taller today than they would have been a century ago. This increased height is part of our personal history during which more nutritious food became available (Floud et al., 1990)

49

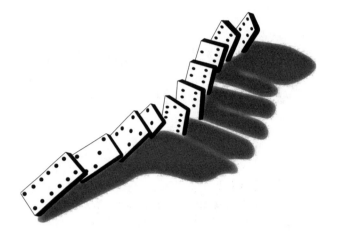

FIGURE 3.1 A Metaphor for Evolutionary and Personal History. The toppling of the initial dominoes represents evolutionary history, which topple later dominoes that represent personal history. The 10th or last domino represents motivated behavior in the present.

and is analogous to the fall of later dominos. In other words, the current height of men and women resulted from the interaction between our evolutionary and personal past. Although determined in the past, men and women's current height has an effect on their current behaviors. For example, during conversation women might gaze slightly upward while men gaze downward, women pass more easily through small doorways while men must stoop, and women may need a stool to reach the top shelf that men can reach flat footed. In addition, compared to a century ago, today's beds are longer, clothes are bigger, and doorways are higher all because of our increased height. Just as these differences in height affect certain behaviors, so too other unspecified characteristics affect behavior. For example, if the couple were ballroom dancing, then the man would lead and the woman would follow.

The purpose of this section is to describe how our evolutionary history and our personal history interact to affect motivation and emotion. There will be an emphasis on the uniformity of certain motives despite the variety of environmental and cultural situations in which people live.

Evolutionary History and Personal History

Just as human evolutionary history has shaped the difference in height between men and women, it has also shaped psychological characteristics that determine what does and does not motivate people.

Evolutionary history as a source of motivation focuses on what behaviors humans have in common in spite of vast social and cultural differences. For instance, all humans have brains and faces, but each brain and face is different. All humans are motivated by incentives, but the same incentive does not motivate everyone. All humans laugh and cry, but what triggers these behaviors may differ among humans. **Human nature** refers to the behavioral, motivational, and emotional similarity among people that results from their common evolutionary history. It is their disposition to behave in a particular fashion, depending on the situation. Human nature is most striking when similarities occur in spite of environmental and cultural differences. It is shaped by natural selection and is genetically transmitted from one generation to the next. It is universal, which means it is the same in societies all over the world. Finally, the behavioral expression of human nature tends to be innate—that is, it is influenced little by experience. The term **universal motives** will be reserved for the commonality of motives amoeng humans that has evolved over their evolutionary history. For example, this term refers to the commonality in what motivates sexual behavior, fear, food preferences, and music enjoyment.

Evolutionary and Personal History Interact. Evolutionary history created human nature, which in turn interacts with our personal history much like the fall of later dominoes depend on the fall of earlier ones (Figure 3.1). The interaction between evolutionary history and personal history is another way of stating that the interaction between heredity (nature) and environment (nurture) motivates behavior. The nature of this interaction was recognized more than 125 years ago by Sir Francis Galton (1883). He claimed that it was difficult to distinguish between that part of human character that results from education and circumstances and that which results from the human constitution. Today, it is accepted that both heredity and environment interact to determine behavior (Plomin et al., 2001).

The relative contribution of heredity and environment is different for various behaviors. Some behaviors are genetically disposed to occur and thus require little environmental experience. Other behaviors are genetically neutral and require much environmental experience to occur. For instance, learning to eat is almost automatic, whereas it takes a lot of practice to master long division. The interaction between heredity and environment in motivating behavior is illustrated in Figure 3.2 by a series of rectangles (Plomin et al., 2001). A rectangle's length and width both contribute to its area, since Area = Length × Width, although the relative contribution of each may vary. Similarly, heredity and environment both contribute to behavior, but their relative contributions may also vary. Changes in the contribution of heredity and environment are illustrated by

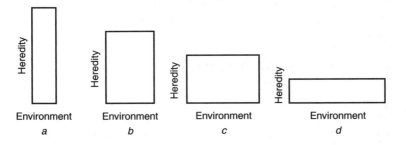

FIGURE 3.2   Relative Contributions of Heredity and Environment. Length and width both contribute to the area of a rectangle, since Area = Length × Width. The relative contribution of length decreases, and width increases from *a* to *d,* yet both length and width still contribute to the total area of each rectangle. Similarly, heredity and environment both contribute to the motivation of behavior. The relative contribution of heredity decreases and that of environment increases from *a* to *d,* yet both heredity and environment still contribute to the motivation of behavior.

rectangles *a* through *d* in Figure 3.2: the contribution of length (heredity) decreases, and the contribution of width (environment) increases. Although the change from rectangle *a* to rectangle *d* represents a decrease in heredity and an increase in environment, both heredity and environment contribute to behavior. Behaviors that are strongly influenced by heredity (rectangle *a*) are known as *innate,* which means not taught or not benefitting from experience.

It is important to remember, however, that heredity can influence behavior in more than one way. First, inherited physical features affect a person's behavior, such as the relationship between the thumb and fingers. How difficult would it be to write, tie a ribbon, or grasp a ball without the use of either a thumb or fingers? Or consider how size and strength differences between men and women contribute to a general division of labor. Men, on average, are bigger and physically stronger and so tend to do heavy work, such as farming, mining, and construction. Women, on average, are smaller and have less muscle mass and so tend to do lighter work, such as cooking and clerical tasks. Second, the hereditary nature, or innateness, of certain feelings or motives disposes humans to react in one way rather than another to various stimuli. The influence of these seemingly innate feelings becomes apparent in the prevalence of sexual behavior, certain fears, a baby's taste preferences, and the universal pleasure of music.

Experience and Motives.   As the rectangles in Figure 3.2 illustrate, even behaviors that appear to be totally innate may actually require at least some minimal environmental experience in order to occur (rectangle *a*). Other behaviors require the benefit of additional experiences (rectangles *b* through *d*). To illustrate, we might think of walking as being innate, but some prior experience in sitting upright and crawling appears necessary for walking to occur in a timely manner (Dennis, 1960). Other examples of behaviors that occur with little experience are an infant's crying to indicate hunger or distress. This behavior is fairly complete immediately following birth. As new parents quickly learn, their baby requires little if any practice at this activity. Facial reactions to taste stimuli also seem to be in place in the first few hours of an infant's life. Little practice, if any, is needed to indicate whether something is tasty or awful (Menella & Beauchamp, 1998; Steiner, 1977).

Finally, an individual's innate disposition and personal experience usually operate in tandem, which happens for example in the development of gender roles. Thus, infants identified as girls and boys are nurtured along feminine and masculine roles, respectively.

Evolutionary Psychology

Human minds are not blank slates at birth upon which experience begins to write. Neither are minds passive recipients of experience. Instead, human minds have been shaped by evolution to adapt to their environment. Our evolutionary past interacts with people's experiences to determine current motivation. This interaction is the view of evolutionary psychology, which analyzes universal motives in the context of evolution. According to evolutionary psychology, **psychological mechanisms** have evolved through natural selection to solve specific problems of adaptation to the environment (Buss, 1995, 1999, 2005). Several of these psychological mechanisms are represented by universal motives. Fear of snakes, for instance, evolved to motivate behavior to escape or avoid such dangerous creatures. Food preferences for sugar and fat evolved to ensure a person liked food that provided sufficient calories. Women evolved a preference for mates who had the economic resources to provide for them and their children. Male attraction to beauty and desire for sexual variety evolved to ensure the selection of fertile mates and to motivate the seeking of more sexual partners. The function of male sexual jealousy developed to increase a man's confidence regarding the paternity of his children. Each human motive can be considered an instance of a psychological mechanism that evolved because it aided humans in adapting to their environment.

> ➤ To learn more about evolutionary psychology go to http://www.psych.ucsb.edu/research/cep/

Universal Motives.   For a motive to be considered universal it must occur in all countries and cultures of the world even though it might be expressed differently. Different geographical regions, climates, societies, cultures, and customs exist around the world. These differences produce differences in the foods people eat, in social customs, and in educational practices. In spite of these geographical, climatic, and societal differences, universal motivation and behavior are presumably the same for food, custom, and learning. The existence of universal needs or motives was noted by the anthropologist Bronislaw Malinowski (1941), who derived a list of basic needs that he believed existed in societies all around the world. The existence of these needs pushed cultures into ways of satisfying them, although the manner by which this was accomplished varied from culture to culture. Thus, the need for food was satisfied by hunting, gathering, and today a sophisticated system of farming, ranching, and the commerce of bringing food to market. Other bodily needs such as sex, physical comfort, and safety resulted in marriage, shelter, health practices, and systems of laws and justice.

Brown (1991) uses the term *universals* to describe traits that are found in almost all cultures and societies the world over. Some items in his list can be categorized together for their relevance to universal motives and universally valued incentives (see Table 3.1). Emotional behaviors seem to predominate the list as reflected by the presence of fears, emotions, and their accompanying facial expressions. The social nature of human motives is

TABLE 3.1   Categories of Universal Motives

Universal Motive/Incentive	Characteristics
Aesthetics:	art, hygiene, music, standards of beauty
Control environment:	fire, mood altering substances, shelter, tools
Emotions:	anger, contempt, disgust, fear, happy, sad, surprise
Facial expressions:	for emotions, for communication, and are modifiable
Fears:	loud noises, snakes, strangers in childhood
Goal setting:	predict and plan for the future
Self-concept:	self as subject, object, and different from other person
Sexual interactions:	attraction, sexual jealousy, and regulation
Social milieu:	live in social units, rights, obligations of membership, and status

Source: Based on *Human Universals* by D. E. Brown, 1991, Chapter 6.

exhibited in categories of sexual interactions and the social milieu. Universals with external characteristics express themselves in terms of controlling the environment and setting goals, which contribute to the prevention and alleviation of stress. Universals that seem more removed from human biology are beliefs about aesthetics and concepts about the self. The universal motive categories in Table 3.1 are taken for granted. We forget that entire institutions and customs have developed in order to satisfy these motives or attain these valued incentives in today's societies.

Inherited Structures for Behavior, Motives, and Emotions.   How can universal motives, such as fear or food preferences, evolve and pass on to succeeding generations? They do so by way of natural selection (see Chapter 2), which operates at the level of the individual. In turn, an individual's genes transmit universal motives to the next generation (Mayr, 2001). **Genes** are those parts of a person's DNA content that provide the information necessary for the construction of proteins, which form the building blocks of the various neurophysiological structures that make up the brain and nervous system. Humans receive one-half of their genes from each parent at conception. At this time the sperm containing the male's genetic information unites with the ovum (egg), which contains the female's genetic information. The resulting combination contains information from each parent, which in turn came from their parents, and so on. Our genes or our genetic past do not influence motivation or behavior directly. Genes provide the information for the building of proteins that are used to create "the skeletal system, muscles, the endocrine system, the immune system, the digestive system, and most important for behavior, the nervous system" (Plomin et al., 2001, p. 47). To say that genes or heredity influence behavior is really a shorthand way of stating that genes are the recipes for various proteins, which in turn produce neurophysiological systems that determine the particular reaction to environmental stimulation (Plomin et al., 2001). Thus, the seeming genetic inheritance of motives or psychological mechanisms simply means that the brain or body appears sensitive to the stimuli evoking or satisfying those motives. For example, different neurons in the tongue and brain react to sweet and bitter stimuli such that infants prefer sweet taste. Genes carry the information for how the tongue's neurons and the brain's structure are constructed. At a more global level, however, it appears that variation and selection occur at the level of behavior. After all, behavioral and environmental events are visible, while genes are not; only their end results are visible.

Section Recap

The motivation for current behavior has its roots in our evolutionary and personal history. Evolutionary history refers to a person's genetic makeup or nature, and personal history is the person's experiences or nurture. Both nature and nurture contribute to what motivates behavior just as length and width both contribute to the area of a rectangle. Usually tendencies that are part of human nature operate in tandem with personal experiences as in the development of gender roles. Evolutionary history created *human nature*, which encompasses all the behavioral, motivational, and emotional characteristics that all people have in common despite different environmental and cultural differences. Evolutionary psychology supposes that part of human nature consists of *psychological mechanisms*, which have evolved to solve problems of adaptation to the environment. Universal motives are psychological mechanisms that refer to similarities in what motivates people, such as a set of basic needs, valued incentives, and social interactions. Societies developed in order to satisfy universals, which are traits found the world over such as fears, emotions, facial expressions, environmental control, goal setting, and beliefs about aesthetics and the self.

Genes are DNA segments that provide information from each parent on how to build the child's neurophysiological structures. These structures, in turn, are the physical basis for psychological mechanisms or universal motives that, according to evolutionary psychology, evolved to meet environmental problems that humans faced in their evolutionary past.

Universal Motives of Sex, Fear, Food, and Music

Much like early dominoes caused the fall of the final domino, natural selection operating in the evolutionary past caused the development of psychological mechanisms and universal motives. These universal motives in turn are satisfied in the current environment. This section examines four major categories of evolved universal motives. One is the motive for sexual behavior in the context of short- and long-term relationships. A second is the motive to prefer certain basic foods and reject others. A third motive concerns the survival value of fear and the stimuli that humans avoid as a consequence. Finally, there is the puzzle of music. Why do people the world over enjoy music? These motives from our evolutionary past push individuals to seek satisfaction, which is achieved in their environment.

Selecting a Mate

"They stroke, kiss, nip, nuzzle, pat, tap, lick, tug, or playfully chase this chosen one. Some sing. Some whinny. Some squeak, croak, or bark. Some dance. Some strut. Some preen. Some chase. Most play" (Fisher, 2004, p. 27). In her book *Why We Love*, Fisher gives many behavioral examples of various animals engaging in behaviors that we can anthropomorphize as romantic love. In addition to this love play, animals, like humans, exhibit a choosiness and do not mate indiscriminately with members of the other sex. A further similarity is that animals, like humans, appear possessive and guard their mates closely as if they are motivated by jealousy. This section examines what factors determine mate choice in humans and how jealousy affects human relationships.

The point of natural selection is to ensure survival and longevity. However, living a long time because of natural selection may benefit an individual but may not benefit the species. For a species to receive the benefits of natural selection, adaptive traits must be passed on to succeeding generations. This requires short- and long-term cooperation between men and women. Short-term cooperation is required for sexual intercourse that leads to conception, and long-term cooperation is necessary for care of any infants. Consequently, a major area of interest in evolutionary psychology concerns the establishment and maintenance of human relationships. In terms of pull motivation, what characteristics do men and women look for or select in the other sex to establish a relationship and what do they look for or select to maintain that relationship?

Darwin (1859/1936) used the term **sexual selection** to refer to the "struggle between males for possession of the females; the result is not death to the unsuccessful competitor, but few or no offspring" (p. 88). The male could be very aggressive and fight off all other males, thereby having a harem of females all to himself. However, if he could not be the most aggressive then maybe he could be the most charming and attract the most females in that manner. In such cases, the female acts as the selecting agent because it is what she likes about the male that determines whether she allows him to mate with her. For example, the number of copulations performed by a peacock correlates positively with the number of eyespots he has on his train of tail feathers. The greater the number of eyespots, the more likely a peahen is to consent to copulation (Petrie et al., 1991).

➤ Pictures of a peacock's tail feather display to a peahen are at http://www.pbase.com/ lesliej/peafowl

Mate Value.   The possession of characteristics that are desired by the other sex defines a person's **mate value.** The higher your mate value, the greater your appeal. The *Mate Value Inventory* in Table 3.2 is one way to measure one's self-perceived physical attractiveness and psychological characteristics that may be valued by the other sex (Kirsner et al., 2003). Notice that a person's mate value consists of physical features, psychological characteristics, and a value system. Physical features are immediately noticeable in a person but fade with time and are ones to which the other person habituates. Psychological characteristics, however, take time to discover and are less likely to fade. Finally, when interests and values are shared, it increases people's attraction to each other.

Facial attractiveness is one physical indicator of mate value in Table 3.2 that is of great interest to evolutionary psychologists (Rhodes, 2006). What makes a face attractive to the other sex? One feature is that a more attractive face is more symmetrical, which means the right and left half of a face match up. Another feature is that an attractive face also represents the average of many facial configurations that occur in the population. It is a face that has average lip, eye, and nose size, for example. A final feature that contributes to facial attractiveness is sexual dimorphism, which refers to differences in the form or structure between men and women. More attractive male faces show greater masculinity and more attractive female faces show greater femininity (Rhodes, 2006).

If facial and physical attractiveness are determinants of mate value, then one obvious question is whether increases in attractiveness do indeed increase one's chances of attracting a mate. Rhodes and coresearchers (2005) investigated this question in an Australian sample of men and women. As a measure of success in attracting a mate, the researchers asked the

TABLE 3.2   Mate Value Inventory

Describe yourself as accurately as possible on the traits listed below. Use the following scale:

extremely low on this trait = −3 −2 −1 0 +1 +2 +3 = extremely high on this trait

Ambitious _____	Faithful to partner _____	Kind & understanding _____
Attractive face _____	Financially secure _____	Loyal _____
Attractive body _____	Good sense of humor _____	Responsible _____
Desire for children _____	Generous _____	Shares my values _____
Emotionally stable _____	Healthy _____	Shares my interests _____
Enthusiastic about sex _____	Independent _____	Sociable _____

Note: To compute your mate value, sum your scores on all of the items. The total score reflects the amount of a person's mate value.

Source: Adapted from "Self, Friends, and Lovers: Structural Relations among Beck Depression Inventory Scores and Perceived Mate Values" by B. R. Kirsner et al., 2003, *Journal of Affective Disorders, 75,* pp. 135, 147.

individuals to report their number of sexual partners, age of first intercourse, and the length of each relationship. The photos of the participants were rated for attractiveness, sexual dimorphism, averageness, and symmetry by a separate group of people. Do these indicators of physical attractiveness correlate with sexual experience? The results showed that they did. Individuals with higher physical mate values had more relationship experiences. Men with attractive faces and attractive and masculine bodies had more sexual partners and also became sexually active at an earlier age. Women with attractive faces became sexually active at an earlier age and had more relationships that exceeded 12 months. The results provide some evidence that as one's mate value increases, the likelihood of attracting others also increases.

> ➤ Research on attractiveness can be found at http://www.beautycheck.de/english

Good Genes Hypothesis.   It is probably safe to state that both women and men prefer attractive partners. But what is the reason for this preference? One answer is that attractiveness is a universally valued incentive that arose during our evolutionary past as a result of sexual selection. The member of the other sex selects an attractive individual based on the assumption that attractiveness signals genes for health, fertility, and intelligence according to the **good genes hypothesis.** A person with an attractive face presumably has genes for high intelligence, health, a good immune system, and for potentially good parenting skills (Rhodes, 2006). Consequently, if a person selects an attractive long-term mate, then they will produce more offspring, who are more intelligent, healthy, and have the benefit of good parents. Their children would have an increased chance of survival. However, evidence that attractiveness signals health, for example, has been difficult to establish partly because modern medicine and grooming practices obscure a person's attractiveness and hence any relationship with health (Weeden & Sabini, 2005).

An inverse to the good genes hypothesis is that individuals reject those people whose physical appearance suggests the possibility of bad genes—that is, genes that signal potential disease and low intelligence (Zebrowitz & Rhodes, 2004). The emphasis is on rejecting people, not attracting them. Zebrowitz and Rhodes (2004) tested this hypothesis with longitudinal data from individuals for whom facial photos, intelligence test scores, and health indicators were available at ages 10, 11–15, 17, and 30–40 years. The photos were rated for facial quality, such as attractiveness, symmetry, averageness, and sexual dimorphism. The individuals were also judged for intelligence and health on the basis of their photos. In order to examine whether people with unattractive faces are rejected, the researchers divided the photos at the median based on attractiveness. Individuals categorized below the median were judged as less attractive at all ages, had less facial symmetry, and male faces showed less masculinity. The researchers reasoned that if facial attractiveness correlates with health and intelligence, it is likely to be exhibited in faces below the median. In other words, to be selected as a mate one must possess a face with a minimal level of attractiveness, which would indicate some minimal level of health and intelligence. The results showed a positive correlation between facial attractiveness, intelligence, and health, but only for individuals whose faces were below the median. For these faces, as rated attractiveness decreased, judgments of the individuals' health and intelligence decreased correspondingly. This relationship was also true when actual indicators of health and intelligence were used: faces with lower attractiveness were associated with poorer health and lower intelligence. Thus, according to the bad genes hypothesis, people avoid mating with individuals who have extremely poor physical appearance or low facial attractiveness. In regard to sexual selection, it is not that people are pulled toward a face with high mate value but instead are repelled by one with poor mate value—that is, one that signals poor health and low intelligence.

Universality of Beauty and Health.   Facial attractiveness evolved through sexual selection. Consequently, the basis of attractiveness and its relationship to health is assumed to be universal and not culturally specific. This claim is based on research that has resulted in several convincing conclusions (Langlois et al., 2000). First, people agree on who is beautiful and who is not within their culture. Second, people agree on the standards of beauty for faces in cultures other than their own. Third, people agree on the degree of attractiveness among children. Presumably, then, the association between an evolved set of features and physical health or intelligence should be similar everywhere. For example, a runny nose and watery eyes that are linked to a cold would be assumed to be unattractive compared to the same face when a person does not have a cold. However, there may be instances of cultural standards of beauty that are not linked to health. For example, thinness in women is associated with beauty and health, although extreme thinness is associated with poor health (Weeden & Sabini, 2005).

Sex Differences in Long-Term Mate Selection.   Once mates are selected and relationships are formed, then the birth of offspring and parenthood is frequently the next step. Thus, other aspects of mate value besides physical beauty are important for relationships. These aspects are important because evolutionary success is based on leaving the most number of surviving offspring. Furthermore, the biological differences between men and women determine what mate values are important. What are these differences?

First, men and women differ in the time investment they make in their offspring (D. M. Buss, 1989). After sexual intercourse, a woman invests an additional 38 weeks as the baby develops so that at birth the woman already has invested much more time in the child than the man. In addition, since she can produce many fewer children than a man, it is more important that a woman help each child that is born to survive; by doing so, she increases her reproductive success. Since a man is capable of having innumerable children, he may not invest as heavily in each individual child as a woman would. He increases his reproductive success by having intercourse with as many women as possible, thereby conceiving many children. Thus, the strategies a woman employs to ensure the survival of her children and hence the perpetuation of her genes is different than the strategies a man employs for the perpetuation of his genes. Consequently, we would expect a woman to look for characteristics in a man that indicate greater commitment and help in raising children. Men should prefer characteristics related to reproductive value, such as a woman's physical health and youth. In mating with a fertile woman a man can maximize his reproductive success by having many children with her (D. M. Buss, 1989).

This difference in what men and women value in long-term mates is assumed to have universal appeal and has led evolutionary psychologists to concentrate on three mate-value characteristics: good financial prospect, ambition and industriousness, and good looks (D. M. Buss, 1989). If differences in sexual preferences among men and women are universal, then ratings of these characteristics should differ in societies all over the world. This is exactly what D. M. Buss (1989) attempted to show by surveying men and women in 37 different countries. Figure 3.3 shows the results of six different countries: Japan, India,

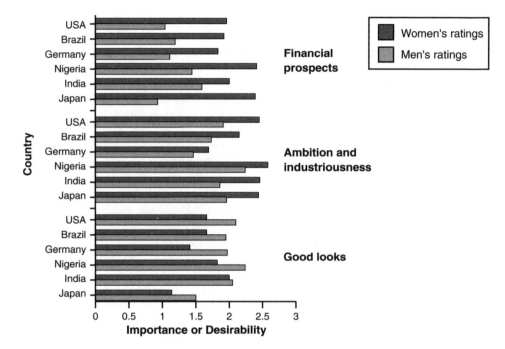

FIGURE 3.3 Preferences for Mate Characteristics. *Top:* The importance of good financial prospects in a long-term mate was rated more important by women than by men. *Middle:* The importance of ambition and industriousness in a long-term mate was rated more important by women than by men. *Bottom:* The importance of good looks in a long-term mate was rated more important by men than by women. There is no significant difference regarding the importance of good looks between men and women sampled in India.

Source: Adapted from "Sex Differences in Human Mate Preferences" by D. M. Buss, 1989, *Behavioral and Brain Sciences, 12,* table 2, p. 6 (top); table 3, p. 7 (middle); table 5, p. 10 (bottom).

Nigeria, Germany, Brazil, and the United States. These countries were selected for display because they seem culturally diverse.

Figure 3.3 (top) shows that in all countries women rate "good financial prospect" as more important in a mate than men rate it. Figure 3.3 (middle) shows that women rate "ambition and industriousness" more important than men rate them. These characteristics are good ones for a woman to look for if she expects her mate to be mature enough to commit to the relationship and to be a good provider of material things necessary for family life. Figure 3.3 (bottom) shows that men rate "good looks" to be more important than women consider them when searching for a long-term mate. If young age and good looks are considered signs of health and fertility, then men consider these important because they imply that the woman is capable of producing many children.

Maintaining Relationships

Once a relationship is established, then what motivates processes that promote conception and maintenance of the relationship? This section examines the function of sexual pleasure and jealousy in these matters.

Function of Sexual Pleasure.   What motivates sexual intercourse, which is necessary for conception? It is as a result of intercourse that the male sperm unites with the female egg, which may eventually lead to conception and eventually the birth of a baby. However, animals or people might well consider sexual intercourse as requiring too much effort or time or as being too dangerous if there were not some kind of immediate reward. Orgasm is that reward; it is the incentive and reinforcer for sexual intercourse (Gould, 1987). For males, the pleasure of orgasm is usually always associated with ejaculation, at which time semen and sperm are expelled from the penis. Even though men may achieve orgasm close to 100% of the time during sexual intercourse, women experience orgasm much less frequently. In a summary of 32 published reports, Lloyd (2005, p. 36) concludes that as a result of sexual intercourse 25% of women always have orgasm, 55% have it more than half the time, 23% sometimes do, 33% rarely or never do, and 5–10% never do. Thus, although men are reinforced consistently for sexual intercourse, the reward for women is inconsistent, which may be the reason why the value of orgasm for women has been pondered more extensively (Lloyd, 2005; Symons, 1979). Several interpretations have been proposed to account for female orgasm.

One interpretation is based on a functional view of evolution, which holds that all body parts must be accounted for in terms of their survival value. This view encounters difficulty in explaining, for example, why men have nipples, which have no function. Another view, however, is that not all body parts have survival value and are merely by-products of the evolution of some other part. In this view, male nipples might be considered the by-products of the evolution of female nipples, which are necessary for nursing children (Gould, 1987). Following this way of thinking, natural selection resulted in the development of the penis as the organ for sexual intercourse and orgasm. Although orgasm is highly pleasurable for women, the clitoris is not the result of natural selection but is instead an evolutionary by-product of the development of the penis (Gould, 1987). In other words, while the penis has an adaptive function, the clitoris does not. According to Gould (1987), the clitoris and penis developed out of the same homologous anatomical structure. At the tenth week of fetal development, for example, the clitoris and penis look very much alike (Van De Graaff, 1988). Eventually, the penis becomes larger and capable of consistently producing orgasm as a reward for ejaculation, while the clitoris remains a nonadaptive by-product of the development of the penis.

Not everyone accepts this view, of course, and several interpretations have been proposed to account for the clitoris and female orgasm. One such interpretation is that female orgasm is very important because it helps promote pregnancy. Since orgasm is pleasurable, it encourages a woman to seek sexual intercourse, especially with a man who can help her achieve it, thereby increasing the chances of pregnancy (Alcock, 1987; Fisher, 1992; Levin, 1992). A woman's orgasm signals her satisfaction to a man, thereby assuring him that she is less likely to seek sexual intercourse with another man (Fisher, 1992; Rancour-Laferriere, 1983). This information increases his confidence that he is the father of any children. Much like a big meal, orgasm also has a satiating effect in that a woman remains calm and in a prone position, which may also increase her chances of conception (Fisher, 1992). Finally, the mechanical action of orgasm itself may increase the likelihood of pregnancy by promoting the transfer of sperm from the vagina into the uterus. The timing of orgasm is also important, as discovered by Baker and Bellis (1993). They found that a woman retained the most sperm when she climaxed any time between one minute before the man ejaculated and up to 45 minutes afterward. The lack of orgasm or one that occurred more than one minute before the man ejaculated resulted in a much lower level of sperm retention.

Even though women might not attain orgasm during sexual intercourse, they still enjoy it because it provides excitement and feelings of intimacy and closeness with their male partners (Lloyd, 2005). Thus, another interpretation for the pleasure of sex is that it is associated with the development of a relatively strong lasting relationship or pair bond (Symons, 1979). This relationship is important, because by remaining together the couple can jointly raise any children that result and thus increase the chances of the children's survival. A couple that parts soon after sexual intercourse will greatly decrease the likelihood of any child from that union surviving. Feelings of sexual arousal and orgasm contribute to pair bonding and the accompanying emotion of *romantic love*. This emotion is characterized by intense attraction to another person, often involving strong sexual desires. Jankowiak and Fischer (1992) consulted ethnographic files of 166 societies from around the world. In 88.5% of these societies they were able to document the occurrence of romantic love, implying that this emotion is universal among humans.

Romantic love and sexual desire are strongly associated in the minds of women and men (Regan & Berscheid, 1999). The presence of one feeling corresponds to the presence of the other. For example, Regan and coresearchers (1998) had men and women university students list those features that they felt defined romantic love. The second-highest-ranked feature of romantic love was sexual desire, which was listed by almost 66% of the respondents. To expand on this connection, Regan (2000) asked 25 heterosexual dating couples to rate the amount of sexual desire and passionate love they felt for their partners. Partners were also asked how frequently in the past week they thought of ending their relationships, starting new ones, or had actually cheated (infidelity). Analyses of the ratings indicated that those individuals who felt the greatest amount of sexual desire for their partners also disclosed the most passionate love. In addition, these individuals were also less likely to have thoughts of ending their relationships, starting new ones, or having cheated. In conclusion, orgasm has been naturally selected as the reinforcer for sexual intercourse, at least in men, and increases the chances of pregnancy in women. It also promotes the development of pair bonds and, along with sexual desire, enhances the development of romantic love.

Guarding Relationships. However, a relationship can end as a result of external factors. It can end through death but also from desertion, especially when someone has stolen one's partner. **Mate poaching** refers to the attempt to attract someone who is already in a romantic relationship in order to form either a short-term or long-term relationship with the poached individual (Schmitt et al., 2004). Mate poaching occurs worldwide based on a survey of nearly 17,000 mostly college students from North and South America; Western, Eastern, and Southern Europe; the Middle East; Africa; Oceania; and South, Southeast, and East Asia. In the survey, nearly 60% of men and 40% of women have reported attempts at poaching. In addition, men are more likely than women to succumb to the temptations of short-term poaching. Thus, individuals who are currently in a romantic relationship need to be on guard for potential poachers. Perhaps the necessity for a guard against poachers was the evolutionary reason for jealousy.

Jealousy. Known as the "green eyed monster" (Shakespeare's *Othello*), **jealousy** is a negative emotion triggered by an actual or suspected loss of a mate's sexual services or a mate's affection. These two losses produce different degrees of jealousy in men and women because of the biological fact that a woman is always certain of her maternity but a man is less certain of his paternity. According to evolutionary psychology, the reproductive strategies for men require knowing that they fathered the children they are helping to raise. Hence, a man is worried about any *sexual infidelity* on the part of his mate. If she was sexually unfaithful, then he is in doubt about his paternity of the children; they may not be carrying his genes. Since a woman obviously knows that her baby is carrying her genes, her major reproductive concern lies in successfully raising it. Hence, a woman is worried about any *emotional infidelity* on the part of her mate. To illustrate the differences between jealousy in men and women, imagine being asked some questions regarding the person with whom you are in love or with whom you are in a committed romantic relationship. One day you discover that your partner has become interested in another person. Which of the following statements from each pair would upset you more—that is, evoke the most jealousy?

> *Emotional infidelity:* "Imagining your partner forming a deep emotional attachment to that person."
>
> *Sexual infidelity:* "Imagining your partner enjoying passionate sexual intercourse with that other person."
>
> *Sexual infidelity:* "Imagining your partner trying different sexual positions with that other person."
>
> *Emotional infidelity:* "Imagining your partner falling in love with that other person." (Buss et al., 1992, p. 252; Buunk et al., 1996, p. 360)

Both pairs of statements contrast sexual infidelity with emotional infidelity. The prediction, based on evolutionary psychology, is that men should be more distressed regarding sexual infidelity. In these situations a man would be more uncertain of being the father and thus may be supporting children that are not carrying his genes. Women, however, should consider the emotional infidelity scenario to be more distressing. It represents the possibility of losing her mate's parental investment, protection, and commitment. When these questions were asked of male and female students, the results showed that men consider imagining sexual infidelity to be more distressing, whereas women consider imagining emotional infidelity to be more distressing (Buss et al., 1992).

To demonstrate the universality of these findings, Buunk and associates (1996) presented these choices between sexual and emotional infidelity in three different countries: the United States, Germany, and the Netherlands. The results, presented in Figure 3.4a, clearly show that in all three countries men are more distressed when they suspect their partners of sexual infidelity rather than emotional infidelity. Women, in contrast, are much more distressed by emotional infidelity (Buunk et al., 1996). These findings regarding sex differences in jealousy have been replicated in three other countries. Researchers asked university students in Korea and Japan (Buss et al., 1999) and in Sweden (Wiederman & Kendall, 1999) whether emotional or sexual infidelity was more distressing. The results in Figure 3.4b again show that for men, in all three countries, sexual infidelity was more distressing than emotional infidelity while for women, in all three countries, the reverse was true.

Biosocial Theory

Remember that behavior depends on both nature (heredity) and nurture (environment) like the area of a rectangle depends on length and width. The discussion of sexual relationships

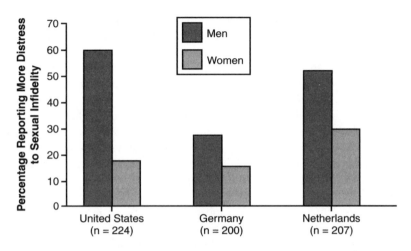

FIGURE 3.4a   Sexual versus Emotional Infidelity. Percentage of subjects reporting that they would be more distressed by imagining their partner enjoying passionate sexual intercourse with another person than by imagining their partner forming a deep emotional attachment to that person. Results are shown separately for men and women from the United States, Germany, and the Netherlands.

Source: From "Sex Differences in Jealousy in Evolutionary and Cultural Perspective: Tests from the Netherlands, Germany, and the United States" by B. P. Buunk et al., 1996, *Psychological Science, 7,* figure 1, p. 361. Copyright 1996 by Blackwell Publishers. Reprinted by permission.

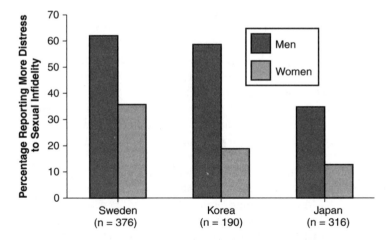

FIGURE 3.4b   Sexual versus Emotional Infidelity. The percentage of students who reported more distress from imagining their partner enjoying passionate sexual intercourse with another person than by imagining their partner forming a deep emotional attachment to that person. Results are shown separately for men and women from Sweden, Korea, and Japan.

Source: Adapted from "Evolution, Sex, and Jealousy: Investigation with a Sample from Sweden" by M. W. Wiederman & E. Kendall, 1999, *Evolution and Human Behavior, 20,* p. 127. And from "Jealousy and the Nature of Beliefs About Infidelity: Tests of Competing Hypotheses About Sex Differences in the United States, Korea, and Japan" by D. M. Buss et al., 1999, *Personal Relationships, 6,* pp. 139, 141.

has emphasized the nature part—that is, how our human evolutionary past determines current sexual relationships. However some psychologists maintain that we are emphasizing our evolutionary past too much. Instead, more emphasis should be given to a person's current environment in the formation of sexual relationships (Eagly & Wood, 1999; Wood & Eagly, 2002). **Biosocial theory** stresses the interaction between social experiences and the evolved sex differences of strength and reproductive capacity. This interaction helps explain gender differences in long-term mate preferences and jealousy. What is important in biosocial theory is that men are physically bigger and stronger and that women can bear and nurse children. What is not relevant in this theory are the evolved psychological mechanisms that are postulated by evolutionary psychology. According to Wood and Eagly (2002; Eagly & Wood, 1999), the biological sex differences in strength and in reproductive capacity interact with societal expectations that men should have greater power and status while women should accommodate to a lesser role. One consequence is that in adjusting to these expectations, men become providers and heads of households, while women become homemakers, cooks, and primary child-rearers. Thus, the biological differences between men and women contribute to the increase in psychological differences, because each sex tries to adjust to their expected social roles. According to biosocial theory, this adjustment is based on the cost-benefit analysis that typical sex roles provide greater satisfaction with lesser effort than would nontypical sex roles. Thus, it is less costly and more beneficial for men to enter male-dominated occupations like construction worker, farmer, and warrior and for women to enter female-dominated occupations like office manager, nurse, and child-care worker. However, the bulk of professions in our society may be staffed equally well by both sexes. Furthermore, although male and female genetic dispositions remain constant, society's views are changing. As a consequence, men and women may begin to enter professions that have been dominated by the other sex.

The evolutionary psychology explanation of why women prefer industrious men has also been challenged on the basis of biosocial theory and how society affects the earning power of men and women (D. M. Buss, 1989; Caporael, 1989; Tattersall, 1998; Wiederman & Allgeier, 1992). According to the **structural powerless hypothesis,** both men and women want the same financial resources. However, since women are relatively powerless to achieve these in the working world, they do so in one of the ways available—that is, by marrying men who have these resources. If this is the case, reasoned Wiederman and Allgeier (1992), then as women earn more money, the prospect of a man's financial prospects should become less important to them. However, based on a sample of working women, the researchers found no relationship between how much money women personally earned and the importance to them of good financial prospects in a prospective mate. In other words, all women regardless of their income wanted a long-term mate who had good financial prospects. Eagly and Wood (1999) have challenged these results by reexamining some of the data from D. M. Buss's (1989) original survey of 37 countries. Do men's preferences for good housekeepers and cooks and women's preferences regarding earning potential depend on the degree of inequality in power and earnings between the sexes? Using various indicators, Eagly and Wood found that as gender equality increases, differences in preference decrease. For example, in countries with greater equality, men's preference for mates with good housekeeping and cooking skills decreases and women's emphasis on a spouse's income potential decreases.

Fear as a Universal Motive

Fear is an excellent example of a universal motive that evolved to push individuals to avoid and escape dangerous stimuli. Fear springs from the interaction between evolutionary history and personal history with dangerous stimuli. Evidence for the evolution of fear comes from the observation that it is a universal emotion experienced by people in every country (Hupka et al., 1999; Scherer, 1997). In addition, fear can occur spontaneously to a seemingly dangerous event with prior experience (Marks, 1987). Fear is also conditionable, which means it can result from experience but only for some stimuli.

Occurrence of Fears. "What do you fear most?" (Muris et al., 1997, p. 929). In response to the question, 9- to 13-year-old Dutch children responded with a number of fears, the top 10 of which are listed in Figure 3.5. These fears ranged from being burglarized to encountering spiders. When 11- to 14-year-old Australian children listed their three greatest fears they duplicated five of the ones from Figure 3.5: parents dying, being hit by a car or truck, snakes, the dark, and spiders (Lane & Gullone, 1999). When American adults were asked to pick their fears from a list presented to them, snakes and spiders were selected (Roper Report, 1984). Several fears included in these three surveys are attributable to our evolutionary past: spiders, the dark, snakes, heights, death of a loved one, thunder and lightning. One interesting feature that came out in the survey with the Dutch children was that many

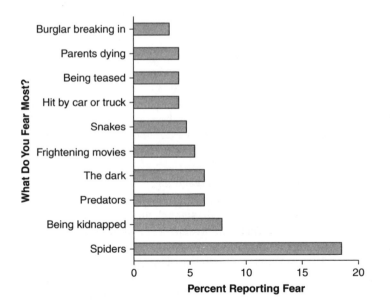

FIGURE 3.5 What Do You Fear? The percentage of children who responded with one of the 10 shown fears to the question "What do you fear most?" Notice that 23% of the children responded with either a fear of snakes or spiders.

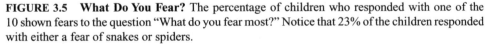

Source: Adapted from "Common Childhood Fears and Their Origins" by P. Muris et al., 1997, *Behaviour Research and Therapy, 35*, table 2, p. 932.

of them did not know how their fears began (Muris et al., 1997). For example, 33% did not know how their fears originated when asked, "How did your fear of ... begin?" (p. 931). In addition, 46% did not know how their fear of spiders began. Either the children did not remember what conditioning experiences produced these fears or the fears were innate and resulted from natural selection.

Survival Value.   Fear has an evolutionary history that helped animals adapt to survival problems that occurred in their environment (Öhman & Mineka, 2001; Plutchik, 1980). First, fear induces the preparation for escape or avoidance responses. Depending on the species, escape may consist of scrambling, freezing, flying, or running away. Second, animals have evolved to fear specific stimuli. The prevalence of a fear of reptiles, for example, may be an archaic remnant of when mammals tried to avoid being eaten by dinosaurs (Öhman, 1986). Öhman (1993) speculates that "feature detectors" in the brain are naturally selected because of their sensitivity to stimulus characteristics of reptile predators. These feature detectors may be located in the amygdala, a part of the brain that is sensitive to stimuli that are ambiguous or that predict probable threat (Whalen, 1998; see also Chapter 14). Sensitivity to fear-relevant stimuli was demonstrated in an experiment in which human participants were asked either to identify snakes or spiders in a background array composed of flowers or mushrooms or to identify flowers or mushrooms in a background array of snakes and spiders (Öhman, Flykt, & Esteves, 2001). Participants identified the fear-relevant snakes and spiders more rapidly than they identified flowers and mushrooms. Furthermore, individuals who feared snakes identified them more rapidly than an individual who did not. A similar result was obtained for individuals who feared spiders.

Preparedness.   One characteristic of universal motives is that some can occur without prior experience, as illustrated in case studies of fear. Marks (1987), in his book *Fears, Phobias, and Rituals,* reports on his 2½-year-old son's reaction to seaweed on the beach. The seaweed skeins looked like tiny snakes. As soon as his son saw them "he screamed in terror and clutched me tightly, trying to stop me from sitting on the sand. When I touched the seaweed he shrieked and refused to do the same. His panic increased when gentle waves rolled the seaweed nearby or when I held him over the water to show him the moving fronds" (p. 40).

Do all fears occur the first time a threatening or dangerous stimulus appears, or is some minimal experience required? After conditioning his daughter to fear a caterpillar after only a single association with a loud whistle, Valentine (1930) concluded that fear is an *"an instinct lurking ready to appear when the occasion arises"* (p. 404; italics in original). In this case, the instinct was a fear of woolly caterpillars that could be awakened when paired with a loud sound from a whistle. This awakening idea is similar to Seligman's (1971) concept of prepared learning, or **preparedness,** to describe the ease with which a behavior is learned. Behaviors for which humans are prepared are ones that occur easily as a result of experience, as if they are disposed toward learning them. *Contraprepared* behaviors are ones that occur with difficulty and only after much experience. Thus, to assume that certain fears are the result of evolution means that there are things of which humans are prepared to become afraid. If humans are prepared to become afraid of snakes, then it will take little experience to learn to fear them. Humans are probably contraprepared to become afraid of flowers. Seligman (1971) points out that humans are more likely to fear insects, heights, and the dark rather than their pajamas, grass, electrical outlets, and hammers.

Preparedness and Observational Fear Conditioning. The concept of preparedness also connotes the possibility that fear of naturally dangerous stimuli can occur indirectly; that is, by observational conditioning. This possibility received support from experiments in which monkeys were conditioned by observation to fear snakes and crocodiles but not flowers or other neutral objects (Cook & Mineka, 1990; Mineka, 1992; Mineka & Cook, 1993). The experiment involved two main groups of monkeys: *models* and *observers*. The model monkeys were videotaped acting calmly or acting fearfully. Spliced underneath the videotaped scene of the model monkey were different stimuli, such as a toy or real snake or silk flowers. This resulted in different videotaped scenes of the model monkey acting calmly or fearfully in the presence of one of these stimuli (see Figure 3.6). An observer monkey watched one of the videotapes. Would the observer monkey become afraid of both stimuli to which the model monkey acted fearfully, or would the observer become afraid of only one stimulus, such as the snake? Following the viewing of a video, an observer monkey was placed in an apparatus in which it could obtain a food treat. To reach this treat, however, the observer monkey had to reach over an open box containing a snake or a flower. The indication of fear was how long (latency) it took the observer

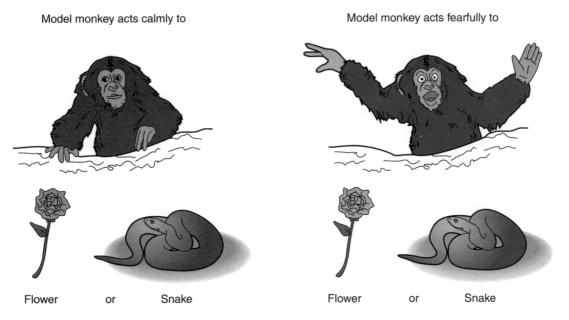

Model monkey acts calmly to   Model monkey acts fearfully to

Flower   or   Snake   Flower   or   Snake

FIGURE 3.6   Preparedness and Fear. The design of the experiment involved four video versions of a model monkey acting calmly or fearfully in reaction to a flower or a snake. The observer monkey watched one of these four versions.

Source: Adapted from "Selected Associations in the Observational Conditioning of Fear in Rhesus Monkeys" by M. Cook and S. Mineka, 1990, *Journal of Experimental Psychology, 16.*

monkey to reach for the food. Other indicators of fear included disturbance behaviors, such as withdrawing, clutching the bars, shaking the cage, staring at the stimulus, or making a grimace or threat.

Observer monkeys learned to fear snakes but not flowers from watching the behavior of model monkeys. The observer monkeys' reactions to the snake or flower were affected by the model monkeys' fear behavior in the presence of a snake but not by that behavior in the presence of a flower. For instance, it took the observer monkeys longer to reach over the open box containing a toy snake when the model monkey had acted fearfully toward the snake. The observer monkeys' reachings were not affected by the flower or by how the model monkeys had acted toward the flower. The observer monkeys also acted more disturbed in the presence of a snake compared to a flower, again provided that the model monkeys acted fearfully toward the snake. The observer monkeys were not disturbed in the presence of a flower even when the model monkeys had acted disturbed. Thus, monkeys appear to be prepared to fear snakes but not harmless stimuli like flowers. The fear of snakes may have been a universal motive that evolved to aid survival.

Preparedness of Classical Fear Conditioning in Humans.   A series of experiments performed by E. Cook and associates (1986) show that humans are also prepared to fear some stimuli more readily than others. The researchers compared fear conditioning to pictures of phobic stimuli like snakes and spiders versus neutral stimuli like flowers and mushrooms. During the conditioning procedure, one phobic stimulus was paired with an uncomfortable shock to the forearm, whereas the other phobic stimulus was presented alone, without a shock. For example, the picture of a snake was paired with the application of a shock, while the picture of a spider was presented without a shock. Conditioning with neutral stimuli involved pairing a flower with a shock and a mushroom with no shock. Heart rate was used as an indicator of fear. Increased heart rate prepares a person to fight or flee from a danger stimulus, such as an approaching snake or spider. The results of a series of experiments showed that humans were more reactive to phobic stimuli compared to neutral stimuli. Accelerated heart rate only occurred when phobic stimuli (snakes, spiders) were paired with a shock. Neutral stimuli (flowers, mushrooms) did not produce an accelerated heart rate even when paired with a shock. Thus, like monkeys, humans are prepared to fear snakes and spiders, which may have been an important survival reaction during our evolutionary past.

Sensitivity and preparedness to phobic stimuli are so great that humans even react when those stimuli are presented below awareness (Öhman & Mineka, 2001). During the conditioning phase of one experiment, Katkin and coresearchers (2001) presented a slide of a snake or spider very briefly, which was then followed by another slide so as to obliterate any visual memory of the first one. Using this procedure, the presentation of a snake slide (conditioned stimulus) was paired with a moderately painful electric shock (unconditioned stimulus) to the nondominant forearm, while a spider slide was paired with the absence of a shock. For another group, this procedure was reversed: spider slides were paired with shock and snake slides, with the absence of shock. Fear (conditioned response) evoked by a conditioned stimulus was measured by the magnitude of the skin conductance responses, which is an indicator of autonomic nervous system arousal. Also, after a slide was presented, participants rated the likelihood that a shock would actually follow. As a result of conditioning, participants made stronger fear responses to the conditioned stimulus that was paired with shock than to the conditioned stimulus not paired with shock. The ability to predict the onset of shock, following a slide, depended on the participant's sensitivity to her visceral activity (heart rate). More sensitive individuals were better able to predict that shock would follow a conditioned stimulus slide. Thus, when phobic stimuli are presented below the level of conscious awareness, individuals are still sensitive to them at another level. They associate them with shock and can predict their occurrence based on sensitivity to their own heart rate.

In summary, fear has been used to illustrate a universal motive that is shaped by evolution. It is a prepared tendency or psychological mechanism in mammals that is ready to occur in response to certain stimuli, such as reptiles or the dark. The evolutionary value of fear is that it increases an animal's chance of survival. Fear motivates the analysis of unusual stimuli and motivates escape and avoidance behaviors like fleeing, hiding, or freezing.

> ➤ More information about fears and phobias is available at http://www.helpguide.org/ mental/phobia_symptoms_types_treatment.htm

Liking and Preferences for Foods

Another universal motive that humans possess is exhibited in their food preferences. The characteristics of this motive are uncovered from examining young children's innate dispositions toward and away from edible substances. The reason for studying children is that their preferences are not yet unduly influenced by the food environment that parents provide. The effects of this environment are immediate, since in making the transition from milk, infants are disposed toward learning to accept the foods associated with their country and culture (Birch, 1992). Food acceptance is possible because humans are **omnivorous,** which means that they are able to eat a variety of foods. In fact, nutritionists recommend that people should do this to obtain all the nutrients that they need. Being omnivorous allowed humans to make use of whatever food sources a geographical area had to offer, in spite of any innate taste preferences.

Food Neophobia.   As an introduction, there are several generalizations regarding innate food preferences. First, as many parents have discovered, in the transition from milk to solid foods, children often show **food neophobia,** which is the tendency to avoid novel foods and prefer familiar foods. Second, children innately prefer sweet and later salty foods. They avoid sour and bitter foods. Third, children are prepared to avoid food associated with negative digestive consequences and prefer those with positive consequences (Birch, 1999). Fourth, humans have a preference for fatty foods (Birch, 1992).

Would you like to eat some hummus, halvah, or funistrada? A "no" answer may be indicative of the universal motive of *food neophobia.* People vary in their degree of this neophobia and hence their willingness to try new foods. Pliner and Hobden (1992) constructed the *Food Neophobia Scale* to measure the extent individuals avoided or were reluctant to eat novel foods. Individuals who scored in the upper 15% of the *Food Neophobia Scale* were labeled neophobics, and those who scored in the lower 15% were labeled neophilics (individuals willing to try new foods). Raudenbush and Frank (1999) asked neophobics and neophilics about their potential reactions to familiar foods (yogurt, icing, applesauce, and peanut butter) and unfamiliar foods (hummus, a chickpea paste; halvah, crushed sesame seeds in honey; and funistrada, a fictitious food). Their reactions to these foods were measured on a 12-point scale on several dimensions: willingness to try, expected liking, actual liking, and willingness to try the foods again. Analyses of the ratings indicated that both neophobics and neophilics were less favorably disposed toward novel foods than toward familiar foods. The unfavorable ratings for novel foods were very apparent for neophobics. Compared to neophilics, neophobics were less willing to try novel foods, expected and actually liked novel foods less, and were less willing to try them again. Also, both groups ate less unfamiliar than familiar food, and neophobics ate significantly less than neophilics.

An explanation for neophobia is based on its survival value. Neophobia protects a person from eating a toxic substance that can cause illness and even death (Birch, 1999). By avoiding novel foods, an individual is less likely to be poisoned or to become very ill. However, neophobia also has some negative consequences. It can be a problem for individuals required to make dietary changes in support of good nutrition. Individuals may be reluctant to switch from familiar foods to new foods that provide diet and health benefits. Nevertheless, the extent of food neophobia diminishes with the amount of experience a person has with other foods (Birch, 1999).

Innate Preference and Aversion for Substances.   The innate human preference for sweet and aversion for sour and bitter becomes apparent during the first few hours and days of life. Evidence for this comes from observing facial expressions made by newborn infants to various taste stimuli. To illustrate, Figure 3.7 shows the distinctive facial reactions of a 3-day-old infant to sweet-, sour-, and bitter-tasting stimuli but its indifference to salt (Mennella & Beauchamp, 1998). Although the infant in Figure 3.7 is indifferent to salt, by 4 months of age a salt preference has developed (Birch, 1999). Additional evidence for innate taste preferences comes from research by Steiner (1977), who showed that infants were sensitive to the taste of sweet, sour, and bitter prior to their first feeding. He placed a drop of flavored liquid on the tongues of infants, who clearly showed whether they liked it or not. Compared to a resting face or the reaction to distilled water, the sweet stimulus produced a

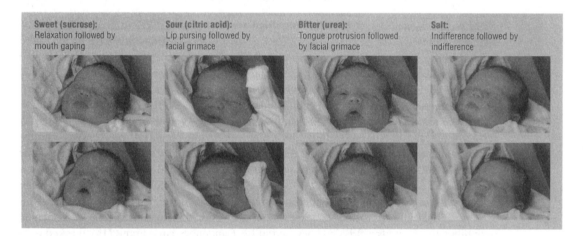

FIGURE 3.7   Innate Preference and Aversion of Tastes. Sequence of facial expressions elicited from 3-day-old infant in response to tasting different substances.

Source: From "Early Flavor Experiences" by J. A. Mennella and G. K. Beauchamp, 1998, *Nutrition Reviews, 56,* p. 207. Baby pictures were reprinted with permission from *Pediatric Basics, 82,* Winter 1998, Gerber Products Company.

retraction of mouth corners resembling a smile, a sucking response, and a licking of the upper lips. The reaction to the sour stimulus, however, produced a pursing of the lips, wrinkling of the nose, blinking of the eyes, and increased salivation. The reaction to the bitter stimulus produced protrusion of a flat tongue, salivation, spitting, and an expression resembling dislike and anger. The instinctive or innate nature of these expressions is also demonstrated by the finding that infants do not rely on higher cortical brain processes. Steiner (1977) tested four infants born without a cortex and with only a brain stem and midbrain. They reacted to taste stimuli in a fashion similar to that of normal infants: a preference for sweet and an aversion for sour and bitter.

Evolutionary Value of Tastes and Facial Expressions. In addition to showing positive reactions to sweets, infants will also eat more of a sweet-tasting substance. Desor and associates (1973) offered 1- to 3-day-old infants plain water or sugar solutions of varying degrees of sweetness. Infants drank more of a sugar water solution than a plain water solution; the sweeter the solution, the more they drank. In fact, one way parents make adult food acceptable to infants is to add sugar (Jerome, 1977). However, infants will eat less of a substance the more bitter or sour it tastes. Desor and associates (1975) found that putting sufficient citric acid in a sugar solution to give it a sour taste led to a reduction in the amount infants drank. However, adding urea for a bitter taste or sodium chloride for a salty taste did not seem to suppress the amount of drinking. Perhaps bitterness is a more complex taste, although the infant in Figure 3.7 (Mennella & Beauchamp, 1998) and Steiner's (1977) research clearly show that infants make an aversive response to bitter tastes.

Liking sugars and disliking sour or bitter foods are assumed to result from our genetic past for several reasons. First, the facial expressions reflecting infants' likes or dislikes are likely innate, or *inborn*, to use Steiner's (1977) term. It does not seem possible that these expressions are learned by infants during their first few hours of life or while in the womb. However, this possibility does exist. For instance, Mennella and Beauchamp (1998) summarized the results of research showing that infants can detect and prefer the odor of their own amniotic fluids during their first few days of life. (Amniotic fluid surrounds the unborn fetus in the mother's uterus.) Second, even infants lacking a cortex for learning more complex material are able to make these facial expressions. Third, there is an evolutionary advantage to liking sweets. In our evolutionary past sugar was only available in fruit, berries, or honey. It did not come neatly packaged in cakes, pies, ice cream, and soft drinks. A sweet taste is associated with ripe fruits, berries, some vegetables that are ripe, and mothers' milk (Mennella & Beauchamp, 1998). The sweet taste comes from complex carbohydrates, which are an essential nutrient for the body's growth, repair, and maintenance. Thus, by eating more sweet-tasting substances, early humans obtained essential nutrients, which aided in their survival. Sour and bitter tastes are associated with bark, dirt, and unripe fruits, berries, and vegetables that are not ready to eat. If eaten, these things are likely to make a person ill. In addition, a bitter-tasting substance is probably associated with toxins or poisons that can kill an individual. Thus, a bitter taste serves as a warning to avoid bad food.

In addition to innate taste preferences, the accompanying facial expressions also have survival value. A newborn infant is totally dependent on its mother for nutrients and can only communicate its likes and dislikes using facial expressions. These expressions are readable (see Figure 3.7) and clearly resemble the reactions made by adults if they were to taste identical stimuli. Steiner (1977) demonstrated this by having a panel of observers interpret what emotion the infant was showing when tasting various stimuli. The panel viewed either a videotape or still photograph of the infant's facial expression. The expression elicited by the sweet stimulus was interpreted as appreciation, enjoyment, or liking. The expression elicited by the bitter stimulus was interpreted as disgust, aversion, or dislike. Thus, it appears that an infant "knows" what is good based on the idea that what an infant likes is nutritious and what an infant does not like is not nutritious.

The various facial responses that accompany different tastes also serve other functions (Rosenstein & Oster, 1988). Sucking responses in reaction to sweet stimuli are a means of ingesting what is presumably a nutritive substance. The increased salivation to a sour stimulus may be an attempt to dilute its concentration, thereby making it less aversive. In an experiment with 2-hour-old infants, Rosenstein and Oster (1988) observed infants' attempts to block swallowing a bitter liquid by allowing it to drain from their mouths. These responses presumably are an adaptive way to get rid of bitter substances. These investigators also tested infants using a salty substance and found no distinctive facial responses. The lack of distinctive responding may have occurred because infants cannot consume enough salt to be dangerous or because they have not yet developed a taste for salt.

Early Experience Interacts with Innate Preference.   Innate taste preferences are presumably a function of our evolutionary past. However, taste may be affected by very early flavor experiences, which could affect food preferences later. Some flavors from foods that pregnant mothers eat may come to reside in the amniotic fluid that surrounds their babies. Consequently, when unborn babies swallow amniotic fluid they experience these flavors. What is the evidence that this early flavor experience affects an infant's later food preferences? In order to answer this question, Mennella and coresearchers (2001) had pregnant women drink either water or carrot juice during their last three months of pregnancy or during the first month of breastfeeding their babies. Other mothers drank water both during their pregnancy and during breastfeeding. The question was: When ready to eat cereal, would infants prefer carrot-flavored over plain-flavored cereal? The infants' preference was measured in three ways. One made use of infants' negative facial expressions while eating, such as nose wrinkling or head turning. Presumably fewer negative expressions implied greater acceptance of a cereal. A second measure involved the mothers' ratings of their infants' enjoyment of the cereal on a scale from 1 (not at all) to 9 (very much). Third was the amount of cereal the infants ate. The results in Figure 3.8 indicate that the mothers' intake of carrot juice while pregnant or nursing increased their infants' acceptance of carrot-flavored cereal. Infants made fewer negative facial responses, showed more enjoyment, and ate more of the carrot-flavored cereal than the plain-flavored cereal. However, the amount eaten did not differ significantly among the three groups. An important implication of this finding is that this initial exposure to a flavor, even prior to birth, disposes an infant to accept the solid foods of its culture and may smooth the transition from nursing to eating solid foods (Mennella et al., 2001).

Fat Preference.   Texture, taste, and smell contribute to our preferences for a food (Schiffman et al., 1998); for example, the higher the butter fat content of vanilla ice cream, the more it is preferred (Pick et al., 1990). To illustrate the power of human fat preferences, in 1991 the McDonald's Corporation introduced the McLean hamburger to provide a more nutritious choice on its menu. This new hamburger contained half the fat and had 100 fewer

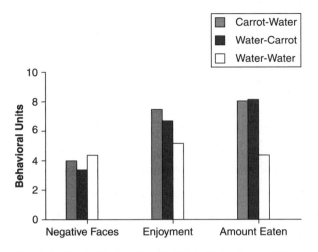

FIGURE 3.8 Effects of Early Taste Experience. When mothers drank carrot juice while pregnant (carrot-water) or during nursing (water-carrot) their infants preferred carrot-flavored cereal over plain cereal. When mothers drank water while pregnant or during nursing (water-water), their infants preferred carrot-flavored cereal less. Amount eaten is reported in decagrams.

Source: Adapted from "Prenatal and Postnatal Flavor Learning by Human Infants" [Electronic version] by J. A. Mennella et al., 2001, *Pediatrics, 107, e88,* table 2, p. 3.

calories than their quarter-pounder hamburger. The McLean hamburger fell in the acceptable range of daily fat consumption, with 30% of its calories derived from fat (Burros, 1991). In spite of its nutritional value, however, the consuming public did not want it, and eventually it was taken off the market (Gibson, 1996). Part of the reason may have been taste, since the McLean did not taste quite the same as other hamburgers. Fat provides flavor, and substitute flavors put into the McLean hamburger may not have provided the same taste. The decline of the McLean hamburger illustrates that people do not necessarily eat what is good for them but instead eat what tastes good.

Universal Appeal of Music

The position of evolutionary psychology is that the function of psychological mechanisms is to solve problems of survival. Psychological mechanisms evolved through natural selection or sexual selection because they increased the survival chances of individuals and their offspring. However, there are also some evolutionary puzzles—mechanisms that evolved as by-products but do not seem beneficial for survival on their own. For example, what is the survival value of male nipples? Music may be in this category of mechanisms for which the evolutionary benefits are not obvious.

Possible Evolution of Music. As Darwin (1871/1981) noted, music arouses emotions that are usually positive (like love) and not negative (like fear or rage). Yet, what is the function of these positive feelings? Perhaps one function is that music can be used as a means of mood regulation: alleviate negative moods and boost positive moods (North et al., 2004; Thayer, 2001). A second possibility is that those feelings promote group or social bonding that can occur while listening to or creating music. Examples would include listening to patriotic music during Fourth of July celebrations or singing the happy birthday song. However, music may have evolved as a by-product in the evolution of other pleasures or motives (Peretz, 2006). In this case, music is an artificial stimulus that people discovered could evoke pleasurable feelings. Another interpretation, however, is that music is the result of sexual selection rather than natural selection. In the words of Darwin (1871/1981), the purpose of music was to charm the other sex. Thus, individuals who could make music were more likely to be sexually selected based on their ability to charm or instill positive feelings in the listener.

Music as Part of Human Nature.   What is music? According to one definition, music refers to an organized movement of sound that is both regular and periodic. This organized movement allows an individual to keep time, which is what distinguishes music from other patterns of sound, such as speech (Cross, 2001). In addition, music seems to be part of human nature. Peretz (2006) describes several reasons why this is so. First, music is not a recent invention but has been part of human culture for at least 30,000 years. Second, music, although in different forms, is present in all cultures the world over. Third, the human response to music seems innate—that is, learning how to respond is not necessary. For example, infants respond to music and early on they can discriminate between music and other sounds while most animals cannot. Fourth, music is functional in that it is a source of pleasure for most members of a culture, which is especially the case for popular music.

Infants Enjoy Music.   The claim that the appreciation of music is innate comes from observing infants. First, this appreciation appears early in the life of infants. Second, infants are calmer and pay greater attention to their mothers when the latter are singing rather than speaking to their infants (Nakata & Trehub, 2004). Third, infants prefer consonant (harmony) over dissonant (non-harmony) music. Zenter and Kagan (1998) tested this last claim by presenting 4-month-old infants with either a consonant (harmonious) melody or a dissonant melody. (Undergraduates who listened to the dissonant version described it as "hurting their ears.") Preference for a melody was based on how much time infants fixated on the speaker-source of the melody. Dislike for a melody was based on the infants' motor activity, such as flexion or movement of arms or legs. Infants seemed to like consonant music and dislike dissonant music. They spent more time visually fixating on the speaker when it transmitted consonant rather than dissonant melodies. Infants also made more motor movements and fretted more in the presence of dissonant melodies. Furthermore, the greater preference for consonant over dissonant music occurs for infants as early as two months of age (Trainor et al., 2002).

How should these results be interpreted? One interpretation favors the idea that humans have an innate bias in favor of consonance over dissonance in musical notes. Perhaps humans evolved a motive to like musical instead of nonmusical sound. How this preference developed is not clear. Another possibility is that infants are neutral at birth in their preference regarding possible patterns of sound. They learn to like whatever they are exposed to immediately after being born, which happens to be consonant rather than dissonant music.

Section Recap

Relationships between members of each sex, the arousal of jealousy, the emotion of fear, and food preferences are all categories of universal motives that resulted from natural selection or sexual selection. Music enjoyment may be a by-product of the evolution of other processes. According to Darwin's concept of *sexual selection*, relationships are formed by members of one sex choosing individuals of the other sex based on the latter's characteristics. *Mate value* includes those characteristics of a person that are desired by the other sex, such as attractiveness, intelligence, common interests, and parental possibilities. According to the *good genes hypothesis*, beauty, as a universal trait, signals that the person has genes for good health and intelligence. Individuals select others either because their attractiveness signals good genes or reject individuals whose unattractiveness signals bad genes for these traits. In the case of sexual selection for long-term relationships, women universally prefer ambitious and industrious men because they will provide the material means to support a family. Men usually prefer young and beautiful women because these features signal fertility.

There are several systems in place to maintain relationships. Orgasm evolved through natural selection and is one of the rewards for sexual behavior and for the development of romantic love as a help in forming pair bonds. It increases the chances of pregnancy. *Mate poaching* occurs when an outsider attempts to attract someone who is already in a romantic relationship. Thus, poaching is a threat to the maintenance of a relationship and jealousy may have evolved to provide the motivation to protect against it.

Jealousy is an emotion that has been sexually selected. According to evolutionary psychology, women become more jealous about the suspected or actual loss of affection, since it implies that they may lose their partners' resources. Men are more jealous about their partners' sexual infidelity, since men are uncertain about being the father of their partners' children. According to *biosocial theory*, gender differences are the result of biological differences between men and women in physical strength and reproductive capacity. These biological differences interact with societal expectations for men and women to take on sex-relevant social roles. The consequence of adapting to these roles is to increase the psychological difference between men and women. These increased psychological differences account for gender differences in preferred mate characteristics and in jealousy. According to the *structural powerless hypothesis*, women are ineffectual in obtaining the same level of financial resources in the working world as men. Therefore, women can gain access to resources by marrying men who can provide these.

Survey research indicates that some fears are more prevalent than others, especially ones that have survival value, such as the fear of snakes and spiders. Not all fears occur the first time in a dangerous situation but can arise quickly, with little previous experience, depending on the preparedness of the behavior. *Preparedness* refers to the ease with which behavior is conditioned. In cases of conditioning, some stimuli are easy to condition (prepared), such as fear stimuli, whereas other stimuli are difficult to condition (contraprepared). The preparedness to fear a particular stimulus is shown with *classical conditioning*, which is the procedure by which a neutral stimulus (e.g., a tone) signals a biologically significant unconditioned stimulus (e.g., an electric shock to forearm). Following several trials, the tone (conditioned stimulus) will evoke a response (conditioned response) that mimics the original unconditioned response to the shock. Monkeys and humans are prepared to become conditioned to fear snakes and spiders. Fear can also develop from observing a fear reaction in other individuals. Humans are extremely sensitive to fear-relevant stimuli, even when these are presented below the level of awareness.

Another set of universal motives revolves around our interaction with food. Humans exhibit *food neophobia*, which is the tendency to avoid novel foods and select familiar foods. Another related universal motive is the human preference for sugar and fat, which indicate high caloric value. Work with infants just a few hours old shows that they prefer sweet substances over sour and bitter substances. Early taste preferences may also result from flavors that babies experienced from their mothers' amniotic fluid or breast milk. Fortunately, humans are *omnivorous*, which means they can eat a variety of foods to obtain the necessary ingredients for growth and maintenance.

The universal appeal of music is also part of human nature. Music is patterned sound that people can keep time with. It is capable of eliciting emotions and is enjoyed all over the world in its many forms. Music may have evolved as a by-product of the evolution of other psychological mechanisms or may have evolved through sexual selection. Infants prefer their mothers' singing to speaking and as early as two months of age, they prefer consonant melodies over dissonant melodies.

ACTIVITIES

1. Ask friends and acquaintances what things they fear. Then ask them how their particular fear developed. Is there any commonality in the fears people report (e.g., tornadoes in the Midwest, earthquakes in California, or hurricanes in the Southeast)? Did the fear develop in the absence of any experience with the feared object? Did fear of the object develop as a result of its association with a traumatic experience? Did the fear develop from watching someone else show a fear reaction to that stimulus?

2. What foods do you like and dislike? What is the source of these likes and dislikes? Is there anything that liked foods have in common or that disliked foods have in common?

3. Can you determine from watching a friend's facial expressions if she likes what is being eaten?

4. Ask some friends of each sex how important the following characteristics are for choosing a husband, wife, or long-term mate. Use this rating scale:

   Good financial prospect: 0 = Irrelevant or unimportant, to 3 = Indispensable

   Ambition and industriousness: 0 = Irrelevant or unimportant, to 3 = Indispensable
   Good looks: 0 = Irrelevant or unimportant, to 3 = Indispensable

   How do your findings compare to the results presented in Figure 3.3? Imagine the type of person with whom you would like to form a long-term relationship or with whom you already have a relationship. Is your choice the result of a biological destiny, society's expectations, or the interaction between biology and society? In other words, do you think the evolutionary psychologists are correct, or are social psychological explanations more accurate, e.g., structural powerless hypothesis?

5. List situations that would make you jealous. Compare your list with a member of the other sex. Are there any differences between the two lists? Which was the greater cause of jealousy: sexual infidelity or emotional infidelity? Did your results support evolutionary psychology?

4 Addictions and Addictive Behaviors

Tobacco surely was designed
To poison and destroy mankind.

—Philip Freneau, 1786

Thou hast the keys of Paradise, O just, subtle, and mighty opium!
—Thomas De Quincey, 1821

■ Some feelings and the substances or activities that produce them are so motivating that little else seems to matter. This observation, along with the following questions, can guide an understanding of the concepts in this chapter:

1. What can drugs of abuse, electrical stimulation, and exercise tell us about the brain as a source of motivation?

2. How do drugs differ from natural incentives in motivating behavior?

3. Why are there pleasure centers in the brain and how do they work?

4. What are the psychological theories for starting and maintaining drug use?

5. Why do strenuous exercise and gambling become addictive behaviors?

Drugs of Abuse and Addiction

A young man has just left his mother's apartment and is strolling around his old neighborhood. He is delighted to be free after having been in prison for one year. While walking, he reflects on the time he spent there undergoing heroin detoxification. This very unpleasant process left him free of any drug cravings. As he walks along familiar streets and sees familiar buildings, however, his intestines begin to rumble, his eyes begin to water, and he starts yawning. He also begins to sweat and becomes nauseated, as symptoms of his old withdrawal agony start returning. These are symptoms that he has not experienced for over a year. "How is this possible?" he asks himself. "I haven't felt this way for so long." Although feeling panicky and anxious, he knows how to alleviate this old sickness. He turns the corner and begins walking toward a familiar apartment building where relief awaits.

A young woman drives her car uptown to visit her girlfriend. Inside her friend's apartment she notices a mirror lying face up on the coffee table. She can't take her eyes off the mirror; it elicits a mounting excitement in her that seems to take over her body. Does her

friend have any cocaine, she wonders? Her whole body tingles in delightful waves of anticipation. She can almost taste the cocaine at the back of her throat. "If I am feeling a rush just
from seeing this mirror, why do I bother using cocaine at all?" she thinks. The reason, she answers herself, is that there is no substitute for the drug. "Nothing in any way, shape, or form
can make me feel this good."

The purpose of this section is to describe the effects of selected legal and illegal psychoactive drugs, how they differ from natural incentives, and why people are motivated to
use them. A **psychoactive drug** is any chemical substance that alters a person's mood and
behavior as a result of the drug's effect on the function of the brain.

Psychoactive Drugs

People are motivated to consume psychoactive drugs because the immediate pleasurable results seem to outweigh the long-term negative consequences. The drugs described in this
section are controlled substances, which means their manufacture, possession, and distri-
bution are regulated by the federal government of the United States. The only exception is
caffeine, which may even be used by children in soft drinks.

Caffeine.   "Caffeine is the most widely consumed psychoactive substance in the world"
(Strain & Griffiths, 2005, p. 1201). It is consumed in coffee, tea, chocolate, sodas, and energy drinks. Caffeine has a stimulating effect that is deemed pleasurable especially among
caffeine drinkers. Even when caffeine is disguised in a novel fruit tea or in capsule form,
consumers report feeling more alert, energetic, lively, and clear-headed, and experience
greater well-being (Schuh & Griffiths, 1997; Yeomans et al., 1998). Furthermore, fruit tea
and juice that contain caffeine are preferred more than those same liquids without caffeine
especially for individuals who are caffeine deprived (Yeomans et al., 1998). Common caffeine withdrawal symptoms begin 12 to 24 hours after the last caffeine drink. The symptoms include headache, fatigue, decreased energy, depressed mood, and decreased alertness
(Juliano & Griffiths, 2004).

Alcohol.   Ethanol is the **alcohol** in a drink. It consists of carbohydrates that serve as
the active ingredient in beer, wine, and distilled spirits (whiskey, vodka, rum, gin). The
amount of alcohol that reaches the brain depends on a number of factors, including
the drinker's body size, whether the stomach is empty or full, and whether other liquids
are also being taken. Although the size of a typical drink may vary, the alcohol content
remains constant. That is, about 0.5 ounces of alcohol is contained in a 12-ounce mug of
beer, a 4-ounce glass of wine, and a 1.25-ounce cocktail of 80-proof liquor (Fishbein &
Pease, 1996). At low amounts, alcohol produces good feelings, such as euphoria, and releases inhibitions. This can result in increased talkativeness, aggression, belligerence,
and promiscuity.

Nicotine.   Tobacco use in the form of cigarettes, cigars, pipes, and smokeless tobacco de-
livers nicotine to the brain. **Nicotine** is the major psychoactive drug in tobacco. In addition
to nicotine, however, smoke contains ammonia (an ingredient in kitchen cleaners), arsenic
(rat poison), and cyanide (a very deadly poison with the smell of bitter almonds). Some cigarette packs inform users that smoke gives off carbon monoxide, a colorless, odorless,

highly poisonous gas that prevents the blood from utilizing oxygen. A person's initial reaction to smoking is quite negative, including coughing, dizziness, nausea, and vomiting. These symptoms eventually disappear, and seasoned smokers report that smoking is mood enhancing and relaxing. If a person tries to quit smoking after becoming addicted, she experiences a set of negative symptoms, including irritability, restlessness, anxiety, depression, hostility, difficulty concentrating, and hunger (Fishbein & Pease, 1996).

Amphetamines.　　Originally a form of this stimulant was available from the khat plant but now it is produced synthetically from various chemicals. Known by street names like speed and crystal meth (or ice), amphetamines produce alertness, euphoria, and well-being more effectively than does cocaine (Jaffe et al., 2005). Methamphetamine is derived from amphetamine and produces even greater psychoactive effects. Ecstacy is a drug similar to methamphetamine. It is one of the more commonly used hallucinogenic drugs, and is especially notable on university campuses (Goldstein, 2001). When taken orally in capsule or tablet form, an ecstacy-produced high can last five hours and includes feelings of spirituality and closeness (Schuckit, 2000).

Cannabis.　　This category of psychoactive drugs includes marijuana and hashish. Tetrahydrocannibol (THC) is the psychoactive component of these drugs and is derived from hemp (cannabis) plants. Smoking marijuana produces a "high" that includes feeling euphoric, relaxed, drowsy, and experiencing a dreamlike state of disconnectedness from the world (Goldstein, 2001). Withdrawal symptoms after heavy marijuana use have included fatigue, anxiety, concentration problems, yawning, change in appetite, depression, and sleeplessness (Schuckit, 2000).

Cocaine.　　Coca paste is derived from the leaves of the coca plant found in South America. **Cocaine** (cocaine hydrochloride) is the odorless white powder that is processed from coca paste. Crack cocaine is made by mixing cocaine hydrochloride with water and baking soda. When the water evaporates, the mixture turns into a crystalline lump that is smoked in a special pipe. Some of the positive effects felt from cocaine include euphoria, increased sense of energy, increased mental acuity and sensory awareness, and a "full body orgasm" (Gold, 1992). These effects are short-lived, often lasting just 15 to 30 minutes. Abusers often go on cocaine binges, which means that they indulge in extremely high use for a day or two, only quitting when their drug supply runs out. During a binge, tolerance quickly develops, and when the effects of cocaine wear off, a person "crashes," experiencing negative symptoms such as depression and anxiety and the need for sleep (Gawin & Kleber, 1986).

Opiates.　　Opium is obtained from the sap that comes from the seed of the opium poppy. This sap is processed into **opiates,** such as morphine, codeine, and heroin. Morphine and codeine serve as painkillers and are also used to treat diarrhea and coughs. Heroin is an even more potent drug derived from opium. Opiate users experience a "rush," which has been likened to sexual orgasm. In addition, there is an elevation of mood ("a high"), a sense of euphoria, a decrease in anxiety, and an increase in self-esteem (Jaffe, 1992). Swallowing is one route of opiate ingestion but not because of any taste that it provides.

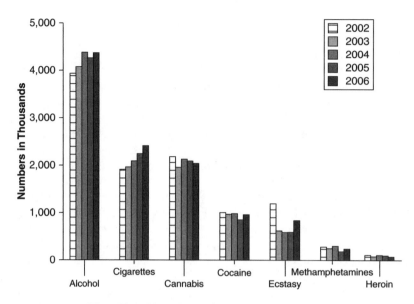

FIGURE 4.1   First-Time Drug Use. The estimated number of individuals age 12 years or older who tried various drugs for the first time during the 2002 to 2006 period. Cannabis includes marijuana and hashish. The method of recording methamphetamine use for 2006 changed and is not comparable to previous years.

Source: Table G.26, SAMSHA, Office of Applied Studies, National Survey on Drug Use and Health, 2002–2006. http://www.oas.samhsa.gov/NSDUH/2k6NSDUH/AppG.htm. Methamphetamines data comes from Table 8.46 at http://oas.samhsa.gov/nsduh/2k6nsduh/tabs/Sect8peTabs46.pdf

Extent of Drug Use

Annual surveys help indicate the extent people are motivated to experiment, use, and eventually abuse psychoactive drugs. The National Survey on Drug Use and Health tracks yearly trends in the use of many psychoactive drugs. Figure 4.1 shows the number of people 12 years or older who had their first drug experience during the years 2002 to 2006. The most frequently tried drug is alcohol followed by cigarettes. Heroin is experimented with least frequently. A certain percentage of the individuals in Figure 4.1 will become addicted to the drug or drugs with which they experimented. The reason for people's experimentation and subsequent addiction are many and will be described in this chapter.

➤ More extensive statistics on psychoactive drug use can be obtained at http://www.oas. samhsa.gov

Characteristics of Addiction

This initial experimentation occurs for various reasons and for any pleasures the drugs produce. From this point forward, however, some individuals will stop, continue to use occasionally, or become involuntarily addicted. For instance, following experimentation with smoking or drinking alcohol, some people quit or continue to use in moderation, as in social drinking or occasional smoking. However, others become involuntarily addicted and develop intense uncontrollable cravings for the drug and cannot stop using it. Let us examine the characteristics of drug addiction: craving, tolerance, and the unpleasantness of withdrawal.

Craving. Do you eat because you want to get rid of your hunger or because you want to attain the pleasure derived from delicious food? **Craving** is an almost overpowering, uncontrollable urge for the drug the person has been using. However, is craving the desire to rid oneself of the negative symptoms associated with withdrawal or is craving the desire for the strong euphoric effect a drug provides? To find an answer to this question, drug researchers asked alcohol, opiate, and cocaine patients what the feeling of craving meant to them. Their answer seemed to depend on the drug the patient chose. For alcoholics and opiate patients, craving was associated more with getting rid of negative withdrawal symptoms and less with any positive feelings the drug may have provided. However, for cocaine patients, the pattern of findings was reversed. For them craving was associated more with getting the positive feelings derived from cocaine and less with removing negative feelings (Childress et al., 1992). Thus, on the whole, craving seems linked to reducing unpleasant feelings or negative drug effects as well as with a desire to experience a drug's specific euphoric effects.

Tolerance and Withdrawal. Drug addiction or dependence is addressed in the *Diagnostic and Statistical Manual of Mental Disorders* of the American Psychiatric Association (2000), which states that drug dependence is characterized by tolerance and withdrawal. **Tolerance** means that the body habituates to the effects of a drug because of repeated experiences. Tolerance is a case of stimulus (drug) habituation and is manifested as an increase in the amount of drug dosage needed to achieve the same desired effect. Figure 4.2 shows increased dosages

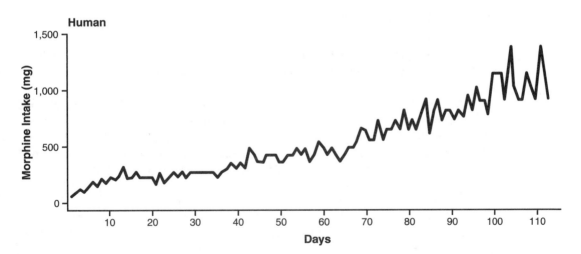

FIGURE 4.2 Drug Tolerance. Patterns of opiate intake in a human under conditions of continuous drug availability. The graph shows the amount of the drug taken over consecutive days.

Source: From "Similarities in Animal and Human Drug-Taking Behavior" by R. R. Griffiths et al. (figure 3, p. 17), 1980, in N. K. Mello, Ed., *Advances in Substance Abuse*, Greenwich, CT: JAI Press. Copyright 1980 by JAI Press, Inc. Reprinted by permission.

needed to offset the tolerance developed by a human addicted to morphine (Griffiths et al., 1980). The data in Figure 4.2 come from a study by Wikler of an individual with a history of drug abuse (cited in Griffiths et al., 1980, p. 17). This individual was allowed to request any drug as often and in any amount he wished. He chose intravenous morphine injections for 112 consecutive days, after which he was instructed to detoxify himself.

A **withdrawal syndrome** is a second characteristic of drug dependence. It refers to a drug-opposite effect. A drug produces a rush or pleasant experience. However, when the drug wears off a person experiences feelings that are by contrast the opposite and negative of what the drug initially produced. Withdrawal can range from mild to extreme and depend on the length of time since the last drug use. Caffeine withdrawal may result in a headache and lack of energy while opiate withdrawal may involve dysphoria, depressed mood, nausea, and feelings of distress. In addition, there are increased cravings for the drug that produced the withdrawal.

Additional characteristics of drug dependence involve an inordinate amount of time spent in obtaining the substance at the expense of other activities, unsuccessful attempts to reduce consumption, and continued use despite resulting physical and psychological problems. The everyday term **addiction** is usually employed in place of the term *dependence*. Addiction has come to mean an intense craving, seeking out, and use of a particular drug. Extended drug use may be accompanied by abuse, which involves the inability to maintain social roles such as family, school, or work. It involves drug use in dangerous situations, such as drunk driving or sharing needles. Drug abuse continues in spite of legal problems and persistent interpersonal problems, such as arguments at home. These characteristics of abuse may become part of addiction in which use of a particular drug occurs in spite of the adverse physical and social consequences that result.

Initiation into Drug Use

Why do a percentage of individuals who experimented with drugs become dependent on them? Genetic dispositions, personality traits, and a condition known as reward deficiency syndrome all seem to contribute to an individual's tendency to become addicted.

Genetic Disposition.   "Everyone in my family smokes" and "Alcoholism runs in my family" are observations that imply a **genetics of addiction.** This field employs methods from behavioral genetics in order to determine how people's genetic inheritance determines their susceptibility to move from experimentation to addiction. Behavioral genetics is based on the assumption that drugs have their effects on structures in the brain. These structures are genetically transmitted from one generation to the next. Furthermore, greater genetic similarity between two individuals is associated with greater similarity in their brains and nervous systems, which in turn is associated with corresponding resemblances in their vulnerability to drugs of abuse (Goldman et al., 2005; Plomin et al., 2001).

Genetic evidence indicates that dependence on the substances in Figure 4.1 are heritable (Kendler et al., 2003; Li et al., 2003) as is dependence on caffeine and gambling (Goldman et al., 2005; Lessov et al., 2004). Heritable means that as the genetic similarity between individuals increases, their similarity in drug-use habits increases. However, genes do not imply that a person is destined to become addicted to psychoactive drugs. In addition to the effects of genes, the general environment, and environmental effects unique to the individual also contribute to drug dependence (Lessov et al., 2004; Turkheimer, 2000).

Personality Disposition. In addition to examining the genetic dispositions, psychologists have also examined personality traits and their association with drug use. It is important to note that there is no single addictive personality but that there are several personality traits that are associated with addiction (Ball, 2005). Two such personality traits are sensation seeking and impulsiveness. *Sensation seeking* refers to a trait that is associated with seeking varied, intense, and novel sensations and the willingness to take various risks to experience those sensations (Zuckerman, 1994). In a review of the literature, Zuckerman (1994) concluded that sensation seekers because of their curiosity and need for novelty seemed motivated to experience a variety of drugs. Disinhibition is a characteristic of sensation seeking that seems particularly associated with the use of alcohol and nicotine. Disinhibition is characterized by reduced social restraint, which is associated with the tendency to party, gamble, and engage in sexual activities. Hittner and Swickert (2006) in a review of studies on sensation seeking that involved over 37,000 participants discovered that disinhibition is the strongest predictor of alcohol use. Nicotine use is also associated with disinhibition. Perkins and coresearchers (2000) administered a nasal spray of nicotine to nonsmokers who varied in sensation seeking. The intensity of the individuals' positive and negative reactions to the spray depended on the level of sensation seeking. Also, individuals high in disinhibition reacted to the spray with more pleasure, a greater head rush, tension, confusion, and arousal. These differences in the initial reaction to nicotine may help explain why high-sensation seekers are more likely to end up as smokers, compared to low-sensation seekers (Zuckerman et al., 1990).

　Impulsiveness is the other personality trait associated with psychoactive drug use. **Impulsiveness** consists of two components: heightened sensitivity to rewards and lack of foresight and planning (Dawe et al., 2004). Impulsive individuals are more sensitive to the rewarding pleasures that drugs provide. But they are also less aware of any negative consequences of their drug use. These two components are responsible for the relationship between impulsiveness and the use of drugs like alcohol, nicotine, and cannabis (Dawe et al., 2004). The *Barratt Impulsiveness Scale* (Patton et al., 1995) is one method that psychologists use to measure an individual's degree of impulsiveness. Five items sampled from this 30-item scale are presented in Table 4.1. Impulsiveness is the inverse of self-control as measured by the *Brief Self-Control Scale* (see Chapter 2; Tangney et al., 2004). Does the *Barratt Impulsiveness Scale* show a difference between individuals who abuse psychoactive drugs and those who do not? It does. Substance abuse patients, for example, scored significantly higher than did a large sample of university students. Other studies have also indicated that individuals who score higher on the *Barratt Impulsiveness Scale* are more prone to abuse drugs. For example, patients who became dependent or abused alcohol before and after age 25 were compared on their impulsiveness scores. Individuals who developed alcohol problems prior to age 25 had higher impulsiveness scores than those who developed problems after age 25 (Dom et al., 2006). Smoking is also affected by impulsiveness. Greater impulsiveness in beginning smokers was associated with greater expectations of the positive and negative reinforcing effects of smoking. More impulsive individuals expected smoking to be very pleasurable, would smoke more frequently, and would be less motivated to quit (Doran et al., 2007).

TABLE 4.1   Items from the 30-Item Barratt Impulsiveness Scale

I "squirm" at plays or lectures.
I act on impulse.
I plan tasks carefully.*
I like to think about complex problems.*
I often have extraneous thoughts when thinking.

Source: Adapted from "Factor Structure of the Barratt Impulsiveness Scale" by J. H. Patton et al., 1995, *Journal of Clinical Psychology, 51,* table 1, p. 771.
Rate how true each item is of you: 1 = rarely/never, 2 = occasionally, 3 = often, 4 = almost always/always.
*means reverse score: 1 = 4, 2 = 3. Sum your scores. A higher score means greater impulsiveness.

➤ The complete Barratt Impulsiveness Scale may be found on the website of the *International Society for Research on Impulsivity*; http://impulsivity.org/BIS-11

Personality traits like sensation seeking and impulsiveness are not psychological abstractions but are heritable—that is, they have a genetic basis. Thus, although these personality traits are associated with drug use, they are also under the partial control of our genes (Hur & Bouchard, 1997; Zuckerman, 2002). Genes help contribute to a person's level of sensation seeking and impulsiveness, which then makes those individuals susceptible to drug experimentation and abuse (Goldman et al., 2005).

The **reward deficiency syndrome** is another characteristic that may influence drug experimentation and use (Blum et al., 1996, 2000). This syndrome refers to sensory deprivation of the brain's pleasure area because of a low number of receptors that are sensitive to a neurotransmitter known as **dopamine** (a chemical related to pleasure). Individuals with this syndrome may also be less sensitive to dopamine when it is released during activities that are pleasurable for most people. The shortage of dopamine pleasure receptors motivates individuals to seek out the more intense forms of pleasure that are provided by both illicit and licit drugs and gambling. As a consequence, they are more likely to take drugs and are more likely to become alcoholics, drug abusers, smokers, or compulsive gamblers (Blum et al., 1996, 2000).

Section Recap

There are both legal and illegal *psychoactive drugs*, which are chemical substances that can alter a person's mood and behavior. *Caffeine* has a stimulating effect and is the most widely used psychoactive substance in the world. *Nicotine* is the psychoactive drug found in tobacco, and *alcohol* is found in beer, wine, and distilled spirits. Psychoactive drugs include *opiates*, such as morphine, codeine, and heroin; and *cocaine*, a powdery substance derived from coca plants. Smoking marijuana arouses feelings of euphoria and drowsiness. *Amphetamines* and methamphetamines produce alertness, euphoria, and subjective well-being and are seemingly more powerful than cocaine. According to the National Survey on Drug Use and Health of individuals ages 12 years and older, the most frequently tried drug (excluding caffeine) is alcohol and the least frequently tried is heroin.

Drug dependence or *addiction* is characterized by craving, tolerance, and a withdrawal syndrome. *Craving* refers to an overpowering, almost uncontrollable urge for the drug a person uses in order to obtain the euphoric effects or to reduce withdrawal effects. *Tolerance* means that a person habituates to the effects of the drug while the *withdrawal syndrome* refers to a drug-opposite effect that results from drug-use abstinence. Several factors contribute to people's experimentation and subsequent addiction. According to the *genetics of addiction,* the likelihood of a person becoming addicted is heritable, which means that an increase in the genetic similarity between individuals is linked to an increase in their similarity of drug use. Personality traits like sensation seeking and impulsiveness are also associated with drug use. The trait of *impulsiveness* is linked to heightened drug pleasures and a lack of foresight regarding the consequences of drug use. Individuals suffering from a *reward deficiency syndrome* are more likely to become addicted. This syndrome refers to the brain's pleasure center being less sensitive to dopamine, a brain chemical that provides the basis for natural rewards.

Theories of Drug Addiction

The two fictitious anecdotes that opened this chapter illustrate that psychoactive drugs are powerful motivators. Both individuals in these examples feel the effects of stimuli associated with their drug use. A mirror and familiar buildings evoke feelings linked with anticipated pleasure and with drug withdrawal. The motivation for drug-seeking behavior comes from the pull of anticipated positive consequences—that is, anticipated *positive reinforcers*, such as a cocaine high. In the other case, the motivation comes from the push to escape aversive withdrawal symptoms—that is, *negative reinforcers*, such as escape with heroin. During the drug experimentation phase, an individual is presumably motivated by anticipated positive reinforcement: drug "highs" or euphoria. It is only after addiction that drugs are used to escape drug "lows" or aversive withdrawal symptoms.

This section presents explanations for the motivation of drug use. The first explanation involves reductionism. What happens in the brain that is associated with drug euphoria and withdrawal pains? The second explanation involves the association of drug stimuli with pleasurable and aversive feelings that emerge in a person's consciousness.

Discovery of Pleasure Centers in the Brain

In 1953 pleasure centers were discovered in the brain of a rat when James Olds implanted electrodes in the hypothalamus. Quite by accident an electrical impulse was delivered while the rat happened to be in a certain location. As a consequence of this stimulation, Olds observed the rat returning to this same location as if it was searching for whatever produced the electrical stimulation (Olds, 1958, 1977). Subsequently, Olds undertook a series of experiments to more closely examine the role of electrical brain stimulation as a reinforcer and as a source of pleasure (Olds, 1958, 1977). Rats were placed in an operant chamber, which is a small cage with a lever on one end. The rats could move freely about the chamber, and when they pressed the lever, a small electrical current was delivered through a chronically implanted electrode, thus stimulating that part of their brain. Olds discovered that the rats were very motivated to attain this stimulation, depending on the part of the brain being stimulated.

Pleasure Emerges from the Brain

There are several implications from Olds' discovery that will help us understand the motivation that leads to addiction.

Drugs and Natural Incentive Effects.   First, artificially produced psychoactive drugs have the ability to provide pleasurable effects that are unmatched in nature. The ingestion of drugs provides no pleasurable sensory effects like those of natural incentives (Stewart et al., 1984). Only when drugs reach the brain do they have rewarding effects. Certain foods and drinks provide pleasure by their smell and taste, and the touch of the right person is pleasure to our skin. Drugs, however, do not provide pleasure to our taste buds and touch receptors. In fact, their routes of administration can be downright unpleasant. Cocaine powder is inhaled into the nose to penetrate the nasal membrane. Hypodermic needles allow addicts to inject drugs (morphine, heroin) directly into their veins for transport to the brain. Nicotine is absorbed into the bloodstream from the lungs when tobacco is smoked. In the 1800s, opium was smoked in specially made pipes, as is crack cocaine today. Alcohol is a drug taken by swallowing and is one that humans flavor heavily. Putting powder up the nose, pricking the skin, and filling the lungs with smoke are unpleasant experiences. Yet, individuals are willing to endure these procedures in order for drugs to reach the brain.

Neurons and Neurotransmitters.   A second implication of Olds's research is the compulsive and uncontrollable nature of both brain stimulation and drug use. Perhaps only by examining what occurs in the brain will it be possible to understand the powerful nature of drug addiction. Toward this end, scientists have discovered that identical brain sites are involved in electrical stimulation and in the action of psychoactive drugs. Prior to embarking on these implications, it is necessary to provide a brief description of the mechanics and processes of the brain that allow drug-induced pleasure to emerge.

   The brain is composed of billions of **neurons,** which are cells that specialize in conducting electrical impulses. Neurons receive external information, process it, and move it along. Neurons represent information as impulses, which are brief electrical changes. Impulses travel along neurons, which are connected to one another in a complex communication network. Neurons come in a wide variety of sizes and shapes, but all contain several important parts: dendrites, cell body, axon, and terminals (see Figure 4.3). *Dendrites* receive impulses from sense organs (eyes, ears, nose, touch receptors) or from other neurons. If a sufficient number of impulses from the senses or other neurons arrive at the dendrites in a certain period of time, then the neuron fires. The neuron sends its own impulse traveling down its *axon* to the end, where the axon begins to divide like branches of a tree. These branches end in little knobs known as *terminal buttons*, which come very close to the dendrites of other neurons without actually touching them (see Figure 4.3). Thus, neurons are one-way channels of communication: they receive impulses from the dendrites of sending neurons and then act like receiving neurons. A receiving neuron also becomes a sending neuron, since its nerve impulses are transmitted to other neurons, to glands, or to muscles.

   At the end of the terminal button, the nerve impulse comes to a halt because there is a *synapse* or *cleft* between the sending neuron and the receiving neuron. It is impossible for the electrical impulse to jump the cleft in order to stimulate the next neuron (see Figure 4.3). This problem is handled by switching from electrical to chemical communication. When the nerve impulse reaches the terminal buttons, it releases a chemical or **neurotransmitter** from containers known as synaptic vesicles. The molecules of this chemical substance diffuse across the synapse and bind with receptor sites on the receiving neuron (see Figure 4.3). Neurotransmitters fit into the receptor sites of the receiving neuron like a key into a lock. When

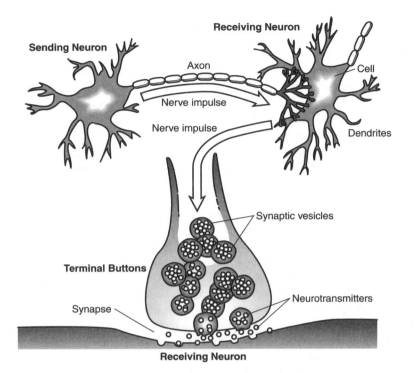

FIGURE 4.3   The Neuron and the Nerve Impulse. A nerve impulse travels down the length of the axon from the sending to the receiving neuron. When the impulse reaches the terminal buttons, it releases a neurotransmitter, which diffuses across the synapse and binds with the receiving neuron. The neurotransmitters then cause the receiving neuron to fire. Psychoactive drugs travel to synapses and affect neurons directly or indirectly by influencing the neurotransmitters that are already there.

enough neurotransmitter is released and binds with receptor sites, then the receiving neuron will fire its own impulse. Once the neurotransmitter has done its job, it is reabsorbed into the terminal button through a process known as *reuptake*. The reason for this brief digression into the action of nerve impulses is because drugs of abuse can fire certain neurons that compose areas of the brain called pleasure centers, which are described next.

Common Brain Pathway.   Each psychoactive drug has its own specific effect. For example, cocaine, nicotine, and caffeine stimulate the central nervous system so that people feel excited, energetic, and more alert. Alcohol, in contrast, is a depressant, which means it slows the function of the central nervous system. Alcohol makes a person feel less anxious, lowers stress, lowers social inhibitions, and increases relaxation. In addition, drugs differ in their method of ingestion and hence sensory stimulation—that is, by smoking, drinking, or injecting it. However, drugs also have a common effect, which refers to the pleasurable feelings that they create. These feelings range from mild euphoria to a rush and emerge from neuronal activity in specific areas of the brain.

In spite of their different routes of administration, drugs share a common brain reward system where they produce their general pleasure (Nestler, 2005; Self, 2005; Wise, 2004). This reward system is referred to as the **mesolimbic dopamine system,** which has two characteristics. First, it is composed of neurons in the middle of the brain that connect differ-ent sites, such as the *nucleus accumbens* and the *ventral tegmental area*. These two sites are responsible for much of the euphoric effects that come from using drugs. Second, dopamine is the neurotransmitter that fires the neurons that make up the mesolimbic dopamine system. Psychoactive drugs travel to the synapses of neurons in the mesolimbic dopamine system where they either directly stimulate the neurons of the nucleus accumbens and ventral tegmen-tal area or they influence the actions of dopamine that is already there. Drugs cause either the release of dopamine or prevent the reuptake of dopamine. In either case, dopamine increases the level of activity in the system, from which emerges feelings of pleasure and euphoria.

The different psychoactive drugs work various ways to produce their ultimate effects (Kelley & Berridge, 2002; Nestler, 2005; Self, 2005; Wise, 2004). Cocaine works by blocking the reuptake of dopamine into the terminal buttons of axons located in the nucleus accumbens. Hence, dopamine remains constantly available to stimulate the neurons there. Opiates (mor-phine and heroin) act differently than cocaine to produce pleasure. When an opiate is injected into the bloodstream, it reaches the brain and attaches to neurons that use a set of neurotrans-mitters known as opioids (resembling opium). The opioid neurons in turn release the neuronal brake that inhibits the release of dopamine. With the brake off, more dopamine is released, and pleasure is the result. Opiates can also stimulate the nucleus accumbens directly, which also results in feelings of pleasure (Goldstein, 2001; Nestler, 2005; Self, 2005). Drinking moder-ate amounts of alcohol also seems to take the brakes off of the release of dopamine. Nicotine is able to activate the release of dopamine in both the nucleus accumbens and the ventral tegmental area (Nestler, 2005). Thus, cocaine, opiates, alcohol, and nicotine evoke pleasur-able feelings because of their ability to stimulate the mesolimbic dopamine system.

> ➤ A video of the actions of cocaine is available at http://www.pbs.org/wnet/closetohome/ animation/coca-anim2-main.html

> ➤ A video of the actions of heroine is available at http://www.pbs.org/wnet/closetohome/ animation/opi-anim2-main.html

It is important to remember the natural function of dopamine and the mesolimbic dopamine system. Recall from Chapter 2 Spencer's (1899) claim that behavior that is im-portant for survival is pleasurable. Dopamine and the mesolimbic dopamine system help carry out that function for the individual and the species. Dopamine is the neurotransmitter responsible for the reinforcing effects provided by natural rewards, such as food for hungry animals, water for thirsty animals, and the opportunity for sexual intercourse by sexually receptive animals (Wise & Rompre, 1989).

Blocking Drug Effects.   If psychoactive drugs could be blocked from binding with their appropriate neurons, then their pleasurable effects should be reduced. Consequently, any behavior motivated by the delivery of those drugs should decline also. This blocking effect is made possible by drugs known as **antagonists.** Pimozide is an antagonist of dopamine. For example, de Wit and Wise (1977) found injecting rats with pimozide reduced their re-sponsiveness for a cocaine reinforcer. It was as if the antagonist blocked any pleasure that the cocaine provided. Naltrexone is an antagonist of heroin. Stewart and Wise (1992) dis-covered that rats injected with naltrexone exhibited a decline in their lever pressing for a heroin reinforcer. Again, it seems that the antagonist reduced the pleasure that heroin pro-vided. Consequently, the rats' motivation for heroin declined.

Naltrexone shows promise in helping humans curb their cravings in order to overcome various addictions (Johansson et al., 2006; O'Brien, 2005). In one experiment, O'Malley and coresearchers (2002) investigated the effects of naltrexone on 18 alcohol-dependent individuals, who consumed 20 to 40 drinks per week. During a 6-day period prior to the experiment, half the participants took either a daily dose of naltrexone while the other half took a daily placebo (non-drug control). Six hours after the last dose, they were tested in a laboratory for their alcohol craving with the *Alcohol Urge Questionnaire* (Bohn et al., 1995). Next, in order to prime the desire for alcohol, participants were provided drinks of their favorite alcohol mixed with fruit juice. A test for any priming effects required the participants to make a choice eight times between receiving a drink now or receiving $3 tomorrow. Thus, the participant could consume a maximum of eight drinks or earn up to $24. If naltrexone effectively reduced the reinforcing value of alcohol, then the naltrexone participants should consume fewer drinks than the placebo participants should. This prediction was confirmed. The results in Figure 4.4 show that naltrexone reduced the urge for a drink and reduced the number of drinks that were consumed. In addition, naltrexone had the effect of making individuals drink more slowly. The researchers concluded that naltrexone reduced the reinforcing value of alcohol for alcohol-dependent individuals.

➤ The complete *Alcohol Urge Questionnaire* is available at http://www.ncbi.nlm.nih.gov/ books/bv.fcgi?rid=hstat5.section.51977

Psychological Theories

In contrast to explanations that focus on the brain, psychological theories concern an individual's feelings of cravings and pleasures that drugs provide. A major distinction among these theories is their emphases on different aspects of addiction.

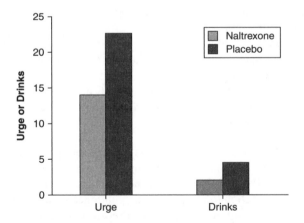

FIGURE 4.4   Effects of Naltrexone on Alcohol. Six consecutive days of naltrexone reduced the urge for a drink of alcohol and reduced the number of drinks consumed during a 2-hour period.

Source: Adapted from "Naltrexone Decreases Craving and Alcohol Self-Administration in Alcohol-Dependent Subjects and Activates the Hypothalamo-Pituitary-Adrenocortical Axis" by S. S. O'Malley et al., 2002, *Psychopharmacology, 160,* table 1, pp. 22, 24.

Opponent-Process Theory.   This theory integrates psychological characteristics of drug motivation (Solomon & Corbit, 1974; Solomon, 1980). According to this theory, the initial positive hedonic process produced by a drug is opposed or counteracted by a negative hedonic process. The positive process is always the same and quickly subsides while the opponent process is slow to take effect and continues after the drug wears off. The opponent process counteracts the disruptive effects of a drug reaction and is an attempt to restore homeostasis (balanced internal environment; see Chapter 5). Subjectively, an individual experiences the algebraic sum of these two processes. For example, inhaling nicotine from tobacco produces a positive hedonic feeling. This positive feeling, however, produces an opponent process to counteract the effects of nicotine. When the nicotine wears off, the positive feeling ceases and the negative opponent feeling becomes dominant, which is felt as withdrawal (Solomon & Corbit, 1974). Repeated drug experiences strengthen the opponent process, while the strength of the initial positive process remains constant.

Incentive Sensitization Theory.   Have you ever had a strong craving for some substance but then not enjoy it as much as expected? Is the degree of craving or wanting a drug linked with the amount of pleasure that is derived from consuming the drug? One line of thinking is that craving or wanting a drug is independent of the actual drug experience. According to **incentive sensitization theory,** craving or wanting results from the drug's incentive value and not from its hedonic value (Robinson & Berridge, 2000, 2003). As a result of repeated drug experiences, the addict's brain becomes sensitized to drugs and associated drug stimuli, which affect wanting a drug more (incentive value) but not liking it more (hedonic value). Sensitization affects that part of the brain that leads to compulsively wanting and seeking drugs. Sensitization does not affect that part of the brain involved in liking drugs. In fact, the pleasure and euphoria from drug use actually decline slightly.

Conditioning Theories

Craving is a major source of motivation for drug use. Thus, it is important to know what promotes craving and how it develops. Opponent-process theory implies that withdrawal and drug cravings eventually cease (Solomon & Corbit, 1974). However, this picture is incomplete. Although the young man in the example that opened the chapter was drug-free for over a year, his withdrawal symptoms returned. In the other example, the young woman's craving for cocaine, dormant at the time, was suddenly activated on seeing the mirror. Thus, although an addict is not using drugs, craving in one form or another can be reinstated by the appropriate reminders.

Classical Conditioning.   Classical conditioning combined with opponent-process theory can explain the return of withdrawal symptoms and druglike euphoria. In his experiments on conditioned reflexes, Pavlov (1927) reports how a dog's reaction to morphine is conditionable. A dog's natural reaction to morphine (unconditioned stimulus) is salivation, nausea, vomiting, and sleep (unconditioned responses). Preparation for the injection, such as seeing the removal of the syringe from its container, becomes the conditioned stimulus. After several days of repeated injections, the conditioned stimulus produces salivation and nausea (conditioned responses) before the actual injection. According to Solomon and Corbit (1974), during the process of repeated drug experiences, stimuli in the environment can become associated with a moderate degree of euphoria, as in the young woman's case and also with withdrawal symptoms, as in the young man's case. Consequently, addicted individuals become motivated for their drug of choice.

Conditioned Compensatory versus Conditioned Druglike Responses. How is it possible that conditioned responses can be similar to withdrawal symptoms at one time yet be similar to drug-unconditioned responses at another? The answer lies in the nature of the conditioned response. In classical conditioning the conditioned response and the unconditioned response are usually the same. However, there sometimes occurs what is called *paradoxical conditioning* in which the conditioned response is the opposite of the unconditioned response (Black, 1965). These conditioned responses are called *conditioned compensatory responses*. Thus, two types of drug-conditioned responses are possible. One conditioned response is the opposite of a drug reaction, while the other one mimics a drug reaction. According to a **conditioned compensatory response model,** a conditioned drug response is in the opposite direction of the unconditioned drug response. The compensatory response offsets the effects of a drug (such as morphine) and returns the body to its normal state to maintain homeostasis. According to the **conditioned druglike response model,** conditioned drug stimuli are reminders that elicit conditioned responses similar to those evoked by the drug itself (Stewart, de Wit, & Eikelboom, 1984). In either model, the desire for drugs returns.

Events That Lead to Drug Relapse

The motivation for drugs comes and goes. Even when an individual has quit using drugs for a time, she can *relapse*, which means going back to using drugs. A few major factors play a role in drug relapse: priming and the relief from stress.

Drug Priming with an Unconditioned Stimulus. "I'll bet you can't eat just one" is the slogan of a potato chip commercial. The slogan implies that the first bite increases your craving so strongly that further resistance is impossible. **Priming** means that a strong craving for a drug can be reinstated with a single dose of alcohol, nicotine, cocaine, or heroin. Kirk and de Wit (2000) demonstrated priming with alcohol for social drinkers. During each experimental session, 22- to 25-year-old university undergraduates drank either a nonalcoholic beverage (placebo) or one containing a 0.2-, 0.4-, or 0.8-gram dose of alcohol mixed with tonic water and lime juice. Participants were not informed what the beverage contained. After drinking it, the participants rated their reactions for "feel" the effect, "like" the effect, feel "high," and "want more" on a visual scale that ranged from 0 = Not at all or Dislike a lot to 100 = A lot or Very much. The results showed that all the ratings of the beverages increased above the placebo as the amount of alcohol increased. Participants felt the effects of the alcohol more, liked it more, experienced a greater high, and wanted more. All these effects are indicative of priming (Kirk & de Wit, 2000).

In addition, the effects of alcohol priming seem greater for heavy drinkers compared to light drinkers. Myrick and coresearchers (2004) compared individuals who averaged eight drinks per day (heavy drinkers) with those who averaged two drinks per day (light drinkers). Both a sip of alcohol and a picture of an alcoholic drink produced greater increases in craving among heavy drinkers than for the light drinkers.

Human addicts who are trying to quit their drug habit also run into the problem of priming. A single cigarette, drink of alcohol, or drug injection can reestablish craving and reestablish the drug habit. For example, following their participation in a stop smoking program, participants smoked their first cigarette 58 days later. They smoked their second cigarette only 9 days after that, with about half of the participants smoking their second cigarette within 24 hours after the first (Brandon et al., 1990). The first cigarette primed a craving for more cigarettes. Thus, it appears that in trying to stop drinking, smoking, or using illegal drugs, one drink, smoke, or drug injection elicits the urge for another and another (Stewart, de Wit, & Eikelboom, 1984). In other words, the motivation for the person's drug of choice returns.

Priming with a Conditioned Stimulus.   Priming is also possible with conditioned stimuli that are intimately associated with the drug-taking procedure. In this chapter's opening vignette, the buildings and mirror on the coffee table are examples of conditioned stimuli associated with the use of heroin and cocaine. Drug-associated stimuli have been incorporated into virtual reality technology, which refers to a realistic environment created on a computer screen. Individuals interact with the environment visually but also through sound via headphones and by means of a mouse, keyboard, or joystick. Baumann and Sayette (2006) primed the desire for cigarettes by embedding them in a virtual reality neighborhood scene. They had smokers navigate a virtual environment that began from an apartment building to the street, past a news stand, and then into a restaurant-bar filled with patrons. During the first run through the virtual environment, cigarette-stimuli were absent but those stimuli were present during the second run. On the second run, participants saw an open pack in the apartment, smokers on the street, cigarettes for sale at the news stand, and entered the bar filled with patrons who smoked. The participants rated their urge to smoke at the start and end of each run and at specific locations where cigarettes were either absent or present. The smoking urge was measured with a 100-point scale that ranged from *0 = absolutely no urge* to *100 = the strongest urge I have ever experienced*. The smoking-associated stimuli indeed increased the urge to smoke. Figure 4.5 shows that even when

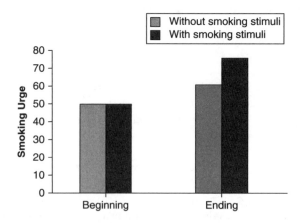

FIGURE 4.5   Priming Effects of Smoking Cues. Smokers traveled through a virtual neighborhood on a computer screen. When they encountered cues associated with smoking or cigarettes, their craving for a cigarette increased.

Source: Adapted from "Smoking Cues in a Virtual World Provoke Craving in Cigarette Smokers" by S. B. Baumann & M. A. Sayette, 2006, *Psychology of Addictive Behaviors, 20,* table 2, p. 487.

cigarette stimuli were absent, the urge to smoke increased from the beginning to the end of the virtual run. Many participants mentioned that in spite of the absence of cigarettes "there were many numerous unintentional and idiosyncratic cues that triggered their urges" (p. 486). Figure 4.5 also shows that the increase in the urge to smoke was greater when the virtual reality scenes were filled with the presence of cigarettes. The strongest smoking urges occurred in the presence of the bar scene that contained patrons who smoked. In a similar use of virtual reality, visits to a crack house evoked reactions to conditioned stimuli associated with cocaine use (Saladin et al., 2006). There was a tendency for most scenes involving cocaine to increase cravings for cocaine. Most effective were virtual reality scenes that portrayed dealing and using crack cocaine.

Stress and Drug Cravings. The motivation for drugs comes and goes partly as a result of priming. In addition, individuals can relapse as a result of stressful experiences. In these cases, drugs are consumed in order to alleviate stress. One line of evidence for this claim is based on *comorbidity*, which refers to the association between posttraumatic stress disorder (PTSD) and substance abuse (Brady et al., 2004). PTSD is the result of exposure to extremely traumatic events, such as physical and sexual abuse or combat. Subsequent PTSD experiences involve physiological arousal, intrusive thoughts about the original trauma, and avoidance of stimuli associated with it (American Psychiatric Association, 2000). Comorbidity refers to the fact that people who suffer from PTSD are also more likely to be substance abusers than are members of the general population. According to the **self-medication hypothesis,** this association is the result of PTSD sufferers attempting to reduce the negative feelings that arise when prior traumatic memories are relived (Brady et al., 2004). Longitudinal research shows that substance abuse occurs after PTSD has developed and not the reverse. Chilcoat and Breslau (1998) found that individuals who suffered from PTSD had a greater likelihood of becoming substance abusers than individuals who did not have PTSD. Furthermore, exposure to traumatic events that did not result in PTSD did not increase the likelihood of subsequent substance abuse. However, an alternative possibility suggested by Goeders (2004) is that the distress experienced during a PTSD episode sensitizes an individual to the effects of a drug. As a result the reinforcing value of the psychoactive drug increases.

Drug-Use Reinforcement

What is experienced by an individual who has been subjected to priming or distress? Do drug-associated stimuli produce reactions that are opposite of the reaction evoked by the drug itself (Siegel, 2005) as in the conditioned compensatory-response model? In this case, the individual is motivated to reduce these feelings. Or do drug-associated stimuli elicit feelings similar to those evoked by the drug itself (Stewart, de Wit, & Eikelboom, 1984) as in the conditioned druglike response model? The addicted individual is motivated to intensify these feelings. There has been much debate whether drug use is motivated by escaping from drug lows or pursuing drug highs. We will examine these two possibilities next.

Positive Reinforcement. As described in the section on drugs of abuse, drugs make a person feel good, high, and euphoric, which are positive reinforcers for their continued use. A direct test of the positive feeling produced by caffeine and nicotine was performed by Garrett and Griffiths (2001). They gave different concentrations of caffeine, nicotine, or a placebo (nondrug) to their participants. Next, they asked the participants questions that pertained to positive reinforcement, such as "How high are you?" and "Do you feel a rush?" The results showed that stronger doses of caffeine and nicotine were associated with reports of greater "highs" and "rushes."

Negative Reinforcement. Drug abstinence produces withdrawal symptoms felt as negative affect, such as bodily distress, headaches, fatigue, dysphoria, anxiety, irritability, and sadness (APA, 2000; Baker et al., 2004). Drug-seeking behavior and use is negatively reinforced because it reduces withdrawal-generated negative affect according to the **affective model of negative reinforcement** (Baker et al., 2004). Several considerations support the model. First, negative affect characterizes a general withdrawal process along with drug-specific withdrawal symptoms. Specifically, alcohol withdrawal may involve tremors and sweating, cocaine withdrawal may involve fatigue and increased appetite, while nicotine withdrawal involves anxiety and insomnia (Jaffe et al., 2005). Accompanying these withdrawal symptoms is a craving for the very drug that produces the withdrawal. Thus, negative affect along with craving motivates seeking and using a variety of drugs. Second, withdrawal symptoms that are the basis for negative affect can occur early in drug use. A person need only use drugs for a short period of time in order to experience negative affect during withdrawal. For example, unpleasant withdrawal symptoms can occur after a first time use of an opiate like heroin (Harris & Gewirtz, 2005). Consequently, negative reinforcement as a motivator for drug use may accompany positive reinforcement early in the process of drug experimentation. Third, the intensity of negative affect increases with the duration of abstinence from drugs. As abstinence increases, there is greater relief from negative affect—that is, a greater amount of negative reinforcement.

Negative reinforcement implies escape, not avoidance behavior. The addict escapes or reduces negative affect that results from drug withdrawal. However, the anticipation of negative affect can motivate drug use as a case of avoidance behavior. An addict uses a drug in order to prevent negative affect. One possibility is that an addicted individual is motivated to reduce the frequency with which withdrawal occurs (Herrnstein, 1969). Addicts may not be able to avoid withdrawal every time but they can reduce the frequency of it happening. Furthermore, the affective model of negative reinforcement states that the process of addiction involves many repetitions of the following cycle: drug levels drop in the body, negative affect follows, and drug use reduces negative affect. An addict becomes sensitive to the drop in drug levels and experiences it as bodily cues. These cues signify the initial emergence of negative withdrawal into conscious awareness. Consequently, these bodily cues set the occasion for drug use in order to avoid aversive withdrawal symptoms (Baker et al., 2004).

Cognition and Addiction

The descriptions of drug addiction given thus far have been mostly mechanistic, with no mention of the role of cognitive processes. The addicted individual was described as reacting to stressful events and to drug-associated stimuli that evoke craving or withdrawal symptoms. The person was not seen as making an active attempt to approach or avoid these situations. Furthermore, mechanistic models minimize the possibility of a person willfully quitting. Therefore, trying to reduce or eliminate drug dependence would be difficult to accomplish. Bandura's (2006) agentic theory (see Chapter 1) may be a way out of this difficulty. According to this theory, humans can intentionally create their circumstances. Thus, an individual has control over whether she wants to continue exposing herself to drugs.

A feature of the interplay between cognition and addiction is the **motivation for change** (DiClemente, 1999; DiClemente et al., 2004). This motivational factor represents various stages of change from a person willfully contemplating change, to preparing for it, acting on it, and maintaining that change. For instance, a drug abuser begins by contemplating a change in his drug use by considering the pluses and minuses of such an action. Next, an individual might commit to change. As part of that commitment, for example, he might say, "I am planning to reduce my cigarette consumption by 10% beginning next month." Then when the time arrives, he initiates the plan and maintains his reduced cigarette intake, perhaps quitting eventually. His plan might be to start the day with a certain self-imposed cigarette allotment. If those are smoked prior to the end of the day, he will not seek more cigarettes. DiClemente (1999; DiClemente et al., 2004) points out that the success of motivation for change and eventually quitting depends on the incentives that are employed at each stage. Incentives imposed from outside are less effective than self-imposed ones. For example, court-ordered drug treatment is less effective than if a person decides for himself to seek treatment. Personal reasons for quitting are much more effective.

Section Recap

The motivation for drug use is based on attaining pleasure (positive reinforcement) or reducing withdrawal symptoms (negative reinforcement). These reinforcing events emerge from the activation of neurons at critical locations in the brain. The brain is composed of billions of neurons, which are cells that send and receive information by way of electrical nerve impulses. *Neurotransmitters* are chemicals at the end of sending neurons that diffuse across a synapse or gap and stimulate receiving neurons, which then send out their own nerve impulses. Dopamine is the neurotransmitter that activates neurons in the *mesolimbic dopamine system* from which feelings of pleasure and euphoria emerge into consciousness. The euphoric effects produced in the mesolimbic dopamine system are powerful, since rats will work long and hard to have these areas electrically stimulated. Psychoactive drugs produce their pleasurable effects when they reach the mesolimbic dopamine system. There the drugs increase the amount of dopamine by either blocking the reuptake or promoting the release. More dopamine is associated with greater pleasure. The natural function of dopamine is to provide pleasure for survival activities, such as eating, drinking, and sex. *Antagonists* are substances capable of blocking the pleasurable effects of psychoactive drugs. As a consequence, the motivation for cocaine, heroin, or alcohol can be reduced with the use of appropriate antagonists.

There are a number of psychological theories that stress various aspects of priming, craving, and euphoria. According to *opponent-process theory*, the initial pleasurable reaction to a drug is held in check by an opponent process or drug-opposite effect characterized by dysphoria and withdrawal. The strengthening of the opponent process is responsible for drug tolerance and withdrawal. *Incentive sensitization theory* emphasizes that individuals are motivated by a drug's incentive value (anticipated pleasure) and not by its hedonic value (actual pleasure). For the *conditioned compensatory response model*, stimuli associated with drugs evoke conditioned responses that are the opposite of drug-unconditioned responses. The *conditioned druglike response model*, however, states that the conditioned drug response is similar to the unconditioned drug response. Either model accounts for *priming*, which refers to the development of cravings whether by being exposed to the drug itself or to stimuli associated with the drug. Craving increases the likelihood of drug use or relapse. Craving and drug use also occur in order to relieve distress, depression, anxiety, or boredom. Thus, there is the tendency for comorbidity, which is the joint occurrence of distress from PTSD, for example, and drug use. According to the *self-medication hypothesis*, individuals with PTSD take psychoactive drugs in order to reduce negative feelings that are evoked by traumatic memories.

Positive reinforcement effects of drug use are the pleasurable euphoric effects. In contrast, negative reinforcement refers to the alleviation of unpleasant withdrawal symptoms. According to the *affective model of negative reinforcement*, repeated drug use allows addicts to be sensitive to the symptoms that predict withdrawal. As a consequence, drug use occurs in order to prevent the anticipated negative effect. Based on agentic theory a person can effect a motivation for change. This change represents the stages from willfully planning to reducing drug use.

Behavioral Addictions

This is the case of a 20-year-old woman who had been running since age 10 and was now in leg casts because she severely sprained both ankles:

> I would sit all day and let my thoughts build up—I would go out at night to drink, I became so frustrated and confused I didn't realize what was important anymore. I ended up sick in bed for 2½ months because of my involvement in drinking and drugs because of my inability to run. (Morgan, 1979, p. 63)

This individual is addicted to running rather than drugs. She craves running, suffers withdrawal when unable to run, and runs despite adverse consequences.

The purpose of this section is to examine whether principles of drug addiction can account for exercise addiction and gambling addiction.

Exercise Addiction and Drug Addiction

Drugs are considered *negative addictions* because their use has long-term negative consequences. **Positive addiction** (Glasser, 1976), however, refers to compulsive behaviors that result in positive health consequences. This is a term applied mainly to runners and strenuous exercisers. Like drug use, running or strenuous exercise produces a *runner's high* or **exercise high.** This refers to a state of euphoria involving exhilaration, mood improvement, and eventually relaxation. People can become addicted to this feeling, and the effect of compulsive running or exercise can be equated with drug addiction.

Reinforcers.   The rewards for running are the consequences that maintain this activity. Summers and associates (1983) asked marathoners who had been running about two years why they ran. Their reasons fell into three categories: physical health (being physically fit, losing weight), psychological health (feeling relaxed, enjoying life), and goal achievement (meeting a challenge, training for a marathon). Some reasons were classified as negative reinforcers, such as relieving depression and tension. The most rewarding consequence, however, was runner's high, which occurred in the latter part of or when finished with a run.

Some runners reported experiencing "spin out," which is a detached dreamy state of mind (Carmack & Martens, 1979; Summers et al., 1982). The length of a run seemed to correlate with the feelings characteristic of spin out. For example, runners who ran 40 minutes or more experienced spin out with a greater frequency than those who ran a shorter length of time. Other exercisers report "feeling high" or feeling like being "on speed" following periods of intense training (Griffiths, 1997).

The relationship between exercise intensity and "feeling high" has been verified in the laboratory. For instance, Blanchard and coresearchers (2002) had female university students exercise for 15 minutes on a stationary bicycle. Students felt significantly more positively engaged (happy, enthusiastic, upbeat) and revitalized as a result. These positive feelings seemed to increase with exercise intensity. Cox and coresearchers (2006) had women run on a treadmill for 33 minutes at either 60% (low intensity) or at 80% (high intensity) of their maximum aerobic capacity. Post-exercise, the participants rated their positive well-being on a seven-point scale. The ratings showed that as exercise intensity increased, positive well-being increased compared to a non-exercise control condition. In addition, positive well-being remained significantly high even 80 minutes post-exercise.

Exercise Tolerance. While drug tolerance refers to the diminishing effects of a constant drug dose, running tolerance means a decline in the euphoric effects that result from running. One cause of this decline is that a person becomes physically conditioned so running becomes less stressful. To experience the same level of runner's high, a runner has to increase the mileage, frequency, or pace of running (Morgan, 1979). The upper limit of this increase, however, is the body's ability to tolerate such stress. When mileage increases, running injuries develop (e.g., hip pain, knee and back injuries, stress fractures, Achilles tendon, and foot problems). For example, a woman who appeared addicted to jiujitsu exhibited exercise tolerance. She started training once a week, but after five years she now exercises every day of the week for longer and longer periods of time (i.e., six hours) (Griffiths, 1997).

The concept of tolerance points out one fundamental difference between exercise addiction and drug or alcohol addiction. Exercise addiction requires the individual to make considerable physical and mental effort in contrast to what is required for drug or alcohol addiction (Cockerill & Riddington, 1996). In the case of exercise, an individual must become physically fit in order to experience euphoria, whereas drug or alcohol addiction requires less effort for the individual to experience any positive effects. Furthermore, when individuals are forced to withdraw from exercise due to injuries, they are not likely to quickly resume their exercise addiction. It will be necessary for them to retrain to achieve a level of fitness necessary to again experience any euphoric effects (Cockerill & Riddington, 1996).

Withdrawal. For individuals who chronically exercise, exercise deprivation results in symptoms akin to physiological and psychological withdrawal. These symptoms appear to reflect a dependence on exercise (Adams & Kirby, 2002). In the case of runners, Morgan (1979) notes that when they cannot run, addicted runners feel depressed, anxious, and irritable and also suffer from muscle tension, decreased appetite, and constipation.

In an actual exercise-withdrawal experiment performed by Mondin and coresearchers (1996), individuals who exercised (running, jogging, or swimming) six to seven days per week were paid $50 not to exercise on Tuesday, Wednesday, and Thursday. Participants filled out various psychological scales each day of the week in order to measure various indicators of their moods before, during, and after their exercise deprivation. The results showed that state of anxiety, tension, and depression increased from Monday to Wednesday and then decreased. These three indicators of the negative effects of exercise deprivation were greatest on the second day of deprivation, which indicates that withdrawal symptoms begin to occur after 48 hours. The decline in anxiety, tension, and depression on Thursday may indicate the participants' awareness that they could resume exercising the next day (Mondin et al., 1996).

In another exercise-withdrawal experiment, one group of regular male runners was paid not to run for two weeks. A control group of regular runners continued their usual running routine (Morris et al., 1990). Both groups filled out questionnaires measuring anxiety and depression before and during the enforced abstinence interval and after running resumed. The two groups did not differ in anxiety and depression before the abstinence interval and after running resumed. The effect of running deprivation became apparent during the second week, when the deprived runners reported greater anxiety and depression. In addition, the deprived runners complained of more social dysfunction and somatic symptoms that developed during their first week of deprivation (Morris et al., 1990).

Addiction.   Running is considered addicting if a person craves a runner's high, organizes his life around opportunities to run, and runs as much as possible in spite of negative consequences. Runners report being addicted to running (Summers et al., 1983). Using case studies, Morgan (1979) illustrated the addictive nature of running by observing that addicted runners feel compelled to exercise daily. When unable to do so, they feel withdrawal symptoms, including anxiety, irritability, and depression. The individual insists on running despite deteriorating interpersonal relationships in social settings, the workplace, or even at home. For example, spouses may complain about being neglected because their mates spend so much time running. In addition, the addicted individual continues running in spite of injuries. Some runners only stop after the pain from their injuries becomes unbearable.

There are several factors that exhibit a person's dependence on or addiction to exercise in general. Ogden and associates (1997) uncovered eight factors with the development of their *Exercise Dependence Questionnaire*. Three of the factors involve interference, withdrawal, and insight. The interference factor reflects the extent exercise interferes with one's family, social, and work life. For instance, a person would report missing work in order to exercise. The withdrawal factor describes the negative feelings that are experienced when a person misses exercising for some reason. For example, a person would report being agitated or irritable when an exercise session is missed or hating being unable to exercise. The insight factor indicates that people are aware that their dependence on exercise is causing a problem. The person would report feeling guilty about the amount he exercises and would realize it is ruining his life but feel unable to cut back. Ogden and associates (1997) found that these factors became more severe with either an increase in the number of years of exercise or an increase in the number of weekly hours of exercise.

Another scale, named the *Exercise Dependence Scale*, contains 21 questions that measure additional components of exercise addiction (Hausenblas & Downs, 2002). For instance, an individual's continuance and lack of control are probed by the extent he continues to exercise despite physical problems and the extent he feels unable to reduce his frequency. A question relevant for exercise tolerance asks the extent a person feels a lack of benefit from his current level of exercise.

> ➤ The *Exercise Dependence Scale* is available at http://www.personal.psu.edu/dsd11/EDS/index.html

Endorphins and Exercise-Induced Euphoria

As documented in the section on reinforcers, exercise induces positive feelings. Are these feelings of an exercise high related to the neurotransmitters associated with the brain's pleasure centers? One hypothesis revolves around a set of opioid neurotransmitters of which endorphins are a special case. The term *endorphin* refers to internal morphine (*endo* for endogenous or internal and *phin* for morphine). Endorphins are primarily located in the pain pathways and are responsible for reducing the negative effects of pain stimuli and stressors. Perhaps that is why endorphins are implicated in a runner's high because running is a stressful activity. The **endorphin–exercise high connection** holds that endorphins released during strenuous exercise act on pleasure neurons and those that are linked to pleasure neurons (Adams & Kirby, 2002). One possibility is that running-induced endorphins eventually affect the mesolimbic dopamine system where feelings of pleasure occur (Nestler, 2005).

According to the endorphin–exercise high connection, exercise-induced mood changes should correlate with endorphin changes. Harte and associates (1995) examined positive and negative mood changes and β-endorphin-level changes in elite runners before and after a hard 15-kilometer (9.3 mile) run. Their findings show that following the hard run, positive mood increased and negative mood decreased. The researchers also found that β-endorphins in the runners' blood also increased over the course of the run. Thus, β-endorphin-level increases were accompanied by mood changes resembling runner's high. Wildmann and associates (1986) also showed that a feeling of pleasantness correlated with blood β-endorphin values of male runners who had completed two 10-kilometer (6.2 mile) runs. Higher levels of β-endorphin circulating in a runner's blood accompanied greater feelings of pleasure. However, the fact that endorphin changes correlated with mood changes in these studies does not mean that endorphin changes caused the mood changes. A third variable besides endorphins may be responsible for runner's high.

Gambling Addiction

Gambling is another example of a behavioral addiction that some people find difficult to control. In fact, the first step in a 12-step recovery program for addicted gamblers requires individuals to admit that they are powerless over gambling (www.gamblersanonymous.org). Addicted gamblers can become so involved with gambling that their behavior resembles drug addiction. Addicted gamblers constantly seek out opportunities to gamble and are not sensitive to any negative financial and social consequences. When gambling reaches the level of an addiction, negative behaviors ensue, which are detrimental to a person's well-being.

The incidence of gambling addicts in society has grown as a result of increased gambling opportunities over the last two decades. Whereas previously illegal, now most states allow casinos, lotteries, and scratch-off cards. Gambling has also attained more social acceptance, especially when states use their gambling profits for the greater social good, such as education and counseling for gambling addicts. Shaffer and colleagues (1999) examined estimates of the prevalence of individuals with gambling problems. Prior to 1993, an estimated 0.84% of surveyed adults reported experiencing pathological gambling problems during the preceding year. This estimate rose significantly to 1.29% after 1993. Estimates of less severe gambling problems also rose significantly during this time.

Characteristics of Addicted Gamblers. One strategy for determining the powerful motivational effects of gambling is to uncover characteristics of addicted gamblers and the psychological costs incurred. With these goals in mind, Grant and Kim (2001) interviewed 131 individuals who had been diagnosed as pathological gamblers. These individuals played slot machines, cards, blackjack, and the lottery for an average of 16 hours per week and had lost an average of 45% of their annual income during the preceding 12 months. Interview results in Figure 4.6 attest to the addictive nature of gambling by showing the percentage of gamblers who experienced various negative consequences. Notice that nearly two-thirds had maxed out their credit cards. After losing nearly all of their assets, nearly one-fourth of the addicted gamblers engaged in at least one form of illegal activity, such as writing bad checks, embezzling money at work, and committing tax fraud. Negative social consequences involved lying to friends and family members and experiencing marriage or work difficulties.

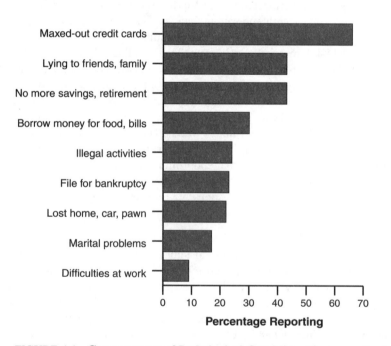

FIGURE 4.6   Consequences of Pathological Gambling. These negative behaviors attest to the addictive nature of gambling. The most frequent consequence was a maxed-out credit card, and the least frequent consequences were difficulties at work.

Source: Adapted from "Demographic and Clinical Features of 131 Adult Pathological Gamblers" by J. E. Grant and S. W. Kim, 2001, *Journal of Clinical Psychiatry, 62,* pp. 959–960.

Gambling Priming.   Gambling urges and behavior can be primed much like drug cravings can be. Environmental stimuli that evoke gambling urges include television and billboard advertisements, thoughts of winning, receiving payment, hearing conversations about gambling, and the sight and sounds of a casino (Grant & Kim, 2001). In addition to priming, gambling-associated stimuli increase a compulsive gambler's level of arousal. This is a pleasant feeling that helps reinforce gambling behavior (Sharpe, 2002). Furthermore, just as stressful events can produce drug cravings, so can they produce urges to gamble. For example, boredom, loneliness, depression, stress, and anxiety all contribute to gambling urges (Grant & Kim, 2001).

Dopamine and Gambling.   Like drugs and running, the pleasure derived from gambling may also depend on the extent that this activity activates the mesolimbic dopamine system (Blum et al., 2000; Sharpe, 2002). However, not much is known about how gambling relates to dopamine. Gambling addiction does not occur in isolation but is often associated with other drug activities. For example, DeCaria and colleagues (1996) cite studies that compulsive gamblers are also likely to have problems with alcohol and illicit drugs. In their survey of 131 pathological gamblers, Grant and Kim (2001) found that 27% also suffered from alcohol dependence or abuse and 8.4% suffered from other forms of drug dependence or abuse. This association between pathological gambling and other forms of licit and illicit drug use warrants the search for a common brain substrate.

   The drug naltrexone has been used effectively to help curb a person's appetite for heroin, cocaine, and alcohol (Goldstein, 2001; O'Brien, 2005). Naltrexone has also been employed to curb compulsive gambling. Kim and coresearchers (2001) tested the hypothesis that pathological gambling is triggered by its potential reward, which involves the actions of dopamine. Therefore, if naltrexone inhibits the release of dopamine, the impulse to gamble should decrease. The researchers gave one group of pathological gamblers a daily pill of naltrexone for 11 weeks, while another group of pathological gamblers received a placebo. Weekly evaluations showed that naltrexone reduced the symptoms of pathological gambling more than the placebo did. Naltrexone reduced the urge to gamble and reduced the subjective pleasure that gambling provided. The results of this study and the association of gambling with alcohol and other drugs support the idea that the mesolimbic dopamine system is involved in gambling addiction.

> ➤ The home page of Gamblers Anonymous is at http://www.gamblersanonymous.org. The home page for Alcoholics Anonymous is at http://www.aa.org

Section Recap

The use of psychoactive drugs is a negative addiction, while repeated strenuous exercise is a *positive addiction* because of the supposed health benefits. However, extensive exercise also has characteristics of negative addiction. Exercise addiction has several similarities with drug addiction. Humans can develop a tolerance for exercise, show withdrawal symptoms when unable to exercise, and behave as if they are addicted. There are exercise-dependence scales that measure the extent of a person's addiction. Strenuous exercise provides several positive reinforcers, with the major one being the *exercise high*, which involves feelings of euphoria, exhilaration, positive mood, and relaxation. According to the *endorphin–exercise high connection*, strenuous exercise releases endorphins, which bind with neurons that are eventually responsible for the feelings of euphoria and exhilaration.

Gambling is another addictive behavior that is pleasurable because it activates the mesolimbic dopamine system. This claim is based on the association between gambling behavior and drug or alcohol use. It is also based on the curbing effects that naltrexone has on gambling urges and pleasures.

ACTIVITIES

1. Consider conducting the following experiment on yourself in order to understand craving:

   a. Hide a piece of your favorite chocolate from view, and while it is hidden think about eating it.
   b. Next, place the chocolate in front of you and stare at it.
   c. Then unwrap it and deeply inhale the chocolate's aroma for a minute or two.
   d. Finally, nibble at the chocolate and try to maximize the flavor sensation that you feel.

   Under each condition a through d, rate your desire or craving for the piece of chocolate using a nine-point scale:
   No desire at all = 0
   Very strong desire = 9

   Did the intensity of your craving increase through steps a through d? People vary widely in their ratings, especially in steps c and d. Why do you think that happens? What does it mean to be a "chocaholic"? What factors influence one person to become a chocaholic and another to be indifferent about chocolate?

2. Do you engage in any strenuous exercise, such as biking, running, swimming, or race-pace walking? If so, do you experience any feelings resembling an exercise high? Is this feeling part of what motivates you to continue exercising?

CHAPTER
5 Homeostasis: Temperature, Thirst, Hunger, and Eating

A hungry stomach will not allow its owner to forget it, whatever his cares and sorrows.

—*Homer, 800 B.C.*

Hunger is the first course of a good dinner.

—*A French proverb*

■ The motivation of behavior would not be possible if there were not an energetic body capable of being motivated. Thus, what is necessary for the motivation of body maintenance? This question and the following ones are presented for your consideration in this chapter:

1. What internal physiological changes motivate humans to adjust their body temperature, fluid balance, and food energy levels?

2. How do the psychological sensations of being cold, hot, thirsty, or hungry motivate behavior toward temperature regulation, drinking, and eating?

3. Is hunger the only motivation for eating, or do food characteristics also determine what and how much people eat?

4. Are there individual differences among people and their situations that also determine what and how much they eat?

Internal Factors of Body Regulation

Individual accounts of extreme food or water deprivation provide insights into hunger and thirst motivation. In the late 1800s, for example, the explorer Sven Hedin suffered the tortures of thirst on a journey across a desert during which men and camels died due to lack of water. What follows is his emotional reaction when he finally discovers a pool of water:

> I stood on the brink of a little pool filled with fresh, cool water—beautiful water! It would be vain for me to try to describe the feelings which now overpowered me. They may be imagined; they cannot be described. Before drinking I counted my pulse: it was forty-nine. Then I took the tin box out of my pocket, filled it, and drank. How sweet that water tasted! Nobody can conceive it who has not been within an ace of dying of thirst. I lifted the tin to my lips, calmly, slowly, deliberately, and drank, drank, drank, time after time. How delicious! What exquisite pleasure! The noblest wine pressed out of the grape, the divinest nectar ever

103

made, was never half so sweet. My hopes had not deceived me. The star of my fortunes shone as brightly as ever it did. . . . I felt how that cold, clear, delicious water infused new energy into me. Every blood-vessel and tissue of my body sucked up the life-giving liquid like a sponge. My pulse, which had been so feeble, now beat strong again. . . . In a word, I felt my body was imbibing fresh life and fresh strength. It was a solemn, an awe-inspiring moment. (Wolf, 1958, p. 144)

Hedin's strong pleasurable reaction to finding and drinking water indicates the interplay between his physiological and psychological demand for water, on the one hand, and the extreme satisfaction that water can provide, on the other.

The purpose of this section is to describe the physiological changes and psychological sensations that motivate temperature regulation, thirst and drinking, and hunger and eating.

Homeostasis

The belief that internal demands of the body serve as a source of motivation begins with an idea formulated by the French physiologist Claude Bernard (1878/1961). He hypothesized a stable *milieu interieur* (internal environment) of fluids that bathe the body's 60 to 100 trillion cells. Many of the vital functions of life are conducted at this level, such as metabolism, growth, repair, and reproduction. In addition, he discovered that blood vessels constrict or dilate in response to temperature changes. Cold weather causes constriction, while warm weather causes dilation, and these processes maintain a constant internal temperature. Walter Cannon (1939), a Harvard physiologist, expanded the work of Bernard and coined the term **homeostasis** (*stasis* meaning staying and *homeo* meaning the same) to describe the constant conditions maintained in the body. Disturbances from both inside and outside the body, such as fluid loss by sweating or environmental temperature change, are counteracted by body processes to maintain a stable internal environment. Cannon considered homeostasis as part of the "wisdom of the body."

Negative Feedback System

These illustrations from Bernard and Cannon, attest to the body's wisdom for maintaining homeostasis—that is, a constant internal environment. The maintenance of homeostasis depends on a **negative feedback system,** a self-correcting process that reduces the discrepancy between a desired state and an actual state. A desired state or *set point* is a condition crucial for life, comfort, or safety. The actual state of the system is compared to the set point, and if a discrepancy is detected, a self-correcting process is initiated. The process ends when the discrepancy reaches zero. A household furnace is a common example (see Figure 5.1). The set point is the desired room temperature—for instance, 68°F. A comparator in the thermostat compares actual room temperature to the set point temperature, and a discrepancy between the two causes the furnace to be turned on. The heat from the furnace raises the room temperature, which is continuously fed back to the comparator for comparison to the set point temperature. When the discrepancy reaches zero, the comparator turns the furnace off. If an open door lets in cold air and lowers the room temperature, then another discrepancy results, causing the comparator to turn the furnace on again.

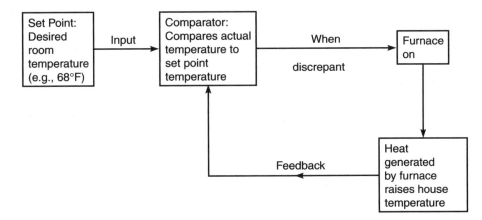

FIGURE 5.1   Negative Feedback Mechanism. The operation of a house furnace illustrates how the negative feedback mechanism operates.

Usually, set point temperature does not remain constant during the year. It varies within a comfort zone ranging from cool at a lower set point to warm at an upper set point. A more complex house temperature control system would include an air conditioner as well as a furnace. For example, an open door in the winter lets in cold air, causing the temperature to fall below the lower set point. The furnace comes on to produce heat and raise the temperature. An open door in the summer, however, lets in hot air, causing the house temperature to rise above the upper set point. The air conditioner comes on to produce cold air to lower the temperature. Between the lower and upper set points is the comfort zone.

Effects of Deviation from Set Point

How does the negative feedback system apply to homeostasis? Humans have set points for various physiological states like body temperature and amount of water, food, and various nutrients. A discrepancy between the set point and the actual physiological state defines a **physiological need.** For example, humans have a physiological need to maintain a constant body temperature, salt concentration, fluid level, and blood glucose level.

Incentives that aid in reducing a need or in restoring homeostasis can also increase pleasure. Cabanac (1971) discovered that whether temperature, odor, and taste stimuli produced pleasant or painful sensations depends on the person's internal state. Stimulus sensations are judged pleasant if they decrease deviations from homeostasis but are judged unpleasant if they increase the deviation from homeostasis. Cabanac coined the term **alliesthesia** (*ethesia* meaning sensation and *allios* meaning changed) to refer to changes in a person's *milieu interieur* that determine whether a stimulus is judged as pleasant or unpleasant. Hedin's description of drinking water as "delicious" and as "exquisite pleasure" illustrates how his strong need for water—that is, his changed internal state—caused water to have this sensation. Alliesthesia motivated him to drink to restore his body's water level. Similarly, food is delicious to a hungry person and induces eating to restore the body's energy supply.

Thermoregulation

During the summer an individual is more likely to feel hot and in winter to feel cold because actual body temperature deviates above and below the body's set point temperature of 98.6°F. This thermal set point is crucial for life and is registered in one part of the hypothalamus of the brain. Actual temperature at many different sites of the body is measured by *thermoreceptors*, and this information is received by another part of the hypothalamus, where this information is integrated (Breugelmann, 1989; Franck et al., 1989). A discrepancy between set point temperature and actual temperature results in both involuntary and voluntary attempts to restore homeostasis. When a person is hot, blood vessels involuntarily dilate to dissipate heat, and sweating occurs for cooling by evaporation. When a person is cold, blood vessels constrict to conserve heat, and shivering occurs to produce heat. Sensations about being hot or cold drive voluntary behavior. When feeling cold, a person voluntarily puts on a sweater to reduce the cold sensation, or because "it feels good" to warm up. When feeling hot, a person voluntarily takes off a sweater to reduce the hot sensation, or because "it feels good" to become less hot. Whether the sweater feels good on or off depends on the person's internal state, according to the alliesthesia concept.

Alliesthesia also plays a role in body temperature regulation by humans. To illustrate, Mower (1976) made male participants *hypothermic* (cold) by placing them up to their shoulders in a bath of cool (15 to 18°C) water or *hyperthermic* (warm) by placing them in a bath of warm (41 to 43°C) water. This procedure resulted in the participants' core body temperatures decreasing or increasing by at least 1°C. Other participants were kept at normal body temperature. Next, participants dipped their hands into baths ranging from cool to warm and rated these baths on an unpleasantness-pleasantness scale. Ratings of the water baths depended on the participants' core body temperature (see Figure 5.2). When participants were hypothermic (cold), they judged cooler baths as unpleasant and warmer baths as pleasant. When participants were hyperthermic (warm), however, they judged cooler baths as pleasant and warmer baths as unpleasant. Participants with normal core temperature judged a water bath as unpleasant only when it deviated greatly from normal skin temperature. Baths that restore body temperature to homeostasis are those that feel pleasant (Cabanac, 1971). Baths are felt to be unpleasant if they cause actual body temperature to deviate further from set point temperature.

Thirst and Drinking

Exercising on a hot day or eating salty foods soon reminds a person of the need for water. The sensation of thirst may drive an individual to drink more water.

Cellular Thirst. A cell is the smallest structure of the body capable of carrying out the functions necessary for life. In order for the trillions of cells composing the body to work properly, the amount of fluid they lose must be replaced by an equal amount. Water replaces lost fluids and is obtained through drinking and eating. **Intracellular fluid** refers to the 67% of water contained within the body's cells. **Extracellular fluid** refers to the remaining water that helps provide the external environment around the cells. Both intracellular and extracellular fluids contain concentrations of salt particles (sodium and potassium) that are necessary for cells to carry out their functions. The concentration of salt on both sides of the cell walls must be carefully maintained. If the concentration of salt is too high inside the cells, then water will enter the cells; if it is too low, then water will exit (Memmler et al., 1992). Thirst can result from a loss of intracellular fluids caused by excessive salt in the extracellular fluid. For

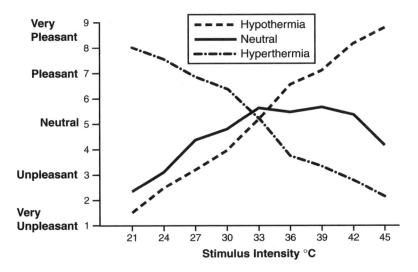

FIGURE 5.2   Core Body Temperature and Thermal Pleasantness. This figure shows group mean category judgments of thermal pleasantness of water baths as a function of stimulus temperature under three conditions of internal body temperature.

Source: From "Perceived Intensity of Peripheral Thermal Stimuli Is Independent of Internal Body Temperature" by G. D. Mower, 1976, *Journal of Comparative and Physiological Psychology, 90*, figure 2a, p. 1154. Copyright 1976 by American Psychological Association. Reprinted by permission.

example, eating a salty meal increases the salt concentration in the extracellular fluids. To restore the ideal state of salt concentration, fluids are drawn from within the cells, thereby decreasing intracellular fluids. The hypothalamus detects the cellular dehydration and registers it as thirst (Memmler et al., 1992). Thirst and drinking can also be prompted by loss of extracellular fluids surrounding the cells by evaporation from the skin, sweating, bleeding, urination, diarrhea, and exhalation. The hypothalamus also detects the loss of extracellular fluid and registers it as thirst. Besides the action of thirst to instigate drinking, the body also has automatic mechanisms to conserve water (Memmler et al., 1992; Pinel, 1997).

Thirst Sensations. The body's need for water is registered as thirst, which regulates drinking. To investigate thirst sensations, Engell and associates (1987) dehydrated male participants by forcing them to lose 3, 5, or 7% of their body water weight. The researchers accomplished this by restricting the men's drinking and eating and by having them do light exercise in a hot, dry environment. Participants' ratings of the intensity of their local sensations (dry mouth and throat, scratchy throat) and general sensations (thirsty, tired, weary, dizzy) increased with deprivation. In other words, the inducement to drink became stronger and stronger. Early researchers thought that thirst resulted from a dry mouth and throat (Wolf, 1958) and that sensory loss to that area would eliminate thirst sensations. However, although patients who have had their larynx (upper part of windpipe containing vocal cords) surgically removed are less aware of thirst in that area, they nevertheless still experience thirst as a general sensation (Miyaoka et al., 1987).

Water Deprivation and the Hedonics of Drinking. Research has shown that the pleasure of replenishing fluids depends on the amount of fluid loss and on the temperature of the water. Hedin's experience of drinking as "exquisite pleasure" resulted from his having suffered severe dehydration in the desert and because the water was cool. Sandick and associates (1984) had army personnel exercise on some days and rest on other days (the control). Following exercise or rest, participants were presented with water samples for drinking that ranged from cool, to room temperature, to warm. On exercise days participants preferred the cooler temperature more than the warmer temperature, whereas on control (rest) days these differences in preference were less pronounced. Participants also drank significantly more of the cooler water following exercise than following a rest day, although this difference disappeared with warmer water samples. Preference or hedonic ratings of the water (how much the water was liked) decreased as the temperature increased. The amount of water all participants drank followed their preference ratings, meaning that as preference decreased, the amount of water participants drank decreased. Cool water reduces core body temperature sooner than warm water and, hence, according to alliesthesia, is preferred.

Inhibitors of Thirst.   The quenching of thirst from drinking occurs several minutes before water replenishes the cells. This observation implies that whatever physiological mechanism starts thirst, a different mechanism stops it, since water has not yet arrived where it is needed. Drinking is triggered by thirst and stopped by feedback from the mouth, throat, stomach, and eventually the absorption of water into the cells. In a series of experiments, Blass and Hall (1976) investigated the contribution these areas make to inhibiting drinking. In one experiment, they deprived rats of water for 12, 24, or 48 hours and then had them *sham drink*. In this procedure, water was not allowed to enter the stomach, since it was drained out by a fistula (a surgically implanted tube) before it reached the stomach. Rats sham drank twice as much following 48 hours of deprivation than following 12 or 24 hours. Since water only contacted the mouth and throat, the sensitivity to hours of deprivation showed that those areas play some role in eventually inhibiting drinking. The contribution of the stomach to inhibiting drinking was investigated by comparing sham drinking to drinking when water reaches, but is not allowed to leave, the stomach. Blass and Hall (1976) placed a noose around the exit portion of the rat's stomach and tightened or loosened it to prevent or allow water to leave. When water remained in the stomach, the rats drank less compared to sham drinking but more compared to when water entered the intestines. The capacity of the stomach to hold water also inhibits drinking, since the rats drank less when water reached the stomach compared to sham drinking. The least amount of drinking occurred when water left the stomach, which shows that absorption into the cells from the intestines also inhibits drinking. Thus, feedback from the mouth, the stomach, and the intestines contributes to the inhibition of drinking before water reaches the cells.

Besides physiological signals of satiety, there are psychological ones that change with drinking (Engell et al., 1987). After being dehydrated (made thirsty) to different degrees, participants were given one hour to consume as much of a fruit-flavored drink as they wanted. The amount participants drank increased with the amount of dehydration but stopped before they were fully rehydrated. The disappearance of a dry mouth, chalk-like taste, and thirst inhibited drinking. For participants who had been the most severely dehydrated, the feeling of a full stomach also inhibited further drinking. Sandick and associates (1984) had U.S. Army enlisted personnel exercise for about 30 minutes and then allowed them to drink as much water as they wanted. Drinking stopped when the sensations that begin and maintain drinking were alleviated. For example, there was a tendency to quit drinking with the disappearance of a dry mouth, feeling warm, and sweating. Finally, as Hedin's description in the opening paragraph implies, as the "deliciousness" of water diminishes, drinking stops.

The Body's Energy Requirements

I have, on rare occasions, discovered the consequences of failing to attend to the gasoline gauge. As the fuel tank level indicator plummets below E, the car stutters and eventually comes to a stop. I have also discovered that feelings of fatigue follow failing to attend to lunch. The analogy here is that the human body, like a car, also requires fuel. Furthermore, "feelings of hunger," like the fuel gauge, are indications that energy reserves are running low and that it is time to eat. This analogy between a car's fuel requirements and the body's energy requirements will help in understanding hunger motivation. Energy released from food is measured in terms of calories. A calorie is the amount of heat energy required to raise one gram of water one degree Celsius. College-age (18 to 22 years old) men require roughly 2,600–2,800 calories and college-age women require roughly 2,000–2,200 calories per day.

Metabolism.   The body's energy requirements can be divided into three components: resting metabolism, thermic effects, and physical activity. Energy used for **resting metabolism** is analogous to using gasoline to keep the engine idling while the car is in neutral. Resting metabolism refers to the use of energy for body maintenance, the pumping of blood by the heart, oxygen utilization, the work of individual cells, and neural activity in the brain. Resting metabolic rate is measured by the body's heat production or oxygen consumption while a person is inactive and has not eaten for at least 12 hours. The **thermic effect** is analogous to the heat produced by running the car's engine. It refers to the energy cost of digesting, storing, and absorbing food. Thermic or heat production can continue for several hours after a meal. The energy used for **physical activity** is analogous to the energy used in moving the car. Physical activity involves voluntary movement, which includes behaviors from studying to running. As individuals become more physically active, they expend more energy. Also included is spontaneous activity, such as fidgeting and the maintenance of body posture (Levine et al., 1999). Estimates of average energy expenditure for a 154-pound man follow: 60 to 75% is expended during resting metabolism, 10% is due to the thermic effects of food, and 15 to 30% is expended on physical activity (McArdle et al., 1996). Resting metabolism slows down at approximately 2% per decade as humans get older. Energy requirements for physical activity also decline with age as people become less active (McArdle et al., 1996; Van Itallie & Kissileff, 1990).

Energy Storage and Use.   People do not eat constantly, but energy must always be available because our brain, heart, lungs, and cells are constantly working even during sleep. Consequently, energy is derived from recently eaten food or from reserves in the stomach, intestines, liver, and muscles and from fat storehouses. Thus, there must be a balance between energy intake, in the form of food, and various forms of energy expenditure. This balance is known as **energy homeostasis** (Woods et al., 2000). Energy stores are out of balance when food intake exceeds energy expenditure (weight gain) or falls short of energy expenditure (weight loss). A major source of energy is glucose, a simple sugar obtained from food carbohydrates. Insulin released from the pancreas aids in transporting glucose into the cells to be used for energy. Insulin also aids in the conversion of excess glucose to **glycogen,** which consists of glucose molecules linked together for storage in the liver and muscles. Glucose can also be converted to fat and stored in adipose (fat) cells. After several hours, however, a person runs out of easily available energy from the stomach and intestines. Now the person begins to rely on stored muscle glycogen, which is reconverted there to glucose and used as energy. Glycogen from the liver can also be reconverted to glucose and released into the bloodstream. During longer periods of not eating or famine, a person can run completely out of glycogen. Consequently, the body converts its stored fat into fatty acids for energy use (McArdle et al., 1996; Sizer & Whitney, 1997).

Short- and Long-Term Energy Regulation

Fuel for a car's engine is regulated by both short- and long-term supplies. Gasoline in the fuel tank represents a short-term supply, while gas waiting to be obtained from the local gas station represents a long-term supply. For the body, glucose levels are a short-term energy supply, while the amount of body fat is a long-term supply.

Glucose and Short-Term Regulation.   As a short-term energy source, the amount of blood glucose is associated with hunger and eating. Campfield and associates (1985) suggest that a decline in blood glucose, at least in rats, may be causally related to eating. In a series of experiments, they continuously monitored blood glucose in rats who were allowed to eat freely. From this monitoring they found a correlation between a fall and rise in blood glucose with eating and food-related behaviors. For example, after blood glucose had reached its lowest level and then began to rise, rats searched for food and ate if food was available. However, if the glucose concentration had risen back to its normal level before finding food, then the rats would not eat (Campfield et al., 1985; Campfield & Smith, 1990). Should the decline in blood glucose be interpreted as a cause of eating? To test this possibility, Campfield and associates (1985) reasoned that if they could prevent the decline in blood glucose, then the rats should not be inclined to eat. In their experiment, when they detected the onset of a decline in glucose, they prevented further decline by injecting the rats with glucose. A control group of rats was injected with a saline solution that should have no effect in eliminating a decline in glucose. A third group was not injected with anything to determine the time between a declining glucose concentration and eating. The results showed that when a drop in blood glucose was prevented, eating was delayed for several hours. When blood glucose was allowed to decline normally in the other two groups, feeding occurred in about 12 minutes. These results imply that a decline in glucose instigates eating, while a sufficiently high level of glucose inhibits eating. Furthermore, only small fluctuations in glucose, not life-threatening changes, are needed by the brain in order to govern eating behavior (Woods et al., 2000).

Set Point Model and Long-Term Regulation.   Long-term energy stores rely on a set point for either body weight or body fat. In his **set point model,** Keesey (1986) assumes that either body weight or body fat is set at a specific value, with a discrepancy below set point instigating hunger. This model is based on the assumption that the set point for a person's body weight remains constant over a long period of time. For example, many people who have lost weight by dieting will tend to return to their prediet weight when ending their diet. One method the body uses to guard its set point from restricted food intake is to decrease its resting metabolic rate (McArdle et al., 1996). To illustrate, Elliot and associates (1989) measured the resting metabolic rate of obese women before, during, and after a weight-reducing diet. Although the women lost weight and body fat, their resting metabolic rate also decreased. Their bodies defended the fat set point from reduced food intake by decreasing energy consumption. A consequence of this decreased metabolic rate was that individuals regained the weight they lost when they resumed their normal diet (Begley, 1991; Keesey & Hirvonen, 1997). Their energy intake had once again exceeded the amount of energy expended.

The reverse can also happen. Some individuals who are forced to gain weight by eating high-calorie meals return to their former weight when resuming their normal diet. An increased thermic effect is responsible, because overfeeding can lead to increased heat production in the digestion of food (Ravussin & Danforth, 1999). The excess calories are simply burned off, resulting in a return to normal weight. Other individuals when overfed burn off excess calories by increased fidgeting and spontaneous muscle contraction and by maintaining their body posture (Levine et al., 1999). The **carrying cost** is another factor that contributes to body weight set point. As an individual gains weight, more energy is required to carry that extra weight (Van Itallie & Kissileff, 1983). Carrying cost levels off an individual's weight because the amount of energy required to carry the excess weight equals the amount of food energy that is consumed. Whether jogging, bicycling, swimming, or walking, a heavier person will burn more calories doing these activities than will a lighter person (McArdle et al., 1996, Appendix D).

Energy Reservoir Model and Long-Term Regulation. Another interpretation of long-term energy regulation is Van Itallie and Kissileff's (1990) **energy reservoir model** of stored body fat. A reservoir containing a town's water supply is analogous to our body's fat storage. First, the amount of stored water depends on the size of the reservoir just as the amount of fat depends on the size and number of a person's fat cells. Second, the amount of water stored in the reservoir will depend on the amount of rainfall. As rainfall increases, the amount of water available for storage increases. Similarly, as the amount of food intake increases, so does the amount that can be stored as fat in adipose tissue. Furthermore, as the reservoir begins to empty due to excessive water use or little rainfall, people begin to conserve water. They conserve water not because of an attempt to maintain a certain water level but so as not to run out completely. Similarly, when food supply is low during a diet, the amount of stored fat becomes lower and energy is conserved by reducing resting metabolic rate. Finally, when much water is used by the community, which is often the case in summertime, the level of the reservoir drops. Similarly when human energy expenditure is high, such as during long-distance running, fat deposits become quite low. Thus, the amount of body fat held in reserve depends on the amount of food minus the amount used for energy, just as the water level in a reservoir depends on the amount of rainfall minus the amount used by the town.

Hunger Sensations

A car has a single indicator that shows when the fuel supply is low. The body, in contrast, has many indicators to show when food energy is low.

Sensations Indicating Energy Depletion. Subjective sensations of hunger inform us that we are running low on energy. These sensations, although differing in intensity, are not located in one place but instead have varied locations (Friedman et al., 1999; Monello & Mayer, 1967). Friedman and coresearchers (1999) devised intensity ratings for sensations related to hunger and appetite, such as the ones in Table 5.1. They also devised intensity ratings for sensations that are associated with hunger, such as anxiety, dizziness, dry mouth,

TABLE 5.1   Ratings of Hunger and Related Sensations

Rate the intensity of your hunger and related sensations that you feel right now:

Hunger: Not at all hungry = 0 1 2 3 4 5 6 7 8 9 = As hungry as I have ever felt

Desire to eat: Very weak = 0 1 2 3 4 5 6 7 8 9 = Very strong

How much could you eat: Nothing at all = 0 1 2 3 4 5 6 7 8 9 = A large amount

How full is your stomach: Not at all = 0 1 2 3 4 5 6 7 8 9 = Very full

headache, stomachache, stomach growling, and weakness. Do the intensities of these sensations change with hours of food deprivation? To answer this question, the researchers recruited male and female participants to go without food for 22 hours from 6:00 P.M. to 4:00 P.M. the following day. At six different times during the 22 hours, participants rated the intensity of their sensations as listed in Table 5.1 and the intensity of other hunger-associated sensations. Participants rated their sensations twice at 4:00 P.M., just before and right after their meal. Figure 5.3 shows that sensations of hunger, the desire to eat, and the amount expected to eat all increased with hours of food deprivation and decreased after the meal. Ratings of stomach fullness showed the reverse pattern. Ratings of hunger-associated sensations showed similar patterns. For example, weakness, headache, dizziness, and stomach growl and ache increased with deprivation and then decreased after the meal.

Hunger Indicates Size of Energy Stores.   Could the stomach be analogous to a car's gasoline tank? Could hunger sensations indicate the number of calories remaining in the stomach, much like a car's fuel gauge indicates how much gasoline is in the tank? To investigate this possibility, De Castro and Elmore (1988) correlated people's hunger sensations with the number of calories of food they had in their stomachs. They asked men and women to record when, what, and how much they ate and drank for seven days and to record their degree of hunger before each meal. The amount of available energy in a person's stomach was calculated from the fact that food leaves at a known rate. This rate is faster for large amounts of food and slower for small amounts. For example, if lunch consisted of a 12-ounce cola beverage (152 calories) and a quarter-pound hamburger (403 calories), then the person would have stored 555 calories. However, as time passes the stomach begins emptying so that fewer and fewer calories of food energy remain available. Thus, knowing the number of calories a person ate and the rate of stomach emptying, the stomach's caloric content could be estimated before a participant's next meal. De Castro and Elmore's calculations showed that as stomach content decreases, hunger sensations increase. The energy content level of the stomach also correlates with the size of the next meal. Returning to the car analogy, as the gauge approaches E, it is time to fill up. Similarly, as hunger sensations become stronger, then it is time to eat. The link between hunger and needing calories, however, breaks down for long periods of fasting. People who go for days or weeks without food (Wolf, 1958) report that hunger sensations do not become more intense but instead disappear. As in a car, once the fuel tank is empty, the gas gauge is not going to fall further past the empty mark.

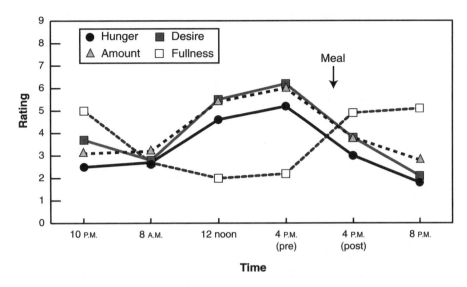

FIGURE 5.3   Hunger and Related Ratings. Ratings of hunger, desire to eat, and amount expected to eat increased with hours of deprivation and decreased with eating. Ratings of stomach fullness showed the reverse trend.

Note: Values are means + *SEM* of 14 subjects.

Source: From "A Figurative Measure of Subjective Hunger Sensations" by M. I. Friedman et al., 1999, *Appetite, 32,* figure 3, p. 399. Copyright 1999 by Elsevier. Reprinted by permission.

Feedback Mechanisms for Satiety

If hunger motivates us to eat, then what motivates us to stop? One answer is **satiety,** which refers to gratifying hunger, feeling content, and replenishing energy stores. Multiple physiological changes are associated with satiety.

Feeling Full.   The stomach contributes to satiety especially when it is full or distended with food. In one experiment, Deutsch (1990) and coresearchers used a noose to close the exit portion of a rat's stomach so that no milk could exit into the lower intestines. Some rats but not others were injected with a saline solution into their stomachs via tubes. Rats who had the extra solution injected into their stomachs quit drinking milk sooner regardless of whether the noose was open or closed. Deutsch and associates concluded that the upper limits of the stomach's capacity to hold food, or stomach distension, is what inhibits eating. Humans similarly report that stomach distension inhibits eating. In a series of surveys asking college students why they usually stop eating a meal, the most common answer given was when "I feel full" (Mook & Votaw, 1992, p. 72).

Calorie Detectors.   Besides stomach distension, sensing the caloric or energy value of food in the stomach is also effective in the inhibition of hunger. Deutsch and Gonzales had rats drink as much as they wanted of a high-calorie substance. When saline was pumped into the rats' stomachs, however, they still drank the same amount of this high-calorie food compared to when saline had not been given. The results of this experiment show that rats sense the food energy content of food in their stomachs regardless of the volume that is there (Deutsch, 1990). Human infants have also developed the ability to alter their volume of intake based on the number of calories contained in their formulas. Fomon and associates (1969) provided mothers with a 3- to 4-day supply of infant formula that had either low- or high-caloric density. Mothers, without knowing the caloric density of the formula, were instructed to feed their infants until their children were satisfied. The infants drank more of the low-calorie than the high-calorie formula. In comparing the number of calories consumed, however, there was no difference. A larger volume of low-density formula was necessary to match the number of calories provided by a lesser volume of the high-density formula (Fomon et al., 1969). It appears from these experiments that the amount of food energy in the stomach is also monitored and inhibits hunger. Personal experience verifies this, since some meals are more filling than others, for example, pastas and rich desserts versus salads.

Hormones.   Blood carries food nutrients to where they are needed but may also carry substances that promote either hunger or satiety. To investigate this possibility, Davis and associates (Davis et al., 1967, 1969) transfused blood from a hungry rat to a satiated one. They reasoned that perhaps a hungry rat carries a substance that produces hunger. However, this turned out not to be the case, since the satiated rat did not eat more following a blood transfusion from the hungry rat. Davis and associates also reversed the procedure and transfused blood from a satiated rat to a hungry rat in case there was a substance that inhibited hunger. In this instance, the hungry rat ate less compared to when it had not been given a blood transfusion. The researchers concluded that the blood of satiated animals contains a substance that inhibits eating in food-deprived animals. One possible explanation of these results is that following eating, a hormone is released into the bloodstream to inhibit further eating. It turns out that indeed there are hormones that inhibit but also stimulate hunger and eating.

Cholecystokinin (CCK) is a hormone released in the upper part of the small intestine after food intake and is involved in the short-term regulation of food energy. In an early experiment, injection of CCK in rats inhibited feeding (Gibbs et al., 1973). In further experiments, Canova and Geary (1991) found that the more CCK that was injected, the less milk the rats drank. Similar results were obtained with humans. Higher levels of CCK in the bloodstream were associated with higher degrees of satiety (Holt et al., 1992). CCK interacts with the amount of food to inhibit hunger and eating. Muurahainen and associates (1991) had male participants eat either 100 or 500 grams of soup followed by either an infusion of synthetic CCK or saline as a control substance. Next, the participants were allowed to eat as much as they wanted of a test meal of macaroni and beef. The amount participants ate depended both on CCK and on the size of the premeal soup. The CCK significantly inhibited eating of the test meal for those participants who had preloaded with the larger portion of premeal soup. The CCK, however, did not inhibit eating of the test meal for those participants who had the smaller amount of premeal soup. Thus, CCK may have an inhibitory effect on hunger but perhaps only when coupled with other satiety cues, such as feeling full.

Leptin is a hormone released by adipose tissue. Unlike CCK, which is sensitive to hunger and satiety, leptin is involved in the long-term regulation of energy as registered in adipose tissue or body fat (Baile et al., 2000; Friedman & Halaas, 1998). The amount of leptin circulation in the bloodstream correlates with the amount of body fat. For instance, leptin declines as individuals lose weight. Obese individuals have greater levels of circulating leptin than lean individuals. It is thought that obesity may result from an insensitivity to leptin (Considene et al., 1996; Friedman & Halaas, 1998). Areas of the hypothalamus detect concentrations of leptin in the bloodstream and in turn help institute various changes to maintain the body fat set point. Thus, a decrease in leptin is associated with changes designed to conserve energy, such as a decrease in basal metabolism and an increase in appetite. An increase in leptin, however, is associated with changes designed to increase energy expenditure and decrease food intake (Baile et al., 2000; Friedman & Halaas, 1998).

Ghrelin, introduced in Chapter 1, is a hormone that stimulates hunger, eating, and images of food (Geary, 2004). Ghrelin is released into the stomach and rises to its highest point just prior to breakfast, lunch, and dinner. It then declines rapidly after eating, only to begin rising again until prior to the next meal. Furthermore, when humans receive an injection of ghrelin, they report greater hunger and eat more (Schmid et al., 2005; Wren et al., 2001). In addition, the success of gastric bypass surgery for the treatment of severe obesity is due in part to a reduction in the release of ghrelin. Thus, with lower levels of ghrelin, it is easier for these individuals to control their hunger and eating (Kojima & Kangawa, 2005). Hunger, eating, and satiation are partly a product of the complex interaction among these three hormones. They send signals to the brain regarding the energy status of the body. Ghrelin stimulates eating and CCK inhibits eating in the short run while leptin appears to have a more long-term involvement (Geary, 2004).

Section Recap

We have examined what physiological changes motivate adjustment in body temperature, fluid balance, and energy levels. We have also investigated how corresponding psychological sensations motivate behavior to regulate these variables. The body attempts to maintain a stable internal environment or *homeostasis*, which is accomplished with the aid of the *negative feedback system*. This system places the optimal set point for body temperature, fluid levels, and food energy stores within an upper and lower boundary. Deviations from set points define a *physiological need* for the incentive that will restore homeostasis. Changes in a person's physiological interior alter sensations (*alliesthesia*) to stimuli that are relevant for restoring homeostasis. Incentives that restore homeostasis are pleasant, while those that disrupt homeostasis further are unpleasant. Different physiological systems are maintained under homeostasis. A drop in body temperature below set point produces involuntary shivering and blood vessel constriction to raise temperature. A rise in body temperature produces involuntary sweating and blood vessel dilation to lower temperature. In addition, the accompanying sensations of feeling cold and hot can result in voluntary actions like putting on or removing layers of clothing.

Thirst results from a loss of *intracellular fluids*, which occurs when water within the cells is drawn out due to a higher concentration of salt in extracellular fluid. Thirst also results from the loss of *extracellular fluid* through sweating, exhaling, and urinating. Cellular dehydration detectors are located in the hypothalamus, which on detecting fluid loss triggers thirst. Specific and global thirst sensations intensify with dehydration and cease with drinking even though fluids have not been completely replaced. Experiments with *sham drinking* indicate that receptors located in the mouth, stomach, and intestines monitor water intake.

Food energy measured in *calories* comes primarily from *glucose*. It is used during *resting metabolism* for maintaining the body, during *thermic effects* for digesting and storing food energy, and for *physical activity* or behavior. Heavier people burn more calories because the *carrying cost* of their weight is greater. Since we do not eat constantly, food energy is stored by converting glucose to *glycogen* as a short-term energy source. Fat storage is a long-term energy source regulated by the *set point model* for a specific amount of body fat. The *energy reservoir model*, however, likens level of fat stores to the amount of water in the town's reservoir. Hunger sensations are experienced in the stomach and abdomen but also as dizziness, headache, and weakness. These sensations increase with hours of food deprivation and are linked to a fall in blood glucose, running out of food in the stomach, and running out of energy. Hunger motivates eating, and *satiety*, or feeling replenished, inhibits eating. Other factors that affect eating are a rise in blood glucose, an increased supply of calories, feeling full, and the release of the hormones *cholecystokinin* (*CCK*), *leptin,* and *ghrelin*.

Food Characteristics and Eating

By perusing photos in cookbooks, a person realizes that food must also be pleasing to the eye as well as to the taste buds. Restaurant chefs do not slop food into a bucket to give to their patrons. Instead, they arrange food on a plate and add garnish to make the meal look attractive to diners. The whole practice of meal planning emphasizes the importance of color, form, variety, texture, temperature, and flavor of food. These considerations to the details of food make it apparent that there is more to eating than just reaching satiety. People often eat beyond satiety, especially when it involves their favorite food or dessert.

The purpose of this section is to describe those food characteristics that also determine what and how much people eat.

Cephalic Responses

Food has the power to make us eat. It can evoke a set of physiological responses that are preparatory to eating, digesting, metabolizing, and storing food (Nederkoorn et al., 2000). **Cephalic responses** to the smell and taste of food involve the secretion of saliva, gastric juices, and insulin from the pancreas (Powley, 1977). In addition, food can also evoke hunger sensations and the desire to eat. To illustrate, Bruce and associates (1987) evoked a cephalic response in their participants following an overnight fast. They presented them with a combination of sweetened gum, sweetened water, and the sight and smell of an appetizing breakfast. Ingesting the sweet stimuli plus the sight and smell of food raised the participants' insulin and lowered the level of blood glucose. Furthermore, the more glucose levels dropped in the participants, the more appetizing they rated the anticipated breakfast. Nederkoorn and associates (2000) exposed their participants to their favorite foods and measured the cephalic response. As a result of the exposure, participants' hunger ratings and cravings increased along with their heart rate, blood pressure, salivation, and gastric activity. Marcelino and colleagues (2001) had participants visually inspect and smell four pizzas that differed in visual quality. Another group was not exposed to the pizzas. Appetite ratings were higher for individuals who saw and smelled the pizzas. Furthermore, the desire to eat a pizza also increased with its visual quality and the participant's degree of hunger.

Palatability and Amount of Food

Both the quality and amount of food determine the urge to eat and the amount that is eaten. One type of food quality is referred to as **palatability,** which refers to its hedonic value as determined by variety, texture, temperature, aroma, and flavor (Young, 1961). Highly palatable food is appetizing, delicious, and a pleasure to eat. For example, Moskowitz and associates (1974) showed that palatability depends on flavor intensity. In their experiment, they varied the sucrose concentration, or sweetness intensity, of vanilla pudding, yellow cake, and a cherry-flavored beverage. Pleasantness ratings of these foods at first increased but then decreased as they became sweeter and sweeter. In other words, people like their desserts to be sweet but not too sweet.

Not only does sugar enhance palatability, but fat does also. Drewnowski and colleagues (1983, 1985) determined the contribution sweet and fat make to palatability for both fed and fasted participants. They had participants taste 20 different substances by a sip-and-spit technique, followed each time by rinsing the mouth. The 20 substances varied in five levels of fat (ranging from skim milk to heavy cream blended with safflower oil) and four levels of sweetness. Participants rated each substance for sweetness, fatness, creaminess, and for liking. Ratings of sweetness, fatness, and creaminess increased as fat and sugar content increased, demonstrating that participants were sensitive to these factors. Liking ratings, however, increased and then decreased as the sugar and fat content of the substances increased. The best-liked substance consisted of about 21% fat and about 8% sugar (Drewnowski et al., 1985). Thus, people like things sweet and fat but not too sweet and not too fat. Not only do we have a "sweet tooth" we also have a "fat tooth."

In addition to palatability, quantity also factors into the motivating effects of food. One observation is that as the size of food portions increase, the amount eaten increases correspondingly. There is experimental evidence to support this claim. Rolls and coresearchers (2002) presented their male and female participants a lunch of macaroni and cheese in one of four different portions: 500, 625, 750, or 1,000 grams. Participants were instructed to eat as little or as much as they wanted. Prior to eating, the four groups did not differ in their hunger, thirst, and the amount they thought they could eat. Portion size, however, determined the amount they did eat. The results presented in Figure 5.4 show that amount consumed increased as portion sizes increased. This increase occurred equally for both men and women although men ate significantly more than women for all portion sizes. Increased portion sizes of meals provided in restaurants or in packaged foods have been blamed for the increase in the percent of overweight and obese individuals (see Figure 12.7, Harnack et al., 2000).

Sensory-Specific Satiety

Quantity interacts with food variety in determining eating. As suggested in many cookbooks, eating will be a more pleasurable experience if a variety of palatable foods are served in a fashion appealing to the eye (Crocker, 1961). Serving only one dish or eating the same food repeatedly is enough to blunt anyone's appetite, which is the result of a process known as **sensory-specific satiety.** This process refers to a decreased liking and consumption of a particular food based on sensory characteristics, such as flavor, texture, and appearance (Raynor & Epstein, 2001). In an early experiment conducted by Rolls and associates (1981), participants tasted and then rated their liking of a number of foods, among which was

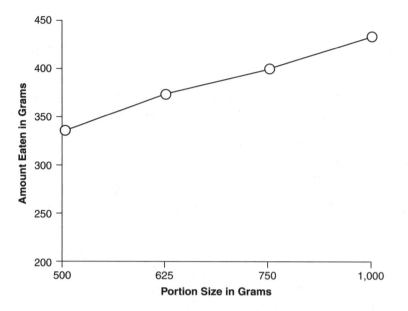

FIGURE 5.4 Portion Size Determines Amount Eaten. The amount eaten of a macaroni and cheese lunch increased as the serving portion increased. This increase occurred for both men and women. In addition, men ate more than women at all portion sizes.

Source: Adapted from "Portion Size of Food Affects Energy Intake in Normal-Weight and Overweight Men and Women" by B. J. Rolls et al., 2002, *American Journal of Clinical Nutrition, 76,* p. 1210.

cheese on crackers or sausage. Half of the participants had a lunch of cheese on crackers, while the other half had a lunch of sausage. Two minutes after the meal, participants were unexpectedly given a second course, which was either the same as the first course (cheese on crackers or sausage) or different (sausage or cheese on crackers). Participants also rated the liking of these foods during their second course. The ratings showed that the same food was liked less compared to a different food. In addition, if participants ate the same food during the second course as they did during the first, they tended to eat less than if the food was different between courses. For example, participants liked sausage less during the second course and ate less of it if they had also eaten sausage during the first course. Sensory-specific satiety means that satiety is specific to a food and does not generalize to other foods. Thus, although a person may quit eating one food, she will eat other foods, thereby ensuring that several varieties are eaten during one meal. A greater variety at meals provides greater enjoyment and increases the likelihood that a nutritionally balanced meal is eaten.

Food Preferences

Your innate dispositions toward food and the eating environment your parents provided jointly determined your current food likes and dislikes. In other words, food preferences result from the interaction between innate dispositions and environmental experiences (Birch, 1999).

Innate Food Preferences.   As described in Chapter 3, humans are born liking certain tastes and foods and not others. For instance, Mennella and Beauchamp (1998) and Steiner (1977) showed that infants innately prefer sweet substances and reject bitter and sour substances. Thus, humans appear innately ready to eat sweet-tasting foods, which are relatively high in calories, and reject bitter or sour-tasting foods, which are associated with poison and being spoiled. Rats show different facial gestures depending on their being exposed to sweet or bitter stimuli (Grill & Norgren, 1978). Rats also show an innate preference for salt (Schulkin, 1991). The same is true for humans. Leshem and colleagues (1999) induced salt loss through perspiration in one group by having them exercise, compared to a control group who did not exercise. When allowed to flavor a cup of tomato soup to their liking, exercisers preferred more than a 50% increase in salt (NaCl) compared to what nonexercisers preferred. These results support the notion that salt preference increases as salt level in the body decreases. Young infants, however, are indifferent to the taste of salt, while infants 4 to 24 months of age prefer salt solutions over plain water. Children 3 to 6 years old, although rejecting salty fluids, prefer salted soups (Beauchamp et al., 1986). Thus, rats and humans appear sensitive to and prefer food substances that are necessary for body growth, maintenance, and repair.

Conditioned Food Preferences.   The recommendation that a variety of foods promotes appetite should not detract from the contribution that familiarity makes in liking certain foods. People often prefer the foods they ate while growing up simply because of their exposure to them. According to Zajonc's (1968) **mere exposure effect,** people increase their positive evaluation of a stimulus because of repeated exposures. To illustrate this concept, Pliner (1982) had participants taste and swallow four different tropical fruit juices from zero to 20 times, each time rating their bitterness. Following the tasting, participants rated the juices for liking (from dislike to like). The rating outcomes were in accord with the mere exposure effect such that liking increased with the number of times a juice had been tasted. However, this effect did not last longer than one week. In another experiment, Birch and Marlin (1982) presented preschool children with three novel foods that consisted of sweet, salty, or plain tofu (soybean curd). The children tasted the foods up to 20 times over a series of days and each time rated how much they preferred them. Again, in accord with the mere exposure effect, as number of food tastings increased, preference ratings increased.

Liking a particular food can also be enhanced by associating it with a hedonically pleasant taste. Zellner and associates (1983) likened this association to a classical conditioning procedure. In their experiment, the flavor of tea served as a conditioned stimulus for either the presence or absence of sugar in the tea. Sugar was the unconditioned stimulus, which evoked an unconditioned response of a hedonically pleasant taste. After drinking either the sweetened or unsweetened teas, the participants rated the teas, now without any sugar, for how much they liked them. The flavors of the teas that had been sweetened were liked better than those teas that had not been sweetened. This effect was still present one week later. The fact that sugar enhances the liking for food has not been lost on parents. In many different cultures, sugar is added to the food of infants so that they will eat it more readily (Jerome, 1977). Boxes of some breakfast cereals at the grocery store list sugar as their second-highest ingredient.

The degree that food restores energy homeostasis also determines how much it is liked. For instance, both animals and humans learn to prefer the flavors of foods that are associated with restoring the body's energy. In an illustrative animal experiment, Fedorchak and Bolles (1987, exp. 2) deprived some rats of food (hungry) and provided free food to others (not hungry). In addition, on some days both hungry and non-hungry rats had orange-flavored water available while on other days grape-flavored water with ethanol was available. The orange flavor became associated with the absence of calories, since water does not provide any calories. The grape flavor became associated with the presence of calories, which were provided in the ethanol. The question was which flavor do rats learn to prefer: orange flavor associated with the absence of calories or grape flavor associated with the presence of calories? To answer this question, the rats were later given a choice between orange-flavored water versus grape-flavored water (ethanol was now absent). The results of the preference test showed that when hungry, rats chose the grape flavor that had been associated with calories from ethanol. They did not prefer the grape flavor simply because of its prior association with ethanol, since when not hungry they preferred both flavors equally.

Similar research with humans has led to the same conclusion. Appleton and coresearchers (2006) had one group of individuals report to the laboratory immediately after breakfast or lunch. This group was defined as having low-energy requirements—that is, they were not hungry. Another group of individuals reported to the laboratory immediately prior to lunch or prior to the evening meal. They were defined as having high-energy requirements—that is, they were hungry. In the laboratory, participants ate one of four novel-flavored yogurts that had either a low or high energy content. This procedure was repeated over a five-day period, during which non-hungry or hungry participants ate a low- or a high-energy yogurt. Prior and during conditioning, participants rated the yogurts for liking and pleasantness of taste. An analysis of these ratings showed that all flavors received higher liking and pleasantness ratings when they had been consumed under high-energy (hungry) compared to low-energy (not hungry) requirements. This finding was especially true for yogurt with a high energy content. These results replicate the experiments just cited with rats. Novel flavors that participants experienced while hungry were preferred over novel flavors that were experienced while not hungry.

The mere energy content of the food is also important for the development of taste preferences. In one illustrative experiment, Brunstrom and Mitchell (2007) had female participants eat two novel and distinctly flavored desserts: one with a high and the other with a low energy content. The desserts were eaten on alternate days over a six-day period. After eating a dessert, participants rated it for liking, desire, and enjoyment. Following the taste experiences, participants then tasted each dessert again. Both now had an intermediate level of energy. Did the preference for a particular dessert depend on its former energy content? Yes, the high-energy dessert was preferred. Initially, there were no differences in dessert preferences as shown by ratings collected on the first day. However, by the test day participants liked, enjoyed, and desired the high-energy flavored dessert more than the low-energy one. The pairing of a flavor with a high-energy content resulted in a preference for that flavor. The results of these experiments imply that people's preferences develop as a result of a food's ability to restore energy, which occurs when a hungry person eats high-energy food.

It is also common, however, for a person to not eat a particular food because of a strong **taste aversion.** This refers to a strong dislike because of the food's association with nausea, which developed through classical conditioning (Bernstein, 1978; Garcia et al., 1966). Taste aversion in humans has several characteristics (Logue et al., 1981). First, the taste and smell of food and drink rather than their texture or appearance generally have more of an influence on taste aversion. Second, an aversion is more likely to develop to an unfamiliar or less-preferred food. Third, it does not matter whether nausea was the result of spoiled food or the stomach flu. Even if individuals do not know why they became ill, an aversion still develops. Aversion may also result from overindulgence, as in the case of alcohol. In a sample of university students,

Logue and associates (1981) found that approximately one-fourth had developed an aversion to alcohol. Of these aversions, approximately 69% were to hard liquor while 17% and 14% were to wine and beer, respectively. Lastly, once developed, an aversion can last for years. Although most prevalent in children, conditioned taste aversion does not last forever and declines with age (Garb & Stunkard, 1974). Eating the aversive food is a quicker way to overcome the aversion rather than just waiting for the passage of time (Logue et al., 1981).

Section Recap

This section addressed the question whether there are factors besides hunger that determine how much people eat. The answer is a definite "yes." The *palatability* of food is a key factor, and refers to its appearance, texture, aroma, and flavor in creating a pleasurable taste experience. As food becomes more palatable it evokes greater *cephalic responses*, such as salivation and gastric secretions. Merely being exposed to food evokes cephalic responses and also increases the desire for food. Hunger levels also intensify cephalic responses. Humans have innate food preferences, especially for sweets and fat but also for salt, which becomes apparent when they are deprived of salt. Finally, repeated experiences with food also determine liking. *Sensory-specific satiety* refers to how eating a particular food decreases our preference for more of that particular food but not for all foods. The *mere exposure effect,* in contrast, refers to the finding that liking foods stems from our exposure to them. In addition, some foods are liked because they have become associated with pleasurable hedonic tastes. Animals and people also learn to prefer the novel flavors of foods that restore energy homeostasis—that is, foods that have a high-energy content and are eaten while hungry. Some foods are disliked because of *taste aversion,* an extreme dislike for a particular food because of the association of aroma and taste with nausea or illness.

Person Characteristics and Eating

When I eat something fattening it is easier to eat at night. So I look forward to eating a cookie, my one cookie, late at night—I eat it really slow, and I have to eat by myself. I wait until the night after I have eaten a big dinner. I am not hungry for the cookie, I'm still thinking about it: "Oh, that is the time when I get to eat my cookie, even if I'm not hungry for it." . . . I get my only happiness from eating that cookie. Then I think I'm going to start eating to be happy. That gives me the fear that I will be unhappy about everything, and be happy about eating a cookie. Then it makes me afraid that I'm going to cure all my unhappiness by eating and eating cookies all the time, because my greatest fear is to lose control and to become fat. (Bruch, 1988, pp. 151–152)

These are the fears expressed by a young woman who suffers from anorexia nervosa, which is a disease characterized by emaciation because of extreme dieting.

The purpose of this section is to explore whether there are differences among people and situations associated with how much is eaten.

Boundary Model of Eating

As described earlier, the set point in the negative feedback system is located between two boundaries that define a comfort zone. For example, when the house temperature drops below the lower boundary in winter, the furnace heats the house. When the temperature goes above the upper boundary in summer, the air conditioner cools the house. Between these two boundaries there exists a comfort zone. Herman and Polivy (1984) used this zone idea in their **boundary model** of hunger (lower boundary) and satiety (upper boundary). According to this model, if a person drops below the lower boundary, then she experiences aversive feelings of hunger, weakness, and an empty stomach; the further below the lower boundary, the greater the impetus to eat. Above the satiety (upper) boundary, a person stops eating when aversive physiological conditions begin to prevail, such as a full stomach. In between (upper and lower boundaries) is the *zone of biological indifference*, where instead of physiological reasons, social factors and the palatability of food determine how much is eaten.

The zone of biological indifference is different for normal eaters, dieters, binge eaters, and people with anorexia nervosa. Physiological factors largely govern when normal eaters start and stop eating. Dieters, however, have a wider zone of biological indifference. They strive to rely on a cognitively imposed *diet boundary* that determines how much they eat, often falling short of their satiety boundary (Herman & Polivy, 1984). For them, trying to lose weight, fitting into clothes, or achieving society's ideal body image are factors that also control their eating. Herman and Polivy (1980) use the term **restraint** to refer to the cognitive effort used to resist the urge to eat. They have devised a 10-item *Revised Restraint Scale* (see Table 5.2) that measures the extent people restrain their eating. Individuals who

TABLE 5.2   Revised Restraint Scale

1. How often are you dieting? Never, rarely, sometimes, often, always (scored 0–4)
2. What is the maximum amount of weight (in pounds) that you have ever lost within one month? 0–4, 5–9, 10–14, 15–19, 20+ (scored 0–4)
3. What is your maximum weight gain within a week? 0–1, 1.1–2, 2.1–3, 3.1–5, 5.1+ (scored 0–4)
4. In a typical week, how much does your weight fluctuate? 0–1, 1.1–2, 2.1–3, 3.1–5, 5.1+ (scored 0–4)
5. Would a weight fluctuation of 5 lbs. affect the way you live your life? Not at all, slightly, moderately, very much (scored 0–3)
6. Do you eat sensibly in front of others and splurge alone? Never, rarely, often, always (scored 0–3)
7. Do you give too much time and thought to food? Never, rarely, often, always (scored 0–3)
8. Do you have feelings of guilt after overeating? Never, rarely, often, always (scored 0–3)
9. How conscious are you of what you are eating? Not at all, slightly, moderately, extremely (scored 0–3)
10. How many pounds over your desired weight were you at your maximum weight? 0–1, 1–5, 6–10, 11–20, 21+ (scored 0–4)

For self-scoring, sum your responses to the 10 questions.

Note: With their female participants, Herman and Polivy (1975) obtained a median of 17 and Spencer and Fremouw (1979) obtained a median of 16. A score below 16 falls in the "unrestrained" or "low-restraint eater" category. A score above 17 falls in the "high-restraint eater" category.

Source: Copyright © 1975 by The American Psychological Association. Adapted with permission. The official citation that should be used in referencing this material is Herman, C. P., & Polivy, J. (1975). Anxiety, Restraint, and Eating Behavior. *Journal of Abnormal Psychology, 84,* p. 669.

score high on the scale are defined as restrained eaters. They constantly think about what and how much they eat and then feel guilty when they have exceeded their diet. People who score low on the scale, however, are unrestrained. They eat when and however much they want. Restrained eaters, who are usually dieters, are described as having lower hunger boundaries and higher satiety boundaries than unrestrained eaters. For example, it takes a greater amount of food deprivation for them to admit being hungry, and they eat less food after equivalent periods of deprivation. Perhaps dieters become accustomed to experiencing hunger and to eating less than unrestrained eaters (Herman & Polivy, 1984).

Some dieters also binge on occasion and thus are described as having a wider zone of biological indifference than normal eaters. These individuals usually have an all-or-none view of their diet so that when they break it, bingeing results. *Binge eating* refers to the inability to stop eating, only doing so when running out of food, being interrupted, or reaching physiological capacity (Wilson et al., 1996). Polivy and Herman (1985) claim that bingeing is a likely consequence of dieting because of the possibility that dieting may make a person chronically hungry.

Cognitive Release of Diet Restraint

The diet boundary is set cognitively rather than physiologically. When the cognitive boundary or restraint is lifted, the result is overeating or bingeing for some previously restrained eaters (Herman & Polivy, 1984; Polivy & Herman, 1985; Ruderman, 1986). In one experimental demonstration, Fedoroff and coworkers (1997) divided individuals into unrestrained and restrained eaters based on their scores on the *Revised Restraint Scale*. Participants were informed that the study was about food preferences and that they would be asked to taste and to give their opinion on various foods. Prior to tasting and rating pizzas, half of the restrained and unrestrained eaters were exposed to the odor of baking pizza for 10 minutes, or were told to think about pizza for 10 minutes. The other half of the restrained and unrestrained eaters were not exposed to the pizza odors and could think about whatever they chose. Afterward, all participants were asked to taste and rate the quality of the pizza. As you might imagine, both the odor of the baking pizza and thinking about pizza increased pizza consumption, but this was only true for restrained eaters. The restrained eaters also reported an increased liking, craving, and desire to eat pizza as a result of the pizza cues. The unrestrained eaters were not affected by these temptations.

Stress-Induced Eating

In the paragraph opening this section, the young woman expressed her fears that eating cookies would be her only source of happiness. For some people eating is a way to relieve stress. What stress seems to do is to remove the diet boundary and cause eating, especially in restrained eaters, regardless of whether they are of normal weight or obese (Greeno & Wing, 1994; Ruderman, 1986). In a representative investigation, Ruderman (1985) tested whether failure-induced stress would inhibit dietary restraint. First, she measured the degree of dietary restraint in her female participants using the *Revised Restraint Scale*. During the experimental phase, half of her participants succeeded or failed at a concept-formation task. In the next phase, participants rated crackers for saltiness, knowing that afterward they could help themselves to any remaining crackers. The effects of failure and the degree of restraint affected the number of crackers eaten. The high-restraint participants

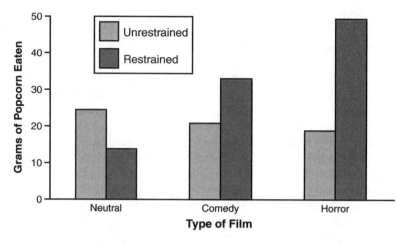

FIGURE 5.5   Stress and Eating Behavior. Restrained eaters ate less popcorn than unrestrained eaters did while watching the neutral film. However, restrained eaters ate more than unrestrained eaters during the comedy film and ate even more during the horror film.

Source: Adapted from "Emotional Arousal and Overeating in Restrained Eaters" by J. Cools et al., 1992, *Journal of Abnormal Psychology, 101,* p. 349.

in the failure group ate more crackers. Low- and high-restraint participants in the success group, however, did not differ in the number of crackers they ate.

Although distress can remove diet boundaries, positive mood can also remove the diet boundary, at least in female restrained eaters. In one interesting experiment, Cools and associates (1992) had women watch a 20-minute film that was either neutral, comic, or of a horror genre to induce a neutral, positive, or negative mood. The researchers provided popcorn, since many people eat popcorn while at the movies. The real purpose in providing the popcorn was to determine how much of it would be eaten based on the type of film that was being watched. Figure 5.5 shows the amount of popcorn eaten during each film type by restrained or unrestrained eaters. Restrained eaters ate the most popcorn while viewing the horror film and the least while viewing the neutral film. They also ate more popcorn than unrestrained eaters during the comedy film and even more during the horror film. Unrestrained eaters, however, ate a similar amount of popcorn during each type of film.

Hunger Boundary

Is your hunger boundary well defined? Do you know the difference between hunger sensations and feelings of distress? Is your mind pushing your "start eating" boundary in one direction only to be opposed by your body pushing it in the other direction?

Physiological Pressures.   Restrained eaters struggle between physiological pressures to eat and their cognitively placed diet boundary. Dieting makes this struggle more intense, since it may make an individual even more susceptible to eating, especially when faced with palatable foods. Klajner and associates (1981) had dieters and nondieters go without eating for five hours and then presented them with freshly baked chocolate chip cookies. For half the participants, the cookies were made unpalatable by having added green food coloring during preparation. Dieters salivated more to the palatable cookies than to the unpalatable ones, while nondieters salivated the same amount to both types of cookies. In a prior experiment, dieters also salivated more to freshly baked pizza compared to nondieters. Dieters experience stronger cephalic responses to palatable food, perhaps making them more susceptible to eating than nondieters.

Internal Cues and Eating Disorders.   The boundary model also describes individuals suffering from **anorexia nervosa,** who impose a very stringent diet boundary on themselves, even lower than that of regular dieters. Individuals most at risk for this condition are young women (15 to 29 years old), who comprise approximately 90% of the cases. They restrict their eating to the extent that they weigh less than 85% of what is normal for their age and height (American Psychiatric Association, 2000; Polivy & Herman, 2002).

There are risk factors that may eventually lead to anorexia nervosa in some women (Polivy & Herman, 2002; Stice, 2001). First, there are societal pressures that promote being thin and disparage being fat. This pressure comes from the media but may also come from parents and peers. Second, to the extent that thinness is accepted as a personal ideal, a young woman often develops a dissatisfaction with her own body. Third, this dissatisfaction can lead to dieting and, in more extreme cases, also purging. Women who diet so extensively as to develop anorexia nervosa (and fall below 85% of normal body weight) also have a distorted body image and usually view themselves as normal or fat when in actuality they have an emaciated appearance (Polivy & Herman, 2002). Depressed moods may also accompany body dissatisfaction, which may also lead to further dieting (Stice, 2001).

In her work with patients suffering from anorexia nervosa, Bruch (1988) observed that her patients were confused about their body sensations. For example, they might confuse anxiety or distress with hunger and respond with eating (Rebert et al., 1991). Women with anorexia nervosa who only restrict their food intake and those anorexics who also binge and purge are not as sensitive to internal signals of hunger and satiety. To illustrate, Halmi and Sunday (1991) examined the course of hunger and fullness during a meal for patients with eating disorders and for normal individuals. Following a 10-hour fast, these individuals rated how hungry and full they were immediately before, during, and after drinking a liquid breakfast meal. For normal eaters, as the meal progressed, they became more full and less and less hungry. Anorexic patients who restricted their diet rated themselves as full and not hungry at the start, during, and end of the meal. It was as if neither the 10-hour fast nor eating the liquid breakfast had any effect on their sense of hunger or satiety. Anorexic patients who also binged and purged showed an up-and-down hunger-fullness pattern during and after the meal. It was as if they had trouble detecting when they were hungry or full. Patients who specifically exhibited these abnormal hunger-fullness patterns also ate less of the liquid meal than patients who showed normal hunger-fullness patterns.

Patients with anorexia nervosa also develop adverse reactions to eating food, which is a condition known as the **refeeding syndrome.** As a result of extreme food deprivation, the body loses its ability to digest and absorb food. For example, food deprivation produces a sharp decline in phosphorous, which is an essential mineral within the body's cells. With refeeding, there is a sudden uptake of phosphorous, which can set off a cascade of life-threatening complications, such as heart failure, coma, and breathing problems. In addition, because of food deprivation, the intestines become intolerant to food, which can result in nausea and diarrhea when food is eaten (Solomon & Kirby, 1990). These adverse reactions may mean that in regards to eating, food has a very low incentive value. However, food can have a positive incentive value when it comes to manipulating, handling, and preparing it but not for eating it. The incentive value for eating food may be so low that an anorexic individual is unable to become motivated enough to eat (Pinel et al., 2000).

> ➤ Information about anorexia nervosa and links to other relevant sites are available from the U.S. Department of Health & Human Services at http://womenshealth.gov/faq// easyread/anorexia-etr.htm

Section Recap

People differ in the extent they limit their eating. The *boundary model* defines the zone of biological indifference as situated between a hunger boundary and satiety boundary. Dieters and individuals suffering from anorexia nervosa have a hunger boundary that is lower and a satiety boundary that is higher than that of normal eaters. Dieters or restrained eaters also place a cognitive restraint, or *diet boundary*, on themselves, which is lower than their physiological satiety boundary. Unrestrained eaters, by contrast, rely on a higher physiological boundary for when to eat. Cognitive restraint can be released by making individuals break their diet boundary. The result is overeating. Both positive and negative stress can release diet restraints and lead to overeating in restrained individuals. In addition, dieting makes individuals more susceptible to eating palatable foods. Finally, young women suffering from *anorexia nervosa*, typified by extreme weight loss, distorted body image, and confused body sensations, have trouble distinguishing when they are hungry or full. As a result of extreme food deprivation, anorexics develop a negative reaction to eating food known as the *refeeding syndrome*. In addition, eating food attains a very low incentive value, so an individual is not motivated to eat.

A C T I V I T I E S

1. Both before and after a meal, rate yourself on the various indicators of hunger given in Table 5.1. Is cessation of eating simply the result of a change in these four sensations, or is it more than that? Are there changes in other body sensations? Is food less tasty?

2. Before the first bite of a meal, consider whether hunger merely results from the passage of time or whether food also has the ability to evoke hunger. Again, monitor the intensity of your hunger and its bodily symptoms at various intervals prior to that first bite. Was the change in hunger gradual, or was there a sharp increase in intensity that resulted from the sight and aroma of food?

3. Have you ever experienced taste aversion? If so,
   a. How long after eating the food did you become ill?

   b. How long has your taste aversion existed?
   c. How could you overcome this taste aversion? Do you even want to?

4. There are several other factors, not presented in this chapter, that determine what foods an individual eats. To illustrate, consider what factors determine whether or not you will eat a particular food.
   a. Cultural beliefs: For instance, you are a vegetarian or people in your culture do not eat horses or steak tartare.
   b. Religious beliefs: Certain foods are not to be eaten or they are not to be eaten during certain times of the year.

6 Behavior, Arousal, and Affective Valence

The body of man is a machine which winds its own spring.
—*J. O. De La Mettrie, 1748*

Music hath charms to soothe a savage beast,
To soften rocks, or bend a knotted oak.

—*William Congreve, 1697*

■ While taking an exam, a student is unable to retrieve an answer from memory. However, as soon as she exits the classroom, the answer comes to mind. Could the anxiety that was aroused by the exam have interfered with recall of the answer? This question and the following ones are provided as guides for understanding the concepts in this chapter:

1. In what ways is arousal similar and different from motivation?
2. What produces arousal?
3. Does arousal affect how well a person performs a task? If so, how?
4. Is arousal linked to the quality of our feelings? If so, what is the nature of this link?
5. How do incongruous events produce arousal? Do their resolutions contribute to the enjoyment of humor, music, and suspense?

Arousal and Performance

Whether pushed by a motive or pulled by an incentive, physiological and psychological arousal accompanies behavior. In one case, arousal is in the background and affects the efficiency of ongoing behavior. In the other case, arousal is in the foreground felt as an affective experience. The following two quotes describing people's experiences help clarify this distinction. The first quote illustrates the effects of arousal on performance.

My math anxiety started because of a teacher that I had for math in the third grade. We were learning our times tables, and she didn't have any sympathy for the kids that were a little slower than the others. We would play a flash card game in front of the class, and if you got it wrong, she made you look like an idiot. So my anxiety comes from being afraid of being wrong in front of a group, and looking stupid. (Perry, 2004, p. 322)

This next quote illustrates how arousal serves as an affective experience.

> To her, the tension-and-release cycle that accompanies cinematic terror brings about some-thing like a gambler's high. "It's not that I'm a self-mutilator," she [Ms. Gauh] said, "but it's just a powerful rush when you can overcome some pain." . . . "It's the adrenaline," said Sarah Stark, a movie theater manager in Lima, Ohio, explaining her long time interest in gory movies. For her, she said, violent horror movies amount to something of a personal endurance test, a bit like white-water rafting—the sheer terror of which clears the mind and, briefly, seems to reduce all of life down to a single exhilarating moment. (Williams, 2006, ¶ 12, 28)

The first quote by a student with math anxiety typifies the relationship between arousal and performance on a task. When arousal is high, as in the case of math anxiety, per-formance is low. If only math anxiety could be reduced, but not totally, then a student might perform better when solving math problems or taking a math test. The second quote is from individuals who enjoy watching horror movies. For them, movie scenes create a level of arousal that is optimal for creating a sense of pleasure, like a rush or moment of exhilaration.

The purpose of this chapter is to describe how these two functions of arousal help us to understand motivation. The intent of this first section is to describe arousal, its an-tecedents, and outcomes. It also covers how the quality of a person's performance depends on the interaction between the level of arousal and the difficulty of the task being performed.

Categories of Arousal

Arousal refers to the mobilization or activation of energy that occurs in preparation or dur-ing actual behavior. "My heart is pounding" implies physiological arousal while "I feel tense and anxious" implies psychological arousal. In combination with neurological or brain arousal, these are the different categories of arousal that have been studied.

Physiological Arousal.   If you raced through your presentation during speech class with clammy hands, pounding heart, and dry throat, then you were physiologically aroused. **Physiological arousal** refers to those bodily changes that correspond to our feelings of being energized, such as sweaty palms and increased muscle tension, breathing, and heart rate. These changes indicate that the body is getting ready for action much like starting a car's engine means that it's ready to move. The autonomic nervous system controls physiological arousal and is divided into two branches: the sympathetic nervous system and the parasym-pathetic nervous system. The *sympathetic nervous system* is responsible for arousing or preparing the body for action. It stimulates the heart to pump blood more effectively. It causes glucose, epinephrine (adrenaline), and norepinephrine (noradrenaline) to be released in the bloodstream. The sympathetic nervous system also makes rapid breathing possible, which increases oxygen intake. The parasympathetic nervous system, however, is concerned with conserving the body's energy. It is active during quiet periods and tends to counteract the arousing effects of the sympathetic system.

Brain Arousal.   The activation of the brain, ranging from deep sleep to wakefulness to alertness, is referred to as **brain arousal.** Different areas of the brain are aroused depending on the operations being performed. Just as a car uses more fuel when it is moving, various areas of the brain also use more energy when active. This energy is in the form of glucose and oxygen. Two techniques for measuring brain activity make use of the fact that energy consumption increases in areas of the brain. Positron emission tomography (PET scan) is a procedure that produces a three-dimensional picture indicating areas of the brain that are most active. The picture is obtained by measuring positrons. These are particles with a positive charge that are emitted by radioactive substances injected into a person's bloodstream and carried to the brain. These radioactive particles concentrate in those brain areas that have the highest blood flow or highest utilization of glucose. Another method for detecting brain activity makes use of functional magnetic resonance imaging (fMRI). This technique is used for obtaining high-resolution images of the brain from energy waves that are emitted from hydrogen atoms, which are released when the brain is surrounded by a strong magnetic field. The energy waves are influenced by the amount of oxygen in the blood of brain tissue. Just as our muscles need oxygen to work, increased blood flow and hence oxygen are provided to that part of the brain that is activated. Brain arousal is relevant for understanding subjective emotional experiences that map onto neural networks in the brain. This topic of affective feelings corresponding to brain activities is described in greater detail in Chapter 13.

Psychological Arousal. Is the anticipation felt prior to getting an exam back the same as the anticipation felt when opening a birthday present? *Psychological arousal* refers to how subjectively aroused an individual feels. An alternative strategy to relying on physiological indicators of arousal is to ask a person how subjectively aroused he feels. "I'm full of pep," "I'm all psyched up," or "I'm tired and have no energy" are verbal reports of various degrees of subjective arousal or activation. In researching subjective arousal, Thayer (1989) developed a theory of arousal that involves two dimensions: energetic arousal and tense arousal. **Energetic arousal** is a dimension characterized by a range of feelings from tiredness and sleepiness at the low end to alert and awake at the high end. High levels of energetic arousal are associated with a positive affective tone and optimism. For instance, energetic arousal could be associated with planning a vacation trip. **Tense arousal** is a dimension characterized by a range of feelings from calmness and stillness at the low end to tension and anxiety at the high end. High levels of tense arousal are associated with a negative affective tone. The student's description of math anxiety in the opening example is a case of tense arousal while the report from the horror-movie goers suggests their experience is a mixture of tense and energetic arousal.

The *Scale Measuring Energetic Arousal and Tense Arousal* in Table 6.1 provides a way of determining the intensity of each type of arousal that a person is momentarily experiencing. The items in Table 6.1 indicate that energetic arousal is associated with positivity and pleasantness while tense arousal is associated with negativity and unpleasantness (Schimmack & Reisenzein, 2002). In validating these two types of arousal, Thayer (1978) found that students rated themselves more jittery and fearful (high tense arousal) on the day of an exam compared to a typical class day. Conversely, they were more likely to rate themselves as being more placid and calm (low tense arousal) on a typical class day than on an exam day. Thayer also found that taking a brisk 10-minute walk elevated energetic arousal compared to sitting restfully for a similar amount of time. Resting, however, reduced an individual's level of tense arousal compared to walking.

➤ An older, more exhaustive measure of energetic and tense arousal is Thayer's *Activation-Deactivation Checklist*, which is available at http://www.csulb.edu/~thayer/thayer/adacl.htm

TABLE 6.1   Scale Measuring Energetic Arousal and Tense Arousal

The six dimensions below describe arousal, energy, or activation levels. Please circle the number of each dimension that indicates how you feel at this moment.

Energetic Arousal
sleepy = 0 1 2 3 4 5 6 7 8 9 = awake
tired = 0 1 2 3 4 5 6 7 8 9 = alert
drowsy = 0 1 2 3 4 5 6 7 8 9 = wakeful

Tense Arousal
at rest = 0 1 2 3 4 5 6 7 8 9 = restless
relaxed = 0 1 2 3 4 5 6 7 8 9 = tense
calm = 0 1 2 3 4 5 6 7 8 9 = jittery

Note: Sum all of your energetic arousal and tense arousal scores separately. The value of each score indicates the amount of each type of arousal that a person experiences at the moment.

Source: Based on "Experiencing Activation: Energetic Arousal and Tense Arousal Are Not Mixtures of Valence and Activation" by U. Schimmack and R. Reisenzein, 2002, *Emotion, 2,* p. 414.

Sources of Arousal

Does loud music, the promise of a bonus, or playing a game energize you? These are examples of stimuli, incentives, and behavior that all contribute to arousal and energization.

Stimuli.   Someone calls out your name and you orient yourself toward the source of the sound. The sound of your name has both a cue function and an arousing function (Hebb, 1955). The cue function determines the type of response, and the arousing function determines the intensity of the response. The arousal function of a stimulus is apparent from the energizing properties of music, which are described later in this chapter.

In addition to arousal from a specific stimulus, background stimuli also affect a person's level of arousal. These stimuli, not the focus of an individual's attention, consist of time of day, caffeine, and the process of being evaluated. Time-of-day effects are most obvious from people's sleep-wake cycles: low arousal during sleep and high arousal when awake. Clements and associates (1976) had students in university classes that met at various times of the day fill out a scale that measured energetic arousal. The results showed that energetic arousal followed an inverted-U relationship with time of day. Arousal began low for 8 o'clock classes, rose to its highest levels for 12 and 2 o'clock classes, and then declined to its lowest value for evening classes. Other studies have also shown that psychological arousal increases from shortly after 8 A.M. to noon and 2 P.M. and then declines, reaching its lowest point prior to bedtime (Thayer, 1967, 1978). More subtle are changes in body temperature, which increases from 8 A.M. to 8 P.M. and then declines, as do changes in subjective alertness, which increases from 8 A.M. to around noon (Monk & Folkard, 1983). Caffeine from a cup of coffee boosts many people's energetic arousal in the morning. As described in Chapter 4, the arousing effects of caffeine are considered pleasurable. Finally, we live in an age when many people suffer from evaluation anxiety, which occurs during exams, sports competition, and social situations (Zeidner & Matthews, 2005). Perhaps most pertinent to the reader is test anxiety and math anxiety, which are aroused in statistics courses.

Collative Variables. In addition to stimulus intensity, other variables also affect arousal. Berlyne (1960) proposed the term **collative variables** to refer collectively to stimulus characteristics that include novelty, complexity, and incongruity. A *novel* stimulus is one that is new and different from the stimuli to which a person has become accustomed. For instance, given a choice between two stimuli that differ in novelty, grade school children are more likely to choose the more novel one. It is assumed that a more novel stimulus is also more arousing (Comerford & Witryol, 1993).

The *complexity* variable is determined by the number of elements and the dissimilarity of those elements in a stimulus array. The *incongruity* variable refers to the difference between a single element in the stimulus array that conflicts with or is discrepant from accompanying stimulus elements or from previous elements. Collative variables also affect an individual's curiosity. Looking time increases as complexity of various stimuli increases, such as drawings, photographs, and works of art (Faw, 1970; Leckart & Bakan, 1965; Nicki & Moss, 1975).

Tasks. Arousal has also been linked to how much energy a person is willing to expend in order to successfully complete a task or attain an incentive (Brehm & Self, 1989; Duffy, 1962). The degree of arousal or *energization* for getting ready to act is based on three factors: (1) the severity of the person's need, (2) the value of the incentive being pursued, and (3) the likelihood that successfully completing the behavior will actually result in the incentive (Brehm & Self, 1989). For example, a person may become little energized if the value of the incentive is low. A person may become greatly energized, however, if the incentive is high and if the chances of earning the incentive are moderate—that is, not too easy and not impossible. To illustrate, people who think they have a good chance at winning a coupon from a fast-food restaurant show an increase in heart rate and blood pressure in anticipation of the task required to earn the coupon (Wright & Dill, 1993). The increase in heart rate and blood pressure, which indicates energization, was greatest when participants were doing a difficult task but one they thought was achievable. Participants who thought they had little chance to succeed showed a smaller increase in heart rate and blood pressure on the difficult task. After all, why get energized over a task that cannot be accomplished?

Arousal and Behavior

Psychologists are interested in how arousal affects the performance of a person working on various tasks. The next several pages examine the relationship between arousal and behavioral efficiency.

Arousal-Performance Relationships. Personal introspection leads to conflicting conclusions about the relationship between arousal and performance efficiency. For example, a person might conclude that it is good to be somewhat aroused while giving a speech, although too much arousal results in poor delivery. However, even the mildest arousal might prevent a person from falling asleep while extreme arousal is necessary to run across the street to avoid being hit by a car. Perhaps the relationship between arousal and behavior depends on the nature of the task that is being performed. Let us examine two experiments on how arousal affects performance on different tasks: basketball free throws and reaction time. Is the efficiency of these two behaviors affected by arousal in the same way? For basketball free-throw behavior, Wang and coresearchers (2004) had participants shoot 20 free throws in low- and high-pressure conditions designed to produce low and high arousal. First, participants shot free throws in the low-pressure condition, during which only one person was present who scored the shots and returned the ball. Next, in the high-pressure condition, participants shot their free throws while being videotaped in the presence of student spectators. In addition, participants received $1 for every shot they made plus an additional $4 was added or subtracted for every shot that exceeded or fell short of the number made in the low-pressure condition. In order to determine if all of these manipulations increased arousal, participants completed a scale that measured their cognitive anxiety and bodily anxiety. The high-pressure manipulations had the intended effect: cognitive and bodily anxiety were greater in the high-pressure than in the low-pressure condition. How was free-throw performance affected? Figure 6.1 shows that participants made significantly fewer free throws while more highly anxious. The main conclusion is that as arousal (anxiety) increases, free-throw performance declines.

In the case of simple reaction time, Smith and coresearchers (2005) manipulated arousal with varying amounts of caffeine. On different days and in the space of 90 minutes, participants drank two beverages either both without caffeine, one with and one without caffeine, or both with caffeine. The simple reaction time task consisted of participants pressing a key as soon as they saw a square appear on the computer screen. Did caffeine-induced arousal affect reaction time? Figure 6.2 shows that a greater amount of caffeine produced faster reaction times. The main conclusion is that as caffeine-induced arousal increases, reaction time becomes faster.

Yerkes-Dodson Law.   Notice that these two experiments provide different conclusions regarding the effects of arousal on performance. In one case (Figure 6.1) increases in arousal reduces performance while in the other case (Figure 6.2) it improves performance. Two hypotheses suggest themselves for these results. First, some arousal helps performance but too much arousal hinders it. Second, the amount of arousal depends on the nature of the task, such as free throws versus reaction time. The first hypothesis describes an **inverted-U**

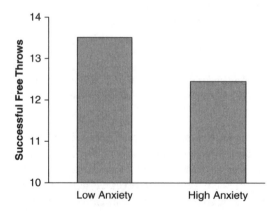

FIGURE 6.1   Anxiety and Free Throws. As anxiety increased, there was a decrease in the number of successful basketball free throws out of 20 attempts.

Source: Adapted from "Coping Style and Susceptibility to Choking" by J. Wang, D. Marchant, & T. Morris, 2004, *Journal of Sport Behavior, 27,* table 1, p. 83.

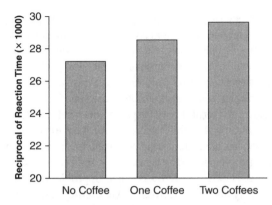

FIGURE 6.2 Caffeine and Reaction Time. Reaction speed became faster with an increase in the amount of caffeinated coffee that participants drank. Reciprocals of reaction times (× 1000) were computed in order to associate taller bars with faster reaction times. The RTs were 366, 353, and 343 milliseconds for no, one, or two coffees, respectively.

Source: Adapted from "Effects of Repeated Doses of Caffeine on Mood and Performance and Fatigued Volunteers" by S. A. Smith, D. Sutherland, & G. Christopher, 2005, *Journal of Psychopharmacology, 19,* table 1, p. 624.

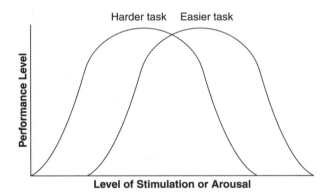

FIGURE 6.3 Yerkes-Dodson Law. Each curve shows the inverted-U arousal-performance relationship. As arousal increases, performance increases and levels off; further increases in arousal lead to decreases in performance. According to the Yerkes-Dodson law, the optimal level of arousal is lower for harder tasks than for easier tasks. The optimal level of arousal is associated with the best performance at a task.

arousal-performance relationship: as arousal increases, performance increases, levels off, and then decreases (Hebb, 1955; Malmo, 1959). The two inverted-U curves in Figure 6.3 show that for each task an intermediate level of arousal is considered optimal—that is, the level that is associated with the best performance.

The second hypothesis suggests that the optimal level of arousal changes with the nature of the task being performed. In other words, the optimal level of arousal is not fixed but depends on the complexity or difficulty of the task being performed. This complication was an early discovery in the history of psychology by Yerkes and Dodson (1908). They trained mice to discriminate between a white box and a black box at three levels of difficulty. In the process of learning, if the mouse made the wrong choice, it received an electric shock, which varied in intensity from weak to medium or strong. The strong electric shock "was decidedly disagreeable to the experimenters and the mice reacted to it vigorously" (pp. 467–468). The intensity of the shock has come to be equated with the level of arousal, although Yerkes and Dodson did not interpret their experiment in terms of arousal but in terms of the intensity of (electrical) stimulation. The results of their experiment show that performance on the discrimination problem depended on problem difficulty and on shock intensity. For easy discrimination problems, performance increased across all levels of shock intensity and almost never declined. For difficult discrimination problems, however, performance increased with shock intensity and then decreased. Medium-difficult discriminations showed the most pronounced inverted-U relationship. These findings became known as the **Yerkes-Dodson law:** low arousal produces maximal performance on difficult tasks, and high arousal produces maximal performance on easy tasks. This law is diagrammed in Figure 6.3.

Zones of Optimal Functioning.   Experiments showing inverted-U relationships between arousal and task performance have been scarce, however (Neiss, 1988). A reason for the shortage of evidence is that individuals have different optimal levels of arousal. The same general curve does not apply to everyone. The **zone of optimal functioning hypothesis** in sports psychology postulates individual inverted-U curves each with a zone of optimal arousal where an athlete performs best (Hanin, 1989). Arousal below or above this zone leads to poorer performance. The zone applies to different psychological variables and has been tested most frequently with cognitive anxiety and somatic anxiety. *Cognitive anxiety* refers to negative expectations and mental concerns about performance in a competitive situation. *Somatic anxiety* refers to the self-perception of physiological arousal associated with nervousness and tension. In a test of the zone of optimal function hypothesis, Krane (1993) examined the relationship between cognitive anxiety and somatic anxiety and the performance of women players during soccer matches. Each player filled out the two anxiety scales about 20 minutes prior to each of the season's 12 soccer matches. A player's optimal zone for cognitive anxiety was defined as between one standard deviation below and above her season's cognitive anxiety mean. Her somatic anxiety zone was also defined as between one standard deviation below and above her season's somatic anxiety mean. At the end of the season, each player's soccer match performance was classified as below, within, or above her optimal zone for cognitive and for somatic anxiety. Krane found partial support for the hypothesis. A player performed best when she was within but also below her optimal zone and played worst when above her zone.

The zone of optimal functioning for cognitive anxiety and somatic anxiety has also been examined with swimmers. Davis and Cox (2002) measured cognitive anxiety and somatic anxiety 10 minutes prior to a highschool swimmer's preferred event. Each swimmer's mean and standard deviation for cognitive anxiety and for somatic anxiety was computed for the season. In this study, a swimmer's optimal zone was defined as between one-half standard deviation below and above the mean for the season. The results for cognitive anxiety, but not for somatic anxiety, supported the zone of optimal functioning hypothesis. Swimmers swam faster when in their optimal zone for cognitive anxiety and slower when below or above their zone. Swimming times did not differ for the three somatic anxiety zones.

Section Recap

Arousal refers to energy mobilization and activation of a person prior to or while engaged in behavior. Arousal occurs in several modes. *Physiological arousal* refers to excitement of the body, as reflected by sweaty palms and increased muscle tension, breathing, and heart rate. The sympathetic nervous system is responsible for stimulating the heart to pump blood more effectively, the liver to release glucose, the release of epinephrine (adrenaline) and norepinephrine (noradrenaline), and increased oxygen uptake. *Brain arousal* refers to activation of various areas of the brain as a person performs various activities. Brain arousal is measured by *positron emission tomography* (*PET scan*), which is a procedure that produces a three-dimensional brain picture indicating areas that are most active. Brain arousal is also measured with a *functional magnetic resonance imaging (fMRI)* procedure that provides an image showing the degree of activity in a particular brain area. A third mode of arousal is *psychological arousal*, which refers to how subjectively aroused an individual feels. Psychological arousal is composed of *energetic* and *tense* dimensions. Energetic arousal is associated with positive affect, while tense arousal is associated with anxiety and fearfulness.

Arousal itself stems from several sources. A stimulus, for example, has an arousing function and a cue function. In addition, background stimuli which do not capture a person's attention also increase arousal. Arousal varies with time of day, being highest around noon and lower in the morning and evening. Coffee boosts arousal as does the process of being evaluated during exams or sports competition. Arousal also depends on *collative variables*, including characteristics like novelty, complexity, and incongruity. A task also can be a source of arousal, since it energizes or activates a person even before he begins working on it. Task-induced arousal is based on a person's need, value of the task's outcome, and chances of success. Sometimes arousal increases behavioral efficiency and in other instances decreases it. This inconsistency is handled by an inverted-U relationship and the Yerkes-Dodson law.

According to the *inverted-U relationship*, as arousal increases, performance on a task increases and then decreases. According to the *Yerkes-Dodson law,* the high point of the inverted-U or arousal-performance relationship depends on the complexity of the task being performed. Low arousal produces maximal performance on difficult tasks, and high arousal produces maximal performance on easy tasks. According to the *zone of optimal functioning hypothesis*, each individual has her preferred zone of arousal based on cognitive or somatic anxiety. Athletic performance is better within the zone and worse below and above it.

Theories about the Performance-Arousal Relationship

Several theories have been proposed to explain the inverted-U arousal-performance relationship. The classic Hull-Spence drive theory emphasizes how arousal affects performance with little regard for any cognitive awareness on the part of the individual. The cusp catastrophe model in sports psychology, the cue utilization hypothesis, and the processing efficiency theory are more concerned with the cognitive aspects of arousal and how this affects behavioral efficiency. The purpose of this section is to describe each theory along with some exemplary evidence for its support.

Hull-Spence Drive Theory

What determines whether arousal aids or hinders performance? The answer depends on whether arousal is energizing a correct response or an incorrect response. For instance, correct responses occur more readily with easy tasks, while incorrect responses are initially more likely with difficult tasks. Spence and his associates (1956a, 1956b) employed Hull's (1943, 1952) drive concept to account for the finding that high drive or arousal aids in the performance of easy tasks but hinders the performance of difficult tasks. For Hull, drive was a persistent internal stimulus or pushing action of a physiological need. The stronger the drive, the greater the pushing action on all responses. Thus, for a simple task as drive increases, the strength of the correct response increases, as does the difference between the correct and the wrong responses. In a complex task, however, the most dominant response is often not the correct one. As drive increases, the strength of wrong responses increases, as does the difference between these responses and the correct one. For the correct response to occur in these situations, the incorrect response must be weakened and the correct one strengthened.

To test this hypothesis, Spence and associates compared the learning of simple versus difficult paired associate tasks (Spence et al., 1956a, 1956b). In paired associate learning, a participant must learn to associate two words together such that a stimulus word cues the participant to say the associated response word. The simple paired associate task involved such pairs of words as *complete-thorough* and *empty-vacant*. It is easy to learn the response *thorough* to the stimulus *complete*, since these words have similar meanings. With these pairs, an increase in drive should make the occurrence of the dominant but correct response more likely, and hence learning should be faster. The difficult task involved pairs such as *quiet-double* and *serene-headstrong*. These pairs are more difficult to learn because the responses *double* and *headstrong* are going to compete when the stimuli *quiet* or *serene* are presented. The reason is because *quiet* and *serene* are similar in meaning and thus will evoke the same response. An increase in drive in this case should also increase the likelihood of the dominant response, which is now the wrong response. This development should make learning more difficult. Drive or arousal in this experiment was defined by the participant's level of trait anxiety as measured by an anxiety scale. Participants low in trait anxiety were defined as low drive, and those high in trait anxiety were defined as high drive. The results confirmed the prediction: high-drive participants learned the easy paired associate task faster than did low-drive participants. High-drive participants, however, learned the difficult paired associate task slower than did low-drive participants (Spence et al., 1956a, 1956b).

Cusp Catastrophe Model

Sports is one of those endeavors in which it is very important to control arousal in order to maximize performance. Arousal factors that determine athletic performance are addressed in the **cusp catastrophe model** from sports psychology, which holds that there are two types of arousal: cognitive anxiety and physiological arousal (somatic anxiety) (Hardy, 1996a, 1996b). At low physiological arousal, increases in cognitive anxiety produce a slight improvement in athletic performance while at high physiological arousal, increases in cognitive anxiety produce a decline in performance. Also, at lower levels of cognitive anxiety, increases in physiological arousal lead to small gradual increases and then decreases in athletic performance resembling a flattened inverted-U curve. However, at midrange or higher levels of cognitive anxiety, increases in physiological arousal lead to a cusp where performance is best. Here an athlete is described as a "clutch" player. Increases in physiological arousal beyond this cusp, however, result in a sudden and dramatic drop in performance. At this point the athlete "chokes" and performs very badly.

One implication of the cusp catastrophe model is that the drop in performance can be so drastic that it is manifested as freezing—that is, the individual ceases all behavior. Freezing, also known as **tonic immobility,** refers to a lack of behavior that occurs in reaction to extremely stressful circumstances. Tonic immobility is characterized by the absence of movement, lack of responsiveness, the tendency to maintain the same posture, remaining silent, an unresponsiveness to pain, and yet a tendency to remain alert (Moskowitz, 2004). Freezing occurs in many animals but also in humans during stressful situations. It has been induced in a variety of birds, chickens, and rats by holding them on their backs for 15 to 30 seconds (Gallup et al., 1970; Ratner, 1967). Freezing occurs in animals when they are attacked by predators, at which time tonic immobility serves as an adaptive strategy. If the prey animal has unsuccessfully tried to escape or fight back, then it freezes as if it were feigning death (Ratner, 1967). Marks (1987) comments on the evolutionary significance of freezing by noting that many predators only attack and kill moving prey. When prey freezes, predators lose interest and their attention lapses, which provides an opportunity for prey to escape. Hawks, for example, do not eat dead animals and would starve if not provided with moving prey to eat (Marks, 1987).

However, when freezing occurs in humans it is usually in situations where it is not adaptive, especially in emergency situations. Leach (2004) provides some descriptions of people's behavior during emergency situations. For example, the passenger ferry MV *Estonia* sank in September 1994 in the Baltic Sea. While sinking, passengers were seen standing still as if paralyzed, exhausted, or in shock. Or they were just sitting incapable of doing anything. In another case, a North Sea oil platform exploded as a result of natural gas accumulation in July 1988. Leach reports that many workers made no attempt to leave the platform and one worker just slumped down unable to move. Another emergency example is the case of an airplane that returned to a Manchester, England, airport in 1985. Upon landing it was discovered that one of the engines was on fire. Unfortunately, there were delays in evacuating the plane because many passengers froze; in fact, ". . . several people were seen to remain in their seats until they became engulfed in flames" (Leach, 2004, p. 540).

According to evolutionary psychology (Chapter 3), human nature evolved because it had survival value. Is freezing a case of evolutionary old behavior intruding into frightening emergency situations in the present? Yes, according to Moskowitz (2004), who wrote that tonic immobility in humans is a holdover from our evolutionary past during which time humans were also prey. Just like animals today freeze in order to increase their chances for survival, so did humans long ago. Thus, freezing that occurs in emergency situations like sinking ships or burning airplanes are really remnants of this behavior that once provided a survival advantage. Unfortunately, in such situations, freezing is incompatible with the behavior that is required for escape.

Cue Utilization Hypothesis

A cognitive explanation of the inverted-U arousal–performance relationship is provided by Easterbrook's (1959) **cue utilization hypothesis,** which holds that the number of cues or amount of information utilized by a person in any situation tends to decline with an increase in arousal. Usually, the use of peripheral and irrelevant cues is reduced, while the use of central and relevant cues is maintained. In the case of simple tasks, irrelevant cues are more likely to be excluded with increasing arousal; thus, more attention can be given to task-relevant cues. Complex tasks, however, involve many cues. Arousal involves the exclusion of task-relevant cues as well, and consequently performance declines. One reason for the reduction in utilizing task-relevant cues comes from the attention-grabbing nature of autonomic nervous system arousal (Mandler, 1975, 1984). A pounding heart and butterflies in the stomach compete for attention, allowing less attention to be devoted to the task at hand; as a consequence, performance declines.

Research on memory and emotionally arousing events has supported Easterbrook's cue utilization hypothesis. For example, arousal should enhance the memory for major or central details of an event but not for peripheral or irrelevant details. In two questionnaire studies, Christianson and Loftus (1990) asked university students to recall the most traumatic events in their lives. Students were asked how many central and peripheral details they remembered. *Central details* are relevant and directly associated with the traumatic event, while *peripheral details* are neither relevant nor directly associated. Students were also asked how strong their emotional feelings were during the event and how strong their emotional feelings were in recalling the event. The results showed that participants remembered more central details than peripheral details. Furthermore, the more intense their emotional feelings about the event, the more likely they were to remember central but not peripheral details.

Are there some events, such as the events of September 11, 2001, so ingrained in our memories that we will never forget them, even if we want to? Is the memory for extremely emotional and arousing events somehow different than the memory for the more mundane things of life? One answer to these questions is based on a theory about the relationship between arousal and a shift in memory systems. This theory, by Metcalfe and Jacobs (1998), postulates the existence of two memory systems, with the level of arousal determining which system is operating. Such a theory postulates the existence of a **cool memory system** and a **hot memory system,** each in a different area of the brain. The cool system, which is localized in the hippocampus, serves the memory of events occurring in space and time. For example, this system would help a person to remember the location of her residence and that her car is parked in a different spot today than yesterday. The hot system, which is localized in the amygdala, serves as the memory of events that occur under high arousal. The hot system is responsible for the intrusive memories of individuals who have experienced extremely traumatic events years earlier.

The level of activation of the cool and hot memory systems depends on the level of arousal (Metcalfe & Jacobs, 1998). The degree of activation or efficiency of the cool system follows the inverted-U curve shown in Figure 6.3. As arousal increases, activation of this memory system increases, levels off, and then decreases. The system is most efficient at intermediate levels of arousal but inefficient at very high levels. The hot memory system, however, shows increasing levels of activation with increasing amounts of arousal. This system is least efficient at low levels of arousal but most efficient at very high levels of arousal. Both systems interact to determine a person's total memory. However, the cool system is most functional at low and intermediate levels of arousal, while the hot system is most functional at high levels. Thus, where the cool system leaves off, the hot system takes over. Metcalfe and Jacobs further theorize that the hot system is geared up for remembering the details of stimuli that predict the onset of highly stressful or arousing events, such as events that predict danger.

Processing Efficiency Theory

Evaluations occur in many facets of life, such as exams, sports competition, and social settings, and can become sources of anxiety in those situations (Zeidner & Matthews, 2005). However, the level of anxiety individuals experience in evaluative situations depends on their disposition to become anxious—that is, some people become anxious quicker than others. So, imagine being evaluated for speed and accuracy for attempting to solve "in your head" problems like: $478 + 59 = ?$ Does your level of math anxiety, in this case, affect your problem solving efficiency?

Trait vs. State Anxiety.   Anxiety is not a single entity but instead consists of two parts: trait and state. **Trait anxiety** is an individual difference measure of the disposition to perceive environmental events as threatening and to respond anxiously. **State anxiety** refers to the actual feelings of apprehension, worry, and sympathetic nervous system arousal that are evoked by threatening situations (Spielberger, 1975). In other words, trait anxiety is the propensity to react with state anxiety in threatening situations, such as evaluation that occurs during exams, sports competition, and social settings. For example, trait anxiety is the disposition to become anxious (state anxiety) during a math test. In general, state anxiety is damaging to performance especially on tasks that are complex (Zeidner & Matthews, 2005). But, how does anxiety affect performance?

Anxiety and Processing Efficiency.   According to **processing efficiency theory,** anxiety expresses itself as worry, which is a preoccupation with evaluation and concerns about performance. Worry, in turn, takes up working-memory capacity and with less working-memory available performance on cognitive tasks declines (Eysenck & Calvo, 1992). Anxiety and accompanying worry are especially telling in their effects on math problems. For instance, solving the problem $478 + 59$ requires a person to retain intermediate solutions (7 and "carry 1") in her working memory. According to processing efficiency theory, the capacity of working memory to retain an intermediate solution decreases because of the presence of intrusive thoughts of worry. Experimental evidence is provided by Ashcraft and Kirk (2001), who compared low, medium, and high math anxiety students for accuracy in working math problems. Some problems did not require "carrying operations" $(15 + 2)$ and other problems did $(23 + 18)$. The effects of anxiety was only apparent with problems that required carrying operations. As math anxiety increases and uses more working memory space, problem solving efficiency decreases for problems that require carrying operations.

Math anxiety appears to be unique. Ashcraft and Kirk (2001, exp. 3) hypothesized that math anxiety only affected the working-memory capacity for numbers but not for letters. In their experiment, they compared the effects of anxiety on working-memory capacity for numbers versus working-memory capacity for letters. A participant's level of math anxiety was measured with a scale similar to the *Abbreviated Math Anxiety Scale*. With this scale, participants answer questions about how much anxiety is evoked in situations relevant to mathematics (Hopko et al., 2003). Examples may include using a table in a math book, listening to a lecture in math class, or being given a "pop" quiz in math class. During the actual

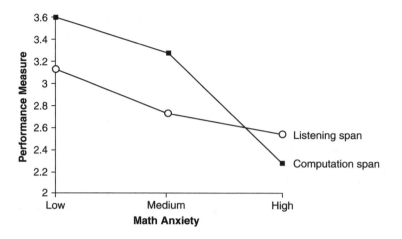

FIGURE 6.4   Math Anxiety and Performance. As math anxiety increased, working-memory capacity for arithmetic decreased. Specifically, as math anxiety increased computation span with numbers decreased while listening span for letters did not decrease significantly.

Source: Adapted from "The Relationship among Working Memory, Math Anxiety, and Performance" by M. H. Ashcraft and E. P. Kirk, 2001, *Journal of Experimental Psychology: General, 130,* table 3, p. 233.

experiment, the researchers used a listening-span task to measure the working-memory capacity for letters and used a computation-span task to measure the working-memory capacity for numbers. For the listening span, participants heard a number of simple sentences, answered a question about each, and were required to remember the last word of each sentence. For example, "It rained yesterday." When? "The dog sat on the porch." Where? After hearing and answering a number of such sentences, participants were asked to recall the last word in each sentence in the correct order (e.g., *yesterday, porch*). The mean number of words recalled correctly defined the letter-span size. The computation-span task resembled the listening-span task. The participant heard a series of simple problems, such as $7 - 3 = ?$ followed by $2 + 6 = ?$ They were required to solve each problem and also to remember the last number of each. At the recall, participants had to name the last number of each problem in the correct order (e.g., 3, 6). The amount recalled correctly defined the working-memory capacity for numbers. Ashcraft and Kirk reasoned that on the basis of processing efficiency theory, math anxiety should negatively influence working-memory capacity for numbers but not for letters. Their results in Figure 6.4 show that as anxiety increased, working-memory capacity for numbers (computation span) decreased while the capacity for letters (listening span) was affected slightly, although not significantly. If working memory is not used to capacity, then anxiety has little effect on math performance. However, when used to capacity as in this experiment, anxiety has a detrimental effect on math performance.

Section Recap

There are several theories that help explain the inverted-U arousal-performance relationship. According to the *Hull-Spence theory*, arousal magnifies the intensity of all responses. In a simple task, arousal magnifies the dominant response, which is usually the correct one. Arousal of the dominant response in complex tasks is most likely to be the incorrect response. According to the *cusp catastrophe model*, performance efficiency is based on the interaction between physiological (somatic) anxiety and cognitive anxiety. At low cognitive arousal, performance increases moderately as physiological arousal increases and then decreases. At high cognitive arousal, however, performance increases and then catastrophically drops as physiological arousal increases. During extremely arousing and dangerous situations a person may exhibit *tonic immobility*, which refers to freezing. This behavior was adaptive in our evolutionary past to escape predators but today that behavior interferes with escape from danger, such as in the case of sinking ships or burning airplanes. According to the *cue utilization hypothesis*, the amount of information utilized in a situation declines as arousal increases. In simple tasks there is a decline in the use of irrelevant cues, and in complex tasks there can also be a decline in task-relevant cues as arousal increases. According to memory research, as arousal increases there is better recall of central detail and a decrease in the recall of peripheral detail. One theory is that a *cool memory system* works best under moderate arousal, while a *hot memory system* works best under high arousal. Thus, as arousal increases there is a shift from a cool to a hot memory system.

Many individuals suffer from evaluation anxiety, which occurs during exams, sports competition, and social situations. *Trait anxiety* is an individual difference variable to respond negatively and with worry to the environment in general, while *state anxiety* refers to feelings of apprehension activated by a particular situation. According to *processing efficiency theory*, state anxiety—especially in math—expresses itself as worry, which takes up working-memory capacity. As a result of increasing state anxiety, solving math problems declines in efficiency, especially when carrying operations are involved.

Arousal and Affective Valence

When considered an independent variable, arousal affects performance: some arousal aids performance but too little or too much hinders it. When considered a dependent variable, arousal depends on the collative variables of novelty, complexity, and incongruity. Humans are both pushed and pulled toward experiencing arousal at a certain intensity and valence. Arousal experiences are provided by collative variables like novelty in new fashions; complexity in art, music, or movies; and incongruity in jokes. This section examines the motivation that humans have for two components of arousal: intensity and valence.

Variation in Affective Valence

Can a person be aroused or energized but still feel subjectively neutral? Or is arousal always accompanied by a positive or negative feeling (Thayer, 1989)? Riding a roller coaster, watching a suspenseful movie, or attending a good party are arousing and provide positive affective experiences. A near traffic accident, witnessing a violent crime, or being insulted are arousing and produce negative affective experiences. While being performed, strenuous exercise may feel negative and arousing, but when completed it feels pleasant while some arousal still remains. Thus, arousal is not neutral but instead has a positive or negative feel to it (Thayer, 1989; Watson & Tellegen, 1985). In trying to determine how the level of arousal regulates behavior, it may be difficult to separate affective valence from arousal (Neiss, 1988). Consequently, both arousal and associated affective valence must be kept in mind when describing behavior.

Optimal Level of Stimulation Theory

What is the relationship between levels of arousal and affective valence? Zuckerman (1969) described the relationship as an inverted U in his **optimal level of stimulation theory.** One postulate of this theory is that every person has an optimal (best) level of stimulation or arousal that is associated with the highest positive affective valence. This optimal or preferred level of arousal is not fixed but changes with personality, age, time of day, and experience. Another postulate is that the optimal level of stimulation and arousal is usually at a moderate level—not too low and not too high. A third postulate is that deviations in either direction from this optimal level decrease positive affective valence. If arousal increases or decreases from the optimal level, then affective valence decreases. Finally, affective valence becomes negative when levels of stimulation and arousal are very low or very high (Zuckerman, 1969). Figure 6.5 graphically shows optimal level of stimulation theory (Berlyne, 1960; Hebb, 1955; Zuckerman, 1969). According to Zuckerman (1969), people are motivated to position themselves at the intermediate level of stimulation that provides the highest positive affective valence. When arousal is low, increases in arousal are positively reinforcing. Thus, a person seeks stimulation, such as loud music with a beat, a party with friends, or an action TV program. When arousal is high, decreases in arousal are negatively reinforcing. Consequently, a person then seeks a decrease in stimulation, such as listening to soft music, being alone, or resting. Increases in arousal above the optimal level or decreases in arousal below the optimal level are punishing. Very low levels of arousal are associated with boredom and with a feeling that "there is nothing to do," while very high levels of arousal are associated with stress and a feeling that "I can't get everything done."

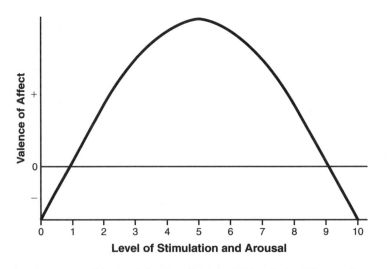

FIGURE 6.5   Graph of Optimal Level of Stimulation Theory. A person's affective valence depends on the level of stimulation and arousal. As the level of stimulation and subsequent arousal increases to a moderate level, affective valence increases. Further increases in the level of stimulation and arousal produce a decrease in affective valence. Very low and very high levels of arousal are associated with negative affective valence.

When Arousal Is Too Low. Boring situations are characterized by repetitiveness, simplicity, and a general lack of stimulation. Consequently, people try to avoid and escape boring situations (Jones, 1969; Zubek, 1973; Zuckerman, 1964). Experiments designed to test the effects of low levels of stimulation have employed a technique known as **sensory deprivation.** This involves reducing sensory stimulation from touch, sound, and light to the lowest possible level. To accomplish this, participants are confined to dark soundproof chambers, where they lie quietly on a mattress with their arms and hands confined in cardboard tubes, thereby eliminating tactual stimulation. Earplugs and goggles may also be used to further reduce the level of stimulation. A variation of this procedure known as *perceptual deprivation* allows the participant to see and hear to some extent, but only diffuse and nonpatterned light and static noise, such as the hum of a fan (Zubek, 1973).

The aversive nature of sensory deprivation is illustrated in experiments performed by Smith and associates (1966, 1967). In the sensory deprivation condition, the researchers confined participants alone in a dark soundproof room. Other than a bed, there was nothing else in the room, and there was nothing to do. In the control condition, participants were confined in a similar room but had access to light, TV, music, books, magazines, writing paper, playing cards, and the possibility of conversation with another participant in an adjacent room. The aversive nature of sensory deprivation became apparent from several findings. First, people were reluctant even to participate in the study. Only 74% agreed to participate after it was explained that they would have to live for seven consecutive days and nights in the room. Of the 40 participants who began the seven days of sensory deprivation, only little more than half (21) completed all seven days. Thus, the aversive nature of sensory deprivation is shown by the fact that many participants dropped out. Only one out of 20 participants dropped out of the control condition, and that was due to illness. Zuckerman (1964) also notes that approximately one-third of all participants drop out of sensory deprivation experiments like the one described here. It does not seem to matter if the sensory deprivation lasts 2, 4, 7, or 14 days.

Hedonic Reversal. At first glance, it might seem that optimal level of stimulation theory (Figure 6.5) applies only to stimuli that have a positive valence. As positive stimuli increase in intensity their pleasurable effects increase. Do negative stimuli show a reverse effect? As their intensity increases, is there an associated increase in unpleasantness? It appears that is not always the case. **Hedonic reversal** refers to the eventual liking of stimuli that were initially aversive or feared (Rozin, 1999). For example, people develop a liking for bitter-tasting beverages, which they initially disliked, such as beer or coffee. Chili peppers that were initially painful are now enjoyed for the burn they provide. Rozin and Schiller (1980) documented how with increasing exposure to chili in their food, individuals eventually learn to enjoy the burn that is produced. The researchers reasoned that the burn is the body's early warning system regarding a harmful stimulus. However, the burn intensity does not reach the level of being harmful. Some individuals also learn to enjoy the experience of fear at low intensities. Fear which should motivate escape and avoidance behavior is now enjoyed in controlled settings, such as scary movies and roller coaster rides. Many people enjoy feelings of suspense and fear when they view actors on screen being attacked, physically injured, or terrified by other individuals or by supernatural beings (Hoffner & Levine, 2005).

Stimulus Complexity and Affective Valence

Have you ever seen a movie more than once because you did not understand it fully the first time? Do some outfits have the wrong combination of plaids and colors, creating a look that's "too busy"? Is some music too atonal or harsh for enjoyment? Each one of these questions addresses the role of stimulus complexity in determining feelings of pleasure. Complexity refers to the number of dimensions that characterize a stimulus. Individual stimuli can vary in intensity, duration, size, and predictability, while objects can vary in the number of individual stimuli that compose them. The degree of complexity determines the level of arousal and valence, which is associated with the amount of pleasure a person experiences.

Liking Increases, Decreases with Complexity.   Preferences for aesthetic stimuli depend on their arousal potential, which is based on complexity (Berlyne, 1970). Preference changes in an inverted-U fashion, with increases in stimulus complexity (see Figure 6.5). Moderately complex stimuli are preferred more, while stimuli of low and high complexity are preferred less. For instance, the inverted-U relationship applies to architectural stimuli, such as the complexity of house facades. Imamoglu (2000) presented students with eight drawings of Turkish house facades that varied in complexity. The simplest drawing showed only the essential elements, while the most complex drawing included additional elements, articulations, and surface treatments. After students examined each drawing, they selected two drawings they liked most and two they liked least. Their choices followed the inverted-U complexity relationship described in Figure 6.5. Students mostly preferred facades of intermediate complexity and preferred fewer facades of lesser or greater complexity.

In addition to visual stimuli, the appreciation of poetry is also affected by its complexity. Kamman (1966) categorized poems into one of five levels of complexity. University students then evaluated the poems for their goodness and desirability for memorization. The results followed the inverted-U pattern of Figure 6.5. Poems of intermediate complexity received higher goodness ratings and were preferred for memorization compared to poems that were either less or more complex.

Does liking for artificial music also depend on complexity? Vitz (1966) defined different levels of complexity by creating six sequences of tones varying in terms of pitch, duration, and loudness. The simplest tone sequence involved two different pitches at one duration and one volume setting. The most complex sequence involved 18 pitches, with eight different durations, and involved four levels of loudness. Vitz played each of the six tone sequences to his participants and asked them to rate how much they liked each sequence. The results followed the inverted-U relationship. As complexity of the tone sequence increased, liking increased and then decreased.

The inverted-U relationship in Figure 6.5 between complexity and liking is also descriptive of actual music. In a supporting experiment, North and Hargreaves (1995) had university students rate for subjective complexity 60 different excerpts of nonvocal New Age music. A different sample of students rated how much they liked each of the same 60 excerpts. An inverted-U relationship provided the best fit for the relationship between complexity ratings and liking ratings of the 60 musical excerpts. As shown in Figure 6.6, as music complexity increases, liking increases, levels off, and then decreases.

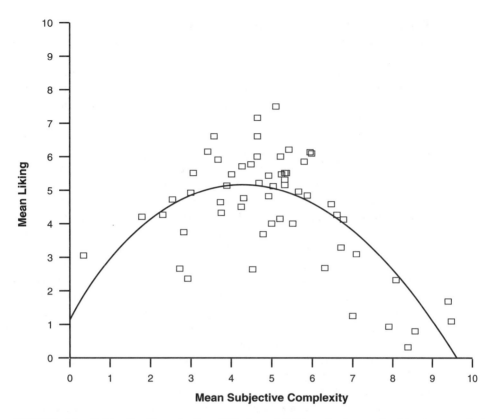

FIGURE 6.6 Subjective Complexity of Music and Liking. As the rated subjective complexity of music increased, liking for that music increased, leveled off, and then decreased.

Source: From "Subjective Complexity, Familiarity, and Liking for Popular Music" by A. C. North and D. J. Hargreaves, 1995, *Psychomusicology, 14,* figure 1, p. 82. Copyright 1995 by Psychomusicology. Reprinted by permission.

The inverted-U complexity-liking relationship also occurs when music is played in a natural setting. North and Hargreaves (1996) played short selections of low, moderate, or high complexity of New Age music in the cafeteria at a student union building. Diners rated the music on a scale ranging from "dislike very much" to "like very much." Their ratings showed that they liked music of moderate complexity more than that of either low or high complexity. Furthermore, when asked "what they would like to change about the cafeteria" (p. 497), diners were more likely to recommend changing the music when it was of low or high complexity. In other words, moderately complex music was preferred most while having lunch. People who are knowledgeable about music, such as music majors, also prefer music of moderate complexity. Burke and Gridley (1990) presented four piano compositions that covered a large range of perceived complexity as rated by music professors. The piano selection rated least complex was Bach's *Prelude and Fugue*, and Boulez's *Piano Sonata No. 1* was rated most complex. The four piano selections were played either to musicians, who were music majors, or to nonmusicians. Analyses of the ratings indicated that as the complexity of the piano pieces increased, both groups showed increases and then decreases in their liking.

Experiences, Complexity, and Liking.   Perceived complexity is subject to stimulus habituation. Consequently, preferred levels of complexity do not remain constant, but instead change. Specifically, repeated exposure decreases the perceived complexity of stimuli that are at or below optimal complexity. Thus, their appeal decreases. Repeated exposure also decreases the perceived complexity of stimuli that are above their optimal complexity. These stimuli have now shifted closer to the optimal level and hence their appeal increases. To illustrate, Smith and Dorfman (1975) exposed participants 1, 5, 10, or 20 times to visual stimuli of low, medium, or high complexity. Liking ratings decreased consistently for low complexity stimuli and increased consistently for high complexity stimuli over 20 exposures. However, liking ratings increased for medium complexity stimuli during the first 10 exposures and then decreased with further exposures.

Advertisements provide a real-world example of the effects of repeated exposures. The intent of an advertisement is to produce a favorable attitude toward a product and motivate people to buy. However, repeated advertisements of certain products can have the opposite effect. Cox and Cox (2002) presented participants with three different dresses that had either a simple design or a complex design. After one, two, or four exposures, participants rated the dresses for complexity and liking. Repeated exposures resulted in decreased complexity ratings. The simple-design dresses moved away and the complex-design dresses moved toward the optimal level of complexity. As a result, liking ratings decreased for simple-design dresses and increased for complex-design dresses. Thus, motivation toward or away from stimulus changes with experience.

Preferences for music also depend on level of complexity and amount of exposure. Specifically, listening experience determines what level of complexity of music is most enjoyable (Steck & Machotka, 1975). Sometimes liking for a piece of music increases with repeated listenings, and sometimes it decreases. These changes depend on whether the music was below or above a person's preferred level of complexity. To illustrate, Heyduk (1975) had participants listen to four different piano compositions at four different levels of musical complexity. By playing each selection over and over, participants' liking for the music changed. If complexity of the music was below a participant's preferred level, then liking decreased. There were no new incongruities to resolve and no arousal; consequently, less enjoyment was derived from the music each time. If the complexity of the music was above the participant's optimal complexity level, then liking increased. In the process of repeated listenings, new incongruities were discovered and resolved each time, thereby creating arousal and pleasure. With more complex music there is something new to discover each time, while less complex music is too predictable—there is nothing left to discover. Thus, with greater experience, more complex music is enjoyed.

Further evidence for this generalization comes from research by Tan and coresearchers (2006), who used short classical piano compositions that were initially near or above the listeners' perceived optimal level of complexity. Moderately complex were intact compositions, which consisted of 1-minute selections from classical piano works. Highly complex were patchwork compositions, which were composed of 20-second segments from three different classical works. Two music professors independently rated the patchwork compositions as highly complex and the intact compositions as moderately complex. The research participants listened to the intact and patchwork compositions plus filler compositions up to four times: twice on Tuesday and twice on Thursday. After each listening, they rated the compositions on several dimensions, such as liking. The results indicated that liking ratings for the intact compositions overall declined slightly over the four hearings while the ratings of the patchwork piece increased. Initially the patchwork compositions exceeded the optimal level of complexity whereas the intact compositions were optimally complex. Repeated hearings reversed this difference. Patchwork compositions presumably approached the optimal level of complexity while intact compositions decreased below that level. As a result liking ratings increased for patchwork and decreased for intact compositions.

There is a problem with the conclusion that repeatedly listening to the same piece of music eventually reduces its enjoyment. On the contrary, people enjoy hearing their favorite piece of music over and over. For example, radio stations play music from the past (golden oldies), and people buy CDs in order to hear the same music repeatedly. So why doesn't your favorite piece of music "get old"? One hypothesis is that a part of our brain functions like a **musical grammar processor** (Jackendoff, 1992). This processor has a primitive schema about a basic musical grammar by which it resolves musical notes. Regardless of whether the music is novel or highly familiar, the musical grammar processor works the same way each time to assimilate musical notes into its primitive schema. Each rehearing brings pleasure because the processor is sealed off from long-term memory and so does not benefit from having heard the music before. It responds as if it has heard a familiar piece of music for the first time. Thus, each time it assimilates a novel or familiar musical note, enjoyment results.

Incongruity Resolution in Music, Humor, and Suspense

Collative variables such as novelty and incongruity evoke arousal and determine the valence of a person's affective reaction. A novel or incongruous event is an unexpected outcome—that is, a specific event was expected but something else occurred instead. When these events are resolved or understood, positive affect results. If not, surprise, confusion, or puzzlement remains. The resolution or understanding of novel and incongruous events serves as the bases for amusement, the pleasure of music, and the thrill derived from suspense and horror films. A feature of incongruity-resolution is that the punchlines, the musical notes, or the suspenseful ending are assimilated into pre-existing knowledge structures known as **schemas.** These are mental representations of environmental regularities that an individual has experienced. They range from the abstract and general to the concrete and specific. Schemas can be thought of as scripts, recipes, maps, or concepts that help direct a person's attention, form hypotheses, develop expectations, and understand novel and incongruous events. An attend-class schema is known by every student and involves entering the classroom, taking a seat, taking notes on the professor's lecture, and leaving at the end. This schema guides a student's behavior regarding what to expect and what to do.

Valence and intensity of affective reactions depend on the degree of incongruity and on the resolution of the incongruous events. Mandler's (1984) **schema incongruity model** describes how the degree of incongruity affects both the valence and intensity of an emotional reaction. First, the degree of incongruity determines the degree of arousal and also determines whether or not the incongruous event is resolvable. If it is resolvable, then a positive affect results; if it is not, then a negative affect results. Events congruous with our expectations are ones that occur as expected. For example, if the traffic light is red, then we expect a car to stop. According to the schema incongruity model, congruous events produce no arousal and are considered familiar and in no way out of the ordinary. A slightly incongruous event produces some arousal and is pleasurable because it is easily assimilated into an available schema. For example, a person does not receive any mail even though a letter was expected. However, this incongruity is resolved when he realizes that it is a national holiday and thus there is no mail delivery. When incongruity is more severe, assimilation into a current schema may not be possible and a search for an alternative schema is then necessary. This process, for instance, occurs in resolving the incongruity created by the punch line of a joke. In this example, the arousal is greater but the pleasure resulting from resolution is also greater, as might occur in events that are pleasantly surprising. Some severe incongruities may not be resolvable because the individual has no relevant schema into which the event can be assimilated. The result of such an experience may alter existing schemas or lead to the development of new ones. Severe incongruities produce high arousal that is tinged with negative affect if they are not successfully resolved, as, for example, when a young child fears an object that is outside her range of experience.

Music

The pleasures derived from listening to music are innate, although the evolutionary significance of music is unclear (McDermott & Hauser, 2005). However, one thing is clear. People the world over enjoy music. In an attempt to determine why people value music, North and coresearchers (2004) sent text messages once per day for two weeks to 346 cell phone owners in England. On receipt of the message, participants were asked a series of questions concerning the reason they were listening to any music. Individuals reported they heard music on 39% of the occasions. Figure 6.7 summarizes the reasons that individuals gave for listening. Enjoyment was the most frequently cited reason. However, as North and coresearchers

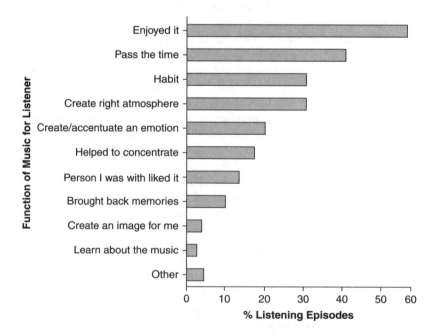

FIGURE 6.7   Reasons for Listening to Music. This graph shows the percentage of occasions that people gave for listening to the music they had selected. Enjoyment was the most frequent reason; to learn more about the music was the least cited reason.

Source: Adapted from "Uses of Music in Everyday Life" by A. C. North et al., 2004, *Music Perception,* table 18, p. 72.

(2004) note, music served mostly as background stimulation and common functions of listening to music were habit, to pass the time, and to help create the right atmosphere.

Music Regulates Arousal.   When you hear John Philip Sousa's *Stars and Stripes* played on July 4th, do you get an impulse to march? Does swing music produce the impulse to swing and waltz music the impulse to waltz? And years ago, did your parents lull you to sleep with a lullaby? Composers have written music to arouse and to relax us. In a review covering 120 years of the physiologically arousing and calming effect of music, Bartlett (1996) concluded that music had the intended consequence of producing physiological arousal. Most studies showed that stimulating music produced increases in heart rate, muscle tension, electrodermal responses, respiration rate, and blood pressure. Calming music had the opposite effect. The type of music and its tempo can affect psychological arousal. For instance, Kellaris and Kent (1994) played either a classical composition for flute, horn, bassoon, and cello or pop music with a "Paula Abdul-type dance beat" (p. 386). The music was played at a slow, moderate, or fast tempo. Participants rated the music for psychological arousal, such as stimulating/soothing, arousing/calming, and soft/loud. Their findings showed that arousal ratings were greater for the pop music than for the classical music. In addition, as tempo increased, arousal ratings increased for pop but not for classical music.

　　Occasionally you might listen to a musical passage that evokes a sudden increase in arousal, known as a **chill.** This is a unique physiological reaction characterized by goose bumps, shivers, or tingles. Chills are accompanied by electrodermal responses, which reflect sweating and blood flow (Grewe et al., 2007; Guhn et al., 2007). Finally, as one might expect, musical passages that evoked chills were perceived as pleasant (Grewe et al., 2007). Furthermore, not only can music produce arousal as in the case of chills, but it can also produce emotions (Davies, 1994). Music can make us feel sad or happy, and many researchers employ classical music as a mood induction procedure. Halberstadt and associates (1995) induced a happy mood by having participants listen to "happy" music (Mozart's *Eine Kleine Nachtmusik*) and a sad mood by having participants listen to "sad" music (Mahler's *Adagietto*). Music rated as being elating or depressing can be played to induce positive and negative moods (Pignatiello et al., 1986). Lyrics can also affect mood. Stratton and Zalanowski (1994) found that a musical melody accompanied by sad lyrics was more depressing than either melody or lyrics alone. As shown in Figure 6.7, on 20% of the listening occasions people reported that listening to music "helped create or accentuate an emotion" (North et al., 2004, p. 72).

Incongruity Resolution and Music Appreciation.   Although the pleasure derived from music may be an innate reaction, it also depends on the incongruity-resolution process. According to Gaver and Mandler (1987), listening to music activates various schemas, such as the progression of notes in a melody; the harmony, chords, or combination of tones; and the type of music, such as rock, blues, or symphonic. One suggestion is that a music schema is based on an innate expectation about repetition—that is, if it happened twice, then it should happen a third time. In the case of a sequence of musical notes, we expect them to repeat (Rozin et al., 2006). Thus, activation of the schema leads to expectations about the next note, chord, or progression of the melody in general. However, as Rozin and coresearchers (2006) point out, the listener would soon habituate to the same sequence of notes and become bored. Listening pleasure is maintained, however, when the next sequence of notes is repeated but with a change in loudness or pitch, for example. The next note, although incongruous, is easily assimilated into the prevailing music schema and hence enjoyed. For example, the onset of chills occurs where there is an incongruity or the beginning of something novel like a change in loudness, tempo, or entry of a voice or their combination (Grewe et al., 2007).

Incongruity Resolution and Humor

The concept of incongruity-resolution can be extended for the understanding of humor. Inevitably the punch line of a good joke elicits smiles, laughs, and amused feelings. The schema incongruity model specifies how punchlines are able to evoke humor.

Consider the following joke: "A mechanical engineer, an electrical engineer, and a computer software engineer were riding in a car when it broke down. 'It's probably a valve,' said the mechanical engineer. 'It's probably a spark plug,' said the electrical engineer. 'I know,' said the computer software engineer, 'let's all get out of the car and get back in again'" (Crossen, 1997). The stem of the joke activates a schema that aids the processing and comprehension of information contained therein. The stem constrains the reader to expect an ending such as the following: "'The car's computer system has probably malfunctioned,' said the computer engineer." According to the actual punch line, however, the computer engineer suggests that everyone get out of the car and then get back in. In other words, the computer engineer's actual suggestion is incongruous with what one would expect to be the diagnosis of the car's problem. In a joke, the punch line disrupts cognitive processing of the stem material and produces surprise and arousal (Mandler, 1984). For instance, the onset of the punch line brings an increase in electrodermal activity (Godkewitsch, 1976) and muscle tension (Chapman, 1976). If the punch line is unresolved—that is, "I don't get it"—then the affective value of the incongruity remains puzzling and negative. The incongruity is resolved, however, by assimilating the punch line into an alternative, less obvious schema also residing in the stem. For example, the computer engineer's "computer solution" schema replaces the "car solution" schema. In this way, the punch line of "get out and get back in again" is assimilated into the "computer solution" schema. Thus, the punch line is understood when a person realizes that computer users fix their computers by turning them off and then on again (Deckers & Avery, 1994; Raskin, 1985; Suls, 1983). The resolution of the punch line results in smiles, laughs, and amused feelings. Ruch (1993) has used the word *exhilaration* to describe that increase in arousal that is specifically linked to humor. Exhilaration comes from the Latin *hilarare*, meaning to gladden or to make merry. That is one of the functions of humor: it arouses and gladdens us simultaneously.

Resolution of Suspense

The enjoyment of suspenseful movies also requires resolution as a successful outcome according to a **theory of suspense enjoyment** (Zillmann, 1991). Several developments must occur before a viewer enjoys the resolution of suspense, however. First, there must be the possibility that some calamity or harm is going to happen to the protagonist in the story or movie. There is some likelihood, as Zillmann (1991) states, that the heroine is in danger of being humiliated, threatened, beaten, raped, strangled, stabbed, shot, severely injured, or even killed by her human assailant or a supernatural being. If the probability of these tragic events happening is perceived as too low, then no tension or suspense accumulates. Also, if the probability is perceived as too high, then these bad events are a foregone conclusion and the viewers may begin to experience sadness or some other dysphoric (unhappy) emotion. Second, the anticipated tragic event will not lead to a buildup of suspense if the viewer is not favorably disposed or does not identify with the protagonist in the movie. The viewer has to care what is going to happen to the character in the story. Third, viewing the anticipated demise of the protagonist produces physiological arousal brought on by the sympathetic nervous system, such as an increase in heart rate and muscle tension. The viewer experiences these reactions as unpleasant, a feeling labeled as *empathetic distress* (Zillmann, 1991). Finally, the uncertainty in the tense situation is resolved when there is a turn of events in which the heroine avoids or escapes the dangerous situation or successfully thwarts her assailant. The resolution produces a switch from dysphoria to euphoria as the viewer or reader experiences relief along with any gratification that the protagonist is now safe. Furthermore, according to the theory of suspense enjoyment, the amount of pleasure experienced during the resolution phase is based on the remaining amount of arousal that had accrued earlier.

Section Recap

Arousal is tinged with positive and negative affect. *Optimal level of stimulation theory* presents affective valence as changing with the level of arousal in an inverted-U relationship. As the level of stimulation and subsequent arousal increases, affective valence becomes more positive. But with further increases, affective valence becomes less positive and more negative. Paradoxically, repeated exposure to unpleasant stimuli at weak intensities eventually evokes positive affect according to the concept of *hedonic reversal*. This concept refers to the eventual liking of initially aversive or dangerous stimuli as a result of repeated exposures. *Sensory deprivation* is a way of creating extremely low levels of stimulation. In this condition, participants lie quietly on a mattress in dark soundproof chambers. The inverted-U curve also describes the relationship between stimulus complexity and preference for visual stimuli, dresses, and music. Stimuli that are less or more complex than the optimal level are preferred less. However, repeated exposure decreases perceived stimulus complexity. The result is decreased liking of simple stimuli and moderately complex stimuli and increased liking for complex stimuli. In the case of the *musical grammar processor*, however, people never tire of their favorite melody because the processor responsible for the resolution of musical notes has no memory.

Incongruity-resolution provides the link between arousal and affect in music, humor, and suspense. Musical notes, punch lines, and suspenseful situations are enjoyed when elements from those domains are incorporated into known *schemas* by a process known as *assimilation*. Schemas are representations of knowledge about regularities in the world, such as musical patterns, scripts, or concepts. An incongruous element is understood when it is resolved by fitting (assimilating) it into a prevailing schema. The degree of incongruity determines the valence and intensity of an emotional reaction, according to the *schema-incongruity model*. Positive arousal increases with the degree of incongruity as long as the incongruity is resolvable. Extreme incongruities that are not resolvable result in reactions that are both intense and aversive. The enjoyment of music stems from the listener's ability to assimilate the next note or musical phrase into an activated musical schema. Some musical passages produce a *chill* (goose bumps, shivers), which are physiological reactions that occur when an incongruous or novel event occurs in the music. Jokes are enjoyed when the punch line is assimilated into an alternative schema inspired by the stem of the joke. The enjoyment of suspense in movies takes place when the incongruity in the seemingly dangerous situation produces physiological arousal. According to the *theory of suspense enjoyment*, pleasure, as relief from arousal, occurs when the incongruity is resolved—that is, when the danger has passed and the protagonist is safe.

ACTIVITIES

1. Fill out the *Scale Measuring Energetic Arousal and Tense Arousal* in Table 6.1 at various times during the day, and each time compute your score for energetic arousal and for tense arousal. Did you detect any variation in your score as a function of time of day? Did your scores differ as a function of the type of activity, like getting an exam back, getting ready for a date, or at the end of an exhausting day?

2. Describe the situation in which you experienced heightened arousal. For example, you were auditioning for the school band or were giving a speech in front of a class.
   a. What physiological symptoms of arousal did you experience, such as butterflies in the stomach, dry mouth, pounding heart, and trembling?
   b. Describe your feeling of psychological arousal. Was it an instance of tense arousal or of energetic arousal?
   c. Did arousal affect your behavior? For example, because of the arousal, did you do much better, better, worse, or much worse

than you usually do? Or was there no effect on your behavior?
   d. Locate your performance on the task on the inverted-U arousal-performance curve (Figure 6.3).

3. Does your exam performance depend on the time of day a class meets? Do you think that you could do better on an exam if it was given between noon and 2 P.M. rather than at 8 A.M. or in the evening?

4. Try your hand at joke resolution. Next time you hear a joke, assimilate the punch line into the alternative, less obvious schema that was derived from the joke stem. Proceed by developing an ending from this alternative schema and comparing that with the actual punch line. Does the ending from the alternative schema coincide with the punch line? If so, the joke is resolved.

5. As a check on your hot memory system, do you remember where you were and what you were doing when you heard the news of the September 11th terrorist attack?

CHAPTER
7
Stress, Coping, and Health

The blessings of life are not equal to its ills, though the number of the two may be equal; nor can any pleasure compensate for the least pain.

—*Pliny the Elder, 77 A.D.*

Life is not merely being alive, but being well.

—*Martial, 95 A.D.*

■ Simply put, stress moves people into action. It motivates them to manipulate stressors so as to alter their impact. And it also motivates people to support behavior aimed at diminishing or removing stressors (Baum & Posluszny, 1999). This is the main theme of this chapter, and the following questions can help guide your understanding:

1. When are life events stressful, and when are they not?
2. How do stressors affect people physically, psychologically, and behaviorally?
3. Can the appraisal of life events alter their impact on a person's well-being?
4. How can a person cope with life events and the stress they evoke?
5. Do people differ in the way they appraise and cope with stressors and stress?

Relationship between Life Events and Stress

Have you ever had days like this?

> If one more thing goes wrong today, I'll scream. I overslept this morning because my alarm did not go off. Then I tried to make it to my first class but my car wouldn't start. Consequently, I was late for my psychology exam and did poorly. I received an e-mail message stating "We need to talk," which can only mean the end of my romantic relationship. A friend borrowed a textbook and has not returned it and I need to study from it tonight. Of course this may not matter, since my boss called to say I had to fill in this evening for a sick coworker. In addition, I've had this lingering cold and sore throat that I cannot seem to shake. I feel as if I am in a vicious cycle: the more things go wrong, the more frustrated, tense, irritable, and sick I become, and this in turn makes things go wrong even more. Things have got to get better; they cannot get any worse.

The purpose of this first section is to examine the nature of stress, the characteristics of the life events or stressors that are responsible, and the stressor-stress relationship.

153

Demands, Strain, Coping, and Stress

The previous tale of woe illustrates how life events make demands on an individual's motivation and behavior. Completing projects, preparing for final exams, and considering career goals are examples of positive demands that motivate an individual to achieve them. A broken printer and a car that needs repair are negative events that motivate a person to remedy them. The death of a friend, a "broken heart," or being in a bad traffic accident are severe negative events that require adjustment necessary for recovery. Background stimulation from noise, light, and overcrowding plus invisible germs motivate action that taxes the body's adaptation energy. Action to meet the demands of life requires the appropriate resources. Does a person have enough time, tangible resources, adaptation energy, and motivation? **Strain** occurs when resources are not adequate for a person to achieve positive events or to avoid or escape negative events. For instance, a student runs out of time before assignments are due and a low grade results. Fixing the printer or car strains a person's budget and means giving up buying other things. When family, friends, or counselors are not available for listening and advice, the student may be unable to dispel grief or make career decisions. Strain also results, for example, when inadequate resources mean losing a romantic relationship, failing to recover from an accident, or being unable to fight off germs. **Coping** refers to behavior that is motivated to meet life's demands and their consequences. **Stress** results when life demands strain-coping resources either because the demand is too great or the resources are inadequate (Lazarus & Folkman, 1984). Stress endangers a person's well-being and shows up as negative feelings, physiological arousal, psychophysiological disorders, illness, or maladaptive behaviors. For example, a person can feel depressed, have trouble sleeping, develop headaches, catch a cold, and drink too much alcohol trying to alleviate negative feelings and stress.

Characteristics of Stress

Do you eat a lot of your favorite ice cream when you feel under pressure? Have you been troubled by the inability to sleep or to slow down? Have you felt anxious or depressed lately? Do you have a cold or flu? Are you trying to fight off various low-grade infections? A "yes" to any of these questions may indicate stress, which manifests in three domains: physical or psychological symptoms and maladaptive behaviors (see Table 7.1).

Physical Symptoms of Stress.   Physical symptoms of stress involve a cold, influenza (flu), headache, sleep disturbance, and being unable to slow down (see Table 7.1). These symptoms are measured by inventories, such as the *Cohen-Hoberman Inventory of Physical Symptoms* (Cohen & Hoberman, 1983) and the *Hopkins Symptom Checklist* (Derogatis et al., 1974). In addition to these self-reports, studies are conducted of the lives of patients with actual physical ailments, such as tuberculosis, heart problems, or skin diseases (Mittleman et al., 1995; Rahe et al., 1964). Visits to the campus health center or infirmary also serve as indicators of physical symptoms (Crandall et al., 1992), as do days absent from school or work.

Psychological Symptoms of Stress.   Psychological symptoms of stress consist of negative feelings like anxiety, depression, and hopelessness (see Table 7.1). These and other psychological symptoms are measured by self-report scales, such as the *Positive and Negative Affect Scale*, which measure the intensity of an individual's positive and negative

TABLE 7.1 Symptoms Indicating Stress

Physical Symptoms	Psychological Symptoms	Maladaptive Behaviors
Allergies	Anxiety	Drinking more alcohol
Colds	Boredom	Drinking more coffee, cola
Diarrhea	Depression	Taking drugs (cocaine, heroin, marijuana)
Flu	Feeling helpless	
Headaches	Feeling hopeless	Eating poorly (poor diet, too many sweets)
Inability to slow down, relax	Forgetfulness	Resting badly (not enough rest, sleeping more than usual)
Indigestion	Irritableness	
Infections (low grade)	Low self-confidence	Filling time passively (too much TV watching, sitting and staring)
Nausea, vomiting	Low self-esteem	
Neck/shoulder aches	Negative emotions (anger, disgust, fear, sadness)	
Psychophysiological disorders	Negative mood	
Stomach aches		
Sweating (nervous)		
Sleep disturbance		

mood (Watson et al., 1988). Positive mood reflects the degree to which a person feels alert and enthusiastic about life, while negative mood indicates feelings of subjective distress. The *General Health Questionnaire* measures depression, anxiety, insomnia, social functioning, and anhedonia, which is a lack of pleasure from things usually enjoyable (Goldberg et al., 1976). The *Perceived Stress Questionnaire* presented in Table 7.2 assesses the amount of stress a person experiences in general (Fliege et al., 2005). The questionnaire covers three components of psychological stress. One component refers to worries like anxiety about the future and feelings of desperation and frustration. A second refers to tension like uneasiness, exhaustion, and a lack of relaxation. A final component refers to a lack of joy as shown by the absence of energetic arousal and low feelings of security. In testing this questionnaire, Fliege and coresearchers (2005) found, for example, that hospital patients with psychosomatic disorders, such as affective, eating, and personality disorders, experienced the most stress, followed by patients who suffered from tinnitus (hearing a ringing or buzzing). Medical students experienced the next most stress while healthy adults experienced the least stress. Finally, as the health of patients improved, their level of worries and tension decreased.

Behavioral Symptoms of Stress.   Drinking to forget, seeing a funny movie to alleviate the blues, eating "comfort foods," or talking to a sympathetic friend are behavioral indicators of stress and coping (see Table 7.1). In some instances, however, these behaviors can themselves be stressful. For instance, coffee drinkers and cigarette smokers increase their consumption when their job stress increases (Conway et al., 1981). Witnesses of terrorist attacks have reported an increase in their smoking, alcohol consumption, and marijuana use (Vlahov et al., 2002). Certain individuals, when faced with stress, tend to overeat

TABLE 7.2   **Perceived Stress Questionnaire**

In general, rate the extent the following 15 statements apply to you using this 4-point scale:

1 = almost never,   2 = sometimes,   3 = often,   4 = usually

The extent of your worries
You are afraid for the future.
You have many worries.
Your problems seem to be piling up.
You fear you may not manage to attain your goals.
You feel frustrated.

The extent you feel tension
You feel tense.
You feel rested. (R)
You feel mentally exhausted.
You have trouble relaxing.
You feel calm. (R)

The extent you feel joy
You feel you're doing things you really like. (R)
You enjoy yourself. (R)
You are lighthearted. (R)
You are full of energy. (R)
You feel safe and protected. (R)

Note: To score, first reverse the numbers of the items designated with an (R) so that 1 = 4, 2 = 3, 3 = 2, and 4 = 1. Sum the numbers to obtain your level of stress. Higher scores mean more stress.

Source: Adapted from "The Perceived Stress Questionnaire (PSQ) Reconsidered: Validation and Reference Values from Different Clinical and Healthy Adult Samples" by H. Fliege et al., 2005, *Psychosomatic Medicine,* *67,* table 1, p. 81. Copyright 2005 by Lippincott Williams & Wilkins. Reprinted by permission.

(Greeno & Wing, 1994). These coping behaviors are maladaptive and add to stress that is already there. For example, caffeine produces insomnia, cigarettes are linked to cancer, drugs produce addiction, and overeating leads to obesity.

Characteristics of Stressors

Many demands in life motivate an individual to make adjustments. Passing university courses, fixing your car, and working are dealt with effectively by most people. Demands that are not dealt with effectively, however, become **stressors;** that is, they produce stress. In the words of Hans Selye (1976), one of the originators of the stress concept, "A *stressor* is naturally 'that which produces stress'" (p. 78). If you lost sleep worrying about getting the money to fix your car, then the broken car is a stressor. If you lost no sleep, then the broken car was not a stressor but merely a demand to be coped with. This definition is circular, since the demand is defined as a stressor only after knowing that stress resulted. In spite of this circularity, however, certain characteristics are likely to make events stressful: when they have a negative valence, when too many have accumulated, when they are of a large magnitude, and when they are unpredictable or uncontrollable (Lazarus & Cohen, 1977; Perkins, 1982).

Negative Life Events as Stressors.   Both positive and negative life events motivate coping actions. Repairing a printer, tolerating a neighbor's noisy stereo, or suffering disappointment are negative events a person would like to escape. Starting a romance, accepting new responsibilities at work, or planning a surprise birthday party are positive events that motivate a person to act. Early stress researchers often disregarded whether an event was positive or negative; both were considered stressful (Holmes & Rahe, 1967; Selye, 1976). Physiological arousal that resulted from positive events was called **eustress** (Selye, 1976), especially if the level of arousal was just right—not too low or not too high. Eustress is a concept similar to the ideal level of arousal described in Zuckerman's (1969) optimal level of stimulation theory (see Chapter 6). **Distress,** in contrast, is the opposite of eustress and occurs when arousal is too low or too high. Moreover, distress has additional symptoms consisting of negative feelings, physical ailments, diseases, and maladaptive behavior. Thus, stress usually means distress. In comparing positive and negative life events, Zautra and Reich (1983) found what they refer to as the **same domain effect.** Negative events produce distress and reduce the quality of life. Positive events, however, increase positive feelings and increase the quality of life. For instance, Cohen and Hoberman (1983) discovered that positive events reduced students' psychological and physical symptoms resulting from a number of negative events. Blair and associates (1981) showed that negative events in the lives of counselors and social workers increased job burnout, which is a form of occupational stress. Positive life events, in contrast, did not increase job burnout but instead reduced the likelihood of its occurrence. Finally, Myers and associates (1974) found that an increase in undesirable life events is associated with a worsening of physical and psychological symptoms. A decrease in negative events or an increase in positive events, however, is linked with a decrease in symptoms.

Predictability and Controllability of Life Events.   Would you like to know when an important exam is coming up, when a violent thunderstorm covers your campus, or when people will argue in your presence? Predictability, or lack thereof, is another life event characteristic that determines the severity of stress. Individuals prefer predictable over unpredictable stressors. Imagine taking part in the following experiment on how people deal with the predictability of an aversive event (Badia et al., 1974). Your task is to avoid an electric shock to the forearm by pressing a button located on your right. When you do so the shock is postponed for 15 seconds; otherwise, it is delivered once every three seconds. This avoidance task can be carried out under one of two conditions: In the unsignaled avoidance condition you will not know when the shock will be delivered. In the signaled avoidance condition, a light comes on signaling the delivery of shock. You can trigger this signal by pressing a button on the left. Would you prefer to know when the shock is coming? Most participants in this experiment clearly favored signaled avoidance and pressed the left button. In a second experiment, participants could only turn off (escape) but not avoid the shock. Again a participant could choose to be in an unsignaled escape or signaled escape condition. By pressing the right-hand button, a participant could turn off (escape) the shock. But by also pressing the left button, a light would come on signaling the delivery of shock. In this experiment, although nothing could be done to avoid shock, escape was possible. The results of this experiment also showed that participants preferred signaled shock over unsignaled shock (Badia et al., 1974). Most of the work on the predictability of stressful events like electric shock comes from animal research, which shows that rats, like humans, prefer knowing when they will be shocked even if they cannot do anything about it (Badia et al., 1979; Harsh & Badia, 1975).

Two hypotheses have been proposed to account for the preference of signaled shock over unsignaled shock. The **preparatory response hypothesis** states that a signal preceding a biologically relevant event allows the organism to prepare for that event (Perkins, 1955). By knowing when the shock is coming, an animal or person can prepare and thus reduce the aversive event. In the college student experiment, knowing when the shock would be delivered helps a person avoid it. If the shock cannot be avoided, then knowing when it will be delivered allows a person to prepare, which may decrease its aversiveness and allow for more rapid escape. For instance, by knowing when an exam or storm is coming a person can prepare for it and thus reduce any stress that may result. As an alternative, the **safety hypothesis** maintains that it is crucial to distinguish safe intervals when shock is not being delivered from unsafe intervals when it is (Seligman, 1971). Thus, rats and humans choose signaled shock because it allows for discriminating safe periods from unsafe ones. In the college student experiment, participants could relax during the safe period and only worry about shock when the signal light came on. Thus, safe periods are those days when exams are not scheduled, when a tornado warning has not sounded, or when people indicate that they are not about to fight. A person can relax during these safe times. Unsafe periods consist of those intervals signaling an exam, a tornado, or a forthcoming argument. These intervals are times of stress and anxiety. In daily life perhaps both hypotheses can explain human behavior. If we know when a negative life event is coming, then perhaps we can do something about it. Perhaps we can avoid it or reduce the negative impact it will have. And according to the safety hypothesis, we can relax during those times when no negative life events are signaled.

Stressor-Stress Relationship

In addition to magnitude, the effects of a life event also depend on its position in the accumulation of stressors. Was the event among the first or the last? Even a small stressor at the end of a line of stressors can act like "the straw that broke the camel's back." This occurs because the effects of stressors are cumulative (Singer & Davidson, 1986). If they keep coming, they eventually overtake the individual's resources to cope. However, the cumulative effects of life events at the level of daily hassles may not be stressful until some threshold has been exceeded (Lloyd et al., 1980; Perkins, 1982). For example, for students this threshold may occur toward the end of the semester when projects and papers are due, final exams are to be studied for, and plans to vacate residence halls or apartments are made. Although the stress curve keeps rising, it eventually levels off, indicating that after a certain point additional stressors will not have much impact (Perkins, 1982).

Determining the Impact of Stressors.   Life's demands require adjustments. At what magnitude, however, do demands become so great that the required adjustments exceed a person's coping resources? A serious car accident versus a fender bender, flunking out of university versus flunking an exam, or the end of a long versus a brief romantic relationship illustrate demands that involve different levels of adjustment. One assumption is that greater demands require more adjustment and potentially more stress. In order to determine the shape of the stressor-stress relationship, it is necessary to quantify the impact of life demands and any subsequent stress. To this end, psychologists have employed both objective and subjective measures of stressor magnitude. With both measures, individuals indicate if the event happened to them. In the case of *objective measures*, the degree of adjustment already has an assigned value. For *subjective measures*, however, individuals assign their own value to the degree of adjustment.

An example of an objective measure comes from early stress research performed by Holmes and Rahe (1967) when they developed their concept of the **life change unit.** Each unit equals a degree of adjustment considered necessary to cope with a life change event (Holmes & Masuda, 1974). Adjusting to different life events, however, requires different numbers of life change units. Holmes and Rahe (1967) had a large sample of participants rate various life events for the number of life change units they considered necessary for adjustment. These ratings were summarized into the *Social Readjustment Rating Scale*, which consists of 43 items ranging from death of a spouse (100 adjustment units) to minor violations of the law (43 adjustment units). (These point values were obtained by dividing the original ratings points by 10.) Since publication of this scale, several other life event rating scales have been developed (Miller, 1993). The *Social Readjustment Scale* contains many items pertinent to the general population, such as a mortgage, trouble with in-laws, change in line of work, being fired, or retirement. However, most of these items have little relevance to the life of college students. Life event items pertinent to university students can be found in the *Undergraduate Stress Questionnaire* (Crandall et al., 1992). It contains a number of items that have been rated for the severity of their stressfulness. Some example items, in order of decreasing stressfulness, are "had a lot of tests, had a class presentation, registration for classes, and got to class late."

> ➤ A complete version of the *Undergraduate Stress Questionnaire* without the severity scores is available at http://www.utulsa.edu/cpsc/undergraduate_questionnaire.htm

Objective ratings scales, however, imply that the same life event is equally severe or stressful for every person. Yet, one life event may require a great deal of adjustment on the part of one individual and little adjustment for another. Being interrupted from studying might be very annoying for one student but be judged a welcome relief by another. Other stress scales take into account the possibility that the same stressor does not impact everyone the same. For instance, the *College Students Life Events Scale* in Table 7.3 requires a student to assign a numerical value to both the degree and duration of tension created by a particular demand. The combination of tension and duration indicates the subjective impact a demand has on an individual. The accumulation of a greater score on this scale implies more life demands and thus a greater likelihood of stress. Finally, most stress questionnaires like the one in Table 7.3 make hardly any reference to positive events. Most stressors have a negative valence, which supports the idea described earlier that stressors are composed mainly of negative, not positive, events.

Stressor Magnitude and Stress. A cataclysmic stressor or traumatic event that threatens a person or others with death or serious injury can result in an **acute stress disorder** and later a **posttraumatic stress disorder (PTSD).** With this disorder, a person reacts with intense fear and helplessness to a traumatic event and may continue to experience intrusive and distressing recollections, thoughts, dreams, and physiological reactivity after the event.

TABLE 7.3   College Students Life Events Scale

Instructions:

Tension: Indicate how much tension you felt while the most recent occurrence of the event was going on. By feelings of tension we mean feeling worried, anxious, irritable, or depressed. Such feelings may be accompanied by difficulty in sleeping or concentrating on other things. Use the following scale:

1	2	3	4	5	6	7
None	Slight	Some	Moderate	Significant	Severe	Almost Unendurable

Duration: If there was tension associated with the event, think about how long the tension associated with the event lasted (or has lasted if it is still going on). Use the following scale:

1	2	3	4	5	6	7
Less than 1 day	More than 1 day, but less than 1 week	More than 1 week, but less than 1 month	About 1 month	About 6 weeks	About 2 months	More than 2 months

Tension	Duration	
————	————	**1.** Increase in normal academic course load (e.g., more academic work than previously, much harder work, etc.)
		2. Increased conflict in balancing time for academic-social activities
————	————	**3.** Struggled with decision about major or career goal
————	————	**4.** Inability to get desired courses or program
		5. Received much poorer grade than expected on a test or in a course
		6. Repeated arguments, hassles with cohabitants (e.g., racial, sexual, religious, personal idiosyncracies, financial, etc.)
————	————	**7.** Living arrangements consistently too noisy (to study, to sleep)
————	————	**8.** Moved to new quarters on or off campus
		9. Realized that finances are increasingly inadequate to meet living expenses
		10. Significant increase in level of debt (e.g., took out large loan, charged more than can easily pay, gambling debts, etc.)
————	————	**11.** Serious attempt to stop, decrease, or moderate use of drugs, alcohol, or smoking
————	————	**12.** Significant increase in use of alcohol, resulting in problems in school, work, or other areas of life
		13. Increased attendance or participation in religious services or practices
		14. Decreased attendance or participation in religious services or practices
————	————	**15.** Increased commitment or participation in political or social activism
————	————	**16.** Began sexual unfaithfulness to a partner to whom you are not married
		17. Engaged in initial sexual intercourse
		18. Engaged in sex act without use of birth control measures (i.e., feared pregnancy)
————	————	**19.** Became pregnant out of wedlock or partner became pregnant out of wedlock

TABLE 7.3 *(Continued)*

_____ _____ **20.** Experienced rejection of a more than casual sexual overture
_____ _____ **21.** Unable to find a satisfactory sex partner
_____ _____ **22.** Divorce or separation of parents
23. Death of member of immediate family (e.g., parent, sibling, grandparent, etc.)
24. Parental remarriage
_____ _____ **25.** Decided for the first time not to go home for major holiday
_____ _____ **26.** Increased conflict with parent (e.g., sex, drug use, dress, religious practices, lifestyle, sleeping out of home, etc.)
27. Increased peer pressure to experiment with sex, drugs, etc.
28. Lost a friend due to personal conflict
_____ _____ **29.** Lost a good friend or friends because you or they moved, or transferred, etc.
30. Realized necessity to make new friends
31. Got married
_____ _____ **32.** Entered new, serious relationship with boyfriend or girlfriend (e.g., engaged, living together, etc.)
_____ _____ **33.** Boyfriend or girlfriend broke up your relationship
34. You broke up with boyfriend or girlfriend
35. Increased conflict with boyfriend or girlfriend (e.g., over sex, drugs, alcohol, independence, recreation, division of responsibilities, etc.)
_____ _____ **36.** Deeply attracted to someone who showed no interest in you
37. Important date was disappointing
38. Your friend went out with someone you were interested in
_____ _____ **39.** Struggled with decision to break up with boyfriend or girlfriend
_____ _____ **40.** Increased job responsibilities
_____ _____ **41.** Increased hassles on the job with boss or supervisor
42. Quit job
43. Realized job responsibilities interfered with academic work
_____ _____ **44.** Victim of assault
_____ _____ **45.** Busted for drug related activity
46. Victim of robbery or burglary
47. Involved in auto accident as driver, without injury
_____ _____ **48.** Involved in auto accident as passenger, without injury
_____ _____ **49.** Illness or injury kept you out of school for one week or more
50. Car broke down
51. Activity run by your group was a flop (e.g., play, team lost game, no one came to your party, etc.)
_____ _____ **52.** Realized responsibilities in extracurricular activities interfered with school work
_____ _____ **53.** Unable to find adequate recreational or athletic outlets

Source: Adapted from "College Students Life Events Scale" by Murray Levine, University at Buffalo, and David Perkins, Ball State University. Printed with their permission.

161

The person also tries to avoid stimuli associated with the trauma, experiences persistent arousal symptoms (e.g., sleep difficulty), and suffers social impairment. In the case of acute stress disorder, the symptoms must occur and subside within four weeks of the traumatic stressor. If the symptoms continue, the diagnosis changes to PTSD (American Psychiatric Association, 2000).

Both acute and posttraumatic stress disorders resulted from the terrorist attacks perpetrated against the United States on September 11, 2001. Two airplanes crashed into the World Trade Center in New York City, a third airplane crashed into the Pentagon, and a fourth crashed in a Pennsylvania field. The combined terrorist attacks killed an estimated 3,000 people and destroyed billions of dollars worth of property. In addition, the attacks and media replays produced psychological havoc in the form of fear, anxiety, a sense of vulnerability, and uncertainty about the future (Susser, Herman, & Aaron, 2002). In one nationwide random telephone survey three to five days after the attack, respondents were asked the extent they felt the following stress reactions: (1) feeling very upset by reminders of the events, (2) disturbing memories, (3) difficulty concentrating, (4) trouble falling or staying asleep, and (5) feeling irritable or having angry outbursts (Schuster et al., 2001). The survey showed that 44% of the adults reported at least one of the stress symptoms, and 35% of their 5- to 18-year-old children did also. Even individuals thousands of miles from the attack site experienced stress symptoms, which may have resulted from the images being shown repeatedly on televison (Schuster et al., 2001). Five to eight weeks after the attack, a random telephone survey of New York City adults living within eight miles of the World Trade Center showed that overall, 7.5% of the respondents experienced PTSD. Figure 7.1 shows that

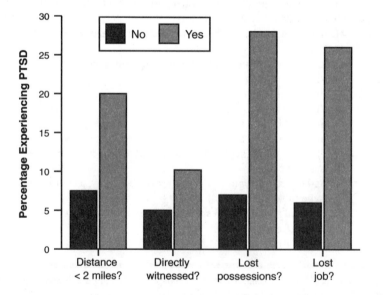

FIGURE 7.1   PTSD from Terrorist Attacks. The incidence of PTSD from the September 11th terrorist attack increased with closeness to the site, directly witnessing the attack, and losing possessions or employment as a consequence.

Source: Adapted from "Psychological Sequelae of the September 11 Terrorist Attacks in New York City" by S. Galea et al., 2002, *New England Journal of Medicine, 346*, table 1, p. 984.

the likelihood of suffering PTSD increased with being close (< 2 miles) to the attack site, directly witnessing the attack, and losing one's possessions or job (Galea et al., 2002).

Cumulative Effects of Stressors. Do demands pile up at the end of the semester? Does something need repair the same time you are low on money? Is there so much to do and too little time to do it? In order to determine the cumulative effects of stressors, Holmes and Masuda (1974) tabulated life changes for a large group of physicians and recorded the occurrence of illness or health changes that occurred within a two-year period following a cluster of such changes. Their results, in Figure 7.2, show that as life change units increase, health changes increase also. In a prospective study, life change scores of resident physicians covering the previous 18 months were correlated with illnesses occurring in the next 9 months. The relationship was positive: the percentage of individuals getting ill was greater for those with a larger number of life change units (Holmes & Masuda, 1974). Other research shows that as the number of life change units increases over a period of years, the likelihood of tuberculosis, heart disease, and skin diseases also increases (Rahe et al., 1964). In reviewing this research, Holmes and Masuda (1974) conclude that life change events require adaptive effort by the individual, or what Selye (1976) calls *adaptation energy*. A decline in adaptation energy lowers the body's resistance and thereby increases the likelihood of disease.

In addition to affecting illness, life changes can also depress behavior such as academic performance and GPA. Lloyd and colleagues (1980) assessed life changes among college students by having them indicate what changes had occurred in their lives. For instance, students were asked if they had experienced changes in sleeping, eating, recreation and family get-togethers, living conditions, or moving; or injury, illness, or the death of a friend or family member. Students were also asked to subjectively weigh each life change in regard to the amount of adjustment each required. Two measures were of interest: the total number of events that occurred in the previous year and the subjective weighted event total, which involved the

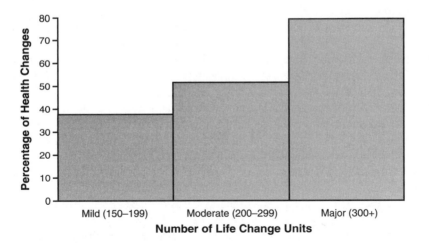

FIGURE 7.2 Accumulated Stress and Health. As the number of life change units increases, the percentage of health changes also increases.

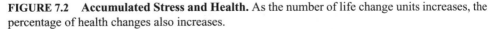

Source: Adapted from "Life Change and Illness Susceptibility" by T. H. Holmes and M. Masuda, 1974, in B. S. Dohrenwend and B. P. Dohrenwend, Eds., *Stressful Life Events*, table 1, p. 61, New York: John Wiley.

subjective impact of a change. The life change measures were associated with a declining GPA: as life change scores went up, GPA went down. This finding was especially true for the subjective weighted event total. In addition, life changes in recreation, in work responsibilities, and in changing to a new line of work had a greater impact on students with lower GPAs.

The cumulative effects of traumatic stressors can be very detrimental for the mental health of people. One group of individuals to whom this has happened are soldiers and Marines, who have experienced ground combat or dangerous security duty in places of war. In one study, Hoge and coresearchers (2004) gave an anonymous survey to returning soldiers and Marines, who had experienced combat or other dangerous duty in either Afghanistan or Iraq. The survey included questions that covered depression, generalized anxiety, and PTSD. A checklist from the Department of Veteran Affairs was used to diagnose PTSD. The checklist contained 17 items that were rated on a scale *1 = not at all* to *5 = extremely.* For example, how much in the past month have you been bothered by "Repeated, disturbing memories, thoughts or images of a stressful military experience?" Other questions addressed stressful experiences that were of a noncombat origin (National Center for Posttraumatic Stress Disorder, 2008). In order to be diagnosed with PTSD, the individual had to score above the midpoint on the checklist. The survey examined a multitude of traumatic stressors. These included being in firefights, which is an exchange of gunfire between combatants and can include being ambushed; shot at by artillery, rockets, or mortar fire; and shooting the enemy in return. Stressors also included killing enemy combatants, seeing and handling dead bodies, knowing someone who was killed or seriously injured. A final set of stressors included being wounded, injured, or having a close call with death, saving someone's life, but also being unable to save the lives of others (Hoge et al., 2004).

The general results of the survey showed that mental health problems increased as a result of being deployed in Afghanistan and Iraq. Furthermore, there was a direct relationship between the incidence of PTSD and the number of firefights. As Figure 7.3 indicates, the greater the number of firefights that individuals had experienced, the greater their likelihood of being diagnosed with PTSD. Even without participating in a firefight, 4.5% of the Marines and soldiers experienced PTSD as a result of their deployment in either Afghanistan or Iraq.

Racism as a Stressor.   Stressors also accumulate by virtue of an individual's minority group membership. Based on physical characteristics, people may be members of minorities, such as being an African American in the United States. As a member of a minority group, individuals often experience the stresses of discrimination and racism. Utsey and Ponterotto (1996) developed the *Index of Race-Related Stress*, which measures the impact of four categories of racism (see Table 7.4). Cultural racism results from the practices of one group being imposed on another, while institutional racism stems from the policies ingrained in an organization. Individual racism is experienced personally, while collective racism occurs when an entire organization discriminates against an individual (Utsey & Ponterotto, 1996). The stressful nature of racism, as measured by the index in Table 7.4, was demonstrated in two ways. First, cultural and individual racism scores on the *Index of Race-Related Stress* correlated positively with scores obtained with the *Perceived Stress Scale* (Cohen & Hoberman, 1983). In other words, the more upset individuals were as a result of cultural and personal racism, the more stress they experienced. Second, African Americans scored significantly higher on all four racism categories measured by the index than did a group of nonblacks (whites and Asian Americans), which indicates African Americans experience more racism than do other groups.

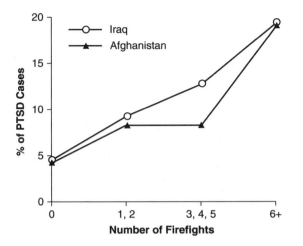

FIGURE 7.3 Cumulative Effects of Traumatic Stressors. The likelihood of a soldier or Marine developing PTSD increased as their participation in firefights increased. Firefights refer to an exchange in gunfire, artillery, rockets, or mortar fire between combatants.

Source: Adapted from "Combat Duty in Iraq and Afghanistan, Mental Health Problems, and Barriers to Care" by C. W. Hoge et al., 2004, *The New England Journal of Medicine, 351*, p. 17.

TABLE 7.4 Four Illustrations of Racism from the *Index of Race-Related Stress*

If the following events happened to you, to what extent were you upset by them (Not bother me, Slightly upset, Upset, Extremely upset)?

Cultural Racism
"You notice that crimes committed by White people tend to be romanticized, whereas the same crime committed by a Black person is portrayed as savagery, and the Black person who committed it, as an animal."

Institutional Racism
"You have discovered that the White/non-Black person employed in the same capacity as you with equal or less qualifications is paid a higher salary."

Individual Racism
"While shopping at a store or when attempting to make a purchase, you were ignored as if you were not a serious customer or didn't have any money."

Collective Racism
"You were the victim of a crime and the police treated you as if you should just accept it as part of being Black."

Source: Adapted from "Development and Validation of the Index of Race-Related Stress (IRRS)" by S. O. Utsey and J. G. Ponterotto, 1996, *Journal of Counseling Psychology, 43,* table 1, pp. 494–495.

Experiencing racism is associated with psychiatric symptoms. Landrine and Klonoff (1996) developed the *Schedule of Racist Events* to assess the effects of racist discrimination in the lives of African Americans. A sample from this schedule is "How many times have you been treated unfairly by *strangers* because you are Black?" (Never, to Almost all of the time) (p. 162). Evidence for the stressful effects of racism came from examining the relationship between the schedule scores and stress-related psychiatric symptoms obtained from the *Hopkins Symptoms Checklist* (Derogatis et al., 1974). Analyses showed that the schedule scores were positively correlated with symptoms like obsessive-compulsive disorders, depression, anxiety, and physical symptoms. In addition, people who were more stressed from racist events, as measured by the schedule, were also more likely to use smoking as a stress reducer.

Finally, there are also ethnic differences in hypertension. For instance, African Americans have a higher incidence of hypertension (high blood pressure) than white Americans. Racism is thought to be one factor responsible for this (Barnes et al., 1997). However, as a note of caution, it is not possible to say that perceived racism is a cause of stress, although the two variables are associated together. Perhaps laboratory research will allow psychologists to determine whether one causes the other (for example, see Vrana & Rollock, 1998).

Section Recap

At times a person is motivated to do too many things at once because of the many demands made on an individual. This can result in *strain*, which means that a person's resources are inadequate to meet those demands. *Stress* is the reaction to strain. It is detrimental to a person's well-being and is manifested by negative feelings, excessive physiological arousal, psychophysiological disorders, illness, and maladaptive behavior. *Coping* behaviors are motivated by the necessity of managing life's demands and the resulting stress. *Stressors* consist mainly of negative life events that produce stress. Positive life events produce a type of arousal known as *eustress*, especially if the level of arousal is optimal. Stress usually means *distress* and is the opposite of eustress. According to the *same domain effect*, negative events produce distress, while positive events produce positive feelings and increase the quality of life and eustress. Stressors vary in magnitude.

Both animals and humans prefer to know when a stressor, such as shock, is coming. According to the *preparatory response hypothesis*, knowing when a shock is coming allows the organism to prepare for it. According to the *safety hypothesis*, it is important to distinguish shock from shock-free intervals, since a shock-free interval allows the person to relax and feel safe. In general, as the magnitude of the stressor increases and as stressors accumulate, stress increases. Scales have been developed to measure the impact of various stressors and the amount of adjustment they require. Some scales measure stress in terms of *life change units*, which refer to the amount of adjustment a stressor requires. Extremely traumatic events, such as the terrorist attacks of September 11, 2001, result in an *acute stress disorder*, which if it persists more than four weeks is diagnosed as a *posttraumatic stress disorder (PTSD)*. These disorders are characterized by distressing dreams, flashbacks, psychological distress, and behaviors reminiscent of the original event. The effects of extreme stressors can accumulate as observed in the increased incidence of PTSD among soldiers and Marines who participated in more and more firefights. Finally, racism as experienced by African Americans and other minority groups is associated with stress and higher levels of psychiatric symptoms.

Bodily Effects of Stress

BODY: What a fine mess you've gotten me into. I'm stuck here in bed with a fever and achy joints. Why didn't you defend me?

IMMUNE SYSTEM: I did the best I could. Can I help it that you expose yourself simultaneously to the viruses of many individuals? A drafty classroom on a winter's day is really not the place for you to be when I am so weak. My defenders did the best they could, fighting the viruses when they invaded. But they were overwhelmed by the onslaught. Besides, you have only yourself to blame.

BODY: Now it's my fault, is it? What did I do wrong?

IMMUNE SYSTEM: Yes it's your fault. You are motivated in too many directions at once. You spend too many hours attending classes, studying, working, recreating while at the same time not getting enough sleep and not eating properly. As a result, I suffer. If you were a bit less active, I would be stronger and thus better able to fight off an attacking virus. Now you will just have to kill them off with heat by raising your temperature. If you decrease your activity level a bit, I will become stronger. However, do not become totally inactive because that will also decrease my strength below an optimal level.

This imaginary conversation shows that some stress is good for the immune system, while too little or too much is bad. The purpose of this section is to describe how stressors affect the physiological system, the immune system, and ultimately a person's well-being.

Physiological Effects of Stressors

General Adaptation Syndrome. One of the earliest and major investigators of the physiological consequences of stressors was Hans Selye (1976, 1993). As a medical student in 1936, he discovered how a variety of different stressors produced similar physiological stress reactions. Regardless of whether the stressors included cold, heat, trauma, hemorrhage, or nervous irritation, the body's physiological reaction was the same. He coined the term **general adaptation syndrome (GAS)** to refer to the observation that stress involved the whole body as it went through three stages: alarm reaction, stage of resistance, and stage of exhaustion. The *alarm reaction* is the body's first and generalized response to a stressor. During this phase sympathetic nervous system arousal increases, and stress hormones are released, such as epinephrine, norepinephrine, and glucocorticoid. These hormones can enlarge the adrenal glands, shrink the thymus gland, and produce stomach ulcers. In addition, there is a tendency to suppress the body's immune system, thus making the body more susceptible to disease. The initial decrease in resistance to stressors is followed by the *stage of resistance*, during which the body is successfully controlling the stress. Stress hormone production is no longer necessary and drops back to normal. The body's response to fighting stress also goes from being generalized to being localized to where the stressor impacts the body. At this stage the body is more resistant to the original stressor while at the same time being more vulnerable to new stressors. During this time, a person is using *adaptation energy* in defending against a stressor and adjusting to its effect. In the final stage, the *stage of exhaustion,* a person runs out of adaptation energy, and the ability to combat stress becomes completely exhausted, resulting in death. During this stage, the level of stress hormones rises in the bloodstream, and they become sources of stress themselves (Selye, 1976).

Psychological Stressors and Physiological Responses.   Physiological stressors are capable of producing physiological responses. Strenuous exercise (e.g., distance running or bicycling) increases the release of stress hormones (Davies & Few, 1973; Farrell et al., 1983; Luger et al., 1988). However, psychological stressors like public speaking, being evaluated in a job interview, or doing mental arithmetic also release stress hormones. Meyerhoff and associates (1988) investigated the effects a voluntary promotion interview had on soldiers when conducted by superior officers. Heart rate and stress hormone levels were measured before, during, and after the interview. All these indicators of stress increased from before to during the oral interview and then decreased afterward. These results confirm one of Selye's (1976) main points: regardless of the nature of the stressor, the stress reaction is the same.

Stressors and Psychophysiological Disorders

Certain medical diseases are caused or made worse by stressors. According to the *Diagnostic and Statistical Manual of Mental Disorders* (DSM-IV), general medical conditions combined with psychosocial and environmental problems lead to diagnoses termed "psychological factors affecting medical condition" (APA, 2000). Stressors adversely affect medical conditions by intensifying, delaying recovery, interfering with treatment, or adding additional health risks. **Psychophysiological** or **psychosomatic disorders** is another name given to these medical conditions, including such classic examples as asthma, headaches, heart disease, hypertension, and ulcers.

The news "broke my heart." This statement implies that a single psychological stressor is capable of producing a strong psychophysiological reaction characterized by heart attack symptoms. Evidence for this claim comes from an analysis of 19 (18 were women) healthy patients with a median age of 63 years, who reported to a hospital with symptoms of chest pain, heart failure, hypotension (extremely low blood pressure), or difficult and labored breathing (Wittstein et al., 2005). The patients had reacted to the death of a loved one (nine cases), surprise party or reunion (two cases), a car accident, fear of a procedure, argument, court appearance, fear of choking, and tragic news. These case studies illustrate how a psychological stimulus can cause severe psychophysiological distress.

Stressors that bring on bouts of anger have also been linked to the onset of heart attacks. In one study conducted by Mittleman and colleagues (1995), coronary patients were interviewed an average of four days after their heart attacks. They were asked to rate the intensity of any anger episodes they may have experienced during the 26 hours preceding their attacks on a scale using the following anger descriptors: calm, busy, mild, moderate, very, furious, or enraged. The 26-hour interval allowed the researchers to compare the incidence and intensity of any anger episodes occurring two hours before the onset of a heart attack with the same two hours on the day previous to the attack. A comparison of the two intervals showed that a heart attack was twice as likely to follow within two hours of a very angry, furious, or enraged episode. Family members, work conflicts, and legal problems were the most frequently reported causes of anger.

Stressors and the Immune System

When you catch a cold or flu, does it happen at a time when there are many demands in your life? Are you more likely to be ill at the end of the semester than at the beginning? If so, this may not be your imagination. A relatively new field known as **psychoneuroimmunology** concerns the relationship between psychological stressors, the immune system, and disease. Scientists working in this field examine how stressors and stress are detrimental to the immune system and whether or not this increases an individual's susceptibility to diseases such as colds and flus (Cohen & Herbert, 1996; Kiecolt-Glaser et al., 2002; Kiecolt-Glaser & Glaser, 1995).

The body's **immune system** is the line of defense against invading microorganisms, such as bacteria and viruses, that are responsible for various diseases. The body defends itself against these infectious invaders in various ways. One line of defense consists of a particular type of white blood cells, known as *phagocytes*, that roam the bloodstream ingesting any and all invading microorganisms. Another type of white blood cells are *natural killer cells*. They have the job of detecting and killing damaged or altered cells like infected or cancerous ones. Yet another line of defense involves recognizing and attacking any microorganisms that have invaded the body previously. Important for this process are white blood cells known as *B cells* and *T cells*. B cells originate in bone marrow as do T cells, but these then mature in the thymus gland. When the same microorganism invades again, the body sends out B and T cells, which are capable of recognizing the invader and attack it and only it (Benjamini et al., 1996).

Stressor Effects on the Immune System. To the extent that stressors can reduce the effectiveness of the immune system, the likelihood of a particular disease will be increased (Cohen & Herbert, 1996; Cohen & Williamson, 1991; Kiecolt-Glaser et al., 2002). Life changes or stressors affect the nervous system, hormonal responses, and behavior. All of these, in turn, can affect immune system functioning and thereby increase the likelihood of disease. The central nervous system affects the immune system, since some of its nerve endings terminate at the organs where B cells and T cells develop. The sympathetic nervous system is instrumental in the release of stress hormones like epinephrine and norepinephrine, which briefly decrease some of the T cells in the bloodstream and also depress the action of phagocytes. Selye (1976) discovered that one consequence of prolonged stressors was a notable shrinkage of the thymus gland, where T cells mature. He also found a dramatic shrinkage of the lymph nodes, which cluster in the neck, armpits, abdomen, and groin. The nodes serve as a kind of home base for lymphocytes in their fight against infectious invaders. Thus, through these intermediate steps, stressors alter the immune system, thereby increasing susceptibility to disease (Black, 1995; Cohen & Herbert, 1996; Kiecolt-Glaser & Glaser, 1995). Behavioral changes may also affect the immune system, since people under stress often engage in bad health practices by drinking too much alcohol, maintaining a poor diet, smoking more, and sleeping less (Cohen & Williamson, 1991; Conway et al., 1981).

Open Window Hypothesis. Strenuous exercise is a behavioral stressor that has been examined to determine how stress affects the immune system. One finding is that exercise affects the immune system in a J-shaped fashion (Nieman, 1994). The left tip of the J represents the likelihood of a respiratory infection as a result of being sedentary (no exercise).

Then as the amount or intensity of exercise increases to a moderate amount, the likelihood of a respiratory infection decreases, as indicated by the bottom part of the J. Further increases in exercise, however, begin to increase the likelihood of infection to the point where high amounts of intense exercise are associated with the greatest risk of respiratory infection (upper right of the J) (Nieman, 1994; Pedersen & Ullum,1994). To account for this J relationship, Pedersen and Ullum (1994) postulated the **open window hypothesis,** which states that a few hours after strenuous exercise the immune system is suppressed and allows an "open window" when natural killer cell activity is low and when there is greater opportunity for a virus or bacteria invade and infect the body. Thus, too much physical exercise, such as running, can actually increase one's likelihood of respiratory diseases. For instance, Nieman (1994) reports that 12.9% of participants in the Los Angeles (26.2 mile) marathon developed respiratory infections compared to only 2.2% of similar runners who did not participate in the marathon. Also, during the two months prior to the marathon, the more miles per week an individual ran in training, the more likely she was to develop a respiratory infection.

Many psychological stressors also follow the J curve. In the case of short-term psychological stressors that are studied in the laboratory, there appears to be an increase in immune system functioning (downward slope of the J curve). Stressors like doing mental arithmetic while being harassed, naming the color that a color name is written in (Stroop task), or placing one's hands in very cold water show an initial increase in natural killer cell activity, which then subsides minutes after the stressor ends (Delahanty et al., 1996; Herbert et al., 1994). Long-term stressors, however, seem to downgrade the immune system. For instance, residents living near a nuclear power reactor that broke down were compared with a group of control residents living in an area more than 80 miles away. The report of this accident was very stressful because it raised the possibility of radioactive contamination for people living nearby. Analyses of blood samples from both areas showed lower immune system functioning up to six years later among residents living near the reactor. They had fewer B cells and fewer natural killer cells than residents from the control town (McKinnon et al., 1989).

Stressors, Immune System, and the Common Cold.   Although stressors can downgrade the immune system, additional evidence is required to show that stressors also contribute to the occurrence of disease. In one investigation, Cohen and associates (1998) investigated how the duration of chronic stressors interacted with the ability of cold viruses to produce colds. Healthy volunteers with no chronic stressors and those with various types of chronic stressors lasting more than two years received two different types of respiratory cold viruses. The percentage of volunteers experiencing cold symptoms and getting colds was greater for those who had experienced at least one month of stressors compared to those with no stressors. In addition, the longer the duration of the chronic stressor the more likely a volunteer would catch cold, especially if the stressor lasted more than two years. Finally, the likelihood of catching a cold was greater for those with interpersonal or work stressors compared to other types of stressors or no stressors. These results indicate that a virus causes a cold provided that the person is undergoing enough stress to downgrade her immune system. In addition to colds, stressors have been implicated in the onset of a variety of infections, such as hepatitis, upper respiratory infection, herpes, and mononucleosis (Black, 1995; Peterson et al., 1991).

Section Recap

Regardless of the type of stressor, the body's adaptive physiological reaction or *general adaptation syndrome* is generally the same. The first stage is known as the alarm reaction, which is the body's initial generalized response to the stressor. The sympathetic nervous system is aroused and stress hormones are released. During the second stage, or stage of resistance, the body successfully controls the stress by localizing its response to where the stressor impacts the body. Adaptation energy is used in defense against a stressor and adjusting to its effect. During the final stage, or stage of exhaustion, a person exhausts his adaptation energy, his ability to combat stress and disease declines, and death results. Diseases caused or worsened by stressors have been referred to as *psychophysiological (psychosomatic) disorders*, such as asthma, headaches, heart disease, hypertension, and ulcers. Tragic news, unexpected events, and anger can worsen coronary heart disease and even precipitate heart attacks.

Psychoneuroimmunology is a field that examines how psychological stressors degrade the immune system, making disease more likely. The body's *immune system* defends against invading microorganisms, such as bacteria and viruses, which are responsible for various diseases. A J-shaped curve describes the relationship between stressors and the integrity of the immune system. As stressors increase, the immune system becomes stronger and then weaker. According to the *open window hypothesis*, strenuous exercise such as marathon running can so weaken the immune system that it provides an "open window" of opportunity for foreign agents to invade and infect the body. Psychological stressors, when of sufficient magnitude, can also degrade the immune system. The consequence of this increases the likelihood of becoming ill from some invading virus.

Variables Moderating the Impact of Life Events

When life hands you a lemon, do you turn sour or do you make lemonade? In a letter to Ann Landers, one distraught reader wrote that her husband left her for another woman. The writer claimed that as a result she suffered a heart attack even though she was only in her 40s. She went on to write, "Since then my life has taken a 360-degree turn. I no longer smoke. I joined [a weight loss organization] and lost 58 pounds. I watch my salt, cholesterol and fat intake and exercise daily. How do I feel? Wonderful! . . . It's tough to admit, but I owe this new-found happiness to my ex-husband who dumped me. What I thought was the worst tragedy of my life turned out to be a blessing." Ann Landers responded by writing, "When life hands you a lemon, make lemonade." The idea of making lemonade out of life's lemons illustrates the fact that people's reactions to life change demands are not fixed but variable. Stress depends on the appraisal of the life event and on characteristics of the individual.

This section describes the process from appraising a life event to coping with it. An individual appraises a life event and inventories her coping strategies. The outcome determines how the individual copes with both the event and the accompanying stress, if any. Along the way, social support and personality traits are important factors that determine the outcome of the appraisal process and coping.

Appraisal of Life Events

When plotting time changes in the course of stress, Tice and Baumeister (1997) discovered that students differed in the number of symptoms at semester's end. Some students reported more stress than others. How could this be possible if there is a precise relationship between the accumulation or magnitude of life events and stress? It turns out that the accumulation of life events is only mildly correlated with the level of stress (Rabkin & Struening, 1976). Why is the number or magnitude of previous life change events so weakly predictive of stress? The reason is a set of **moderator variables,** which are characteristics of the environment or of the person that alter the relationship between stressors and stress. These variables can make the person either more or less vulnerable to life events. For example, not everyone interprets a life event the same way—that is, some individuals turn sour, while others make lemonade. One individual may be thankful he was not killed in a traffic accident, while another is bitter about the loss of his car. Two individuals may experience the same number of negative life events, but one may also experience positive life events to help alleviate stress. One individual may be a member of a close-knit family where she can turn for help, while another may not have this resource available. Finally, there may be personality traits like sense of humor and hardiness that help people weather stressors. Figure 7.4 previews how these moderator variables influence the impact of a stressful life event.

Appraisal and Stress.   Appraisal is the process whereby initial negative life events can be viewed positively or even more negatively. The metaphor of making lemonade from life's lemons illustrates how appraisal can turn negative events into positive ones. Appraisal alters the meaning of a life change event and consequently how an individual reacts (Folkman & Lazarus, 1985; Lazarus & Folkman, 1984). Does a student look

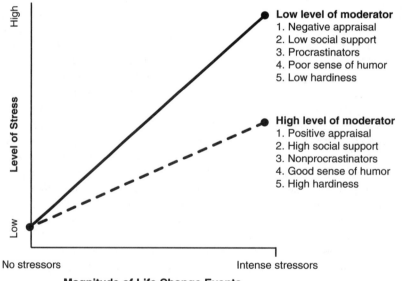

Magnitude of Life Change Events

FIGURE 7.4 Moderators of Stressors and Stress. As the level of life changes or stressors increases, the level of stress increases. The increase in stress, however, is significantly less for individuals who possess some moderator variables. Less stress is experienced by individuals who appraise events positively, have good social support, do not procrastinate, have a good sense of humor, and are hardy.

forward to writing a course paper as a challenge or as a threat? Does the rejected lover dwell on what might have been or view the end of the romantic relationship as a new beginning? In **primary appraisal** a potential event is evaluated as to whether or not it is relevant, benign, positive, or stressful. If the event is judged irrelevant, then a person may have little reaction to it. Benign or positive events produce little reaction or result in positive emotions but provide little if any stress. An event is appraised as stressful, however, if it implies a threat, challenge, or has the potential for harm or loss. Threat refers to the potential for harm or loss, while challenge means that an event, although potentially damaging, is controllable.

Assessing what strategies can meet the demands of life events illustrates **secondary appraisal** (Folkman & Lazarus, 1985; Lazarus & Folkman, 1984). First, an individual can take an inventory to determine if she has the appropriate resources to cope with the event. She can decide what coping strategy to employ and evaluate the likelihood that it will succeed. For example, a student realizes that she will not have enough time to complete a course paper of the quality she would like. What can be done in this situation? Should she turn in the paper and earn a lower grade than she is capable of earning? Should she curtail other activities in order to finish her paper? Should she ask for an extension? What is the likelihood that it will be granted? All of these considerations are part of secondary appraisal.

Appraisal as a Moderator.   The possibility that appraisal can affect an individual's level of stress was demonstrated in a classic series of experiments by Lazarus and associates (Lazarus & Alfert, 1964; Lazarus et al., 1965; Speisman et al., 1964). Lazarus combined several stressful films with soundtracks designed to affect the viewer's cognitive orientation toward the various scenes in the films. One film depicted primitive subincision rites showing deep cuts being made into the penises of adolescent boys. Another stressful film showed workshop accidents of fingers being cut off. Soundtracks that fostered denial, intellectualizing, and trauma orientations accompanied all films except the control. In the denial orientation, the harmful aspects of subincision were minimized; instead the event was emphasized as a happy one for the boys. In the denial orientation, the soundtrack of the shop accident film emphasized that the events were acted, the blood was fake, and no one was injured. In the intellectual orientation, the soundtrack offered a technical description, thus providing emotional distance from the scenes shown. For example, in the film on job accidents the shop foreman was described as training workers in safety procedures. In the trauma orientation, the emphasis was on the pain and terror the boys must have experienced during subincision. As a control, another group of participants watched these films without soundtracks. Electrodermal (skin conductance) and heart rate responses were used as indicators of arousal and stress. The results of these experiments showed that denial and intellectual orientations produced lower levels of physiological arousal or stress compared to the control group. The trauma orientation, however, increased the level of arousal. The moderating variable in this research was the viewer's orientation in appraising the films. Appraised one way, as in trauma orientation, stress increased; appraised another way, as in denial or intellectualization, stress decreased.

Coping and Behavior

We can infer from her letter to Ann Landers that the woman coped with her husband's departure and with the stress that resulted. Coping has two functions: trying to deal with a life change demand and with any distress the demand produces (Folkman & Lazarus, 1985;

Lazarus & Folkman, 1984). **Problem-focused coping** involves trying to identify the problem more clearly and to consider potential solutions. **Emotion-focused coping** involves managing the negative reactions of the accompanying stress. There are a number of emotion-focused coping strategies. *Wishful thinking* is the desire that the problem would somehow go away or that the person would feel differently about it. *Distancing* refers to biding one's time before doing anything or trying to forget about the problem. Coping by *emphasizing the positive* means interpreting the problem in a positive light—that is, "making lemonade when life hands you lemons." *Self-blame* as a way of coping refers to the realization that you are responsible for your actions and their consequences. Smoking, drinking, drug taking, eating, and jogging are *tension reduction* coping strategies that make the person feel better. Finally, some people employ *self-isolation* in which they keep other people ignorant of their problems or avoid people in general (Folkman & Lazarus, 1985).

Coping strategy depends on the controllability of the stressor. Controllable events are more likely to elicit problem-focused coping, while events requiring acceptance and adaptation elicit more emotion-focused coping. Problem- and emotion-focused coping can occur together. For example, a person might seek the advice of a career counselor to learn about potential careers for which she is suited and thereby also reduce anxiety about an uncertain future.

Appraisal and subsequent coping are processes rather than static events (Folkman & Lazarus, 1985; Lazarus & Folkman, 1984). As part of a process, how an event is appraised determines the coping strategies that will be used. To demonstrate this dynamic process, Folkman and Lazarus (1985) studied coping strategies employed by students two days before a midterm exam, five days later but before grades were announced, and five days after grades were announced. They found that problem-focused coping was highest before the exam and decreased afterward, since nothing more could be done. The emotion-focused coping strategy of wishful thinking also decreased after the exam and again after grades had been posted. Wishful thinking as a way of reducing negative emotions (fear, anxiety) is most beneficial when those emotions are at their highest just before the exam. Wishful thinking was also stronger for students with lower grades than those with higher grades. After all, a student is not likely to wish for something else if she earns an A. Wishful thinking is more likely to be employed when a student earns a D in order to help alleviate feelings of disappointment or guilt. Emphasizing the positive also decreased after the exam but did not decline significantly after that. Coping by distancing was greatest while waiting for grades, which was at that point an uncontrollable outcome. Although seeking social support occurred in each exam phase, it also depended on the grade a student had earned. Students who earned a lower grade were more likely to seek social support. For example, a student who earns a D is more likely to experience harmful emotions, such as disappointment, guilt, or disgust, and to therefore seek social support as a way of alleviating these emotions.

Coping strategies that students employ to deal with the stresses of college life may depend on their level of academic experience. Toray and Cooley (1998) compared first-year and upperclass female students regarding their coping strategies during finals week. Both groups of students did not differ in their stress levels during this time or in their perceived test-taking abilities. However, they did differ in their coping strategies. First-year students were more likely to use distancing and self-isolation as a coping strategy compared to their upper-class counterparts. Upper-class students, however, were more likely to employ problem-focused and self-blame coping during the week. Perhaps they had learned that by attacking the problem and holding oneself responsible final exams are less stressful. The students also differed in regard to an aspect of coping by tension reduction. Upper-class students reported a greater likelihood to think about food and to eat in anticipation of finals. Perhaps they were more likely to eat "comfort foods" to help them alleviate their stress.

Social Support as a Moderator

When you need help, is it available? Do you have someone to go to for money, for practical help, or to talk to when troubled? Social support is provided by a network of helpful individuals during both primary and secondary coping. According to the **buffering hypothesis,** various forms of social support buffer or protect an individual from the harm of potential stressors (Cohen & Wills, 1985). Having a friend you can talk to about a forthcoming job interview, for example, can act as a buffer against feelings of anxiety and lack of confidence. The lack of social support from friends and family or of professional help increases the likelihood that a stressor will have a negative impact on the individual.

As a test of the buffering hypothesis, Cohen and Hoberman (1983) measured the extent to which social support protects students against the stressors of college life. Different scales assessed the level of various stressors experienced by students during the previous year, along with depressive and physical symptoms. Other scales measured students' level of social support from friends and family and the availability of physical resources like money. Other scales measured the availability of people in whom an individual could confide and also the extent she felt esteemed, respected, and valued by others. The results showed that as the number of negative life events increased, both depressive and physical symptoms increased. However, social support and physical resources buffered the effect of negative life events. Stress symptoms were less pronounced for individuals who had a greater amount of social support and physical resources, greater feelings of belonging, and higher self-esteem. In a one-semester prospective study, Demakis and McAdams (1994) found that introductory psychology students who reported being highly satisfied with their social support network were more satisfied with university life and tended to have lower negative affect compared to students less satisfied with their social support. Finally, the likelihood of developing PTSD from the September 11th terrorist attack was lower for people who had a high compared to a low level of social support (Galea et al., 2002).

Social support also buffers the immune system and physical health against stressors. It is linked to lowering blood pressure and better immune system functioning (Uchino et al., 1999). For instance, Kiecolt-Glaser and associates (1984) investigated the effects previous life changes and course exams had on the immune system of medical students. Analyses showed that the number of prior life events and the exams contributed to a decrease in natural killer cell activity in the immune system. Buffering effects were observed, however, based on how lonely the students felt. Students who reported being lonely showed a greater decline in natural killer cell activity than students who reported being less lonely. Taft and associates (1999) examined the relationship between social support, PTSD, and the physical health of Vietnam veterans. Social support was measured by inquiring if the veterans had friends and relatives who could provide psychological assistance and practical help, such as lending a car. Veterans benefitted from social support, since those who received it suffered less from combat-related PTSD and from poor physical health. Uchino and associates (1999) theorized that social support lessens the impact of stressors on physical health in several ways. First, the support of others may lessen the impact of a stressor. For example, sympathetic others may serve as a buffer against college- or job-related stress. Being able to complain to a sympathetic roommate about a boring professor or to a sympathetic spouse about a demanding boss may be great stress relievers. Second, even in the absence of stressors, friends and family affect physiological processes by influencing one's self-esteem, feelings of self-efficacy, and mood. Third, social support may increase health-enhancing behaviors and decrease health-impairing behaviors. Thus, with the encouragement of others an individual may be more likely to eat well and exercise and be less likely to smoke and eat an unhealthy diet. Of course, not all social relationships are positive and thus buffers against stress. Housemates and spouses who are hard to get along with are more likely to be a source of stress than buffers against it.

Personality Differences as Moderator Variables

People differ in their outlook on life. One person may react quite negatively to minor life changes, while another might bear up well even under severe setbacks. These different reactions are related to personality traits that are linked to appraisal and coping. This section examines the personality traits of procrastination, sense of humor, and hardiness as ways of accounting for differences in people's stress reactions. These traits, as examples of moderator variables, are illustrated in Figure 7.4.

Procrastination.   Are you good or lousy at time management? Do you study for exams and complete course assignments well in advance, or do you put them off until the last moment? These questions address differences in the tendency to procrastinate. Tice and Baumeister (1997) questioned whether student procrastination was beneficial, harmless, or harmful at various times in the semester. They divided students into nonprocrastinators and procrastinators and then examined the students' level of stress early and late in the semester. Figure 7.5 shows that procrastinators benefitted early in the semester from putting things off. The end of the semester was a different story, however. At that point, procrastinators reported more stress, more physical symptoms, and more visits to health care professionals. Stressors that naturally occur at the end of the semester add to those that have accumulated from procrastination, which results in greater stress. Procrastination illustrates a personality variable that worsens the impact of time-related stressors, since the strategy of putting things off leads to stressor accumulation.

Sense of Humor.   "A cheerful heart is a good medicine" (Proverbs 17:22). It has long been known that a sense of humor can moderate the impact of negative life events. **Sense of humor** has no clearly agreed-on definition but does involve the propensity to habitually smile, laugh, and be amused in a variety of situations (Deckers & Ruch, 1992; Martin & Lefcourt, 1984). To measure sense of humor, Martin and Lefcourt (1984) developed the *Situational Humor Response Questionnaire*, which measures people's reaction to life events that are both common and unusual, pleasant and unpleasant. People responded to these statements on a 1 to 5 scale ranging from 1 = "I wouldn't have found it particularly amusing," to 5 = "I would have laughed heartily." Using this five-point scale, how likely are you to respond with humor to such negative events as "You are eating in a restaurant with some friends and the waiter accidently spills a drink on you" or to such positive events as "You are having a romantic evening alone with someone you really like." Martin and Lefcourt (1984) assumed that a greater likelihood of laughing in such situations indicates

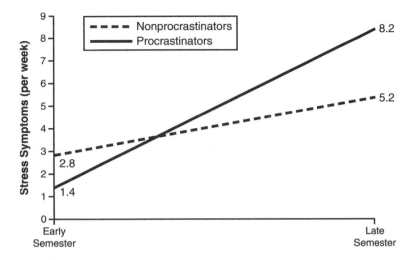

FIGURE 7.5   Procrastination as a Stressor. The number of stress symptoms reported rose more sharply for procrastinators than for nonprocrastinators as the semester progressed.

Source: From "Longitudinal Study of Procrastination, Performance, Stress, and Health" by D. M. Tice and R. F. Baumeister, 1997, *Psychological Science, 8,* figure 1, p. 456. Copyright 1997 by Blackwell Publishers. Reprinted by permission.

a greater sense of humor. The *Coping Humor Scale* was designed specifically to measure how humor is used for coping (Martin & Lefcourt, 1983). Examples of items from this scale are "I have often found that my problems have been greatly reduced when I tried to find something funny in them" and "I can usually find something to laugh or joke about, even in trying situations."

> *Situational Humor Response Questionnaire* is available at http://www.umm.edu/news/releases/humor_survey.html

Is there any empirical evidence for the ancient wisdom that humor moderates stress? According to a review by Lefcourt and Thomas (1998), "there is enough evidence to encourage the belief that humor can have positive effects in alleviating distress" (p. 201). For instance, Lefcourt and Martin (1986) examined how sense of humor affected the relationship between negative life events and mood disturbance (anger, anxiety, and depression). Using the *Situational Humor Response Questionnaire, Coping Humor Scale,* and other sense-of-humor measures, they found that as the number of experienced negative life events increased, mood disturbance increased. However, this increase in stress was much greater for students with a low compared to a high sense of humor. Later research examined the possibility that sense of humor affects both appraisal of and coping with life events. Kuiper and associates (1993) compared students with high and low senses of humor on the strategies they used in appraising and coping with an exam. Students who scored higher on the *Coping Humor Scale* appraised the exam more as a positive challenge. They were also more likely to use distancing as a form of coping as well as to use confrontive coping by meeting the exam head on.

Laboratory research has also supported the hypothesis that sense of humor moderates the appraisal of life events. In one study, participants had to appraise for challenge and threat the task of drawing "a person on a winter day." Participants with a higher sense of humor appraised the task as more challenging and slightly less threatening (Kuiper et al., 1995). Newman and Stone (1996) examined how a humorous interpretation of a stressful event affects physiological distress. They had male participants create a humorous monologue to go along with an industrial accident film, while control participants created a serious monologue. Physiological distress, as indicated by electrodermal responses, heart rate, and skin temperature, was lower for participants who created a humorous monologue than for those who created a serious monologue. Although sense of humor appears to moderate the stress of mild life events, its efficiency has been questioned for very negative life events. For example, DesCamp and Thomas (1993) found that sense of humor did not buffer nurses from job stress such as work load, meeting the emotional needs of patients and their family members, and exposure to dying and death. Nevertheless, when tragedy occurs, people can lessen its negative impact somewhat by seeing the humorous aspects of the situation. Can you think of your ex spilling soup on herself? Can you think of a humorous event you shared with a deceased friend? Humor in these examples may provide momentary relief from feelings of disappointment and grief.

Several possibilities exist for why humor is a stress reducer (Martin, 2001). First, humor may simply be one of several positive emotions that is beneficial in counteracting stress (Folkman & Moskowitz, 2000; Salovey et al., 2000). Laughing and feeling amused enhance positive moods, which are incompatible with feelings of distress. Also, humor moderates stress through the appraisal process. Examining life change events from a humorous outlook may be part of a larger appraisal process by which events can be viewed either more positively or less negatively. An additional benefit comes from the social nature of humor. People with a good sense of humor attract more individuals to them. In this way, they have a greater network of social support to rely on when experiencing stress.

Hardiness.   When it comes to withstanding stressors and stress, some individuals just seem stronger or hardier than others. **Hardiness** is a personality trait composed of three characteristics: control, commitment, and challenge. The hardy individual perceives herself to be in control of life's events, is committed or involved in daily activities, and views unexpected events, whether threatening or positive, as challenging rather than as aversive (Kobasa, 1979). In a scale measuring hardiness (Kobasa, 1984), *control* was assessed by statements that hard work makes a difference. *Commitment* was depicted by statements indicating that one is enthusiastic about working on the day's projects. A willingness to forgo financial security in order to do something challenging was a statement designed to measure *challenge*. In one study, Kobasa (1979) examined 200 executives who had experienced a high number of life change events during the past three years. Using her questionnaire, she concluded that hardiness was the factor that differentiated the low- from the high-stress group. Independent of income, age, wealth, or level of education, the hardier executives were ill less frequently than the less hardy executives. Hardy executives viewed the events in their lives as challenges to be met head on rather than trying to avoid or escape any anxiety the events created. In addition, they felt in control of the life events or stressors rather than being controlled by them.

Hardiness has also been shown to moderate the relationship between combat exposure, PTSD, and subsequent physical health conditions. Taft and associates (1999) measured the intensity of combat exposure experienced by both men and women during their Vietnam experience. They examined the intensity of such exposure by asking veterans whether they had been fired on, had fired a weapon, or had observed "Americans being killed or wounded" (p. 8). The intensity of combat predicted the degree of PTSD and physical health, such as high blood pressure, ulcers, asthma, or joint stiffness. More intense experiences were associated with greater PTSD and greater negative health symptoms. However, hardiness moderated or served as a buffer against the intensity of combat. Taft and associates found that the severity of PTSD and physical health were negatively related to hardiness. In other words, although combat produces PTSD and ill health, hardier male and female Vietnam veterans had been better able to withstand the stressors of combat. As a consequence, they experienced lower levels of PTSD and less serious adverse health consequences.

The influence of hardiness can be observed during primary appraisal. Allred and Smith (1989) required low- and high-hardy participants to work on either a threatening or non-threatening task, which consisted of difficult analogy questions and the mental rotation of various cubes. To create high stress, half of the participants were told that their performance predicted success on a variety of academic and vocational activities. To create low stress, the other half of the participants were told that the accuracy of their answers was not important. As a way of assessing task appraisal, the researchers inventoried the positive and negative thoughts that occurred to the participants. An example of a positive thought is "I think I am performing well," while a negative thought is "I am thinking lower of my ability" (p. 260). The effects of hardiness were seen in the high-stress condition. Hardy participants reported more positive thoughts during the task than did less hardy participants. Thus, hardiness moderates the effects of a stressor through such cognitive strategies as appraising an event in a positive manner.

Section Recap

The effect of a stressor is regulated by *moderating variables*. These variables are features of the environment or person that transform the stressor-stress relationship. How a life event is appraised is one type of moderating variable. In *primary appraisal* an event is analyzed for whether it is positive, negative, or irrelevant for the individual's well-being. If appraised as negative, then an individual uses *secondary appraisal* to inventory the resources that can be used to manage the event. Following appraisal, an individual can cope with either the original stressor or with the stress. *Problem-focused coping* involves clarifying and trying to solve the stressor, while *emotion-focused coping* requires alleviating the accompanying distress. Social support is another moderating variable. The *buffering hypothesis* states that social support provided by other individuals cushions or protects an individual from the harm of potential stressors. The tendency to procrastinate, sense of humor, and hardiness are personality traits that also affect life event appraisal and stress. *Sense of humor* is the habitual inclination to smile, laugh, and be amused by various events. Humor is a feeling incompatible with distress, alters stressor appraisal, and draws people to us to provide social support when needed. *Hardiness* is a personality trait manifested by seeing life events as challenging, feeling in control of those events, and being committed to various activities.

➤ Helpful information about stressors, stress, and coping is provided at The American Institute of Stress, http://www.stress.org/, and at HELPGUIDE, http://www.helpguide.org/mental/stress_signs.htm

A C T I V I T I E S

1. To make the relation between life demands, resources, strain, and stress more concrete, think of a situation in your life where these factors might apply.

   a. What are some demands? Describe these demands (e.g., final exams, getting a job over the holidays, bills that are due).

   b. What are some of your *resources* to meet those demands (e.g., study time, job prospects, money)?

   c. Is there any *strain* (i.e., resources are not enough to meet demands)? Describe the strain you feel (e.g., not enough time for studying, no job prospects, lack of money).

   d. Describe any *stress* you are experiencing in the psychological, physiological, or behavioral domains (see Table 7.1).

2. When is the next exam for this course? List strategies that would be part of primary appraisal and problem-focused coping in preparing for the exam. In what circumstances would you use secondary appraisal and emotion-focused coping after the exam is completed?

3. Recall the last time you were ill. Did this occur during a time when you were experiencing stress? Can you use the magnitude and number of stressors to predict when you will be sick? Describe a specific instance.

4. Of the people you know, think of those that have little sense of humor and those that have a good sense of humor. Do they differ in the number of stress symptoms that they exhibit? Are these symptoms related to their sense of humor? Although sense of humor alleviates stress, can the reverse happen? In other words, can stress depress one's sense of humor? If so, how?

PART THREE

Psychological Properties of Motivation

Can two individuals be both the same and different in what motivates them? Do people with different needs, traits, and concerns know they are motivated by different things? The themes of this section are population thinking, differences between motives and traits, awareness of what is motivating, and self-concept as a motivational system. Population thinking emphasizes the notion that every person is different. Chapter 8 (Drives, Needs, and Awareness) shows people differ in the intensity of their psychological needs. Individuals with stronger psychological needs or motives are pushed harder toward satisfaction. Chapter 9 (Personality and Self in Motivation) stresses population thinking by emphasizing differences in personality traits. Trait differences explain why people are attracted or repelled by different incentives.

What is the motivational distinction between psychological motives and personality traits? One distinction is that motives like drives and psychological needs push behavior, whereas traits do not. Drives are created through incentive deprivation. For example, food deprivation creates a hunger drive, which pushes or motivates a person to seek, attain, and eat food. Psychological needs are persistent deficits that push an individual toward activities or incentives that provide satisfaction. If left unsatisfied, needs produce psychological ill health. Thus, people are motivated from within to satisfy their needs and attain psychological health. The need to belong or affiliate, for example, pushes people to join clubs, organizations, fraternities, and sororities in order to satisfy this need. Personality traits, however, determine whether incentives are valued positively or negatively. To illustrate, for the trait of extraversion, extraverts positively value and are pulled to attend large, noisy parties. Introverts, in contrast, negatively value those parties and decline to attend.

Are people aware that they are motivated by their psychological needs and personality traits? Although needs and traits affect the motivation of behavior, people may not be aware of the source of that motivation. They seem to act automatically but with limited insight as to why. This lack of awareness may result from the fact that needs and traits are considered stable and unchanging. Stable needs and traits cannot explain why the same person behaves differently at different times. However, people differ in needs and traits, and this can account for differences in their behavior.

Does how you view yourself in the present and in the future motivate your behavior? A person's view of him- or herself defines self-concept, which is an organized system of knowledge about the self. Envisioned future selves may serve as positive or negative incentives. A positive future self motivates approach behavior toward that end while a negative future self motivates avoidance behavior, which is designed to prevent a negative self from happening. Self-esteem, however, refers to the outcome of an evaluation about the self. Self-esteem depends on the outcome of evaluations that occur in critical domains. Positive evaluations in important domains boost self-esteem and negative evaluations lower self-esteem.

8 Drives, Needs, and Awareness

By annihilating desires you annihilate the mind. Every man without passions has within him no principle of action, nor motive to act.
—*Claude Adrien Helvetius, 1715–1771*

Body cannot determine mind to think, neither can mind determine body to motion or rest or any state different from these, if such there be.
—*Benedict de Spinoza, 1677*

■ The focus of this chapter is on motives—that is, the internal source of motivation. Keep that idea in mind as you consider the following questions, which introduce the contents of this chapter:

1. What are the differences among physiological needs, drives, and psychological needs?
2. What is the relationship between psychological needs and incentives?
3. Can needs be categorized and ranked for their potential to motivate behavior?
4. What are some of the major psychological needs that motivate behavior?
5. Is awareness of a need or incentive necessary before it can motivate behavior?

Drives and Needs as Internal Sources of Motivation

How does one become a world renowned actor, a popular musician, a Nobel-prize winning scientist, or a gold medal-winning athlete? To reach this level of achievement, it is probably necessary to be a genius, such as an acting, musical, scientific, or athletic genius. With this provision in place, one source of motivation for these achievements is the value placed on financial rewards, fame, winning, or the adoration received from others. The philosopher Schopenhauer (1851/1970), however, suggests that these incentives are not enough. The money may not be worth it and fame is too uncertain. In addition, the possibility that these incentives will be the result of one's actions is vague, uncertain, and far in the future. Schopenhauer instead suggests that there are processes inside these individuals that will explain their motivation. He reasons that these individuals possess some inner force or drive that compels them toward their achievements. Schopenhauer likens this inner drive to an innate instinctual process that compels these individuals into action toward their goals as if they had no choice in the matter. This inner force is today labeled drive because it refers to

183

TABLE 8.1   **Internal and External Motivation and Likelihood of Behavior**

	Strength of Internal Motive	
Strength of External Incentive	**Weak**	**Strong**
Weak	Behavior not likely	Behavior likely
Strong	Behavior likely	Behavior very likely

Note: The combined effects of internal and external sources of motivation must be strong enough to exceed the threshold in order for behavior to occur. For example, eating depends on the palatability of food (external) and the degree of hunger (internal).

that internal push, urge, or force that moves a person into action. It could also refer to psychological needs such as a very high need for achievement, competence, or autonomy. What internal drives and psychological needs do humans possess that motivate their behavior?

The purpose of this section is to contrast internal with external sources of motivation, with a major emphasis on internal sources such as drives and physiological and psychological needs. The section will conclude with a description of Maslow's hierarchy of needs and an evaluation of that hierarchy.

Interaction of Push and Pull Motivation

As emphasized in Chapter 1, motivation comes from internal sources that push and from external sources that pull an individual. Internal motivation refers to drives and physiological and psychological needs, while external motivation concerns incentives and goals. The combined push and pull effects of internal and external sources must exceed some threshold for behavior to occur, as described in Table 8.1. When above the threshold, behavior occurs; when below, it does not (Kimble, 1990). Behavior can result from little external motivation, provided that there is a lot of internal motivation. For example, the food may not be very tasty but a hungry person will eat it. Or behavior can occur with little internal motivation, provided there is a lot of external motivation. For example, even though a person may not be very hungry, he will still eat a bowl of delicious ice cream. Internal motivation is the disposition to perform a particular action. It can be created through depriving an organism of an incentive such as food, water, or visual stimulation. In other instances, the disposition to respond is dormant, and a situational stimulus will arouse it. For instance, a psychological need such as the need for power could be activated by being a member of the police force, which allows for the legitimate exercise of power.

Physiological Needs and Psychological Drives

There is a very important difference between physiological and psychological needs that is anchored in the distinction between materialism and mentalism. Physiological needs refer to deficits that exist in the material body or brain. **Psychological needs,** however, do not have any material existence and are mental or psychological in nature. There is reference to a deficit of some psychological entity; a discrepancy between a desired level and a current amount. In some cases, psychological needs are assumed to emerge into consciousness from physiological needs. Murray (1938), for instance, assumed that psychological needs emerged from processes that occurred in the brain. However, the possible physiological origin of psychological needs is usually ignored.

Need as the Physiological Basis for Motivation. Homeostasis (see Chapter 5) describes the maintenance of constant conditions within the body. Motivation theorists who emphasize internal events, such as Clark Hull (1943, 1951, 1952) and Judson Brown (1961), accepted the idea that a set of ideal internal conditions was necessary for survival. Deviation from these conditions defines **physiological need** and is responsible for pushing an organism into action. The need for food can correspond to a low amount of glucose in the blood. The need for putting on a sweater corresponds to a drop in body temperature below 98.6°F. The need for iron exists when the amount in the body is so low so that the blood's capacity to carry oxygen is reduced. This condition results in feeling tired and weak and being unable to perform manual work without extensive feelings of fatigue (Sizer & Whitney, 1997). Thus, a physiological need implies that it is possible to specify a deficit in a physiological state that is detrimental to a person's physical well-being. Another category of need refers to sensory stimulation that exceeds a certain intensity thereby causing pain or harm. Excessive sensory stimulation occurs when french fries are too hot, the volume on the stereo is too loud, or the light in one's eyes is too bright. Sensations of pain or discomfort are warnings of possible tissue damage and prompt the need to escape and avoid such stimulation.

Hull's Drive Theory. Related to physiological need is psychological **drive,** which is a motivational construct that results when an animal is deprived of a needed substance (Hull, 1943, 1951, 1952). Drive is the persistent internal stimulus or pushing action of a physiological need. Drive has several properties or characteristics (Hull, 1943, 1951, 1952). First, it energizes behavior by intensifying all responses in a particular situation. The more intense the drive, the more intense the behavior (Hull, 1943, 1952). This point is illustrated in an experiment by Hillman and associates (1953), who deprived two groups of rats of water for either 2 or 22 hours and then measured how long it took them to run a 10-unit T maze for a water reward. After 10 trials, one-half of each group remained at the original deprivation level, while the other half switched to the other deprivation level. For example, group 2-2 and group 22-22 remained at 2 and 22 hours of water deprivation, respectively, throughout the experiment. Group 2-22 switched from 2 to 22 hours of water deprivation after the first 10 trials, while group 22-2 switched from 22 to 2 hours of water deprivation. According to Hull's theory, 22 hours of water deprivation corresponds to high thirst drive, while 2 hours of water deprivation corresponds to low drive. High drive should multiply or intensify instrumental behavior much more than low drive. As shown in Figure 8.1, the rats took less time to run the maze under high drive than under low drive. The interpretation based on drive theory is that high drive is a more intense source of internal motivation than low drive.

A second characteristic is that each drive has its own unique internal sensations that serve as internal stimuli for guiding behavior. For example, hunger and thirst feel different and provide the basis for knowing when to eat and when to drink. Leeper (1935) used thirst and hunger drives as cues for rats to choose the correct goal box when water or food deprived. In his experimental apparatus, rats had to make a choice between an alley leading to food and another alley leading to water. The rats learned to choose the alley leading to

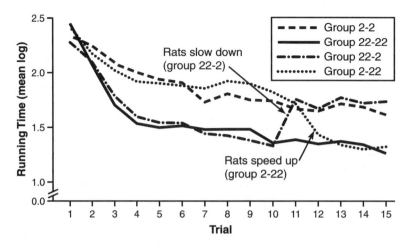

FIGURE 8.1   Intensity of Drive and Running Behavior. Effects of deprivation time on mean log time to run a 10-unit T maze for a water reward by water-deprived rats. Note the increase in running time immediately after the 22-2 hour shift and the decrease in running time after the 2-22 hour shift.

Source: From "The Effect of Drive Level on the Maze Performance of the White Rat" by B. Hillman et al., 1953, *Journal of Comparative and Physiological Psychology, 46*, figure 1. Copyright 1953 by American Psychological Association. Reprinted by permission.

food on food-deprived days and to choose the alley leading to water on water-deprived days. Thus, hunger drive stimuli became associated with the location of food, and thirst drive stimuli became associated with the location of water. A third characteristic of drive is that it motivates the individual to behave in order to reduce its intensity. Hull considered drive to be unpleasant. In fact, he felt that "Bentham's concept of *pain* is equated substantially to our own [Hull's] concept of *need*" (Hull, 1952, p. 341). Recall from Chapter 2 that Bentham (1789/1970) is the utilitarian philosopher who claimed that people are under the governance of two masters: pain and pleasure. Humans are motivated to reduce drive—that is, to get rid of any painful or unpleasant feeling. Since drive is characterized as being painful, then the behavior that reduces it will be more likely to occur. Eating reduces an unpleasant hunger drive, and drinking reduces an unpleasant thirst drive. The importance of Hull's drive concept is that drive motivates the voluntary behavior that restores homeostasis. Drive motivates an individual to reduce feelings of hunger, thirst, or internal temperature deviation, thus maximizing the conditions necessary for well-being and life.

Characteristics of Psychological Needs

The definition of psychological needs parallels that of physiological needs since both center on the notion of a deficit. In the case of a psychological need, there is a deficit between a person's desired or set point level and the current level of the matching incentive or behavior.

Chronic or Temporary Psychological Needs.   Psychological needs are chronic if a person desires some incentive or behavior of which she is habitually deprived. For example, if a person has a large appetite for social inclusion then she might be chronically unsatisfied if the current social environment does not provide enough social inclusion. A person might have an enduring need for cognition if she is consistently deprived of her daily opportunity to solve Sudoku or crossword puzzles. However, psychological needs can also be temporary and are aroused occasionally. In this case, it is as if psychological needs are preexisting but remain dormant until aroused by the appropriate stimulus situation. When aroused, the psychological need serves as a motive that reminds a person of the discrepancy between his current situation and a final desired state (McClelland et al., 1953). **Redintegration** describes the process by which a need is activated or restored (Murray, 1938). For example, a safety need is aroused or redintegrated when an unlighted parking lot late at night is discrepant from a person's ideal level of lighting. The aroused safety need produces a hurried pace to reach one's car and drive away. The need to achieve is activated or redintegrated by the sight of a textbook, reminding a student of the discrepancy between his current knowledge and the amount necessary to succeed on an exam. The resulting need state or achievement motive leads to studying a textbook to reduce the discrepancy. Stimuli activate, redintegrate, or restore psychological needs because they have been associated with the arousal characteristics of needs in the past (McClelland et al., 1953). To illustrate, the presence of people arouses the need for affiliation, and textbooks arouse the need to achieve, because in the past these stimuli have been associated with feelings of affiliation and achievement.

Using Needs to Explain Behavior.   A final consideration involves demonstrating the relationship between need intensity and need-satisfying behavior. Do people differ in their intensities of psychological needs? How is a person's level of need intensity measured? These questions cannot be answered by measuring behavior that is instrumental in satisfying the need, since this behavior could have resulted from other factors. For example, if a person's residence hall room is neat and tidy, does that mean she has a high need for order (Murray, 1938)? Or could it be she is just expecting company or likes being able to find things easily? If the concept of need is used to explain behavior, then two steps are necessary: measuring need intensity and showing its relationship with behavior satisfying the need. First, psychologists measure need level with a valid scale or questionnaire. Just as the number on the bathroom scale reflects the amount a person weighs, the score on a need scale reflects the intensity of a need. Second, need scale scores must correlate with behavior instrumental in satisfying the need. Thus, when need is high, there must be a greater amount of need-satisfying behavior than when need is low. For example, the greater a person's measured need for affiliation, the more friends he visits and telephones (Lansing & Heyns, 1959). In the next few sections, we will examine how various psychological needs are measured and the relationship between specific needs and behavior.

Maslow's Theory of Needs

Are all needs equally important or are some more potent than others? One view is that there are categories of needs that differ in their potency to motivate behavior.

Abraham Maslow (1970) constructed a **hierarchy of needs:** *physiological, safety, belongingness, esteem*, and *self-actualization*. These needs are organized into five tiers whereby the lower tier of needs is more likely to be acted on first, followed by needs at higher tiers (see Figure 8.2). Notice that in ascending the hierarchy, needs have been

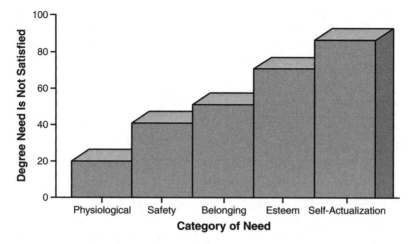

FIGURE 8.2   Maslow's Hierarchy of Needs. Physiological needs are most readily satisfied, and self-actualization needs are least easily satisfied. A person works to satisfy these needs in a hierarchical fashion, with the most time spent on the most potent need, which is lowest on the hierarchy, then working up the hierarchy to the next potent need.

satisfied less and less. Physiological needs are based on homeostasis and include food, water, and a generally balanced internal state. Maslow also includes sexual, sleep, and activity needs in this category. Once physiological needs are addressed, then safety needs begin to emerge. Safety needs refer to the absence of fear, anxiety, and chaos and the presence of security, stability, dependency, and law and order. With the satisfaction of safety needs, next on the hierarchy are the belonging needs. In order to satisfy these needs, humans seek to establish social relationships with friends, lovers, and family members. Without these relationships the individual feels rejected and lonely. Next on the hierarchy are esteem needs, which concern the respect of self and the respect of others. These needs involve achievement, adequacy, mastery, and competence plus the prestige, fame, and glory derived from the recognition of others. Finally, at the top of the hierarchy is the most elusive of all needs, the need for self-actualization. This refers to the need to fulfill and utilize one's abilities and talents to the fullest in whatever area one chooses.

The *Need Satisfaction Inventory* (Lester, 1990) in Table 8.2 provides a possible means for testing whether needs are indeed arranged in this hierarchy. The inventory measures the degree to which a person has satisfied each need category. The inventory has face validity, which means that its items appear to measure what they are supposed to (i.e., "on the face of it"). Thus, question 36, regarding the amount of exercise, would help determine the satisfaction of your physiological needs, while question 10, regarding whether life has meaning, is valid for determining satisfaction of your self-actualization needs. If Maslow's (1970) theory is correct, then Lester's inventory should show a decreasing amount of need satisfaction going up the hierarchy. In other words, a person's physiological and safety needs should be satisfied more than her esteem and self-actualization needs.

TABLE 8.2   Need Satisfaction Inventory

For the 50 statements listed below, use the scale to indicate the extent you agree with each statement. Read each statement carefully and answer with your first impulse.

$-3 = $ *Strongly disagree* $-2 = $ *Disagree* $-1 = $ *Slightly disagree*
$0 = $ *Neither disagree nor agree*
$+1 = $ *Slightly agree* $+2 = $ *Agree* $+3 = $ *Strongly agree*

Physiological Needs
  1. I never have trouble getting to sleep at night.
  6. I have an income that is adequate to satisfy my needs.
11. I get an adequate amount of rest.
16. I have a satisfactory sex life.
21. In general, my health is good.
26. In winter, I always feel too cold. (R)
31. I eat enough to satisfy my physiological needs.
36. I get an adequate amount of exercise.
41. There's usually some part of my body that is giving me trouble. (R)
46. The summers are too hot for me ever to feel comfortable. (R)

Safety and Security
  2. I think the world is a pretty safe place these days.
  7. I would not walk alone in my neighborhood at night. (R)
12. My anxiety level is high. (R)
17. I feel secure about the amount of money I have and earn.
22. I feel safe and secure.
27. I am afraid to stay in my house/apartment alone at night. (R)
32. My life is orderly and well-defined.
37. I can depend on others to help me when I am in need.
42. I am often worried about my physical health. (R)
47. My life has a nice routine to it.

Belonging
  3. I know my family will support me and be on my side no matter what.
  8. I am involved in a significant love relationship with another.
13. I feel rootless. (R)
18. I have a group of friends with whom I do things.
23. I feel somewhat socially isolated. (R)
28. I have a few intimate friends on whom I can rely.
33. I feel close to my relatives.
38. I am interested in my ethnic roots and feel a kinship with others in my ethnic group.
43. I am religious and consider myself to be a member of a religious group.
48. I am able to confide my innermost thoughts and feelings to at least one close and intimate friend.

Esteem
  4. I feel dissatisfied with myself much of the time. (R)
  9. I feel respected by my peers.

continued

TABLE 8.2   (*Continued*)

14. I seldom have fears that my actions will cause my friends to have a low opinion of me.
19. I can stand on my own two feet.
24. I feel confident in my present field of endeavor.
29. I would describe myself as a self-confident person.
34. I have earned the respect of others.
39. I do not spend much time worrying about what people think of me.
44. I feel that I am a worthy person.
49. In groups, I usually feel that my opinions are inferior to those of other people. (R)

Self-Actualization
5. I have a good idea of what I want to do with my life.
10. My life has meaning.
15. I am uncertain about my goals in life. (R)
20. I feel I am living up to my potential.
25. I am seeking maturity.
30. I find my work challenging.
35. I know what my capabilities are and what I cannot do.
40. I feel I am doing the best I am capable of.
45. I feel that I am growing as a person.
50. My educational achievements are appropriate given my ability.

Note: To score, first reverse your answer for the items followed by an (R). For example, change a -2 to a $+2$ and change a $+1$ to a -1. Sum your score in each category. A higher score means a greater amount of need satisfaction for that category.

Source: From "Maslow's Hierarchy of Needs and Personality" by D. Lester, 1990, *Personality and Individual Differences, 11*, p. 1188. Copyright 1990 by Elsevier Science Ltd. Reprinted by permission.

Section Recap

The body requires an ideal set of internal conditions for its well-being, and any deviation from these conditions produces a *physiological need*. Whenever an organism is deprived of a needed substance, a psychological *drive* results. This hypothetical construct is felt as unpleasant and thus motivates and guides the organism to search for the appropriate incentive that reduces the drive. A *psychological need* is an internal motive to achieve a desired endstate. Needs exist permanently because the environment does not provide the means for satisfaction. Or needs lie dormant until activated by the appropriate stimulus situation through a process known as *redintegration*. There are two requirements for using psychological needs to explain behavior. One is to measure the intensity of a psychological need; the second is to show that this intensity correlates with the magnitude of need-satisfying behavior. A very influential need theory is Abraham Maslow's *hierarchy of needs*, which includes physiological, safety, belongingness, self-esteem, and self-actualization needs. Needs must be satisfied from the lower tier on up. For example, physiological and safety needs must be satisfied to some extent before a person can begin satisfying needs higher up in the hierarchy.

Some Important Psychological Needs

As described in Chapter 2, from Georges Le Roy in 1764 to Henry Murray in 1938, students of human motivation have speculated on the existence of a wide variety of needs. Of these needs, seven have become important for the motivation of behavior: *achievement, power, cognition, esteem, autonomy, competence*, and *relatedness*. This last need has also been labeled the need to affiliate or to belong. The purpose of this section is to describe these needs in more detail.

Achievement Motivation

The motive or need to achieve has been a theme in popular literature. In a long series of books described as "rags to riches stories," the 19th-century author Horatio Alger, Jr., implied that the road to success is by way of persistence and hard work. The main theme of all of Alger's stories is the motive to achieve or need to achieve (Tebel, 1963). Beginning with Murray (1938), the need to achieve has also been a popular theme with researchers and has probably received more attention from psychologists than any other psychological need.

Need to Achieve and Need to Avoid Failure. The **need to achieve** or motive to achieve success (Ms) is a disposition to engage in task-oriented behavior or achievement behavior. It is characterized by doing things better than before or surpassing a high external or internal standard of excellence. The standards can be defined on the job, in sports, or in school and are based on the performance of others or on the person's own standards. The achievement motive is assumed to be dormant until activated by an associated achievement cue (McClelland et al., 1953), such as the sight of textbooks, instruments, or tools.

Do all individuals concentrate on achievement, or do some simply want to avoid failure? In addition to the motive to achieve success (Ms), people also vary in their motivation to avoid failure. The **motive to avoid failure** is the opposite of the need to achieve and inhibits a person from attempting achievement tasks (Atkinson, 1957/1983). Motive to avoid failure (Maf) is characterized by anxiety and fear about failing a task. The strength of Ms and Maf combine to determine the tendency to attempt an achievement task (Atkinson, 1974). On the one hand, Ms motivates an individual to engage in the task, while on the other, Maf motivates the individual to avoid tackling the task. Individuals in whom Ms is greater than Maf (Ms > Maf) are more likely to pursue achievement tasks, while individuals in whom Maf is greater than Ms (Maf > Ms) are more likely to avoid them (Atkinson, 1958/1983). Thus, individuals are attracted to and repelled from achieving a task to a degree consistent with the strength of these two motives. For example, in selecting a major or a final career goal, students are driven toward their choices by their Ms but at the same time are inhibited from pursuing those choices by their Maf. For instance, if a student has a career goal to become a marriage and family counselor, then her Ms pushes her toward that goal while at the same time her Maf pushes her away from it.

Measuring the Need to Achieve and Need to Avoid Failure. Claims about the relationship between Ms and Maf and achievement behavior are based on the measurement of each construct. How does a psychologist determine the extent of an individual's Ms and Maf? This section examines various procedures that are used to measure each construct.

If the need to achieve is dormant, then the test used to measure it must also activate it. This is one of the reasons different projective tests have been employed to measure the

FIGURE 8.3   Picture Resembling One from Thematic Apperception Test. The picture shows two women in lab coats and resembles one of the actual TAT pictures. Need to achieve is measured by evaluating respondents' answers to questions about this and other pictures in the test.

Source: Photo © The Stock Market Agency/William Taufic.

need to achieve (Fineman, 1977). In a **projective test** a person verbally responds to an unstructured stimulus, such as an inkblot, in a manner that is presumably consistent with her activated motives. McClelland and associates (1953) adapted a projective test procedure pioneered by Murray (1938) known as the *Thematic Apperception Test* (TAT). The TAT consists of a series of pictures of people in ambiguous but potential achievement settings. The respondent is instructed to tell a story, which the picture may hint at but does not contain. Figure 8.3 resembles the TAT picture of two women in lab coats (McClelland, 1975, p. 387). To a series of such pictures, participants are asked the following questions:

1. "What is happening? Who are the persons?"
2. "What has led up to this situation? That is, what has happened in the past?"
3. "What is being thought? What is wanted? By whom?"
4. "What will happen? What will be done?" (McClelland et al., 1953, p. 98)

What determines whether a person tells a story with an achievement theme? The analyses provided in Table 8.1 provide the basis for the answer. Whether a story is indicative of achievement motivation depends on the strength of a person's dormant achievement motive and the instigating force of the TAT card (Tuerlinckx et al., 2002). If either motive strength or TAT card force increases, then the likelihood of an achievement story increases. An individual with a strong need to achieve, however, is more likely to respond with achievement imagery regardless of the force of the TAT card. Answers to the TAT-relevant questions are scored for achievement motivation based on references to competition with a standard of excellence, a unique accomplishment, or long-term involvement. For example, a protocol might state that the two women in lab coats have been working for many years (long-term involvement) developing a vaccine that has no negative side effects (high standard of excellence), which no one has ever accomplished before (unique accomplishment).

The TAT as a measure of the achievement motive has not escaped criticism. Entwisle (1972) challenged the reliability of the TAT pictures used to measure the need to achieve. The TAT has low reliability, which means that each picture is not measuring the need to achieve consistently. However, this is to be expected, since not every picture is equally forceful in evoking achievement imagery (Tuerlinckx et al., 2002). Also, test-retest reliability of the pictures is low, which means that from one week to the next, for example, individuals' need-to-achieve scores seem to fluctuate. This is an important point because the need to achieve is assumed to be a stable motive. Additional criticism comes from Klinger (1966), who questioned the validity of TAT measures. He found many studies showing no relationship between TAT measures and achievement-relevant behavior such as school grades. However, more recent analyses by Spangler (1992) indicate that a large number of studies found a positive correlation between TAT measures of achievement motivation and achievement behavior. Furthermore, many psychologists researching the area maintain that the TAT is a valid measure not only of the need to achieve but also of the need for affiliation and the need for power (Smith, 1992).

One solution to the problems of reliability and validity inherent in projective tests is to construct questionnaires that are structured and less open to interpretation. Objective tests serve that purpose. The *Achievement Motives Scale* is a short questionnaire, revised by Lang and Fries (2006), that was designed to measure both the motive to achieve success and the motive to avoid failure. For example, to what extent do you agree with the statements: "I am attracted to tasks, in which I can test my abilities" and "If I do not understand a problem immediately, I start to feel anxious" (p. 221)? The first statement measures the motive to achieve success while the second statement measures the motive to avoid failure. Several studies verified that the *Achievement Motives Scale* was a valid measure of the motive for success (Ms) and the fear of failure (Maf).

Factors That Affect Achievement Motivation

Individuals high in Ms or Maf show their differences in three important aspects of achievement behavior: difficulty of a task, probability of achieving a task, and persistence in trying to achieve a task.

Probability and Incentive Value of Task Success. Whether a person pursues an achievement task also depends on estimates of the probability of successfully achieving the task and on the incentive value of that success. In other words: "What are the chances I can do it, and what is the value of doing it?" The probability and incentive value of success can be portrayed as opposite sides of the same coin. Atkinson (1957/1983, 1974) assumed that the incentive value of a task is inversely related to how difficult it is to achieve. The greater the difficulty of succeeding at a task, the higher its incentive value. The difficulty of a task is based on a person's subjective estimate of the probability of successfully achieving it. To illustrate, imagine a course that has a reputation of being very easy; almost everyone earns an A. A student might rate the probability of earning an A to be very high, and so the incentive value of earning an A is quite low. Imagine a different course that has the reputation of being tough; very few students earn an A. A student might rate the subjective probability of earning an A to be very low, and so the incentive value of earning an A is quite high. Thus, in general as the subjective probability of success (Ps) decreases, the incentive value of success (Is) increases according to the formula:

$$Is = 1 - Ps$$

The incentive value of failure, however, is just the opposite. Imagine that you do not earn an A in a course where just about everyone else does. The negative incentive to avoid this outcome is quite high. However, it is not so bad if a student did not earn an A in the course where most other students also did not earn an A. The negative incentive to avoid this outcome is not so high. Thus, as the subjective probability of failure (Pf) increases, the negative incentive value failure ($-$If) decreases according to the formula:

$$-If = Pf$$

(The minus [$-$] sign means that failure [f] has negative incentive value.)

Consequently, whether an individual approaches or avoids an achievement task is based on both the probability and incentive value of either success or failure. Furthermore, Ms > Maf and Maf > Ms individuals are affected differently by these factors such that they act in opposite ways.

The outcomes of various research investigations show that tasks having a medium probability of success (around p = 0.50) are preferred by individuals for whom Ms > Maf but avoided by individuals for whom Maf > Ms. Atkinson and Litwin (1960) had male students stand any distance from the peg in a ring-toss game. It was assumed that intermediate distances should approximate a probability of 0.50 for successfully making a ring toss. The results indicated that Ms > Maf students selected the intermediate distances more than Maf > Ms students did. In another relevant investigation, Karabenick and Youseff (1968) examined learning performance in participants who were both low and high in Ms and Maf. Participants for whom Ms > Maf performed better on a learning task of intermediate difficulty (P = 0.50) than did participants for whom Maf > Ms. The Ms > Maf and Maf > Ms students, however, did not differ in their learning of a task that was either very easy or very difficult. Vocational choice or aspiration is also governed by the variables in achievement motivation theory. Mahone (1960) found that Ms > Maf students were more realistic in their vocational choices when they were based on their interests and abilities. Students with Maf > Ms, however, were more likely to make unrealistic choices. Morris (1966) examined the preferences for easy and difficult occupations of high school seniors as a function of the strength of their Ms and Maf. Seniors with high-achievement motivation preferred occupations at an intermediate probability of success; those with low-achievement motivation, however, preferred occupations that had either a low or high probability of success.

In validating the *Achievement Motives Scale*, Lang and Fries (2006) found that higher achievement motive scores were associated with setting high but realistic goals—that is, ones that were still achievable.

Achievement Motivation and Behavioral Persistence.   Success at a task, project, or job depends on how long an individual persists. Individuals high in achievement motivation are expected to be more persistent, which is more likely to lead to success. In an early investigation of the need to achieve, Lowell (1952) found that high-Ms participants solved more anagrams during a 20-minute period than did low-Ms participants. When using addition problems, Lowell (1952) again found that high-Ms participants solved more problems than low-Ms participants. Sherwood (1966) had male and female students take the TAT for achievement motivation early in the semester and then participate in achievement tasks near the end of the semester. The achievement tasks required solving anagrams and addition problems. The results for both the male and female students showed that their output of solutions increased with their need to achieve. In another study, Atkinson and Litwin (1960) timed how long students spent taking their final exam in a psychology course. Students for whom Ms > Maf spent more time working on their final exams and earned higher scores than did students for whom Maf > Ms.

Lang and Fries (2006), using the *Achievement Motives Scale,* also showed that motive for success scores correlated positively with goal performance, digit substitution, and reasoning-task performances, and most importantly with persistence. Fear of failure, however, correlated negatively with goal setting and reasoning-task performance. In addition, as expected, high fear of failure was associated with anxiety and worry.

An Achievement Goal Framework

Further research on the need to achieve (Ms) and to avoid failure (Maf) has led to the discovery that each need can be divided into different facets (Elliot & McGregor, 2001). The first facet concerns valence or value. Success has positive valence and its anticipation motivates approach behavior. For example, a student enrolls in a course with the expectation of passing—a positive outcome. By contrast, failure has a negative valence and its anticipation motivates avoidance behavior. A student may hesitate to enroll in a course in which failure or a low grade is anticipated—a negative outcome.

The second facet concerns goal achievement as representing a person's competence, which is based on absolute and personal standards, on the one hand, and relative standards, on the other. Absolute standards refer to whether a person has successfully achieved a task, such as passed a course or earned a driver's license. Personal standards refer to whether a person improved her performance on a task. As Elliot and McGregor (2001) note, personal standards may refer to acquiring new knowledge or skills, such as learning a computer application. Relative standards base success on comparing one's performance with others, as in the case of percentile ranks or one's position at the end of a contest, such as first, second, or third place. **Mastery goals** are ones that involve absolute or personal standards—that is, they involve the accomplishment, improvement, or greater understanding of a task. **Performance goals** are based on relative standards, which involve a comparison with others—that is, the level of goal achievement depends on surpassing or outperforming others.

Positive and negative valence combined with performance and mastery goals result in four separate goal categories: performance-approach, performance-avoidance, mastery-approach, and mastery-avoidance. The *Achievement Goal Questionnaire* in Table 8.3 provides a way of measuring each goal category (Elliott & McGregor, 2001). The questions indicate the meaning of each goal and the rating scale defines the measurement procedure. As the scale indicates, performance-approach goals imply a need to outperform other students while performance-avoidance goals imply a fear of doing worse than others. Mastery-approach goals indicate a desire for self-improvement by learning the course material while mastery-avoidance

TABLE 8.3   Achievement Goal Questionnaire

Indicate the extent each item is true of you on the scale below:

Not at all true of me = 1   2   3   4   5   6   7 = Very true of me

Performance-Approach

1. It is important for me to do better than other students.
2. It is important for me to do well compared to others in this class.
3. My goal in this class is to get a better grade than most of the other students.

Mastery-Avoidance

4. I worry that I may not learn all that I possibly could in this class.
5. Sometimes I'm afraid that I may not understand the content of this class as thoroughly as I'd like.
6. I am often concerned that I may not learn all that there is to learn in this class.

Mastery-Approach

7. I want to learn as much as possible from this class.
8. It is important for me to understand the content of this course as thoroughly as possible.
9. I desire to completely master the material presented in this class.

Performance-Avoidance

10. I just want to avoid doing poorly in this class.
11. My goal in this class is to avoid performing poorly.
12. My fear of performing poorly in this class is often what motivates me.

Note: To score yourself, find the mean of each of the three items under each category. To see how you scored, compare your scores against the following norms based on 190 students who filled out the scale. Performance-Approach mean = 4.82, Mastery-Avoidance mean = 3.89, Mastery-Approach mean = 5.52, Performance-Avoidance mean = 4.49 (table 2, p. 504).

Source: Copyright © 2001 by the American Psychological Association. Adapted with permission. The official citation that should be used in referencing this material is Elliot, J., & McGregor, H. A. (2001). A 2×2 achievement goal frame work. *Journal of Personality and Social Psychology, 80*, p. 504.

goals indicate fear of being incapable of learning the course material. The importance of both mastery and performance goals were associated with academic achievement: higher mastery-approach or performance-approach goals were associated with higher course grades and exam scores while higher performance-avoidance goals were associated with lower course grades and exam scores. Mastery-avoidance goals were not associated with academic performance (Elliot & McGregor, 2001; Finney et al., 2004).

Need for Power

Why would anyone want to be president of the United States, of your university, or of a university club? Is it for the money, the fame, or to satisfy some inner drive or need? Consider the following "get ahead or get along scenario": A worker is offered a promotion to manager that will require supervising former coworkers who are friends. By declining the promotion, she can remain in a situation that provides the opportunity for being with her friends. By accepting the promotion, however, she gains the opportunity to exercise authority. Would a person with a strong need for power accept this promotion?

Measuring Need for Power.　To exert influence over other people, to be in charge, to be noticed, and to have "high" status are all characteristics of the **power motive** (Winter, 1988, 1992). Look again at the picture of the two women in lab coats (see Figure 8.3). A story written in response to this resemblance of a TAT picture is scored for the power motive if the response contains phrases related to power, giving unsolicited help, or trying to influence or impress people. Another power motive characteristic is a reference that the person's actions produce a strong emotional response in others. A character in the story might perform an action that produces gratitude on the part of the helped individual. Finally, a power motive involves a concern with reputation or image. For example, the women in the TAT picture might be described as having graduated from a top medical school and are now working for a well-known drug company (Veroff, 1992; Winter, 1992).

Characteristics of Need for Power.　There are various ways people satisfy their need for power (Winter, 1988, 1992). One way is to place themselves in legitimate positions of power. Both men and women with a high need for power are more likely to be office holders or be in positions to make decisions affecting others. As students, they are more likely to be residence hall counselors or student government officers. A high power motive is associated with entering power-related careers, such as being teachers, business executives, mental health workers, psychologists, and journalists. The power motive is satisfied in these occupations because the person has the legitimate right and duty to direct the behavior of the people she is in contact with. Individuals with a moderate to high power motive are more likely to succeed as managers and executives of large corporations, especially when this motive is coupled with a low affiliation motive (McClelland & Boyatzis, 1982). Since power means being visible to others, individuals with a high need for power strive to do so. Students with a high power need are more likely to write letters to the editor of the school newspaper and to put their names on their residences. Another demonstration of a high power motive is owning trappings of power, such as high-tech stereo equipment, expensive wines, elite credit cards, fancy cars, or valuable pictures or wall hangings. Power-motivated women, more than men, are interested in using clothing as a show of power (Winter, 1988, 1992). Finally, men and women with a high need for power place greater importance on status and wealth than do those with a low need for power (Parker & Chusmir, 1991).

　　Individuals high in power motivation are also more likely to have autobiographical memories of peak experiences that involve power themes (McAdams, 1982). They like to take extreme risks, provided this occurs in situations where they can draw attention to themselves (McClelland & Watson, 1973). People with a high power motive are more likely to exploit members of the opposite sex and to drink, gamble, and use drugs (Winter, 1988). College-educated men with a high power motivation, compared to men with a low power motivation, have wives who are less likely to have professional careers of their own (Winter et al., 1977).

Expressing Need for Power.　Psychological needs may be interpreted as categories of incentives. Thus, a person who seemingly has a need for power is really one who prefers power-related incentives. If this is the case, then individuals with a need for power should enter and remain in situations that provide those incentives. Jenkins (1994) investigated this possibility in a longitudinal study tracking the career development of women who varied in need for power. Power motive scores were collected on these women when they were college seniors and then correlated with various aspects of their professional careers at age 35. Several of Jenkins's findings showed that women with a high need for power were sensitive to situations that allowed for expression of their power motives. First, they were more likely to have entered and remained in power-relevant careers (teacher, psychotherapist, business executive, journalist) than women with a low need for power. Second, their degree of job satisfaction was related to the opportunity to exercise interpersonal power. Third, they were more likely to progress professionally provided they were in power-relevant jobs. When in non-power-relevant jobs, however, professional progress seemed absent. A conclusion of this study is that people with various needs are sensitive to the incentives that satisfy those needs. Consequently, we should not be surprised that they enter situations or professions that satisfy their needs. In the "get ahead or get along" scenario, a person with a high need for power probably would accept the promotion to manager.

Need for Cognition

A more recently postulated need resembling Murray's (1938) need for understanding is the **need for cognition** (Cacioppo & Petty, 1982; Cohen et al., 1955). This has been defined as "a need to structure relevant situations in meaningful, integrated ways. It is a need to understand and make reasonable the experiential world" (Cohen et al., 1955, p. 291). In an early demonstration of the validity of this need, Cohen and associates (1955) measured the need for cognition in students and then had them read either a structured or ambiguous story about a person's interview with a potential employer. Students then rated the story for interest, liking, and understanding in addition to their effort in trying to understand it. Those with a high need for cognition rated the ambiguous story as less interesting and enjoyable than the structured story. Students with a medium or low need for cognition, however, did not differ in their ratings of the stories (Cohen et al., 1955). Using this research as a foundation, Cacioppo and Petty (1982) felt that a more precise measure of the need for cognition was necessary. Thus, they developed the *Need for Cognition Scale*, which contains statements measuring a person's enjoyment in thinking and solving complex problems (Cacioppo et al., 1996). For example, to what extent does a person enjoy thinking abstractly, coming up with new solutions to problems, putting forth mental effort, or watching educational programs?

A high need for cognition describes individuals who are disposed to engage in and enjoy analytical thinking. Thus, these individuals should pay closer attention to attitude change messages. To illustrate, imagine a situation in which you are asked to read and evaluate the proposal that "seniors be required to pass a comprehensive exam in their major as a requirement for graduation" (Cacioppo et al., 1983, p. 807). This proposal was presented to students as an editorial written by a journalism student. One version presented a weak set of arguments, and the other version a strong set of arguments. Students either low or high in the need for cognition read either the weak or strong editorial version and evaluated it for effectiveness, liking, and convincingness. The students also rated themselves for how much cognitive effort they put into evaluating the editorial and were asked to recall as many arguments as they could remember. The results showed that students with a high need for cognition were affected more by the strength of the editorial than those with a low need for cognition. They evaluated the strong argument more positively and the weak argument more negatively. They also reported expending more effort thinking about the editorial and recalled more messages than did students with a low need for cognition.

Need for cognition is also associated with **attitude polarization,** which means that as a result of thinking, favorable attitudes become more favorable and unfavorable attitudes become more unfavorable (Tesser, 1978). For example, if you are mildly in favor of comprehensive exams, then thinking about them makes you even more favorable toward them. However, if you have a mildly unfavorable attitude toward comprehensive exams, then thinking about them will make your attitude even more so. Leone (1994) reasoned that people low in the need for cognition would be more subject to attitude polarization, since they do not especially enjoy thinking. They are less likely to consider both the pros and cons of an issue. Instead they follow the easiest path and think only about information that is already consistent with their initial attitude, thereby strengthening their beliefs. For example, they might only think about the con side of comprehensive exams and develop an even more negative attitude toward them. However, people high in the need for cognition, because they enjoy thinking about an issue, would more likely weigh additional pros and cons about an issue. These considerations are more likely to lead to a balancing out, whereby they would not change their initial attitude on this subject. Leone gave participants the *Need for Cognition Scale* and then divided them into two groups: one low and the other high in the need for cognition. Next, participants rated the extent they agreed or disagreed with a series of issues. Afterward they were asked to think about those issues on which they had only mildly agreed or disagreed. As predicted, polarization was greater for participants low in need for cognition than for those high in the need for cognition.

Feelings of boredom also vary with need for cognition. Watt and Blanchard (1994) have shown that participants low in need for cognition are more susceptible to boredom than those high in need for cognition. The reason is that people high in need for cognition enjoy thinking. They are more likely to rely on their own internal stimulation and therefore are less likely to become bored.

➤ The *Need for Cognition Scale* is available at http://fp.dl.kent.edu/fcubed/modules/modules/learningstyles/need%20for%20cognition.html

Self-Esteem, Relatedness, Autonomy, and Competence

As described previously, psychological needs do not have identifiable body or brain correlates. The validity of psychological needs is based on the mental impressions they make on individuals. In an attempt to determine the validity of ten postulated psychological needs, Sheldon and coresearchers (2001) instructed their participants to "bring to mind the *single most personally satisfying event* that you experienced" (p. 327). Their hypothesis was that gratifying an important psychological need is very satisfying, just like eating a delicious meal when hungry is very satisfying. Participants rated their satisfying events on need-relevant dimensions with a scale that ranged from 1 (not at all) to 5 (very much). For instance, if hunger were a psychological need, then some statements about eating that a participant might rate are:

1. During this event [eating] I felt that my body was getting just what it needed.
2. During this event [eating] I felt intense physical pleasure and enjoyment.

The strength by which a statement is endorsed reflects the strength of the psychological need. Participants also compared all psychological needs with one another in order to determine

TABLE 8.4   Psychological Needs and Their Associated Feelings

Psychological Need	Characteristic Feeling of Each Psychological Need
Self-esteem	You are a worthy person who is as good as anyone else rather than feeling like a "loser."
Relatedness	You have regular intimate contact with people who care about you rather than feeling lonely and uncared for.
Autonomy	You are the cause of your own actions rather than feeling that external forces or pressures are the cause of your actions.
Competence	You are very capable and effective in your actions rather than feeling incompetent or ineffective.

Source: Adapted from "What Is Satisfying about Satisfying Events? Testing 10 Candidate Psychological Needs" by K. M. Sheldon et al., 2001, *Journal of Personality and Social Psychology, 80*, appendix, p. 339.

the strength of each need. The outcome of these comparisons indicated that the four strongest psychological needs were self-esteem, relatedness, autonomy, and competence. Table 8.4 provides a definition of each need, based on the feelings each produces (Sheldon et al., 2001).

These four psychological needs have several implications for motivation. First, they are a main source of internal motivation. Second, the amount of pleasure and satisfaction attained from fulfilling a need depends on need intensity. More intense needs provide more fulfillment and satisfaction than less intense needs. Thus, satisfying their esteem, relatedness, autonomy, and competence needs should provide people a great amount of satisfaction. Third, each psychological need provides its own unique feeling of satisfaction when it is fulfilled, much like eating provides a unique pleasurable experience (see Table 8.4). Fourth, the need-relevant experiences were salient and easy for individuals to bring to mind. This finding implies that these needs are also prominent in people's lives. Fifth, the opportunity to fulfill a psychological need is related to feelings of positive affect. Positive mood is one consequence of consistently being able to satisfy psychological needs.

Need for Affiliation and Intimacy

The work by Sheldon and coresearchers (2001) and Reis and coresearchers (2000) verified that the need for relatedness is one of the top psychological needs. This need has also been referred to as the need for affiliation and belonging and has received extensive attention from psychologists beginning with Murray (1938, see Table 2.2) and Maslow (1970, see Table 8.2). The need for affiliation is also captured in the "get ahead or get along" scenario described previously. In this case, would a person who has a strong need for affiliation accept or decline the promotion?

Measurement and Characteristics of Need for Affiliation.   Imagine writing stories in response to several TAT pictures. Your story is scored according to its indication of having a social relationship, desiring a relationship, or feeling bad following the termination of a social relationship. Such imagery reflects a **need for affiliation,** which refers to the motive to establish, maintain, or restore positive social relationships with other individuals or groups (McClelland & Koestner, 1992). Like other psychological needs, the need for affiliation is latent until relevant environmental conditions arouse it, such as the presence or availability of other individuals. Shipley and Veroff (1952) aroused the affiliation motive in college fraternity members by having each member stand up in a group gathering and then be rated by his fellow members on various personality characteristics. A control group was questioned about food preferences, which was assumed not to arouse the affiliation motive. Stories written in response to TAT pictures depicting people in various poses contained a greater number of affiliation statements from fraternity members in whom the affiliation motive had been aroused compared to the control group. Affiliation statements contained references to loneliness, separation, rejection, or ways of preserving social relationships.

People with a need for affiliation do what the need suggests: they affiliate in order to satisfy that need. Students with a high need for affiliation work harder and receive higher grades in classes taught by teachers who call students by their names and take a personal interest in them (McKeachie et al., 1966). Presumably such students will then strive harder to earn good grades to please and affiliate with the teacher and with other students. Those with a high need for affiliation are better able to recognize photographs of faces that have been presented below the recognition threshold (Atkinson & Walker, 1956). They also tend to make more personal telephone calls and write more letters to friends and relatives compared to individuals with a low need for affiliation (Lansing & Heyns, 1959). In addition, people with a high need for affiliation prefer to work on a task with incompetent friends over competent strangers (French, 1956). In the "get ahead or get along" scenario, a person with a need for affiliation would probably turn down the promotion so as to remain with friends.

Intimacy Motive.   The affiliation motive may reflect a fear of rejection rather than a striving to attain positive social interactions (McClelland, 1985). For instance, individuals high in the affiliation motive fear disapproval and are anxious about their social relationships. Consequently, they seek others for continual reassurance, which reduces their popularity (McClelland, 1985). Instead of focusing on the negative aspects of affiliation or fear of rejection, McAdams (1992a) postulated an **intimacy motive** to emphasize the positive feelings that exist between the individuals in a social relationship. This motive refers to a "readiness for experiences of warm, close, and communicative interactions with other persons" (McAdams, 1992a, p. 224). McAdams (1980) presented TAT pictures of actual intimate situations, such as a celebration initiating new members into fraternities or sororities, people at a large dance party, or couples who reported being in love. Participants' stories about the TAT pictures were scored for the intimacy motive if they included themes about positive relationships or dialogue between individuals. The intimacy motive might concern two people sharing an encounter that involved feelings of love, friendship, happiness, or peace or tender behavior. In their dialogue, the individuals may sit and talk, confide in one another, or have a friendly argument (McAdams, 1992b).

Differences in the intimacy motive among individuals show up in terms of differences in their social behavior. McAdams and Constantian (1983) contacted students seven times a day for a week using a beeper. Each time the students recorded what they were thinking and doing. They also rated their degree of affect in connection with other people, such as being alert, carefree, content, friendly, happy, and sociable. Students with a high intimacy motive thought more about other people, had a greater number of conversations, and were more likely to be writing letters. As shown in Figure 8.4, students with a high intimacy motive experienced

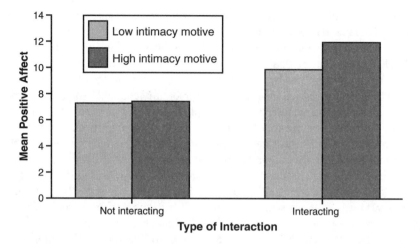

FIGURE 8.4   Intimacy Motive and Social Interaction. During a social interaction, positive affect ratings were higher for students with a high intimacy motive compared to students with a low intimacy motive. There were no differences in mean affect scores during nonsocial interactions.

Source: Adapted from "Intimacy and Affiliation Motives in Daily Living" by D. P. McAdams and C. A. Constantian, 1983, *Journal of Personality and Social Psychology, 45,* table 1, p. 857.

greater positive affect during their social interactions compared to those with a low intimacy motive. It is important to notice also that when not interacting with others, low and high intimacy motive students did not differ in their affective feelings. Apparently, people with a high intimacy motive enjoy their social interactions more than people with a low intimacy motive. In a second study, McAdams and associates (1984) had university students describe recent 15- to 20-minute-long interactions with friends. Their findings showed that higher intimacy motivation was associated with a greater frequency of interactions with friends, greater levels of self-disclosure, and higher levels of listening during conversations.

Self-Determination Theory

As described earlier, physiological needs imply a deficit between a fixed set point for a substance and the actual amount, such as a need for vitamin C or iron. Similarly, psychological needs are also indicative of a lack or deficit in the opportunity to reach a psychological set point. However, for psychological needs the set point may not be static but is marked by growth and development, especially for needs of autonomy, competence, and relatedness. Furthermore, if unsatisfied, these needs produce conditions akin to diseases, such as impaired well-being and stunted psychological growth (Deci & Ryan, 2000).

In order to account for these suppositions, psychological need theories view the motivation for behavior as coming from within, as if an individual is the source, cause, or origin of his or her own behavior. This view is the claim of **self-determination theory,** which holds that psychological needs are innate, universal, and serve as the basis for a variety of experiential activities (Deci & Ryan, 2000). The motivation for these activities is autonomous, freely chosen, and does not stem from external demands. In other words, they are self-determined. Self-determination theory is not concerned with varying amounts of each need nor in the relationship between the amount of need deficit and the corresponding motivational strength. However, the satisfaction of autonomy, competence, and relatedness needs are necessary for good psychological health.

> ➤ A website devoted to self-determination theory is at http://www.psych.rochester.edu/SDT/index.html. Click on *questionnaires* to access the *Basic Psychological Needs Scale* (BPNS), which measures the needs of autonomy, competence, and relatedness.

Consequences of Unfulfilled Needs. What is the evidence that unfulfilled needs are associated with impaired psychological health? Reis and coresearchers (2000) examined whether increased satisfaction of the needs of autonomy, competence, and relatedness during daily activities was associated with increased daily well-being. Satisfaction of the need for autonomy was analyzed from ratings that concerned whether an activity was done out of free choice or was imposed on the individual by external factors. Satisfaction of the need for competence was based on how capable a person felt in doing an activity. Fulfillment of the need for relatedness came from analyzing social interactions during the day. The extent a person felt "close and connected" to others during social interactions indexed the degree of need satisfaction. How do these measures of need satisfaction relate to well-being? To answer this question, students were asked to rate their positive affect (happy, fun), negative affect (depressed, worried), and vitality (feel alive, energized). They also filled out a symptom checklist about ailments like a runny nose, breathing difficulties, and soreness. In general, the results supported the hypothesis that as need satisfaction increased, indicators of well-being also increased. Favorable changes in the satisfaction of autonomy and competence needs were accompanied by favorable changes in well-being. Increases in the satisfaction of the relatedness need were associated with increases in positive affect and vitality but unassociated with changes in negative affect and symptoms.

Balanced Psychological Needs. Nutritional advice is often in the form of "eat a balanced diet." Too much of one nutrient will not compensate for too little of another. The same idea applies to the satisfaction of the needs for autonomy, competence, and relatedness. Does a balance among the satisfaction of psychological needs result in greater well-being beyond that provided by the average level of satisfaction? This question refers to the **balance hypothesis,** which was examined in several studies by Sheldon and Niemiec (2006). In one investigation (study 2), participants were evaluated several times during the semester to the extent their basic needs were satisfied. Balance was based on calculating the difference between pairs of needs and summing the absolute values. Higher scores indicated a greater imbalance in satisfaction among the three needs. Participants' well-being was measured at the end of the semester with two scales. One was the *Positive and Negative Affect Schedule* (Chapter 13), which measures two types of affect. Positive affect refers to the extent a person feels active, enthusiastic, and strong while negative affect refers to the extent a person feels afraid, irritable, or upset. The second scale was the *Satisfaction with Life Scale,* which involves such questions as "I am satisfied with my life." The scores from both scales were combined to form an overall well-being score.

> ➤ The *Satisfaction with Life Scale* is available at http://www.psych.uiuc.edu/~ediener

The results showed that increases in overall well-being were associated with increases in the satisfaction of the needs for autonomy, competence, and relatedness. Furthermore, as the degree of balance in need satisfaction increased, subjective well-being also increased. This finding supported the balance hypothesis. The association between greater balance and subjective well-being encourages varied experiences. It is better to seek satisfaction in all domains of autonomy, competence, and relatedness rather than concentrating on one need while ignoring others.

Section Recap

This section described seven psychological needs or motives: achievement, power, cognition, esteem, autonomy, competence, and relatedness (affiliation, belonging). Achievement motivation is guided by two internal sources of motivation: the *need to achieve,* or motive for success, and the *motive to avoid failure.* The need to achieve is characterized by wanting to do things well, being persistent, and having a high standard of excellence. In contrast, the motive to avoid failure is characterized by fear and anxiety about failing at a task. Achievement motivation theory has been expanded to include additional determinants of achievement behavior, such as the probability of success and failure and the incentive value of success and failure.

Achievement motivation theory has been elaborated into a framework that postulates two aspects of goals: valence and achievement. Positive valence refers to anticipated success, which is a good outcome, while negative valence refers to anticipated failure, which is a bad outcome. People are motivated to achieve success and to avoid failure. Achievement motivation involves *mastery goals,* which refer to absolute standards of accomplishment or improvement, and *performance goals,* which refer to comparing one's achievements to those of others. The combination of valence and achievement results in four categories of goals: performance-approach, performance-avoidance, mastery-approach, and mastery-avoidance.

To show that psychological needs motivate behavior, it is first necessary to independently measure the existence and intensity of a need. Next, it is necessary to show that the measured intensity of the need correlates with behavior motivated to satisfy that need. Both projective and objective tests exist for this purpose. In *projective tests* a person verbally responds to an unstructured stimulus in a manner that is presumably consistent with her psychological needs. One type of projective test is the TAT, which consists of a series of pictures of people in ambiguous settings. Stories written in response to these tests have been scored for the need to achieve as well as the need for affiliation (belonging) and power. An example of an objective test is the *Achievement Motives Scale* which was designed to measure the motive for success and the motive to avoid failure.

The *power motive* is the wish to influence the lives of other individuals, to be in command, to have high status, and to be noticed. People with a power motive are more likely to be successful in occupations that allow for the legitimate exercise of power. The *need for cognition* refers to a desire to understand one's experiences and things in the world through thinking. The need for cognition has an effect on *attitude polarization*, which means that a person's attitudes become more extreme after he has thought about them. People with a high need for cognition show less attitude polarization, because in thinking about an issue they are more likely to consider both the positive and negative aspects of a proposal.

Four important sources of internal motivation are the psychological needs of self-esteem (self-worth), autonomy (self-determination), competence (capability and effectiveness), and relatedness (affiliation, belonging). Each need provides its own unique feeling of satisfaction. Their fulfillment is linked to positive affect and well-being. Relatedness, or the *need for affiliation*, is the desire to initiate, maintain, and restore a positive social relationship with another person or group. A specific aspect of affiliation involves the *intimacy motive,* which emphasizes the shared positive feelings between two individuals.

Self-determination theory views individuals as the source, cause, or origin of their own freely chosen behavior, which is necessary for the satisfaction of autonomy, competence, and relatedness needs. The satisfaction of these three needs is necessary for good psychological health. According to the *balance hypothesis*, greater equality in the level of satisfaction among these three needs is associated with better psychological health.

Motivation without Awareness

Are people aware that psychological needs motivate their behavior? Can psychological needs be activated without an individual being aware of it? According to Freud's theory about the workings of the unconscious, this is indeed possible (see Chapter 2). For example, people can laugh at jokes about sex or aggression without being aware that they are satisfying associated instinctual impulses.

The purpose of this section is to describe the role of awareness in motivation and a current elaboration of how this may be possible according to the idea of reflexology and the auto-motive hypothesis.

Reflexology

According to the ancient Roman poet Ovid (43 B.C.–A.D. 17), "The cause is hidden but the effect is known." This statement could be interpreted to mean that humans may not be aware of some of the events that motivate their behavior. For instance, in not being aware of the motivational source, a person may consider thoughts or intentions to be responsible for her behavior. According to the Russian physiologist Ivan Sechenov (1863/1965), this would be an error. Sechenov reasoned that stimulation from an external stimulus may produce thought and behavior simultaneously or may produce thought with behavior being inhibited. These joint occurrences lead to the belief that thought and behavior are two separate entities and that one causes the other, especially when the source of stimulation is unknown. Sechenov's view is called **reflexology** and assumes that all human action, both involuntary and voluntary, is reflexive in nature—that is, in response to external stimulation and not in response to thought or intention. Although humans are consciously aware of the link between thought and behavior, they may be unaware of the original stimulus that triggered thought. Thus, the motive available in consciousness is given as the reason for behavior, while in actuality it may be an external event that was responsible (Nisbett & Wilson, 1977).

Auto-Motive Hypothesis

It is possible that individuals may not always be aware that a particular need has been activated or that they have been sensitized to a certain class of incentives. It may be as Freud believed, namely that an individual is unaware of the psychological need that evoked his behavior (Uleman 1987; Vollmer, 1993). When an individual is asked the reason for his behavior, he might reply, "I am not certain why I did that." Furthermore, in addition to not being aware of the stimulus that activates a motive, a person may also be unaware that his behavior is an attempt to satisfy that motive. Bargh (1990) considers these possibilities in his **auto-motive hypothesis,** which describes the nonconscious activation of motives and intentions by environmental stimuli and the subsequent effect of those motives and intentions on behavior. First, environmental stimuli activate mental representations of motives and goals. This activation is possible because the stimuli and their mental representations have been frequently associated together in the past. Second, these motives and goals reside in the preconscious, and the person is not aware of them, since they have not yet captured the attention of the conscious. Third, when activated these motives and goals arouse behavioral strategies or plans designed to satisfy them. Finally, in the appropriate context these strategies or plans then manifest themselves as behavior in an environment that allows for the satisfaction of a motive or the achievement of a goal.

Priming Achievement Behavior.   Research on nonconscious motivation involves activating a motive, without a person's awareness, to determine if that motive affects behavior. In one demonstration, Bargh and coresearchers (2001) primed participants without their awareness for a high-performance goal—that is, a goal or motive to do well on a puzzle task. To prime this goal, participants worked on a word-search puzzle that required finding words embedded in a 10×10 matrix of letters. Words designed to prime a high-performance goal included *win, compete, succeed, strive, attain, achieve,* and *master*. When participants found these words, it was assumed that this would prime a high-performance motive. In the neutral prime control condition, participants solved a word-search puzzle that contained words such as *ranch, carpet, river, shampoo, robin, hat,* and *window*. A high-performance motive was assumed not to be activated in this condition. After completing one of these initial puzzles, participants were instructed to work on three additional puzzles that contained words related to foods, bugs, and colors. Performance on these puzzles during a 10-minute period served to measure the different effects produced by the prior high-performance versus neutral priming procedures. The results showed that participants primed for a high-performance goal discovered significantly more solution words than did the neutrally primed participants. Furthermore, in a postexperimental debriefing, no participant reported being aware of the relationship between the priming nature of the first puzzle and performance on the second set of puzzles. These results imply that a nonconsciously primed high-performance goal elevates achievement performance, at least in the case of puzzle-solving behavior.

Priming an Action.   Further evidence for Bargh's (1990) auto-motive hypothesis comes from experimental procedures that nonconsciously activate motives that are relevant for social behavior (Bargh et al., 1996). In their first experiment, Bargh and associates (1996) primed participants to be either rude, polite, or neither in a social setting. Priming of the motive was accomplished by asking participants to construct a grammatically correct sentence from a list of five randomly presented words. To prime the rude motive, synonyms and words implying rudeness were employed. To prime the polite motive, synonyms for politeness were used. Although participants were aware of creating the sentences, they were not aware that this was priming a motive to be either rude or polite. The participants were told that when finished with the sentence task, they were to walk to another room to find the experimenter so that they could complete another experiment. Now, suppose you are the participant and you find the experimenter engaged in conversation with another person. How long will you wait before interrupting so that you can receive instructions about what to do next? Will how soon you interrupt depend on whether you have been primed with the

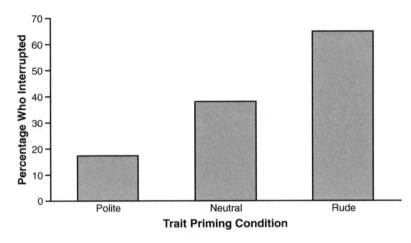

FIGURE 8.5   Priming the Motive and Behavior. Percentage of participants who interrupted the experimenter within the 10-minute period was highest among students primed with the rude motive condition.

Source: From "Automaticity of Social Behavior" by J. A. Bargh et al., 1996, *Journal of Personality and Social Psychology, 71*, experiment 1, figure 1, p. 235. Copyright 1996 by American Psychological Association. Reprinted by permission.

rude or polite motive? Figure 8.5 shows that participants who had a motive for rudeness activated were most likely to interrupt, while participants who had a motive for politeness activated were least likely to interrupt. Furthermore, of those who interrupted, rude participants were more likely to interrupt sooner, while polite participants waited longer.

In a second experiment, Bargh and associates (1996) primed a stereotype of the elderly and assumed that participants would act in accordance with characteristics of that stereotype. The scrambled sentence task primed an elderly stereotype by using such words as *worried, Florida, old, lonely*, and *gray*. A control group was primed with a set of neutral words. Following the task, participants were debriefed, thanked for their participation, and monitored for how fast they walked away. The hypothesis was that participants with the activated stereotype of the elderly would walk away more slowly than participants in the control group, since presumably slow walking is a trait of the elderly. The results supported the hypothesis. Participants primed for the elderly stereotype took longer to walk down a corridor than participants in the neutral primed condition. In other words, participants acted in accordance with the stereotypic trait that had been activated without their awareness.

Imperceptive Effects of Mimicry.   Psychologists have long been aware of people's motivation to associate with others as formulated in the need for affiliation, relatedness, and the intimacy motive. James (1890/1950) postulated a love instinct, Murray (1938) postulated a need for affiliation, and Maslow (1970) did the same for the need to belong. A way to satisfy those needs and be liked by others may be to mimic the individuals with whom one is interacting. Is a person aware of being mimicked? And does mimicry actually lead to greater liking and to smoother and more pleasant social interactions? To test this possibility, Chartrand and Bargh (1999) matched people's behavior, with the use of mimicry, to determine if it increased liking and the feeling that their interaction went smoothly. In their experiment two participants (one was actually a confederate of the experimenters) described what they saw in a series of photographs. The alleged purpose of this task was to evaluate the photographs for their possible use in a *Thematic Apperception Test*. During the mimic condition, the confederate mimicked the participant's mannerisms, while in the control condition, the confederate acted in a neutral fashion with regard to the participant. After the photograph evaluation task, participants were asked how likeable was the other participant (the confederate) and how smooth was their interaction with him. Mimicked participants liked the confederate more than control participants. Mimicked participants also rated the interaction as going more smoothly than did control participants. Were participants aware that being mimicked led to higher ratings about the confederate? The answer to this question seems to be "no." When questioned, participants reported not being aware of being mimicked by the confederate. Thus, being mimicked without awareness increased participants' liking of the confederate and increased the apparent smoothness of social interaction.

Section Recap

Reflexology is the idea that external stimulation is responsible for all motivated action, both involuntary and voluntary, regardless of whether individuals are aware of the source of motivation. Current research on the awareness of motivation has led to the formulation of the *auto-motive hypothesis*. Accordingly, environmental stimuli can activate motives and goals, accompanying strategies, and subsequent behaviors to satisfy them. This all happens without the person's awareness. Research has shown that when a motive is activated in this manner, participants behave in a manner consistent with that motive. The nonconscious activation of motives has been shown to affect the behavior of achieving a high-performance goal, of social interactions, and mimicry.

ACTIVITIES

1. *Hierarchy of Needs.* Fill out Lester's *Need Satisfaction Inventory* in Table 8.2 of this chapter. Was your level of satisfaction in agreement with Maslow's theory—that is, highest satisfaction for physiological needs and lowest satisfaction for self-actualization needs? Do you think your results would be affected by any of the following:

   a. You are on a tight budget so you cannot meet some of your physiological needs easily.
   b. The campus is a place to make new friends and lifelong partners, thereby easily satisfying your need for belonging. (So far, during my teaching career three couples met in my classes and married.)
   c. The four years you spend at the university are filled with feedback about progress toward your goals, thereby contributing to

   meeting your need for self-esteem and self-actualization.

   Do you think your other-sex counterpart has the same level of satisfaction of the need for safety as you?

2. *Achievement Motivation.* In our society we often emphasize intelligence over achievement motivation as a predictor for success. For example, to apply to the university you must take the SAT; to apply to graduate school, the GRE; and law, business, and medical schools also have their aptitude tests. Yet you probably know people who are smart but not motivated and people who are not smart but very motivated. Do you think it would be worth the effort to construct a test like the SAT that would measure achievement motivation, which could then be used to

predict success in college? Would it even be possible? Do you think your high school grades partly reflect your achievement motivation?

3. *Affiliation or Relatedness Motive versus Power Motive.* The phrase "get ahead or get along" pits the need for power (get ahead) against the need for affiliation or intimacy (get along). Do you think to be successful at your profession you will have to exercise your need for power at the expense of your need for affiliation or intimacy? Or can you satisfy those needs in different domains of your life?

4. *Need for Cognition.* Are some people thinkers and others doers? Do thinkers go on to the university, while doers go to vocational schools or apprentice on the job? Are thinkers philosophy and art majors and doers accounting and physical education majors? How would you classify yourself?

9 Personality and Self in Motivation

Fierce eagles do not produce timorous doves.

—*Horace, 13 B.C.*

With a good heredity, nature deals you a fine hand at cards; and with a good environment, you learn to play the hand well.

—*Walter C. Alvarez, M.D.*

■ Different things motivate different people. The last chapter showed that different motivators could be organized according to various psychological needs. This chapter examines whether different motivators can be grouped according to people's personalities. Is it possible that people with similar personality traits are alike in their motives and in their preferred incentives? This chapter presents possible answers to this and the following questions:

1. What is the difference between temperament and personality?

2. Are personality traits real?

3. How do personality traits affect a person's reaction, selection, and manipulation of a situation?

4. Do personality traits influence the manner in which psychological needs are satisfied?

5. Can a person's concept of herself serve as a source of motivation?

Personality Associated with Motivation

After being separated since infancy for 39 years, identical twins Jim Springer and Jim Lewis were reunited. Even though they were adopted and reared by different families, there were some uncanny similarities between the twins. Each had been married twice, had a son named James, and had a dog named Toy during childhood. In regards to personal habits, both smoked and drank lite beer, bit their fingernails, and vacationed in the same beach area in Florida. Both twins had worked part time as sheriffs, owned light blue Chevrolets, and wrote love notes to their wives (Segal, 1999, pp. 116–118). How can two individuals reared in different environments be so similar? Is it due to chance or due to their similar temperaments and personalities, which were shaped by their genes?

The purpose of this section is to show that temperament and personality traits are real and that they are a source of motivation. These sources motivate people to react differently to the same situations and also to seek out or avoid different situations.

Temperament, Personality, and Behavior

People differ in both temperament and personality, and these differences have an impact on what motivates them. Were you active and outgoing as a child, or were you quiet and shy? To what extent are you the same or different today? **Temperament** refers to consistent individual differences in emotionality and is a result of genetically inherited characteristics. **Personality** is a consistent way of behaving as a result of the interaction between temperament characteristics and social experience. Although both imply long-term behavior dispositions, there are distinctions between them (Strelau, 1985, 1987). First, hereditary and biological factors play more of a role in determining temperament, whereas social factors are involved in determining personality. Temperament manifests itself earlier in childhood, while personality develops later. Temperament can refer to behavior differences, for example, among different breeds of dogs, as Gosling and John (1999) suggest. These researchers also noted differences in personality within the same breed. Finally, temperament is more or less fixed, while personality is modifiable by experience. Insight into temperament can be gained by considering different breeds of dogs. For example, a basset hound is slow and easygoing, whereas a poodle is more active. A collie is timid, while a Scottish terrier tends to be feisty (Mahut, 1958). Although a trainer may be able to alter the temperament of an individual dog by varying its experience, that dog will still behave much like its breed. Perhaps a trainer can enliven the temperament of a basset hound to be more like a poodle. Yet a basset hound will still retain most of the behavioral characteristics of its breed.

Fearfulness and sociability are two frequently studied temperament traits in dogs (Jones & Gosling, 2005). Fearfulness characterizes a dog's approach or withdrawal behavior to novel stimuli or strangers. It is also reflected in general activity, wariness, startle reactions to loud sounds, and heart rate changes. Fearful dogs have also been labeled as shy. Sociability can be contrasted with aloofness. Sociable dogs tend to show an interest in people and other dogs as opposed to a lack of interest. It is associated with initiating friendly interactions, affection, attention seeking, and being more amenable to obedience training. Sociability may be parallel to extraversion in humans.

Personality Traits as Categories or Causes of Behavior

Do people show consistency in their behavior from one time to the next or from one situation to the other? **Personality traits** refer to the consistency in a specific set of behaviors across time and across relevant situations. A trait is also defined by the relationship among different behavioral habits. The trait of sociability, for example, consists of such behaviors as going to parties, liking to talk, preferring listening to reading, and being bored when alone (Eysenck, 1990). Sociability indicates that a person shows these behavioral characteristics from one time to the next and from one social situation to the other.

Personality traits help answer two important questions. First, why do people react differently to the same situation? Second, why do people differ in the situations they approach or avoid? Consider the physical trait of being left-handed versus right-handed. Left-handed individuals find it more awkward to take notes sitting in classroom desk chairs designed for right-handed people, to swing golf clubs designed for right-handers, and to shift a manual transmission. They are also more likely to be bumped by the right-handed individual when seated in the middle of a crowded dinner table. In all of these situations, left-handed individuals might feel less comfortable and efficient than right-handed persons. And if given a choice, a left-handed person might prefer a left-handed desk chair or golf clubs, shifting a gearshift with his left hand, and sitting on the far left of the dinner table.

Being left- or right-handed illustrates that differences between people are associated with differences in their reaction to and preferences for different situations. Similarly, people with different personality traits also react to situations differently and prefer to be in different situations. For example, the extravert may look forward to a large party, while anticipation of a party may make the introvert anxious. The high-sensation seeker may explore a new restaurant in town, while the low-sensation seeker will stay with her familiar eating place. However, to use personality traits as an explanation of why people differ in what motivates them, some assumptions are necessary. Are traits categories of behavior only, or can they also serve as causes of behavior? Revelle (1987), and John and Robins (1993) describe traits as categories of behavior and also as causes of behavior. People can be categorized as left- or right-handed, but handedness also "causes" people to prefer different situations.

Personality Traits for Motivation

Five-Factor Model.   This chapter examines several personality dimensions for their capacity to motivate behavior. One set of critical dimensions comes from the **five-factor model** of personality: *openness, conscientiousness, extraversion, agreeableness,* and *neuroticism* (John, 1989, 1990a, 1990b; McCrae, 1989; McCrae & Costa, 1985, 1987). These five factors spell the acronym OCEAN, which helps to remember the factors. Each factor can be considered a dimension, which ranges from low to high. Table 9.1 lists some trait descriptors that help define each end of the five personality dimensions (John, 1989). Extraversion and neuroticism have been studied the most extensively in their relationship to motivation. They also comprise two of three major factors in Eysenck's theory of personality (Eysenck, 1967, 1990). Personality dimensions are important for motivation

TABLE 9.1   Dimension Descriptors of Personality

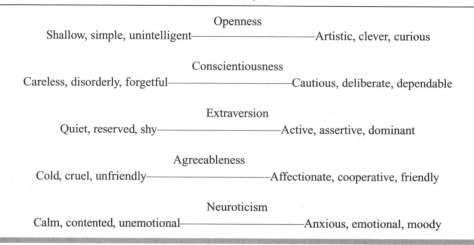

Openness
Shallow, simple, unintelligent————————————Artistic, clever, curious

Conscientiousness
Careless, disorderly, forgetful————————————Cautious, deliberate, dependable

Extraversion
Quiet, reserved, shy————————————Active, assertive, dominant

Agreeableness
Cold, cruel, unfriendly————————————Affectionate, cooperative, friendly

Neuroticism
Calm, contented, unemotional————————————Anxious, emotional, moody

Source: Adapted from "Towards a Taxonomy of Personality Descriptors" by O. P. John, 1989, in D. M. Buss & N. Cantor (Eds.), *Personality Psychology: Recent Trends and Emerging Directions*, table 19.2, p. 265. New York: Springer Verlag.

because they help explain why people are motivated by different incentives, situations, and activities. Individuals at one end of a dimension may be motivated differently than individuals at the other end. For example, an extravert is motivated to attend a large party, while an introvert is motivated to stay home. An individual high in neuroticism may be easier to induce into a bad mood, while an individual low in neuroticism is not.

> More information about the five-factor model is available at http://www.uoregon.edu/ ~sanjay/bigfive.html

Sensation Seeking. This is another personality trait that is linked to differences in motivation. It is usually considered separately from the five-factor model. **Sensation seeking** "is a trait defined by the *seeking* of varied, novel, complex, and *intense* sensations and experiences, and the willingness to take physical, social, *legal*, and *financial* risks for the sake of such experience" (Zuckerman, 1994, p. 27). Risk taking is an accompaniment of sensation seeking, since it is the consequence of the rewarding sensation or experience. For example, people may experiment with drugs to obtain a certain sensation or experience. The consequence, however, is that the drug may kill them (physical risk) or may cause them to get arrested (legal risk) or fined (financial risk). In addition, they may have their names published in the local paper for all to read (social risk). Yet, high-sensation seekers are willing to take greater risks only because of the rewards provided by the sensation-seeking activities and experiences. Low-sensation seekers, however, are not willing to take such risks because those same sensation-seeking activities are not rewarding to them. Zuckerman (1994) has provided a rich source of evidence indicating that, in comparison to low-sensation seekers, high-sensation seekers have engaged in a wide variety of behaviors that provide these intense sensations and experiences. For example, high-sensation seekers are more likely to engage in high-risk sports (sky diving, mountain climbing); to have had a greater variety of sexual experiences; and to have used tobacco, alcohol, and other drugs.

Sensation seeking is not one large trait, however, but instead consists of four factors. *Thrill and adventure seeking* is the desire for sensations induced by participating in risky activities, such as sky diving and fast driving. Although people may not have participated in these activities, they express a desire to do so. *Experience seeking* is the desire for mental and sensory stimulation from art, travel, drugs, and music. These individuals are characterized by desiring a more unconventional lifestyle. *Disinhibition* reflects the desire for variety attained by drinking, partying, gambling, sexual activity, and other hedonic pursuits. These people can be characterized as extraverted sensation seekers in that they seek other individuals as a source of stimulation. Finally, *boredom susceptibility* is an aversion to boredom resulting from repetitive experiences and the absence of stimulation from activities and other people. Individuals with this factor have a low tolerance for boredom and become restless in such situations (Zuckerman, 1979).

Biological Reality of Traits

Are personality traits real? Imagine people who have large feet versus those who have small feet. One could almost say that having large feet causes a person to buy large shoes and that having small feet causes a person to buy small shoes. These individuals are doing nothing more than buying shoes that fit. After all, good-fitting shoes allow the wearer to walk comfortably and efficiently, while poor-fitting shoes make this difficult. The point is that the foot is a real biological entity and not some hypothetical construct postulated to account for differences in shoe size among people. Applying this reasoning to personality traits, it is assumed that personality traits are real entities that account for differences in behavior among people.

The reality of personality traits is verified in several ways. First, operational definitions of personality traits refer to the procedures by which the traits are measured. This usually involves a valid psychological paper-and-pencil scale. Second, other people's appraisal externally validates the existence of a personality trait. For example, if you rate yourself as an extravert and a sensation seeker, then another person, such as a good friend, will agree with your assessment. Third, personality traits have biological correlates. Neural activity in the brain and physiological reactivity correlate with operational measures of personality traits. Finally, the biological correlates of personality traits are genetically transmitted—that is, traits run in families. The following subsections examine some trait-verification procedures.

Operational Definitions.   It is important to separate measures of a personality trait from the behavior the trait is supposed to explain. To reason that a person frequently attends parties because she is an extravert and then use frequent party attendance as evidence for extraversion provides little understanding about the motivation for party attendance. Frequent party attendance cannot serve both as evidence for the trait of extraversion and as the behavior to be explained by extraverison. Instead, it is necessary to measure a personality trait independently of the behavior that is to be explained. The existence of a personality trait is validated by how it is measured—that is, its **operational definition.** The *NEO Personality Inventory* is used to measure the five personality factors presented in Table 9.1 (Costa & McCrae, 1985, 2001). The inventory consists of 243 items that a person rates on a five-point scale, which ranges from Strongly disagree to Strongly agree. The *Mini-Marker Set* is a much briefer scale, which involves a list of 40 adjective markers that are descriptive of the big five personality factors (see Table 9.2; Saucier, 1994, 2003). A person endorses each adjective in the set according to how accurately it reflects his personality. The more accurate an adjective is rated, the more indicative it is of a person's personality trait.

The *Sensation Seeking Scale* was developed to measure the four factors of the sensation-seeking trait (Zuckerman, 1978, 1979, 1994). A person receives one score for each factor ranging from zero to 10 and a total score equal to the sum of the four factors. The *Sensation Seeking Scale* assesses the thrill-and-adventure-seeking component with preferences for activities like sky diving, mountain climbing, or motorcycle riding and assesses the experience-seeking component with whether a person would like to be hypnotized, try new foods, or experiment with drugs. The disinhibition component is measured by one's preference for emotionally expressive individuals, liking to get high, or observing sex scenes in movies. Finally, the boredom-susceptibility component is measured by whether or not one gets bored seeing the same old faces, watching the same movie again, and preferring unpredictable friends.

> ➤ A complete version of the *Sensation Seeking Scale* developed by Zuckerman (1979, 1994) can be found at http://www.bbc.co.uk/science/humanbody/mind/surveys/sensation/index.shtml

Psychophysiology and Neuropsychology.   Another method by which to validate personality traits is to examine their correlation with physiological responses. Carl Jung (1924),

TABLE 9.2   The 40-Item Mini-Marker Set: How Accurately Can You Describe Yourself?

Please use this list of common human traits to describe yourself as accurately as possible. Describe yourself as you see yourself at the present time, not as you wish to be in the future. Describe yourself as you are generally or typically, as compared with other persons you know of the same sex and of roughly your same age. Before each trait, please write a number indicating how accurately that trait describes you, using the following rating scale:

1	2	3	4	5	6	7	8	9
Extremely Inaccurate	Very Inaccurate	Moderately Inaccurate	Slightly Inaccurate	Neither Inaccurate nor Accurate	Slightly Accurate	Moderately Accurate	Very Accurate	Extremely Accurate

The eight words underneath each of the big five personality traits are descriptive markers of that trait.

OPENNESS	CONSCIENTIOUSNESS	EXTRAVERSION	AGREEABLENESS	NEUROTICISM
Uncreative–	Careless–	Bashful–	Cold–	Relaxed–
Unintellectual–	Disorganized–	Quiet–	Harsh–	Unenvious–
Philosophical	Inefficient–	Shy–	Rude–	Envious
Complex	Sloppy–	Withdrawn–	Unsympathetic–	Fretful
Creative	Efficient	Bold	Cooperative	Jealous
Deep	Organized	Energetic	Kind	Moody
Imaginative	Practical	Extraverted	Sympathetic	Temperamental
Intellectual	Systematic	Talkative	Warm	Touchy

Note: A negative sign after a word indicates reverse scoring: 1 = 9, 2 = 8, 3 = 7, 4 = 6, 5 = 5, etc. Sum the scores for each personality trait. A higher score indicates a greater degree of that personality trait.

Source: Adapted from The *40-Item Mini-Marker Set* by G. Saucier available at http://www.uoregon.edu/~gsaucier/gsau41.pdf

a one-time collaborator with Freud, was one of the first to propose that a personality trait was real in the sense that it had a biological basis. In regard to the particular disposition of a person, "It may well be that physiological causes, inaccessible to our knowledge, play a part in this" (p. 416). Gordon Allport (1937b, 1966), one of the originators of the trait theory of personality, also believed that traits are real, meaning that they have direct counterparts in the brain. Accordingly, a personality trait refers to behavioral consistencies and to neurological structures or processes in the brain. *Psychophysiology* is a field that relates changes in psychological variables with changes in physiological variables. Examples of physiological variables are heart rate, electrodermal activity, and changes in muscle activity, which are measured by electrical signals. Differences in personality traits correspond to differences in physiological responding (Andreassi, 1989). Using sense of humor as an example, electrical changes in facial muscles from smiling at cartoons may be greater for individuals with a good sense of humor compared to those with little sense of humor. Another method that attempts to demonstrate the reality of traits relates differences in personality to differences in brain characteristics. In the study of *neuropsychology*, an investigator would attempt to relate differences in brain activity and neurotransmitters with differences in personality (Zuckerman, 1991).

The study of the psychophysiology and neuropsychology of extraversion has been carried out extensively. Differences in the degree of extraversion are associated with central and peripheral nervous system differences (Eysenck, 1990). The cortex of an introvert is chronically more aroused than that of an extravert, due to greater levels of excitation produced by the introvert's reticular activating system (Eysenck, 1967). To test this hypothesis, Bullock and Gilliland (1993) measured brain stem auditory-evoked responses in reaction to a click sound for both introverts and extraverts. Introverts exhibited faster brain stem auditory responses to these sounds than did extraverts. The results were interpreted as supporting Eysenck's theory in that the activity level in the auditory pathway in the reticular activating system was greater for introverts. There are also differences between introverts and extraverts in physiological responding. Introverts are more physiologically reactive than extraverts in response to various kinds of intermediate levels of stimulation. Electrodermal and auditory-evoked responses to tones of different loudness or frequency also tend to be greater in introverts than extraverts (Stelmack, 1990). The cortex of an introvert is assumed to be habitually more aroused than that of an extravert (Eysenck, 1967, 1990).

Sensation seeking is based on inherited differences in the central nervous system and in brain chemistry. Zuckerman (1985, 1990, 1994) relies on the brain enzyme **monoamine oxidase (MAO)** as a reliable marker for sensation seeking in humans. The enzyme MAO correlates negatively with scores on the *Sensation Seeking Scale* (Zuckerman, 1994). High-sensation seekers are low in MAO, while low-sensation seekers are high in MAO. The apparent function of MAO is to break down brain neurotransmitters such as serotonin, norepinephrine, and dopamine (Zuckerman, 1985, 1990, 1994). Dopamine energizes or activates behavior toward biological rewards and the search for such rewards. (The role of dopamine as a brain reward system was described in Chapter 4.)

MAO and suspected neurotransmitter differences between high- and low-sensation seekers is revealed in their physiological responses to various stimuli (Zuckerman, 1990, 1994). For example, Neary and Zuckerman (1976) presented a simple visual stimulus at random intervals to extremely low- and high-sensation seekers. Following habituation to this stimulus, the participants were presented with a novel stimulus of a complex colored design. The intensity of electrodermal responses to the initial simple stimulus and to the complex novel stimulus was stronger for high- than for low-sensation seekers. High-sensation seekers also give stronger electrodermal responses than low-sensation seekers to words that have a strong aggressive or sexual connotation (Smith et al., 1989). The effects of high- versus low-sensation seeking, especially the disinhibition factor, are also apparent in orienting responses. These are "What is that?" reactions. High-disinhibition participants show heart rate deceleration (orienting response) to visual and auditory stimuli, whereas low-disinhibition participants show heart rate acceleration (defense response) (Zuckerman et al., 1988). High-disinhibition participants also show stronger cortical-evoked potentials (brain wave responses) to a flashing light and loud tones presented at short intervals (Zuckerman et al., 1974).

Behavioral Genetics.   Another method of demonstrating the reality of traits is through **behavioral genetics,** which is the science of the genetic inheritance of biological traits that are relevant to behavior. The use of this method is based on the assumption that the intricate structures and components of the brain and nervous system are genetically transmitted. Furthermore, greater genetic similarity between two individuals is associated with greater similarity in their brains and nervous systems, which, in turn, is associated with corresponding resemblances in their personality traits (Plomin et al., 2001). For instance, identical, or monozygotic (MZ), twins come from a single fertilized egg that splits in half, resulting in two genetically identical individuals who have 100% of their genes in common. Fraternal, or dizygotic (DZ), twins and siblings represent two different eggs fertilized by two different sperm, resulting in two individuals who share an average of 50% of their genes. Finally, a parent and his or her biological child have 50% of their genes in common, while a parent with an adopted child has no genes in common. In regards to the similarity of personality traits, identical twins should be more similar than fraternal twins and siblings. In addition, fraternal twins, siblings, and parents with biological children should be more similar in personality traits than two unrelated individuals. For example, twins should be more alike in extraversion (sociable, outgoing) and sensation seeking (daring, adventuresome) than siblings, who should be more alike on those traits than unrelated children.

Evidence for genetic influences on the five personality dimensions comes from Riemann and coworkers (1997) in Germany, who used *NEO Personality Inventory* scores obtained from identical and fraternal twins. They computed the correlations between the five personality dimension scores for 660 identical twins and for 200 same-sex fraternal twins. The results in Figure 9.1 show higher correlations for identical twins (MZ) than for same-sex fraternal (DZ) twins. In other words, individuals who are 100% alike genetically

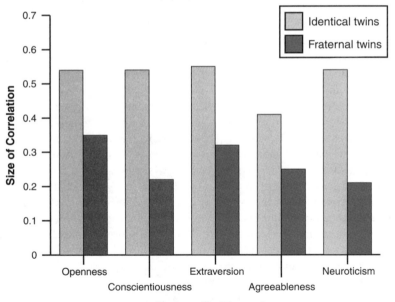

FIGURE 9.1   Personality Traits of Identical and Fraternal Twins. The graph shows the correlations for all big five personality factor scores between identical (MZ) twins and same-sex fraternal (DZ) twins. Correlations were higher for MZ twins than for DZ twins on all five personality dimensions.

Source: Adapted from "Genetic and Environmental Influences on Personality: A Study of Twins Reared Together Using the Self- and Peer Report NEO-FFI Scales" by R. Riemann et al., 1997, *Journal of Personality, 65,* table 2, p. 461.

are more similar on all five personality dimensions than individuals who are 50% alike genetically (Bouchard & Loehlin, 2001; Loehlin, 1992; Plomin et al., 2001).

One could make the argument, however, that this greater similarity among identical twins is the result of rearing practices. Perhaps identical twins are treated more alike than are fraternal twins, resulting in greater behavioral similarities between identical twins. One answer to this criticism is to compare twins who have been reared together with those who have been reared separately. If the environment has an effect, then twins reared together should be more alike than twins reared separately. This comparison is possible when twins are adopted by different families and reunite years later, as was true for the "Jim" twins in the case that opened this chapter. Loehlin (1992) summarizes the similarity in extraversion and neuroticism of twins reared together or separately in Finland, Sweden, the United States, and Great Britain. These analyses show that the correlations for both extraversion and neuroticism are greater for identical twins (MZ) than for fraternal twins (DZ), regardless of whether the twins were reared together or apart. Thus, even when rearing environments differ, greater genetic similarity corresponds to greater similarity in extraversion and neuroticism. Identical twins reared together are also more similar than identical twins reared apart, which implies that rearing conditions have some effect on extraversion and neuroticism.

There is also strong evidence for a genetic contribution to sensation seeking (Zuckerman, 2002). The closer the genetic relationship between individuals, the greater their similarity in sensation seeking. Hur and Bouchard (1997) examined the correlation between separated MZ and DZ twins on the four traits that comprise sensation seeking. The correlations, shown in Figure 9.2, indicate greater similarities between MZ twins than DZ twins on all traits of sensation seeking except thrill and adventure seeking. Even when identical twins were reared separately in different environments, they were still similar on all four sensation-seeking traits.

Other researchers have also contributed evidence for the effects of genes on sensation seeking. In analyzing a large set of sensation-seeking scores obtained from identical and fraternal twins, Fulker and associates (1980) found stronger correlations for identical twins than for fraternal twins. The authors concluded that the similarity in twins for sensation seeking is more the result of heredity than it is of environmental similarities. Tellegen and coresearchers (1988) compared scores of identical and fraternal twins on a *constraint factor*. High scorers on this factor are similar to low-sensation seekers in that they "describe themselves as being restrained, cautious, avoiding dangerous kinds of excitement and thrills, differential and conventional" (p. 1034). Low scorers on this factor, by contrast, are similar to high-sensation seekers in that they show "impulsiveness, fearless sensation seeking, and rejection of conventional strictures on their behavior" (p. 1034). The degree of relationship between scores on the constraint factor was strongest and practically identical for MZ twins reared together or apart, much weaker for DZ twins reared together, and nonexistent for DZ twins reared apart (Tellegen et al., 1988). Thus, the results of this study also indicate that similarity in sensation seeking is more the result of genetic similarity among pairs of twins than it is the result of environmental similarity, such as where the twins were reared. Bear in mind, however, that "personality traits are not inherited as such; only the biological structures coded in the DNA are inherited" (Zuckerman, 1994, p. 295). There is also evidence for genetic influences on sensation seeking and its biological marker MAO. In a summary of twin studies regarding measures of MAO, Zuckerman (1991, table 11.3)

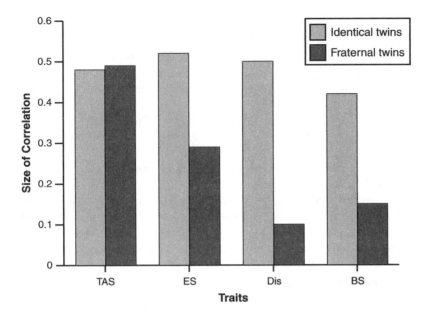

FIGURE 9.2 Sensation Seeking of Separated Identical and Fraternal Twins. Correlations are presented between identical (MZ) and fraternal (DZ) twins for the four traits that comprise sensation seeking: TAS = Thrill and adventure seeking, ES = Experience seeking, Dis = Disinhibition, BS = Boredom susceptibility. Correlations were higher for MZ twins than for DZ twins on all sensation-seeking factors except for thrill and adventure seeking.

Source: Adapted from "The Genetic Correlation between Impulsivity and Sensation-Seeking Traits" by Y-M Hur and T. J. Bouchard, Jr., 1997, *Behavior Genetics, 27,* table III, p. 460.

shows that there is a positive correlation in MAO levels between sets of twins. This leads to the conclusion that MAO is almost totally under genetic control.

Section Recap

To show that personality is a source of motivation, it is first necessary to show the origin of personality traits, how they are studied, and that they are real. *Temperament* is a consistent individual difference in emotional responding resulting from inherited genetic features. *Personality* stems from temperament. It is a consistent individual difference in behavior resulting from the interaction of temperament and social experience. A *personality trait* refers to consistency in a specific set of behaviors across relevant situations from one time to the next. A trait can serve as a category for similar behaviors but also as a cause of why people differ in their reactions to, and in their approach and avoidance of, different situations. Traits represented in the *five-factor model* important for motivation are represented by the acronym OCEAN: openness (shallow–curious), conscientiousness (careless–dependable), extraversion (quiet–active), agreeableness (unfriendly–friendly), and neuroticism (calm–moody). Another trait important for understanding motivation is *sensation seeking*. This trait is characterized by seeking intense sensations and experiences and the willingness to take risks and incur costs for the sake of such experiences.

Several procedures help validate the reality of personality traits. First, *operational definitions* refer to the use of psychological scales to measure the extent of personality traits in a person. The *NEO Personality Inventory* and the *Mini-Marker Set* are two ways to measure the big five personality factors. Second, the appraisal of traits by other individuals correlates with a person's self-assessment of those traits. Third, personality traits have biological correlates. Psychophysiology studies the relationship between personality in terms of physiological and psychological variables. Neuropsychology studies differences in brain structure, chemistry, and function to determine how these relate to personality and behavior. For instance, the cortex of the introvert is chronically more aroused than the cortex of the extravert. For sensation seeking, *monoamine oxidase (MAO)* is an important brain enzyme that breaks down neurotransmitters. A greater amount is present in low-sensation seekers, and a lower amount is present in high-sensation seekers. Fourth, *behavioral genetics* is the science of the inheritance of behavioral characteristics and helps validate the existence of traits. Identical twins, whether reared together or apart, are more alike than fraternal twins on all big five personality traits and on sensation seeking.

Personality Traits Affect Motivation

The previous sections demonstrated that personality traits have a real existence. The purpose of this section is to describe how personality traits affect motivation.

Personality and Environment

Two concepts from behavioral genetics, gene-environment interaction and gene-environment correlation (Loehlin, 1992; Plomin et al., 2001), will help us understand the influence of personality traits on motivation. These two concepts will be translated with an emphasis on personality traits: trait-environment interaction and trait-environment correlation. **Trait-environment interaction** means that how a person reacts to the environment depends on the amount of a particular trait she possesses. Individuals with different levels of a personality trait react differently to environmental situations. For example, an extravert enjoys a large party while an introvert does not. An individual high in neuroticism may be more upset by unfavorable weather than an individual who is low in neuroticism. Finally, a high-sensation seeker enjoys the latest scary movie, while the low-sensation seeker thinks of leaving in the middle of it.

A **trait-environment correlation** means that traits and environments are associated in their effects on behavior, because personality traits determine the situations a person chooses. Individuals with different personality traits select different situations, while those with similar personality traits seek out similar situations. Snyder (1983) suggests that people "may choose to enter and spend time in situations that facilitate behavior expressions of their characteristic dispositions" (p. 502). These situations allow for the satisfaction of motives that are characteristic of those personality traits. In addition, people manipulate the situations in which they find themselves (Buss, 1987, 1992; Buss et al., 1987). For example, extraverts seek out large parties, while introverts seek out small gatherings. Or, when given a choice of videos, a high-sensation seeker may select a scary movie, while a low-sensation seeker may choose a comedy. In other words, when traits are different, choices are different. But when traits are similar, choices are similar. The Jim twins, presumably having similar personality traits, selected the same vacation spots, cars, cigarettes, and part-time law enforcement work.

Effects of Extraversion on Motivation

The following questions illustrate the relationship between extraversion and motivation. (1) Trait-environment interaction: How would you react at a party where you did not know most of the guests? Would you dominate a group's conversation at a party, or would you speak individually to only one other person? (2) Trait-environment correlation: On Saturday night would you prefer to attend a large party or watch a video with a few friends? The answer to each question depends on a person's degree of extraversion. As described next, extraverts would do one thing, and introverts another.

Extraversion-Environment Interaction.   The differences between introverts and extraverts account for the variation in their reactions to the same situation. To illustrate, extraverts are easier to put into a good mood than introverts. Larsen and Ketelaar (1989, 1991) had extraverts and introverts imagine as vividly as possible either a pleasant or unpleasant experience happening to them. The pleasant experience consisted of imagining that they had won a $50,000 lottery and were taking a vacation in Hawaii. The unpleasant experience consisted of imagining being expelled from school in an embarrassing manner and also having a close friend die. A control group of introverts and extraverts were asked to imagine visiting a supermarket and taking a car trip on the highway. Following this, participants were asked to rate their level of positive mood and their level of negative mood. Extraverts developed a greater positive mood than did introverts as a result of imagining the pleasant experience. The result of imagining the unpleasant experience, however, did not necessarily put introverts in a more negative mood than it did extraverts. Other research has shown that extraverts, compared to introverts, seem to be in a better mood consistently. For instance, Ruch and Köhler (1998) have found that extraverts tend to be consistently more cheerful and less often in a serious or a bad mood.

How individuals react to the opportunities and confines of a relationship depends on their level of extraversion. Watson and colleagues (2000) measured the degree of relationship satisfaction of married couples and of heterosexual-dating couples and correlated these measures with each member's level of the big five personality factors. Extraversion correlated positively with relationship satisfaction. Extraverted wives and husbands were more satisfied with their relationship than were introverted wives and husbands. For dating couples, extraverted men were more satisfied than introverted ones. However, there was no difference between extraverted and introverted women.

Extraversion is also a factor in work success. Seibert and Kraimer (2001) administered the *Mini-Marker Set* (Table 9.2) to a sample of employees in a variety of organizations and occupations. Employees identified as high in extraversion had received a greater number of promotions and higher salaries than employees identified as low in extraversion. In addition, extraverted employees also enjoyed greater intrinsic career satisfaction, such as feeling that they made progress toward their goals.

Extraversion-Environment Correlation.   Extraverts and introverts voluntarily choose to participate in different activities. Extraverts participate in social activities such as noisy parties, debates, dancing, and meeting new people. Introverts, however, are more likely to avoid these activities (Argyle & Lu, 1990). When seeking recreation, extraverts, rather than introverts, are more likely to seek out social situations involving other people (Diener et al., 1984). In an extension of these latter findings, Emmons and associates (1986) tried to assess whether personality traits determined which situation people selected. At the end of each day, participants were asked to indicate how much time they spent in a particular situation that ranged from 15 minutes to over 2 hours. The situations were of the participants' own choosing, such as being alone, semisocial (studying in library), or social (interacting with others in recreation, family, or work). In addition, participants were asked if the situation was imposed (you had to be there—e.g., go to class) or chosen (you decided to have lunch with a friend). Their results indicated that extraversion was positively related to the percentage of time spent in chosen social situations and negatively related to time spent in imposed social situations. Extraversion also correlated with the time spent in recreation that was freely chosen but was uncorrelated with imposed recreation. Thus, extraverts, more than introverts, are motivated to seek social stimulation.

Differences between introverts and extraverts are exhibited in a variety of other situations and activities. In the library, extraverts prefer areas containing easy chairs and large tables, where the opportunity for socialization is greater. Introverts prefer small tables or individual study desks, with limited opportunities for socialization. In addition, in the library extraverts prefer a higher noise level than do introverts (Campbell & Hawley, 1982). Extraverts prefer to participate in group-oriented or team sports such as basketball or soccer rather than solitary-type sports such as running or swimming. In addition, extraverts have a greater preference for highly competitive sports than for less competitive ones (Kirkcaldy & Furnham, 1991). Extraverted men and women have different occupational preferences than do introverted men and women (Costa et al., 1984). Extraverted men prefer occupations like advertising executive, manufacturer's representative, marriage counselor, and sales manager. Extraverted women prefer occupations of concert singer, advertising executive, sports promoter, symphony conductor, and freelance writer. As Costa and associates (1984) note, these occupations require the use of the extraverts' assertive and somewhat exhibitionistic tendencies. Extraversion also plays a role in the choice of dating partners.

Extraversion and the Channeling of Motives.   Psychological needs are stable individual differences that have motivational properties. They push individuals into action. Personality traits are also stable individual differences in behavior but have no motivational properties. Traits, however, determine the different values that people place on incentives. Both needs and traits are examples of Darwin's population thinking. Need differences produce behavior differences. People behave differently because they have different intensities of psychological needs to satisfy. Trait differences are also associated with behavior differences. People behave differently because of the differently valued incentives that they hope to attain.

A reason for the motivational distinction between needs and traits is that their studies have separate histories in psychology. However, there are attempts to link the effects of needs and traits for the motivation of behavior. An example is to link extraversion to the need for affiliation and to the need for power. Winter and associates (1998) express this idea in their **channeling hypothesis,** which states that personality traits channel or convey how psychological motives are represented and satisfied. To support their theory, they used the results of important longitudinal studies to illustrate how extraversion channels the expression of the affiliation motive and the power motive. The use of longitudinal data makes it possible to show how over a long period of time extraversion channels motive expression.

How would introverts and extraverts differ in their attempts to satisfy their affiliation motives? Winter and associates (1998) hypothesized that extraverts would channel the expression of their affiliation motive by doing volunteer work. Such activity would provide the means for satisfying their affiliation motive along with the opportunity for meeting new people. Introverts with a high affiliation motive, however, would shy away from volunteer work as a way of satisfying their need for affiliation, since they do not particularly enjoy meeting new people. A low need for affiliation also would not motivate introverted and extraverted women to do volunteer work. In studies consulted by these researchers, Mills College women had their need for affiliation and for power measured with the TAT at age 21 and their level of extraversion measured at age 43. Radcliffe College women had their need for affiliation and for power measured with the TAT at age 18 and their level of extraversion measured at age 43. The results confirmed the predictions for both the Mills and Radcliffe samples. Extraverted women with a high affiliation motive sought to do volunteer work at age 43, while introverted women with a high affiliation motive shied away from it.

How would an extravert and an introvert differ in their attempts to satisfy the power motive? Entering an impact career such as business, education, psychotherapy, or journalism is a way of expressing one's power motive (Jenkins, 1994; see Chapter 8). Winter and associates (1998) hypothesized that extraverts with a high power motive would enter high-impact careers, since these provided opportunities for interacting with other individuals. Introverts with a high power motive, however, would shy away from such careers and would channel their power motive in some alternative career direction. The results show that extraverted Radcliffe graduates with a high need for power selected high-impact careers. Introverted Radcliffe graduates did not use high-impact careers to satisfy their power motives. For Mills women graduates, however, impact careers were selected by both introverts and extraverts to satisfy their power motives. One reason for this difference between the two college samples is that Radcliffe women entered more traditionally "male" impact careers (psychiatrist, professor), while Mills women entered more traditionally "female" careers (social worker, elementary school teacher) (Winter et al., 1998).

Effects of Neuroticism on Motivation

Neuroticism refers to a complex of trait dimensions that ranges from being characteristically nonemotional (calm, contented) at the low end to being emotional (anxious, quickly aroused) at the high end.

Neuroticism-Environment Interaction.   Individuals high in neuroticism are easier to put in a negative mood than those low in neuroticism. Rusting and Larsen (1997) had participants imagine pleasant scenes, like winning the lottery, or unpleasant scenes, like having a friend die of cancer. Follow-up mood measures showed a greater degree of negative mood in high- compared to low-neuroticism individuals. Neuroticism did not correlate with the degree of positive mood that had been induced in the participants. Suls and associates (1998) had male participants who resided in the community record the occurrence of problems and moods several times per day over eight days. The degree of negative mood depended both on daily problems and on the level of neuroticism. Daily problems put everyone in a negative mood, but the level of negative mood was greater for the more neurotic men. In a study described earlier regarding relationship satisfaction, Watson and colleagues

(2000) found that, at least for women, neuroticism correlated negatively with satisfaction. Women high in neuroticism were less satisfied with their married or dating relationship than were women low in neuroticism. However, neuroticism had no effect on men's satisfaction. Neuroticism also has a negative impact on career satisfaction. Employees high in neuroticism tended to evaluate their careers more negatively than employees low in neuroticism (Seibert & Kraimer, 2001).

Neuroticism-Environment Correlation.   A person's level of neuroticism determines the extent he chooses to engage in risky behavior to enhance his positive feelings or lessen his negative feelings. For instance, Mohr and coresearchers (2001) examined the link between negative interpersonal exchanges and drinking over a 30-day period in a community sample of adults. Negative exchanges were measured by the answers to such questions as, Did anyone yell at you, take advantage of you, or prevent you from working on your goals today? If any of these negative social events happened, then how likely is an individual to have a drink alone that evening? The results showed that individuals high in neuroticism coped with negative events by drinking alone more frequently than individuals low in neuroticism. Figure 9.3 provides a clear indication of a trait-environment correlation. High-neuroticism individuals chose to increase their number of solitary drinks in response to an increase in the number of negative interpersonal exchanges they experienced. Low-neuroticism individuals did not show this increase.

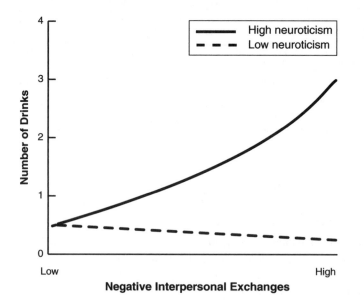

FIGURE 9.3   Neuroticism and Drinking Alone. The impact of negative interpersonal exchanges is different for individuals high in neuroticism compared to those low in neuroticism. High-neuroticism individuals choose to increase their solitary drinking as the number of negative interpersonal exchanges increases. Low-neuroticism individuals are unaffected.

Source: From "Daily Interpersonal Experiences, Context, and Alcohol Consumption: Crying in Your Beer and Toasting Good Times" by C. D. Mohr et al., 2001, *Journal of Personality and Social Psychology, 80,* figure 2, p. 496. Copyright 2001 by American Psychological Association. Reprinted by permission.

Emotional distress and negative mood states characterize neuroticism. Individuals high in neuroticism also choose to use other risky behaviors, besides drinking, to cope (Cooper et al., 2000). For example, Trobst and coresearchers (2002) measured the big five personality factors of individuals engaged in risky sexual practices (anal sex, no condoms) and shared needles. Their results revealed a trait-environment correlation—that is, a positive relationship between the level of neuroticism and the degree of risky behavior. Neurotic individuals were more likely to choose to engage in highly risky sexual and drug behaviors than were nonneurotic individuals.

Effects of Conscientiousness on Motivation

A person with a high level of conscientiousness is competent, orderly, dutiful, achievement-striving, self-disciplined, and deliberate in her actions. These characteristics should show their mark on various behaviors, such as academic work and health-related behaviors. In the case of academic work, Noftle and Robins (2007) examined the relationship between conscientiousness and GPA at two different University of California campuses. The major finding in all cases was that conscientiousness correlated with GPA even after indicators of scholastic aptitude were factored out. Simply put, more conscientious students earned high grades! Furthermore, students who became more conscientious as their academic careers progressed over the four years were also inclined to earn higher grades. The increase in grades with conscientiousness were the results of what the researchers termed *academic effort*. For example, students were asked, "On average, how many hours a week (outside of class time) have you spent on school work the current semester [quarter]?" (p. 121). More conscientious students reported that they put forth more academic effort, which was associated with earning higher grades (Noftle & Robins, 2007).

Conscientiousness is associated with lifestyle behaviors that promote healthful living and disassociated with unhealthy lifestyle choices. Bogg and Roberts (2004) examined numerous studies that covered the relationship between conscientiousness and health-related behaviors. On the whole, the authors found that increases in the level of conscientiousness was associated with decreases in excessive alcohol use, illicit drug use, unhealthy eating, risky driving, risky sex, and tobacco use. Individuals lower in conscientiousness were more likely to engage in these health-threatening behaviors. Conversely, individuals higher in conscientiousness are more likely to engage in health-promoting behaviors.

Effects of Agreeableness on Motivation

Individuals high in agreeableness tend to be trusting, compliant, and helpful. So would they be more likely to help individuals in distress? Consider the following common scenario: Imagine driving and seeing an individual whose car has broken down along the side of the road. How likely is it that you will risk being late somewhere in order to help this individual if he or she was a stranger, a friend, or one of your siblings? Consider the following extraordinary scenario: How likely would you enter a burning house at the risk of death in order to save the life of the occupant if that person were a stranger, a friend, or one of your siblings? Are individuals high, compared to low, in the trait of agreeableness more or less likely to help? Graziano and coresearchers (2007) presented these two scenarios to university students in order to answer this question. Based on a personality questionnaire, participants were divided into two groups: low agreeableness and high agreeableness. The results

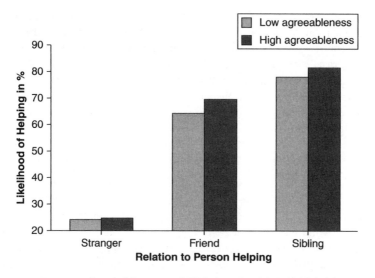

FIGURE 9.4   Agreeableness and Helping. Participants high in agreeableness were more likely to help a stranded motorist when that person was a friend or sibling. There was no difference between low and high agreeableness in the likelihood of helping strangers.

Source: Adapted from "Agreeableness, empathy, and helping: A person × situation perspective" by W. G. Graziano et al., 2007, *Journal of Personality and Social Psychology, 93,* 583–599, p. 586.

for the first scenario are shown in Figure 9.4. Individuals high in agreeableness reported a greater willingness to be late in order to help a stranded motorist provided that individual was a friend or sibling. There was no difference in the likelihood of helping a stranger. However, when it came to saving strangers from a burning house, high-agreeable people were a bit more likely to do so than low-agreeable people would. Low- and high-agreeable individuals were equally likely to save friends and siblings from burning buildings. Thus, agreeable people are more likely to help individuals who are in distress. However, helping also depends on the situation and on the relationship between the helper and the person helped. Individuals in grave danger are helped nearly equally by low- and high-agreeable people. However, when helping creates an inconvenience, such as being late, highly agreeable people are more likely to help.

Effects of Multiple Traits on Motivation

The motivation of behavior comes from multiple sources. In the case of personality traits, multiple sources imply that several traits combine to determine a person's reactions to and choices of situations and activities. This section examines some behaviors and how they are affected by multiple personality traits.

Internet Usage.   Does the extent of Internet usage correlate with an individual's personality traits? This question was examined in university students by Landers and Lounsbury (2006). Students could indicate their Internet usage along eight incremental steps that ranged from less than 1 hour per week to more than 10 hours per day. Internet usage could involve communication (e-mail or chat), leisure (music, shopping, games), and academics (research, course participation). Agreeableness, conscientiousness, and extraversion correlated negatively with Internet usage. However, in the case of conscientiousness, Internet usage for academic purposes increased. Overall, the researchers concluded that " . . . more introverted, less agreeable, and less conscientious students engaged in higher levels of Internet usage" (p. 288). Perhaps less agreeable students find that fewer demands for cooperation are placed on them when they use the Internet. High conscientiousness may discourage use of the Internet for leisure because these individuals spend more time in structured-student activities like sports or clubs. In addition, being high in conscientiousness increases the motivation to use the Internet for academic purposes. Finally, extraverted students may enjoy real social encounters in place of the more solitary encounters that the Internet provides (Landers & Lounsbury, 2006).

Prejudice.   What is your attitude to groups or individuals who are different from you? This question taps into an individual's prejudices. The definition of prejudice usually involves negative attitudes and feelings about a social group or its members. Jackson and Poulsen (2005) reasoned that prejudice could be tempered by the amount of favorable contact that a person has with another group or individual. This contact, however, may depend on the strength of certain personality traits. Based on the **selection hypothesis,** an individual's personality determines the type of contact sought with members of other groups. The selection hypothesis is an instance of trait-environment correlation, since personality is associated with the amount of group contact. Jackson and Poulsen (2005) hypothesized that individuals high on openness to experience would be more likely to seek contact with minority group members, such as African Americans or Asian Americans. Furthermore, they reasoned that the quality of contact should be greater with increases in openness but also with agreeableness. In their investigation, after the big five personality traits were assessed, students described the amount of their contact experiences with either African Americans or Asian Americans, followed by an assessment of their level of prejudice toward those groups. The results indicated that as the trait of openness increased, the frequency of group contact increased. In addition, as openness and agreeableness increased, the quality of contact also increased. Individuals high in openness and high agreeableness had lower negative attitudes and higher positive attitudes toward those groups as a result of their contact experiences (Jackson & Poulsen, 2005). It is important to note that individuals high in openness to experience are more willing to initiate contact with members of other groups. As a result, they, along with people high in agreeableness, report those experiences as positive, friendly, and pleasant.

Happiness and the Big Five Personality Traits

As described earlier, personality stems partly from temperament and is under genetic control. These factors, over which an individual has little control, imply that personality is determined and is not created by free will. This conclusion has implications for the dependence of happiness on personality. Are individuals free to be as happy as they want to be or are they constrained by their personality traits? Diener and Seligman (2002) have examined the relationship between personality factors and happiness. They identified 22 (top 10%) very happy and 24 (bottom 10%) very unhappy university students out of an initial sample of 222. The classification of whether one is happy or unhappy depended on a screening procedure that involved four psychological scales, memory for positive and negative events, and the

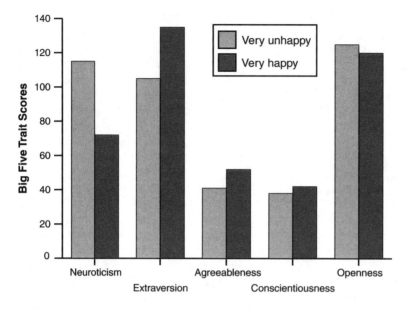

FIGURE 9.5   Happiness and Personality. Students classified as very happy were significantly lower in neuroticism and higher in extraversion and agreeableness than were students classified as very unhappy. They did not differ in conscientiousness and openness.

Source: Adapted from "Very Happy People" by E. Diener and M. E. P. Seligman, 2002, *Psychological Science, 13,* table 3, p. 84.

evaluation by people who knew the students. The results in Figure 9.5 clearly show that very happy and unhappy individuals differ on three of the personality factors. Very happy students were significantly lower on neuroticism and higher on extraversion and agreeableness. They did not differ in conscientiousness and openness. Figure 9.5 shows that neuroticism and extraversion appear to be the most influential personality factors governing happiness.

The specific association between extraversion and happiness may result from extraverts deriving greater positive affect from their social activities. Ratings of happiness, enjoyment, and satisfaction are generally greater for extraverts than for introverts in social situations (Argyle & Lu, 1990; Diener et al., 1984; Pavot et al., 1990). Extraverts seek out social situations because they add to their happiness and subjective well-being (Pavot et al., 1990). Emmons and associates (1986) asked their participants to rate whether their mood was positive or negative in a particular situation. The researchers found that affect ratings correlated with extraversion in social situations. Extraverts experience more positive affect than introverts when in a social situation of their choosing and less when they are required to be in a solitary situation. Extraverts also feel more negative affect when required to be alone and less negative affect when in a social situation of their choosing. Argyle and Lu (1990) studied how much time and how much enjoyment extraverts derive from various common activities, such as going to a bar or having a quiet conversation with a friend. Their findings showed that extraverts enjoy and participate more in social activities, while introverts have a greater preference and enjoyment for solitary activities.

Effects of Sensation Seeking on Motivation

What are your sensation-seeking tendencies like? Would you like to sample some raw oysters or escargot? Would you enjoy the newest roller coaster ride at an amusement park? Do you consider tattoos and body piercing attractive? A person's answers to these questions depend on his level of sensation seeking.

Differences in motivation can stem from differences in sensation seeking. The sensation seeking–environment interaction implies that the sensation experienced as pleasurable by a high-sensation seeker may be aversive to a low-sensation seeker. And a pleasurable sensation for a low-sensation seeker may be aversive for a high-sensation seeker. Also, since sensations result from activities, high- and low-sensation seekers engage in different activities in order to attain their most pleasurable level of sensation. In addition, different behaviors are selected, depending on whether the person is seeking sensation from thrill and adventure seeking, experience seeking, disinhibition, or boredom susceptibility. Zuckerman (1994) has provided a rich source of evidence indicating that in comparison to low-sensation seekers, high-sensation seekers have engaged in a wide variety of behaviors that provide intense sensations and experiences. Many high-sensation behaviors, however, are illicit, such as substance abuse, reckless driving, theft, vandalism, and risky sexual behavior (Wagner, 2001).

A small sample of activity differences between high- and low-sensation seekers is provided next in order to develop a flavor for this area. Individuals who participate in high-risk sports are more likely to be high- rather than low-sensation seekers. Freixanet (1991) compared alpinists (those who had participated in several expeditions to the Himalayas), mountaineers (mountain climbers and skiers), other sportsmen (scuba divers, water skiers, white-water canoeists, sky divers, race car drivers), and a control group of individuals who did not participate in any sports. All three sports groups scored higher on thrill and adventure seeking and experience seeking and had higher total sensation-seeking scores than did the control group. A major finding of this study was that the biggest difference was between sports groups and the controls; also, there was little difference among the sports groups. In comparing hang gliders, auto racers, and bowlers, Straub (1982) found that hang gliders and auto racers scored higher on all components of the sensation-seeking scale. Men and women who canoe and kayak white-water rivers involving long rapids and moderate waves have higher thrill-and-adventure-seeking scores than the general population. Higher thrill-and-adventure-seeking scores also are associated with lower anxiety levels prior to launching into the river (Campbell et al., 1993).

Sensation seeking is associated with stimulus preference. For instance, high- and low-sensation seekers differ in the type of humor they prefer. Using factor analysis, Ruch has classified humor into three factors: incongruity-resolution, nonsense, and sex (see Ruch & Hehl, 1998). Incongruity-resolution humor involves jokes and cartoons in which the incongruity is completely resolvable. Nonsense humor contains incongruities that are either not or only partially resolvable or create new incongruities on resolution. The sex factor refers to jokes and cartoons having a sexual theme. Ruch (1988) found that participants high in experience seeking and boredom susceptibility prefer nonsense humor over incongruity-resolution humor. Participants high in disinhibition preferred humor based on sexual content more than did participants low in disinhibition. High- and low-sensation seekers also differ in their preference for eroticism. For example, Zuckerman (1978) found that high-disinhibition and experience-seeking participants prefer viewing erotic films more than low-disinhibition and experience-seeking participants.

Section Recap

Realizing that people differ in personality traits helps us to understand why they are motivated by different incentives and goals. First, individuals with a high level of a particular trait act as the trait name implies: open to experience, conscientious, extraverted, agreeable, and neurotic. Sensation seekers are individuals willing to take risks in order to experience varied, novel, complex, and intense sensations and experiences.

Individuals with different levels of traits react differently but also choose to be different in different situations. Based on the *trait-environment interaction*, individuals at one end of a personality dimension react differently to various situations than do individuals at the other end. Thus, for each of the big five personality traits and sensation seeking, people with high levels of each trait react or respond differently to a situation than do those with low levels of each trait. According to the *trait-environment correlation*, individuals at one end of a personality dimension seek out, create, or modify situations differently than do individuals at the other end. In this case, for each big five trait and sensation seeking, high trait levels are associated with seeking, creating, or modifying situations in ways that are different from those of individuals with low levels of each trait. The task of psychology is to determine what those situations and behaviors are. In some representative findings, extraverts are easier to put in a good mood. Extraverts are more likely than introverts to seek social stimulation in a variety of situations. According to the *channeling hypothesis*, extraversion channels or conveys how psychological motives like power and affiliation are expressed and satisfied. Extraverts are more likely than introverts to do volunteer work when expressing their affiliation motive and to enter high-impact careers when expressing their power motive.

Other traits have also been examined for how people react and select or modify different situations. Individuals high in neuroticism are easier to put in a bad mood and are less satisfied with their relationships and careers. They are also more likely to choose to drink in solitude following negative social exchanges. Individuals high in conscientiousness earn higher grades and are more likely to engage in health-enhancing behaviors. High agreeableness is associated with a greater likelihood of helping friends and siblings in distress. Frequently a composite of trait levels are associated with a particular behavior. For instance, students low in extraversion, agreeableness, and conscientiousness spend more time using the Internet. According to the *selection hypothesis*, individuals high in openness to experience sought out minority contact more and reported less prejudice as a result as did individuals high in agreeableness. Happiness is associated with high levels of extraversion and agreeableness and low levels of neuroticism.

High sensation seekers respond positively to risky events, drugs, and unusual experiences, while low sensation seekers respond negatively. High sensation seekers are more likely to seek out and engage in risky sports, prefer unusual stimuli and situations, and experiment with things out of the ordinary.

Self as a Motivational System

In a personality trait analysis of motivation, a person is viewed as reacting, selecting, and changing situations in a consistent fashion from one time to the next. Another type of consistency in motivation is a person's self-image. Individuals try to maintain a consistent but also adaptable view of themselves depending on their role in a situation (Pervin, 1984, p. 171). To illustrate:

> Looking-glass, Looking-glass, on the wall,
> Who in this land is fairest of all?

The looking glass answers:

> Thou, O Queen, are the fairest of all!

The mirror's answer certainly gratifies the queen, because here is independent verification of her self-image that she is the most beautiful person in the land. Six years later the queen asks again:

> Looking-glass, Looking-glass, on the wall,
> Who in this land is fairest of all?

The glass answers:

> Thou art fairer than all who are here, Lady Queen.
> But more beautiful still is Snow-white, as I ween [imagine]. (Grimm, 1884/1968)

This time the queen is quite displeased with the mirror's answer because now there is a large discrepancy between the queen's self-conception of her beauty and the mirror's conception.

This familiar fairy tale illustrates a unique psychological need: concern with self. As in the case of the queen, a person is motivated to have a positive image of herself. This need is similar to Maslow's (1970) esteem need, since it involves holding yourself in respect (see Table 8.4). Concern with self also resembles Rogers's (1959) concept of the need for self-regard, which refers to a person's desire to feel positive about himself.

The purpose of this section is to examine how the image of the self and the evaluation of the self serve as a unique source of human motivation.

Self-Concept

When you look into a mirror, do you see someone staring back at you? The person doing the staring is the *I* of the self and the person staring back is *me*. In introducing the concept of self into psychology, James (1892) described the *I-self* as the observer, knower, or subject and the *me-self* as the observed, the known, or the object. Just as a person's image is reflected back in a mirror, the self as object is also reflected back from others, according to Cooley (1902/1964). He maintained that other individuals can serve as mirrors from which the self is reflected back. Cooley felt that "in imagination we perceive in another's mind some thought of our appearance, manners, aims, deeds, character, friends, and so on, and are variously affected by it" (p. 184). Through analysis of the self and from the feedback of others, an individual develops a **self-concept.** This is a person's knowledge of herself organized into a schema or framework and from which information about the self can be retrieved and evaluated. A self-schema might be organized around such domains as appearance, performance, and social interactions with others (Heatherton & Polivy, 1991). For example, a student might identify himself as a male with red hair and freckles (appearance domain) who is good at math but bad at dancing (performance domain) and who enjoys talking about basketball with other students (social domain).

Motivation Regarding Self-Knowledge.   The development of a self-concept depends on gaining knowledge about oneself. To this end, Baumeister (1998) postulates three categories of motivation regarding self-knowledge. *Self-enhancement* is the foremost motive, which refers to the desire to learn positive things about the self. For example, a person would like to learn that she is good, moral, attractive, pleasant, and capable. The *consistency* motive refers to the desire for information that confirms or is congruous with current knowledge. For example, if a person perceives himself as having a good sense of humor, then information confirming that perception is accepted, while contrary information tends to be rejected. Finally, the *appraisal* motive refers to the desire to learn about oneself. Based on feedback from different people in different situations, a person learns about different characteristics of self. Although people wish appraisal to be accurate, they mostly want it to be enhancing and consistent with what they already think of and know about themselves.

Possible Selves as Incentives.   In addition to the current self, people can also think of what they would like or not like to become (Markus & Nurius, 1986). These future *possible selves* are based on past selves and serve as guides for what to strive for and what to avoid. "I am now a student but can picture myself as a marriage and family counselor." "I now hold a part-time minimum wage job yet I do not foresee myself as ever being on welfare." One important motivational role of possible selves, according to Markus and Nurius (1986), is that they serve as incentives for behavior. When perceived as positive, the possible self is an incentive or goal that the individual strives for, such as picturing oneself as being successful in a future career. When perceived as negative, a possible self is an outcome to be avoided, such as picturing oneself on long-term unemployment. Incentives and goals are usually treated as things or distinct entities; possible selves as incentives or goals, however, are seen as actual roles in which people visualize themselves. The process of visualizing possible selves includes cognitive elaboration of the future self, envisioning accompanying plans, and experiencing associated affect (Markus & Nurius, 1986).

What are the characteristics of possible future selves? By asking this question, Markus and Nurius (1986) found that students thought more about possible selves in the future than about past selves. Students were much more likely to consider and think about positive selves in comparison to negative selves. For example, they were more likely to see themselves as happy and confident rather than depressed and lazy and as being sexy and in good shape in contrast to being unattractive and flabby. Furthermore, students were more likely to think that positive selves were more probable to happen than negative selves. The incentive nature of a future possible self also depends on the nature of the current self. For example, Carver and associates (1994) found that optimistic students considered it more likely that they would attain their positive future selves compared to pessimistic students.

Self-Esteem

Consider, for example, a student who sees himself as a future nurse, but is not accepted into the nursing program at the university. What would be the consequences of this rejection for the future self? If the student had been accepted, how would this affect his future self?

Defining Self-Esteem.   **Self-esteem** is a case of *I* evaluating *me*, which results in either a positive or negative judgment (James, 1892). Thus, a person feels good about herself (positive self-esteem) if her current self compares well against possible selves, or she feels bad about herself (negative self-esteem) if the comparison is unfavorable. An insightful way of defining self-esteem was provided by James (1892, p. 187) through his formula:

$$\text{Self-esteem} = \frac{\text{Success}}{\text{Pretensions}}$$

In this context, pretensions could be thought of as imagined possible selves: to become a rock star, to become rich, to receive a $45,000-a-year starting salary, to become immensely popular as a motivational speaker, to earn a 4.00 GPA. Success is defined through achieving these possible selves or pretensions. For example, success means a student earned a 4.00 GPA and received a $45,000-a-year job offer on graduation. Lack of success, however, means most people considered the student's guitar playing and singing awful, and his motivational speeches put people to sleep. According to James, an individual can raise her level of self-esteem by either reducing the number of possible selves (pretensions) or by increasing the number of successes. Self-esteem is lowered, however, by decreasing the number of successes or increasing the number of possible selves (pretensions).

Self-Esteem Depends on the Contingency of Self-Worth.   The term *pretensions* in James's self-esteem formula has been transformed into the modern-day concept of **contingencies of self-worth** (Crocker et al., 2003). This term refers to specific domains in people's lives that they consider important for their self-esteem. High self-esteem or self-worth depends on success in those self-defined domains while low self-esteem is associated with failures. A person's endeavors that fall outside of those domains of contingency have no effect on self-worth. Crocker and coresearchers (2003) have hypothesized seven domains of contingencies of self-worth: others' approval, appearance, competition, academic competence, family support, virtue, and God's love. The domains are described in Table 9.3. An individual's level of contingent self-worth in each domain is measured with the 35-item

TABLE 9.3   Domains of Contingencies of Self-Worth

Contingency	Self-Esteem Depends on These Characteristics
Others' approval	The opinion, approval, or acceptance by other people in general
Appearance	A person's physical appearance of face and body
Competition	Outperforming or doing better than others in competitive tasks
Academic competence	Academic performance, high grades, doing well in school, or high on teachers' evaluations
Family support	Approval, acceptance, care, and love of family members
Virtue	Follow ethical principles or abide by a moral code
God's love	Belief that one is loved and valued by God; feeling of religiosity

Source: Adapted from "Contingencies of Self-Worth in College Students: Theory and Measurement" by J. Crocker et al., 2003, *Journal of Personality and Social Psychology, 85,* pp. 895, 896, and table 2, p. 899.

Contingencies of Self-Worth Scale (Crocker et al., 2003). A higher score indicates a greater level of contingent self-worth in a particular domain.

> ➤ The *Contingencies of Self-Worth Scale* is available at http://www.rcgd.isr.umich.edu/ crockerlab/scales/CSWscale.pdf

Self-esteem depends on the domain of contingent self-worth in which a person experiences success or failure. Crocker and coresearchers (2002, 2005) tested this hypothesis in the domain of academic competence. They measured the level of students' contingent self-worth with items from the *Contingencies of Self-Worth Scale*. A sample item from this domain is "My self-esteem is influenced by my academic performance" (Crocker et al., 2003, p. 899). Students rated themselves on this and similar items with the scale 1 = strongly disagree to 7 = strongly agree. Students one standard deviation below and above the mean on the *Scale* were defined as low and high in contingent academic self-worth, respectively. An important indicator of achievement in this domain is whether students are accepted to graduate schools. Does the rise or fall of a student's self-esteem depend on receiving a letter of acceptance or rejection and on whether they have high compared to low contingent self-worth in the domain of academic competence? In order to answer these questions, college seniors filled out a measure of self-esteem on days that a letter of acceptance or rejection was received and twice per week on regularly scheduled days when no news was received. The *Rosenberg Self-Esteem Inventory* was used to measure the level of self-esteem on all days.

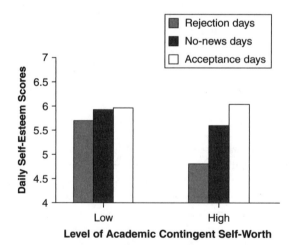

FIGURE 9.6   **Self-Esteem Depends on Academic Contingent Self-Worth.** Students low and high in academic contingent self-worth were affected differently by rejection from or acceptance to graduate school. Self-esteem dropped more with rejection and rose more with acceptance for students with a high academic contingent self-worth.

Source: Adapted from "Hopes Dashed and Dreams Fulfilled: Contingencies of Self-Worth and Graduate School Admissions" by J. Crocker et al., 2002, *Personality and Social Psychology Bulletin, 28,* p. 1280.

> The *Rosenberg Self-Esteem Scale* is available at http://www.bsos.umd.edu/socy/Research/rosenberg.htm

Measured self-esteem on a particular day depended on the type of letter received and on the level of contingent self-worth as shown in Figure 9.6. For students with high contingent self-worth, a letter of rejection lowered their self-esteem while a letter of acceptance raised their self-esteem compared to no-news days. For students with low contingent self-worth, letters of acceptance had no effect on self-esteem and a letter of rejection had a small negative effect on self-esteem compared to no-news days (Crocker et al., 2002, 2005). These results and others suggest that people's self-esteem rises and falls with successes and failures but only in those domains that they consider important.

Section Recap

Self-concept refers to a person's knowledge of herself organized into a schema or framework from which information about the self can be retrieved and evaluated. Self-concept develops through analysis of the self and from the feedback of others. The motivation for knowledge about the self is based on the assumption that the information be self-enhancing, consistent with current self-knowledge, and accurate. A person is motivated to aspire to a possible self that is more valued than the current self. *Self-esteem* refers to the evaluative feelings a person has about the self. According to James, self-esteem depended on how many possible selves (pretensions) a person has achieved or become. A contemporary view of pretensions is the concept of a *contingency of self-worth*, which can occur in various domains, such as academic competence. Successes in a domain boost self-esteem and failures lower self-esteem provided the individual has a high degree of contingent self-worth in that domain. Successes or failures in domains of low contingent self-worth have little effect on self-esteem.

ACTIVITIES

1. Measure your level on each of the big five per- factors by completing *The 40-Item .arker Set* in Table 9.2. Take the test ƆƆiological parent and try to determine if ilarity between your scores, if any, is the ƆƆf heredity, rearing, or their interaction. ~ preferences and behaviors seem to de- .hose personality factors on which you ᶇigh? In other words, does your person- ᶒtermine your motivation?

2. hink members of fraternities and soror- nore likely to be extraverts compared ᶇmbers? Why? Are there any other ac- groups on campus that introverts or would be more likely to do or join?

3. One characteristic of extraverts is that they smile and laugh more. If smiling and laughing is an outward sign of happiness, then it may be that extraverts are happier than introverts. In fact, some research indicates that they are. What do you think?

4. Body piercing (multiple earrings, nose rings, and lip rings) is a fashion in our society. Which component of sensation seeking do these individuals characterize: thrill and adventure seeking, experience seeking, disinhibition, or boredom susceptibility? Are there any other activities that would differentiate low- from high-sensation seekers on your campus? For example, art majors versus accounting majors,

smokers versus nonsmokers, drinkers versus nondrinkers. Can you add any other examples?

5. Based on James's formula (Self-esteem = Success/pretensions), you can have high self-esteem by having very few pretensions. If you advise people to raise their self-esteem by lowering pretensions, are you basically saying they should reduce their achievement motivation? Is there an inconsistency here?

6. Do you think people can raise their self-esteem by thinking about their successes and lower their self-esteem by thinking about their failures? Do people with low self-esteem dwell more on their failures, while those with high self-esteem dwell more on their successes? What do you think?

PART FOUR

External Sources
of Motivation

Have you noticed how much of your behavior is based on anticipated outcomes? Is behavior motivated to make some consequences happen and other consequences not happen? These consequences refer to the anticipated incentives or goals that a person's behavior brings. Incentives (Chapter 10) and goals (Chapter 11) motivate either approach or avoidance behavior. Positive incentives, such as a high GPA or a raise in pay, motivate approach behavior, which is designed to make these consequences happen. Negative incentives, however, such as failing grades or a cut in pay, motivate avoidance behavior, which is designed to prevent these consequences. People commit to goals that they plan to achieve. An incentive provides extra motivation on the way toward achieving a goal. A university degree, for example, is a goal for students, while course grades are incentives to motivate students along the way.

What determines the motivational strength of incentives and goals? The answer is linked to the concept of value and utility. Value refers to quantity while utility refers to usefulness. Thus, $100 has greater value than $10 but also has greater utility, since more services and goods can be bought with $100. As incentive or goal value increases, motivation increases. In addition, positive and negative values motivate opposing behaviors at different intensities. Loss has a stronger impact than does an identical gain. People are motivated more to prevent negative events like a loss, failure, or lower status.

Is behavior always performed for extrinsic reasons—that is, for anticipated consequences? Can't behavior also simply occur for its own sake without external rewards? Yes, sometimes behavior is motivating in its own right, which is referred to as intrinsic motivation (Chapter 10). Recreation, hobbies, and leisure time activities occur because these behaviors are enjoyed for their own sake.

How is motivation affected by the delay interval between the present and a future goal? The delay interval reduces the motivating effects of future incentives compared to immediate ones. For example, an exam one day away provides more motivation for study than does an exam one week away. Also, do you ever estimate the likelihood that you can achieve your chosen goal? Motivation is also affected by the likelihood that a goal will be achieved. As likelihood increases, motivation increases. Among goals of equal value, likely goals are more motivating than unlikely ones.

Do some goals seem more expensive to achieve than others in terms of response, time, and energy costs? Chapter 12 (Economics of Motivation) describes how various costs affect goal achievement. Incentives and goals are like the items available at the store. Some are more expensive than others just like some goals are more difficult to achieve than others. They require more behavior, time, and effort. Usually, as the cost of goals increase, the demand for them decreases. Fewer people try to achieve expensive goals, such as a 4.00 GPA, an Olympic gold medal, or the presidency. However, people have motivation resources with which to achieve their goals, such as their behavior, time, and energy.

CHAPTER

10 Extrinsic and Intrinsic Motivation

A thing is worth whatever the buyer will pay for it.

—Publius Syrus, 50 B.C.

Let not the enjoyment of pleasure now within our grasp be carried to such excess as to incapacitate you from future repetition.

—Seneca, 4 B.C.–65 A.D.

■ In the push/pull metaphor of motivation, motives are within the person and push while incentives are outside the person and either pull or repel. What qualities determine their strength of attraction or repulsion? How does this strength wane with temporal distance after which the incentive becomes available? These considerations are rephrased in the following questions for you to think about:

1. How do incentives differ from reinforcers and punishers in motivating behavior?
2. What characteristics influence the value of an incentive?
3. How does incentive value affect the motivation of behavior?
4. Are some behaviors freely chosen—that is, not coerced by incentives?
5. Can behavior be motivating in its own right—that is, be intrinsically motivating?
6. How do extrinsic and intrinsic sources interact to motivate behavior?

Extrinsic Motivation and Incentive Value

According to the familiar axiom of "wanting more," to have something desirable is good, and to have more of it is better, and to have still more is better yet; to have less is worse. One corollary of the axiom of wanting more is that the more frequently a desirable event occurs, the better it is, and the less frequently it occurs the worse it is. A second corollary is that the sooner a desirable event occurs the better it is, and the later it occurs the worse it is. The reverse, then, is likely to be true: to have something undesirable is bad, to have more of it is worse, and to have still more is worse yet; to have less is better. A corollary of this axiom is that the more frequently an undesirable event occurs, the worse it is, and the less frequently it occurs the better it is. A second corollary is that the sooner an unpleasant event occurs, the worse it is and the later it occurs the better it is.

239

These axioms, or self-evident truths, describe some major features of extrinsic motivation: often more and larger incentives are preferred—though not in the case of negative incentives—and are more motivating than fewer and smaller incentives.

The purpose of this section is to describe what characteristics determine the value of an incentive and how this affects a person's choices and behavior.

Reinforcers and Punishers versus Incentives

How does a student know which behaviors result in good grades? How does a worker know how to earn a year-end bonus? Why does the prospect of good grades or a bonus motivate certain behaviors and not others? These questions address the difference between reinforcers and punishers, on the one hand, and positive and negative incentives, on the other. The difference is based on the effects of past events versus the anticipation of future events. In the past, attending class, studying, or working diligently resulted in a good grade or year-end bonus. When anticipating the future, a good grade or year-end bonus motivates behavior.

Selecting versus Motivating Behavior.   Learning what to do and actually doing it illustrate the separate effects of reinforcers and incentives (Cofer & Appley, 1964; Tolman, 1955; Tolman & Honzik, 1930). Learning what to do results from the action of **reinforcers**. These are stimuli that select appropriate behaviors and make them more likely to occur in a situation (see Skinner, 1938, 1953; Staddon & Simmelhag, 1971). Learning what *not* to do results from the action of **punishers** that select against behaviors and make them less likely to occur (Skinner, 1953). Thus, attending class and studying are selected for by good grades (reinforcers), while skipping classes and not studying are selected against by failing exams and courses (punishers). **Incentives** are the external stimuli that motivate or induce behavior to occur (Bolles, 1975; Logan & Wagner, 1965). A *positive incentive* motivates the behavior that is instrumental in attaining the incentive. For example, the incentive of a good grade motivates studying. A *negative incentive* motivates avoidance behavior, which is instrumental in averting or preventing the incentives from happening. For example, the negative incentive of failing a course motivates a student to avoid skipping classes.

Past versus Future.   Reinforcers and punishers are the actual consequences of behavior, whereas positive and negative incentives are the anticipated consequences. Incentives influence behavior based on their anticipation (Bolles, 1975; Karniol & Ross, 1996). Both mechanistic and cognitive accounts have been provided as explanations. According to one mechanistic explanation, anticipation of an incentive consists of minuscule responses that resemble the final consummatory response of the incentive (Hull, 1952). For instance, a person salivates driving to a restaurant and then, when there, he salivates more intensely while eating. Or a student smiles in anticipation of receiving congratulations from family members at graduation. According to a cognitive explanation, people visualize themselves in a future incentive situation (Markus & Nurius, 1986). For instance, a student cognitively represents the incentive of a university degree as "my earning a B.A. or B.S." The cognitive representation bridges the present to the future and motivates a person's behavior. Thus, a student may form a mental image of her professor giving an exam, which in turn motivates the student to study for the exam.

TABLE 10.1   Distinction between Reinforcers and Punishers versus Positive and Negative Incentives

	Outcomes of Behavior: Past Events	Anticipated Outcomes of Behavior: Future Events
Positive Stimulus	Reinforcer: Behavior is selected for and becomes more likely. Example: Past passing grade, parental approval, and pride	Positive Incentive: Motivates approach behavior to attain the incentive Example: Anticipated passing grade, parental approval, and pride
Negative Stimulus	Punisher: Behavior is selected against and becomes less likely. Example: Past failing grade, parental disapproval, and shame	Negative Incentive: Motivates avoidance behaviors to prevent occurrence of incentive Example: Anticipated failing grade, parental disapproval, and shame

Some incentives are derived from their association with reinforcement and punishment. If a response consistently results in a reinforcer, then that reinforcer becomes a positive incentive; it will be sought out or approached. If a response consistently results in a punisher, then that punisher becomes a negative incentive; it will be avoided or prevented (Bolles, 1975; Logan, 1960). In some instances, however, prior experience seems unnecessary for a stimulus to act as an incentive. A new car, for example, serves as an incentive to save money even if an individual has never owned a new car. A person also avoids touching a hot stove even if she has never been burned by one before. Table 10.1 summarizes the distinctions between reinforcers and punishers and positive and negative incentives.

Progress through a university illustrates the distinctions in Table 10.1. Studying and attending class produce passing grades, parental approval, and a feeling of pride. These consequences are reinforcers, provided they increase or maintain those behaviors. As anticipated consequences these outcomes serve as positive incentives that motivate a student to attend class and study. Not attending class and not studying produce failing grades, parental disapproval, and perhaps a feeling of shame. These consequences are classified as punishers, provided they decrease those behaviors. As anticipated consequences these outcomes are negative incentives if they motivate a student to avoid them by not missing class and not neglecting to study (see Table 10.1).

Objective and Subjective Incentive Value

An incentive refers to the motivational properties of a reinforcer. The value of an incentive determines its preference and motivational strength. Terms like *more, bigger*, and *better* usually indicate increased value of a positive incentive, while *less, smaller*, and *worse* usually indicate decreased value. **Incentive value** refers to the attractiveness of an incentive and is based on objective properties like the number or the amount. Objective incentive value refers to physical properties of an incentive, while subjective incentive value refers to an individual's appraisal of the objective value. The distinction between the objective and subjective value of economic goods serves as a case in point. According to economists, subjective value is synonymous with **utility**, which refers to the satisfaction, pleasure, or usefulness of an economic good. A pencil has a certain objective value based, say, on how much it costs, but it also has a great deal of utility. It is a very useful instrument (try attending school without one). Utility rather than objective value provides a better understanding of why economic goods such as cars, clothes, and computers are satisfying.

What is the nature of the relationship between the objective and subjective value or utility of an incentive? One answer was provided by Fechner (1860/1966), who explored the relationship between stimulus intensities and corresponding psychological sensations. He showed that equal increases in stimulus intensity produce smaller and smaller increases in sensations. For instance, equal increases in a tone's loudness produce increases in the sensation of loudness but in diminishing amounts. This relationship became known as **Fechner's law.** Several economists in the late 1800s noted that the relationship between amount of money and its utility followed Fechner's law (Stigler, 1950). Even earlier, in 1738, the French mathematician Bernoulli made a similar proposal about money and its utility (Stevens, 1972). Figure 10.1 shows such a relationship: as the number of dollars increases, the utility of those dollars increases but in diminishing amounts. (Utility is measured in utils, units employed at one time by economists to indicate the utility of economic goods.) Thus in Figure 10.1, the first $10 corresponds to 10 utils of satisfaction, whereas the next $10 corresponds to approximately 9 more utils of satisfaction. Although $20 is twice as much as $10, $20 does not have twice as much utility as $10. Equal increments in

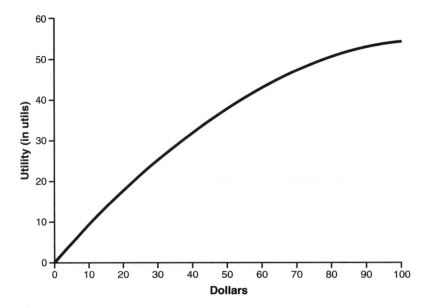

FIGURE 10.1   Dollars and Utility. The relationship between the number of dollars and their utility is such that as the dollar amount increases, utility increases, but in smaller and smaller amounts. The graph is only an approximation of the true dollar-utility relationship.

dollar value lead to smaller and smaller increases in utility. Perhaps the most general statement we can make about money and its utility is that more is better.

Incentives as Losses and Gains

Suppose there is very little time remaining in a very exciting game and your team has the ball. Will your team score and win the game or fail to do so and lose? The outcome of any game ends with a change in status for each team. One team attains a positive incentive or win, while the other team fails to prevent a negative incentive or loss. Which outcome has the greater psychological effect? The win or the loss?

Losses Loom Larger Than Gains. Rather than considering incentives as absolutes, think of them as gains and losses (Kahneman & Tversky, 1979, 1982). With this thought, positive incentives become gains, and negative incentives become losses. For instance, a *B* grade earned in a course is a positive incentive if it increases a student's GPA but a negative incentive if it decreases GPA. Furthermore, the impact of incentives as gains and losses, although opposite, are not equal. **Losses loom larger than gains,** which means losses are more dissatisfying than gains are satisfying (Kahneman & Tversky, 1979, 1982). For instance, a \$100 loss produces a greater decrease in subjective value than a \$100 gain produces an increase. In other words, a \$100 loss is more dissatisfying than a \$100 gain is satisfying.

Buyer and Seller Experiments. A technique for determining the effects of losses and gains involves using identical measuring units to assess both outcomes. Money is a good measure because it reflects how much a person pays to gain (buy) an item and how much a person receives for the loss (sale) of an item. Using this approach, Kahneman and associates (1990) conducted a marketing experiment during which they randomly gave half the students in a class some attractive coffee mugs imprinted with the name of the university. The new owners were informed that the mugs were theirs to keep or they could sell them. The nonowners were told to examine their neighbors' mugs and that they could offer them any price in order to buy one. Owners (potential sellers) had to decide at what price they were willing to sell their mugs. Nonowners (potential buyers) had to decide how much they were willing to pay for the mugs. The purpose of the individual price setting was to determine the subjective value of the loss of a mug when sold and the subjective value of the gain of a mug when bought. To summarize:

> Willingness-to-accept price = Subjective value of a loss of the mug
> Willingness-to-pay price = Subjective value of a gain of the mug

If losses are more dissatisfying than gains are satisfying, then the sellers' prices should be higher than the buyers' prices. In other words, the decrease in value from losing (selling) a mug would be greater than the increase in value from gaining (buying) a mug. To make these experiments as realistic as possible, Kahneman and associates (1990) also let students barter for pens and folding binoculars in addition to coffee mugs. Students had been told to bring their own money to class in order to make any purchases, and provisions were made for extending credit and for making change. The results of several experiments are shown in Figure 10.2. For all commodities, a typical seller's willingness-to-accept price exceeded a typical prospective buyer's willingness-to-pay price (Kahneman et al., 1990).

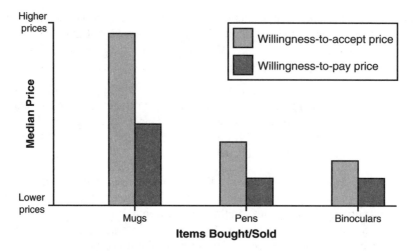

FIGURE 10.2   Loss/Gain and Buyer/Seller Behavior. Typical median willingness-to-accept prices were greater than median willingness-to-pay prices for mugs, pens, and binoculars. When seller and buyer agreed on price, money and goods changed hands.

Source: Adapted from "Experimental Tests of the Endowment Effect and the Coase Theorem" by D. Kahneman et al., 1990, *Journal of Political Economy, 98,* table 2, p. 1332, and table 3, p. 1334.

This difference in price indicates that the loss of a particular item was more dissatisfying than the gain of the same item was satisfying.

Section Recap

Prior reinforcers and punishers provide the knowledge and anticipated incentives provide the motivation for what behavior to carry out in a particular situation. *Reinforcers* select a particular behavior, making it more likely to occur in the appropriate situation. *Punishers*, however, select against a particular behavior, making it less likely to occur. *Incentives* are external stimuli that induce or motivate the behavior to occur in a particular situation. People are motivated toward positive and away from negative incentives.

The degree an incentive motivates behavior depends on its *incentive value,* which is based on objective properties such as number or quantity. Subjective value or *utility* is based on the pleasure, satisfaction, or usefulness of the incentive. As objective incentive value increases, subjective value or utility increases but in smaller and smaller amounts, as described by *Fechner's law.* Positive incentives can be interpreted as gains and negative incentives as losses. According to the view that *losses loom larger than gains,* the loss of an incentive is more dissatisfying than the gain of an incentive is satisfying.

Factors That Affect Incentive Value

Storewide Clearance: 40% to 50% off original prices
One Day Sale: Fantastic Storewide Savings
Up to 50% Off Sale
Every car, truck, and van in stock MARKED DOWN

Sale notices bring customers into stores and motivate them to buy. If a shirt has a sign marked "33% off the original price," then shoppers are more likely to buy it than if it is listed for the same price but without the sale sign. For example, they are more likely to buy a shirt advertised at "$20, marked down from $30" than to buy it when simply priced at $20. Is it just the lower price or also the contrast between the original and the sale price that motivates shoppers to buy?

The purpose of this section is to describe some of the properties of incentives that motivate behavior.

Amount

An important feature of incentive motivation is **incentive amount,** which refers to the quantity or number of incentives. Crespi (1942) demonstrated the effect of incentive amount on how fast rats would run down a straight alley to a goal box holding either 16, 64, or a whopping 256 food units. His rats ran fastest for 256 food units and slowest for 16 units. Kraeling (1961) provided rats with 2.5, 5.0, or 10.0% sucrose solutions as incentives for running down an alley. Her results indicated that rats ran consistently faster for the 10.0% sucrose concentration and slower for the 2.5% sucrose concentration, with an intermediate speed for the 5.0% concentration. Clearly, running, which is instrumental in obtaining the incentive, increases with an increase in the amount of the incentive.

Incentive value also affects the motivation for behavior not to occur. For instance, incentives have been used to reduce smoking in university students. Correia and Benson (2006) recruited smokers in order to examine the motivating effects of incentive amount on smoking abstinence. Participants reported to the laboratory twice per day for one week and were paid in cash if their carbon monoxide level was below the criterion amount. Carbon monoxide is obtained from a person's breath and indicates the amount a person has smoked recently along with reports of the number of cigarettes smoked and hours of not smoking. The amount paid defined the incentive value for not smoking: up to $40 versus $80 for the week. The results indicated that the larger incentive was more effective in reducing smoking than the smaller incentive. Carbon monoxide levels and the number of cigarettes smoked were lower for smokers who received the larger incentive. In addition, they also reported a greater number of hours of not smoking.

Rate of Reinforcement

The frequency of an incentive or reinforcer also affects motivation. Rate of reinforcement is studied in situations where an animal is given a choice between two responses, one of which is reinforced more frequently. For example, pigeons are presented with two response keys to peck. Pecking one key yields 30 reinforcers per hour while pecking the other key yields 15 or 45 reinforcers per hour. If reinforcement rate affects motivation, then the pigeon should peck whatever key produces the higher rate. To verify this prediction, Herrnstein (1961) varied the rate of reinforcement between the left and right response keys. For example, pecking the left response key yielded 27 reinforces per hour while the right key yielded 13 reinforcers per hour. The results showed that pigeons chose the left response key more than the right one, since the former provided a higher rate of reinforcement. Humans are also affected by the rate of reinforcement. Neef and associates (1992) reinforced special education students for working on math problems from one of two stacks situated on the students' right and left. When students worked on one stack of problems they were reinforced with a nickel or token every 30 seconds, on average, compared to every 120 seconds from the other stack. The rate of reinforcement affected their choice. Students spent more time working math problems from the stack that provided a higher rate of reinforcement. Thus, animals and humans shift to activities that provide higher rates of reinforcement (de Villiers, 1977). **Melioration** refers to a shift toward an activity that is more lucrative or provides a greater rate of reinforcement (Herrnstein, 1990). For example, if the rate of reinforcement declines for one activity, then a person switches to another activity that provides a higher rate. To illustrate, a person may switch credit cards to one that offers a lower interest rate, go to another restaurant because the food is better, or change into a clean shirt.

One implication of melioration is that a faster rate of responding will produce a faster rate of reinforcement. Imagine a hungry rat in a Skinner Box that is reinforced with food each time it presses a lever. Faster rates of responding result in faster rates of reinforcement. A similar relationship exists in the "real world" between the amount of responding and the magnitude of the reinforcer. For example, enrolling in more courses results in quicker graduation, studying more results in higher grades, and working more hours produces larger paychecks. Lippman (2000) provided experimental demonstrations of this relationship. In order to earn points (reinforcers), participants pushed a button. All that was required for a fixed amount of reinforcement was to push the button once at the conclusion of a 15-second interval. However, additional button presses during the 15 seconds increased the size of the reinforcer in one condition while it decreased the size of the reinforcer in another condition. As might be expected, response rate increased when it provided for a larger reinforcer and decreased when it produced smaller reinforcers. Lippman's (2000) experiments showed that the amount of the anticipated incentive determines the rate of responding.

Contrast Effects

How effective is showing the sale price alongside the old price in motivating shoppers to buy? How motivating is a wage of $10 per hour? Well that depends. Did the worker just receive a raise from $8 per hour or a pay cut from $12 per hour?

Contrast of Incentive Amount.   The phenomenon of **contrast effects** means that the ability of an incentive to motivate behavior depends on how it differs from prior incentives. *Positive incentive contrast* refers to an upward shift in value, which increases behavior above what is considered normal. For example, after receiving a substantial raise, workers perform more efficiently. *Negative incentive contrast* refers to a downward shift in value, which decreases behavior below what is considered normal. For instance, after their salaries were cut, workers performed less efficiently. Evidence for the effects of incentive contrast comes mainly from animal research. Pieper and Marx (1963) made either a 4, 11.3, or 32% sucrose solution available to rats in their cages. The sucrose concentration became the rat's neutral point to which subsequent sucrose concentrations were contrasted. In the next phase of the experiment, rats were required to lever press in order to earn an 11.3% sucrose reinforcer. For the rats accustomed to a 4% solution, 11.3% was an increase in incentive amount. They lever pressed at a faster rate than the rats accustomed to the 11.3% concentration. For the rats accustomed to a 32% sucrose solution, 11.3% was a decrease in incentive amount. They lever pressed slower than the 11.3% group. Thus, the motivating effects of an 11.3% sucrose solution depended on its contrast with the previous amount of sucrose.

Increases in incentive amount increased motivation, and decreases in incentive amount decreased motivation. However, although negative contrast has been observed consistently, the reliability of positive contrast has been questioned (Bolles, 1975; Dunham, 1968). For instance, if an animal is responding at close to maximum effort, then it would be difficult to show an increase with an upward shift in incentive amount. Similarly, if a salesperson has been working very hard already, it may not be possible to show an increase in sales with a pay raise.

Hedonic Contrast.   Results of incentive contrast experiments bear a striking resemblance to the **law of hedonic contrast,** which Beebe-Center (1932/1965) attributed to the German psychophysicist Fechner (1876). According to this law, the pleasure a stimulus gives will be greater if it contrasts with sources of lesser pleasure or displeasure. Similarly, the displeasure a stimulus gives will be greater if it contrasts with sources of greater pleasure or less displeasure. Contrast effects, however, also depend on how those other sources are categorized. Are they from the same or a different category? Zellner and coresearchers (2003) investigated the effects that category membership had on the hedonic evaluation of fruit drinks. Three groups of participants evaluated the pleasantness of eight fruit-flavored drinks followed by two diluted test drinks. The test drinks were either from the same or a different category than the prior eight. One group was told that all 10 solutions were commercial drinks from England—that is, the two test drinks were from the same category as the first eight drinks. Another group was informed that only the last two solutions were drinks from England—that is, the last two drinks were from a different category. A control group only evaluated the two diluted test drinks.

Contrast effects were apparent in two ways. First, the two diluted drinks were rated lower in pleasantness when they followed the eight full-strength solutions as compared to being the only two drinks. In addition, the test drinks were rated as more unpleasant when they were labeled as being from the same category compared to a different category. Zellner and coresearchers (2002) found similar results for coffee and beer. The contrast effect of ordinary coffee compared to gourmet coffee was greater when all coffees were labeled as belonging to the same compared to different categories. Contrast effects were also greater for beers from the same category than from different categories. These category effects imply that people's stimulus preferences can be manipulated through comparison with other stimuli. The contrast effects will be greater if people are told the comparison stimuli are from the same category rather than a different category.

Contrast effects also depend on a person's expectations. For instance, students have experienced changes in their feelings as a result of the contrast between the exam grade they expected and the grade they received (Shepperd & McNulty, 2002). Imagine a class where you have taken an exam and that you expected an *A*. When the professor returned the exam, you found that you earned an *A* (or *C*). How does that make you feel? Or, imagine that you expected a *C* on the exam and found that you earned a *C* (or *A*). How does that make you feel? More precisely, how unhappy or happy would you feel about expecting an *A* and receiving an *A* or *C* and expecting a *C* and receiving a *C* or *A*? Use the following scale: 1 = Very unhappy to 7 = Very happy. The hedonic contrast effects found in such an experiment as this are presented in Figure 10.3 (Shepperd & McNulty, 2002). An *A* grade produces the greatest happiness if contrasted with an expected *C* rather than an expected *A*. And a *C* grade produces the least happiness if contrasted with an expected *A* rather than an expected *C*.

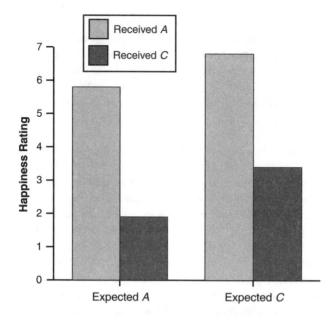

FIGURE 10.3   Happiness and Expected Grades. Happiness ratings were highest when the received grade was higher than the expected grade (expected *C*, received *A*). Happiness ratings were lowest when the received grade was lower than the expected grade (expected *A*, received *C*). Ratings were intermediate when the received grade matched the expected grade, although an *A* produced greater happiness than a *C*.

Source: Adapted from "The Affective Consequences of Expected and Unexpected Outcomes" by J. A. Shepperd and J. K. McNulty, 2002, *Psychological Science, 13,* table 1, p. 86.

Temporal Motivation Theory

You have known for two weeks that there will be an exam on this material but you have not started studying in earnest until two days before. Why is that? One answer is that incentives are based in the future. This feature has tremendous negative impact on incentive value. Although incentive value increases with amount, it decreases with delay. How do these two features combine to determine the value or utility of a future incentive? Remember that value refers to the amount of an incentive while utility refers to its usefulness. Thus, $50 has greater value than $10 but it also has greater utility, since more goods and services can be purchased with $50.

Incentive Utility from Amount and Delay.   Several mathematical formulas express how the utility of an incentive changes with delay (Green & Myerson, 2004; Mazur, 1987; Steel & König, 2006). As part of their temporal motivation theory, Steel and König (2006) provide the following formula:

$$\text{Utility} = \frac{\text{Expected incentive value}}{(1 + \text{Delay interval})}$$

Temporal motivation theory integrates how incentive utility changes temporally (with time) (Steel & König, 2006). Utility in this formula refers to the ability of a positive incentive to motivate approach behavior and a negative incentive to motivate avoidance behavior. The term *expected* in the formula refers to the likelihood that the incentive will occur. The expectation is that the incentive is promised or likely to happen although not guaranteed. For example, a job interview may result in a job and diligent studying may result in an *A*. However, the job or the *A* are not guaranteed. Finally, the denominator of the formula represents the temporal distance to the incentive—that is, the incentive delay interval.

This *interval* refers to the time between current behavior and the availability of a future incentive. For example, there is a delay between a telephone call for a date and the actual date or between studying and taking an exam. The Saturday night date (the incentive) occurs some time after (the delay) the telephone call. The exam is scheduled some time after a student has studied. As a consequence of this delay, incentives lose value. A future incentive is represented in the present at a marked-down value by a process known as **delay discounting** or temporal discounting (Green & Myerson, 2004; Myerson & Green, 1995). The amount of discounting increases with the length of the delay interval. For instance, the value of a Saturday night date or an exam depends on how far in the future they are. The later they occur, the lower their value in the present. However, as their due time approaches, their value increases. As Saturday night approaches, the value of the date increases, and as exam time approaches, the value of the exam increases.

According to the utility formula, as the incentive delay interval decreases (approaches 0), the utility of the incentive increases for both positive and negative incentives. Figure 10.4 illustrates this relationship. The increase in utility is the result of a decline in delay discounting. When the incentive is reached, the delay interval equals zero (delay = 0), and the incentive value equals the amount of the incentive. At this point, a positive incentive becomes a reinforcer, and a negative incentive becomes a punisher (Rachlin, 1989). However, their values are not equal. The absolute value of a negative incentive is greater than the absolute value of an identical positive incentive. The reason for this is based on the concept *losses loom larger than gains*, which was described earlier. Thus, the negative-incentive curve in Figure 10.4 declines more steeply than the positive-incentive curve rises (Knetsch & Sinden, 1984; Miller, 1959).

Some experiments illustrating delay discounting require participants to make a choice between two monetary values. For example, they might be asked to choose between $800 right now or $1,000 after six months and between $600 right now or $1,000 after one year. By examining the pattern of choices, researchers have determined the discounted value of $1,000 and $10,000 after delay periods ranging from zero to 25 years (300 months) (Green et al., 1994a; Myerson & Green, 1995; Rachlin et al., 1991). The curve of discounted values across delay periods resembles the positive-incentive curve in Figure 10.4. In other words, as the delay interval of receiving $1,000 or $10,000 increases, the discounted value of that money decreases. Delay discounting indicates that participants are more likely to accept a smaller amount immediately rather than larger amounts after a delay. In other words, we want our money immediately rather than waiting, even if it means receiving less.

Preference Reversal.   Have you ever planned to do one thing only to change your mind later? For example, you planned to get up early to study for an exam but when the alarm went off you decided to remain in bed. This example illustrates a reversal of incentive or

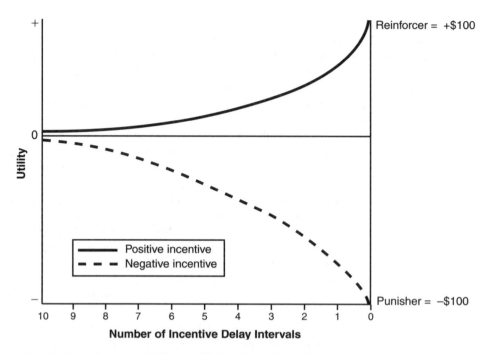

FIGURE 10.4 Incentive Utility and Delay. The values of both a positive incentive (+$100) and a negative incentive (−$100) increase as their delay intervals decrease. When the incentives are reached (zero delay), the positive incentive equals the reinforcer (gain $100), and the negative incentive equals the punisher (lose $100). The subjective absolute value of the negative incentive is greater than that of the positive incentive.

reward preferences. Generally, people prefer large incentives over small incentives and immediate incentives over delayed incentives. When amount and delay are combined, however, a person may prefer a small immediate incentive (sleep) over a larger delayed incentive (good grades). Then, as the delay interval lengthens, preference shifts from the small immediate incentive to the large delayed incentive. This process is known as **preference reversal** (Green et al., 1994a; Green & Myerson, 2004; Steel & König, 2006). For example, the night before a student prefers a good grade (the larger, more delayed incentive) over extra sleep (the smaller, less delayed incentive). However, the next morning a student prefers extra sleep (the smaller incentive) because it is available immediately (no delay). Figure 10.5 illustrates preference reversal between time *x* and time *y*. During time *x*, the larger delayed incentive has a higher value, but as the delay interval decreases, the smaller immediate incentive attains a higher value during time *y*. Thus, preference reversal occurs because of the change in value between two incentives over time.

In a demonstration of preference reversal, participants were presented with choices between different dollar amounts that were available after various delays (Green et al., 1994a). The choices pitted smaller against larger dollar amounts, such as $20 versus $50, $100 versus $250, and $500 versus $1,250. The choices also pitted shorter delay intervals

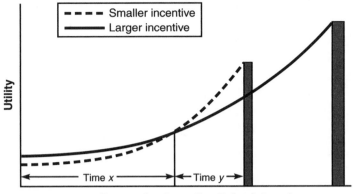

Decreasing Incentive Delay Interval

FIGURE 10.5   Changes in Incentive Value or Utility Over Time. During time x, the larger incentive has a greater value than the smaller incentive. As the delay interval decreases, the smaller incentive attains the higher value during time y.

against longer delay intervals ranging from zero to 20 years. As an illustration, decide between each of the following six choices:

Choice 1. $25 now	versus	$50 now
Choice 2. $25 now	versus	$50 in 2 weeks
Choice 3. $25 now	versus	$50 in 4 weeks
Choice 4. $25 now	versus	$50 in 6 weeks
Choice 5. $25 now	versus	$50 in 8 weeks
Choice 6. $25 now	versus	$50 in 10 weeks

Assume that a hypothetical individual preferred $50 on choice 1 and also preferred $50 on choices 2 through 4—that is, he preferred the larger delayed reward over the smaller immediate reward. If on choices 5 and 6 the person selected $25, then he reversed and preferred the smaller immediate reward over the larger delayed reward. This preference reversal occurred between choices 4 and 5 because the larger reward of $50 was discounted at the longer delay intervals so that its value fell below the value of an immediate $25.

Procrastination.   Waiting until the last hour to file a federal tax return, not studying for an exam until the last opportunity, or finishing a paper until late the night before it is due are examples of procrastination. However, is procrastination merely putting off until later what can be done now? One perspective is that "to procrastinate is to delay an intended course of action despite expecting to be worse off for the delay" (Steel, 2007, p. 66). This definition indicates that procrastination depends on the temporal distance of the important activity and the state of being "worse off." For example, an essay that is due in one week has high positive utility and being "worse off" is also high. Not writing the essay in this case would be an instance of procrastination. Steel (2007) presents a hypothetical illustration of student procrastination, which is summarized in Figure 10.6. A student is assigned an essay on September 15 that is due on December 16, a 92-day delay. The expected

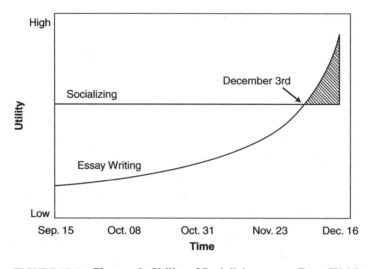

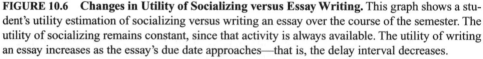

FIGURE 10.6   Changes in Utility of Socializing versus Essay Writing. This graph shows a student's utility estimation of socializing versus writing an essay over the course of the semester. The utility of socializing remains constant, since that activity is always available. The utility of writing an essay increases as the essay's due date approaches—that is, the delay interval decreases.

Source: From "The Nature of Procrastination: A Meta-Analytic and Theoretical Review of Quintessential Self-Regulatory Failure" by P. Steel, 2007, *Psychological Bulletin, 133,* figure 1, p. 72. Copyright 2007 by American Psychological Association. Reprinted by permission.

incentive value of the essay is based on its letter grade and the likelihood that the student's efforts will produce it. However, how high should the utility of the essay be so that a student will work on it compared to other activity-related utilities? In Figure 10.6, socializing is always available either down the hall, across the campus, or with a phone call. So a student socializes because its utility is higher than essay writing. However, on December 3, 12 days before the essay is due, its utility exceeds that of socializing and the student begins to work.

The formula [Utility = (Expected incentive value) / (1 + Delay interval)] helps show what factors will affect procrastination. First, the lower incentive value of a task, the more people will procrastinate on it. For example, students are more likely to procrastinate on assignments they consider less interesting (Ackerman & Gross, 2005). Second, as indicated in Figure 10.6, when procrastinating on a task individuals are doing something else, such as socializing. Thus, procrastination should increase for alternative activities that have greater value. For example, students procrastinate with activities that they consider more pleasant, less stressful, and less difficult than their assignments (Pychyl et al., 2000a). They procrastinate by watching TV, sleeping, talking, playing, eating, or working.

What are some examples of being "worse off" that result from procrastination? One obvious illustration is that procrastination results in less time in which to accomplish one's goal, assignment, or project. One way of defining procrastinators is to use various available psychological scales such as Lay's (1986) *General Procrastination Scale.* Students identified as procrastinators, for example, tend to predict that they will study less for an exam and do so. In addition, they are more likely than nonprocrastinators to cram by squeezing more of their study time into the last three days (Pychyl et al., 2000b). In general, investigations have concluded that procrastination does make a person worse off. Rothblum and associates (1986) found that students identified as procrastinators had lower GPAs for the semester, delayed taking self-paced quizzes, and had more anxiety or anxiety-related symptoms that accompanied their pro-crastination. Tice and Baumeister (1997) also showed that procrastinators as defined by Lay's (1986) *General Procrastination Scale* turned in their papers later or late, earned lower scores on their papers, and earned lower exam scores in the course. In addition, procrastination took its toll on the procrastinators at the end of the semester. Procrastinators reported more stress, more symptoms, and more health center visits than did nonprocrastinators (see Figure 7.5).

➤ Lay's (1986) *General Procrastination Scale* is available at http://www.yorku.ca/rokada/psyctest/prcrasts.pdf

Section Recap

Incentive amount refers to the objective quantity or number of stimuli that serve as incentives. Usually, as incentive amount increases, indicators of motivation also increase. Incentives also affect choice behavior, as shown by the fact that an animal or person will shift to a better in-centive if one is available. According to the concept of *melioration* a person keeps shifting to alternatives that provide a higher rate of reinforcement than the current one. The phenomenon of *contrast effects* means that the motivational effects of an incentive depend on the organism's experience with prior incentives. Positive incentive contrast refers to a sudden increase in the incentive that results in a sudden upward shift in motivation. Negative incentive contrast, however, refers to a sudden decrease in the incentive that results in a sudden downward shift in motivation. The *law of hedonic contrast* refers to the subjective feelings that accompany incentive contrasts. Positive contrast produces pleasant feelings, while negative contrast produces unpleasant feelings.

According to *temporal motivation theory*, the utility (usefulness) of an incentive de-pends on the value of the expected incentive and when it becomes available in the future. This relationship is expressed in the formula: Utility = (Expected incentive value) / (1 + Delay interval). The incentive delay interval represents the time span between the present and the availability of the incentive in the future. *Delay discounting* is the process by which the future incentive is represented in the present but at a reduced (discounted) value. Thus, longer delays result in greater discounting, which can result in *preference reversal*. This means that initially an individual prefers incentive A over B, but as the delay interval de-creases, preferences reverse and incentive B is now preferred over A. Procrastination is a form of preference reversal. The important task has been discounted to the extent that an immediate alternative activity is preferable.

Intrinsic Motivation

Not all behavior is done for extrinsic incentives. Many activities are done for no apparent external reasons. To illustrate, consider author John Irving's motivation for writing:

> The unspoken factor is love. The reason I can work so hard at my writing is that it's not work for me. Or, as I said before, work is pleasure to me. I work, and always have, quite obsessively. I can't just write for four or five hours and then turn the book off. I wake up in the middle of the night and I'm writing it. (Amabile, 1989, p. 56)

Consider the motivation for dancing to rock-and-roll music expressed by a dancer:

> When you feel [the music] resonating through you, it really helps. Cause when it's loud, like when you're dancing to a rock group, you can really feel yourself vibrate almost. And also, the louder it is, the more it blocks out other noises, so it's more of a total immersion in the music, which is also a very good sensation and is also conducive to just dancing and being part of the music—almost incorporating it. (Csikszentmihalyi, 1975, p. 105)

In these examples, the motivation for writing or dancing seems inherent in the activity. External incentives are not apparent.

The purpose of this section is to examine differences between motivation for an activity that seems inherent or intrinsic to that activity and motivation that is external or extrinsic to the activity. Another purpose is to describe how these two types of motivation interact.

Differences between Extrinsic and Intrinsic Motivation

For what reasons are you reading these pages? To earn a good grade on the exam or to please your parents? To feel good about yourself or to reduce anxiety about a forthcoming exam? To learn the material so that it can be put to future use? To act in accord with your self-concept as a student? To satisfy curiosity or because the material is interesting?

The source of motivation defines whether behavior is extrinsically or intrinsically motivated. **Extrinsic motivation** comes from an external source, such as money, good grades, or the approval of others. **Intrinsic motivation,** in contrast, does not come from an external source but instead is inherent in the activity being performed. Extrinsically motivated behavior is coerced (forced) by environmental contingencies, while intrinsically motivated behavior is freely chosen (Deci & Ryan, 1985). Money forces a person to work. A passing grade on an exam forces a student to study. Intrinsically motivated behavior, however, is not forced by environmental events. The activity is performed because the person seemingly wants to experience the activity for its own sake. Thus, individuals may play tennis, bowl, or watch a movie simply for the sake of doing that activity and not because they were forced to do it in order to obtain something. A distinction also should be made between psychological needs (Chapter 8) and intrinsic motivation. For instance, a person could be motivated to play tennis to satisfy needs of achievement, affiliation, and power. Tennis played for these reasons would be extrinsically motivated, however, since satisfying these psychological needs is external to playing the game. However, playing tennis for the enjoyment that the game provides would be an instance of intrinsic motivation.

Could a student who enrolled in a course because it was required end up liking it? Is it possible that although the original reason for doing an activity is no longer relevant the person still performs the activity anyway? Behavior that began for extrinsic reasons later can be performed for its own sake—that is, for intrinsic reasons. This shift in motivation describes Allport's (1937a) concept of the **functional autonomy of motives.** Allport characterizes the idea as "what was a means to an end has become an end in itself" (Allport, 1937a, p. 150). Allport uses the example of doing fine work. An individual may feel compelled to do an excellent job even though job security or pay are no longer dependent on performance as was originally the case. In the case of college work, a student may enroll in a course to please her parents or because it comes at a convenient hour. Yet the course may prove to be so interesting that the student decides to major in the field and make it her life's profession.

Purpose of Intrinsically Motivated Behavior

Is intrinsically motivated behavior an end in itself? Or is it linked to other sources of motivation? For instance, intrinsically motivated behavior may be in service to satisfying curiosity and developing competence and self-determination. Curiosity provides the motivation to learn about the environment (Woodworth, 1958), while motives for competence and self-determination provide reasons to control the environment (White, 1959).

Curiosity.   Can you avoid eavesdropping on a conversation about someone's sexual escapades at the next table? Can you put off opening a first-class letter you received or not bother answering your telephone? These questions illustrate the power of curiosity to intrinsically motivate behavior (Loewenstein, 1994). A stimulus situation can evoke an intense feeling of curiosity. For example, a suspenseful mystery novel is difficult to put down. Curiosity also makes people act impulsively in their desire to seek information, even against their better judgment. For example, a person might eavesdrop on the conversation at the next table at the risk of being rude and being embarrassed if caught. Furthermore, curiosity can make people act against their own self-interest. For example, a person may experiment with an illegal and potentially dangerous drug. Although curiosity can be classified as an instance of intrinsic motivation, it is linked to a person's desire to know. Curiosity results when the amount a person wants to know about a situation exceeds his current knowledge. A situation evokes curiosity to the extent it has the capacity to resolve this gap in knowledge (Loewenstein, 1994). The conclusion of the mystery novel provides the "who done it." The letter provides information about its content. By answering the telephone or using "caller ID," a person will discover the identity of the caller. Thus, satisfying one's curiosity is the motive for exploring and learning about the environment.

Effectance Motivation.   A person plays games, pursues hobbies, or spends time with friends simply because these activities are pleasurable or intrinsically motivating. However, intrinsic motivation is also in service to the development of competence. Intrinsically motivated behavior guides an animal or child to act effectively on its surroundings—that is, to become competent (White, 1959). The increase in competence is gained from such activities as exploring novel objects, playing, crawling, walking, speaking, writing, and thinking. These activities result from **effectance motivation,** which is the motive to actively interact and control one's environment (White, 1959). For example, Piaget (1951/1976) refers to a child's *mastery play* resulting from the mere joy of conquering a particular behavior. A child plays to make things happen and gain control over those happenings.

   A simple experiment illustrates effectance motivation in infants who were eight weeks old at the start of the two-week experiment (Watson, 1972/1976). One thing the infants could do at that age was to press their heads back against their pillows, and so this response was used in the experiment. Watson (1972/1976) devised a mobile that was placed above the infants in their crib at home. Some mobiles moved and others did not when the infants pressed their heads back against their pillows. In the contingent condition, pressing against the pillow caused the overhead mobile to turn. In the noncontingent condition, the pillow pressing response had no effect on turning the mobile. Although the mobile moved on occasion, it did so independent of any pillow pressing by the infant. In the stable condition, the mobile remained stationary regardless of what the infant did. Thus, in the contingent condition the infant caused the mobile to move, while in the noncontingent condition, the infant did not cause the mobile to move; it moved on its own. Being able to have an effect on the mobiles motivated the infants. They increased their frequency of pillow pressing in the contingent condition only, not in the noncontingent and stable conditions. In addition, infants in the contingent condition began cooing and smiling as if they were enjoying their mastery over the movements of their mobiles. Infants in the other conditions cooed and smiled much less at their mobiles. Thus, infants as young as 8 to 10 weeks are intrinsically motivated to have an effect on their environments.

Flow.   Competence is also gained by pushing oneself successfully to the limits of one's capability. To illustrate, on more than one occasion I have heard a student say, "I work hard in a course I like." Couldn't the reverse also be true? That is, "I like a course because I work hard in it." The fit between a person's efforts and success at an activity produces **flow** (Csikszentmihalyi, 1975, 1988; Csikszentmihalyi & Rathunde, 1993). Flow refers to the desirable subjective state a person experiences when completely involved in some challenging activity that matches the individual's skills. The activity has a clear goal and provides immediate feedback regarding the caliber of one's performance. In addition, a person is enjoyably concentrating all attention on the activity so that time, fatigue, and everything else is disregarded (Csikszentmihalyi, 1975, 1988; Csikszentmihalyi & Rathunde, 1993). Flow also has been used as a metaphor to describe the feelings experienced by artists, athletes, composers, dancers, scientists, and others when engaged in their favorite activities of doing something for the sake of doing: "they are in their flow."

What happens when personal capabilities exceed or fall below the demands of a task? The answer is that individuals are now out of their flow. People are aware of opportunities that challenge them as well as their capabilities of handling that challenge. When the challenges of the task exceed the person's capabilities, then stress is felt as anxiety and worry. However, when the challenges of the task are easily met, then a person feels bored. Flow, however, is experienced when the individual's skills fit with the demands of the task (Csikszentmihalyi, 1975, 1988; Csikszentmihalyi & Rathunde, 1993). To illustrate, canoeing, skiing, and playing chess can be performed at various levels of difficulty. However, whether any of these activities produce flow depends on the match between the difficulty level and the person's capability. If the water is too swift, the slope too steep, or the opponent too skilled, then the canoeist, skier, or chess player experiences stressful reactions like anxiety and worry. However, when the water is too slow, the slope too flat, and one's opponent less skilled, then the person generally experiences boredom. These activities, however, provide maximum enjoyment and flow occurs when there is a match between the challenge of the activity and the person's capability level (Csikszentmihalyi, 1975, 1988; Csikszentmihalyi & Rathunde, 1993). The personality psychologist Gordon Allport (1937a) also noted the positive relationship between ability and interest. He remarked, "A person likes to do what he can do well" (p. 150).

Interaction between Extrinsic and Intrinsic Motivation

What happens when extrinsic and intrinsic motivation combine? When amateur athletes become professionals, does money make them enjoy their sports more or less? Do retired professional athletes still play their sport for fun? The combination of extrinsic and intrinsic motivation affects the enjoyment and performance of behavior differently (Tang & Hall, 1995; Wiersma, 1992).

Extrinsic Reward and Intrinsic Motivation. According to one major league outfielder, "I used to enjoy playing baseball until I started getting paid for it" (Arkes & Garske, 1977, p. 251). This quote previews some findings regarding the effects of extrinsic rewards on intrinsically motivated behavior (Deci, 1971, 1972a, 1972b). In his research, Deci tested the effects of extrinsic rewards on the intrinsic motivation for solving interesting and challenging three-dimensional puzzles. In general, the research involved three different reward conditions. In the contingent payment condition, participants were told they would be paid for each puzzle completed. In the noncontingent payment condition, participants were unexpectedly paid after the puzzle-solving session ended. The amount paid, however, did not depend on the number of puzzles solved. In the no-payment condition, participants did not receive any money for solving the puzzles. At the end of the puzzle session, the experimenter left the room on some pretext for several minutes, during which time participants were given a choice: they could smoke, read magazines, do nothing, or continue working on the puzzles, although now no money was given. During this time the participants were unobtrusively observed to see what they would do. Deci reasoned that participants would continue working on the puzzles during this time to the extent such activity was intrinsically motivating. The results confirmed this supposition. Participants in the contingent payment condition spent less time working on the puzzles than participants in the noncontingent payment and no-payment conditions. The conclusion was that when payment was contingent on performance, intrinsic motivation decreased, whereas noncontingent or no payment did not affect intrinsic motivation. Deci (1972a, 1972b; Deci & Ryan, 1985) interpreted these findings in terms of **cognitive evaluation theory.** According to this theory, a person's intrinsic motivation for a task depends on what is perceived to be the reason for the behavior. If the reason is perceived as external, as in the case of being paid for a task, then a person perceives the reward as the basis for doing the task. Consequently, when payment ceases, the behavior ceases. In this case, intrinsic motivation declines, since the individual reasons that his behavior is externally rather than internally controlled. However, when no contingent external rewards are perceived, then the person concludes that her behavior is under self-control, which means it is freely chosen and is intrinsically motivating. Extrinsic rewards can also undermine the intrinsic enjoyment in children. For instance, Lepper and associates (1973) found that children who had been rewarded for drawing would spend less time drawing on a future occasion compared to children who had not been rewarded.

Extrinsic Reward, Intrinsic Motivation, and Performance. The decline in intrinsic motivation from extrinsic rewards comes from experiments in which a person is given a choice at the end of the contingency payment session. Besides choice, motivation is also reflected in performance measures of behavior. Although extrinsic reward undermines intrinsic interest, it facilitates performance measures of motivation (Wiersma, 1992). For example, what would happen to performance on an intrinsically motivated task if the person started receiving contingent pay? Such a question was asked by Harackiewicz and associates (1984, study 2) in their investigation of students who engaged in the intrinsically motivating task of playing pinball. The expected-reward group was offered and received a reward (movie pass) if its pinball playing performance was at the 80th percentile level. The unexpected-reward group was not told anything about a reward (movie pass) and unexpectedly received it anyway at the end of the game. A no-reward group neither expected nor received any kind of reward for its playing. At the conclusion of one game of pinball, the

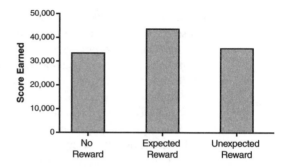

FIGURE 10.7a Extrinsic Reward and Interest. The graph shows mean number of pinballs played during a free period. Fewer balls were played during the expected-reward condition, which indicates that extrinsic reward undermined intrinsic interest of the game.

Source: Adapted from "Rewarding Pinball Wizardry" by J. M. Harackiewicz et al., 1984, *Journal of Personality and Social Psychology, 26*, p. 294.

FIGURE 10.7b Extrinsic Reward and Performance. The graph shows scores earned playing pinball during a free period. Pinball Performance was greatest in the expected-reward condition, which indicates that an extrinsic incentive can enhance performance based on intrinsic motivation.

Source: Adapted from "Rewarding Pinball Wizardry" by J. M. Harackiewicz et al., 1984, *Journal of Personality and Social Psychology, 26*, p. 294.

experimenter informed each participant they had performed at the 80th percentile. The experimenter then left the room on some pretext. Before leaving, however, the experimenter suggested that participants play some more pinball or just relax while waiting. While gone, the number of balls that were played, the score achieved, and the enjoyment of any playing was recorded. The number of balls played and enjoyment measures are indicators of intrinsic interest, while the score achieved is a performance measure of motivation. Figure 10.7a shows that fewer balls were played in the expected-reward condition than in the unexpected-reward condition. Thus, being rewarded for playing decreased the intrinsic motivation for pinball. However, ratings indicating enjoyment did not differ among the three conditions. The performance measure of motivation in Figure 10.7b shows that participants in the expected-reward condition, however, achieved higher scores for playing than participants in the unexpected-reward and no-reward conditions. Thus, when a performance measure is used, extrinsic motivation enhances performance that is based on intrinsic motivation (Wiersma, 1992). Similarly, regardless of what effect salaries have on the enjoyment of their sport, professional athletes still play extremely well when paid millions of dollars.

Extrinsic and Intrinsic Motivational Orientations

Activities like schoolwork and employment are done for reasons of both extrinsic and intrinsic motivation. When performing such activities, individuals differ in their **motivational orientation,** which refers to being consistently directed toward an extrinsic or an intrinsic source of motivation. A person is extrinsically oriented when studying is done solely for a grade or working is done solely for money. A person is intrinsically oriented when studying or working are done solely for their own sake. Of course, an individual could be motivated both intrinsically and extrinsically to various degrees. And a student may be motivated extrinsically in one course and intrinsically in another and be motivated by both in a third. Workers may need to make a living but at the same time may enjoy what they do. Amabile and associates (1994, 1995) saw motivational orientation as a consistent outlook on the part of the individual. These researchers attempted to measure an individual's motivational orientation by developing the *Work Preference Inventory* (see Table 10.2). The inventory measures the extent to which people feel extrinsically or intrinsically motivated in what they do. The statements in Table 10.2 measure students' external and internal orientations toward their schoolwork, although the complete scale also includes orientation toward work in general. For example, "I am strongly motivated by grades I can earn" measures a student's extrinsic motivation for schoolwork. But the statement "I enjoy trying to solve complex problems" measures a student's intrinsic motivation.

Results regarding the *Work Preference Inventory* indicate that extrinsic and intrinsic scale scores were independent, which means that students' scores on one scale were not related to their scores on another (Amabile et al., 1994). It is possible to have a high or low extrinsic orientation and at the same time have a low or high intrinsic orientation. Therefore, a student can be intrinsically motivated to work on a project or in a class while at the same time be trying to earn a good grade or praise. It is also possible for a student to have no intrinsic interest and work just hard enough to pass. In validating the *Work Preference Inventory*, Amabile and associates (1994) correlated extrinsic and intrinsic scores with other behaviors. For example, the intrinsic scale scores were moderately correlated with people's involvement in art, problem-solving activities, and writing. However, for current problem-solving activities, extrinsic motivation also became important, such as working for a grade. Intrinsic scale scores also correlated positively with the *Need for Cognition Scale* scores (Cacioppo & Petty, 1982). The need for cognition means that a person engages in and enjoys analytical thinking. Extrinsic scale scores correlated with how soon introductory psychology students finished their participation in course-required research projects. The importance of the *Work Preference Inventory* is that it indicates that people are motivated both intrinsically and extrinsically for many of the things they do.

Section Recap

Motivation can come from sources external to behavior or from the satisfaction that the behavior itself provides. *Extrinsic motivation* is coerced by an external incentive, such as praise, money, or good grades, while *intrinsic motivation* is freely chosen and is inherent in the activity. Intrinsic motivation may be in service to curiosity and the evolution of competence. In some instances behavior that is performed for extrinsic reasons is eventually maintained by intrinsic motivation, as described by the concept of *functional autonomy of motives*. Curiosity provides the motive for learning about one's environment. Competence results from *effectance motivation*, which provides the impetus for children to interact effectively with their environment so that they can learn to control it. Another feature of intrinsic motivation is *flow*, which is the desirable subjective feeling that results from being involved in a challenging activity that matches one's skills. Adding extrinsic motivation to an intrinsically motivated activity has two effects. On the one hand, extrinsic motivation decreases the intrinsic value of the activity, but on the other, extrinsic motivation enhances the performance of the intrinsic activity. According to *cognitive evaluation theory*, the

TABLE 10.2   Work Preference Inventory Items

Read each item and indicate the extent to which it describes you:
1 = Never or almost never true of me ——— 4 = Always or almost always true of me
The higher the score, the more the item describes you.

Number	Item
1	I am not that concerned about what other people think of my work.
2	I prefer having someone set clear goals for me in my work.
3	The more difficult the problem, the more I enjoy trying to solve it.
4	I am keenly aware of the goals I have for getting good grades.
5	I want my work to provide me with opportunities for increasing my knowledge and skills.
6	To me, success means doing better than other people.
7	I prefer to figure things out for myself.
8	No matter what the outcome of a project, I am satisfied if I feel I gained a new experience.
9	I enjoy relatively simple, straightforward tasks.
10	I am keenly aware of the GPA (grade point average) goals I have for myself.
11	Curiosity is the driving force behind much of what I do.
12	I'm less concerned with what work I do than what I get for it.
13	I enjoy tackling problems that are completely new to me.
14	I prefer work I know I can do well over work that stretches my abilities.
15	I'm concerned about how other people are going to react to my ideas.
16	I seldom think about grades and awards.
17	I'm more comfortable when I can set my own goals.
18	I believe that there is no point in doing a good job if nobody else knows about it.
19	I am strongly motivated by the grades I can earn.
20	It is important for me to be able to do what I most enjoy.
21	I prefer working on projects with clearly specified procedures.
22	As long as I can do what I enjoy, I'm not that concerned about exactly what grades or awards I can earn.
23	I enjoy doing work that is so absorbing that I forget about everything else.
24	I am strongly motivated by the recognition I can earn from other people.
25	I have to feel that I'm earning something for what I do.
26	I enjoy trying to solve complex problems.
27	It is important for me to have an outlet for self-expression.
28	I want to find out how good I really can be at my work.
29	I want other people to find out how good I really can be at my work.
30	What matters most to me is enjoying what I do.

Note: To score yourself on extrinsic motivation, find the mean of items 1 (reverse score), 2, 4, 6, 10, 12, 15, 16 (reverse score), 18,19, 21, 22 (reverse score), 24, 25, 29.
To score yourself on intrinsic motivation, find the mean of items 3, 5, 7, 8, 9 (reverse score), 11, 13, 14 (reverse score), 17, 20, 23, 26, 27, 28, 30.
To see how you scored, compare your score against the following norms based on 1,323 students who took the scale. Intrinsic scale mean = 2.99, SD = .37; Extrinsic scale mean = 2.56, SD = .41

Source: Copyright © 1994 by the American Psychological Association. Reprinted by permission. The official citation that should be used in referencing this material is Amabile, T. M., Hill, K. G., Hennessey, B. A., Tighe, E. M. (1994). The work preference inventory. *Journal of Personality and Social Psychology, 66,* 956.

reason for the decline in intrinsic interest is that motivation for a task depends on the perceived reason for the behavior. If the reason is perceived as external, as in the case of an external incentive, then removal of the incentive leads to a decline in motivation. Finally, individuals differ in their consistent *motivational orientation* toward extrinsic and intrinsic motivation. A person can be high or low on either type of motivational orientation. When extrinsically oriented, a person works for grades or money, but when intrinsically oriented, a person works for the inherent satisfaction the activity provides.

ACTIVITIES

1. Determine the "value" of the course for which you are using this textbook. For example, how much is the tuition for this course? What happens if you fail and must take it or another course over again? What is its value in terms of future career goals or earnings or in terms of self-esteem? Are there things in life for which value cannot be determined?

2. Boy and girl meet. Boy and girl have romantic relationship. Boy loses girl, and vice versa. According to the concept of "losses loom larger than gains," where will feelings be felt most strongly? In the meeting phase or in the losing phase?

3. Think of a recent instance when you procrastinated. Can you explain your procrastination in terms of preference reversal? In other words, as the time to the task or incentive decreases, a small reward becomes overly important or valuable compared to the larger, more important one.

4. Fill out the *Work Preference Inventory* and compare yourself to the norms listed at the bottom of Table 10.2. What do you think should determine a student's major field of study: extrinsic interest, like earning potential, or intrinsic interest, like pleasure resulting from learning the material? To what extent do you think college graduation depends on having the requisite amount of extrinsic and intrinsic motivation?

11 Goal Motivation

In all human affairs there is always an end in view—of pleasure, or honor, or advantage.

—Polybius, 125 B.C.

Our plans miscarry because they have no aim. When a man does not know what harbor he is making for, no wind is the right wind.

—Seneca, 4 B.C.–65 A.D.

■ Whereas incentives are potential motivators, goals are actual ones. For example, a goal of reading this chapter can be to find and understand the answers to the following questions:

1. Where do people's goals originate?
2. What goal characteristics are important for motivation?
3. What factors determine whether a goal should be pursued?
4. How do goals motivate behavior?
5. How are goals achieved, and what happens when they are not?

Origins of Goals

"Skating takes up 70% of my time," Michelle says. "School about 25%. Having fun and talking to my friends 5%. It's hard. I envy other kids a lot of things, but I get a guilt trip when I'm not training" (Swift, 1998, p. 117). These are the words of Michelle Kwan, whose goal was to win a gold medal in the 1998 winter Olympics. To achieve this goal she divided her time as described above. In addition, she never took a day off, skated when tired, took no vacations, and even skated on Christmas day. She has also skated with a sore throat, runny nose, flu, and chicken pox. Michelle even turned down her father's offer of $50 for every day she did not skate. She is a person totally committed to her goal. (Swift, 1998, p. 118)

The purpose of this section is to describe how goals differ from incentives and the various sources that give rise to goals.

Incentives versus Goals

There are many similarities between incentive motivation (discussed in the last chapter) and goal motivation. There are also differences.

Differentiating Characteristics. When faced with choices on how to spend time and effort to obtain an outcome or incentive, the outcome or incentive that is chosen becomes the **goal** (Klinger, 1977). For example, Michelle Kwan's goal was to become an Olympic skater rather than to become a successful water skier. There are other differences between incentive and goal motivation. First, goals are portrayed as larger and more important in scope than incentives. The goal of winning an Olympic gold medal, for example, also entails such aspects as personal achievement, worldwide recognition, and possibly product endorsements. Second, goals are usually more complex than incentives and have both positive and negative features to be approached and avoided, respectively. For example, in a risky investment, a person could earn a lot of money but she could also lose it. Third, goals involve the cognitive realm of motivation. A person cognitively evaluates the worth of a goal and the chances of achieving it and then formulates the necessary plans for doing so. Michelle, for instance, made long-range plans to try to achieve her goals (Swift, 1998). Fourth, a person's goals are usually one-time events that will not be repeated. Incentives, in contrast, occur over and over. For example, the goal of a university degree happens once, while a monetary incentive occurs repeatedly in different situations. Fifth, incentives can serve as assists toward the achievement of a goal. For example, a profit-sharing incentive motivates sales personnel to achieve the company's goal of the number of units sold for the year. Finally, it is also possible to have more than one goal. A person may work toward one goal and then shift direction and work toward another goal.

From Incentives to Goals. Consider the following alternatives facing a hypothetical student on a Saturday afternoon:

1. Wash dirty clothes. (Clean clothes have a great utility.)
2. Prepare for a psychology exam on Monday. (An *A* in this class is important for achieving a desired career in psychology.)
3. Decide whether to go to a party that evening and whom to ask as a date. (Enjoying oneself and looking for a romantic partner are important to a sense of well-being.)

One task in the psychology of motivation is discovering what incentives people pursue (Karniol & Ross, 1996). In this example, what factors determine the incentives the student is going after: clean clothes, an *A* on Monday's exam, or the party? If the student decides on clean clothes, then washing clothes becomes a goal. If the student decides on an *A* on the exam, then earning the *A* becomes a goal. If she decides on the party, then going to it becomes a goal. Which incentive is selected, however, depends on several factors. First, the value of an incentive affects whether it will be selected as a goal. Washing clothes competes with studying for the exam. Doing well on the exam may be more important than clean clothes, but since clean clothes are needed in a few hours and the exam is still two days away, clean clothes may have higher value. Second, all other things being equal, the incentive with the highest probability of success will be selected as a goal. The probabilities of getting a date, going alone, or staying home determine whether the student decides to go to the party. The time and effort to achieve a goal are also factors in the decision. If incentives are valued equally, then the one requiring the least amount of time and effort is pursued (Hull, 1943; Tolman, 1932). Perhaps the student will choose to wash clothes, if that requires less time and effort than studying for the exam. Incentive value or utility, probability, and effort are all factors that interact to determine what incentive becomes a goal.

A person persists in trying to achieve a goal, however, until one of three things has occurred: the goal has been achieved, the original goal has been displaced by another goal, or the goal has simply been abandoned (Atkinson & Birch, 1970; Klinger, 1977). A person can also be working on achieving one goal while at the same time be thinking or planning on how to achieve another.

Future Orientation of Goals.   The seeming capacity of the future to motivate present behavior is a feature that goals share with incentives. This capacity is realized when a future positive goal is represented in the present as something a person is motivated to become or motivated to achieve. A negative goal, when visualized in the present, however, is to be avoided and represents what a person does not want to become. It is the current representation of a goal that becomes the occasion for behavioral strategies designed to achieve or avoid it (Karniol & Ross, 1996).

How does a goal's future location affect current motivation? To illustrate, assume that it has become the goal of your psychology department to require a comprehensive exam of all graduating psychology majors. Two positive features of this goal are that the exam is an opportunity for self-evaluation and for departmental evaluation. Two negative features are your distress and the possibility that you may do poorly. How much in favor are you of this comprehensive exam if it were given two or four semesters from now? Goals, like incentives, are affected by their distance in the future, as illustrated in Figure 11.1. The closer an individual comes to her goal, the stronger the motivation to approach its positive features and avoid its negative features (Markman & Brendl, 2000; Miller, 1959). When a long time away,

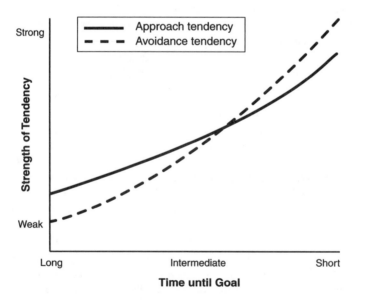

FIGURE 11.1   Goal-Approach and Goal-Avoidance Tendencies. The tendency to approach positive goal features and to avoid negative features increases as a goal draws closer. Changes in the strength of an approach tendency are slower than changes in an avoidance tendency. At distant intervals, the approach tendency is stronger, while at nearer intervals, the avoidance tendency is stronger.

the approach tendency is stronger, but as the goal gets nearer, the avoidance tendency is stronger. In the case of the comprehensive exam, a student supports taking the exam when it is four semesters away because the approach features of this goal are strongest. When the exam is two semesters away, however, a student does not support the goal because now the avoidance features are strongest.

Changes in a goal's motivational strength vary with time to the goal as a result of delay discounting (Chapter 10). Shelley (1994) demonstrated that losses or negative features of a goal are discounted more steeply than are gains or positive features. This difference in discount rate explains why the avoidance curve in Figure 11.1 is steeper than the approach curve. Negative goal features are less motivating than positive features far from the goal, but they are more motivating nearer the goal. In the comprehensive exam example, when it is four semesters away, the negative features of the exam are discounted more than its positive features. When two semesters away, however, the negative features are discounted less than the positive features.

Sources of Goals

Goals motivate behavior because people strive to achieve them. One question for students of motivation concerns the origin of goals. Where do goals come from?

Levels of Aspiration.   This refers to a person's desire to excel, to do better the next time, or to do better than others (Rotter, 1942). Research on the level of aspiration describes people's desires to strive for goals that exceed their current levels (Lewin et al., 1944). It is that part of our human nature that drives us to want more or to improve, not want less or get worse. Setting and pursuing goals is one way to achieve this. For instance, a promotion and raise in salary are likely to be goals while a demotion and cut in salary are unlikely to be.

Association of Goals with Affect.   Asking someone for a date may result in either happiness if the person accepts or disappointment if not. In this example, the goal of getting a date may arise from its association with **affect,** which is the subjective tone of an emotion. Affect can be a positive, pleasant feeling or a negative, unpleasant feeling. Goals producing positive affect are approached, while those producing negative affect are avoided. The idea that goals are associated with affect can be traced back to the ideas of Thomas Hobbes in his book *Human Nature* (1640/1962). In modern terminology, Hobbes would argue that people pursue as goals those things they anticipate will give pleasure and avoid as goals those things they anticipate will bring displeasure or pain. Troland (1928/1967) elaborated this idea by claiming that the present anticipation of future pleasure is pleasant and the present anticipation of future pain is unpleasant. In this manner, present affect determines a future course of action. Modern psychologists also claim that goals are associated with positive or negative affect, which determines whether something is to be approached or avoided (Atkinson & Birch, 1970; Klinger, 1977; Mowrer, 1960; Pervin, 1989). Animal behavior theorists have also used affect to explain goal-approach and goal-avoidance behavior. According to Mowrer (1960) rats felt hope when in the presence of a stimulus that predicted food. They felt fear, however, in the presence of a stimulus that predicted shock. Positive affect like self-satisfaction and negative affect like self-dissatisfaction provide the motivation for personal accomplishments in humans (Bandura, 1991). Bandura and Cervone (1986) showed that self-dissatisfaction increased when goals were not met, whereas self-satisfaction increased when they were. Furthermore, greater self-dissatisfaction favored lowering future goals. Self-satisfaction gained from previous success, however, favored raising the level of future goals.

The emotions a person experiences from goal success or goal failure also determine goal-setting behavior, according to Weiner (1985). Success at achieving a goal produces happiness, whereas failure to achieve the goal is associated with sadness and frustration (Weiner, 1972). In some representative research, Weiner and Kukla (1970) had female student teachers rate what degree of pride and shame they would feel following feedback about various degrees of success on an exam. Feedback about their exam performance was categorized as excellent, fair, borderline, moderate failure, or clear failure. Ratings of pride depended on the amount of success feedback the students received. Pride was lowest for clear failure on the exam and highest for feedback signifying excellent performance. Shame ratings, however, showed the reverse pattern. Shame was highest for feedback indicating clear failure on the exam and lowest for feedback showing excellent performance. Thus, a person may strive to achieve a goal because its accomplishment is associated with pride. A person may avoid pursuing a goal, however, because of the possibility that failure may bring shame.

Goals That Satisfy Needs.   Some substances become goals because they satisfy physiological needs. Feelings of hunger and thirst, for instance, are the reasons that gaining food and water become goals. How does an individual know what substance satisfies a particular physiological need? One idea is that the physiological need increases the attractiveness of the necessary substance but not of other substances. As Tolman (1959) expressed in his principle of purposive behavior, the subjective value, or valence, of a stimulus depends on the animal's or person's motivational or physiological state. Valence, in turn, determines *psychological demand,* how much a stimulus is wanted or desired (Tolman, 1932). According to the valence concept, an incentive with the highest valence is selected as a goal, whereas those with a low or negative valence are avoided. Thus, for a hungry person food has a positive valence and becomes a goal, while watching television or reading a book has either a lower or a negative valence and is avoided.

A psychological need also influences the valence of the incentive that satisfies it. Attaining that incentive, therefore, becomes a goal. Chapter 8 described psychological needs such as for power and cognition. Goals satisfying these needs might include joining the police force or becoming a crossword puzzle developer. There are also needs concerned with affiliation and intimacy. Goals satisfying these needs might include membership on a team or in an organization. Humans prefer to form close intimate relationships, to love and to be loved. In this case, the goal is to interact with individuals who can provide for this need. In addition, there are needs related to our sense of self-esteem, competence, and mastery. The actual process of achieving a goal helps satisfy these needs. As noted in Chapter 9, personality traits also determine what goals become important. The trait of conscientiousness, for example, may determine whether a person considers recycling to be a worthwhile goal. Finally, a person's value system can determine her goals. If a person places a high ethical value on the lives of animals, then being a vegetarian may become a goal.

Goal Setting for Evaluating Self-Efficacy.   Do you think you can make the grade, pass the inspection, or get the job done? Goals serve as a standard for evaluating one's **self-efficacy** (Bandura, 1977, 1991). This is a person's belief about how capable he is in performing the behavior necessary for achieving a specific goal. Self-efficacy is task specific, which means a person evaluates his capability of achieving the task at hand. For example, a professional musician might rate himself as having high self-efficacy for playing an instrument and low self-efficacy for working with a computer. Indications of success and failure at particular tasks raise or lower self-efficacy, which in turn affects a person's future achievement striving. Weinberg and associates (1979) compared high- and low-self-efficacy participants for their ability to perform a leg muscle endurance task. Low self-efficacy was created by telling participants they were competing against a varsity track athlete who had outperformed the participant on a similar task. High self-efficacy was created by telling participants they were competing against someone with a knee injury who had done poorly on a similar task. Measures of the participants' self-efficacy were low when they compared themselves to the athlete and high when they compared themselves to the injured individual. Furthermore, high-self-efficacy participants predicted better performance and also outperformed low-self-efficacy participants on the leg muscle endurance task.

Goal setting also allows for self-efficacy evaluations of cognitive tasks like problem solving. Cervone and Peake (1986) manipulated self-efficacy by asking participants if they could solve more than, equal to, or less than a standard number of anagrams. The standard was either a high or low number. As a rating of their self-efficacy, participants were asked how many anagrams they thought they were capable of solving. Participants exposed to the high standard gave higher self-efficacy ratings than participants exposed to the low standard. Furthermore, during the anagram-solving task, high-self-efficacy participants persisted longer than low-self-efficacy participants. Thus, goal setting allows individuals to test their self-efficacy. Successes and failures can raise and lower self-efficacy, which in turn can raise and lower the motivation to achieve one's goal.

Environmentally Activated Goals. Goals may become associated with stimuli present in the situation in which goal-achievement behavior occurs. If these associations happen frequently enough, then those stimuli may activate goals. Markman and Brendl (2000) provide an example of a person who notices the picture of a check as part of an advertisement displayed in the window of a bank. The check activates the goal that the rent must be paid, which is achieved when the person arrives home. Murray (1938) had a similar idea when he hypothesized that psychological needs can be evoked by environmental demands (see Chapter 2). The possibility that goal-relevant stimuli can activate goals from memory was provided in an experiment by Patalano and Seifert (1997). In the learning phase, they presented participants with a set of goals and with relevant objects that could be used to accomplish those goals. In the recall phase, participants were more likely to recall a goal when a relevant object was presented as a cue. For example, when Vaseline rather than masking tape was presented as a cue, participants were more likely to recall the goal: remove stuck ring from finger. Finally, as noted in Chapter 8, the process by which situational stimuli activate goals can occur without a person's awareness (Bargh & Barndollar, 1996).

Other People as Sources for Goals. A person's relationships with other people also determine his goals (Hollenbeck & Klein, 1987). According to social comparison theory, the level of the goal set by an individual is determined by his standing relative to members in the group (Lewin et al., 1944). For example, imagine a task in which some individuals perform better than the group's average, while others perform worse. In setting future goals, individuals who are above average tend to lower their performance goals, whereas those below average tend to raise theirs. As Locke and Latham (1990) note, the demands other individuals make on a person often become goals. Professors make demands on students. Coaches make demands on players. Children and parents make demands on one another. In addition, the goals of the group become the goals of the individual. To illustrate, the goal of the team is to win games, but this is also the goal of an individual player when she joins the team. In the case of a student, if the professor's goal is to give an exam on Monday, then as a member of the class the student accepts that goal.

Section Recap

Goal motivation refers to the ability of a desired end-state to move a person into action. The *goal* is the incentive a person is motivated to achieve. They are selected from an array of incentives, depending on their scope, complexity, cognitive nature, and their likelihood of being achieved. Goals are one-time accomplishments, although a person may have several concurrent goals. The motivational power of a goal decreases as its distance in the future increases due to discounting. Negative goal features are discounted more steeply than are positive features. People's *level of aspiration,* which refers to their desire to want more and do better, serve as the motivation to set goals that accomplish that. Goals originate from their association with positive or negative *affect,* which is the emotional feeling the anticipated goal produces. Positive affect leads to approaching the end-state, whereas negative affect leads to avoiding the end-state. Goals are the means for satisfying physiological and psychological needs. Obtaining food is the goal for satisfying hunger, and obtaining praise is the goal for satisfying a need for self-esteem. The valence of a goal determines how much it is psychologically demanded or wanted. Goals provide the opportunity for the evaluation of *self-efficacy,* which refers to one's capability to perform the task at hand. Achieving a goal increases self-efficacy, while failing to achieve a goal decreases it. Stimuli can activate goals as a result of the repeated association between goal pursuit in situations that contain those stimuli. People are also sources of goals. For instance, in the case of social comparisons, the goal to which a person aspires depends on how his performance compares to other members of the group. In addition, the goal of the group is also the goal of the individual members.

Goal Characteristics and Expectations

The purpose of this section is to examine various characteristics of goals. A goal motivates behavior consistent with the value of the goal and guides behavior according to the specificity of the goal. But before a person commits, a goal's value and likelihood of being achieved are estimated along with whether the goal is framed as achieving a gain or avoiding a loss.

Characteristics of Goals

Being bored may mean an individual is not working toward any goal at the moment. A goal, however, motivates an individual, produces goal-relevant thoughts, and guides behavior according to how precisely the goal is defined.

Goal Level and Goal Difficulty.   People set goals for themselves at various levels. **Goal level** refers to the rank of a goal in a hierarchy of potential goals. Higher-level goals have higher value or valence, greater utility, and provide greater benefits compared to lower-level ones. One person may have a goal to walk five miles per week, while another individual plans to run 10 miles per week. One student may have a GPA goal of 3.50, while another is satisfied with a GPA just high enough to graduate. Goal level is associated with **goal difficulty,** which means that some goals are harder to achieve than others (Lee et al., 1989; Locke & Latham, 1990). "While high goals may be harder to reach than easy goals, in life they are usually associated with better outcomes" (Locke & Latham, 1990, p. 121). In other words, as the value of a goal increases, the difficulty of achieving it also increases. In an attempt to determine the relationship between goal level and outcomes, Mento and associates (1992) told participants to assume that as undergraduate students their goal was to achieve a GPA close to an *A* (4.00), *B* (3.00), or *C* (2.00). Next, participants were asked to rate what benefits their GPA goal would bring, such as pride, respect, and confidence; job benefits; scholarship and graduate school benefits; and life and career benefits. The results showed a strong relationship between the GPA goal level and benefit ratings. Higher GPA goals were associated with greater benefits. Matsui and associates (1981) had students perform a clerical aptitude test that involved detecting a discrepancy between two lists of numbers. The goal set for the students varied between easy and hard. Prior to working on the clerical task, students were asked to rate the expected valence (value) of their goals for achievement, self-confidence, competence, ability to concentrate, and persistence. The ratings showed that more difficult goals were rated as having higher valence and greater benefits.

Goal Specificity. How important is it for a person to be able to visualize a goal? Is it necessary for a student to visualize herself in her chosen career? One requirement of goal setting is that a person must be able to visualize the goal in some respect (Beach, 1990; Miller et al., 1960; Schank & Abelson, 1977). The clearer the image a person has of his goal, the better he will know if it has been achieved. "Vague goals make poor referent standards because there are many situations in which no discrepancy would be indicated and, therefore, there would be no need for corrective action" (Klein, 1989, p. 154). A goal with a vague image will more likely result in poorer performance, because feedback from a variety of behaviors may appear to have met the goal (Klein, 1989). In contrast is **goal specificity,** which is an important part of the goal-achievement process. It refers to how precise the goal is in contrast to how vague or unspecified it is (Lee et al., 1989; Locke & Latham, 1990). For example, during one minute, list 4, 7, or 12 uses for a coat hanger or as many uses as you can (Mento et al., 1992). Listing 4, 7, or 12 uses is a specific goal, while "as many uses as you can" is a vague goal. In the former case, a person can determine whether the specific goal was met, while it is very difficult to determine whether the vague do-your-best goal was met.

An additional benefit of goal specificity is that it increases planning (Locke & Latham, 1990), as demonstrated by Earley and associates (1987). In their experiment, participants had to present an argument in favor of a certain advertising medium for various products ranging from household goods to business computers. In the do-your-best condition, participants had to present as many arguments as they could in 60 minutes. The goal for these participants was vague, since they did not know when they had done their best. In the assigned goal condition, participants had to present a minimum of four arguments per advertising medium. The goal for these participants was specific. They knew precisely if they had met their goal. Following the completion of the task, the experimenter asked how much planning and energy participants had expended. The results showed that participants with assigned specific goals spent more time planning and expended more effort than participants who were given vague do-your-best goals.

Joint Effect of Goal Level and Goal Specificity. Goal level affects the magnitude of performance, while goal specificity affects the variability of performance (Locke et al., 1989; Mento et al., 1992). Imagine students being asked for ways in which the psychology department at their university could be improved. The number of requested improvements could vary in specificity. For example, imagine being asked to suggest three improvements, which is a specific number, or to suggest several improvements, which is a vague number. The task could also differ in goal level. Students could be asked to suggest many improvements or could be asked to suggest very few. In the Locke and associates (1989) study, some of the students were given vague goals at different levels—for example, "List a small, medium, or large number of improvements." These categories are vague, since a small, medium, or large number is undefined. Other students were given moderately specific goals—for example, "List between one and three, two and four, or three and five ways of improving the department." Other students were provided with very specific goals at three different levels—for example, "Provide exactly two, three, or four ways of improving the department." In the actual study, Locke and associates (1989) asked students to list improvements for the undergraduate business and management programs. The number of proposed improvements should depend on goal level, while variability of the number of improvements should depend on goal specificity. Greater variability is expected for vague goals, because a wider variety of improvements will be accepted as having met those goals. The results in Figure 11.2a show that higher-level, more difficult goals produce a greater number of recommended improvements. The results in Figure 11.2b indicate that variability (standard deviation) in the number of improvements

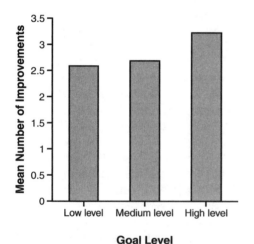
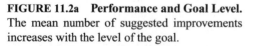

FIGURE 11.2a   Performance and Goal Level. The mean number of suggested improvements increases with the level of the goal.

Source: Adapted from "Separating the Effects of Goal Specificity from Goal Level" by E. A. Locke et al., 1989, *Organizational Behavior and Human Decision Processes, 43,* experiment 2.

FIGURE 11.2b   Performance and Goal Specificity. The standard deviation of the number of suggested improvements decreases as a goal becomes more specific.

Source: Adapted from "Separating the Effects of Goal Specificity from Goal Level" by E. A. Locke et al., 1989, *Organizational Behavior and Human Decision Processes, 43,* experiment 2.

decreases as the stated goal becomes more specific. In other words, as a goal becomes more precise, there is greater agreement on whether it has been achieved. In the coat-hanger study described previously, the vague do-your-best goal produced low achievement, with greater achievement resulting from the goal of listing 7 or 12 coat-hanger uses. In general, research has shown that goals that are both difficult and specific result in more achievement behavior than do vague goals or no goals (Locke et al., 1981; Mento et al., 1992; Tubbs, 1986).

The research on goal level and goal specificity has shown that goals have both energizing and directive functions (Locke et al., 1989). Goal level has an **energizing function** in that it motivates a person to expend effort to achieve a goal. Higher goals lead to greater expenditure of effort. Goal specificity has a **directing function** in that it informs the individual exactly what behavior is acceptable for goal achievement. The greater the specificity of a goal, the more precisely it directs behavior. Thus, one major conclusion is that specific, high-level goals lead to greater performance than do vague, low-level goals.

Expected Utility Theory

What determines whether a person commits to a goal? Is it the goal that has the greatest likelihood of being achieved? Is it the goal with the highest utility (that is, value)? Or does a combination of these two factors determine one's goal?

A person may have her sights set on various incentives trying to decide which one to select as a goal. According to **expected utility theory,** the motivation to select a particular goal is based on the goal's utility and estimated probability of being achieved. Utility refers to the usefulness or the satisfaction that a goal provides. More valuable goals have greater utility—that is, they produce greater satisfaction. However, as in the case of money, as the value of a goal increases, its utility increases but in lesser amounts (see Figure 10.1). In expected utility theory, the utility of a goal is multiplied by its subjective probability of being achieved (Arkes & Hammond, 1986; Edwards, 1961; Shoemaker, 1982). The resulting product is known as expected utility:

Expected utility = Utility × subjective probability

Thus, when faced with a choice among several incentives, a person determines the utility of each and also estimates the probability of achieving each incentive. Whatever incentive has the highest expected utility is the one selected as a goal.

Meaning of Probability.   At this point we should differentiate objective probability from subjective probability. Objective probability refers to the number of times an outcome favoring some event occurs divided by the total number of outcomes that are possible. The probability of obtaining heads in a coin flip is 0.50. This proportion represents the number of outcomes favoring heads (1 in this case) divided by the total number of outcomes (2—heads or tails). Expected utility theory, however, does not rely on objective probability but instead uses **subjective probability,** which is a person's belief that a particular event will occur. This belief can be expressed as a number between 0.00 and 1.00 (Savage, 1954). For example, during his first semester at the university a student may form the belief (subjective probability) that his chances of earning a *B* average is 0.50. Based on first-semester grades, however, his probability estimate can change. If he earns better than a 3.00 GPA, then his subjective probability estimate will be revised upward. An earned GPA below 3.00, however, may produce a decline in subjective probability.

Choice Based on Utility, Probability, or Expected Utility.   How is it possible to separate the effects of utility, probability, and expected utility? One way was demonstrated in an experiment with elementary school children by Gray (1975). She provided them with arithmetic problems that differed in incentive value and probability of a correct solution. The probability of a solution defined a problem's difficulty level. Level-1 problems were the easiest and level-6 problems were the most difficult to solve. The arithmetic problems were written on index cards and placed in six stacks according to their level of difficulty. The children attempted to solve problems from each level and were asked: "If you had to do 10 problems from this deck, and they were all pretty much like the one you tried first, how many do you think you could get right out of 10?" (p. 150). The children's answer to this question was their subjective probability estimate. The utility of correctly solving a problem was defined by the number of red poker chips associated with each difficulty level. If a child solved a problem correctly from the easiest deck, she received one red poker chip. The next easiest deck was worth two poker chips and so on up to six poker chips for the most difficult problem deck. However, if a child did not solve a problem correctly, he had to pay the experimenter the same number of poker chips as the deck's value. Since a child could go into debt, each child received 10 red poker chips at the start of the experiment. During the experiment, a child was given the opportunity to solve 15 arithmetic problems in order to earn as many red poker chips as possible.

The problems children selected to solve could be based on the utility, subjective probability, or expected utility of the solutions. First, the children could select a problem deck based on its utility or value as indicated by the number of red poker chips. Children might choose deck 6, since it would provide the most chips. Second, the children might select problems based on the estimated probability of success. Easier problems might be chosen, since more of them could be solved, thus earning more poker chips. Third, children could make their selections based on the expected utility of a problem. The expected utility would be the child's probability estimate of solving a problem multiplied by the utility of that problem as indicated by the number of poker chips. Different children had different expected utilities for each deck because they gave different probability estimates. For example, one child might estimate deck 4 to have a probability of 0.70, while for another child the probability might be 0.60. Thus, the expected utility for deck 4 (worth 4 chips) for each child would be 2.80 and 2.40, respectively. Gray (1975) examined how the children distributed their choices according to the utility, subjective probability, and the expected utility of a problem deck. The children did not make their choices according to the utility of a deck. Their choices were spread fairly evenly over the different utilities (one to six chips) of the decks. The subjective probability of a correct solution for a problem also had no effect. Their choices were spread fairly evenly over the six subjective probabilities of the decks. The expected utility of a problem deck was the main determiner of the children's choices. As shown in Figure 11.3, children distributed their choices based on the expected utility of solving the problems. Problem decks with the highest expected utility were chosen most often. As the problems deviated more and more from their expected utility, they were chosen less and less.

Expected Utility with Social Incentives.   Expected utility theory also applies to goals involving people. A date's expected utility influences a person's choice. Shanteau and Nagy (1979) examined whether dating choice was affected by attractiveness and probability of

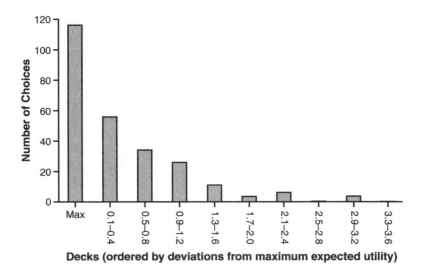

FIGURE 11.3   Choice and Expected Utility. Children made choices based on the expected utility of solving the problem.

Source: Reprinted from *Organizational Behavior and Human Performance, 13,* C. A. Gray, "Factors in Students' Decisions to Attempt Academic Tasks," p. 153. Copyright 1975, with permission from Elsevier.

acceptance. In their experiment, female participants had to choose which of two males they would prefer as a date. The photos of the male students varied from attractive to unattractive. An attractive male is usually preferred and presumably has greater utility (Eagly et al., 1991; Walster et al., 1966). The subjective probability that the male student would accept a date was provided along with the photo. The probability levels were: Sure thing, Highly likely, Fairly likely, Toss-up, Somewhat unlikely, Very unlikely, and No chance. The female participants' preference for a particular male could be determined by the probability of getting a date, by the attractiveness of the male, or by the product of probability times attractiveness. The results indicated that female participants preferred those males with the highest product of these two factors—that is, those with the highest expected utility. For example, moderately attractive males, when paired with "highly likely," were strongly preferred over more attractive males paired with lower probabilities.

Framing

Is a glass half full or half empty? Is an exam the opportunity to earn an *A* or to avoid an *F*? Is a date the opportunity to have fun or a way to avoid a lonely Saturday night? Should a person concentrate on achieving gains or avoiding losses? **Framing** refers to the perspective from which a goal is viewed. A goal can be viewed as either providing the opportunity for making a gain or for avoiding a loss. How a choice is framed coupled with the probability of achieving the outcome determines a person's decision.

Framing and the probability of gaining or losing money affects our choices, according to Kahneman and Tversky (1979). Imagine trying to decide between buying lottery ticket A or lottery ticket B. Which ticket would you buy if the prospects of winning are:

Problem 1
Prospect A1: 90% chance of winning $3,000; expected utility = $2,700

or

Prospect B1: 45% chance of winning $6,000; expected utility = $2,700

Suppose you won the lottery and now have money to invest in a business venture. In this case, concentrate more on the prospects of losing the money during the first year of the business. In which of the two prospects would you invest your money?

Problem 2
Prospect A2: 90% chance of losing $3,000; expected utility = −$2,700

or

Prospect B2: 45% chance of losing $6,000; expected utility = −$2,700

What prediction would expected utility theory make for these two problems? According to it, there should be no difference in the choices a person would make between the pairs of prospects. In problem 1, both prospects have an expected utility equal to $2,700. Therefore, 50% of the participants should choose prospect A1 and the other 50% should choose prospect B1. Similarly, in problem 2 the expected utility equals −$2,700 in both prospects. Again, participants should evenly split their choices. The actual results, however, are not in accord with predictions from expected utility theory (see Figure 11.4). In problem 1, 86% of Kahneman and Tversky's (1979) participants selected the prospect of a 90% chance of gaining $3,000.

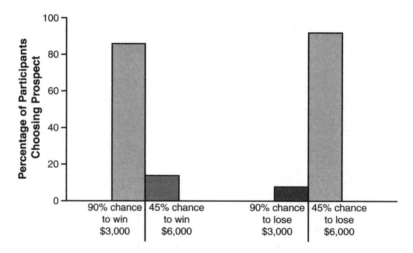

FIGURE 11.4   Expected Utility and Probability of Gain/Loss. People prefer less risk in regard to winning money but are more risk seeking regarding losing money.

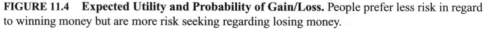

Source: Adapted from "Prospect Theory" by D. Kahneman and A. Tversky, 1979, *Econometrica, 47,* table 1, p. 268.

In problem 2, 92% of the participants chose the prospect of a 45% chance of losing $6,000. The two choices made in problems 1 and 2 are mirror images. People prefer a good chance (90%) of gaining a small reward ($3,000) compared to a nearly even chance (45%) of gaining a large reward ($6,000). In other words, people prefer a sure thing as opposed to a gamble. Regarding losses, however, people are risk seeking. They prefer a nearly even chance (45%) of losing a large amount ($6,000) compared to a good chance (90%) of losing a small amount ($3,000). What prospect a participant preferred depended on how it was framed. When the emphasis was on gaining $3,000, participants preferred a sure thing (90% chance). When the emphasis was on losing $3,000, however, participants preferred to gamble (45% chance). The results indicate that the greater the certainty, the more people want to achieve gains and avoid losses. As the probability of a gain increases, its attractiveness increases even though its expected utility is identical to an alternative, less probable gain. In contrast, a less probable although larger loss is preferable to a more probable although smaller loss.

Consider two more problems for which the prospects of winning the lottery are much, much less. Choose between the following pairs of prospects:

Problem 3
Prospect A3: 0.2% chance of winning $3,000; expected utility = $6.00
or
Prospect B3: 0.1% chance of winning $6,000; expected utility = $6.00

Consider investing in a business but concentrate on the prospects of losing the money during the first year. In which of the two prospects would you invest money?

Problem 4
Prospect A4: 0.2% chance of losing $3,000; expected utility = −$6.00
or
Prospect B4: 0.1% chance of losing $6,000; expected utility = −$6.00

Predictions based on expected utility theory suggest that participants should choose both prospects equally. In problem 3, the expected utility equals $6.00 for both prospects, and so participants should choose each prospect 50% of the time. In problem 4, the expected utility equals −$6.00 for both prospects, and so participants should also choose each prospect 50% of the time. However, the actual results did not confirm predictions from expected utility theory (see Figure 11.5). In problem 3, 73% of Kahneman and Tversky's (1979) participants chose the prospect (B3) of a 0.1% chance of winning $6,000. In problem 3, it appears almost certain (0.2% or 0.1%) that participants will not win; hence, they prefer the larger amount ($6,000). In problem 4, 70% of the participants chose the prospect (A4) of a 0.2% chance of losing $3,000. In problem 4, even though it appears almost certain (0.2% or 0.1%) that participants are not going to lose, they prefer to lose the smaller amount of $3,000 rather than the larger amount of $6,000. These results show no shifting of preference from gains to losses as occurred between problems 1 and 2.

Prospect Theory

The results presented in Figures 11.4 and 11.5 show that people do not behave according to predictions derived from expected utility theory. An alternative, **prospect theory,** is more descriptive of what humans do (Kahneman & Tversky, 1979). According to this theory,

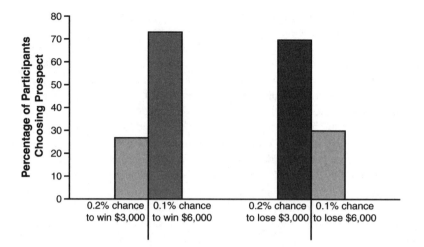

FIGURE 11.5   Expected Utility and Gain/Loss. When very low, probabilities are ignored and decisions are based on the actual value of a gain or loss. People tended to choose the larger gain of $6,000 and choose the smaller loss of $3,000.

Source: Adapted from "Prospect Theory" by D. Kahneman and A. Tversky, 1979, *Econometrica, 47,* table 1, p. 268.

a prospect or goal is appraised with a *decision weight* that determines its value or importance. Prospect theory differs from utility theory in several ways. First, the psychological value of a loss is greater than the psychological value of an identical gain. This observation comes from Chapter 10 with the example that a $100 loss is more dissatisfying than a $100 gain is satisfying. Second, people prefer smaller gains that are highly likely over larger gains that are much less likely (see Figure 11.4). This preference reverses with losses. Larger risky losses are preferred over smaller losses that are less risky (see Figure 11.4). Third, decision weights resemble probabilities but are not identical with them. Risks at very low probabilities are weighted more heavily than the actual probabilities indicate. People are less sensitive at intermediate probabilities, and changes are weighted less heavily. Finally, very low or very high probabilities are weighted as certainties (Hastie & Dawes, 2001). For example, Figure 11.5 shows that with 0.2% and 0.1% chances, people chose to win $6,000 over $3,000 and lose $3,000 over $6,000, even though the expected utilities of the alternatives are identical.

What are some implications of the difference between probabilities and decision weights? Probabilities influence how much an incentive is weighted. The weighted incentive or prospect, in turn, determines the individual's decision. However, when probabilities are very low or very high, people appear to consider them of no consequence. As a result, choice is based on the actual utility of the gain or the actual utility of the loss (Kahneman & Tversky, 1979).

Perhaps the idea that very low probabilities carry no weight may account for some unsafe behaviors. Why would some individuals engage in unsafe sex or not wear seatbelts unless they thought that the resulting negative consequences would "never happen to me"? Things can only never happen that have a probability of 0.00. Dying as a consequence of unsafe sex or dying in an accident from not wearing a seatbelt have probabilities greater than 0.00. On a more positive note, the high probability that good things can happen also impacts certainty. For example, a student may believe with certainty that he will graduate even though the probability is somewhat less than 1.00. A person may believe in the certainty of forming a lifelong partnership, such as marriage, even though the probability of that happening is less than 1.00 also.

Section Recap

Not all goals are of equal value. *Goal level* refers to the value or valence of a goal, with higher levels indicating higher values. As goal level increases, so does *goal difficulty*, which refers to how hard it is to achieve a goal. *Goal specificity* refers to how precisely a goal is conceived. Specific goals, in contrast to vague ones, provide a directive function. Specific, high-level goals lead to better achievement behavior than do vague, low-level goals. Goals have both an *energizing function* that motivates the person toward the goal and a *directing function* that informs the person which behaviors are necessary to achieve a goal.

According to *expected utility theory,* the goal an individual pursues is the one with the highest expected utility. A person arrives at expected utility from judging the utility of a goal and multiplying that by *subjective probability,* which is a personal estimate of the likelihood that a goal can be achieved. Does the person see the goal as a potential gain or as avoiding a loss? This depends also on how the goal is *framed,* which means a goal can be viewed either positively as a gain or negatively as avoiding a loss. People prefer gains that have a higher likelihood of success even if the value of the gain is low. This preference reverses for losses. People prefer losses that have a low likelihood of occurring even if the loss has a higher value. *Prospect theory* maintains that people make decisions based on prospects, which are potential outcomes based on their value and weighted by what is known as a decision weight. Value can refer to a prospective loss or to a prospective gain. Decision weights are based on probabilities but are not identical with them.

Goal Commitment and Goal Achievement

The purpose of this section is to describe the process by which a person commits to a goal and how she is motivated by a goal. It concludes with a description of various goal-achievement behaviors and what happens when a goal is achieved or if it is not.

Committing to a Goal

True or false: "I think I can graduate from this university." If true, then you are committed to a goal of graduation and are in the process of trying to achieve it.

Commitment as a Factor in Goal Achievement. **Goal commitment** is the process whereby a person becomes set to achieve a goal (Klinger, 1977; Locke & Latham, 1990; Locke et al., 1981). It implies a person's willingness and persistent determination to expend time and effort in its pursuit (Locke et al., 1988). In fact, an analysis of a number of investigations support the generalization that greater commitment means a greater expenditure of effort in trying to achieve a goal (Klein et al., 1999). For example, the more committed a student is to achieving a particular GPA goal, the more time the student will spend studying. The effects of commitment, however, are more apparent for difficult goals compared to easier ones. For instance, commitment becomes more important if a student's goal is to earn a 3.50 GPA compared to a 2.50 GPA. Finally, it appears that greater commitment is associated with a goal being more attractive and being considered more achievable (Klein et al., 1999). Continuing the GPA example, along with greater commitment comes more appreciation of the GPA goal's value and of its chances of being reached.

How can goal commitment be measured? One way is to ask how committed an individual is to achieving a particular goal. A second and more precise way is to use the *Hollenbeck, Williams, and Klein Goal Commitment Items* (Hollenbeck et al., 1989a, 1989b; Klein et al., 2001). Items recommended for this inventory are shown in Table 11.1 as a set of self-report statements that measure how dedicated or devoted individuals are to a particular goal (Klein et al., 2001). Do you have a GPA goal this semester and how committed are you to it? If this scale measures commitment, then students who score high should spend more time and effort trying to achieve their goal than students who score low. Hollenbeck and associates (1989b) conducted a study testing this predicted relationship. One group of students had voluntarily committed to the goal of a 0.25 increase in GPA, while another group was assigned this goal. Both the voluntary goal group and the assigned goal group had their level of commitment measured with an earlier version of the *Goal Commitment Items*. The GPA for that quarter improved slightly for students in both groups, but the amount of improvement also depended on the level of commitment. Students who scored higher on the *Goal Commitment Items* came closer to achieving their goal than students who scored lower.

People can increase their level of commitment by announcing their goals publicly (Salancik, 1977). Telling other significant people like friends about the goal should make it more difficult to abandon. Hollenbeck and associates (1989b) also tested this possibility by having half of the students publicly announce their goal of a 0.25 increase in GPA. This announcement was made by distributing to all students a list of names containing each student's GPA goal. In addition, the publicly committed students had to send a statement of their goal to a significant other, usually a parent or sibling. The public commitment manipulation worked. Students who had publicly announced their goals earned higher GPAs than students who had not made a public announcement. Thus, one way you can perform better on the next exam is to announce your exam goal score to a friend. This announcement increases commitment and should motivate you to study harder.

TABLE 11.1   Goal Commitment Scale Items

1. It's hard to take this goal seriously. (R)
2. Quite frankly, I don't care if I achieve this goal or not. (R)
3. I am strongly committed to pursuing this goal.
4. It wouldn't take much to make me abandon this goal. (R)
5. I think this is a good goal to shoot for.

Note: Answer each item with this scale: Strongly disagree = 1 2 3 4 5 = Strongly agree. Items followed by (R) are reverse scored; for example, 1 becomes 5 and 4 becomes 2. The higher the score, the higher the level of goal commitment.

Source: From "The Assessment of Goal Commitment: A Measurement Model Meta-analysis" by H. J. Klein et al., 2001, *Organizational Behavior and Human Decision Processes, 85,* table 1, p. 34. Copyright 2001 by Elsevier. Reprinted by permission.

Negative Feedback Loop. How does a person know if progress is being made toward achieving a goal? Progress toward or away from a goal is represented by a negative feedback loop, as diagrammed in Figure 11.6 (Campion & Lord, 1982; Klein, 1989; Powers, 1973). The diagram is comparable to the thermostat example in Figure 5.1. In this process, the goal box represents a person's desired goal. In the case of a student, the goal is, say, to learn enough to earn an *A* on an exam. The current state box represents a student's current level of knowledge in relation to the goal. For example, the student assesses her current knowledge of the material to be covered on the exam. Information about the current state and the goal state is fed into the comparator box. If the goal has not been achieved, then the comparator detects this as a discrepancy between the current state and the goal state. The discrepancy motivates the person to achieve her goal. For example, if a student determines that her current knowledge is short of what is necessary to earn an *A,* then she will study. If the goal has been achieved, then the discrepancy is zero and achievement behavior ceases. For example, a student quits studying on determining that she knows the material well enough to earn an *A*.

Feedback. How do individuals know if they are making progress toward their goals? Although a goal informs people about what is desired, **feedback** tells them how they are progressing relative to their goals (Locke & Latham, 1990). A goal also provides the information about what instrumental or achievement behavior is necessary. Feedback about the outcome of this behavior is judged in relation to the goal. As shown in Figure 11.6,

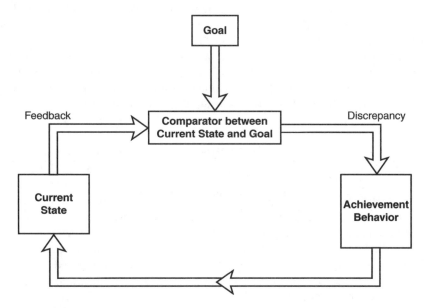

FIGURE 11.6 Negative Feedback Loop of Goal Achievement Behavior. The comparator detects whether there is a discrepancy between the current state and the goal state. When a discrepancy is no longer detected, it means the goal is achieved.

information about a person's current state is fed back into the comparator to determine the discrepancy between the current state and the goal. However, goals do not motivate behavior if feedback is not provided. Bandura and Cervone (1983) demonstrated the joint effect of a goal plus feedback on motivation. They had participants perform an exercise task that required alternately pushing and pulling two arm levers on an exercise machine. The amount of effort expended on this task defined the participants' motivation. Following five minutes of exercise, participants were divided into four experimental groups. The goal-plus-feedback group was to increase their effort by 40% over the next five minutes and was given feedback as to how well they had done. The goal group was given the same goal but was not provided with any feedback at the end of the five-minute period. Without feedback, participants in this group had no way of knowing how close to achieving their goal they had come. The feedback group was not given a goal but was given feedback at the end of the five-minute period. Their feedback was provided as if they had a goal of 40% increased effort. The feedback was meaningless for this group, since they did not know what the goal was. The control group was given neither a goal nor feedback. To determine the effects of a goal plus feedback, goal alone, feedback alone, or neither, participants were to exercise on the machine for an additional five minutes. During this third exercise period, the group that received a goal plus feedback put forth twice as much effort compared to the groups that received only a goal or only feedback. These last two groups did no better than the control group, which received neither a goal nor feedback. Thus, for a goal to motivate behavior, it is necessary to receive feedback.

The necessity of a goal plus feedback on motivation was also demonstrated in an applied experiment on electricity conservation. Becker (1978) recruited households and gave them a goal of reducing their energy by 2 or 20%. Furthermore, half of the households were provided with feedback regarding the amount of electricity they had used every Monday, Wednesday, and Friday. The feedback was given in terms of the percent of energy conserved or wasted since the last reading. The other half of the households in each goal condition were not given any feedback. Without feedback, how would a family know if it was getting closer or farther away from the goal? The results bore out the importance of feedback. There was a significant reduction in electricity consumption only for households with the 20% reduction goal plus feedback. When feedback was not provided or the goal was only a 2% reduction, there was no saving in electricity consumption.

Motivational Features of Goal Setting.   The feedback loop in Figure 11.6 shows two sources of motivation (Locke & Latham, 1990). One source is the goal itself. The motivational aspect of a goal is that it almost always exceeds a person's current state or current level of performance. The second source of motivation illustrated in the feedback loop is the discrepancy between the goal and the current state. Instrumental or goal behavior is an attempt to reduce the size of the discrepancy—that is, to bring the person closer to the goal (Carver & Scheier, 1982; Powers, 1973). Behavior is reinforced when the discrepancy decreases, which means getting closer to a goal. Behavior is punished, however, when the discrepancy increases, which means getting farther away from the goal. There appears to be somewhat of a paradox here. On the one hand, people set goals that exceed and are discrepant from their current state. On the other hand, they behave so as to reduce this discrepancy—that is, to achieve their goals (Locke, 1991).

Goal Thoughts. Have you thought what your first job after graduation will be like? Have you thought how to get that job? Commitment produces thinking about a goal. Klinger (1977) has categorized goal thinking into respondent and operant thoughts. **Respondent thoughts** are elicited by stimulus aspects of the goals. Respondent thoughts intrude into consciousness and are not sought voluntarily. Examples of respondent thoughts would include musing and daydreaming. Klinger and associates (1980) showed that the frequency of goal-related thoughts depended on how committed people were to achieving their goal. The amount of joy or relief a person expected from the goal and the probability of achieving the goal also determined the frequency of respondent thought. Whereas respondent thoughts might be termed fantasies about the goal, **operant thoughts** are similar to problem solving. These thoughts are mental attempts to try out different strategies for achieving a goal. Strategies that mentally seem to work for achieving the goal will be tried in actuality, while those that do not work will be discarded (Dennett, 1975; Klinger, 1977). Thus, a student might think what it is like to have a job after graduation (respondent thoughts) and think of possible strategies for getting a job (operant thoughts).

Subgoals as Achievements toward Final Goals. Are there strategies that can help an individual achieve her goals once operant thoughts are translated into goal-achievement behaviors? One strategy is to achieve a series of subgoals along the way toward the final goal. If reaching the top of a ladder is the final or *distal* goal, then each individual rung is a **subgoal,** sometimes referred to as a *proximal* goal. A person must climb each individual rung in order to reach the top of the ladder. Likewise, goals are arranged in a hierarchical fashion, with the final, distal goal at the top and subgoals below (Miller et al., 1960). To reach a final goal, subgoals must be achieved along the way. Incentives that help individuals reach their final goal become subgoals.

Motivation for the final goal increases with the addition of subgoals that must be achieved along the way (Latham & Seijts, 1999; Locke & Latham, 1990; Weldon & Yun, 2000). For example, Latham and Seijts (1999) had university students participate in a complex simulated manufacturing task during which they were to buy material to build and sell toys. The experiment employed three different groups, each with a different goal regarding the amount of money to be earned. For the do-your-best goal, participants were urged to make as much money as possible. For the distal goal, participants were told to earn more than a specific designated amount. This amount was a difficult goal, according to results from a prior exploratory study. In the proximal-plus-distal goal condition, specific proximal goals were to be achieved along the way toward achievement of the distal goal. The simulated manufacturing task consisted of six 10-minute sessions during which prices changed for the purchase of materials and for sale of the toys. During the sessions, participants had to buy, manufacture, and sell toys while trying to make a profit according to the different goal criteria. Figure 11.7 shows the amount of money earned in each goal condition. The subgoals increased motivation toward the final goal, as shown in the proximal-plus-distal goal condition, in which participants earned the most money. Participants in the proximal-plus-distal goal condition also developed a greater sense of self-efficacy during the course of the six sessions, which helped them perform better—that is, earned a greater profit.

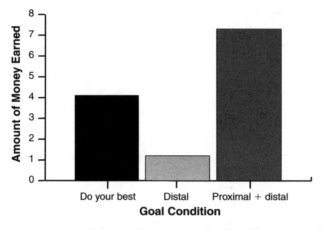

FIGURE 11.7   Subgoals Increase Motivation. The amount of money earned at the end of a simulated manufacturing task was greatest when participants were given subgoals (proximal goals) along with a distal or final goal. A distal goal alone resulted in the least amount of money earned at the end of the task with the do-your-best goal falling in between.

Source: Adapted from "The Effects of Proximal and Distal Goals on Performance on a Moderately Complex Task" by G. P. Latham and G. H. Seijts, 1999, *Journal of Organizational Behavior, 20,* p. 426.

Subgoals provide several advantages for achievement of the distal goal. First, they provide a more immediate source of motivation than the delayed motivation provided by the final goal. Second, subgoals serve as feedback about progress toward the final goal. Third, feedback from subgoals provides information about whether achievement strategies are effective or need to be modified. Fourth, the achievement of subgoals increases a person's sense of self-efficacy, which is associated with increased persistence and effort (Bandura, 1997).

The value of subgoals (proximal goals) also depends on the extent they can help satisfy end goals (Markman & Brendl, 2000). A task that is relevant for the achievement of a final goal should be more valuable than a similar one that is not relevant. For example, college courses that are directly relevant for a student's chosen career should be valued more than other courses. To illustrate the importance of subgoals, take out a sheet of paper. On the left, list all courses you have taken and next to each course indicate how important earning a good grade is for your career plans. Raynor (1970/1974) asked such questions of university students to determine how important they considered a particular course as a subgoal for their final career goal. He expected that the more important a course was for a student's career, the better the grade they earned in that course. Courses rated as very important or important were designated as having high career instrumentality. Courses rated as fairly, not too, or not at all important were designated as having low career instrumentality. The ratings indicated that students earned higher grades in their high-instrumentality courses and lower grades in their low-instrumentality courses. Thus, as the importance of the subgoal increases, the effort to achieve that subgoal also increases. Raynor also found that students earned higher grades in an introductory psychology course when it had high career instrumentality.

Achievement Behaviors

What happens when goals are established but achievement strategies are not in place? For instance, from studying charts, maps, and books, the navigator Christopher Columbus concluded that he could sail west from Spain to reach Asia. He must have been fairly certain of this because he spent nearly eight years trying to find backers for an expedition. Finally, in 1492 Queen Isabella and King Ferdinand agreed to sponsor an expedition. Although his goal was well defined, the method for achieving it was not well planned or was at least based on faulty information. Because of inaccurate maps Columbus never did discover a route to Asia although he did land in what is now known as the Bahamas, Cuba, the Dominican Republic, and Haiti. The lesson here for students of motivation is that the estimated likelihood of achieving a goal is an important element of goal motivation. Also, although a goal should be well defined, it is also necessary to have the correct strategy for achieving it. As indicated in Figure 11.6, achieving a goal proceeds by reducing the discrepancy between the current state and the goal. The process of goal achievement rarely proceeds with trial-and-error or random behavior. Instead, goals are accompanied by knowledge that guides behavior instrumental for achieving a goal.

A current question concerns how goals activate relevant achievement behavior. There are two possibilities. First, according to Bargh and Williams (2006), the *perception-behavior link* refers to the idea that a goal elicits achievement behavior because goals and their achievement behaviors have been associated together many times in the past. Thus, the representation of a goal in consciousness automatically produces relevant achievement behavior. For example, the goal of writing a paper automatically elicits an image of a computer and its available word-processing program. Second, according to Cesario and coresearchers (2006), *motivated preparation* means that the aim of the behavior depends on a goal's valence—that is, whether the goal is negative or positive. Imagine that the concept of a social group has been automatically activated. The perception-behavior link hypothesis predicts that subsequent behavior toward a member of the group is based on the group's characteristics. For example, walk slow in the presence of old people, since they walk slow. The motivated-preparation hypothesis, however, would maintain that behavior also depends on whether the group is evaluated negatively or positively. Negative evaluations might prompt avoidance behaviors while positive evaluations prompt approach behaviors. Thus, how slow or fast a person walks may depend on whether the image of an old person was evaluated negatively or positively. If negative, then walk fast to escape; if positive, walk slow to maintain interaction (Cesario et al., 2006).

Goal Achievement and Goal Failure

Once a goal is achieved, a person receives both extrinsic and intrinsic satisfaction—that is, extrinsic from the goal itself and intrinsic from the feeling that results from having achieved the goal.

Achievement Valence. While goal valence refers to the benefits derived from a goal, **achievement valence** refers to the satisfaction a person receives from achieving it. Higher benefits accompany more difficult goals, but the likelihood of attaining satisfaction actually decreases (Mento et al., 1992). A person is more likely to fail to achieve a difficult goal and thus be disappointed. Failure is less likely when trying to achieve an easy goal. In one experimental demonstration, students were first asked to assume that their personal GPA goal was 4.0, 3.0, or 2.0. Next, to ascertain achievement valence, they were asked how satisfied they would be with an *A, B,* or *C* average. For example, if your goal was a 3.0 GPA and you earned an *A, B,* or *C* average, then how satisfied would you be on a scale from Incredibly dissatisfied to Incredibly satisfied? The results showed that satisfaction ratings decreased as GPA goal increased (Mento et al., 1992, study 7). Satisfaction resulted from an earned GPA exceeding the goal GPA, while dissatisfaction resulted from an earned GPA falling below the goal GPA. A student with a goal of *A* would only be satisfied with an *A* and be dissatisfied with anything less. A student with a goal of *B* would be satisfied with a *B* but would be much more satisfied with an *A* and dissatisfied with a *C*. A student with a goal of *C* would be satisfied with a *C* but would be more satisfied with a *B* and incredibly satisfied with an *A*. Thus, as goal difficulty increases, the likelihood of achievement decreases and attaining satisfaction is less likely. People often set goals as high as possible but not so high that the likelihood of failure exceeds some acceptable level.

Consequences of Success and Failure.   What happens when goals are not achieved was summarized humorously by the comedic actor W. C. Fields. "If at first you don't succeed, try, try, again. Then quit. There's no use being a damn fool about it." One consequence of not achieving a goal is to try, try, again. A second consequence is to quit that particular goal, scale it down, or seek an alternative goal.

The negative feedback loop illustrated in Figure 11.6 implies that a goal, once set, is forever fixed. However, just as a homeowner can alter the desired temperature setting on the thermostat, an individual can change her goals. Goals are altered based on the type of feedback an individual receives regarding goal achievement. If feedback indicates that a person is failing to meet her goal, then one choice is to reduce the level of the goal. Feedback indicating success might mean raising the level of a future goal. Furthermore, success and failure affect proximal goals and consequently distal goals, since the lowering or raising of proximal goals will result in a lower or higher distal goal, respectively. These possible effects were examined in male and female track and field athletes during one season of competition (Donovan & Williams, 2003). Proximal goals referred to performance in an individual competition and distal goals referred to performance over the entire eight-week season. Prior to each competition, the athletes were asked to indicate their goals for the next competition and for the entire season. How did their goals change when they failed, met, or exceeded their goals? The results showed that if athletes failed to achieve their goals, then there was a tendency to lower their goals for the next competition and for the season's distal goal. However, if they met or exceeded their goals, then subsequent competition and season goals were revised upward. Furthermore, the greater the discrepancy between their stated goals and actual performance, the greater the revision of all their future goals (Donovan & Williams, 2003).

Academic goals also change with success and failure feedback. Success and failure affect the level that students set for their proximate goals of individual exams and for the distal goal of the course grade. Campion and Lord (1982) asked university students to report their minimum satisfactory grade for an approaching exam and for the course. As would be expected from level of aspiration, the minimum satisfactory grade goal was about one letter grade higher than performance on a previous exam. However, the level of this goal was also consistent with a student's ability and past performance. So, for example, if a student earned a *D* on the last exam, she might aspire to a *C* on the next one, while another student who previously earned a *B* might aspire to an *A*. In the Campion and Lord (1982) investigation, those students who exceeded their goals were more likely to raise them for the next exam. If a student's goal was a *B* and she earned an *A,* then for the next exam her goal would be raised to an *A*. Furthermore, consistent and repeated success in meeting exam grade goals led to raising course grade goals. Students who failed to reach their exam goals, however, were more likely to lower them for the next exam. If a student's goal was a *B* but he earned a *C,* then he was more likely to lower his goal to a *C* for the next exam. Repeated failures to meet exam grade goals also led to a lowering of course grade goals. Raising goals following achievement and lowering goals following failure was more apparent when examined over the entire academic quarter. Figure 11.8 shows that students were more likely to raise their exam grade and course grade goals following success on exams. However, when students consistently failed to meet their goals, they were more likely to lower their subsequent exam and course grade goals. An important conclusion from this research and that of the athletes is that goals are not static. Goals change as a result of success or failure of earlier goals.

There are exceptions to the preceding generalizations. Following success, a minority of students lowered their goals, while after failure another minority raised their goals (see Figure 11.8). Thus, success or failure is not the sole determiner of whether individuals raise or lower their goals. Raising or lowering a goal is mediated by self-efficacy, which is the belief about how capable a person feels about achieving a particular goal. Bandura and Cervone (1986) showed that despite failure, a person with strong self-efficacy was more

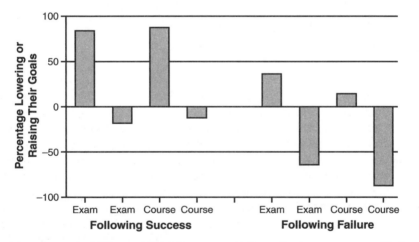

FIGURE 11.8   Effects of Goal Success or Failure. Students were more likely to increase their exam grade goals and their course grade goals following success in meeting a previous goal. They were more likely to lower goals following failure in meeting a previous goal. The data are averaged over four exams given during the academic quarter.

Source: Adapted from "A Control Systems Conceptualization of the Goal-Setting and Changing Process" by M. A. Campion and R. G. Lord, 1982, *Organizational Behavior and Human Performance, 30,* table 4, p. 279, and table 7, p. 283.

likely to try harder the next time, while a person with weak self-efficacy was more likely to decrease effort. Thus, high-self-efficacy individuals are more likely to increase their goal level following failure, while low-self-efficacy individuals are more likely to lower it. In addition, following success, individuals with low self-efficacy did not think they were able to achieve their goal a second time. These individuals were less likely to expend more effort the next time, especially when they had just expended a lot of effort to meet the goal.

Section Recap

Once a goal is selected, the process of *goal commitment* indicates that a person persists in expending time and effort to achieve his goal. The negative feedback loop is a model for goal-achievement behavior. Progress toward a goal depends on *feedback,* which is information about the outcome of achievement behavior in relation to the goal. Goal achievement is not possible without feedback. Achievement behavior is motivated to reduce the discrepancy between the person's goal and current state. Once a person commits to a goal, *respondent thoughts,* which are fantasies about the goal, intrude into consciousness. *Operant thoughts,* however, are mental plans about how to achieve one's goal. Achievement of the final goal is aided by *subgoals* (proximal goals), which are like individual rungs of a ladder that must be climbed to reach the top or final goal.

Most goals come with definite strategies for how to achieve them. According to the *perception-behavior* link, a goal activates the appropriate achievement behavior because the two have been associated many times in the past. According to the concept of *motivated preparation,* goal valence determines the aim of achievement behavior. Positive goals spur approach behavior and negative goals spur avoidance behavior. Associated with goal valence is *achievement valence,* which refers to the satisfaction attained from accomplishing a goal. Following success a goal is usually scaled up, while following failure it is usually scaled down.

ACTIVITIES

1. *Goal Setting:*
   a. Apply concepts from this chapter by setting a high but doable goal for your next exam. As an illustration, let us assume your next exam is 14 days away. Answer the following:

   My goal on this next exam is to earn a score of ____ .

   (This exam score should be higher than the last exam but within reach of your abilities.)

   The benefits I hope to achieve from this goal are

   _____

   _____.

   (By setting a precise score, your goal is specific and high enough to motivate you.)

   My level of commitment to accomplishing this goal is ____ .

   (This score is based on your answers given to the *Hollenbeck, Williams, and Klein Goal Commitment Items,* table 11.1.)

   b. You can increase your commitment to your exam goal as follows:

   1. Tell a classmate about your goal.
   2. Tell the whole class about your goal.
   3. Tell your roommate(s) about your goal.

4. Tell your best friend or a few friends about your goal.
5. Write or telephone your parents, brothers, sisters, and/or grandparents informing them about your goal.

c. In order to achieve your goal, there are subgoals that must be met. To set subgoals, write the number of minutes you plan to study on each of the following days (assume exam is 14 days away).

Day 14 ____	Day 13 ____	Day 12 ____
Day 11 ____	Day 10 ____	Day 9 ____
Day 8 ____	Day 7 ____	Day 6 ____
Day 5 ____	Day 4 ____	Day 3 ____
Day 2 ____	Day 1 ____	Exam day ____

CHAPTER

12 Economics of Motivation

Laziness travels so slowly that poverty soon overtakes him.
—*Benjamin Franklin, 1756*

Work is the price you pay for money.

—*Anonymous*

■ The nature of motivation is to move a person into action. Are there pressures, however, that hinder this from happening? Do antimotivation factors exist? The possibilities of antimotivation factors are examined in this chapter along with answers to the following questions:

1. How are the behavioral costs of need satisfaction and goal achievement measured?
2. Is the expenditure of goal-achievement behavior governed by a principle of least effort?
3. Does behavior that results in need satisfaction or goal achievement resemble an economic transaction such that easy goals are accomplished more than difficult ones?
4. How pervasive is least effort or the economic demand law as a description of motivated behavior?

Motivation Costs and Resources

Once upon a time there was a king, who on his deathbed promised his kingdom to the son who was the laziest. The eldest son proclaimed to be the laziest, since he would not bother to remove a drop of water from his eye in order to sleep. The second son claimed the kingdom, maintaining that he was too lazy to remove his burning heel from a fire. The third son exclaimed that the kingdom should be his because he indeed was the laziest: "If the hangman's noose were already around my neck, then I would be too lazy to cut it with a knife so that I could save myself." Guess who inherited the kingdom? (taken from Grimm, 1884/1968).

This fairy tale portrays a paradoxical goal-achievement scenario. Usually, higher-level or more difficult goals—like acquiring a kingdom—require more work. But in this story achievement was conditional on how little effort was made.

Push and pull motivation require energy. Whether a person is pushed to satisfy a physiological or psychological need, the expenditure of some type of energy is required. Similarly, if a person is pulled toward the achievement of a goal, then this also requires energy. There is a paradox in motivation. Humans value high-level goals, on the one hand, which they hope to achieve with minimal cost, on the other hand. These two preferences are

TABLE 12.1 The Motivational Costs of Typing a 10-Page Paper

Response costs:	Number of responses required to complete the task (e.g., keystrokes)
	Estimated 160,000 keystrokes for 3,000 words (10 pages)
Time costs:	Amount of time required to complete the task (e.g., minutes, hours)
	Estimated 1.50 hours of typing at 30 words per minute
Physical energy costs:	Utilizing oxygen and glucose (e.g., calories burned)
	A 140-pound person will burn 143 calories typing for 1.5 hours
Psychological energy costs:	Self-control to keep on task; not give in to temptation; no units
	Amount of self-control spent depends on degree of temptation
Opportunity costs:	Activities person gave up to type paper (e.g., number of activities)
	Gave up watching TV with friends

incompatible. The achievement of difficult high-level goals requires persistent achievement behavior while easy low-level goals do not.

The purpose of this section is to describe the inclination of animals and humans to expend the fewest motivational resources in attempting to achieve the highest goals possible.

Costs of Motivated Behavior

Your goals are not free. Their achievement depends on motivated behavior that brings the goal closer and closer until finally achieved. There are a variety of cost measures of motivated behaviors. For example, if your goal is to type a 10-page paper, then it will cost you in terms of responses, time, physical energy, psychological energy, and lost opportunities. These costs are laid out in detail in Table 12.1. In general, as need intensity or goal level increases, the cost of satisfaction or achievement increases also.

Response and Time Costs. Responses refer to discrete behavioral units that are required to achieve a goal. The typing example in Table 12.1 classifies keystrokes as responses. Response costs have been studied extensively with animals in a Skinner box. This is a chamber in which a rat, for example, presses a lever in order to earn a pellet of food. The cost of food is set by the number of lever presses, which is controlled by a **fixed ratio (FR) schedule of reinforcement.** For this schedule, an experimenter establishes a ratio between the number of lever presses the rat must make in order to receive one reinforcer. For instance, an FR 10 requires 10 lever presses for one reinforcer, while an FR 100 requires 100 lever presses for one reinforcer. Thus, a food pellet requiring 100 lever presses is more expensive than one requiring 10 lever presses.

A difficulty with the response-cost measure is quantifying the topography and intensity of a response. Is it feasible to count the number of responses in any complex human activity, such as working or studying? In the case of typing, are typing the letters *q* and *z* with the little finger equal to typing the letters *t* and *b* with the index finger? One way out of the difficulty of response measurement is to use *time costs*. Employers compensate workers for time spent working, such as per hour or per month. Thus, the cost of typing a 10-page paper can be measured by how much time was required rather than by how many keystrokes. Time spent working can be translated into an exact dollar amount. Thus, it is possible to translate the dollar-costs of various goods and services into working-time costs. For instance, suppose a worker who earned $7.25 per hour ordered a hamburger, french fries, and a cola drink, which cost $5.00. In terms of time spent working, this meal cost 41 minutes ($5.00/$7.25 × 60 minutes = 41 minutes).

Physical Energy Costs.   The workings of our muscles and brain require the use of glucose for energy either with or without the aid of oxygen. Thus, both glucose and oxygen consumption may be used as cost measures of behavior. The *calorie* is a unit of physical energy that can serve as the cost measure for the duration and intensity of activities. For example, a 140-pound person burns 210 calories walking for one hour at 20 minutes per mile and burns 318 calories walking at 15 minutes per mile. The same individual would burn 143 calories typing a 10-page paper (Table 12.1). Lighter and heavier individuals burn fewer or more calories on these activities, respectively.

> You can calculate the caloric cost of 222 activities with the *Activity Calorie Calculator* available at http://primusweb.com/fitnesspartner/cgi-bin/fpc/actcalc.pl

As described in Chapter 1, the brain is a voracious user of glucose for energy; proportionately way more than the rest of the body. Glucose is used for mental (brain) work, which presumably should deplete some of the brain's glucose. A test of this assumption was conducted by Gailliot and coresearchers (2007), who measured blood glucose levels before and after a mental task that required the control of attention. As part of the research, participants viewed a silent six-minute video of a woman talking, while on the bottom of the screen common words appeared singly for 10 seconds each. Mental effort was manipulated by instructing the participants *not* to look at the words (control attention condition) while other participants were simply allowed to watch the video (watch normally condition). Blood samples were drawn before and after the video presentation in order to measure any changes in glucose. Normally watching the video did not reduce participants' glucose. However, when required to control their attention in order not to look at the words, there was a significant decline in glucose. In other words, the extra mental (brain) effort for the control of attention cost the participants additional glucose.

Psychological Energy Costs.   This general term covers the ability to persist at self-control, decision making, and information processing, such as reading, comprehending, or performing arithmetic. There are no units of psychological energy, like calories, other than some indication of greater or lesser amounts. One type of psychological process is self-regulation or self-control, which is "the overriding or inhibiting of automatic, habitual, or innate behaviors, urges, emotions or desires that would otherwise interfere with goal directed behavior" (Muraven et al., 2006, p. 524). Resisting temptation is an example of self-regulation. Baumeister and coresearchers (1998) showed that when self-regulation energy was drawn on for one task, then less energy was available for another task. For example, the experimenters concluded that participants used more self-regulation energy resisting the temptation to eat chocolate chip cookies than resisting the temptation to eat radishes. This conclusion was based on the finding that participants, who had resisted cookies, did not persist as long at a later puzzle-solving task because they were low in self-regulating energy. As further illustrations, a person may inhibit the urge to nap in order to study, forego dessert so as to maintain a desired weight, or suppress her anger so as not to escalate an argument.

In each example, there is a cost in psychological energy. Self-control has been compared to muscular energy. Self-control energy can be depleted with use and restored with rest, much like our muscles are (Muraven & Baumeister, 2000).

Opportunity Costs. According to economists, the opportunity cost for reading this chapter is the next preferred activity that you gave up. Any lesser preferred activities should not be counted. Perhaps you gave up the opportunity to watch TV, which was your most preferred alternative, while studying for another class was the next alternative. Studying should not be counted as an opportunity cost, since it was preferred less than TV watching. However, Schwartz (2004) points out that choosing one option may involve multiple opportunity costs—that is, foregoing several other alternatives. Perhaps you gave up watching TV with friends and so you also gave up the opportunity to socialize. Opportunity costs can have an effect in different ways (Schwartz, 2004). First, the opportunity cost of a decision increases with the number of abandoned alternatives. For example, the opportunity cost of reading this chapter is greater if you abandoned watching TV with friends rather than watching TV alone. Second, the evaluation of lost opportunities produces regret; an unpleasant feeling brought on by a wrong decision. Regret is more likely from a greater number of abandoned opportunities.

Regret is likely to occur when a person's choice did not fulfill expectations or was a disappointment. Regret depends on the value of the alternatives or opportunities that were rejected. Sagi and Friedland (2007) conducted a series of experiments showing that intensity of regret in such an instance is based on the combination of values of the rejected alternatives. As a way of understanding how the value of rejected alternatives determines the intensity of regret, consider being a participant in their second experiment, which begins with the following vignette.

> After a very busy week you had, at last, a free evening. Knowing that it would be a while before you get a free evening again, you wanted to make the most of it. You could go to the movies, go to bed early, or go to a café, or read a book. (p. 518)

Now imagine that you chose to go to the movie, which turned out to be long and boring; a disappointment. How much do you regret your decision? It depends on the union or combination of values of the alternatives, which are listed in Table 12.2. Prior to the experiment a separate group of participants rank ordered the four activities in Table 12.2 according to their personal preferences. Watching a movie was preferred most, followed by going to a café while going to bed early was preferred least (Table 12.2). In the main experiment, one group was

TABLE 12.2   Regret Depends on the Combined Value of the Alternative Opportunities

Choices	Chose	Value of the Rejected Alternatives		
		Highest Value	**Medium Value**	**Lowest Value**
Set 1: Higher alternative values	Saw movie: disappointing	Go to a local café	Read a book	—
Set 2: Lower alternative values	Saw movie: disappointing	Go to a local café	—	Go to bed early

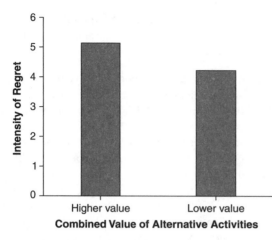

FIGURE 12.1   Intensity of Regret Depends on the Value of the Alternatives. Participants chose to go to a movie that turned out to be a disappointment. Their regret of this decision was more intense when based on the set of rejected alternatives that had a higher combined value.

Source: Adapted from "The Cost of Richness: The Effect of the Size and Diversity of Decision Sets on Post-Decision Regret" by A. Sagi and N. Friedland, 2007, *Journal of Personality and Social Psychology, 93,* p. 518.

asked how much they regretted their movie choice when compared to the alternatives in set 1 while a different group based their regret on the alternatives in set 2. A scale of 1 = Not at all to 7 = Very much was used to measure regret. Notice that for set 1, the alternatives were going to a café or reading a book while in set 2 reading a book was replaced by going to bed early. The combined values of set 1 is higher than that of set 2 and so greater regret was predicted, which is what happened. The intensity of regret shown in Figure 12.1 is higher for set 1 where the combined value of the alternatives was greatest.

The existence of too many alternatives can also result in **choice overload.** This phenomenon refers to the demotivating effect of too many choices on the decision-making process (Iyengar & Lepper, 2000). An individual is initially attracted to a large array of available choices but yet is less likely to make a decision and is more dissatisfied when a decision is made. Iyengar and Lepper (2000) conducted three experiments in which individuals were presented with a limited-choice condition or an extensive-choice condition. In one experiment, shoppers at a grocery store had available for sampling a display of either 6 jams or 24 jams. More shoppers purchased a jar of jam after having visited the limited-choice display of six jams. In the second experiment, university students could write an essay for extra credit from a list of 6 versus 30 topics. More students wrote essays when they were presented with the limited choice of 6 topics rather than the extensive choice of 30 topics. In a third experiment, participants were led to believe that they were in a marketing study that investigated how people selected chocolates based on their names and flavors. They could also select one of the chocolates to eat. Participants either examined a limited-choice display of 6 chocolates or an extensive-choice display of 30 chocolates. The results showed that participants in the limited-choice conditions were more satisfied with their chocolate selection than those in the extensive-choice condition. In addition, as pay for their participation in the research, the participants were given an option of $5 or a box of chocolates ($5 value). More participants from the limited-choice condition chose the box of chocolates instead of $5. The authors note that people enjoy the decision-making process when provided with an extensive set of choices. However, they also feel more responsible for making the best decision and feel more regret when they have made an unsatisfactory decision. Perhaps it is this responsibility of choosing the best option that demotivates them in those situations that provide so many options.

Motivation Resources

When a couple enters a restaurant in order to enjoy a meal, one assumes that they have the resources to pay. Thus, when individuals are pushed to satisfy a need or pulled to achieve a goal, they must have the resources to cover the costs. Otherwise, they will fail. The costs listed in Table 12.1 also serve as categories of motivation resources. For example, a meal costs money but money is also a resource. This section examines whether the likelihood of satisfying a need or achieving a goal depends on the amount of motivation resources a person has available.

Response Resources. Instrumental behavior acts like money (Allison, 1993). Like an amount of money, an amount of behavior determines how much a person accomplishes. For instance, the concept of **reflex reserve** was proposed by Skinner (1938) as a hypothetical entity that refers to the total available activity for obtaining reinforcers. Available activity can refer to the number of lever press responses a rat has in reserve during an experimental session. According to Skinner (1938), reserves are built up during conditioning. Thus, each reinforcement builds up the reserve of lever presses to some maximum amount. Extinction and fatigue, however, reduce the size of the reserve. If lever press responses are no longer reinforced during an extinction session, then the rat eventually quits responding, as if its reserve of responses had run out. Applied to motivation, reflex reserve can indicate a person's persistence in attempting to meet a goal, which is more likely with a greater reserve.

Can something akin to a reflex reserve be built up? Some people are more intelligent, which is a characteristic that helps them achieve their goals. Other people, regardless of their intelligence, are more persistent, determined, and tenacious in trying to achieve their goals. One example of this persistence is the construct of **learned industriousness,** which refers to the acquired ability to sustain effort or be persistent in spite of the buildup of sub-jective fatigue (Eisenberger, 1992). Sustained physical or mental effort produces fatigue, which is an aversive feeling that makes a person quit trying. Effort is qualitatively similar for different behaviors, and the resulting fatigue is similar for different activities. Thus, learning to respond in the presence of fatigue transfers from one behavior to another behavior. However, if effort is sustained in spite of physical or mental fatigue, the animal or individual is eventually more likely to be reinforced by success (Eisenberger, 1992). A prime example of this in animal learning is the *partial reinforcement in extinction effect.* This refers to the greater persistence in responding during extinction by animals who have received prior intermittent reinforcement rather than continuous reinforcement. For instance, Boren (1961) reinforced different groups of rats from once per response to once per 21 responses. Following the delivery of 60 reinforcers, an extinction procedure began during which time no responses were reinforced. Responding during extinction was great-est for the group that had experienced the most nonreinforced responses (the group rein-forced once per 21 responses). These more infrequently reinforced rats persisted longer before giving up completely. According to Eisenberger's (1992) learned industriousness interpretation, a rat's effort during nonreinforced responding was eventually rewarded, which reduced the aversiveness of response-produced fatigue. Because effort is less aversive, an animal with such learning is able to persist longer in the future than is an animal that has had no such experience.

In humans, effort and persistence also occur in cognitive tasks and transfer across such tasks. In one experiment, children with learning disabilities were rewarded with a token every time they learned a spelling word or reading word, whereas other children were only rewarded after learning every fourth or fifth word. The less frequently rewarded children presumably put forth greater effort in the absence of reward, which made their effort more tolerable. Next, when working on a math test, the less frequently rewarded children worked longer on their problems and produced more correct answers than the other children (Eisenberger et al., 1979). The implication is that learned industriousness is a type of motivational resource. All other things being equal, the more industrious person has more of this motivational capital to draw on. As a result he will persist longer, work harder, and expend a greater effort toward completing his goals compared to a less industrious individual.

Another motivational resource and one that resembles learned industriousness is an individual difference variable labeled as **grit** (Duckworth et al., 2007). It refers to the "perseverance and passion for long-term goals" (p. 1087). Individuals with a lot of grit can work hard for years toward distant goals despite setbacks, failures, hardships, and intervals of little progress. The concept of grit is captured by a 1903 remark attributed to the inventor of the lightbulb, Thomas Edison, who said that "Genius is one percent inspiration, ninety-nine percent perspiration." In other words, long hard work is way more responsible for great achievements than brilliance. Duckworth and coresearchers (2007) have developed the *Grit Scale*, which attempts to measure an individual's degree of grit. The scale examines two major attributes of grit: consistency of interests and perseverance of effort. Individuals rate themselves to the extent they agree with each statement on a scale that ranges from 1 = Not at all like me to 5 = Very much like me. For example, consistency of interest is captured by statements such as, "I often set a goal but later choose to pursue a different one" (p. 1090). A high rating on this statement would imply a small amount of grit. Perseverance of effort is reflected in statements such as, "I have achieved a goal that took years of work" (p. 1090). A high score on this statement does reflect a large amount of grit.

> ➤ A complete version of the *Grit Scale* is available from a link on the web page of one of the authors of the scale, Angela Duckworth: http://www.sas.upenn.edu/~duckwort/

Are peoples' scores on the *Grit Scale* indicative of consistent interests and long-term perseverance of effort? Duckworth and coresearchers (2007) examined several achievement behaviors to determine if these were associated with grit. First, there was an indication that higher grit scores were associated with higher levels of education. For example, it takes more grit to complete four additional years of education in order to earn a college degree following high school graduation. Older individuals have more grit than younger individuals. This age effect indicates that your parents possess more grit than you do. Grit is also associated with GPA. Students with higher grit scores had higher GPAs even after the effects of SAT scores were eliminated statistically. Grit scores also predicted long-term achievements, such as for United States Military Academy cadets who successfully completed a demanding summer training program. Finally, participants in the national spelling bee who had higher grit scores spent more time studying and reached later final rounds (Duckworth et al., 2007). Grit is an important motivational resource especially for reaching arduous long-term goals.

Physical Energy Resources. If a person has more energy in the form of glycogen and glucose, does she have a greater potential for motivation? Glucose is obtained from digesting the complex carbohydrates that are in food, such as milk, potatoes, orange juice, rice, pasta, corn, and honey. By being transformed into glycogen, glucose can be stored in the liver and muscles and later used to power the brain and muscles (McArdle et al., 1996; Sizer & Whitney, 1997). Thus, a person's level of motivation depends on the amount of potential energy available for behavior. All other things equal, the more carbohydrates a person has stored, the longer he can persist at an exercise task. Bergstrom and associates (1967) provided participants with a low-, medium-, or high-carbohydrate diet. The low-carbohydrate diet consisted mostly of fat and protein, while the high-carbohydrate diet consisted of foods rich in carbohydrates. The medium-carbohydrate diet consisted of a mixed, uncontrolled diet. Analyses of the participants' muscle fibers showed that the low-carbohydrate diet resulted in the least amount of stored glycogen, while the high-carbohydrate diet resulted in the highest amount. Following their diets, participants were given the motivational task of riding a bicycle ergometer until they were exhausted and could pedal no further. The prediction was that persistence in pedaling depended on the amount of available energy. The results came out as predicted. Participants with the high-carbohydrate diet and more stored muscle glycogen were able to persist longer at the bicycle task. Participants with the low-carbohydrate diet and least amount of muscle glycogen persisted for the shortest time before becoming exhausted. Thus, achieving one's goal depends on the amount of energy one has available. As a resource, the more available physical energy a person has, the more likely her goal will be reached.

Glucose powers our muscles as described in the preceding experiment. However, glucose also powers the brain. Thus, mental tasks performed by the brain should also depend on the amount of glucose available. Gailliot and coresearchers (2007) use the Stroop task to investigate the relationship between glucose availability and mental performance. In the Stroop task, color names are written in a colored ink that does not match the color name. For example, green is written in red ink. Participants are required to respond with the color of the ink and not the name of the color, such as respond with "red." The Stroop task requires control of attention in that a person must inhibit reading the color name (green) in order to respond with the color of the ink (red). The Stroop task should be more difficult for participants with lesser amounts of motivational resources—that is, less glucose. Gailliot and coresearchers (2007) used the video viewing procedure described previously to alter the amount of available glucose. They depleted glucose levels in one group by having it view the video in the control-attention condition—that is, participants viewed the six-minute video but were not to attend to the words at the bottom of the screen. The researchers did not deplete glucose levels of the other group in the watch-normally condition, since its members were not required to control their attention while watching the video. The video task was followed by 80 Stroop-task trials. How does the amount of glucose that remains after the video task affect performance on the subsequent Stroop task? The results indicated that participants who had less glucose performed more poorly on the Stroop task compared to individuals with more glucose. Poorer performance on the Stroop task presumably resulted from the lowered availability of a motivational resource, glucose.

> A sample Stroop task is available at http://www.businessfaculty.utoledo/edu/ddwver/STROOP.HTM

An increase in one's motivation resources, however, should also boost mental performance. Thus, if individuals are given extra glucose, then their performance on the Stroop task should improve. In order to test this possibility, Gailliot and coresearchers (2007) provided half of the participants in the control-attention condition a glass of sugared lemonade in order to replenish their glucose. The other half of the participants drank lemonade that was artificially sweetened, so glucose was not replenished. Participants in the watch-normally condition for whom glucose was not depleted were also provided with sugared lemonade for glucose or artificially sweetened lemonade. A 12-minute interval elapsed before the Stroop task began in order to allow time for glucose to reach the brain. How does the amount of available glucose affect Stroop-task performance? The results presented in Figure 12.2 indicate that the most errors were made when participants' glucose had declined and was not replenished. This occurred for participants in the control-attention condition, who drank artificially sweetened lemonade. The error rate was unaffected when glucose

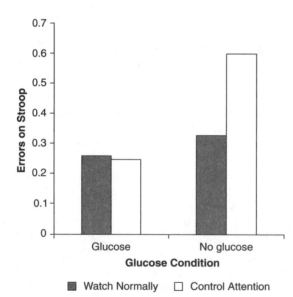

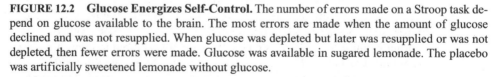

FIGURE 12.2   Glucose Energizes Self-Control. The number of errors made on a Stroop task depend on glucose available to the brain. The most errors are made when the amount of glucose declined and was not resupplied. When glucose was depleted but later was resupplied or was not depleted, then fewer errors were made. Glucose was available in sugared lemonade. The placebo was artificially sweetened lemonade without glucose.

Source: From "Self-Control Relies on Glucose as a Limited Energy Source: Willpower Is More Than a Metaphor" by M. T. Gailliot et al., 2007, *Journal of Personality and Social Psychology, 92,* figure 2, p. 331. Copyright 2007 by the American Psychological Association. Reprinted by permission.

was replenished with sugared lemonade in the control-attention condition or had not declined as occurred in the watch-normally condition. Notice that added glucose only boosted performance when it had been depleted in the control-attention condition. Thus, replenishing an individual's motivational resources boosts performance.

What can we conclude about the function of glucose as an energy source for motivated behavior? First, energy in the form of glucose is required in order for muscles or the brain to perform a task, such as pedaling or the control of attention. Second, the more difficult attention-control task results in a greater decline in glucose. Third, a lower supply of glucose is associated with poorer performance on a task. Fourth, if glucose has decreased but then is resupplied, performance improves.

Psychological Energy Resources. Psychological energy powers the mind to do its work, such as processing information, making decisions, and engaging in self-control. Psychological energies, if there are more than one, have no material base although it has been compared to muscle energy (Muraven & Baumeister, 2000). Does the amount of available self-control energy affect performance on tasks for which self-control is required? In one experiment, the question was whether people's ability to keep their hands in ice water depended on their amount of self-control energy and on conserving that energy for future use. If some self-control energy is depleted, then this cold-water task should be more difficult. However, performance on the cold-water task should also depend on whether self-control is required for a future task. To test these two possibilities, Muraven and coresearchers (2006) reduced self-control strength in some participants by requiring them to "not think about a white bear." Once this instruction is given, it takes self-control to prevent pictures of bears from intruding into one's consciousness. Other participants did not perform the white-bear suppression task and so they presumably had more available self-control energy. Furthermore, if self-control is a resource, then a person might conserve some for future tasks. Half of the participants were led to expect a third self-control task after the cold-water task while the other half was not. The third task would require participants to inhibit their facial expressions of mirth while watching a video of an extremely funny stand-up comedian. Would participants conserve self-control energy for the third task by not keeping their hands in the ice water as long? Following the white-bear suppression task, participants submerged their hands in ice water. The number of seconds their hands remained in ice water depended on the amount of available self-control energy and on the necessity of conserving energy for the third task (see Figure 12.3). First, when some self-control strength had been depleted by "not thinking of a white bear," participants shortened their time in ice water. Second, when expected to perform another (third) self-control task, participants conserved their self-control strength. How? By not keeping their hands in ice water as long as those participants who were not expected to perform the future self-control task.

Section Recap

There are costs for satisfying a motive or achieving a goal. These costs are classified as response and time costs, physical and psychological energy costs, and opportunity costs. Response costs are measurable in a Skinner box with a *fixed ratio (FR) schedule of reinforcement,* which details cost as the number of lever presses per reinforcer. Time costs refer to how long it takes to achieve a desired outcome. Physical energy is derived from glycogen and glucose and is measured in terms of calories. Psychological energy, which

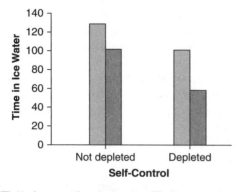

FIGURE 12.3   Effects of Depleted Self-Control. With their self-control energy depleted by controlling their attention, participants shortened the time their hands remained in ice water. When a future self-control task was required, participants shortened their time in ice water as if to conserve energy for the future.

Source: Adapted from "Conserving Self-Control Strength" by M. Muraven et al., 2006, *Journal of Personality and Social Psychology, 91,* table 1, p. 527.

has no material basis, is used for self-control, such as resisting temptation and for the control of attention. Opportunity costs refer to those activities that a person rejected in favor of a more preferred one, such as rejecting the chance to watch TV in order to study. *Choice overload* results when individuals have too many alternatives to choose from. In this case, people become demotivated and less likely to make a choice. Regret results when a choice was disappointing and increases with the combined value of the rejected alternatives. In general, stronger motives and higher goals are more expensive in terms of motivational costs.

People also have motivation resources with which to satisfy their motives and achieve their goals. *Reflex reserve* is a resource that consists of a bank of stored responses that accumulated through reinforcement and are available for attaining future reinforcers. *Learned industriousness* refers to persistence that was acquired as a result of putting forth extended effort that eventually results in reinforcement. *Grit* is an individual difference variable that describes consistent interest in an activity and persistent effort in order to achieve success at it. Physical energy in the form of glucose is required to power our muscles and brain. Psychological energy is the ability to do mental work, such as self-control. As a generalization, greater amounts of either available physical or psychological energy increases the likelihood of motive satisfaction and goal achievement.

Spending Motivation Resources

Which product do you prefer: (1) A state-of-the-art home entertainment system for audio and video or (2) a small TV and radio? Which payment do you prefer: (1) $3,000 or more or (2) $300 or less? The choices illustrate two extensive but incompatible motivational forces. On one hand, motivation is geared to obtain the most valuable incentive possible. On the other hand, humans are motivated to expend the least amount of time and effort necessary to attain these incentives. In other words, we want the most for the least. The purpose of this section is to apply economic principles to motivation. In economics, people spend their money to obtain goods and services. In the case of motivation, people expend their motivation resources in order to satisfy their motives and achieve their goals. This similarity has led psychologists to examine whether principles of economics can help in the understanding of motivation.

Demand Law

From Chapters 10 and 11, we learned that as incentive value or goal level increases, motivation increases. Thus, an *A* grade is more motivating than a *C*, first place in a race is more motivating than second, and $100 is more motivating than $10. However, the ability of an incentive to motivate behavior also depends on the cost of attaining it. In the preceding examples, an *A* costs more study time than a *C*, first place requires more calories for faster running than second place does, and earning $100 requires more work than $10 requires. Thus, the likelihood of achieving a goal depends on its value but also on the cost of achievement. The effect of cost is described by the **demand law** or demand schedule, which refers to the relationship between the quantity of goods a person is willing to purchase (demand) at various prices. When the price of economic goods is raised, less is bought; when the price of goods is lowered, more is bought. In the Skinner box, demand refers to the amount of reinforcement an animal demands or consumes at various lever press prices as set by an FR schedule of reinforcement (Hursh, 1980; Hursh & Bauman, 1987). Figure 12.4 provides two hypothetical curves that illustrate the demand law in a Skinner box. Notice that as FR requirements increase, demand decreases.

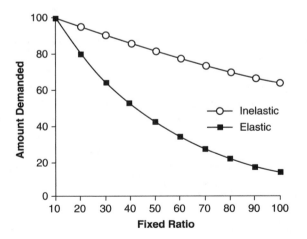

FIGURE 12.4 Demand Elasticity. As the cost of a reinforcer increases from FR 10 to FR 100, the demand for that reinforcer decreases. Decline in demand is shallowest for the inelastic reinforcer and steepest for the elastic reinforcer.

Elasticity

Is the demand for need satisfaction or goal attainment affected equally by price? Are there some needs and goals that humans will quickly abandon if the cost of their satisfaction becomes too high? Are there other needs and goals that humans will attempt to satisfy regardless of the cost?

Elasticity of Demand.   Demand changes as the price for a reinforcer changes but this change is not equal for all reinforcers. In Figure 12.4 notice that as FR requirements increase from 10 to 100, the demand for a reinforcer could decline little (upper curve) or could decline a great deal (bottom curve). The amount of decline depends on the type of reinforcer and if there are alternative reinforcers. When reinforcers decline greatly in demand as FR requirements increase, this is termed **elastic demand.** When reinforcers decline very little in demand as FR size increases, this is termed **inelastic demand.** The demand for inelastic reinforcers is much more resistant to price increases than is the demand for elastic reinforcers. The elasticity of reinforcers or goods is based on their utility. Goods with low utility are known as *luxuries*, such as soft drinks, movies, and CDs. Goods with high utility are known as *necessities*, such as food, computers, and gasoline.

Elasticity and Responses.   Demand for elastic reinforcers declines more than for inelastic reinforcers with an increase in price—that is, an increase in the number of responses, such as from FR 10 to FR 100. The smaller decline for an inelastic reinforcer is because the price increase is offset with an increase in responding. However, for elastic reinforcers, the decline in demand is greater because there is also a decline in responding. In other words, an increase in price or FR requirements leads to an increase in responding for inelastic reinforcers and a decrease in responding for elastic reinforcers (Hursh, 1980; Hursh & Bauman, 1987).

To illustrate, let us compare changes in the demand for colas (a luxury) and gasoline (necessity) with changes in their price. Changes in the demand for colas with changes in price illustrates elastic demands. For example, if a two-liter bottle of cola costs $1.50, then a shopper might buy two bottles for $3. However, if the price of cola were to increase to $2 per bottle, then a shopper might only buy one bottle. Since the utility of colas is low, demand declined a great deal from two to one bottle—that is, by 50%. The large decline is because the amount of money spent decreased from $3 to $2. Changes in the demand for gasoline with changes in its price illustrates inelastic demands. For example, when the price of gasoline is $3 per gallon, then $30 buys 10 gallons. However, when the price of gasoline rises to $4 per gallon, then $36 buys 9 gallons. Since the utility of gasoline is high, demand declined little from 10 to 9 gallons—that is, by 10%. The reason for the small decline is that the amount spent increased from $30 to $36. Differences in demand changes between cola and gasoline illustrate the difference in their utility. The utility of gasoline is so great that the consumer spends additional money in order to buy nearly as much gasoline as previously. The utility of cola, however, is much less and the consumer does not spend additional money in order to buy as much cola as previously.

The relationship between demand elasticity and instrumental responding occurs for a variety of reinforcers and behaviors. For instance, research on smokers responding for puffs on a cigarette have revealed an overall demand curve showing both inelastic and elastic properties. In a series of 17 experiments involving 74 smokers, Bickel and Madden (1999) had smokers pull and reset a plunger at various FR prices in order to earn access to a cigarette to puff on. The initial decline in the demand for puffs on a cigarette was inelastic and decreased moderately. Smokers offset the increase in price up to FR 400 by making more responses in order to access a cigarette. Beyond FR 400, however, cigarette demand became elastic. The price of a puff became too high, demand declined steeply, and the number of responses to earn a cigarette declined also (Madden, 2000).

Reinforcers at the same FR requirements can also differ in elasticity. In a special chamber, Findley (1959) had a monkey work 24 hours a day for food pellets, water, or one minute of overhead illumination from a lightbulb. Food, water, and light were only obtainable by pressing the appropriate button on an FR 5, 40, 80, 160, or 320 reinforcement schedule. At FR 5 the reinforcers were very cheap, while at FR 320 they were very expensive. There was an unequal decline in the demand for all three reinforcers, which indicates their difference in elasticity. This difference was most apparent between FR 5 and FR 80 when there was little decline in the demand for food and water but a steep decline in the demand for light. The small decline in the demand for food and water from FR 5 to FR 80 occurred because the monkey compensated for the increase in price by increasing its response output for those two reinforcers. The monkey was able to acquire most of the food it needed at the three highest prices by making nearly 8,000 responses per day. The monkey did not compensate for the increase in the price of light. In fact, responding for light declined so that the demand for it also declined steeply.

Incentive motivation depends on incentive price. As Hursh and Bauman (1987) point out, when the price is cheap (low FR), light and water appear equal in value, since the number of occasions each is consumed is about equal. When price increases, however, the demand for the light declines much more rapidly than the demand for food or water. Thus, at a higher price the motivation for food or water appears greater than the motivation for light. The lesson here is that motivation for an incentive depends on the price a person has to pay for it. When the cost is low, it is difficult to distinguish which incentive an individual prefers. The person appears to have enough energy and time to obtain both incentives. When the cost increases, however, differences in the preference of one incentive over another become apparent.

Elasticity and the Substitution Effect

When response requirements rise, reinforcer demand declines. Does this mean the individual ceases working for the reinforcer, or will she work for a substitute? The **substitution effect,** in economics, refers to the principle that an increase in the price of one economic good leads to increased demand for a different economic good. Reinforcers can serve as substitutes, complements, or independent commodities (Green & Freed, 1993). Substitutability means that one reinforcer can replace another provided that both have the same function (for instance, exchanging one cola drink for another, one elective course for another, or one roommate for another). Complementary reinforcers are ones that have a joint function, such as toothbrush and toothpaste, paper and pencil, or DVDs and DVD player. Independent reinforcers are ones that serve different and unrelated functions, such as colas and printers, elective courses and toothpaste, or roommates and paper. The function of substitutes is very important for determining the shape of demand curves. Increase the price of a reinforcer, and the demand for it decreases while the demand for its substitute increases. For example, if the price of pepperoni pizza increases, then its consumption decreases while consumption of substitute mushroom pizza increases. Similarly, if the requirement for one elective course becomes too high, students will substitute another elective course in its place.

The effects of price on reinforcer demand depend on the availability of a substitute. Lea and Roper (1977) altered the price of two different foods in two different compartments of a Skinner box. In the main compartment a rat found mixed diet food pellets that could be purchased at varying prices of FR 1, 6, 11, or 16 lever presses. In the alternative compartment, some of the time the rat might find either the same mixed diet pellets, sucrose pellets, or nothing. The price for these two types of pellets was always FR 8. Does a rat prefer lever pressing in the main compartment for the mixed diet pellets when the price is cheap, such as FR 1 or FR 6? And when the price rises to FR 11 or FR 16, does the rat switch to see what is available in the alternative compartment? This strategy makes sense, provided that the same mixed diet pellets are available in the alternative compartment or that a substitute, such as sucrose pellets, is available. If the alternative compartment is empty, however, it would make no sense to quit lever pressing in the main compartment.

The rats behaved like rational shoppers (Lea & Roper, 1977). The number of mixed diet pellets obtained in the main compartment declined with an increase in the FR price for the reinforcer. The decline in demand for pellets, however, was also determined by what was available in the alternative compartment. The decline in the demand for pellets in the main compartment was greatest when identical pellets or mixed sucrose pellets were also available in the alternative compartment. The decline in demand was lowest when the alternative compartment was empty. If no alternative food is available, then the rat must increase its response output in order to eat the amount of food it needs. When substitute food is available, the decline in demand is steeper, since the rat can switch to the alternative food source.

Substitutes can also be independent, such as a visual stimulus serving as a substitute for auditory or social stimuli. Tustin (1994) had mentally disabled men push one of two buttons on a computer joystick to earn one of two available reinforcers. In the case of one man, the choice was between computer-generated visual stimuli versus auditory stimuli or between visual stimuli versus social attention (smile, nod, and praise from a known person). For each choice, the price of the visual reinforcer remained constant at FR 5, while the price of the auditory or social reinforcer ranged from FR 1 to FR 20. The left side of Figure 12.5 shows that as the FR price of the auditory reinforcer increased, its demand decreased while demand for the visual reinforcer increased. The right side of Figure 12.5 shows that as the FR price for the social reinforcer increased, its demand decreased while the demand for the visual reinforcer increased. In other words, the visual reinforcer served as a substitute for either auditory or social reinforcers when their FR requirements became too high.

Section Recap

Principles from economics aid in the understanding of motivation. The number of goals achieved (goals demanded) depends on the price of doing so in terms of motivation resources. According to the *demand law,* when prices go up, demand goes down; when prices go down, demand goes up. For instance, in the Skinner box, demand would refer to the number of reinforcers that a rat obtains at a set price, which is the number of required lever presses. Elasticity of demand defines the amount of decrease in demand with increases in price. *Inelastic demand* means that demand decreases very little as price increases. In this case, the increase in price is offset by increased responding, thereby allowing little decline in demand. Incentives that have high utility (necessities) like gasoline or required courses have inelastic demand. *Elastic demand* means that incentive demand decreases a great deal as price increases. In this case, the increase in price results in decreased responding, thereby

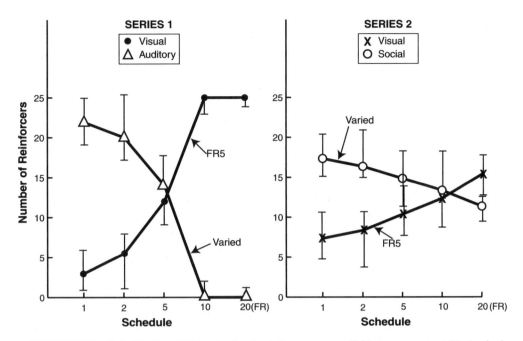

FIGURE 12.5   Substituting Effect. A visual reinforcer was available on a constant FR 5 schedule, while an auditory reinforcer (left side) or a social reinforcer (right side) was available on an FR schedule ranging from 1 to 20. As FR requirements increased for the auditory and social reinforcers, the participant eventually substituted the cheaper visual reinforcer.

Source: From "Preference for Reinforcers Under Varying Schedule Arrangements: A Behavioral Economic Analysis" by R. D. Tustin, 1994, *Journal of Applied Behavior Analysis, 27,* Figure 2, p. 603. Reprinted by permission.

producing a dramatic decline in demand. Incentives that have low utility (luxuries) like soft drinks or elective courses have elastic demand. Also, demand declines steeply if there are substitute reinforcers but declines slowly if there are no substitutes. *Substitution effect* means that as price goes up, a person is more likely to obtain an alternative reinforcer.

Motivation toward Least Effort

There are two main aspects of motivation to keep in mind. First, humans are motivated more to satisfy strong rather than weak needs and to achieve high-level rather than low-level goals. Second, strong needs and high-level goals cost more in terms of motivation resources. The cost factor would not be an issue if everyone had unlimited motivation resources, such as time and energy. However, since resources are limited, there is a tendency to use them in the most economical manner possible. The guiding principle of this section is the inclination of animals and humans to expend the fewest motivation resources possible in order to satisfy motives or achieve goals.

Early Views on Effort and Motivation

During the first half of the 1900s, psychologists recognized that effort and motivation were inversely related. This section describes the views of two psychologists on this relationship.

Two psychologists presented the idea that an animal prefers less rather than more effort in order to achieve a goal. Tolman (1932) described the relationship between effort and motivation in his **principle of least effort** as that "which is found in numerous sciences under a variety of names, when applied to the study of behavior would assert that the final choices between alternative means-routes will always tend to occur in the direction of a minimum expenditure of physical energy" (p. 448). In other words, given a choice between two incentives of equal value, the one requiring the least effort will be selected. In his research, Tolman provided hungry rats a choice of two routes to the goal box at the end of a complex maze. In this situation, the rats tended to choose the shorter and quicker route to the goal. Although Tolman was aware of this principle in the physical sciences, he lacked physiological indicators of effort he could apply to behavior.

Hull (1943) formulated a similar principle, which he named the **law of less work.** "If two or more behavior sequences, each involving a different amount of energy consumption or work (W), have been equally well reinforced an equal number of times, the organism will gradually learn to choose the less laborious behavior sequence leading to the attainment of the reinforcing state of affairs" (p. 294). Hull arrived at this part of his theory by relying on an experiment performed by Mowrer and Jones (1943). In their experiment, hungry rats were required to press a lever in a Skinner box to earn a food reinforcer. After they had learned this task, the rats were divided into three groups, and extinction was carried out during which time lever presses did not produce reinforcers. For one group, the lever had to be pressed with a force of 5 grams; for another group a force of 42.5 grams was required; and for a third, 80 grams. According to Hull (1943), 80 grams of force is more work than 42.5 grams, which is more work than 5 grams of force. The results showed that the number of lever presses decreased as their force requirements increased. When effort was slight, the rats made many more responses during extinction than when effort was hard.

Choices Based on Least Effort

How do economic principles like the demand law and elasticity affect the choices that people make? This section examines how some choices are influenced by these principles.

Romantic Love.   How are romantic choices affected? Economic principles apply to sexual and dating behavior (McKenzie & Tullock, 1981). Sex, for example, can be considered a service that each member of a couple provides for and receives from the other. Dating and sex have both utility and costs. The opportunity cost of dating or spending time with one person means that you cannot be spending time with someone else. Thus, forgoing a date with one individual is your opportunity cost for going out on a date with another. Dating and sex also involve energy costs and time costs of trying to please the other person. Finally, a person's willingness to be romantically involved with a particular individual depends on substitutes like spending time with other dating partners, friends, or family members.

Incentive value, demand, costs, and substitution effects describe why romantic relationships begin, endure, and end. With these concepts, Rusbult (1983) developed an **investment model** for describing people's commitment to each other in a relationship. Investment refers to things people have put into a relationship that they cannot get back if the relationship ends. Examples of investments are shared friends, shared material possessions, and memories (Rusbult, 1983). Commitment to a relationship depends on the rewards provided, the costs, the value of alternative relationships, and how much has been invested.

To test the investment model, Rusbult recruited dating couples early in the academic year when they had been together an average of about four weeks. Every 17 days over the course of the academic year, she asked one member of each couple a series of questions to determine the cost, rewards, alternatives, and investments in the relationship. Some of the questions were:

1. How rewarding is this relationship? (1 = not at all, 9 = extremely)
2. How costly is this relationship? (1 = not at all, 9 = extremely)
3. In general, how appealing are your alternatives (dating another person or other persons, or being without a romantic involvement)? (1 = not at all appealing, 9 = extremely appealing)
4. All things considered, are there objects/persons/activities associated with the relationship that you would lose (or value less) if the relationship were to end? (1 = none, 9 = many) (Rusbult, 1983, p. 106)

At the end of the academic year members of the couples were placed into one of three categories. Stayers were partners who were still involved in their relationship. Leavers were persons who had ended their relationship. The abandoned were people whose partners had ended the relationship. The change in the reward value of the relationship, its costs, the value of a substitute relationship, and investment size were different for stayers, leavers, and the abandoned. Figure 12.6 shows that the reward value increased most for stayers but not at all for leavers. Changes in cost, however, showed the reverse pattern. Stayers' costs increased very little, while leavers' costs increased a great deal over the year. Perhaps it is not surprising that leavers ended their relationship. After all, their costs increased at a high rate, while their reward value remained practically constant over the

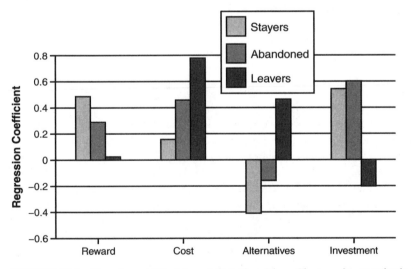

FIGURE 12.6 Investment Model and Relationships. Changes in magnitude of reward, cost, alternative, and investment values in a romantic relationship over the academic year are shown for stayers, the abandoned, and leavers.

Source: Adapted from "A Longitudinal Test of the Investment Model" by C. E. Rusbult, 1983, *Journal of Personality and Social Psychology, 45*, table 6, p. 111.

duration of their relationship. The substitution effect was also apparent during the course of these relationships. For stayers and the abandoned, there was a decrease in the appeal of alternatives. In contrast, for leavers there was an increase in the appeal of their alternatives or substitutes. Leavers ended their relationship when costs increased, perhaps because they had highly attractive substitutes. The abandoned, however, appeared more willing to pay the costs of their relationship, since the attractiveness of substitutes for them had decreased over the year.

While there is a cost of staying in a relationship, there is also a cost for ending a relationship. This cost is reflected in investment size. The more people have invested in a relationship, the more it will cost them to end it. Figure 12.6 shows that the investment size for stayers and the abandoned became larger as the academic year progressed. Thus, for them a breakup would be more costly. The investment size for leavers was negligible and showed no change over the academic year. It was easier for leavers to terminate their romantic relationship, since they had very little invested and so very little to lose.

Body Consequences of Least Effort.   People frequently face such choices as walk or ride, stairs or elevator, and exercise or watch TV. Does the energy cost of each choice bias the decision toward the less-exerting activity? As one might expect, the principle of least effort fosters a sedentary lifestyle rather than an active one. As a consequence, there is an increasing trend for people to become overweight (BMI 25.0–29.9) and eventually obese (BMI $\geq$ 30.0). (BMI refers to body mass index, which is represented as weight/height^2.) A person's BMI increases as her body weight increases. Obesity is accompanied by health problems that include diabetes, high blood pressure, and cardiovascular disease. National Health and Nutrition Examination Surveys (National Center for Health Statistics, 2006) conducted between 1976 and 2004 found an increase in the percentage of adults 20 to 74 years old who were either overweight or obese (see Figure 12.7). One explanation for this increase in obesity is that

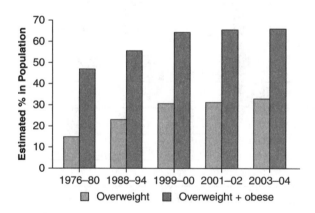

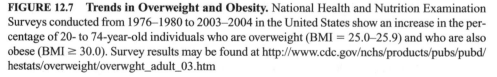

FIGURE 12.7   Trends in Overweight and Obesity. National Health and Nutrition Examination Surveys conducted from 1976–1980 to 2003–2004 in the United States show an increase in the percentage of 20- to 74-year-old individuals who are overweight (BMI = 25.0–25.9) and who are also obese (BMI $\geq$ 30.0). Survey results may be found at http://www.cdc.gov/nchs/products/pubs/pubd/hestats/overweight/overwght_adult_03.htm

it results from a change in energy balance: people's energy intake has increased, and their energy expenditure has decreased over the years (Khan & Bowman, 1999).

> You can compute your body mass index (BMI) at http://nhlbisupport.com/bmi

The principle of least effort contributes to this energy imbalance. For instance, the case has been made, at least in Britain (Prentice & Jebb, 1995), that the energy imbalance results from slothfulness (least effort). Humans evolved during a time that required a much greater expenditure of physical energy than is required today. Currently, we have many labor-saving conveniences that provide a choice between being active or being sedentary. It is now possible to replace physical labor with energy- and time-saving appliances, power equipment, power tools, and motorized transport (Prentice & Jebb, 1995). The principle of least effort induces the use of these machines, which results in a decrease in energy expenditure. This decrease in energy expenditure, however, is not off-set by a decrease in energy intake. Weight gain, obesity, and associated health problems are the consequences.

Behavior and Thought Based on Least Effort

In addition to the principle of least effort determining choice, it also determines people's behavior afterwards. Thus, whatever motive or goal has been chosen to be satisfied or achieved, people tend to economize in the use of their motivation resources to achieve those aims. This section examines some of the ways that people economize with their behavior.

Behavioral Economizing. Why walk if you can drive, take the stairs if there is an elevator, or exercise for pleasure when a couch and TV are available? As these choices imply, opportunities for economizing time and effort occur frequently, such as meal preparation and path creation. For instance, fast-food restaurants, take-out meals, home-food deliveries, and easily prepared meals are often the preferred modes of meal preparation. In fact, the term *fast-food* implies that the time-cost for the meal is low. For another example, when people want to get from one place to another, they try to use the least amount of effort possible, as can be seen by the development of paths on campuses. The campus landscape architect lays out a concrete walk from one building to another by going around a beautifully manicured lawn. However, some individual creates a shortcut, an alternative path, that cuts across the lawn in order to save time, steps, and calories. Indeed, students often create paths across campus precisely to shorten distance and lessen effort. The results of actual way-finding experiments have shown that participants prefer the shortest routes to their destinations, those that require the least expenditure of energy (Butler et al., 1993). Cattle are of a similar mind when it comes to developing trails from one place to another. With the aid of a global positioning satellite, Ganskopp and coworkers (2000) observed that cattle were more likely to develop the easiest trails possible over rugged terrain. The cattle tended to select a combination of the shortest routes with the shallowest slopes—that is, trails that required the least effort to walk from a watering hole to other pasture areas.

Economizing also governs the speed with which individuals reach their destination. Individuals can increase their speed of walking by combining an increase in the length and frequency of their strides. Walking or running at one's preferred stride length is the most economical. If either stride frequency or length increases beyond the person's preferred level, then energy costs will increase (Holt et al., 1995; Sparrow & Newell, 1998). However, it will be less costly to increase the frequency of one's strides than to lengthen them (Holt et al., 1991). Now imagine that you are in a great hurry to get to your destination and you begin to increase your walking speed. At some point, you will break into a run. The transition from walking to running occurs because of a reduction in energy costs—that is, less oxygen and glucose is used. Costs will be higher, however, if a person runs slower than her preferred walking speed (Hanna et al., 2000).

Cognitive Economizing.   What laptop should you buy from, say, six that are available from electronic stores or by shipment from well-known computer companies? A person could perform an exhaustive expected utility analysis that involved the following computer features: desktop or laptop, size of hard drive, size of working memory, operating speed, screen size, game capabilities, features to play and create CDs and DVDs, and price. After an analysis of all computers, the one with the highest expected utility is identified and purchased. Although a person made the best choice, a great deal of time and energy was spent. However, a person could expend much less time and energy and employ **satisficing** (Simon, 1955/1979), which means to find a satisfactory option but not necessarily the best. Using shortcuts and energy-saving procedures, an individual arrives at an acceptable expected utility and bases her decision on that. Instead of comparing computers on all features, only some features are examined provided they have met some minimum standard. For example, a person only examines computers that are available at the local electronics store and that are priced below a certain amount.

   Would you do an expected utility analysis of all computers or would you be more apt to satisfice? The *Maximization Scale* in Table 12.3 measures the extent of an individual's tendency to maximize in order to decide among options (Schwartz et al., 2002). Higher scores on the scale are indicative of a greater tendency to maximize. Both satisficing or maximizing have costs and benefits (Schwartz et al., 2002; Schwartz, 2004). First, satisficing requires less time in order to make a decision. Second, satisficers consider fewer alternatives than maximizers and thus have lower opportunity costs. Third, satisficers have fewer feelings of regret as a result of their lower opportunity costs compared to the regrets of maximizers. Fourth, satisficers are less indecisive regarding a decision whereas maximizers may feel powerless—that is, experience choice overload. Finally, however, maximizers make better choices than satisficers do (Iyengar et al., 2006).

Section Recap

People try to achieve their goals by expending the least amount of time, responses, and energy according to Tolman's *principle of least effort* and Hull's *law of less work.*

   In addition to least effort, the demand law and elasticity explain the choices that people make, such as the choice of convenience foods and shortcuts. In the case of romance, according to the *investment model,* people put resources into a romantic relationship that they cannot get back; this investment determines whether the couple chooses to remain together. In addition, the likelihood of choosing to stay in a relationship depends on the reward, costs, and alternatives (substitutes) that are available to each partner. Our choice to embrace human energy-saving devices (elevator rather than stairs) has led to increases in weight, obesity, and associated health problems.

TABLE 12.3   Maximization Scale

Indicate the extent each item describes you on the scale below:
Completely disagree = 1   2   3   4   5   6   7 = Completely agree

When I watch TV, I channel surf, often scanning through the available options even while attempting to watch one program.

When I am in the car listening to the radio, I often check other stations to see if something better is playing, even if I'm relatively satisfied with what I'm listening to.

I treat relationships like clothing: I expect to try a lot on before I get the perfect fit.

No matter how satisfied I am with my job, it's only right for me to be on the lookout for better opportunities.

I often fantasize about living in ways that are quite different from my actual life.

I'm a big fan of lists that attempt to rank things (the best movies, the best singers, the best athletes, the best novels, etc.).

I often find it difficult to shop for a gift for a friend.

When shopping, I have a hard time finding clothing that I really love.

Renting videos is really difficult. I'm always struggling to pick the best one.

I find that writing is very difficult, even if it's just writing a letter to a friend, because it's so hard to word things just right. I often do several drafts of even simple things.

No matter what I do, I have the highest standards for myself.

I never settle for second best.

Whenever I'm faced with a choice, I try to imagine what all the other possibilities are, even ones that aren't present at the moment.

Source: Copyright © 2002 by the American Psychological Association. Reprinted with permission. Schwartz, B., et al. (2002). Maximizing versus satisficing: Happiness is a matter of choice. *Journal of Personality and Social Psychology, 83,* 1182.

Economic principles also explain motivated behavior and cognition. Behavioral economizing occurs, for example, in the transition from walking to running. Beyond a certain speed, it takes less energy to run than to walk. In the case of cognitive economizing, people *satisfice* rather than maximize. Satisficing means to make a decision on a "that-is-good-enough" criterion as opposed to maximizing, which means doing an extensive expected-utility analysis to determine the best choice. People's tendency to maximize is measured by the *maximization scale*.

ACTIVITIES

1. Do you find yourself obeying the principle of least effort or law of less work? For example, do you drive instead of walk, take the elevator instead of stairs, eat fast-food rather than cook, or take an easy elective course rather than a challenging one?

2. There are few laws in psychology. A law implies that there are no exceptions. Can you think of an exception to the principle of least effort, law of less work, or demand law?

3. Who will be more successful in life: a person with many motivational resources but few intellectual resources, or a person with few motivational and many intellectual resources?

4. Have you ever made choices based on the law of least effort or the demand law, such as enrolling in easy courses or trying to do a minimal job on a class project?

5. If you are currently in a romantic relationship, estimate your rewards, costs, investments, and alternatives. What is your prognosis for the relationship?

6. If your class attendance is not perfect, then consider a cost-benefit analysis. What are the costs and benefits of attending class or of not attending? In doing the analysis, be certain to take both short- and long-term costs and benefits into account. Do these factors explain your behavior of imperfect attendance? Compare your cost-benefit analysis with the quote from Socrates (470–399 B.C.) in Table 2.1.

PART FIVE

The Emotions

Have you ever done something in the heat of an emotion that you would not have done otherwise? Emotions perform like strong motives that induce us into action even when it seems irrational. Whereas incentives and goals require cognitive deliberation before they are committed to and pursued, emotion-induced behavior seems to occur automatically with little forethought. For instance, humans yell in anger and then regret it later. Nevertheless, emotions did not develop haphazardly but instead evolved because of their survival function. The utility of an emotion depends on its ability to mobilize the behaviors that are necessary to cope with recurrent survival problems. Fear, anger, disgust, and love are prime examples of emotions that help promote human survival. Guilt, shame, embarrassment, and pride are the self-conscious emotions that operate in order to maintain group harmony.

Does your heart flutter when you see a certain man or woman? Is that how you know you are in love? Physiological arousal may provide the basis of our emotional feelings. In addition, physiological arousal that is experienced as part of an emotion may indicate that the person is ready for action. One's muscles, heart, and lungs are all ready to do what is necessary to cope with the situation, such as fight or flight. In fact, the aim of emotion is for a person to adapt to the changed situation. Along with physiological arousal, emotions are channeled along subjective feelings, facial expressions, and behavior. These channels move in synchrony, dependently. Furthermore, feelings, expressions, and arousal are not learned in response to the stimulus change but instead seem to pre-exist as if they came about during our evolutionary past. Accompanying behavior, however, could either be innate or the result of experience. For example, rather than yelling when angry, a person may have learned that it is best to walk away. Emotional feelings are linked to behaviors that serve the aim of each emotion. Fear is linked to escape behaviors that lead to safety. Anger is linked with assertive and aggressive behaviors to restore blocked goals. In addition to motivating behavior, emotions also guide cognitive processes in line with the emotional feeling. Thus, when in love, a person spends a lot of time thinking of that other person.

What does a smile or what do tears mean? Do facial expressions, such as these, indicate feelings or signal social motives? Both may be functions of facial expressions: to show emotional feelings or to signal what is wanted from others. For example, tears can indicate sadness or indicate "help me." Facial expressions are innate (not taught), since they occur early in life, are identical the world over, and occur in blind individuals.

Does life seem better when you're happy? New research indicates that positive emotions like happiness can expand thought, motivate behavior, and serve as positive reinforcers. On average, people are at least a little bit happy, which is their set point to which they consistently return. Events like marriage can increase happiness and being stood-up can produce unhappiness, but eventually people return to their usual set point level of happiness. Unfortunately, strong negative events produce long-term unpleasant feelings, such that people may never return to their set point level.

13 Emotions and Moods

The advantage of the emotions is that they lead us astray.

—*Oscar Wilde, 1891*

It is the hardest thing in the world to put feeling, and deep feeling, into words.

—*Jack London, 1899*

■ Emotion is a process closely allied with motivation. Emotions serve as a unique source of motivation that both activates and guides behavior. But first, what characterizes emotion from other sources of motivation? This question, along with the following, are presented for your consideration while reading this chapter:

1. What are the components of emotion?
2. Is there a basic set of prototype emotions?
3. How are subjective emotional experiences labeled in ourselves and described to others?
4. What are moods, and how do they differ from emotions?
5. What is the function of physiological arousal that accompanies an emotional experience?
6. How do various theories explain the function of arousal in emotion?

Characteristics and Categories of Emotions

Can you distinguish between feeling hungry and thirsty, hot and cold, or excited and sleepy? How about feeling the distinction between love and lust or guilt and shame? All of these distinctions concern sensing differences between internal states. The first two comparisons refer to internal feelings that are based on our body's homeostasis and usually arise gradually. The last comparison refers to emotional feelings that arise suddenly in reaction to stimulus changes. Both sets of feelings motivate behavior. Emotions, like hunger and thirst, are motives that can cause approach, withdrawal, or even inaction. An interesting characteristic about emotional feelings is that they are difficult to describe. Descriptions of emotional feelings are heard in song lyrics about a broken heart, feeling blue, and rain falling from your eyes. Lyrics are also more about negatively felt emotions than positively felt ones because, as Descartes noted long ago, there are more negative than positive emotions.

The purpose of this section is to describe what an emotion is and what its different components are. Also, this section will identify the different categories of emotion and how they were discovered.

What Is an Emotion?

First, an **emotion** is a functional reaction to a stimulus event or change, such as an actual or anticipated loss or gain. Second, an emotional reaction is channeled along psychological, physiological, and behavioral dimensions. Third, these channels operate in synchrony for the purpose of coping and adapting to these stimulus changes (Keltner & Shiota, 2003).

Emotion Channels.   As stated, emotions are channeled along various dimensions: affective, facial, physiological, and behavioral, with the brain playing an underlying role. Affect refers to the private subjective experience that floods consciousness. It is experienced directly by an individual but can be conveyed to others verbally. Language is rich with emotion words to convey a person's affective experiences. The words *happy, sad, fear,* and *anger* are descriptors of different affective states. Facial expressions are another channel for emotions and are associated with affect. For example, smiles coincide with happiness, scowls with anger, raised eyebrows with surprise, and tears with grief. Physiological arousal as a channel for emotions received credibility from the first American psychologist, William James (1884/1948), who asked what is fear without "the feelings either of quickened heartbeats nor of shallow breathing, neither trembling of lips nor of weakened limbs, neither of goose-flesh nor of visceral stirrings" (p. 295). Physiological responses are a salient channel for emotions and occur as changes in electrodermal responses, blood pressure, heart rate, respiration rate, skin temperature, and muscle activity (Chapter 6). The source of all of these channels is the brain. Our understanding of emotions will be enhanced if we can determine how neural events that occur in the brain are thought to underlie the other channels. Tomkins (1982, 1984), Damasio (2003), and Barrett and coresearchers (2007) have speculated that neural activity in certain brain areas serve as the material basis from which affective experiences emerge.

Coherence among Channels.   In everyday parlance, emotion refers to a person's private subjective experience or affect that occurs in reaction to some meaningful life event, such as university graduation or job loss. However, psychologists view emotion as a hypothetical construct that serves as a label for the coherence among the various channels. It is possible that each channel acts independently to an emotional event rather than jointly. Thus, affect, physiological reactions, and facial expressions may all be unrelated in their reaction to some emotion stimulus. However, if the reaction is to be termed emotional, then these channels should act in concert—that is, cohere (Barrett, 2006). According to the **response coherence postulate** (Mauss et al., 2005), the channels that underlie emotions are associated together; they do not act independently. Casual observations suggest that this association is indeed the case as in the association of happiness with smiles, fear with fleeing, and anger with yelling.

There have not been many investigations of whether the response coherence postulate is valid. In one investigation, Mauss and coresearchers (2005) measured various emotion channels in participants who were exposed to sad and amusing stimuli. Specifically, women participants viewed a five-minute video composed of an amusing, sad, and final amusing scene three times in succession. Participants continuously rated the segments for amusement and sadness while their facial expressions were videotaped (first segment only). Measurements were also taken of their heart rate, electrodermal responses, and general activity by way of a sensor attached to the bottom of their chair. Evidence in favor of response coherence requires that the various measures correlate positively, which was definitely the case for amusement. Amusement ratings, heart activity, electrodermal responses, and general activity all correlated positively—that is, all cohered together in reaction to the amusing episodes. The case for sadness was mixed. Sadness ratings and facial expressions of sadness correlated positively but each correlated negatively with electrodermal responses. In other words, as feelings of sadness and facial expressions increased together, accompanying electrodermal responses decreased. Finally, as facial signs of sadness increased, participants tended to remain still. All in all, the results of the experiment provided some support for response coherence. However, how tightly emotion channels adhere together may depend on the emotion (Mauss et al., 2005). For example, coupling might be more tight for arousing emotions like anger and fear than for a dampening emotion like sadness. In addition, other influences may affect a particular channel, such as the presence of others who can influence a person's facial expressions.

Methods for Uncovering Basic Emotions

A strategy of science is to classify its subject matter into various categories. Chemists classify basic elements. Botanists classify plants. Zoologists classify animals. Psychologists have classified emotions into basic categories (see Table 13.1). Each category represents a basic emotion, and these cannot be grouped into larger categories without losing some defining characteristics. It is assumed that basic emotions actually exist and that this categorization is not just some convenient classification system that has no correspondence in nature (Ekman, 1992; Izard, 1992; Ortony & Turner, 1990; Russell, 1991; Turner & Ortony, 1992). The emotion words within each category in Table 13.1 are listed in the order of decreasing intensity. For example, happiness ranges from being light-hearted or serene to ecstasy. The emotion categories were derived by various means, such as by making a semantic (meaning) analysis of emotion words, investigating how emotions may have evolved, and analyzing facial expressions.

TABLE 13.1   Basic Emotions Derived from Three Different Methods of Analyses

Category Analysis	Evolution Theory	Facial Expressions	
Happiness/Joy[a,b]	Reproduction	Happiness	
ecstatic	ecstasy	(Emotion intensity increases	
euphoric	*joy*	with facial expression intensity.)	
happy	delight		
carefree	cheerfulness		
light-hearted	serenity		
Love[b]	Incorporation		
passion	*love*		
attraction	liking		
liking	trust		
fondness	tolerance		
tenderness	acceptance		

TABLE 13.1   (*Continued*)

Category Analysis	Evolution Theory	Facial Expressions	
Surprise[b] amazement surprise astonishment	Orientation astonishment *surprise* confusion distraction uncertainty	Surprise (Emotion intensity increases with facial expression intensity.)	
Sadness[a,b] wretched depressed melancholic gloomy wistful	Reintegration grief sorrow *sadness* dejection gloominess	Sadness (Emotion intensity increases with facial reaction intensity.)	
Fear[a,b] terror panicky fearful anxious timid	Fear terror panic *fear* apprehension wariness	Fear (Emotion intensity increases with facial reaction intensity.)	
Anger[a,b] fury irascible irritable touchy grouchy	Destruction fury rage *anger* exasperation hostility	Anger (Emotion intensity increases with facial reaction intensity.)	

TABLE 13.1   (*Continued*)

Category Analysis	Evolution Theory	Facial Expressions	

Disgust[a]
   queasy
   nausea
	Rejection
	   revulsion
	   disgust
	   aversion
	   dislike
	   boredom
		Disgust
		 (Emotion intensity increases
		 with facial reaction intensity.)	

	Exploration
	   anticipation
	   expectancy
	   curiosity
	   inquisitiveness
	   mindfulness		

		Self-conscious emotions[c]
		   embarrassment (negative)
		   shame (negative)
		   guilt (negative)
		   pride (positive)	

[a]Johnson-Laird and Oatley, 1989.

[b]Shaver et al., 1987.

[c]Leary, 2007.

Category Analysis of Emotion Words.   One way of analyzing emotions is to study the meaning of emotion words. This method assumes that words have developed to describe people's emotional experiences. In other words, the reason for words such as *love, hate, sad, happy, afraid,* and *angry* is because each labels a distinctly unique feeling in a particular situation. If people did not experience these distinctly unique feelings, then words designating emotion would not have been invented. Johnson-Laird and Oatley (1989; Oatley & Johnson-Laird, 1990) conducted an extensive analysis of the meaning of 590 English words to determine the various ways or modes that emotions are expressed. One major concern was determining whether a word described a subjective feeling. From their analysis they classified words into emotion categories, with words of similar meaning being classified together. Their semantic analysis produced five basic emotion categories: happiness, sadness, anger, fear, and disgust.

    Another way of classifying emotion into categories is to ask people how they would categorize emotion words in their own minds. Imagine participating in a study designed to answer this question (Shaver et al., 1987). As a participant, you would receive 135 cards, each containing an emotion word along with the following instructions:

> We'd like you to sort these cards into categories representing your best judgments about which emotions are similar to each other and which are different from each other. There is no one correct way to sort the cards—make as few or as many categories as you wish and put as few or as many cards in each group as you see fit. (Shaver et al., 1987, p. 1065)

Each participant classified the emotion words according to his own categorization scheme. However, the degree of agreement among participants showed how people in general categorize emotions. One participant put all 135 words into two categories of positive and negative emotions. For example, *contentment* and *desire* would be placed in the positive category, while *fury, worry,* and *disappointment* would be placed in the negative category. Another participant employed 64 different categories. A statistical analysis, however, indicated that six categories provided the best summary of the participants' classification efforts. These categories were labeled: happiness/joy, love, surprise, sadness, fear, and anger. Each label represents an **emotion prototype,** which suggests the average or typical meaning that all words in the emotion category have in common (Shaver et al., 1987). Each category in turn had a number of subcategories of emotion words. As a note of caution, however, a variation of this sorting procedure has resulted in different category names, such as excitement, lust, melancholy, hate, extreme pain, pain, and low-level hostility (Alvarado, 1998). Nevertheless, evidence for the universal development of emotion categories has also been found. Hupka and associates (1999) looked at 64 different languages for subcategories of emotion under the major categories of joy, love, surprise, sadness, fear, and anger. They found that most languages had all subcategories of emotion words. This led them to conclude that these emotion categories, based on English terms, were relatively similar across languages. The results of Johnson-Laird and Oatley's (1989) semantic analysis and Shaver and associates' (1987) categorization are grouped together in Table 13.1 as seven basic or prototype emotions. Specific instances of an emotion prototype are listed in order of decreasing intensity within a category. Table 13.1 also shows the role of evolution and facial expression in emotion, which are discussed in following subsections.

Evolution Theory.   Another classification approach is based on the idea that emotions aid species survival (Plutchik, 1980). A crucial event evokes a subjective emotional experience, which in turn increases the likelihood of a class of behaviors that promotes survival. The appearance of a predator evokes fear, which in turn leads to escape by running away. The loss of its mother produces sadness and a cry for help in a child. Crying brings aid and comfort from other adults. Feelings of fear and grief produce behaviors that aid survival, because without those feelings the critical behaviors may not have occurred. The eight emotions listed in Table 13.1 (middle column) correspond to eight functions necessary for the survival of animals or humans. The eight functions are reproduction, incorporation, orientation, reintegration, fear, destruction, rejection, and exploration. Examples of emotion in the service of each function are listed in order of decreasing intensity (Plutchik, 1980, 1984).

Facial Expressions.   Another line of reasoning is that each basic emotion has a corresponding facial expression. If there is no distinctive facial expression, then the corresponding subjective state should not be considered an emotion (Ekman, 1984, 1994a; Izard,

1971). Both Ekman and Izard discovered that posed facial expressions of emotions were identified accurately by people of different cultures throughout the world (Ekman, 1984, 1994a; Ekman & Friesen, 1971; Izard, 1971). These findings led Ekman to propose the six basic emotions presented in the right column of Table 13.1, along with representative facial expressions. Ekman (1984) assumed that the intensity of a felt emotion and the intensity of its facial expression increase together. More defined facial expressions accompany more intense emotional feelings.

Happiness, surprise, sadness, fear, anger, and disgust have clearly identifiable facial expressions, as shown in Table 13.1. Nevertheless, Darwin (1873) noted that in addition to facial expressions, humans can also signal emotions vocally and behaviorally through blushes, hiding the face, laughs, screams, and shrugs. It is through these modes of communication that humans can signal self-conscious emotions such as shame, guilt, embarrassment, and pride. The category of self-conscious emotions stems from the evaluation that people think others are making about them. These emotions, in turn, help regulate people's interpersonal relationships (Leary, 2007). Self-conscious emotions are signaled in various ways. The sequence of signals that are involved in embarrassment, for example, involve a downward gaze followed by a close lipped inhibited smile and conclude with the head turning away and perhaps even blushing (Keltner & Anderson, 2000). Shame and guilt show similar expressions (Keltner, 1995). An example of a shame expression is provided in Table 13.1. Pride, which results from a perceived positive evaluation, has distinct facial and behavioral features that involve a slight head tilt, weak smile, and an expanded posture (Tracy & Robins, 2004, 2007). Finally, romantic love, which is considered an emotion in the minds of many people, has behavioral accompaniments. These include sincere smiles, leaning toward one's partner, affirmative head nods, and gesticulations (Gonzaga et al., 2001, 2006).

> ➤ Facial expressions associated with emotions are available at http://www.face-and-emotion.com/dataface/emotion/expression.jsp

Characteristics of Affect

We all experience emotions, and so we can use ourselves as a source of information. Verbal description of another person's affect or conscious feelings should be verifiable by our own experiences. We have a "feel" for what a person is experiencing when she says "I'm in love with," "People who litter anger me," or "I'm anxious about the upcoming exam." The reason we can understand these statements is that we have said similar things. In addition to the subjective feel, emotion words also provide other information about the intensity of the experience and the relation between the person experiencing the emotion and the cause of that emotion. There are also words describing complex emotions (Johnson-Laird & Oatley, 1989).

Private Affective Experience. To what extent do words denoting affect describe a person's private feelings? In a semantic analysis of emotion words, Johnson-Laird and Oatley (1989; Oatley & Johnson-Laird, 1990) considered their emotion categories as representing the most primitive subjective experiences possible. According to philosophers, primitive subjective experiences are known as **qualia.** This means that the emotion words that represent the experiences are not fully describable by other words. Describing a basic emotion is like trying to describe a flavor like strawberry. The same problem is encountered in trying to describe feelings of joy, sadness, fear, anger, and disgust. The problem of qualia becomes apparent if we were to describe our emotions to someone who is emotionally blind (Johnson-Laird & Oatley, 1989) like a very sophisticated robot.

How then do we describe our emotional feelings? One method might be to describe the eliciting conditions for emotions. For example, joy is what you feel when someone accepts your proposal of marriage. Sadness is what you feel when the family dog dies. Anger is what you feel when someone insults you. These eliciting examples, however, would not help emotionally blind individuals understand these emotions, since they would not feel what we feel in those situations.

Affect Emerges from Brain.   From where do affective feelings emerge? The brain provides the material basis for affect and also creates the feelings of affect in a person's consciousness. What are the patterns of neuron activation that parallel the affective feelings that are the signatures of basic emotions?

One finding is that neural circuits for subjective emotional experiences are laid down in the limbic system. One source of evidence for this comes from patients who suffer epileptic seizures involving the limbic system. An epileptic seizure is an excessive discharge of neurons in the brain that can result in rigidity, tremors, convulsions, loss of balance, and even loss of consciousness. Other seizures, however, might only involve subtle changes in thought, mood, or behavior (Pinel, 1997). Persons with epilepsy may experience an **epileptic aura,** which consists of psychological changes preceding the occurrence of an actual seizure. The seizures, localized in the limbic system, are preceded by auras involving feelings of happiness, sadness, fear, anger, disgust, and depression and are often accompanied by facial expressions (Gloor et al., 1982; MacLean, 1986; Williams, 1956). Table 13.2 provides case reports of patients whose auras involved emotional experiences.

A second source of evidence comes from brain-imaging studies using PET scan and functional MRI. The idea is to induce an emotion and measure what portions of the brain are activated and to what extent (Berthoz, Blair, Le Clec'h, & Martinot, 2002). For example, Damasio and coresearchers (2000) used a relived emotions task with their participants to induce either sadness, happiness, anger, or fear. Next, a PET scan measured activity in those brain areas that were hypothesized to correlate with the different affective feelings. The resulting PET scan images showed different patterns of activation and deactivation in different subregions of the brain. The ones involved were mainly deep inside the cerebrum, which makes up the two outer layers of the brain. The different patterns of activation and deactivation provided distinctive neural maps of a person's brain at the time of each emotional feeling. Differences among the neural maps help determine why each emotion has a different affective feel (Damasio, 2003; Damasio et al., 2000). There is a parallel between neural maps for emotions and the James-Lange theory regarding physiological response specificity. The James-Lange theory prompted psychologists to look for physiological response patterns that correspond with the affective component of emotions. Similarly, the neural map idea looks for specific patterns of brain activation that correspond with the affective feel of each prototype emotion.

Emotional Education.   Although it is difficult to describe affect, people have learned to label their own feelings with emotion words through a process known as **emotional education** (Buck, 1988; Fulcher, 1942). Through this process a child learns from people and

TABLE 13.2 **Emotional Experiences during Epileptic Auras**

Emotion	Description
Happiness	Reported by a 41-year-old housewife: "There is a sudden feeling of being lifted up, of elation, with satisfaction, a most pleasant sense. 'I am just about to find out knowledge no one else shares—something to do with the line between life and death.' Her heart pounds, and she is seen to be pale and trembling" (Williams, 1956, p. 57). Experience of a 34-year-old certified public accountant, married with two children: He experienced intense euphoria during his seizures. "On the night before surgery, he reported for the first time, after weeks of evaluation, that he was reluctant to seek definitive therapy for fear of losing the 10–30s [seconds] of intense euphoria (i.e., ecstasy) that he experienced prior to his seizure" (Ervin & Martin, 1986, p. 155).
Sadness	Reported by a 34-year-old woman: "There would be a dramatic onset of depression, always with a thought, half remembered, about 'Death and the World,' and a compulsive urge to suicide; always the feeling about 'Death and the World' comes with a feeling like going under gas" (Williams, 1956, p. 52). Reported by a 28-year-old woman: "The whole attack consisted of a shivering feeling in the abdomen, a general sense of weakness, and the association of 'feeling very sad,' with apprehension" (Williams, 1956, p. 51).
Fear	Reported about a 19-year-old woman: She "had seizures that started with a feeling of intense fear followed by loss of consciousness and automatism in which she acted as if she were in the grips of the most intense terror. She let out a terrifying scream and her facial expression and bodily gestures were those of someone having a horrifying experience" (Gloor et al., 1982, p. 132).
Anger	Reported by a male patient describing one of his auras: "I just get an electrical feeling, and it goes all the way through me; it starts in my head (I'd say both the stomach and head) and then it makes me do things I don't want to do—I get mad" (unpublished records of MacLean & Stevens, cited in MacLean, 1986, p. 76).
Disgust	Reported by an 18-year-old schoolgirl: "A very brief unpleasant throat sensation, a queer unpleasant feeling in the body, and an unpleasant emotional state without fear, which may lead to a major fit" (Williams, 1956, p. 58).

from situations to indirectly label his feelings. For example, consider the process by which a child learns that the name of a certain object is *pencil,* that the name of its color is *yellow,* and that it is used for *writing.* In this instance, the object is visible both to the child and her teacher. Thus, a teacher can point to the object and say, "This is a pencil, its color is yellow, and it is used for writing." A problem in emotional education, however, is that a subjective feeling is not open for public inspection like a pencil. Instead, emotional education takes place by noting the situation in which the emotion presumably occurs, the facial expression of the child, and her behavior and that of other people who may be experiencing the emotion (Buck, 1988; Fulcher, 1942). For instance, a birthday party may produce happiness, or being denied a toy may produce anger. In these situations a parent may label the child's feelings by asking "Are you happy with your presents?" or "Are you angry because you can't have the toy?" Presumably, a child will use these emotion words to label her feelings in future situations that are similar. A parent also assumes that a recognizable facial expression of emotion is linked to a subjective feeling. A crying child versus a laughing child produces different behaviors in the parent. When a child is crying, the mother might ask, "Did you hurt yourself?" or "Why are you so sad?" When a child is laughing, the father might ask, "Why are you so happy?" Presumably, the child will use these emotion words to label her feelings associated with those facial expressions. Behavior may also indicate to a parent whether a child is feeling happy or angry. Jumping up and down may indicate happiness, while shouting "no" may indicate feelings of anger.

Finally, a child can observe the emotional behavior of other people. For example, a child might see the expression of fear on the face of another child as he runs to his mother on seeing a large dog. The child might hear the mother say, "Don't be afraid. The dog won't bite you." The child learns in this instance that the feeling associated with the expression and the running away receives the label *fear* or "I'm afraid." By many such lessons, children eventually learn to use emotion words to label their internal subjective (affective) feelings (Buck, 1988; Fulcher, 1942).

Intensity and Duration of Emotions

Negative and positive emotional feelings can be intense but short while at other times they can be mild but lasting. This observation indicates that negative and positive emotions vary in intensity and in duration. This section describes how the emotion stimuli determine the intensity and duration of emotions.

Emotion Intensity.   First, however, the valence of stimulus change is an important feature that determines the quality of the emotion. The onset of negative stimuli produces unpleasant emotions while the onset of positive stimuli produces pleasant emotions. Second, emotion intensity depends on the degree of stimulus change. According to the **law of change** the "greater the [stimulus] change, the stronger the subsequent emotion" (Frijda, 2007, p. 11). Empirical evidence for the law of change comes from experiments that measure participant's physiological responses to and evaluations of emotion stimuli. In one such experiment, Bernat and coresearchers (2006) presented male participants pictures with negative or positive themes, such as weapons and erotic scenes. Other pictures contained neutral themes, such as unexpressive faces and household objects. Stimulus intensity was manipulated by picture content. For example, a pointed gun is a more intense theme than one not pointed, while a nude female is considered more intense than a clothed one. Participants rated the pictures for pleasantness and arousal intensity, while their frown muscles and skin conductance responses were also measured. Analyses of the results showed that positive pictures were rated more pleasant and the negative pictures were rated more unpleasant compared to that of neutral pictures. In addition, arousal ratings of the positive and negative pictures were higher than those of the neutral pictures. The degree of emotion-stimulus change across pictures also had an effect. For example, a pointed gun was rated more intense in unpleasantness than a side view of the same gun. Frowns and skin conductance were sensitive to the intensity of the pictures and theme content. Frowns became more intense as the pictures became more negative but less intense as the pictures became more positive. Skin conductance responses, however, increased as the picture-theme became either more negative or more positive.

Emotion Duration. There is a negative relationship between the duration and intensity of an emotion—that is, the more intense an emotion, the shorter its duration (Frijda et al., 1992; van Thriel & Ruch, 1994). For example, being ecstatic does not last as long as being cheerful, and being in a rage does not last as long as being hostile. The relationship between emotion intensity and duration was explored by van Thriel and Ruch (1994), who measured the intensity and duration of facial muscle activity that occurred before, during, and after the punch line of a joke. As shown in Figure 13.1, the intensity of facial expression increased, leveled off, and then decreased. At peak intensity the duration of facial muscle activity was shorter, while at a weaker intensity the duration was longer. Duration is a factor defining emotion, according to Ekman (1984), who reasoned that "the great majority of expressions of felt emotions last between ½ second and 4 seconds, and those that are shorter or longer are mock or other kinds of false expressions" (pp. 332–333). Yet each emotion may have its own window of time. Surprise may be an emotion of short duration, while sadness or fear may be of much longer duration.

The duration of an emotion is captured by Frijda's (2007) **law of emotional momentum,** which states that an emotion stimulus can repeatedly elicit the same emotion provided that an individual has not habituated to the stimulus. Thus, each time a reminder of the original

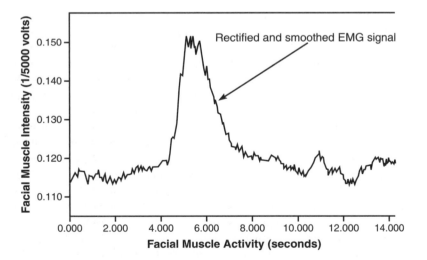

FIGURE 13.1 Emotion Intensity and Duration. Intensity of emotion changes over time. Facial muscle activity increases, levels off, and then decreases in reaction to the punch line of a joke.

Source: From "The Role of Surprise in Humor Appreciation" (p. 3) by C. van Thriel and W. Ruch, 1994, unpublished manuscript, University of Düsseldorf, Germany. Reprinted by permission.

emotion stimulus intrudes into consciousness a person experiences a portion of the emotion all over again. For example, you might recall a joyous occasion spent with friends and as a result a happy smile appears on your face. Or you might recall an embarrassing moment and consequently become embarrassed all over again. Grief is the emotional reaction that occurs with the loss of a person or pet. Even though grief to the original loss has subsided, it can be evoked again by mental intrusions regarding the loss. For example, in one survey of 350 widows and widowers 13 months after the death of their spouses, 14% avoided looking at pictures or belongings of their deceased spouses and 16% found visiting the cemetery too painful. In addition, 20% cried whenever they thought of their spouses and 53% would cry whenever they spoke of their deceased spouse (Shuchter & Zisook, 1993). The researchers concluded that stimuli associated with former spouses acted as triggers for painful feelings of loss.

Emotional stimuli can lose their potency to evoke emotions by the process of habituation. Habituation occurs in the case of romantic love. Initially, one's beloved has the ability to intrude into a person's thoughts, to sexually and physiologically arouse the person, and to evoke the urge to touch. One way habituation becomes evident is in the declining frequency of sexual intercourse over the years of marriage (Call et al., 1995). For example, from the data provided by a sample of 400 married women, Udry (1980) found that their frequency of sexual intercourse per month declined by about 32% over a four-year period. James (1981) examined the frequency of sexual intercourse for newlyweds over a 12-month period. He found that frequency declined from a median of 17.5 times during the first month to 8.8 times during the 12th month of marriage. The high frequency of intercourse early in a marriage or relationship compared to later has been termed the **honeymoon effect** (James, 1981).

Section Recap

Emotion means to be moved along several channels: affect, facial expressions, physiological arousal, brain processes, and a readiness to act. According to the *response coherence postulate* these channels all work in unison during an emotional experience in order to adapt to stimulus change. Emotions that are qualitatively similar are grouped into one of six to eight categories. The label of the category represents the *emotion prototype,* which reflects the most representative emotion of the category. Emotions within a category differ in intensity. The subjective or affective channel of an emotion is difficult to describe to others because of a property known as *qualia.* According to this concept, affective experiences have such basic and primitive qualities that words cannot adequately describe them. The distinctive affective feeling that accompanies each emotion emerges from its corresponding neural map in the brain. Evidence for this comes from examining an *epileptic aura,* which occurs before a seizure in the limbic system and can involve an emotional experience of joy, sadness, fear, anger, or disgust. *Emotional education* is the process by which a person learns to attach emotion labels to his own subjective feelings. This process occurs when a child associates an internal feeling, facial expression, behavior, and situation with the emotion label provided by another individual. Whether an emotion is pleasant or unpleasant depends on whether the emotion stimulus had a positive or negative valence. In addition, according to the *law of change,* the greater the stimulus change the stronger the emotion. The *law of emotional momentum* holds that an emotion-stimulus evokes the same emotion provided a person has not habituated to the stimulus. Habituation occurs to some emotion-stimuli as illustrated by the *honeymoon effect,* which means that the initial passion in a romantic relationship fades in intensity.

The Function of Arousal

Physiological arousal is one of the expressive channels for emotion. But what is its function? Is the pattern of a person's physiological arousal synonymous with the emotional experience? Or does arousal represent a state of alertness for monitoring the environment? Could arousal indicate a readiness for action like attacking, withdrawing, or perhaps doing nothing? The purpose of this section is to examine the function of arousal that is part of the emotion experience.

Changes in various physiological variables are indispensable accompaniments to affective feelings; without them a person might wonder whether an emotion was being experienced. There are several possible connections between physiological arousal and subjective emotional feelings. First, arousal is the source of emotional feeling. Second, arousal is the impetus for attending to and interpreting the environment, with the emotional feeling occurring as a result. Finally, arousal and subjective feelings occur together, with arousal providing a readiness for important activity, such as fight or flight. As described in Chapter 2, philosophers such as Francis Bacon and René Descartes briefly described the correspondence between physiological responses and subjective experiences. Bacon, for example, described anger by paleness, blushing, and trembling, while Descartes described sadness as being accompanied by a feeble, slow pulse and a constriction around the heart. The attention paid to physiological arousal as a factor in emotional feelings attained increased significance in William James's (1884/1948) very influential article "What Is an Emotion?" published in the journal *Mind.*

To set the stage for understanding the relationship between arousal and affective experiences, imagine the following situation: You are in bed ready to doze off, when suddenly you hear the sound of breaking glass. What could this mean? Is someone attempting to break into your apartment, or has your careless roommate broken something? Will you experience fear of a would-be burglar or anger toward your roommate? Table 13.3 presents three possible interactions among arousal and subjective experiences that could result in this situation according to the James-Lange theory, the cognitive arousal theory, and Cannon's theory.

James-Lange Theory

One interpretation of the interaction between arousal and affective experience is derived from the writings of William James (1884) and Carl Lange (1885/1968). According to the **James-Lange theory,** each specific emotion is accompanied by a unique pattern of physiological responses. James reasoned that emotion occurs when we become aware of our body's physiological arousal and emotional behavior in reaction to an exciting stimulus. According to him, "*The bodily changes follow directly the* Perception *of the exciting fact, and that our feeling of the same changes as they occur* Is *the emotion*" (James, 1884/1948, p. 291; italics in original). Suppose you hear the sound of breaking glass (see Table 13.3). From a commonsense view, if this means someone is attempting to break into the apartment, then you become afraid, which produces trembling and a pounding heart. If the sound of breaking glass resulted from your roommate's carelessness, then you become angry, which produces a pounding heart and increased blood pressure. James felt, however, that this commonsense sequence was incorrect. According to him, a person's awareness of his own trembling and pounding heart is the basis for the emotional experience of fear of the would-be burglar.

Table 13.3   Different Views of the Sequence of Events for the Generation of Affective Experience

Theory	Emotion Stimulus	Phase 1	Phase 2
James-Lange Theory	Sound of breaking glass	Arousal: Pulse quickens Muscles tense Breathing arrested Emotion behavior: Escape apartment Call 911 Grab golf club	Affective experience: Anxiety, fear, anger
Cognitive Arousal Theory	Sound of breaking glass	Arousal: Pulse quickens Muscles tense Breathing arrested Appraisal: Orient toward sound Register discrepancy of it Determine meaning of sound	Affective experience: Anxiety, fear, anger Emotion behavior: Escape apartment Call 911 Grab golf club
Cannon's Theory	Sound of breaking glass	Arousal: Pulse quickens Muscles tense Breathing arrested	Emergency response: Fight or flight Action readiness Affective experience: Anxiety, fear, anger

A rise in blood pressure, however, is the source of a person's subjective anger (Levenson, 1992). Thus, in the James-Lange theory, the sequence of events in experiencing an emotion is:

Emotion stimulus ⟶ Physiological response pattern ⟶ Affective experience

The James-Lange theory stimulated extensive research to determine the correspondence between affective experiences and unique physiological response patterns. For James, emotional behavior, such as fleeing from your apartment or setting your jaw tightly in anger, also serves as information. A paper by Lange published in 1885, however, placed great emphasis on autonomic nervous system arousal as the input for subjective affect. Thus, the James-Lange theory (Mandler, 1990) emphasizes physiological arousal to the exclusion of emotional behavior as the determiner of emotional feelings.

Physiological Specificity of Emotion.   The James-Lange theory proposes that each emotional feeling has a unique pattern of physiological responses associated with it. To show this, various criteria must be met (Cacioppo et al., 1993). First, at least two emotions should be induced. The physiological response patterns should differ between them and also differ from the pattern produced by a nonemotional control condition. Second, the presence of any emotion should also be verified using other measures, such as facial expressions or verbal reports. For example, suppose that in a hypothetical experiment procedure H is used to create happiness, such as an unexpected monetary bonus for participating in the experiment, while procedure A is used to create anger by frustrating a participant with unsolvable puzzles. A nonemotional control procedure is used to measure baseline levels of physiological responding in the absence of any emotional experience. Verbal reports or facial expressions would have to verify that participants undergoing procedure H were experiencing happiness, that participants undergoing procedure A were experiencing anger, and that control participants were not experiencing any emotion. During the procedure, two different physiological responses would be measured, such as heart rate and electrodermal responses. Hypothetical results that would support the James-Lange theory are presented in Figure 13.2. Procedure H (happiness) produced a heart rate–electrodermal response pattern that differed from the pattern produced by procedure A (anger). Furthermore, both patterns differ from the pattern accompanying the control procedure. Different patterns presumably provide participants with information for different subjective emotional experiences. If physiological response patterns are similar, then there would be no basis for feeling different emotional experiences, according to the James-Lange theory.

Research on Physiological Specificity of Emotion. Using real life manipulation methods, Stemmler (1989) created fear, anger, and happiness in female medical students to determine if each emotion would be accompanied by different patterns of physiological responses. In the fear condition, participants were in a dimly lighted room while they listened to a dramatic reading of the last part of Edgar Allan Poe's *The Fall of the House of Usher*. This part describes the sounds made by Usher's sister, Madeline, as she awakens from "death" and scratches her way out of the family tomb in an attempt to become reunited

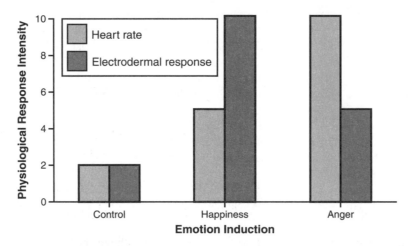

FIGURE 13.2 Physiological Response to Emotion. Hypothetical results of an experiment show a different physiological response pattern for each subjective emotional experience. The pattern for happiness is different than the pattern for anger, and both of these differ from the control pattern.

with her brother. The reading of this scary passage was accompanied by dramatic music. Following the reading, the room was plunged into total darkness and silence for one minute. Participants reported that this procedure was frightening to them. In the anger condition participants were frustrated, insulted, and were also made to talk in an angry voice. They were frustrated by trying to solve anagrams that had no solution. They were insulted when it was implied that failing to solve the anagram task reflected their lack of intelligence. In addition, participants were admonished by having to announce their solutions louder and louder. Participants reported being angry and irritated as a result. In the happiness condition, participants were told the physiological recordings were going well, were treated in a friendly manner by the experimenter, and learned the experiment was almost over. The experimenter also promised a monetary bonus above the amount of money already offered. The happiness manipulation was effective, since participants rated themselves happier in this condition than in the others. In the control condition participants were involved in an auditory-visual number-matching task that was designed not to evoke any emotions.

The results showed that only 6 of the 14 physiological variables discriminated among the three emotion conditions. The fear and anger conditions produced physiological profiles that differed from those of the control condition. The happiness condition profile, however, did not differ from the control profile. Thus, although there are seemingly unique profiles for fear and anger, there did not appear to be a unique physiological profile for happiness. According to this latter result, participants have no physiological response pattern corresponding to the feeling of happiness. Other findings contrary to the James-Lange theory have also been reported. For instance, Stemmler (1989) notes that finger sweating was greater for fear than for anger. However, another investigator (Ax, 1953) reported opposite results. He also noted that in the experiment, finger temperature for fear was high, while other investigators have found finger temperature for fear to be low (Ekman et al., 1983). On the whole, Stemmler's results provide only partial support for the James-Lange theory.

Other research has led to a similar conclusion. In a careful analysis of 22 experiments, Cacioppo and associates (2000) found some specific physiological differences among discrete emotions. For example, heart rate was greater during anger and fear than during happiness and was also greater during fear than during sadness. Diastolic blood pressure was higher in anger than either fear, sadness, or happiness and was also higher during sadness than happiness. Electrodermal responses increased more during fear than during sadness. However, there were also occasions when a physiological variable would not differentiate between two emotions. Nonetheless, a major difference does occur between negative and positive emotions (Cacioppo et al., 2000). This difference stems from greater autonomic nervous system activation during negative emotions than during positive ones. For example, negative emotions are accompanied by greater heart activity (rate and stroke volume) and diastolic blood pressure.

In spite of some response-pattern differences, Cacioppo and associates (2000) concluded that discrete emotions "cannot be fully differentiated by visceral activity alone" (p. 184). In fact, most psychologists studying the physiology of emotions arrive at the same conclusion: it is unlikely that different physiological patterns correspond with different affective experience (Cacioppo et al., 1993; Davidson & Ekman, 1994; Mandler, 1984; Zajonc & McIntosh, 1992). The failure to find specific physiological patterns is probably the result of the nature of the autonomic nervous system. It responds in a global fashion

CHAPTER THIRTEEN / Emotions and Moods

rather than showing specific reactions in an emotion-inducing situation. People are only aware of general changes in their autonomic nervous system rather than of specific changes (Mandler, 1984). Consequently, perception of our body's physiological reactions does not provide enough information to determine the subjective nature of an emotional experience.

Brain Maps and Affective Experiences. If different affective experiences do not have unique corresponding physiological profiles, then another approach is to look for corresponding neural maps in the brain. In this vein, a two-step extension of James's theory is provided by Damasio (2003). First, actual physiological changes in reaction to an emotion-stimulus are mapped onto body-sensing areas of the brain. The brain registers these physiological changes, such as a pang in the heart, an increase of the pulse, or a smile. Second, when the brain maps reach a critical intensity the corresponding emotional feeling emerges into consciousness. The pattern of the brain map determines the qualia of the emotional feeling. These brain maps are analogous to what some emotion researchers call **affect programs** (Tomkins, 1982, 1984). They refer to unique brain maps or networks that when activated produce emotional feelings in consciousness (Ekman, 1999; Phan et al., 2004). For example, a mix of affect programs are activated during an epileptic aura (see Table 13.2). Brain-imaging technology is one research strategy used to identify the brain maps. Functional magnetic resonance imaging and positron emission tomography detect brain activity by measuring changes in blood flow, oxygen, and glucose consumption. The emotion brain maps correspond to areas of greater metabolic activity. Brain-imaging technology has led to the discoveries that different areas are involved with the appraisal of emotion stimuli, the triggering of emotional responses, and the emergence of emotional feelings (Murphy et al., 2003; Phan et al., 2002, 2004; Wager et al., 2003). For example, the amygdala is a crucial site in the brain for processing and experiencing fear.

Cognitive Arousal Theory

A second interpretation of events in Table 13.3 focuses on the interaction between arousal and cognition as described in **cognitive arousal theory** (Mandler, 1984; Reisenzein, 1983; Schachter & Singer, 1962). A specific affective experience results from the interpretation a person gives her physiological arousal, based on the information extracted from the situation. In this theory, arousal is important for several reasons (Mandler, 1984). First, the occurrence of arousal forces the person to focus her attention on the environmental events that may have been responsible. Thus, on hearing glass breaking, all your attention is focused on the source of the sound. Second, arousal leads a person to analyze the meaning of the sound. What could have made that noise: someone breaking in or a careless roommate? Third, arousal enables the person to respond to the environment more effectively. Perhaps you should dial 911; then again, maybe you should tiptoe into the kitchen to assess how much damage your roommate has done. Mandler (1984) refined the original cognitive arousal theory (Schachter & Singer, 1962) by emphasizing two dimensions of emotion: quality and intensity. The quality of an emotional experience depends on the evaluation and subsequent meaning given to the emotion-inducing event. The intensity of the emotional experience, however, depends on the degree of physiological arousal. For example, the subjective emotion produced by hearing the sound of breaking glass depends on the meaning assigned to the noise (see Table 13.3). Is someone breaking in, or has your careless roommate dropped a drinking glass? The first interpretation evokes fear, while the second evokes anger. The sound of breaking glass also produces physiological arousal in both cases.

The intensity of that arousal, however, determines whether a person feels anxiety, fear, or terror of a would-be burglar or mild annoyance to intense anger toward a roommate.

In cognitive arousal theory, the emotion stimulus is the source of information for behavior but also the source of arousal. Recall that according to the law of change, greater stimulus changes produce stronger emotions and hence greater physiological arousal. Thus, when participants are presented with arousing stimuli such as an aimed gun or snake compared to a flower or mushroom, their physiological arousal is greater to the former—that is, to the more arousing stimuli (Bernat et al., 2006; Greenwald et al., 1989).

However, whether the arousal comes from the original stimulus or from elsewhere does not seem to matter based on the findings from **excitation transfer** experiments. In these, physiological arousal induced from one source influences emotional experience and behavior induced by another source (Zillmann, 1978, 1984). For instance, physiological arousal induced by physical exercise or by viewing action-packed films influences emotion induced by another stimulus. To illustrate, consider how an unrelated source of arousal can influence someone's romantic attraction for a person. White and associates (1981) produced low and high levels of physiological arousal in male participants by having them run in place for 15 or 120 seconds, respectively. After 15 minutes of rest, participants viewed a five-minute videotape of a university coed. In one version, she was made up attractively and talked about herself in an energetic fashion. In another version, she was made up unattractively and talked about herself in a generally dull manner. Participants then rated the videotape model for romantic attraction: her physical attractiveness and how much they would like to date her and kiss her. They also rated her for general attraction: how similar they were to her and how much they would like to work with her, get to know her better, and get along with her.

The experiment contained the two features that were necessary for emotion, according to cognitive arousal theory. First, there was the emotional aspect of the model, who was made to look and sound either attractive or unattractive. In evaluating her, the male participants presumably experienced some degree of emotional reaction. Second, there was a low or high amount of arousal that transferred from another source, which was running in place. The interaction between these two features influenced romantic attraction and general attraction ratings of the models. Higher arousal increased the emotional attraction for the attractive model while at the same time decreasing the emotional attraction for the unattractive one. The emotional experience evoked by the model increased because additional arousal transferred from running in place. If the model was unappealing, the added arousal made her more unappealing. If she was appealing, the added arousal made her more appealing. A potential piece of advice for the lovelorn is to take your date to an exciting basketball game or movie. The arousal from the game or movie should transfer over to the arousal being produced by the person. As a consequence of the transferred arousal, people should be even more attracted to their dates.

Cannon's Theory of Arousal

The question opening this section implied that a particular emotion is linked to a certain part of the body (Nieuwenhuyse et al., 1987). For example, sadness is felt as a broken heart and disgust is felt as gagging. For Bacon, "The *Spirits,* in all *Passions,* resort most to the *Parts,* that labour most, or are most affected" (Bacon, 1627/1974, p. 525; italics in original). In other words, the affected part of the body is ready for action during a particular emotional experience. These insights of Bacon are forerunners of the *emergency response* concept, which is a major point of emphasis in **Cannon's theory** (Cannon, 1929/1953). Accordingly, physiological arousal is merely an indication that the organism is ready or prepared for an **emergency response,** such as fighting or fleeing (see Table 13.3). For example, the liver releases glucose for the muscles to use as fuel for running or fighting. The adrenal glands release adrenaline to restore the vigor of fatigued muscles. In addition, blood is shifted to the heart, lungs, and skeletal muscles of the limbs to be of greater service in transporting oxygen. Blood clotting is also more likely during this time, since bleeding might occur in a fatal injury. According to Cannon (1927, 1929/1953) these emergency responses make the organism more capable in dealing with situations that produce fear, rage, and pain. Hearing the sound of breaking glass produces an emergency response. You may need to be prepared to flee from a burglar or to confront your roommate. The emergency response is similar to Frijda's (1986, 2007) **action readiness,** which is a state of preparedness to execute a particular kind of behavior. These states are felt as urges and impulses to act in a certain fashion depending on the emotional experience. Thus, when frustrated a person may have an urge to yell insults or when in love a person may have the impulse to touch another person. Emotions and action readiness are linked together (see Table 13.3). Fear readies you to flee the apartment from the would-be burglar, while anger readies you to yell at your roommate.

Action readiness implies that each discrete negative emotion is a motive for a different type of behavior. Consequently, each emotion requires a different pattern of physiological support. The basic emotion of anger, for example, produces a readiness to fight and act aggressively. Therefore, increased heart rate is necessary to distribute blood more efficiently to the muscles. Fear is also associated with increased heart rate, since that emotion is associated with a readiness to flee. Disgust, however, does not require any extensive activity on the part of a person other than the expulsion of sickening objects. As expected, Levenson (1994) has noted that a higher heart rate accompanies anger and fear, while a lower heart rate accompanies disgust. In a review cited earlier, Cacioppo and others (2000) found that the physiological pattern for disgust did not differ from a nonemotional control pattern. Furthermore, compared to anger, fear is associated with vasoconstriction, lower blood pressure, and less blood to peripheral vessels. Blood instead is redirected to the larger muscles in preparation for flight, which is consistent with the function of fear (Levenson, 1992). In other words, each negative emotion may have a somewhat different physiological profile, since each is linked to a readiness to perform different behaviors.

Section Recap

Three different theories have attempted to account for the function that physiological arousal has for emotions. According to the *James-Lange theory,* each emotion has a specific physiological response profile. Awareness of these profiles provides the information for different affective experiences. Research on finding physiological profiles that match affective experiences has not fared well and question the validity of the James-Lange theory. Instead research has shifted toward using brain imaging technology to find brain maps or *affect programs* that correspond to the processing of emotion stimuli, subsequent affective feelings, and accompanying behavior. According to another theory, *cognitive arousal theory,* arousal forces a person to attend to and interpret the surrounding situation. The interpretation determines the nature of affective experience, while the intensity of the physiological arousal is associated with the intensity of the experience. *Excitation transfer* experiments show that arousal from one source transfers and influences the intensity of the emotional experience induced by another source. Research with excitation transfer experiments illustrates the importance of arousal for interpreting the situation. The intensity of arousal created by the emotion stimulus correlates with intensity of affect. The third theory, *Cannon's theory,* maintains that arousal prepares the person to make an *emergency response.* For example, physiological arousal associated with fear results from glucose and epinephrine being released into the bloodstream so that an emergency response like running away can be executed effectively. Similar to the emergency response is the concept of *action readiness,* which refers to an urge or impulse characteristic of the associated emotion. A conclusion regarding Cannon's theory is that different physiological arousal patterns are linked to the type of emergency response, such as fight or flight, that benefits the organism in an emotion-inducing situation.

Moods

"Are you gloomy, cheerful, grouchy, or serious?" These descriptors refer to an individual's mood. Although moods are similar to emotions, they differ in several characteristics: duration, intensity, and salience of eliciting events.

Differences between Moods and Emotions

Mood is a subjective experience similar to, but not identical with, emotion. First, according to Morris (1992), moods are usually considered to last longer than emotions, although there is no consensus on the duration. Usually, moods are considered to last on the order of hours and days, whereas emotions last for seconds or perhaps minutes (Ekman, 1994b; Goldsmith, 1994). Second, the intensity of moods is less than that of emotions. Moods are more global and diffuse. Watson and Clark (1994a) imply that moods may be milder versions of emotions. For example, *gloomy* is classified in the sadness category (see Table 13.1) and may be a better indicator of mood than of emotion. A person might say, "It is a gloomy day," meaning that the weather is producing a gloomy mood. Similarly, under the happiness/joy (or reproduction) category (see Table 13.1), being carefree and cheerful may be more indicative of moods rather than of low-intensity emotions. Third, a person is less likely to be aware of the stimulus that produced a mood and more aware of the stimulus that produced an emotion. Davidson (1994) claims that moods follow from stimulus events that occur slowly over time, while emotions follow stimuli that occur more quickly. For example, the seasons of the year change slowly, and people's moods change with the seasons (Smith, 1979). An emotion stimulus, however, has a more sudden onset, like the punch line of a joke or friend failing to show up for a date.

Another distinction between mood and emotion relates to a dimension versus a category view of affect. Moods belong in either positively valenced or negatively valenced dimensions in contrast to membership in one of the six to eight categories of emotion presented in Table 13.1 (Watson, 2000; Watson & Clark, 1994b). The dimensional analysis means that moods have no specific affective feel or qualia like prototypical emotions do.

Instead, moods have either a pleasant or unpleasant feel or affect that can vary in intensity. The intensity of positively and negatively valenced affect is measurable with 20 descriptors contained in the *Positive and Negative Affect Schedule—Expanded Form* (PANAS-X) (Watson & Clark, 1994b). The 10 descriptors for the positive dimension depict a tendency to approach and engage in situations and activities, while the 10 descriptors for the negative dimension depict the opposite. To illustrate: for positive affect, participants indicate the extent they felt active, enthusiastic, and strong. For negative affect, participants indicate the extent they have felt afraid, irritable, or upset. This scale and an earlier version have been used extensively in the relationship between mood and other variables.

> The PANAS-X is available at http://www.psychology.uiowa.edu/faculty/clark/PANAS-X.pdf

Time of Day, Day of Week

Moods are linked to systematic changes in the environment, especially time of day (Hill & Hill, 1991). This last statement probably comes as no surprise to students with 8 o'clock classes. Clark and associates (1989) measured the positive and negative moods of college students every three hours from 6 o'clock in the morning to 3 o'clock in the morning (depending on whether the students were awake at that time). The results of their investigation showed that positive mood rose rapidly from 9 A.M. to noon and then remained stable until about 9 P.M. at which time it declined suddenly. Students were energetic and active during the middle of the day and less so in the morning and evening. Negative mood ratings, however, were low and remained relatively stable throughout the day.

In a replication study, Watson and colleagues (1999) had University of Iowa students rate their positive and negative affect and take their body temperature every two hours (odd or even numbered hours) over a period of one week. Figure 13.3 plots their positive and negative affect scores and body temperature as a function of time of day. The graph has been standardized so that the scores represent the number of standard deviations below or above the mean. Zero (0) represents the mean. Positive affect and temperature show similar trends. They are both low early in the morning and late at night, although positive affect peaks between 11 A.M. and 1 P.M. while body temperature peaks between 5 and 7 P.M. Negative affect, however, remained relatively the same throughout the day. The temperature curve in Figure 13.3 is part of a person's *circadian rhythm,* which accounts for the sleep-wake cycle.

In addition to time of day, mood also varies with the day of the week. Watson (2000) had University of Iowa students provide positive and negative affect ratings over a 30-day period. These scores were also standardized, with zero equal to the mean. The results in Figure 13.4 show that positive affect starts low on Sunday and rises through the week to its high point on Saturday. Negative affect shows a reverse trend. Although it rises from Sunday to Monday, it then declines for the rest of the week and reaches its lowest points on Friday and Saturday. The results in Figure 13.4, and that of another sample obtained with university students in Texas, led Watson (2000) to conclude that "the subjective weekend of college students seems to last from Thursday through Saturday" (p. 130).

Seasonal Variation

Moods are also associated with seasons of the year. From being happiest in the spring, positive affect declines slowly in summer and fall to its lowest point in winter. Then there is a

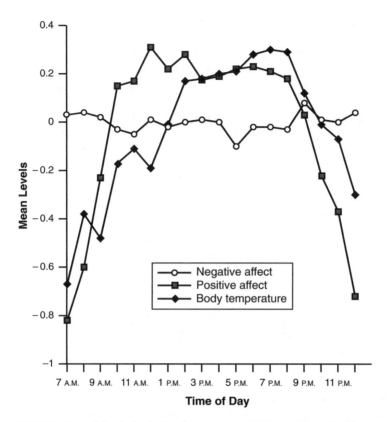

FIGURE 13.3 Mood, Body Temperature, and Time of Day. Positive affect and body temperature increase from morning to late afternoon, remain fairly constant, and then decline in early evening. Negative affect remains fairly constant throughout the day.

Source: From "The Two General Activation Systems of Affect: Structural Findings, Evolutionary Considerations, and Psychobiological Evidence" by Watson et al., 1999, *Journal of Personality and Social Psychology, 76,* figure 6, p. 835. Copyright 1999 by American Psychological Association. Reprinted with permission.

revival of happiness the following spring as the weather warms and the vegetation greens. Negative affect, however, is affected much less by the seasons of the year (Smith, 1979). Some individuals, however, are extremely affected by changes in the seasons. These individuals have a **seasonal affective disorder (SAD),** which is characterized mostly by depression in winter. Some individuals, however, also seem to experience depression in the summer (Wehr & Rosenthal, 1989). Wintertime depression appears associated with a decrease in sunlight, while summertime depression is associated with heat. In addition to extreme changes in affect, there are also changes in people's eating and sleeping habits with the seasons.

Section Recap

Moods are a milder and longer form of emotional experience. Moods are classified as either positively valenced or negatively valenced affect. The PANAS-X can be used to measure the intensity of positive and negative affect. Stimuli producing mood changes appear

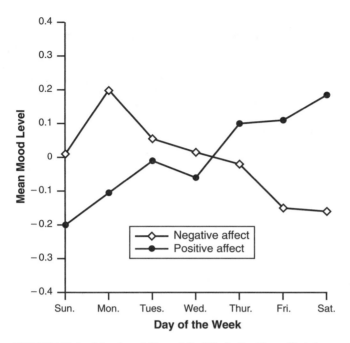

FIGURE 13.4   Mood and Day of the Week. Positive affect rises across the days of the week from Sunday to Saturday. Negative affect rises from Sunday to Monday and then declines across the rest of the week to Saturday.

Source: From D. Watson, 2000, *Mood and Temperament,* figure 4.9, p. 131. Copyright by the Guilford Press. Reprinted by permission.

to have a gradual and subtle beginning. For example, our moods are affected by hour of the day, day of the week, and season of the year. Positive mood is highest during the middle of the day, on the weekend, and during spring. Some individuals experience *seasonal affective disorder (SAD),* which is characterized most by depression in the winter due to lack of sunlight, although depression can occur in summer due to heat.

ACTIVITIES

1. To understand the meaning of qualia, describe to a friend various flavors such as strawberry, chocolate, or vanilla. Be certain to describe your reactions to the food substance. Do not make a stimulus error, which means describing the properties of the stimulus. Can your friend identify the flavor? Now, imagine trying to describe the quale of various emotions.

2. You can rate your general positive and negative affect using the *Positive and Negative Affect Schedule* in tables 1 and 2 of *The PANAS-X Manual for the Positive and Negative Affect Schedule—Expanded Form* at the following web address: www.psychology.uiowa.edu/faculty/clark/PANAS-X.pdf.

Keep track of your moods as a function of time of day or day of the week. Do your mood changes parallel those shown in Figures 13.3 and 13.4?

3. What are some activities that can maintain a positive mood and reduce a negative mood? For example, does being with friends, viewing a comedy, or exercising reduce your negative mood or increase your positive mood?

4. Reflect on the physiological arousal you have experienced during an intense emotion. How did that arousal affect you? Did it provide information about the quality or intensity of the emotion? Or was the arousal merely your body's preparation for action?

CHAPTER

14 Emotions as Motives

The face is the image of the soul.

—*Cicero, 80 B.C.*

A silent face often expresses more than words.

—*Ovid, 2 B.C.*

- How do emotions unfold and for what function? This chapter examines the unfolding and function of emotions in motivating cognition, facial expression, and behavior. The following questions serve as a guide in reading this chapter as these issues are examined:

1. What features of a situation produce an affective or emotional feeling?
2. Does emotion stem directly from the situation or from the situation as appraised?
3. What is the nature of the link between an emotional feeling and a public facial expression?
4. What function do facial expressions serve?
5. How do emotions motivate cognitive activity and behavior?
6. What specific motivational features does happiness provide?

Appraisal of the Emotion Event

As the chapter title indicates, emotions can serve as motives that push an individual into action. As noted in Chapter 2, the French philosopher Descartes (1649/1968) believed that the effect of an emotion first was to instill the goal of the emotion into a person's consciousness. The second effect was to prepare the mind and body to achieve that goal. Descartes' theory implies that fear wills a person to flee toward safety and anger wills a person to fight in order to redress an insult. The observation by Descartes serves to tie emotions to motivation—that is, emotions are an internal source of motivation that push humans into action toward a specific aim.

In trying to describe emotional feeling, a person can describe the situation that induced it. For example, happiness is what you feel when hearing good news, while disappointment is what you feel when someone lets you down. Is it possible that all emotions in the same category are evoked by similar circumstances, while emotions in different categories are evoked by different circumstances?

The purpose of this section is to describe how the characteristics of the situation lead to the unfolding of a particular emotion. Also explored is how appraisal of the situation is important in the unfolding of emotion.

Event-Appraisal-Emotion Sequence

As joke tellers know, a listener's reaction can range from amused laughter to disgusted groans. An explanation of these varied reactions is that individuals appraise jokes differently. In a review of theories concerned with the appraisal of emotion-inducing events, Roseman and Smith (2001) derived some common assumptions. First, different appraisals of the same event produce different emotions. For example, the breakup of their romantic relationship induces sadness in one partner and relief in the other. Second, the same appraisal of different events produces the same emotion. For example, a student who earned a *C* on an exam is as satisfied as one who earned an *A*, provided that both grades were proportional to the amount of exam preparation. Third, the outcome of the appraisal process elicits the involuntary unfolding of emotion. For instance, at times a person cannot help but feel disappointed or elated. Finally, appraisal can occur above and also below an individual's cognitive awareness—for instance, gut-level reactions that occur without knowledge of their cause.

A good overview of the stimulus-appraisal-emotion sequence that incorporates these assumptions is shown in Figure 14.1. The process begins with the occurrence of an emotion-inducing stimulus and ends with the unfolding of the various components of emotion. During the pre-aware phase, there occurs a rough nonconscious appraisal of the negative

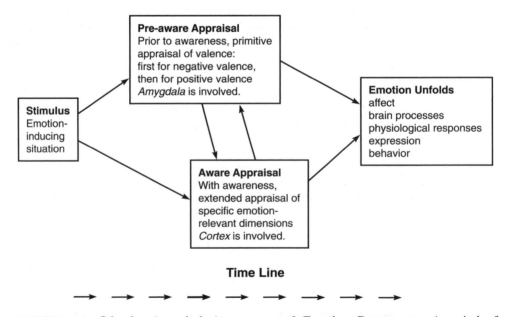

Time Line

FIGURE 14.1 Stimulus Appraisal, Awareness, and Emotion Components. Appraisal of the emotion stimulus can begin prior to awareness. With involvement of the amygdala, negative features receive more emphasis during this initial appraisal process. Appraisal prior to and with awareness results in the unfolding of emotion, with its various components.

and positive aspects of the situation. During this interval, the rough appraisal process is biased to detect negative features prior to any positive ones. Are there any features that are dangerous rather than safe, damaging rather than beneficial, unpleasant rather than pleasant, or to be avoided rather than approached? A few milliseconds later, the situation is appraised cognitively and more extensively, with awareness occurring along emotion-relevant dimensions. This phase includes information obtained during the pre-aware appraisal process. According to Smith and Lazarus (1990), during the awareness phase, a person appraises a situation in a manner consistent with her attitudes, personality, needs, and goals. This process is quite flexible, so there may be no close correspondence between the actual stimulus and the appraised stimulus. Two people who are in the same actual situation may appraise it quite differently. For example, what if the stimulus is receiving a *C* in a course? To one student this may be a cause of happiness, if failure had been expected. To another student, however, a *C* may be a cause of disappointment, if a higher grade had been expected. As Figure 14.1 shows, the outcomes of both appraisal processes elicit the unfolding of emotion.

Characteristics of the Emotion Situation

According to Figure 14.1, the unfolding of an emotion begins with the actual stimulus, and so this is the place to begin in discovering how emotions unfold.

Situational Definitions of Emotions. The **situational definition** approach emphasizes the actual stimulus and its context as the major determiners of emotion. According to this idea, emotions are specified by the conditions that produce them. Mowrer (1960) used this theory in describing an animal's reaction to the gain and loss of positive or negative incentives (see Table 14.1). Mowrer felt that if a stimulus predicted the delivery of food, then a hungry animal would experience the emotion of hope. For example, a family dog becomes hopeful when its master rattles the box of dog biscuits. However, if a stimulus predicts the delivery of food but food does not arrive, then an animal experiences disappointment. Thus, if a dog does not receive a biscuit, it feels disappointed. A stimulus that predicts the delivery of an electric shock evokes fear in an animal. A stimulus that predicts the shock will not occur, however, evokes the feeling of relief. For example, an owner trying to housebreak a puppy punishes it when it has an accident. Now when the puppy sees the owner coming, it experiences fear. However, the puppy experiences relief if the owner signals that punishment is not forthcoming.

TABLE 14.1   Emotions from Gains or Losses of Positive and Negative Incentives

	Positive Incentive Occurs	Negative Incentive Occurs
Stimulus Predicts Positive Incentive	Hope Owner rattles box of dog biscuits.	Disappointment Rattled box is not followed by biscuits.
Stimulus Predicts Negative Incentive	Relief Owner signals punishment not forthcoming.	Fear Puppy sees master coming to punish it for accident.

It is neither ethical nor practical to present or take away meaningful incentives from people in order to study their emotional reactions. As an alternative, however, emotion researchers have asked participants to recall situations when such events have happened to them. How did the participants appraise these situations, and what specific emotions were experienced? By asking these questions, commonalities among emotion-eliciting situations can be discovered.

Emotion-Eliciting Situations.   Describe a situation in which you experienced fear, sadness, anger, or happiness. What prompted your feelings? Having a similar goal, Shaver and associates (1987) attempted to identify various elicitors of different emotions. Respondents in the study were asked to think of incidents during which they experienced emotions such as fear, sadness, anger, joy, or love. They were then to describe in detail the events that led them to experience the emotion. The reports of the participants resembled Mowrer's situational outcomes in Table 14.1. For example, experiencing a positive stimulus or event evokes joy, such as achieving a task, receiving acceptance and love, or attaining what was wanted. Losing a positive incentive or experiencing a negative outcome—such as experiencing rejection, loss of love, or a negative surprise—evokes sadness. A threat to a person's well-being results in fear, especially when the threat is severe and unexpected. For example, participants reported being afraid in the dark or walking alone. The emotion of anger occurred in reaction to blocked goals, losses, and injustices. The positive emotion of love, however, was inspired from the ability of other individuals to induce good feelings in the participant.

Processing of Emotion Stimuli

"I do not like thee, Dr. Fell. The reason why I cannot tell." As the first two lines of the nursery rhyme suggest, like love at first sight, dislike can also occur without the benefit of cognitive appraisal. Is an emotion possible without cognition? Can a person like or not like someone or some situation and not think of the reason why? In other words, how extensively must a situation be appraised before it evokes an emotion?

Separation of Emotion and Cognition.   Emotions can occur automatically or result from appraisal that was primitive and below the level of awareness (Roseman & Smith, 2001; Smith & Lazarus, 1990). For example, one day walking behind two students on a snowy path, I observed that when one fell down, her friend burst out laughing almost instantaneously. The laughter occurred so quickly that any cognitive appraisal of the event must have been very rapid. "You looked so funny," she said to her fallen friend. In another instance, a male and female student were reading a bulletin board in the hall. He was standing behind her left shoulder and out of her line of vision. When turning to leave, she was immediately startled on detecting his presence. Her reaction happened so quickly that any appraisal of him must have been almost instantaneous. About the only thing she could have registered was that someone was there now and had not been earlier. She said, "Oh, you scared me." He replied, "I'm sorry. I didn't mean to."

These examples illustrate the possibility that elaborate cognitive processing is not necessary for emotion. Zajonc (1980) provided several intriguing possibilities why emotions can occur without cognition. First, feelings can occur prior to cognition. The female student was startled seemingly before she even recognized the harmless demeanor of the male student. Second, emotional responses are universal and occur in most species of animals and in humans. Smiling and laughing, for example, occur in all cultures (Ekman, 1973;

Izard, 1971) and may occur in some animals like chimpanzees (Ruch & Ekman, 2001). Third, emotional reactions may accompany cognitive judgments regardless of whether a person wants this to occur or not. The student who laughed at her fallen friend could not stifle her laughter even if it was socially impolite. The startled student was scared even though the hallway was quite safe and the other student's intentions were harmless. Fourth, when affective reactions occur, it is difficult to reverse them. It is difficult to change like to dislike, and vice versa. Even if a person realizes that she should not be amused by her friend's fall, it is difficult to change amusement into serious concern. Fifth, affective judgments about likes and dislikes refer to an individual's feelings and not to properties of actual stimuli. Saying "you looked so funny" suggests that the friend experienced a feeling of amusement. Sixth, it is difficult for people to state the reason for a particular affective judgment. They know what they like or dislike even if they cannot state the reason for it. Stimulus features that induce various components of emotion are often vague, global, and not used in making cognitive judgments. Why laugh when a friend falls? Is it because the fall, although unexpected, was a harmless mishap (Rothbart, 1973, 1976)? Why the sudden fright when the student detected the other individual behind her? Is it because of his size and that he appeared so unexpectedly in her field of vision (Lynn, 1966; Sokolov, 1963)? Finally, affect or feelings are difficult to put into words. Instead, humans communicate their emotions to others via facial expressions and to themselves with the sensations their affective experiences produce.

Appraisal without Awareness.   Have you ever fallen in love at first sight or disliked someone but could not verbalize the reason why? Emotional feelings seemingly can occur without any cognitive processing or from processing of which the person is not aware (Bornstein, 1989; Roseman & Smith, 2001). For instance, Bornstein and associates (1987) used photographs of people as stimuli. These photographs were exposed at intervals below (four-millisecond exposure) or above the level of conscious recognition (48- or 200-millisecond exposure). Afterward, participants were presented pairs of photographs, one new and one old. They were asked to select the previously exposed photograph as well as the one they preferred. The results showed that exposed photographs were preferred more than unexposed photographs no matter whether their exposure was below or above the level of conscious recognition. What happened to stimuli exposed below the threshold of conscious recognition proved most interesting. At the four-millisecond exposure, recognition was no better than chance (48%), while preference was significantly greater than chance (58%). The conclusion from these experiments is that humans can develop a like or dislike for a stimulus even if they are not aware of being exposed to it.

Repeated stimulus exposures below the level of cognitive awareness are also capable of elevating a person's mood and liking of those stimuli (Monahan et al., 2000). Imagine watching Chinese idiographs that are presented on a computer screen so rapidly that you are not consciously aware of them. In one condition, 25 different idiographs are presented one time each, while in the other condition five different idiographs are shown five times each. Immediately afterwards, you are asked to provide three different introspective reports on the extent of your positive mood. One report requires the use of pictures of facial expressions to indicate your mood. Neutral expressions equal 1 and a smile equals 5. A second report requires indicating your mood on a scale that ranges from 1 = Sad to 5 = Happy while a third requires using a scale that ranges from 1 = Depressed to 5 = Upbeat. Is a person's mood affected by the number of subliminal exposures of the same stimulus? The ratings in Figure 14.2 show that this is so. Five repeated exposures of the same idiograph elevated positive mood more

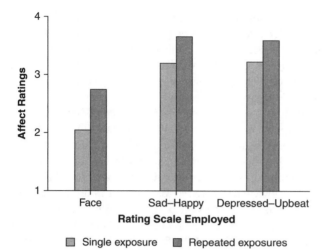

FIGURE 14.2   **Affect from Subliminal Stimulus Exposure.** Stimuli presented repeatedly below cognitive awareness produced greater positive affect than stimuli presented only once below awareness. Facial indicators of mood and sad–happy ratings were significantly higher for the repeatedly exposed stimuli. The depressed–upbeat ratings were almost significantly higher in the repeated-exposure compared to the single-exposure condition ($p = .09$).

Source: Adapted from "Subliminal Mere Exposure: Specific, General, and Diffuse Effects" by J. L. Monahan et al., 2000, *Psychological Science, 11,* p. 463.

than did a single exposure. In a follow-up experiment, imagine that you again are shown, below awareness, 25 different idiographs one time each or five different idiographs five times each. Afterwards, rate each idiograph for how much you like it: $1 = $ Not at all to $5 = $ Quite a bit. The results replicated those of the first experiment. The ratings showed that the idiographs exposed five times were liked more than those exposed just once. One interpretation of these results is based on the idea that the repeatedly exposed idiographs are associated with the absence of aversive events (Zajonc, 2001). As indicated in Figure 14.1, a person is aroused to appraise a stimulus first for any negative features and then for positive ones. Repeated exposures signify the absence of negative features, and thus avoidance tendencies diminish. Approach tendencies remain, however, and become associated with the stimulus that had been presented below awareness. The result is increased positive affect in response to the original stimuli and the situation (Zajonc, 2001).

Priority of Negative Stimulus Appraisal.   The results presented in the previous section indicate that appraisal is possible without cognitive awareness. Furthermore, during this process, appraisal for negative valence occurs prior to appraisal for positive valence (Dijksterhuis & Aarts, 2003). Negative features are evaluated first and longer in order to determine the extent of their negative valence. In a test of this hypothesis, Dijksterhuis and Aarts (2003, experiment 2) required participants to categorize words as possessing either a positive or negative valence. The researchers showed participants 15 positive words (e.g., *baby, friend, happiness*) and 15 negative words (e.g., *cancer, fear, war*) for 13.3 milliseconds each. This exposure speed was so fast that participants were unable to identify the words, and many reported they had not seen anything flash on the screen. If negative stimuli are evaluated first, then more negative than positive words should be categorized correctly. The results confirmed this prediction. Positive words were categorized no better than chance (0.480), while negative stimuli were categorized more accurately than chance (0.563). These results again show that emotion stimuli can be evaluated very rapidly and below the level of cognitive awareness. The results also indicate that appraisal of negatively valenced stimuli take precedence over positively valenced ones. The researchers reasoned that each word evoked an affective reaction but that this reaction occurs sooner to negative stimuli than to positive ones.

These evaluation tendencies occur automatically—that is, without conscious intention and are also associated with behavioral tendencies (Duckworth et al., 2002). Negatively evaluated stimuli are associated with avoidance tendencies (to flee, withdraw), while positively evaluated stimuli are associated with approach tendencies (to contact, enter). One way to determine if stimuli and response tendencies of the same valence are automatically associated together is to see what happens when they are made incompatible—that is, avoidance responses are required to positive stimuli and approach responses are required to negative stimuli. Duckworth and coresearchers (2002) created novel drawings that served as negative and positive stimuli. Drawings considered negative were more chaotic, with jagged lines, while those considered positive were more uniform, with curved lines. Five negative and five positive drawings were presented on a computer screen one at a time to participants. On seeing a drawing, participants either had to push a lever away (avoidance response) or pull a lever toward them (approach response) as quickly as possible. A push-avoidance response should be faster to a negative than to a positive drawing, since avoidance tendencies are associated with negative stimuli. Furthermore, a pull-approach response should be faster to a positive than to a negative drawing, since approach tendencies are associated with positive stimuli. The results supported the hypothesis. Avoidance responses were faster to negative drawings than to positive ones, and approach responses were faster to positive drawings than to negative ones. These results imply that action readiness is automatically attached to the stimulus valence and occurs very early in the unfolding of emotion.

Appraisal Dimensions. The situational definition emphasizes the power of the stimulus event in evoking the emotion. Appraisal, in contrast, emphasizes how the stimulus event as evaluated or as appraised evokes the emotion. Following pre-aware appraisal, people realize they are appraising a situation even though an emotion might follow automatically. Is a situation or event appraised using a universal set of dimensions? Do these dimensions separate emotions from one another? One possible set of dimensions presented in Table 14.2 was examined by Scherer (1997) for its utility in differentiating among emotions. Scherer had respondents from 37 different countries answer questions similar to the ones listed in Table 14.2. The results indicate that there seems to be high agreement around the world on what appraisal dimensions are responsible for evoking emotions. For example, joy was induced by goal-compatible events that could be easily coped with. Sadness, however, was the result of events produced by others that hindered one's goals and that were difficult to cope with. Most indicative of fear was its unpleasantness rating, its external causation, and difficulty in being coped with. Anger-evoking situations were appraised as being unfair and resulting from hindered goals. The most striking appraisal dimension for disgust was its unpleasantness, with external causation also being important.

Other researchers have used similar dimensions to those in Table 14.2, although emphasizing different aspects (Ellsworth, 1994). Novelty, for instance, means the situation

TABLE 14.2   Appraisal Dimensions for Emotion-Inducing Situations

Dimension	Definition
Expectedness	To what extent did you expect the situation to occur?
Unpleasantness	To what extent was the situation unpleasant or pleasant?
Goal hindrance	To what extent did the situation help or hinder your goals or intentions?
Unfairness	To what extent was the emotion-inducing situation unjustified or undeserved?
External causation	Who was responsible for the situation?
Coping ability	How powerful or capable did you feel in coping with the situation?
Immorality	Was the person responsible for the situation acting inappropriately or unethically?
Self-consistency	To what extent did the situation affect your self-esteem?

is new or has yet to be experienced. Mildly novel stimuli evoke interest and orienting responses, while extremely novel stimuli are judged strange and lead to withdrawal. Orienting responses imply that the organism is investigating a novel stimulus, as if asking "What is that?" Extremely novel or strange stimuli, however, evoke defense reactions such as fear and avoidance (Lynn, 1966; Sokolov, 1963). After an initial evaluation of novelty or strangeness, uncertainty about the event may remain. How well can a person predict what is going to happen in a situation? This question relates to the expectedness dimension (see Table 14.2). Ellsworth (1994) feels that uncertain positive situations produce curiosity, interest, and hope, while uncertain negative situations produce anxiety and fear. Ellsworth and Smith (1988) found some evidence that situations of low certainty evoked fear, while highly uncertain situations, especially when involving others, evoked surprise.

Responsibility as an appraisal dimension has also received scrutiny and relates to the external causation dimension. Responsibility means attributing credit or blame to whoever was accountable for the situation. Anger, hope, and anxiety are more likely to result from someone else's being responsible for the event rather than oneself. If the borrower does not return a book as promised, then the lender may feel anger. Guilt, shame, and pride, however, are more likely to result from events for which the person feels responsible. If an individual feels responsible for not returning a book, then she is likely to feel guilty (Ellsworth & Smith, 1988; Manstead & Tetlock, 1989).

Amygdala and Emotion-Event Processing

As described, the processing of stimulus changes that are relevant for emotion can occur rapidly without awareness or more slowly with awareness. Processing occurs in various areas of the brain, with the limbic system playing a crucial role. This system is a bundle of fiber tracts that form a ring (limbus) around the brain stem. An important component of the limbic system is the **amygdala**, which is an almond-shaped region that plays a crucial role in evaluation emotion events. This structure receives visual, auditory, taste, and smell information and uses it to make a quick and rough evaluation of the stimulus change for its relevance to a person's well-being (LeDoux, 1996, 2000a, 2000b; Phan et al., 2004).

Is this information used to protect the individual? A personal example illustrates this possibility. One spring day, while strolling in a field with my dog, I almost stepped on something that resembled a stick, except that sticks are not that color. In an instant, I was frightened, my heart pounded, my muscles tensed, and I began breathing harder. I was ready for action, fight or flight. LeDoux (1996, 2000a, 2000b) uses this type of situation to illustrate the dual nature of emotion-stimulus processing by the amygdala and the cortex. As illustrated in Figure 14.1, the amygdala and the cortex are involved in the processing of emotion stimuli, especially fear-relevant stimuli. Visual and auditory information about an emotion-inducing situation is received by the amygdala for crude and rapid appraisal, with additional information going to the visual and auditory cortex for more elaborate appraisal. Should a person respond based on rapidly processed though crude information provided by the amygdala? Or should a response be based on the slower but more accurate information provided by the cortex? The amygdala rapidly shows us that something is amiss or discrepant and can be life threatening. Slower and more elaborate analysis by the visual cortex indicates that the oddly colored stick is only a small harmless snake. The amygdala errs on the side of danger. It assumes the stimulus is potentially harmful and executes orders for a flight-or-fight response. It is better to make a response that was not needed than fail to make one at all. I jumped over the snake without thinking. There was no harm done other than having wasted some energy. However, what if a person only responds by following the slower analyses of the visual cortex? By then it may be too late, especially if the stimulus is dangerous. In other words, the failure to make a fight-or-flight response is more detrimental to the person than it is to make this response even if not needed (LeDoux, 1996, 2000a, 2000b). Thus, the amygdala is responsible for inducing fast action in a situation appraised as potentially dangerous.

Section Recap

The event-appraisal-emotion sequence refers to the unfolding of an emotion that began with the evaluation of a stimulus and ended with the emotional reaction. Initial appraisal scans for negative features that may denote harm before proceeding with a more extensive analysis. The unfolding of an emotion begins with the appraisal of the stimulus and ends with an emotional reaction. The initial stimulus helps determine the emotion. According to the *situational definition*, an emotion is synonymous with the stimulus event that evokes it. The promise of a positive incentive defines hope, while the failure of the incentive to occur defines disappointment. The anticipation of a negative incentive defines fear, and the failure of its occurrence defines relief. Each basic emotion has eliciting situations in common. Joy stems from gains, love from a close association with other people, sadness with loss, fear with threat, and anger with frustration or threat. Evaluation of the emotion stimulus can occur either very rapidly without awareness or after cognitive appraisal with awareness. These appraisals are carried out along several dimensions. Situation appraisal and consequent emotional feelings involve the limbic system. The *amygdala* carries out a quick and crude appraisal of the situation, while the cortex conducts a more elaborate appraisal. The quick evaluation by the amygdala allows the person to act more swiftly to a potentially dangerous situation instead of relying on information from the slower cortex.

Emotions Motivate Facial Expressions

According to evolutionary psychologists, the response coherence postulate (Chapter 13) is a working assumption regarding the function of emotions. They assume there is a master program that coordinates the many different channels along which emotions operate. This coordination is necessary in order to effectively deal with the environmental demands that people encounter (Tooby & Cosmides, 2005). In some respects, an emotion resembles the conductor of an orchestra as he directs the different musicians so that they all play in an organized manner. Without the conductor's organizational control, the play of the musicians would not be in synchrony and the music would sound awful. Similarly, during an emotional experience, the various channels must interact in a unified manner in order to achieve the aim of the emotion. Disunity among the channels would result in chaos and the aim of the emotion would not be met. For example, a person will more effectively assert her rights when a raised voice is accompanied by an angry expression and matching posture. Who would pay attention to a voice raised in anger when it was accompanied by a smile and a dejected posture? This section examines the role of facial expressions in emotion. The next section examines how emotions motivate thought and actions. However, keep in mind that facial expressions associated with emotion are in synchrony with accompanying thoughts and the behavioral goals of emotions.

Expression-Feeling Link

Facial expressions and emotional feelings (affect) are both components of emotion. According to Izard (1994) they are joined in an **expression-feeling link.** This means that different facial expressions are linked with different emotional feelings (see photos in Table 13.1). Thus, a smile is linked with happiness, and tears are linked with sadness. Furthermore, as the intensity of the emotional feeling increases, the linked facial expressions become more vivid. What is the nature of this link?

One hypothesis is that the affective experience and expression simply correlate with each other. One does not cause the other, but both are in response to an emotion stimulus (Buck, 1984, 1985). For example, viewing sad movie scenes can evoke tears, moist eyes, and the urge to cry along with feelings of depression, sadness, anger, and decreased happiness (Marston et al., 1984; Martin & Labott, 1991). Viewing a playful puppy, however, evokes a smile and feelings of happiness (Ekman et al., 1980a). Viewing cartoons evokes smiles, laughs, and feelings of amusement (Deckers, 1994). Comedy scenes evoke facial expressions showing pleasantness along with pleasant feelings. Unpleasant scenes such as traffic accidents and ritual suicides, however, evoke facial expressions indicating that the feelings induced are unpleasant (Zuckerman et al., 1981). Disgusting odors are considered very unpleasant and evoke facial expressions signifying disgust, while good-smelling odors are considered pleasant and evoke pleasant facial expressions (Kraut, 1982). Furthermore, as the emotion stimulus becomes more intense, the affective experience and expression do also. In humor research, for example, stimulus incongruity is a necessary condition for feeling amusement and exhibiting smiles and laughs. As incongruity of the stimulus increases, smile intensity and funniness ratings increase (Deckers, 1993). Films prerated as more amusing evoke stronger happiness/amusement feelings and greater zygomaticus smile muscle movements than films prerated as less amusing (Hess et al., 1995). A conclusion from these examples is that both affective experiences and facial reactions jointly occur in reaction to the emotion-inducing event.

Another view is that the affective experience produces the facial expression. Feeling happy results in a smile, while feeling sad results in tears. In fact, neural activity in the brain responsible for the subjective feeling is also responsible for movement of the facial muscles. According to the **efference hypothesis,** the activated brain circuit sends information to the facial muscles, which generate the expression that is synonymous with the emotion (Camras et al., 1993; see also Izard, 1993). That is, an activated fear circuit stimulates facial muscles that produce the expression of fear, while a disgust circuit stimulates looks of disgust.

Innateness of Facial Expression of Emotion

Facial expressions are easy to induce. They serve as a universal language that enriches human interaction. In fact, it is difficult to have a face-to-face conversation without attending to the nonverbal cues provided by the face. Facial expressions are largely innate; that is, they occur very early in life, in deaf and blind children, and are the same in all cultures.

Facial Expression in Early Life. Facial expressions occur long before learning could have had much influence. Recall from Chapter 3 that newborn infants made facial reactions to various taste stimuli. In reaction to sweet, sour, and bitter tastes, infants made sweet, sour, and bitter faces (as interpreted by adults). A person might argue that taste sensations are not emotions. However, the infants were making facial expressions consistent with adult taste experiences (Mennella & Beauchamp, 1998; Steiner, 1977).

In addition to reacting to taste, infants show facial expressions of emotion within the first few months of life. Izard and associates (1995) recorded the expressions made by 2.5- to 9-month-old infants during pleasant or mildly stressful interactions with their mothers. During these interactions a mother showed interest and joy while playing with her infant, or she showed a sad, angry, or still expression. Infants at 2.5 months were already sensitive to their mothers. They exhibited facial expressions of interest, joy, sadness, and anger. Furthermore, the infants' expressions also depended on their mothers' emotional expressions. For instance, at 6 months of age, infants expressed sadness, anger, and decreased joy to their mothers' sadness and expressed more anger and interest in reaction to their mothers' anger. However, infants generally showed a much greater frequency of positive expressions in reaction to their mothers' positive expressions.

According to Izard and Malatesta (1987), infant facial expressions are true to the subjective emotion the infant is experiencing. For example, distressful crying accompanies painful sensations, and smiling accompanies feelings of joy. These expressions are important because they influence the infant's caregiver. For example, a sign of disgust alerts the caregiver not to feed the infant a particular food. An infant's smile contributes to the development of attachment and social bonding. Izard and associates (1995) interpret the infants' disposition to smile in response to most of their mothers' expressions as an adaptive behavior pattern, because the smiling infant positively influences the caregiver. Furthermore, the amount of facial area involved in an infant's smile depends on the level of involvement with the mother (Messinger, 2002). Infant smiles were weakest when the mother neither smiled nor gazed at her infant. However, when the mother did smile and gaze at her infant, the infant's return smile involved more facial area—raised cheeks, opened mouth, and contracted muscles around the eyes.

Facial Expression in Deaf and Blind Children. Evidence for the innateness of an expression also comes from deaf and blind children, who exhibit the same facial expressions as seeing and hearing children do. Thompson (1941) compared smiling, laughing, and crying in seeing children with these expressions in children who were totally blind from birth or shortly thereafter. The 7-week-old to 13-year-old children were observed while playing, fighting and arguing, doing schoolwork, listening to music, and being instructed in games and drawing. Smiling, laughing, and crying occurred in situations evoking happiness, anger, annoyance, and sadness in both groups of children. Thompson concluded that maturation was responsible for the development of facial expressions in blind children, since there was no obvious way they could have learned these expressions. She did discover, however, that learning helped stylize facial expressions of seeing children compared to blind and deaf children.

Eibl-Eibesfeldt (1973) studied facial expressions in six deaf and blind children. He observed these children smiling, laughing, crying in distress and anger, frowning, pouting, and showing surprise. Furthermore, the situations producing these expressions were the same for deaf and blind children as for normally developed children. Of particular interest was Sabine, who was born with no eyesight and was totally deaf. Yet she exhibited expressions in much the same manner as a hearing and seeing child. For example, Sabine smiled "when she sat by herself in the sun patting her face with the palms of her hands" (p. 175). She also smiled when she was patted, tickled, or engaged in social play. Sabine also exhibited angry crying when someone persistently presented her an object that she did not like or social contact that she did not want. She would also pout afterward. Sabine exhibited surprise when she sniffed a pungent-smelling object, much like a hearing and seeing person would. Eibl-Eibesfeldt (1973) felt these facial expressions were innate and like Thompson (1941) concluded that learning refines facial expressions. "The deaf-and-blind often lack the minute gradation of an expression. An expression suddenly appears, and equally suddenly wanes without warning leaving a completely blank face" (p. 192).

Learning and Fine-tuning of Expression.   Learning plays some role in the voluntary posing of facial expressions. Ekman and associates (1980b) had 5-, 9-, and 13-year-old children intentionally move the facial muscles appropriate for displaying anger, disgust, fear, happiness, and sadness. The researchers discovered that the ability to make these facial movements increased with age. Blind children, however, did not become better at posing as they got older; they became less adept. Fulcher (1942) photographed seeing children and blind children while they posed with a happy, sad, angry, or afraid expression. Fulcher rated how close the child's pose matched the expression judged to be appropriate for that particular emotion. His ratings showed that facial poses of seeing children were judged to be more adequate than the poses of blind children. The poses of blind children became less precise as they got older, while those of the seeing children became more refined.

More recent research shows that learning allows for fine-tuning of expressions. Rinn (1991; cited in Galati et al., 1997) concluded that blind individuals do not develop suitable control over their facial muscles because they lack practice and do not benefit from feedback. Galati and associates (1997) had individuals blind from birth and normally sighted individuals portray neutral, surprise, anger, joy, disgust, sadness, and fear expressions. A different group of sighted individuals was then asked to identify what emotional expression was being conveyed. The results in Figure 14.3 show that it was easiest for judges to identify the expression of joy. They had more difficulty, however, identifying the expressions of surprise, anger, disgust, and a neutral expression of blind individuals compared to those of sighted individuals. In a later study, with children younger than four years, different facial intensities between positive and negative emotions were also clearer in normally sighted children than in blind children (Galati et al., 2001).

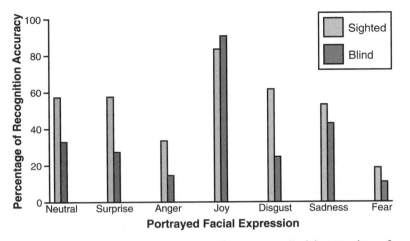

FIGURE 14.3 Recognition of Emotional Expression. Facial expressions of emotions were more difficult to recognize when portrayed by blind individuals than by sighted individuals. The expression of joy or happiness is the exception and was recognized very accurately in both groups.

Source: Adapted from "Voluntary Facial Expression of Emotion" by D. Galati et al., 1997, *Journal of Personality and Social Psychology, 73,* table 5, p. 1374.

Universality of Facial Expression of Emotion. Although societies the world over vary widely, facial expressions are fairly similar. Much work on the universal recognition of facial expressions of emotion has been reported by Izard (1971) and Ekman (1973). Both researchers assumed that each basic emotional experience has a corresponding unique facial expression. Furthermore, since these facial expressions are innate, they should not be affected by any differences that exist among cultures. Izard (1971) and Ekman (1973; Ekman & Friesen, 1971) conducted a series of **emotion recognition** studies in which they asked people in different countries to identify the emotion portrayed by various facial expressions. According to Izard (1971), "The general assumptions underlying these Emotion Recognition studies were as follows: there exist discrete fundamental emotions common to all mankind; and each of these emotions has a characteristic expression or pattern which conveys particular meaning or information for the expresser and the perceiver" (p. 251).

Imagine being a participant in a study that asks you to identify facial expressions of emotion. Slides of facial expressions are shown on a screen, and you are to identify the emotion it portrays from a list containing these options: happiness, disgust, surprise, anger, sadness, and fear. If facial expressions are universal, then participants the world over should agree on what emotions are represented. Ekman's (1973) study employed participants from five different countries representing a variety of cultures and languages: Argentina, Brazil, Chile, Japan, and the United States. They were shown several photographs representing a specific emotion. There was high agreement among members of the different countries in recognizing what emotions each facial expression represented. The greatest agreement was in the identification of happiness, with the least agreement being in the identification of anger and fear. Izard (1971) showed pictures of facial expressions representing eight basic emotions to people from the United States, Europe, Greece, Japan, and Africa. He also found high agreement among the different cultures in identifying these expressions. A person's accuracy in identifying a facial expression of emotion in another person, however, depends on the group membership of each. According to the in-group advantage, an individual is more accurate at recognizing the facial expression of a member from her own cultural group than from a different cultural group (Elfenbein & Ambady, 2002a, 2002b). This finding suggests that learning may play some role in either the recognition or formation of facial expressions.

Could it be possible, however, that people in different countries show identical facial expressions because of contacts among cultures? People are exposed to individuals from other cultures through travel, movies, and television. Thus, learning through observation could be the reason people show similar facial expressions. To answer this question, Ekman and Friesen (1971) did an emotion recognition study with the South Fore people living in South East Highlands of New Guinea, a large island located just north of Australia. Members of the South Fore group had had little if any contact with Westerners. They did not speak English and had never seen a movie or television. South Fore participants were read a story in their own language depicting an emotion and then were asked to identify a picture of a facial expression matching that emotion. For example, happiness and anger were defined as follows: "Happiness: His (her) friends have come, and he (she) is happy. . . . Anger: He (she) is angry; or he (she) is angry, about to fight" (p. 126). The results showed that participants could match the facial expression with the emotion description. Ekman and Friesen (1971) found that South Fore children also showed similar emotion recognition ability. In addition, Ekman and Friesen took photographs of the South Fore people portraying facial expressions of various emotions and showed them to American college students. The students in turn could accurately identify the emotion portrayed by the faces of the South Fore.

> More information about facial expression of emotion is available at http:// face-and-emotion .com/dataface/emotion/expression.jsp

Function of Facial Expression

It is certainly difficult to put one's emotional feelings into words, although this is the work of song writers, poets, and novelists. Feelings are often considered more authentic than words. People often judge us by the nonverbal facial communication of our feelings and not by what we say, as if the face, rather than the words, is a more accurate conveyor of emotional meaning. According to the efference hypothesis (Camras, Holland, & Patterson, 1993), an emotion circuit in the brain sends information to the facial muscles to create an expression. What is the function of these expressions? To answer this question, two hypotheses have emerged.

Two Hypotheses on the Function of Facial Expression. "Pass the salt!" Does this mean I have a craving for salt or that I simply want you to hand me the shaker, since I cannot reach it? Similarly, do tears indicate sadness, or are they a plea for help? Does a smile mean happiness, or is it a reward one friend bestows on another?

According to the **readout hypothesis,** a facial expression conveys an individual's emotional feeling to another individual (Buck, 1984, 1991, 1994; Ekman, 1984). A facial expression is like a dial that registers the emotional feelings, much like the tachometer of a car registers the number of revolutions per minute of the engine. This relationship is the expression-feeling link. According to Buck (1984), "It is useful for social animals to be able to communicate their internal states of anger, fear, interest, sexual excitement, and so forth,

TABLE 14.3   Interpretations of Facial Expressions according to the Readout Hypothesis and the Behavioral Ecology Hypothesis

Facial Expression	Readout Hypothesis Face Communicates	Behavioral Ecology Hypothesis Face Communicates
Smile	Happiness	Friendship, friendliness, no threat
Cry	Sadness, grief	Need for help, readiness to receive help/comfort
Anger	Annoyance, anger, fury	Verbal attack, physical attack
Fear	Worry, fear, terror	Readiness to submit, desire to be rescued
Disgust	Offended, disgusted, sickened	Reaction to bad-smelling or bad-tasting object
Blush	Ashamed, embarrassed	Make amends, reduce salience of others

to their fellows without actually having to engage in overt behaviors associated with those states" (p. 36). Thus, tears communicate sadness, and a smile communicates happiness. However, according to the **behavioral ecology hypothesis,** facial expressions "are issued to serve one's social motives" in a particular situation and need not be linked to emotional feelings (Chovil & Fridlund, 1991; Fridlund, 1991a, 1992, 1994). Fridlund (1991a) points out that "if we exhibit social inclinations and we are emotional, our faces signal the former and not the latter" (p. 69). Table 14.3 compares the meaning of facial expressions according to the readout hypothesis and the behavioral ecology hypothesis. Fridlund provides other examples as well (1994, p. 129).

People are able to infer social motives from the facial expressions that individuals exhibit. Yik and Russell (1999) presented photos of facial expressions that displayed surprise, happiness, disgust, sadness, anger, fear, and contempt. The participants (who were Canadian, Hong Kong Chinese, and Japanese) were required to match the faces with a list of social messages—for example, What face matches the statement "Back off or I'll attack" or matches "Don't hurt me! I give up"? The matching results showed that all groups were able to identify a face with its corresponding social message and also with the emotion a face displayed.

Blushing may not qualify as a facial expression but it has interesting implications for the behavioral ecology hypothesis. It is the one facial signal that is involuntary; it cannot be faked. Blushing is localized in the face and results from increased blood flow (Leary et al., 1992). Generally, undesired social attention is the major circumstance that elicits blushing, such as being evaluated, scrutinized, stared at, criticized, or praised excessively. Blushing also results if the person violated social norms and is considered incompetent, rude, or immoral or if the person has not lived up to a public self-image as a result of criticism or from being overly praised.

There may be two reasons, in accord with the behavioral ecology hypothesis, why people blush: appeasement and escape from unwanted attention (Leary et al., 1992). The appeasement function is to show that the person cares about social norms and wants to repair any social damage that was caused. It is an attempt to admit error, apologize, or placate the offended individuals in order to deter retaliation, aggression, or banishment.

For example, your cell phone sounded during your professor's lecture. The skin of your face became red or darkened in order to appease the professor and surrounding students—that is, you are truly sorry for disturbing the class. The escape function also notes that blushing is often accompanied by the lowering of one's head and averting one's gaze. These actions are designed to escape or deflect the scrutiny of others and thereby make those individuals less salient or noticeable. In this case when the cell phone rings, individuals also avert their gaze from others in order to make the scrutiny of others less salient or noticeable.

Implications of the Readout and Behavioral Ecology Hypotheses.   The presence or absence of other individuals is important when considering the validity of each hypothesis. According to the readout hypothesis, another individual should not influence our facial expressions. The emotion-generated expression should occur whether the individual is alone or with others. According to the behavioral ecology hypothesis, however, the presence of another individual is important for the occurrence of a facial expression, since the other individual is the one most likely to satisfy our social motive.

To what extent does the presence of other individuals affect a person's facial expressions? To find out, Fridlund (1991b) measured the facial expressions and emotional experiences of his participants while they were in the presence of a real or imaginary person. During the experiment, participants viewed videos of cute babies, a playing dog, a sea otter, or the routine of a stand-up comedian while alone, with an imaginary friend, or with a real friend. During viewing, Fridlund made recordings of the participants' zygomaticus muscle, which is the one responsible for smiling. In addition, participants also rated their degree of happiness after viewing a video.

According to the readout hypothesis, smile muscle activity should correspond with happiness ratings such that greater smile activity is associated with greater happiness ratings. For the behavioral ecology hypothesis, however, smile activity should correlate with the sociality of the condition and not necessarily with happiness ratings. The results supported the behavioral ecology hypothesis. Smile muscle activity varied according to the degree of sociality, while happiness ratings did not. Smile muscle activity was greatest when participants viewed the videos with a real friend, next when with an imaginary friend, and least when alone. Happiness ratings, however, did not vary with the sociality of the conditions. According to Fridlund (1991b), when with imaginary friends participants smile while looking at mental images of their imaginary friends doing the same thing. This image is unlikely to occur in the solitary participation condition, since no one else is sharing in a similar task. Thus, Fridlund feels that facial expressions are possible in isolation when a person responds to the mental image of another individual. Furthermore, these expressions are not in response to feelings of happiness, since those ratings were not different across the four conditions.

How did facial expressions gain their ability to motivate other individuals according to the behavioral ecology hypothesis? Is the pattern of the expression arbitrary or did it stem from another function? For example, a fearful face signals submission and so should ward off further assaults by an attacker. An angry face, however, signals attack and so the recipient of the expression might prefer a defense. The reason for these two different behaviors according to Marsh and coresearchers (2005) is that a fear expression resembles a babyish face while an anger expression resembles a mature face. Babyish faces trigger one type of behavior and mature faces another. For example, the ethologist Konrad Lorenz (1971) postulated that a baby face (large eyes, high forehead) has a tendency to elicit caregiving and

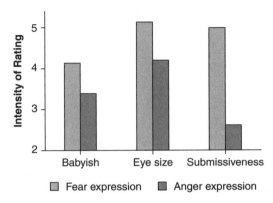

FIGURE 14.4 Fear/Anger Expressions Resemble Baby/Mature Faces. Fearful facial expressions resembled baby faces, had larger eyes, and showed greater submissiveness. Angry facial expressions resembled mature faces, had smaller eyes, and showed less submissiveness.

Source: Adapted from "Why Do Fear and Anger Look the Way They Do? Form and Social Function in Facial Expressions" by A. A. Marsh et al., 2005, *Personality and Social Psychology Bulletin, 31,* table 1, p. 77.

inhibit aggression in adults. Thus, if a fear expression resembles a baby face, then it should suppress further aggression on the part of an attacker. A mature face, however, is indicative of strength and dominance. Thus, if an anger expression resembles a mature face, then it should trigger escape or avoidance behavior when a person sees it.

In their research, Marsh and coresearchers (2005) had participants examine photographs of male and female faces that portrayed either fear or anger in order to determine if such faces had baby or mature features, respectively. The photos were rated with a 7-point scale on a variety of features, which included babyish/mature, eye size, and submissive/dominant (experiment 1). The results in Figure 14.4 show that indeed fear expressions were rated more babyish, with larger eyes and greater submissiveness. Rating of other features showed that fear compared to anger expression was also judged more dependent, feminine, honest, naive, and youthful. The researchers concluded that "something about the way the anger expression changes the facial features may make the face appear more mature, and the same may be true for the fear expressions and babyishness" (Marsh et al., 2005, p. 82). The emotion of fear implies submissiveness and so is associated with a babyish face indicative of submission. The emotion of anger, however, implies dominance and so is associated with a mature face that signals dominance (Marsh et al., 2005).

Display Rules for Facial Expressions. Is that smile real or fake? Are those tears real or fake? These questions imply that a person can shape an expression to serve his or her purpose. People have voluntary control over their facial muscles. Consequently, an expression may not be real if it does not match any feelings and instead is an attempt to manipulate others. Furthermore, there are **display rules** that govern the expressions that individuals must exhibit in public and need not be linked to emotional feelings (Ekman & Friesen, 1975; Matsumoto et al., 2005). According to Matsumoto and coresearchers (2005), "display rules are cognitive representations of social conventions about emotional displays" (p. 29). For example, do you know what expression to display when receiving a gift, when being reprimanded, and when angry with your boss or romantic partner?

TABLE 14.4   Displays from the *Display Rule Assessment Inventory*

Amplify:	Intensify or exaggerate the expression of your feelings
Not inhibit:	Express your feelings naturally
Deamplify:	Reduce the intensity of the expression of your feelings
Qualify:	Express your feelings but add an accompanying expression (e.g., smile)
Neutralize:	Show a neutral face not indicative of any emotional feeling
Mask:	Show a different expression than what you are feeling; cover up with a smile

Source: Adapted from: "Development and Validation of a Measure of Display Rule Knowledge: The Display Rule Assessment Inventory" by D. Matsumoto et al., 2005, *Emotion, 5,* p. 40.

> Complete versions of the *Display Rule Assessment Inventory* are available at http://www.davidmatsumoto.info/research.htm

Matsumoto and coresearchers (2005) have developed the *Display Rule Assessment Inventory* to measure the extent that people feel they should alter their facial expressions in the presence of family members, close friends, colleagues, and strangers in various situations. The *Inventory* describes six different facial management techniques, which are shown in Table 14.4. With the *not inhibit* procedure, individuals display facial expressions that match their emotional feelings. If you see an anger expression on her face, then she is angry with you. If you see a smile on his face, then he is happy to see you. The other procedures, however, are used by the individuals to alter their facial expressions independent of their emotional feelings. For example, a father might feel it is necessary to *amplify* his smile of appreciation when he receives a valentine card from his young son. However, a person might feel she should *deamplify* her expression of anger at a dining companion. Perhaps one feels he should use *mask* technique in order to hide the disappointment when a friend let him down. Finally, the boss reprimands a worker for making an error but feels it necessary to add a qualifying smile in order to indicate absence of anger.

Section Recap

According to the *expression-feeling link*, spontaneous facial expression is linked to the emotional feeling. The *efference hypothesis* holds that the emotion circuit in the brain connects to the facial muscles to generate the expression linked with the emotion. Facial expressions linked to emotion come from our evolutionary past. Spontaneous facial expressions are mostly innate. They occur very early in life, are present in blind and deaf children, and are influenced little by learning, although learning seems to fine-tune them. Based on the results of *emotion recognition* studies, facial expressions of emotion are universal and are recognized the world over. There is also an in-group advantage, which means we can more accurately recognize the facial expression of someone from our cultural group compared to a different group.

Emotions also stimulate facial expressions. The function of facial expression is to communicate a person's emotional feeling according to the *readout hypothesis*. A smile communicates happiness, and tears communicate sadness. Facial expressions can also signal a person's intent or social motive, according to the *behavioral ecology hypothesis*. A person smiles as a signal to maintain contact with another person, or a person blushes as appeasement for having violated a social norm and to repair any social damage. Nonemotional aspects of a situation also determine what facial expression an individual should display. These *display rules* are governed by social custom. For example, an individual smiles when receiving a gift even if the item is considered totally useless. Several factors interact in determining a person's facial expression. The internal emotional state, social motive or intent, and the presence of other individuals all contribute to what the face expresses.

The Motivating Function of Emotions

Emotions motivate behavior toward some designated end, which is the goal or aim of the emotion. This section examines how behaviors and thoughts are channeled in order to achieve the goals of various emotions.

Emotions as Motives for Behavior

If a stimulus is dangerous or disgusting, then wouldn't it be appropriate for the person to run away from danger or spit out the disagreeable product? And if a situation is beneficial, then shouldn't it be preserved? In each of these examples, emotion serves as a **motive for action** to induce the individual to deal specifically with the emotional event (Frijda, 1994). The person is in a state of *action readiness*, which is the impulse or urge to behave in a particular manner (Frijda, 1986, 2007). Some action tendencies in response to emotion are innate, as if they are already wired into the nervous system. Other action tendencies result from learning and occur only after some deliberation (Clark & Watson, 1994; Scherer, 1994).

Different emotions have different goals or aims. Some possible goals of basic emotions and the actions they motivate are summarized in Table 14.5 (Ellsworth & Smith, 1988; Frijda, 1994; Izard, 1993). Joy acts like a reward for achievement and accompanies consummatory behavior. For sadness, the event is appraised as an irrevocable or uncontrollable loss. The goal of sadness is to signal others for help when we cannot help ourselves. In fear, we appraise a stimulus as dangerous and harmful. The goal of fear is to motivate avoidance and escape behavior in order to reach safety. For anger, we appraise a situation or other person as blocking our goal or as detrimental to our well-being. The goal of anger is to motivate a person to remove the obstacle or person who is potentially harmful. The goal of disgust is to avoid becoming ill or contaminated. This is achieved by an active rejection of the repelling substance. Self-conscious emotions of shame, guilt, embarrassment, and pride serve as social motives for a person's interactions with others (Leary, 2007; Tangney et al., 2007). Shame is the result of a self-evaluation that focused on the self as a bad or unworthy person. Guilt is the negative evaluation of some misdeed. The goal of shame is to maintain the respect of others along with one's self-esteem. Shame motivates denying or escaping shame-inducing situations and avoiding and withdrawing from other individuals (Barrett & Campos, 1987). Guilt, however, motivates attempts to make amends, apologies, and in general undo the effects of one's misdeeds (Ellsworth & Smith, 1988; Tangney et al., 2007). Embarrassment results when a person violates a social norm and others derive a negative conclusion of that person (Leary, 2007). The goal of embarrassment is to promote appeasement through withdrawal, apologies, or explanations as the means of restoring harmonious social relations (Keltner & Anderson, 2000). In contrast, pride is a positive emotion that reinforces successful achievement and

TABLE 14.5 Goals of Emotions and the Actions They Motivate

Emotion	Goal	Action Tendency
Joy/happiness	To reward goal achievement To motivate consummatory behavior (eating, sex)[a] To maintain social interaction[b]	Any instrumental behavior achieving goals, leading to consummatory behavior, or maintaining interactions
Sadness	To seek help to make harm or loss easier to bear[c] To bring people together To scrutinize the cause of the sadness[b] To promote disengagement from the lost object/person[a]	Sad facial expression signals others to help;[c] behavioral and thinking activities slow down[b]
Fear	To motivate escape from danger[a,b] To focus attention on stimulus for danger[b,c]	Avoid, escape, freeze, depending on the stimulus and situation
Anger	To motivate to remove obstacle blocking goal[c] To discourage another's anger or aggression[a,b]	Actual removal of goal-blocking obstacle;[c] angry state discourages other's aggression[b]
Disgust	To maintain clean environment for survival[b] To keep person from harmful substances[b]	Nausea, vomiting, turning away from disgusting object
Shame	To maintain respect of others, restore self-esteem[f]	Escape, avoid situation and people[d]
Guilt	To undo effect of one's misdeeds[c,f]	Make amends, apologize[c,f]
Embarrassment	To restore harmonious social relationships[e]	Withdraw, apologize, explain[e]
Pride	To reinforce successful achievement of socially valued behaviors[g]	Act altruistically, treat others well[g]

[a]Frijda, 1994.
[b]Izard, 1993.
[c]Ellsworth and Smith, 1988.
[d]Barrett and Campos, 1987.
[e]Keltner and Anderson, 2000.
[f]Tangney et al., 2007.
[g]Tracy and Robins, 2007.

behaviors that are socially valued. Thus, pride motivates a person to act altruistically and to treat others well (Tracy & Robins, 2007).

Emotions as Motives for Cognitive Activity

As part of achieving their goal, emotions also motivate cognitive activity. The distinctive nature of an emotional feeling informs an individual how a situation was appraised. For example, feeling fear means the situation was appraised as dangerous, while feeling guilt means a person appraised her actions as wrong. In addition, as a **cognitive signaler,** an emotional feeling influences a person's future cognitive appraisal (Clore, 1994; Frijda, 1994, 2007). Emotion can bias the appraisal of a situation. For example, how would being happy or sad influence appraisal? To answer this question, Halberstadt and associates (1995) had participants listen to happy or sad music. While listening to the music at low volume, participants also heard a word, either *bridal/ bridle* or *banned/band*. These words are known as homophones, which means they sound the same but are spelled differently. If happy music causes a positive emotion, then is a person more likely to report hearing *bridal* than *bridle?* If sad music results in a negative emotion, will a person more likely hear *banned* instead of *band?* In other words, will a person's current emotional state alter the manner in which stimuli are appraised? There is some support for this idea. Participants who listened to sad music reported hearing significantly more sad words than did participants who listened to happy music. The type of music did not affect the hearing of happy words.

The happy or sad music may simply have put participants in positive or negative moods. Thus, rather than the specific emotion, it is a person's general mood that influences appraisal and judgment. However, according to Lerner and Keltner's (2000) **appraisal tendency hypothesis,** each emotion has a unique influence on people's judgments. For example, Lerner and Keltner (2001) induced feelings of anger or fear in their participants by having them describe events that made them most angry or most fearful. Next, participants rated hypothetical situations for the extent they would feel in control and for the extent such situations were predictable. Even though both anger and fear are negative emotions, they affected the ratings differently. Angered participants rated themselves as having more personal control and felt the situations were more predictable than fearful participants did.

According to the appraisal tendency hypothesis, the unique feel of an emotion also can affect a person's judgments about unrelated events. In a field experiment, Lerner and coresearchers (2003) had 973 respondents reply to e-mail messages that were designed to induce either fear or anger. Following the inducement, participants were asked to evaluate the likelihood of future risks, such as another terrorist attack on the United States or on themselves. Risk estimates depended on the emotion that had been induced. Angered respondents rated the likelihood of these risks to be lower than frightened respondents did. The respondents were also asked to rate their level of support for the following two government policies: (1) "Deport foreigners in the U.S. who lack valid visas" or (2) "Strengthen ties with countries in the Muslim world." The results presented in Figure 14.5 show that when angered, respondents were more likely to retaliate—that is, more in favor of deporting foreigners who lacked visas. However, when afraid, respondents were more likely to be conciliatory—that is, more in favor of trying to establish better relations with Muslim countries. In addition, feelings of anger that resulted from the actual September 11th terrorist attacks also resulted in greater endorsement of the policy to deport foreigners and less endorsement of strengthening ties with the Muslim world.

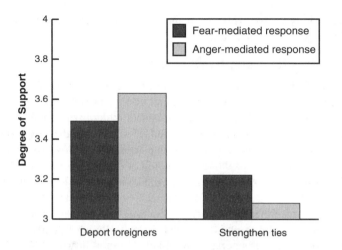

FIGURE 14.5   Emotions and Policy Support. The policy to deport "foreigners who lack a valid visa" received greater support from participants in whom anger had been induced. The policy to "strengthen ties with countries in the Muslim world" received greater support from participants in whom fear had been induced. Participants rated the policies on the following scale: 1 = Strongly opposed to 4 = Strongly support.

Source: Adapted from "Effects of Fear and Anger on Perceived Risks of Terrorism: A National Field Experiment" by J. S. Lerner et al., 2003, *Psychological Science, 14,* table 4, p. 149.

Section Recap

Emotions serve as *motives for action* that have either evolved or were learned in order to achieve the goal of the emotion. Each emotion has a different goal or aim, which is to alter a person's relationship with the emotion-inducing situation. For instance, fear motivates running away in order to reach safety while anger motivates asserting oneself in order to unblock a goal. Self-conscious emotions motivate behavior to restore the goal of group harmony. Emotional feelings inform the individual how a situation has been appraised. For example, fear means danger and sadness means a loss. An emotion also serves as a *cognitive signaler* by influencing the cognitive system in appraisal of the changing situation. According to the *appraisal tendency hypothesis*, a specific emotion influences cognitive judgments in a manner congruent with the emotion's affective feeling.

Motivational Nature of Positive Emotions

Most emotions are negative or unpleasant, which gives them the capacity to serve as negative reinforcers. Emotion-motivated behavior reduces the intensity of a negative emotion and hence its unpleasantness. For example, escape reduces fear, turning away lessens disgust, and an apology relieves guilt. When the intensity of an unpleasant emotion recedes, it ceases to motivate behavior.

Aim of Positive Emotions

Pleasant emotions, in contrast, serve as positive reinforcers, since they maintain the behavior that produced them. Pleasant emotions also act like positive incentives since individuals strive to attain those experiences. The motivational ability of positive emotions is examined in this section.

Positive Emotions Terminate Negative Emotions. Do people schedule an appointment with a psychotherapist because they are too happy? Not likely. When they are depressed? Probably. In other words, the relation between emotion and behavior depends on the valence of the emotion. Positive emotions do not often instigate instrumental behavior. No action readiness, adjustment, or correction is required, since there are no emergencies to meet or unpleasant negative feelings to alleviate. Instead, behavior occurs to arouse a positive emotion rather than to alleviate an emotion. For instance, people might see a comedy to bring about a feeling of amusement or they might purchase birthday gifts for friends to bring about a feeling of pleasure.

One function of positive emotions, according to Levenson (1994), might be to restore the person to a state of physiological calmness, which would happen more rapidly than if negative emotions ran their course. This effect has been referred to as the **undoing hypothesis**—that is, a positive emotion undoes the effect of a negative emotion (Fredrickson, 2001; Fredrickson et al., 2000). For example, amusement might restore calmness more rapidly following fear or anger than would letting fear or anger subside gradually. In a supporting experiment, Fredrickson and coresearchers (2000) induced anxiety in their participants by putting them under time pressure to prepare a speech on why they are good friends. This task increased anxiety as indicated by cardiovascular reactivity, such as increased heart rate and blood pressure. Following this task, different groups were shown a neutral film clip or one designed either to induce amusement or contentment. The time it took cardiovascular activity to return to normal established the effectiveness of each film in reducing anxiety. Both the amusement and contentment films reduced anxiety more quickly than the neutral film. Fredrickson and coresearchers concluded that whereas negative emotions increase cardiovascular activity in preparation for emergency responses, positive emotions undo these effects—that is, they reduce preparedness of the emergency response.

Positive Emotions Expand Thoughts. Positive emotions also have an expanding effect on cognitive activity. According to Fredrickson's (1998, 2001) **broaden-and-build theory,** positive emotions are able to enlarge the availability of thought-action links and to broaden a person's scope of attention. In one experiment (experiment 2), Fredrickson and Branigan (2005) showed their participants video clips that evoked one of two positive emotions (amusement or contentment) and one of two negative emotions (anger or anxiety). A neutral video served as a baseline condition against which to compare the effects of the positive and negative emotions. Following the video, participants were asked to feel the emotion evoked by the video and to strongly imagine being in a situation in which such an emotion would occur. Then participants were instructed that, "Given this feeling please *list* all the things you would like to do *right now*" (p. 320). Does the number of thought-action responses participants provide depend on the valence of their emotions? Examples of thought-action responses include reading or resting, working, exercising, being outside, playing, socializing, visiting, and experiencing positive feelings. Participants generated more thought-action responses in the two positive-emotion conditions and generated fewer in the two negative-emotion conditions in comparison to the neutral condition. Thus, positive emotions broaden and negative emotions narrow the range of thought-action urges.

Subjective Well-Being

Whether reasoning on the basis of hedonism, utility, or positive incentives, people behave in order to attain pleasant affect. For example, a person may work hard for a sense of personal satisfaction, for happiness from a pay raise, or for pride from a job well done. This section examines the neutral point from which positive affect begins and examines the consequences of continuously seeking positive experiences.

Every individual is assumed to have a baseline level of emotional valence, which resembles a set point. It is the level of unhappiness or happiness to which people consistently return—that is, their *set point level of happiness*. Some experiences reduce happiness and others increase happiness. However, eventually people return to their normal level. What is happiness? **Subjective well-being** or happiness is a private experience that an individual strives to bring into consciousness while its opposite or unhappiness is the feeling to be driven out of consciousness. To be happy means that a person is highly satisfied with life and experiences positive affect (glad, cheerful) more frequently than negative affect (anxious, gloomy) (Lyubomirsky et al., 2005). How happy are you at the moment? The *Subjective Happiness Scale* in Table 14.6 is an operational definition of happiness. It is the procedure used to measure how happy a person is currently (Lyubomirsky & Lepper, 1999). Scales that measure happiness are important because they can be used to show what factors determine one's level of happiness and how happiness relates to various behaviors.

➤ Ed Diener's web site provides more information on subjective well-being as well as links to other well-being web sites at http://www.psych.uiuc.edu/~ediener

TABLE 14.6   Subjective Happiness Scale

Instructions to participants: For each of the following statements and/or questions, please circle the point on the scale that you feel is most appropriate in describing you:

1. In general, I consider myself:
    not a very happy person 1   2   3   4   5   6   7 a very happy person

2. Compared to most of my peers, I consider myself:
    less happy 1   2   3   4   5   6   7 more happy

3. Some people are generally very happy. They enjoy life regardless of what is going on, getting the most out of everything. To what extent does this characterization describe you?
    not at all 1   2   3   4   5   6   7 a great deal

4. Some people are generally not very happy. Although they are not depressed, they never seem as happy as they might be. To what extent does this characterization describe you?
    not at all 1   2   3   4   5   6   7 a great deal

Note: To score, first reverse score item 4, which means change 1 to 7, 2 to 6, 3 to 5, 5 to 3, 6 to 2, and 7 to 1. Then sum all of the items. Your score is the measure of your level of happiness with higher scores indicating greater levels. The mean happiness scores for 2,124 university students from eight different American campuses ranged from 4.63 (SD = 1.72) to 5.07 (SD = 1.14).

Source: Springer and *Social Indicators Research, 46,* 1999, p. 151, "A Measure of Subjective Happiness: Preliminary Reliability and Construct Validation," by S. Lyubomirsky and H. S. Lepper, Appendix. With kind permission from Springer Science and Business Media.

Set Point of Happiness.   Psychologists have discovered three factors that determine people's habitual level of unhappiness or happiness (Lyubomirsky et al., 2005). First, the happiness set point is genetically determined. For example, Lykken and Tellegen (1996) report that identical twins are more alike than fraternal twins in well-being or happiness even when identical twins have been raised by different families. Furthermore, these consistencies remain in effect even when measured 10 years apart. Weiss and coresearchers (2008) also found that identical twins were more alike than fraternal twins in subjective well-being. A second factor is that happiness has been linked to some of the big-five personality traits. The traits of neuroticism, extraversion, and agreeableness are definitely associated with happiness (Figure 9.5). The happiest students were those ranked low in neuroticism, high in extraversion, and high in agreeableness (Diener & Seligman, 2002). Weiss and coresearchers (2008) confirmed these findings, especially for extraversion and neuroticism. Well-being correlated positively with extraversion and negatively with neuroticism.

A third factor is the phenomenon that people always seem to return to their set point level of happiness. Events that increase or decrease happiness only have a temporary effect, according to the concept of the **hedonic treadmill.** People return to their set point level of happiness because they habituate to changes in their life circumstances (Brickman & Campbell, 1971). Lyubomirsky and coresearchers (2005) liken the hedonic treadmill to walking up a down-escalator. Walking up resembles trying to improve life's circumstances in order to increase happiness while the descent of the escalator shows that people return to their set point level. However, as Diener and coresearchers (2006) point out, a person's habitual level of happiness is not zero as a neutral point would suggest but is actually a bit higher. Most people are at least a little bit happy. This observation is supported by the happiness norms provided with the *Subjective Happiness Scale* (Table 14.6). Means on this seven-point scale from eight campuses are above 4—that is, above the midpoint of happiness. Furthermore, a return to set point happiness may not always occur. Diener and coresearchers (2006) observe that some negative life events have lasting impacts so that people do not return to their set point. For example, using data from longitudinal surveys, Lucas (2007) found that people do not return to their initial level of life satisfaction after they experience divorce, widowhood, unemployment, or disability even up to seven years after the event.

Subjective Well-Being Can Motivate Behavior.   Psychologists assume that happiness motivates success or leads to successful outcomes. However, does happiness cause success or does success cause happiness? Does hard work produce an *A* grade, which then causes happiness? Or does happiness motivate hard work, which results in the *A* grade? One way out of this quandary is to examine longitudinal studies in which happiness existed well before the occurrence of any behavior that could influence it (Lyubomirsky et al., 2005). To illustrate by analogy, foot size determines the size of shoe a person buys, not the reverse. A person's foot size existed well before she bought a pair of shoes. Success in marriage is a representative finding of the relationship between initial subjective well-being and subsequent behavior. Harker and Keltner (2001) availed themselves of data from a 30-year longitudinal study that involved female university graduates. The researchers measured the extent positive emotions were portrayed in college yearbook pictures of women when they were about 21 years old. At ages 27, 41, and 52 the women were asked a series of questions, which included ones about their marital happiness. The picture indicator of happiness was

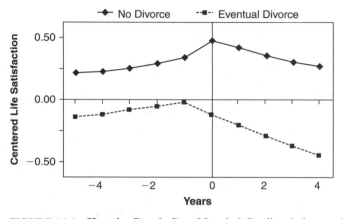

FIGURE 14.6   Happier People Stay Married. Predicted changes in life satisfaction in the years before and after marriage for those respondents who eventually divorced and those who did not. Satisfaction scores are centered. The vertical line (0 years) indicates the year of marriage.

Source: From "Time Does Not Heal All Wounds" by R. E. Lucas, 2005, *Psychological Science, 16,* figure 2, p. 948. Copyright by Blackwell Publishing.

associated with a greater likelihood of being married at age 27, less likelihood of remaining single in mid-adulthood, and greater marital satisfaction at age 52. In other words, happier women were a bit more successful at marriage than unhappier women.

Other longitudinal data also show that prior happiness contributes to marital satisfaction. On a scale from 1 to 10, how satisfied are you with your life? Does this measure of subjective well-being relate to the likelihood of a successful marriage? To answer this question, Lucas (2005, 2007) examined data from a long-term longitudinal study conducted in Germany. Several of his interesting findings are presented in Figure 14.6. First, the mean satisfaction score for each year is set at zero. Thus, people above the 0.00 line are happier than average while those below are less happy than average. Second, notice that the level of happiness prior to marriage predicts marital success. Happier people are more likely to remain married than unhappier people are. Third, happier people experienced a small rise in happiness from marriage while unhappier people did not.

A second type of evidence for the effects of happiness on motivation comes from experiments. Different degrees of happiness are created in different groups in order to see the effects on subsequent behavior. In general, based on experimental research, increases in happiness cause increases in achievement behavior (Lyubomirsky et al., 2005). In one illustrative experiment by Erez and Isen (2002), a small increase in happiness was created in the experimental group by giving its members a bag of candy prior to the start of the experiment. The control group was not given any candy at that time but received candy after the experiment concluded. The candy procedure resulted in greater positive affect in the experimental group than in the control group as measured by the PANAS (Chapter 13). An anagram-solving task was used to measure three effects of happiness: number of anagrams solved, persistence at solving, and future motivational interest in the task. The measure of motivation involved asking participants the extent to which they would look forward to taking the same anagram-solving test in the future. Participants were provided 25 minutes to solve 10 anagrams although only six of them had a solution. The results showed that the positive affect from the candy had a facilitative effect. The experimental group solved more anagrams and persisted longer than the control group did. In addition, the experimental group reported a higher level of future motivation for solving anagrams.

Section Recap

In contrast to unpleasant emotions, pleasant emotions act like positive incentives in that a person behaves to attain pleasant affect. According to the *undoing hypothesis*, positive emotions reduce (undo) more quickly the physiological reactivity that is associated with negative emotions. According to *broaden-and-build theory*, positive emotions increase a person's available repertoire of thought-action links and enhance the scope of attention. *Subjective well-being* or happiness means a person experiences positive affect more than negative affect and is satisfied with life. A person's set point of happiness refers to her habitual level of happiness or unhappiness. The set point depends on a person's genetic makeup, level of extraversion, neuroticism, and agreeableness. Happiness has a stable set point according to the *hedonic treadmill*. Decreases or increases in happiness are temporary, since people habituate to changes in their circumstances. Greater happiness seems to produce positive developments in life in those cases where happiness has existed beforehand; for example, happier people prior to marriage are less likely to divorce. However, major negative life changes like divorce and unemployment can lower one's level of happiness for many years. Experimentally created positive affect increases motivated behavior, such as more success and persistence in an anagram-solving task.

ACTIVITIES

1. Have you ever experienced a like or dislike for someone but were unable to give the reason? Think about what factors may have been involved. Do you think you can consciously change your dislike to like? If so, how could this be accomplished? Along the same line, are people's prejudices of others based on things of which they are not aware? Does this lack of awareness affect the difficulty of trying to reduce people's prejudices?

2. When watching an emotional scene in a movie or on television, pay close attention to the facial expressions of the actors. Are they experiencing the emotion portrayed on their faces, or is it acting without emotion?

3. When you smile in greeting a friend, is it because you are happy to see her, or is it simply a greeting without any feeling?

4. What governs your facial expressions? Is it your felt emotions, your social motives, the person you are with, or display rules in general?

5. Can you think of other goals that emotions serve in addition to the ones listed in Table 14.5?

6. According to the appraisal tendency hypothesis, emotions can influence a person's judgments and decisions. Has this ever happened to you? Have you made judgments, decisions, or commitments during an intense emotion that you would not have made in the absence of the emotion? When is it best to make a judgment or decision: in the presence or absence of an emotional feeling? Why?

REFERENCES

Ackerman, D. S., & Gross, B. L. (2005). My instructor made me do it: Task characteristics of procrastination. *Journal of Marketing Education, 27,* 5–13.

Adams, J., & Kirby, R. J. (2002). Excessive exercise as an addiction: A review. *Addiction Research and Theory, 10,* 415–437.

Adolphs, R., Damasio, H., Tranel, D., Cooper, G., & Damasio, A. R. (2000). A role for somatosensory cortices in the visual recognition of emotion as revealed by three-dimensional lesion mapping. *The Journal of Neuroscience, 20,* 2683–2690.

Alcock, J. (1987). Ardent adaptationism. *Natural History, 4,* 5.

Allison, J. (1993). Response deprivation, reinforcement, and economics. *Journal of the Experimental Analysis of Behavior, 60,* 129–140.

Allport, G. W. (1937a). The functional autonomy of motives. *American Journal of Psychology, 50,* 141–156.

Allport, G. W. (1937b). *Personality: A psychological interpretation.* New York: Holt.

Allport, G. W. (1966). Traits revisited. *American Psychologist, 21,* 1–10.

Allred, K. D., & Smith, T. W. (1989). The hardy personality: Cognitive and physiological responses to evaluative threat. *Journal of Personality and Social Psychology, 56,* 257–266.

Alvarado, N. (1998). A reconsideration of the structure of the emotion lexicon. *Motivation and Emotion, 22,* 329–344.

Amabile, T. M. (1989). *Growing up creative: Nurturing a lifetime of creativity.* New York: Crown.

Amabile, T. M., Hill, K. G., Hennessey, B. A., & Tighe, E. M. (1994). The Work Preference Inventory: Assessing intrinsic and extrinsic motivational orientations. *Journal of Personality and Social Psychology, 66,* 950–967.

Amabile, T. M., Hill, K. G., Hennessey, B. A., & Tighe, E. M. (1995). The Work Preference Inventory: Assessing intrinsic and extrinsic motivational orientations: Correction. *Journal of Personality and Social Psychology, 68,* 580.

American Psychiatric Association (APA). (2000). *Diagnostic and statistical manual of mental disorders* (4th ed., text rev.). Washington, DC: American Psychiatric Association.

Anderson, C. A., Lindsay, J. J., & Bushman, B. J. (1999). Research in the psychological laboratory: Truth or triviality. *Current Directions in Psychological Science, 8,* 3–9.

Andreassi, J. L. (1989). *Psychophysiology: Human behavior and physiological response* (2nd ed.). Hillsdale, NJ: Lawrence Erlbaum.

Appleton, K. M., Gentry, R. C., & Shepherd, R. (2006). Evidence of a role for conditioning in the development of liking for flavours in humans in everyday life. *Physiology & Behavior, 87,* 478–486.

Argyle, M., & Lu, L. (1990). The happiness of extraverts. *Personality and Individual Differences, 11,* 1011–1017.

Arkes, H. R., & Garske, J. P. (1977). *Psychological theories of motivation.* Monterey: Brooks/Cole.

Arkes, H. R., & Hammond, K. R. (1986). General introduction. In H. R. Arkes & K. R. Hammond (Eds.), *Judgment and decision making: An interdisciplinary reader* (pp. 1–11). Cambridge: Cambridge University Press.

Arnold, M. B. (1960). *Emotion and personality: Vol. I. Psychological aspects.* New York: Columbia University Press.

Ashcraft, M. H., & Kirk, E. P. (2001). The relationship among working memory, math anxiety, and performance. *Journal of Experimental Psychology: General, 120,* 224–237.

Atkinson, J. W. (1957/1983). Motivational determinants of risk-taking behavior. In J. Atkinson (Ed.), *Personality, motivation, and action: Selected papers* (pp. 101–119). New York: Praeger.

Atkinson, J. W. (1958/1983). Towards experimental analysis of human motivation in terms of motives, expectancies, and incentives. In J. W. Atkinson (Ed.), *Personality, motivation, and action: Selected papers* (pp. 81–97). New York: Praeger.

Atkinson, J. W. (1974). The mainspring of achievement-oriented activity. In J. W. Atkinson & J. O. Raynor (Eds.), *Personality, motivation, and achievement* (pp. 13–41). Washington, DC: Hemisphere.

Atkinson, J. W., & Birch, D. (1970). *The dynamics of action.* New York: Wiley.

Atkinson, J. W., & Litwin, G. W. (1960). Achievement motive and test anxiety conceived as motive to approach success and motive to avoid failure. *Journal of Abnormal and Social Psychology, 60,* 52–63.

Atkinson, J. W., & Walker, E. L. (1956). The affiliation motive and perceptual sensitivity to faces. *Journal of Abnormal and Social Psychology, 53,* 38–41.

Ax, A. F. (1953). The physiological differentiation between fear and anger in humans. *Psychosomatic Medicine, 15,* 433–442.

Bacon, F. (1627/1974). Sylva sylvarum. In S. Diamond (Ed.), *The roots of psychology* (pp. 523–525). New York: Basic Books.

Badia, P., Culbertson, S. A., & Harsh, J. (1974). Relative aversiveness of signaled vs. unsignaled avoidable and escapable shock situations in humans. *Journal of Comparative and Physiological Psychology, 87,* 338–346.

Badia, P., Harsh, J., & Abbott, B. (1979). Choosing between predictable and unpredictable shock conditions: Data and theory. *Psychological Bulletin, 86,* 1107–1131.

Baile, C. A., Della-Fera, M. A., & Martin, R. J. (2000). Regulation of metabolism and body fat mass by leptin. *Annual Review of Nutrition, 20,* 105–127.

Baker, R. R., & Bellis, M. A. (1993). Human sperm competition: Ejaculate manipulation by females and a function for the female orgasm. *Animal Behaviour, 46,* 887–909.

Baker, T. B., Piper, M. E., McCarthy, D. E., Majeskie, M. R., & Fiore, M. C. (2004). Addiction motivation reformulated: An affective processing model of negative reinforcement. *Psychological Review, 111,* 33–51.

Ball, S. A. (2005). Personality traits, problems, and disorders: Clinical applications to substance use disorders. *Journal of Research in Personality, 39,* 84–102.

Bandura, A. (1977). Self-efficacy: Toward a unity theory of behavioral change. *Psychological Review, 84,* 191–215.

Bandura, A. (1991). Self-regulation of motivation through anticipatory and self-reactive mechanisms. In R. Dienstbier (Series Ed.) & R. Dienstbier (Vol. Ed.), *Nebraska symposium on motivation: Vol. 38. Perspectives on motivation* (pp. 69–164). Lincoln: University of Nebraska Press.

Bandura, A. (1997). *Self-efficacy: The exercise of control.* New York: Freeman.

Bandura, A. (2006). Toward a psychology of human agency. *Perspectives on Psychological Science, 1,* 164–180.

Bandura, A., & Cervone, D. (1983). Self-evaluative and self-efficacy mechanisms governing the motivational effects of goal systems. *Journal of Personality and Social Psychology, 45,* 1017–1028.

Bandura, A., & Cervone, D. (1986). Differential engagement of self-reactive influences in cognitive motivation. *Organizational Behavior and Human Decision Processes, 38,* 92–113.

Bargh, J. A. (1990). Auto-motives: Preconscious determinants of social interaction. In E. T. Higgins & R. J. Sorrentino (Eds.), *Handbook of motivation and cognition* (Vol. 2, pp. 93–111). New York: Guilford Press.

Bargh, J. A., & Barndollar, K. (1996). Automaticity in action: The unconscious as repository of chronic goals and motives. In P. M. Gollwitzer & J. A. Bargh (Eds.), *The psychology of action: Linking motivation and cognition to behavior* (pp. 457–481). New York: Guilford Press.

Bargh, J. A., & Chartrand, T. L. (1999). The unbearable automaticity of being. *American Psychologist, 54,* 462–479.

Bargh, J. A., Chen, M., & Burrows, L. (1996). Automaticity of social behavior: Directed effect of trait construct and stereotypic activation on action. *Journal of Personality and Social Psychology, 71,* 230–244.

Bargh, J. A., Gollwitzer, P. M., Lee-Chai, A., Barndollar, K., & Trötschel, R. (2001). The automated will: Nonconscious activation and pursuit of behavioral goals. *Journal of Personality and Social Psychology, 81,* 1014–1027.

Bargh, J. A., & Williams, E. L. (2006). The automaticity of social life. *Current Directions in Psychological Science, 15,* 1–4.

Barnes, V., Schneider, R., Alexander, C., & Staggers, F. (1997). Stress, stress reduction, and hypertension in African Americans: An updated review. *Journal of the National Medical Association, 89,* 464–476.

Barrett, K. C., & Campos, J. J. (1987). Perspectives on emotional development II: A functionalist approach to emotions. In J. D. Osofsky (Ed.), *Handbook of infant development* (pp. 555–578). New York: Wiley.

Barrett, L. F. (2006). Are emotions natural kinds? *Perspectives on Psychological Science, 1,* 28–58.

Barrett, L. F., Mesquita, B., Ochsner, K. N., & Gross, J. J. (2007). The experience of emotion. *Annual Review of Psychology, 58,* 373–403.

Barrett, L. F., & Wager, T. D. (2006). The structure of emotion: Evidence from neuroimaging studies. *Current Directions in Psychological Science, 15,* 79–83.

Bartlett, D. L. (1996). Physiological responses to music and sound stimuli. In D. A. Hodges (Ed.), *Handbook of music psychology* (pp. 343–385). San Antonio: IMR Press.

Baum, A. & Posluszny, D. M. (1999). Health psychology: Mapping biobehavioral contributions to health and illness. *Annual Review of Psychology, 50,* 137–163.

Baumann, S. B., & Sayette, M. A. (2006). Smoking cues in a virtual world provoke craving in cigarette smokers. *Psychology of Addictive Behaviors, 20,* 484–489.

Baumeister, R. F. (1998). The self. In D. T. Gilbert, S. T. Fiske, & G. Lindzey (Eds.), *The handbook of social psychology* (Vol. II, pp. 680–740). Boston: McGraw-Hill.

Baumeister, R. F., Bratslavsky, E., Muraven, M., & Tice, D. M. (1998). Ego depletion: Is the active self a limited resource? *Journal of Personality and Social Psychology, 74,* 1252–1265.

Beach, L. R. (1990). *Image theory: Decision making in personal and organizational contexts.* Chichester: Wiley.

Beauchamp, G. K., Cowart, B. J., & Moran, M. (1986). Developmental changes in salt acceptability in human infants. *Developmental Psychobiology, 19,* 17–25.

Becker, L. J. (1978). Joint effect of feedback and goal setting on performance: A field study of residential energy conservation. *Journal of Applied Psychology, 63,* 428–433.

Beebe-Center, J. G. (1932/1965). *The psychology of pleasantness and unpleasantness.* New York: Van Nostrand.

Begley, C. E. (1991). Government should strengthen regulation in the weight loss industry. *Journal of the American Dietetic Association, 91,* 1255.

Benjamini, E., Sunshine, G., & Leskowitz, S. (1996). *Immunology: A short course* (3rd ed.). New York: Wiley-Liss.

Bentham, J. (1789/1970). *An introduction to the principles of morals and legislation* (J. H. Burns & H. L. A. Hart, Eds.). London: Athlone Press.

Bergstrom, J., Hermansen, L., Hultman, E., & Saltin, B. (1967). Diet, muscle glycogen and physical performance. *Acta Physiologica Scandinavica, 71,* 140–150.

Berkowitz, L., & Harmon-Jones, E. (2004). Toward an understanding of the determinants of anger. *Emotion, 4,* 107–130.

Berlyne, D. E. (1960). *Conflict, arousal, and curiosity.* New York: McGraw-Hill.

Berlyne, D. E. (1970). Novelty, complexity and hedonic value. *Perception and Psychophysics, 8,* 279–286.

Bernard, C. (1878/1961). *An introduction to the study of experimental medicine* (H. C. Green, Trans.). New York: Collier Books.

Bernat, E., Patrick, C. J., Benning, S. D., & Tellegen, A. (2006). Effects of picture content and intensity on affective physiological response. *Psychophysiology, 43,* 93–103.

Bernstein, I. L. (1978). Learned taste aversions in children receiving chemotherapy. *Science, 200,* 1302–1303.

Berthoz, S., Blair, R. J. R., Le Clec'h, G., & Martinot, J. L. (2002). Emotions: From neuropsychology to functional imaging. *International Journal of Psychology, 37,* 193–203.

Bickel, W. K., & Madden, G. J. (1999). The behavioral economics of smoking. In F. J. Chaloupka, M. Grossman, W. K. Bickel, & H. Saffer (Eds.), *The economic analysis of substance use and abuse* (pp. 31–61). Chicago: University of Chicago Press.

Biner, P. M., & Hua, D. M. (1995). Determinants of the magnitude of goal valence: The interactive effects of need, instrumentality, and the difficulty of goal attainment. *Basic and Applied Social Psychology, 16,* 53–74.

Biner, P. M., Huffman, M. L., Curran, M. A., & Long, K. L. (1998). Illusory control as a function of motivation for a specific outcome in a chance-based situation. *Motivation and Emotion, 22,* 277–291.

Birch, L. L. (1992). Children's preferences for high-fat foods. *Nutrition Reviews, 50,* 249–255.

Birch, L. L. (1999). Development of food preferences. *Annual Review of Nutrition, 19,* 41–62.

Birch, L. L., & Marlin, D. W. (1982). I don't like it; I never tried it: Effect of exposure on two-year-old children's food preferences. *Appetite, 3,* 353–360.

Black, A. H. (1965). Cardiac conditioning in curarized dogs: The relationship between heart rate and skeletal behaviour. In W. F. Prokasy (Ed.), *Classical conditioning: A symposium* (pp. 20–47). New York: Appleton-Century-Crofts.

Black, P. H. (1995). Psychoneuroimmunology: Brain and immunity. *Scientific American: Science & Medicine, 2,* 16–25.

Blair, J., Gold, R. S., & Klein, J. P. (1981). Life events and burnout. *Journal of Psychology, 108,* 219–226.

Blanchard, C. M., Rodgers, W. M., Courneya, K. S., & Spence, J. C. (2002). Moderators of the exercise/feeling-state relationship: The influence of self-efficacy, baseline, and in-task feeling states at moderate- and high-intensity exercise. *Journal of Applied Social Psychology, 32,* 1379–1395.

Blass, E. M., & Hall, W. G. (1976). Drinking termination: Interactions among hydrational, orogastric, and behavioral controls in rats. *Psychological Review, 83,* 356–374.

Blum, K., Braverman, E. R., Holder, J. M., Lubar, J. F., Monastra, V. J., Miller, D., Lubar, J. O., Chen, T. J. H., & Comings, D. E. (2000). Reward deficiency syndrome: A biogenetic model for the diagnosis and treatment of impulsive, addictive, and compulsive behaviors. *Journal of Psychoactive Drugs, 32* (supplement), 1–68.

Blum, K., Cull, J. G., Braverman, E. R., & Comings, D. E. (1996). Reward deficiency syndrome. *American Scientist, 84,* 132–145.

Bogg, T., & Roberts, B. W. (2004). Conscientiousness and health-related behaviors: A meta-analysis of the leading behavioral contributors to mortality. *Psychological Bulletin, 130,* 887–919.

Bohn, M. J., Krahn, D. D., & Staehler, B. A. (1995). Development and initial validation of a measure of drinking urges in abstinent alcoholics. *Alcoholism: Clinical and Experimental Research, 19,* 600–606.

Bolles, R. C. (1975). *Theory of motivation* (2nd ed.). New York: Harper & Row.

Boren, J. J. (1961). Resistance to extinction as a function of the fixed ratio. *Journal of Experimental Psychology, 61,* 304–308.

Boring, E. G. (1965). On the subjectivity of important historical dates: Leipzig 1879. *Journal of the History of the Behavioral Sciences, 1,* 1–9.

Bornstein, R. F. (1989). Exposure and affect: Overview and meta-analysis of research, 1968–1987. *Psychological Bulletin, 106,* 265–289.

Bornstein, R. F., Leone, D. R., & Galley, D. J. (1987). The generalizability of subliminal mere exposure effects: Influence of stimuli perceived without awareness of social behavior. *Journal of Personality and Social Psychology, 53,* 1070–1079.

Bouchard, Jr., T. J., & Loehlin, J. C. (2001). Genes, evolution, and personality. *Behavior Genetics, 31,* 243–273.

Bradley, M. M., Zack, J., & Lang, P. J. (1994). Cries, screams, and shouts of joy: Affective responses to environmental sounds. *Psychophysiology, 31,* Suppl., 29.

Brady, K. T., Back, S. E., & Coffey, S. F. (2004). Substance abuse and posttraumatic stress disorder. *Current Directions in Psychological Science, 13,* 206–209.

Brehm, J. W., & Self, E. A. (1989). The intensity of motivation. *Annual Review of Psychology, 40,* 109–131.

Breugelmann, G. L. (1989). Body temperature regulation. In H. D. Patton, A. F. Fuchs, B. Hille, A. M. Scher, & R. Steiner (Eds.), *Textbook of physiology: Circulation, respiration, body fluids, metabolism, and endocrinology* (Vol. 2, pp. 1584–1596). Philadelphia: W. B. Saunders.

Brickman, P., & Campbell, D. T. (1971). Hedonic relativism and planning the good society. In M. H. Appley (Ed.)., *Adaption level theory* (pp. 287–302). New York: Academic Press.

Briers, B., Pandelaere, M., Dewitte, S., & Warlop, L. (2006). Hungry for money: The desire for caloric resources increases the desire for financial resources and vice versa. *Psychological Science, 17,* 939–943.

Brown, D. E. (1991). *Human universals.* Philadelphia: Temple University Press.

Brown, J. S. (1961). *The motivation of behavior.* New York: McGraw-Hill.

Brown, R., & Herrnstein, R. J. (1975). *Psychology.* Boston: Little, Brown.

Brozek, J., Guetzkow, H., & Baldwin, M. V. (1951). A quantitative study of perception and association in experimental semistarvation. *Journal of Personality, 19,* 245–264.

Bruce, D. G., Storlien, L. H., Furler, S. M., & Chisholm, D. J. (1987). Cephalic phase metabolic responses in normal weight adults. *Metabolism, 36,* 721–725.

Bruch, H. (1988). *Conversation with anorexics* (D. Czyzewski & M. A. Suhr, Eds.). New York: Basic Books.

Brunstrom, J. M., & Mitchell, G. L. (2007). Flavor-nutrient learning in restrained and unrestrained eaters. *Physiology & Behavior, 90,* 133–141.

Buck, R. (1984). *The communication of emotion.* New York: Guilford Press.

Buck, R. (1985). Prime theory: An integrated view of motivation and emotion. *Psychological Review, 92*, 389–413.

Buck, R. (1988). *Human motivation and emotion* (2nd ed.). New York: Wiley.

Buck, R. (1991). Social factors in facial display and communication: A reply to Chovil and others. *Journal of Nonverbal Behavior, 15*, 155–161.

Buck, R. (1994). Social and emotional functions in facial expression and communication: The readout hypothesis. *Biological Psychology, 38*, 95–115.

Bullock, W. A., & Gilliland, K. (1993). Eysenck's arousal theory of introversion-extraversion: A converging measures investigation. *Journal of Personality and Social Psychology, 64*, 113–123.

Burke, M. J., & Gridley, M. C. (1990). Musical preferences as a function of stimulus complexity and listeners' sophistication. *Perceptual and Motor Skills, 71*, 687–690.

Burros, M. (1991, March 13). Weighing in on the nutrition scale. *New York Times*, p. L D9.

Buss, D. M. (1987). Selection, evocation, and manipulation. *Journal of Personality and Social Psychology, 53*, 1214–1221.

Buss, D. M. (1989). Sex differences in human mate preferences: Evolutionary hypotheses tested in 37 cultures. *Behavioral and Brain Sciences, 12*, 1–49.

Buss, D. M. (1992). Manipulation in close relationships: Five personality factors in interactional context. *Journal of Personality, 60*, 479–499.

Buss, D. M. (1995). Evolutionary psychology: A new paradigm for psychological science. *Psychological Inquiry, 6*, 1–30.

Buss, D. M. (1999). *Evolutionary psychology: The new science of the mind*. Boston: Allyn & Bacon.

Buss, D. M. (Ed.). (2005). *The handbook of evolutionary psychology*. Hoboken, NJ: John Wiley & Sons.

Buss, D. M., Gomes, M., Higgins, D. S., & Lauterbach, K. (1987). Tactics of manipulation. *Journal of Personality and Social Psychology, 52*, 1219–1229.

Buss, D. M., Larsen, R. J., Westen, D., & Semmelroth, J. (1992). Sex differences in jealousy: Evolution, physiology, and psychology. *Psychological Science, 3*, 251–255.

Buss, D. M., Shackelford, T. K., Kirkpatrick, L. A., Choe, J. C., Lim, H. K., Hasegawa, M., Hasegawa, T., & Bennett, K. (1999). Jealousy and the nature of beliefs about infidelity: Tests of competing hypotheses about sex differences in the United States, Korea, and Japan. *Personal Relationships, 6*, 125–150.

Butler, D. L., Acquino, A. L., Hissong, A. A., & Scott, P. A. (1993). Wayfinding by newcomers in a complex building. *Human Factors, 35*, 159–173.

Buunk, B. P., Angleitner, A., Oubaid, V., & Buss, D. M. (1996). Sex differences in jealousy in evolutionary and cultural perspective: Tests from the Netherlands, Germany, and the United States. *Psychological Science, 7*, 359–363.

Cabanac, M. (1971). Physiological role of pleasure. *Science, 173*, 1103–1107.

Cacioppo, J. T., Berntson, G. G., Larsen, J. T., Poehlmann, K. M., & Ito, T. A. (2000). The psychophysiology of emotion. In M. Lewis & J. M. Haviland-Jones (Eds), *Handbook of emotions* (2nd ed., pp. 173–191). New York: Guilford Press.

Cacioppo, J. T., Klein, D. J., Berntson, G. G., & Hatfield, E. (1993). The psychophysiology of emotion. In M. Lewis & J. M. Haviland (Eds.), *Handbook of emotions* (pp. 119–142). New York: Guilford Press.

Cacioppo, J. T., & Petty, R. E. (1982). The need for cognition. *Journal of Personality and Social Psychology, 42*, 116–131.

Cacioppo, J. T., Petty, R. E., Feinstein, J. A., & Jarvis, W. B. G. (1996). Dispositional differences in cognitive motivation: The life and times of individuals varying in need for cognition. *Psychological Bulletin, 119*, 197–253.

Cacioppo, J. T., Petty, R. E., & Morris, K. J. (1983). Effects of need for cognition on message evaluation, recall, and persuasion. *Journal of Personality and Social Psychology, 45*, 805–818.

Call, V., Sprecher, S., & Schwartz, P. (1995). The incidence and frequency of marital sex in a national sample. *Journal of Marriage and the Family, 57*, 639–652.

Campbell, J. B., & Hawley, C. W. (1982). Study habits and Eysenck's theory of extraversion-introversion. *Journal of Research in Personality, 16*, 139–146.

Campbell, J. B., Tyrrell, D. J., & Zingaro, M. (1993). Sensation seeking among whitewater canoe and kayak paddlers. *Personality and Individual Differences, 14*, 489–491.

Campfield, L. A., Brandon, P., & Smith, F. J. (1985). On-line continuous measurement of blood glucose and meal pattern in free-feeding rats: The role of glucose in meal initiation. *Brain Research Bulletin, 14*, 605–616.

Campfield, L. A., & Smith, F. J. (1990). Systemic factors in the control of food intake. In E. M. Stricker (Ed.), *Handbook of behavioral neurobiology: Vol. 10. Neurobiology of food and fluid intake* (pp. 183–206). New York: Plenum Press.

Campion, M. A., & Lord, R. G. (1982). A control systems conceptualization of the goal-setting and changing process. *Organizational Behavior and Human Performance, 30,* 265–287.

Camras, L. A., Holland, E. A., & Patterson, M. J. (1993). Facial expression. In M. Lewis & J. M. Haviland (Eds.), *Handbook of emotions* (pp. 199–208). New York: Guilford Press.

Cannon, W. B. (1927). The James-Lange theory of emotions: A critical examination and alternative theory. *American Journal of Psychology, 39,* 106–124.

Cannon, W. B. (1929/1953). *Bodily changes in pain, hunger, fear and rage.* Boston: Charles T. Branford.

Cannon, W. B. (1939). *The wisdom of the body* (2nd ed.). New York: W. W. Norton.

Canova, A., & Geary, N. (1991). Intraperitoneal injections of nanogram CCK-8 doses inhibit feeding in rats. *Appetite, 17,* 221–227.

Caporael, L. R. (1989). Mechanisms matter: The difference between sociobiology and evolutionary psychology. *Behavioral and Brain Sciences, 12,* 17–18.

Carmack, M. A., & Martens, R. (1979). Measuring commitment to running: A survey of runners' attitudes and mental states. *Journal of Sport Psychology, 1,* 25–42.

Carver, C. S., Reynolds, S. L., & Scheier, M. F. (1994). The possible selves of optimists and pessimists. *Journal of Research in Personality, 28,* 133–141.

Carver, C. S., & Scheier, M. F. (1982). Control theory: A useful conceptual framework for personality—social, clinical, and health psychology. *Psychological Bulletin, 92,* 111–135.

Cervone, D., & Peake, P. K. (1986). Anchoring, efficacy, and action: The influence of judgmental heuristics on self-efficacy judgments and behavior. *Journal of Personality and Social Psychology, 50,* 492–501.

Cesario, J., Plaks, J. E., & Higgins, E. T. (2006). Automatic social behavior as motivated preparation to interact. *Journal of Personality and Social Psychology, 90,* 893–910.

Chapman, A. J. (1976). Social aspects of humorous laughter. In A. J. Chapman & H. C. Foot (Eds.), *Humour and laughter: Theory, research, and applications* (pp. 187–214). London: Wiley.

Chartrand, T. L., & Bargh, J. A. (1999). The chameleon effect: The perception-behavior link and social interaction. *Journal of Personality and Social Psychology, 76,* 893–910.

Chilcoat, H. D., & Breslau, N. (1998). Investigations of causal pathways between PTSD and drug use disorders. *Addictive Behaviors, 23,* 827–840.

Childress, A. R., Ehrman, R., Rohsenow, D. J., Robbins, S. J., & O'Brien, C. P. (1992). Classically conditioned factors in drug dependence. In J. H. Lowinson, P. Ruiz, R. B. Millman, & J. G. Langrod (Eds.), *Substance abuse: A comprehensive textbook* (2nd ed., pp. 56–69). Baltimore: Williams & Wilkins.

Chovil, N., & Fridlund, A. J. (1991). Why emotionality cannot equal sociality: Reply to Buck. *Journal of Nonverbal Behavior, 15,* 163–167.

Christianson, S.-A., & Loftus, E. F. (1990). Some characteristics of people's traumatic memories. *Bulletin of the Psychonomic Society, 28,* 195–198.

Clark, L. A., & Watson, D. (1994). Distinguishing functional from dysfunctional affective responses. In P. Ekman & R. J. Davidson (Eds.), *The nature of emotion* (pp. 131–136). New York: Oxford University Press.

Clark, L. A., Watson, D., & Leeka, J. (1989). Diurnal variation in the positive affects. *Motivation and Emotion, 13,* 205–234.

Clements, P. R., Hafer, M. D., & Vermillion, M. E. (1976). Psychometric, diurnal, and electrophysiological correlates of activation. *Journal of Personality and Social Psychology, 33,* 387–394.

Clore, G. L. (1994). Why emotions are felt. In P. Ekman & R.J. Davidson (Eds.), *The nature of emotion* (pp. 103–111). New York: Oxford University Press.

Cockerill, I. M., & Riddington, M. E. (1996). Exercise dependence and associated disorders: A review. *Counseling Psychology Quarterly, 9,* 119–129.

Cofer, C. N., & Appley, M. H. (1964). *Motivation: Theory and research.* New York: Wiley.

Cohen, A. R., Stotland, E., & Wolfe, D. M. (1955). An experimental investigation of need for cognition. *Journal of Abnormal and Social Psychology, 51,* 291–294.

Cohen, S., Frank, E., Doyle, W. J., Skoner, D. P., Rabin, B. M., & Gwaltney, J. M. (1998). Types of stressors that increase susceptibility to the common cold in healthy adults. *Health Psychology, 17,* 214–223.

Cohen, S., & Herbert, T. B. (1996). Health psychology: Psychological factors and physical disease from the perspective of human psychoneuroimmunology. *Annual Review of Psychology, 47,* 113–142.

Cohen, S., & Hoberman, H. M. (1983). Positive events and social supports as buffers of life change stress. *Journal of Applied Social Psychology, 13,* 99–125.

Cohen, S., & Williamson, G. M. (1991). Stress and infectious disease in humans. *Psychological Bulletin, 109,* 5–24.

Cohen, S., & Wills, T. A. (1985). Stress, social support, and the buffering hypothesis. *Psychological Bulletin, 98,* 310–357.

Comerford, B., & Witryol, S. L. (1993). Information metrics for novelty level preference of first- and fifth-grade children. *Journal of Genetic Psychology, 154,* 155–165.

Considine, R. V., Sinha, M. K., Heiman, M. L., Kriauciunas, A., Stephens, T. W., Nyce, M. R., Ohannesian, J. P., Marco, C. C., McKee, L. J., Bauer, T. L., & Caro, J. F. (1996). Serum immunoreactive-leptin concentrations in normal-weight and obese humans. *New England Journal of Medicine, 334,* 292–295.

Conway, T. L., Vickers, Jr., R. R., Ward, H. W., & Rahe, R. H. (1981). Occupational stress and variation in cigarette, coffee, and alcohol consumption. *Journal of Health and Social Behavior, 22,* 155–165.

Cook, E. W., III, Hodes, R. L., & Lang, P. J. (1986). Preparedness and phobia: Effects of stimulus content on human visceral conditioning. *Journal of Abnormal Psychology, 95,* 195–207.

Cook, M., & Mineka, S. (1990). Selective associations in the observational conditioning of fear in rhesus monkeys. *Journal of Experimental Psychology: Animal Behavior Processes, 16,* 372–389.

Cooley, C. H. (1902/1964). *Human nature and the social order.* New York: Schocken Books.

Cools, J., Schotte, D. E., & McNally, R. J. (1992). Emotional arousal and overeating in restrained eaters. *Journal of Abnormal Psychology, 101,* 348–351.

Cooper, M. L., Agocha, V. B., & Sheldon, M. S. (2000). A motivational perspective on risky behaviors: The role of personality and affect regulatory processes. *Journal of Personality, 68,* 1059–1088.

Correia, C. J., & Benson, T. A. (2006). The use of contingency management to reduce cigarette smoking among college students. *Experimental and Clinical Psychopharmacology, 14,* 171–179.

Cosmides, L., & Tooby, J. (2005). Evolutionary psychology: A primer. Retrieved August 30, 2005, from University of California, Santa Barbara, Center for Evolutionary Psychology: http://cogweb.ucla.edu/ep/

Costa, Jr., P. T., & McCrae, R. R. (1985). *The NEO Personality Inventory Manual.* Odessa, FL: Psychological Assessment Resources.

Costa, Jr., P. T., & McCrae, R. R. (2001). *The NEO Personality Inventory.* Retrieved August 9, 2003, from http://www.rpp.on.ca/neopir.htm.

Costa, Jr., P. T., McCrae, R. R., & Holland, J. L. (1984). Personality and vocational interests in an adult sample. *Journal of Applied Psychology, 69,* 390–400.

Cox, D., & Cox, A. D. (2002). Beyond first impressions: The effects of repeated exposure on consumer liking of visually complex and simple product designs. *Journal of the Academy of Marketing Science, 30,* 119–130.

Cox, R. H., Thomas, T. R., Hinton, P. S., & Donahue, O. M. (2006). Effects of acute bouts of aerobic exercise of varied intensity on subjective mood experiences in women of different age groups across time. *Journal of Sport Behavior, 29,* 40–59.

Crandall, C. S., Preisler, J. J., & Aussprung, J. (1992). Measuring life event stress in the lives of college students: The Undergraduate Stress Questionnaire (USQ). *Journal of Behavioral Medicine, 15,* 627–662.

Crespi, L. P. (1942). Quantitative variation of incentive and performance in the white rat. *American Journal of Psychology, 55,* 467–517.

Crocker, B. (1961). *Betty Crocker's new picture cook book* (6th ed.). New York: McGraw-Hill.

Crocker, J., & Knight, K. M. (2005). Contingencies of self-worth. *Current Directions in Psychological Science, 14,* 200–203.

Crocker, J., Luhtanen, R. K., Cooper, M. L., & Bouvrette, A. (2003). Contingencies of self-worth in college students: Theory and measurement. *Journal of Personality and Social Psychology, 85,* 894–908.

Crocker, J., Sommers, S. R., & Luhtanen, R. K. (2002). Hopes dashed and dreams fulfilled: Contingencies of self-worth and graduate school admissions. *Personality and Social Psychology Bulletin, 28,* 1275–1286.

Cross, I. (2001). Music, cognition, culture, and evolution. In R. J. Zatorre & I. Peretz (Eds.), *Annals of the New York Academy of Sciences: Vol. 930. The biological foundations of music* (pp. 28–42).

Crossen, C. (1997, January 31). Funny business. *Wall Street Journal*, pp. A1, A6.

Csikszentmihalyi, M. (1975). *Beyond boredom and anxiety*. San Francisco: Jossey-Bass.

Csikszentmihalyi, M. (1988). The flow experience and its significance for human psychology. In M. Csikszentmihalyi & I. S. Csikszentmihalyi (Eds.), *Optimal experience: Psychological studies of flow in consciousness* (pp. 15–35). New York: Cambridge University Press.

Csikszentmihalyi, M., & Rathunde, K. (1993). The measurement of flow in everyday life: Toward a theory of emergent motivation. In R. Dienstbier (Series Ed.) & J. E. Jacobs (Vol. Ed.), *Nebraska Symposium on Motivation: Vol. 40. Developmental perspectives on motivation* (pp. 57–97). Lincoln: University of Nebraska Press.

Cummings, D. E., Frayo, R. S., Marmonier, C., Aubert, R., & Chapelot, D. (2004). Plasma ghrelin levels and hunger scores in humans initiating meals voluntarily without time- and food-related cues. *American Journal of Physiology: Endocrinology and Metabolism, 287,* E297–E304.

Damasio, A. (2003). *Looking for Spinoza: Joy, sorrow, and the feeling brain*. Orlando: Harcourt.

Damasio, A. R., Grabowski, T. J., Bechara, A., Damasio, H., Ponto, L. L. B., Parvizi, J., & Hichwa, R. D. (2000). Subcortical and cortical brain activity during the feeling of self-generated emotions. *Nature Neuroscience, 3,* 1049–1056.

Darwin, C. (1859/1936). *On the origin of species by means of natural selection*. New York: Random House.

Darwin, C. (1871/1981). *The descent of man, and selection in relation to sex*. Princeton: Princeton University Press.

Darwin, C. (1873). *The expression of the emotions in man and animals*. London: John Murray.

Davidson, R. J. (1994). On emotion, mood, and related affective constructs. In P. Ekman & R. J. Davidson (Eds.), *The nature of emotion* (pp. 51–55). New York: Oxford University Press.

Davidson, R. J., & Ekman, P. (1994). Afterword: Is there emotion-specific physiology? In P. Ekman & R. J. Davidson (Eds.), *The nature of emotion* (pp. 261–262). New York: Oxford University Press.

Davies, C. T. M., & Few, J. D. (1973). Effects of exercise on adrenocortical function. *Journal of Applied Physiology, 35,* 887–891.

Davies, S. (1994). *Musical meaning and expression*. Ithaca: Cornell University Press.

Davis, J. D., Gallagher, R. J., & Ladove, R. F. (1967). Food intake controlled by a blood factor. *Science, 156,* 1247–1248.

Davis, J. D., Gallagher, R. J., Ladove, R. F., & Turausky, A. J. (1969). Inhibition of food intake by a humoral factor. *Journal of Comparative and Physiological Psychology, 67,* 407–414.

Davis, J. E., & Cox, R. H. (2002). Interpreting direction of anxiety within Hanin's individual zone of optimal functioning. *Journal of Applied Sport Psychology, 14,* 43–52.

Dawe, S., Gullo, M. J., & Loxton, N. J. (2004). Reward drive and rash impulsiveness as dimensions of impulsivity: Implications for substance misuse. *Addictive Behaviors, 29,* 1389–1405.

DeCaria, C. M., Hollander, E., Grossman, R., Wong, C. M., Mosovich, S. A., & Cherkasky, S. (1996). Diagnosis, neurobiology, and treatment of pathological gambling. *Journal of Clinical Psychiatry, 57* (supplement 8), 80–84.

De Castro, J. M., & Elmore, D. K. (1988). Subjective hunger relationships with meal patterns in the spontaneous feeding behavior of humans: Evidence for a causal connection. *Physiology & Behavior, 43,* 159–165.

Deci, E. L. (1971). Effects of externally mediated rewards on intrinsic motivation. *Journal of Personality and Social Psychology, 18,* 105–115.

Deci, E. L. (1972a). The effects of contingent and noncontingent rewards and controls on intrinsic motivation. *Organizational Behavior and Human Performance, 8,* 217–229.

Deci, E. L. (1972b). Intrinsic motivation, extrinsic reinforcement and inequity. *Journal of Personality and Social Psychology, 22,* 113–120.

Deci, E. L., & Ryan, R. M. (1985). *Intrinsic motivation and self-determination in human behavior*. New York: Plenum Press.

Deci, E. L., & Ryan, R. M. (2000). The "what" and "why" of goal pursuits: Human needs and the self-determination of behavior. *Psychological Inquiry, 11,* 227–268.

Deckers, L. (1993). On the validity of a weight-judging paradigm for the study of humor. *Humor: International Journal of Humor Research, 6,* 43–56.

Deckers, L. (1994, June). *The relationship between facial reactions of humor and funniness ratings within and across subjects.* A poster presented at the International Humor Studies Conference, Ithaca, NY.

Deckers, L., & Avery, P. (1994). Altered joke endings and a joke structure schema. *Humor: International Journal of Humor Research, 7,* 313–321.

Deckers, L., & Ruch, W. (1992). The Situational Humor Response Questionnaire as a test of sense of humor: A validity study in the field of humor appreciation. *Personality and Individual Differences, 13,* 1149–1152.

de La Chambre, M. C. (1663/1974). Of weeping, fear, and despair. In S. Diamond (Ed.), *The roots of psychology* (pp. 526–528). New York: Basic Books.

Delahanty, D. L., Dougall, A. L., Hawken, L., Trakowski, J. H., Schmitz, J. B., Jenkings, F. J., & Baum, A. (1996). Time course of natural killer cell activity and lymphocyte proliferation in response to two acute stressors in healthy men. *Health Psychology, 15,* 48–55.

Demakis, G. J., & McAdams, D. P. (1994). Personality, social support and well-being among first year college students. *College Student Journal, 28,* 235–243.

Dennett, D. C. (1975). Why the law of effect will not go away. *Journal of the Theory of Social Behaviour, 5,* 169–187.

Dennis, W. (1960). Environmental influences upon motor development. *Journal of Genetic Psychology, 96,* 47–59.

Derogatis, L. R., Lipman, R. S., Rickels, K., Uhllenhuth, E. H., & Covi, L. (1974). The Hopkins Symptom Checklist (HSCL): A self-report symptom inventory. *Behavioral Science, 19,* 1–15.

DesCamp, K. D., & Thomas, C. C. (1993). Buffering nursing stress through play at work. *Western Journal of Nursing Research, 15,* 619–627.

Descartes, R. (1649/1968). The passions of the soul. In E. S. Haldane & G. R. T. Ross (Eds.), *The philosophical works of Descartes.* Cambridge: Cambridge University Press.

Desor, J. A., Maller, O., & Andrews, K. (1975). Ingestive responses of human newborns to salty, sour, and bitter stimuli. *Journal of Comparative and Physiological Psychology, 89,* 966–970.

Desor, J. A., Maller, O., & Turner, R. E. (1973). Taste in acceptance of sugars by human infants. *Journal of Comparative and Physiological Psychology, 84,* 496–501.

Deutsch, J. A. (1990). Food intake. In E. M. Stricker (Ed.), *Handbook of behavioral neurobiology: Vol. 10. Neurobiology of food and fluid intake* (pp. 151–182). New York: Plenum Press.

de Villiers, P. (1977). Choice in concurrent schedules and a quantitative formulation of the law of effect. In W. K. Honig & J. E. R. Staddon (Eds.), *Handbook of operant behavior* (pp. 233–287). Englewood Cliffs, NJ: Prentice-Hall.

de Wit, H., & Wise, R. A. (1977). Blockade of cocaine reinforcement in rats with the dopamine receptor blocker pimozide, but not with the noradrenergic blockers phentolamine or phenoxybenzamine. *Canadian Journal of Psychology, 31,* 195–203.

DiClemente, C. (1999). Motivation for change: Implications for substance abuse treatment. *Psychological Science, 10,* 209–213.

DiClemente, C. C., Schlundt, D., & Gemmell, L. (2004). Readiness and stages of change in addiction treatment. *The American Journal on Addictions, 13,* 103–119.

Diener, E., Larsen, R. J., & Emmons, R. A. (1984). Person X situation interactions: Choice of situations and congruence response models. *Journal of Personality and Social Psychology, 47,* 580–592.

Diener, E., Lucas, R. E., & Scollon, C. N. (2006). Beyond the hedonic treadmill: Revising the adaptation theory of well-being. *American Psychologist, 61,* 305–314.

Diener, E., & Seligman, M. E. P. (2002). Very happy people. *Psychological Science, 13,* 81–84.

Dijksterhuis, A., & Aarts, H. (2003). On wildebeests and humans: The preferential detection of negative stimuli. *Psychological Science, 14,* 14–18.

Dom, G., D'haene, P., Hulstijn, W., & Sabbe, B. (2006). Impulsivity in abstinent early- and late-onset alcoholics: Differences in self-report measures and a discounting task. *Addiction, 101,* 50–59.

Donovan, J. J., & Williams, K. J. (2003). Missing the mark: Effects of time and causal attributions on goal revision in response to goal-performance discrepancies. *Journal of Applied Psychology, 88,* 379–390.

Doran, N., McChargue, D., & Cohen, L. (2007). Impulsivity and the reinforcing value of cigarette smoking. *Addictive Behaviors, 32,* 90–98.

Drewnowski, A., Brunzell, J. D., Sande, K., Iverius, P. H., & Greenwood, M. R. C. (1985). Sweet tooth reconsidered: Taste responsiveness in human obesity. *Physiology and Behavior, 35,* 617–622.

Drewnowski, A., & Greenwood, M. R. (1983). Cream and sugar: Human preferences for high fat foods. *Physiology & Behavior, 30,* 629–633.

Duckworth, A. L., Peterson, C., Matthews, M. D., & Kelly, D. R. (2007). Grit: Perserverance and passion for long term goals. *Journal of Personality and Social Psychology, 92,* 1087–1101.

Duckworth, A. L., & Seligman, M. E. P. (2005). Self-discipline outdoes IQ in predicting academic performance of adolescents. *Psychological Science, 16,* 939–944.

Duckworth, K. L., Bargh, J. A., Garcia, M., & Chaiken, S. (2002). The automatic evaluation of novel stimuli. *Psychological Science, 13,* 513–519.

Duffy, E. (1962). *Activation and behavior.* New York: John Wiley.

Dunham, P. J. (1968). Contrasted conditions of reinforcement: A selective critique. *Psychological Bulletin, 69,* 295–315.

Eagly, A. H., Ashmore, R. D., Makhijani, M. G., & Longo, L. C. (1991). What is beautiful is good, but . . . : A meta-analytic review of research on the physical attractiveness stereotype. *Psychological Bulletin, 110,* 109–128.

Eagly, A. H., & Wood, W. (1999). The origins of sex differences in human behavior. *American Psychologist, 54,* 408–423.

Earley, P. C., Wojnaroski, P., & Prest, W. (1987). Task planning and energy expended: Exploration of how goals influence performance. *Journal of Applied Psychology, 72,* 107–114.

Easterbrook, J. A. (1959). The effect of emotion on cue utilization and the organization of behavior. *Psychological Review, 66,* 183–201.

Edwards, W. (1961). Behavioral decision theory. *Annual Review of Psychology, 12,* 473–498.

Eibl-Eibesfeldt, I. (1973). The expressive behaviour of the deaf-and-blind-born. In M. von Cranach & I. Vine (Eds.), *Social communication and movement* (pp. 163–194). New York: Academic Press.

Eibl-Eibesfeldt, I. (1989). *Human ethology.* New York: Aldine de Gruyter.

Eisenberger, R. (1992). Learned industriousness. *Psychological Review, 99,* 248–267.

Eisenberger, R., Heerdt, W. A., Hamdi, M., Zimet, S., & Bruckmeir, M. (1979). Transfer of persistence across behaviors. *Journal of Experimental Psychology: Human Learning and Memory, 5,* 522–530.

Ekman, P. (1973). Cross-cultural studies of facial expression. In P. Ekman (Ed.), *Darwin and facial expression* (pp. 169–222). New York: Academic Press.

Ekman, P. (1984). Expression and the nature of emotion. In K. R. Scherer & P. Ekman (Eds.), *Approaches to emotion* (pp. 319–344). Hillsdale, NJ: Lawrence Erlbaum.

Ekman, P. (1992). Are there basic emotions? *Psychological Review, 99,* 550–553.

Ekman, P. (1994a). Moods, emotions, and traits. In P. Ekman & R. J. Davidson (Eds.), *The nature of emotion* (pp. 56–58). New York: Oxford University Press.

Ekman, P. (1994b). Strong evidence for universals in facial expressions: A reply to Russell's mistaken critique. *Psychological Bulletin, 115,* 268–287.

Ekman, P. (1999). Basic emotions. In T. Dalgleish & M. J. Power (Eds.), *Handbook of cognition and emotion* (pp. 45–60). Chichester, UK: Wiley & Sons, Ltd.

Ekman, P., & Friesen, W. V. (1971). Constants across cultures in the face and emotion. *Journal of Personality and Social Psychology, 17,* 124–129.

Ekman, P., & Friesen, W. V. (1975). *Unmasking the face.* Englewood Cliffs, NJ: Prentice-Hall.

Ekman, P., Friesen, W. V., & Ancoli, S. (1980a). Facial signs of emotional experience. *Journal of Personality and Social Psychology, 39,* 1125–1134.

Ekman, P., Levenson, R. W., & Friesen, W. V. (1983). Autonomic nervous system activity distinguishes among emotions. *Science, 221,* 1208–1210.

Ekman, P., Roper, G., & Hager, J. C. (1980b). Deliberate facial movement. *Child Development, 51,* 886–891.

Elfenbein, H. A., & Ambady, N. (2002a). Is there an in-group advantage in emotion recognition? *Psychological Bulletin, 128,* 243–249.

Elfenbein, H. A., & Ambady, N. (2002b). On the universality and cultural specificity of emotion recognition: A meta-analysis. *Psychological Bulletin, 128,* 203–235.

Elliot, A. J., & McGregor, H. A. (2001). A 2 × 2 achievement goal framework. *Journal of Personality and Social Psychology, 80,* 501–519.

Elliot, D. L., Goldberg, L., Kuehl, K. S., & Bennett, W. M. (1989). Sustained depression of resting metabolic rate after massive weight loss. *American Journal of Clinical Nutrition, 49,* 93–96.

Ellsworth, P. C. (1994). Some reasons to expect universal antecedents of emotion. In P. Ekman & R. J. Davidson (Eds.), *The nature of emotion* (pp. 150–154). New York: Oxford University Press.

Ellsworth, P. C., & Smith, C. A. (1988). From appraisal to emotion: Differences among unpleasant feelings. *Motivation and Emotion, 12,* 271–302.

Emmons, R. A., Diener, E., & Larsen, R. J. (1986). Choice and avoidance of everyday situations and affect congruence: Two models of reciprocal interactionism. *Journal of Personality and Social Psychology, 51,* 815–826.

Endler, J. A. (1986). *Natural selection in the wild.* Princeton: Princeton University Press.

Engell, D. B., Maller, O., Sawka, M. N., Francesconi, R. N., Drolet, L., & Young, A. J. (1987). Thirst and fluid intake following graded hypohydration levels in humans. *Physiology and Behavior, 40,* 229–236.

Entwisle, D. R. (1972). To dispel fantasies about fantasy-based measures of achievement motivation. *Psychological Bulletin, 77,* 377–391.

Erez, A., & Isen, A. M. (2002). The influence of positive affect on the components of expectancy motivation. *Journal of Applied Psychology, 87,* 1055–1067.

Ervin, F. R., & Martin, J. (1986). Neurophysiological bases of the primary emotions. In R. Plutchik & H. Kellerman (Eds.), *Emotion: Theory, research, and experience: Vol 3. Biological foundations of emotion* (pp. 145–170). Orlando: Academic Press.

Eysenck, H. J. (1967). *The biological basis of personality.* Springfield, IL: Charles C. Thomas.

Eysenck, H. J. (1990). Biological dimensions of personality. In L. A. Pervin (Ed.), *Handbook of personality, theory and research* (pp. 244–276). New York: Guilford Press.

Eysenck, M. W., & Calvo, M. G. (1992). Anxiety and performance: The processing efficiency theory. *Cognition and Emotion, 6,* 409–434.

Farrell, P. A., Garthwaite, T. L., & Gustafson, A. B. (1983). Plasma adrenocorticotropin and cortisol responses to submaximal and exhaustive exercise. *Journal of Applied Physiology, 55,* 1441–1444.

Faw, T. T. (1970). The effects of stimulus incongruity on free looking time of adults and children. *Psychonomic Science, 19,* 355–357.

Fechner, G. T. (1860/1966). *Elements of psychophysics.* New York: Holt, Rinehart and Winston.

Fechner, G. T. (1876). *Vorschule der aesthetik* [Introduction to aesthetics]. Leipzig: Breitkopf & Härtel.

Fedorchak, P. M., & Bolles, R. C. (1987). Hunger enhances the expression of calorie- but not taste-mediated conditioned flavor preferences. *Journal of Experimental Psychology: Animal Behavior Processes, 13,* 73–79.

Fedoroff, I. C., Polivy, J., & Herman, C. P. (1997). The effect of pre-exposure to food cues on the eating behavior of restrained and unrestrained eaters. *Appetite, 28,* 33–47.

Findley, J. D. (1959). Behavior output under chained fixed-ratio requirements in a 24-hour experimental space. *Journal of the Experimental Analysis of Behavior, 2,* 258.

Fineman, S. (1977). The achievement motive construct and its measurement: Where are we now? *British Journal of Psychology, 68,* 1–22.

Finney, S. J., Pieper, S. L., & Barron, K. E. (2004). Examining the psychometric properties of the achievement goal questionnaire in a general academic context. *Educational and Psychological Measurement, 64,* 365–382.

Fishbein, D. H., & Pease, S. E. (1996). *The dynamics of drug abuse.* Boston: Allyn and Bacon.

Fisher, H. (2004). *Why we love: The nature and chemistry of romantic love.* New York: Henry Holt and Company.

Fisher, H. E. (1992). *Anatomy of love.* New York: W. W. Norton.

Fletcher, R. (1966). *Instincts in man.* New York: Schocken Books.

Fliege, H., Rose, M., Arck, P., Walter, O. B., Kocalevent, R.-D., Weber, C., & Klapp, B. F. (2005). The perceived stress questionnaire (PSQ) reconsidered: Validation and reference values from different clinical and healthy adult samples. *Psychosomatic Medicine, 67,* 78–88.

Floud, R., Wachter, K., & Gregory, A. (1990). *Height, health and history.* Cambridge: Cambridge University Press.

Folkman, S., & Lazarus, R. S. (1985). If it changes it must be a process: Study of emotion and coping during three stages of a college examination. *Journal of Personality and Social Psychology, 48,* 150–170.

Folkman, S., & Moskowitz, J. T. (2000). Positive affect and the other side of coping. *American Psychologist, 55,* 647–654.

Fomon, S. J., Filer, L. J., Thomas, L. N., Rogers, R. R., & Proksch, A. M. (1969). Relationship between formula concentration and rate of growth of normal infants. *Journal of Nutrition, 98,* 241–245.

Fortenbaugh, W. W. (1975). *Aristotle on emotion.* New York: Harper & Row.

Franck, J. A. E., Schwartzkroin, P. A., Phillips, J. O., & Fuchs, A. F. (1989). The limbic system. In H. D. Patton, A. F. Fuchs, B. Hille, A. M. Scher, & R. Steiner (Eds.), *Textbook of physiology: Excitable cells and neurophysiology* (Vol. 1, pp. 693–717). Philadelphia: W. B. Saunders.

Fredrickson, B. L. (1998). What good are positive emotions? *Review of General Psychology, 2,* 300–319.

Fredrickson, B. L. (2001). The role of positive emotions in positive psychology: The broaden-and-build theory of positive emotions. *American Psychologist, 56,* 218–226.

Fredrickson, B. L. & Branigan, C. (2005). Positive emotions broaden the scope of attention and thought-action repertoires. *Cognition and Emotion, 19,* 313–332.

Fredrickson, B. L., Mancuso, R. A., Branigan, C., & Tugade, M. M. (2000). The undoing effect of positive emotions. *Motivation and Emotion, 24,* 237–258.

Fredrickson, B. L., Tugade, M. M., Waugh, C. E., & Larkin, G. R. (2003). What good are positive emotions in crises? A prospective study of resilience and emotions following the terrorist attacks on the United States on September 11th, 2001. *Journal of Personality and Social Psychology, 84,* 365–376.

Freixanet, M. G. I. (1991). Personality profile of subjects engaged in high physical risk sports. *Personality and Individual Differences, 12,* 1087–1093.

French, E. G. (1956). Motivation as a variable in work-partner selection. *Journal of Abnormal and Social Psychology, 53,* 96–99.

Freud, S. (1905). Jokes and their relation to the unconscious. In J. Strachey (Ed.), *The standard edition of the complete psychological works of Sigmund Freud* (Vol. 8). London: Hogarth Press.

Freud, S. (1915a). Instincts and their vicissitudes. In J. Strachey (Ed.), *The standard edition of the complete psychological works of Sigmund Freud* (Vol. 14). London: Hogarth Press.

Freud, S. (1915b). The unconscious. In J. Strachey (Ed.), *The standard edition of the complete psychological*

works of Sigmund Freud (Vol. 14). London: Hogarth Press.

Freud, S. (1920). Beyond the pleasure principle. In J. Strachey (Ed.), *The standard edition of the complete psychological works of Sigmund Freud* (Vol. 18). London: Hogarth Press.

Freud, S. (1920/1943). *A general introduction to psychoanalysis.* Garden City, NY: Garden City Publishing.

Freud, S. (1924). The economic problem in masochism. In E. Jones (Ed.), *Sigmund Freud: Collected papers* (Vol. 2). New York: Basic Books.

Fridlund, A. J. (1991a). Evolution and facial action in reflex, social motive, and paralanguage. *Biological Psychology, 32,* 3–100.

Fridlund, A. J. (1991b). Sociality of solitary smiling: Potentiation by an implicit audience. *Journal of Personality and Social Psychology, 60,* 229–240.

Fridlund, A. J. (1992). The behavioral ecology and sociality of human faces. In M. S. Clark (Ed.), *Review of personality and social psychology: Vol. 13. Emotion* (pp. 90–121). Newbury Park, CA: Sage.

Fridlund, A. J. (1994). *Human facial expression: An evolutionary view.* San Diego: Academic Press.

Friedman, J. M., & Halaas, J. L. (1998). Leptin and the regulation of body weight in mammals. *Nature, 395,* 763–770.

Friedman, M. I., Ulrich, P., & Mattes, R. D. (1999). A figurative measure of subjective hunger sensations. *Appetite, 32,* 395–404.

Frijda, N. H. (1986). *The emotions.* Cambridge: Cambridge University Press.

Frijda, N. H. (1994). Emotions are functional, most of the time. In P. Ekman & R. J. Davidson (Eds.), *The nature of emotion* (pp. 112–122). New York: Oxford University Press.

Frijda, N. H. (2007). *The laws of emotion.* Mahwah, NJ: Lawrence Erlbaum.

Frijda, N. H., Ortony, A., Sonnemans, J., & Clore, G. L. (1992). The complexity of intensity: Issues concerning the structure of emotion intensity. In M. S. Clark (Ed.), *Review of personality and social psychology: Vol. 13. Emotion* (pp. 60–89). Newbury Park, CA: Sage.

Fulcher, J. S. (1942). "Voluntary" facial expression in blind and seeing children. *Archives of Psychology,* no. 272, 2–49.

Fulker, D. W., Eysenck, S. B. G., & Zuckerman, M. (1980). A genetic and environmental analysis of sensation seeking. *Journal of Research in Personality, 14,* 261–281.

Gable, S. L., & Haidt, J. (2005). What (and why) is positive psychology? *Review of General Psychology, 9,* 103–110.

Gailliot, M. T., Baumeister, R. F., DeWall, C. N., Maner, J. K., Plant, E. A., Tice, D. M., Brewer, L. E., & Schmeichel, B. J. (2007). Self-control relies on glucose as a limited energy source: Willpower is more than a metaphor. *Journal of Personality and Social Psychology, 92,* 325–336.

Galati, D., Miceli, R., & Sini, B. (2001). Judging and coding facial expression of emotions in congenitally blind children. *International Journal of Behavioral Development, 25,* 268–278.

Galati, D., Scherer, K. R., & Ricci-Bitti, P. E. (1997). Voluntary facial expression of emotion: Comparing congenitally blind with normally sighted encoders. *Journal of Personality and Social Psychology, 73,* 1363–1379.

Galea, S., Ahern, J., Resnick, H., Kilpatrick, D., Bucuvalas, M., Gold, J., & Vlahov, D. (2002). Psychological sequelae of the September 11 terrorist attacks in New York City. *New England Journal of Medicine, 346,* 982–987.

Gallup, Jr., G. G., Nash, R. F., Potter, R. J., & Donegan, N. H. (1970). Effects of varying conditions of fear on immobility reactions in domestic chickens *(Gallus Gallus). Journal of Comparative and Physiological Psychology, 73,* 442–445.

Galton, F. (1883). *Inquiries into human faculty and its development.* London: Macmillan.

Ganskopp, D., Cruz, R., & Johnson, D. E. (2000). Least-effort pathways? A GIS analysis of livestock trails in rugged terrain. *Applied Animal Behaviour Science, 68,* 179–190.

Garb, J. L., & Stunkard, A. J. (1974). Taste aversion in man. *American Journal of Psychiatry, 131,* 1204–1207.

Garcia, J., Ervin, F., & Koelling, R. A. (1966). Learning with prolonged delay of reinforcement. *Psychonomic Science, 5,* 121–122.

Garrett, B. E., & Griffiths, R. R. (2001). Intravenous nicotine and caffeine: Subjective and physiological effects in cocaine abusers. *The Journal of Pharmacology and Experimental Therapeutics, 296,* 486–494.

Gaver, W. W., & Mandler, G. (1987). Play it again, Sam: On liking music. *Cognition and Emotion, 1,* 259–282.

Gawin, F. H., & Kleber, H. D. (1986). Abstinence symptomatology and psychiatric diagnosis in cocaine abusers: Clinical observations. *Archives of General Psychiatry, 43,* 107–113.

Gay, P. (1999, March 29). Sigmund Freud. *Time, 153,* 66–69.

Geary, N. (2004). Endocrine controls of eating: CCK, leptin, and ghrelin. *Physiology & Behavior, 81,* 719–733.

Geary, N., & Schwartz, G. J. (2005). Appetite. In B. J. Sadock & V. A. Sadock (Eds.), *Comprehensive textbook of psychiatry: Volume I* (8th ed., pp. 295–308). Philadelphia: Lippincott Williams & Wilkins.

Gerrards-Hesse, A., Spies, K., & Hesse, F. W. (1994). Experimental inductions of emotional states and their effectiveness: A review. *British Journal of Psychology, 85,* 55–78.

Gibbs, J., Young, R. C., & Smith, G. P. (1973). Cholecystokinin decreases food intake in rats. *Journal of Comparative and Physiological Psychology, 84,* 488–495.

Gibson, R. (1996, February 5). McDonald's decides its McLean burger fails to cut the mustard with diners. *Wall Street Journal,* p. B5.

Gillis, J. R. (1988). From ritual to romance: Toward an alternative history of love. In C. Z. Stearns & P. N. Stearns (Eds.), *Emotion and social change: Toward a new psychohistory* (pp. 87–121). New York: Holmes & Meier.

Glasser, W. (1976). *Positive addiction.* New York: Harper & Row.

Gloor, P., Olivier, A., Quesney, L. F., Andermann, F., & Horowitz, S. (1982). The role of the limbic system in experiential phenomena of temporal lobe epilepsy. *Annals of Neurology, 12,* 129–144.

Godkewitsch, M. (1976). Physiological and verbal indices of arousal in rated humor. In A. J. Chapman & H. C. Foot (Eds.), *Humour and laughter: Theory, research, and applications* (pp. 117–138). London: Wiley.

Goeders, N. E. (2004). Stress, motivation, and drug addiction. *Current Directions in Psychological Science, 13,* 33–35.

Gold, M. S. (1992). Cocaine (and crack): Clinical aspects. In J. H. Lowinson, P. Ruiz, R. B. Millman, & J. G. Langrod (Eds.), *Substance abuse: A comprehensive textbook* (2nd ed., pp. 205–221). Baltimore: Williams & Wilkins.

Goldberg, D. P., Rickels, K., Downing, R., & Hesbacher, P. (1976). A comparison of two psychiatric screening tests. *British Journal of Psychiatry, 129,* 61–67.

Goldman, D., Oroszi, G., & Ducci, F. (2005). The genetics of addictions: Uncovering the genes. *Nature Reviews Genetics, 6,* 521–532.

Goldsmith, H. H. (1994). Parsing the emotional domain from a developmental perspective. In P. Ekman & R. J. Davidson (Eds.), *The nature of emotion* (pp. 68–73). New York: Oxford University Press.

Goldstein, A. (2001). *Addiction: From biology to drug policy.* New York: Oxford University Press.

Gonzaga, G. C., Keltner, D., Londahl, E. A., & Smith, M. D. (2001). Love and the commitment problem in romantic relations and friendship. *Journal of Personality and Social Psychology, 81,* 247–262.

Gonzaga, G. C., Turner, R. A., Keltner, D., Campos, B., & Altemus, M. (2006). Romantic love and sexual desire in close relationships. *Emotion, 6,* 163–179.

Gosling, S. D., & John, O. P. (1999). Personality dimensions in nonhuman animals: A cross-species review. *Current Directions in Psychological Science, 8,* 69–75.

Gould, S. J. (1987). Freudian slip. *Natural History, 96,* 14–21.

Grant, J. E., & Kim, S. W. (2001). Demographic and clinical features of 131 adult pathological gamblers. *Journal of Clinical Psychiatry, 62,* 957–962.

Gray, C. A. (1975). Factors in students' decisions to attempt academic tasks. *Organizational Behavior and Human Performance, 13,* 147–164.

Graziano, W. G., Habashi, M. M., Sheeese, B. E., & Tobin, R. M. (2007). Agreeableness, empathy, and helping: A person × situation perspective. *Journal of Personality and Social Psychology, 93,* 583–599.

Green, L., & Freed, D. E. (1993). The substitutability of reinforcers. *Journal of the Experimental Analysis of Behavior, 60,* 141–158.

Green, L., Fry, A. F., & Myerson, J. (1994a). Discounting of delayed rewards: A life span comparison. *Psychological Science, 5,* 33–36.

Green, L., & Myerson, J. (2004). A discounting framework for choice with delayed and probabilistic rewards. *Psychological Bulletin, 130,* 769–792.

Greene, B. A., DeBacker, T. K., Ravindran, B., & Krows, A. J. (1999). Goals, values, and beliefs as predictors of achievement and effort in high school mathematics classes. *Sex Roles, 40,* 421–458.

Greeno, C. G., & Wing, R. R. (1994). Stress-induced eating. *Psychological Bulletin, 115,* 444–464.

Greenwald, M. K., Cook III, E. W., & Lang, P. J. (1989). Affective judgment and psychophysiological response: Dimensional covariation in the evaluation of pictorial stimuli. *Journal of Psychophysiology, 3,* 51–64.

Grewe, O., Nagel, F., Kopiez, R., & Altenmüller, E. (2007). Listening to music as a re-creative process: Physiological, psychological, and psychoacoustical correlates of chills and strong emotions. *Music Perception, 24,* 297–314.

Griffiths, M. (1997). Exercise addiction: A case study. *Addiction Research, 5,* 161–168.

Griffiths, R. R., Bigelow, G. E., & Heningfield, J. E. (1980). Similarities in animal and human drug-taking behavior. In N. K. Mello (Ed.), *Advances in substance abuse: Behavioral and biological research* (pp. 1–90). Greenwich, CT: JAI Press.

Grill, H. J., & Norgren, R. (1978). The taste reactivity test. I. Mimetic responses to gustatory stimuli in neurologically normal rats. *Brain Research, 143,* 263–279.

Grimm, J. L. K. (1884/1968). *Grimm's household tales* (Vol. I-2; M. Hunt, Ed. and Trans.). Detroit: Singing Tree Press.

Guhn, M., Hamm, A., & Zentner, M. (2007). Physiological and musico-acoustic correlates of the chill response. *Music Perception, 24,* 473–483.

Guthrie, R. V. (1998). *Even the rat was white* (2nd ed.). Boston: Allyn and Bacon.

Halberstadt, J. B., Niedenthal, P. M., & Kushner, J. (1995). Resolution of lexical ambiguity by emotional state. *Psychological Science, 6,* 278–282.

Halmi, K. A., & Sunday, S. R. (1991). Temporal patterns of hunger and fullness ratings and related cognitions in anorexia and bulimia. *Appetite, 16,* 219–237.

Hamilton, E. L. (1929/1931). The effect of delayed incentive on the hunger drive in the white rat. Experiment 1: The obstruction method. In C. J. Warden (Ed.), *Animal motivation: Experimental studies on the Albino Rat* (pp. 81–96). New York: Columbia University Press. (Reprinted with modifications from E. L. Hamilton, 1929,

Genetic Psychology Monograph, 5(2), 137–166.)

Hanin, Y. L. (1989). Interpersonal and intragroup anxiety in sports. In D. Hackfort & C. D. Spielberger (Eds.), *Anxiety in sports: An international perspective* (pp. 19–28). New York: Hemisphere.

Hanna, A., Abernethy, B., Neal, R. J., & Burgess-Limerick, R. (2000). Triggers for the transition between human walking and running. In W. A. Sparrow (Ed.), *Energetics of human activity* (pp. 124–164). Champaign, IL: Human Kinetics.

Harackiewicz, J. M., Manderlink, G., & Sansone, C. (1984). Rewarding pinball wizardry: Effects of evaluation and cue value on intrinsic interest. *Journal of Personality and Social Psychology, 47*, 287–300.

Hardy, L. (1996a). A test of catastrophe models of anxiety and sports performance against multidimensional anxiety theory models using the method of dynamic differences. *Anxiety, Stress, and Coping, 9*, 69–86.

Hardy, L. (1996b). Testing the predictions of the cusp catastrophe model of anxiety and performance. *Sport Psychologist, 10*, 140–156.

Harker, L. A., & Keltner, D. (2001). Expressions of positive emotion in women's college yearbook pictures and their relationship to personality and life outcomes across adulthood. *Journal of Personality and Social Psychology, 80*, 112–124.

Harnack, L. J., Jeffery, R. W., & Boutelle, K. N. (2000). Temporal trends in energy intake in the United States: An ecologic perspective. *American Journal of Clinical Nutrition, 71*, 1478–1484.

Harris, A. C., & Gewirtz, J. D. (2005). Acute opioid dependence: Characterizing the early adaptations underlying drug withdrawal. *Psychopharmacology, 178*, 353–366.

Harsh, J., & Badia, P. (1975). Choice for signalled over unsignalled shock as a function of shock intensity. *Journal of the Experimental Analysis of Behavior, 23*, 349–355.

Harte, J. L., Eifert, G. H., & Smith, R. (1995). The effects of running and meditation on beta-endorphin, corticotropin-releasing hormone and cortisol in plasma, and on mood. *Biological Psychology, 40*, 251–265.

Hastie, R., & Dawes, R. M. (2001). *Rational choice in an uncertain world: The psychology of judgment and decision making.* Thousand Oaks, CA: Sage Publications.

Hausenblas, H. A., & Downs, D. S. (2002). How much is too much? The development and validation of the exercise dependence scale. *Psychology and Health, 17*, 387–404.

Heatherton, T. F., & Polivy, J. (1991). Development and validation of a scale measuring state self-esteem. *Journal of Personality and Social Psychology, 60*, 895–910.

Hebb, D. O. (1955). Drives and the C. N. S. [conceptual nervous system]. *Psychological Review, 62*, 243–254.

Herbert, T. B., Cohen, S., Marsland, A. L., Bachen, E. A., Rabin, B. S., Muldoon, M. F., & Manuck, S. B. (1994). Cardiovascular reactivity and course of immune response to an acute psychological stressor. *Psychosomatic Medicine, 56*, 337–344.

Herman, C. P., & Polivy, J. (1975). Anxiety, restraint, and eating behavior. *Journal of Abnormal Psychology, 84*, 666–672.

Herman, C. P., & Polivy, J. (1980). Restrained eating. In A. J. Stunkard (Ed.), *Obesity* (pp. 208–225). Philadelphia: W. B. Saunders.

Herman, C. P., & Polivy, J. (1984). A boundary model for the regulation of eating. In A. J. Stunkard & E. Stellar (Eds.), *Eating and its disorders* (pp. 141–156). New York: Raven Press.

Herrnstein, R. J. (1961). Relative and absolute strength of response as a function of frequency of reinforcement. *Journal of the Experimental Analysis of Behavior, 4*, 267–272.

Herrnstein, R. J. (1990). Rational choice theory: Necessary but not sufficient. *American Psychologist, 45*, 356–367.

Hess, U., Banse, R., & Kappas, A. (1995). The intensity of facial expression is determined by underlying affective state and social situation. *Journal of Personality and Social Psychology, 69*, 280–288.

Heyduk, R. G. (1975). Rated preference for musical compositions as it relates to complexity and exposure frequency. *Perception & Psychophysics, 17*, 84–90.

Hill, C. M., & Hill, D. W. (1991). Influence of time of day on responses to the Profile of Mood States. *Perceptual and Motor Skills, 72*, 434.

Hillman, B., Hunter, W. S., & Kimble, G. A. (1953). The effect of drive level on the maze performance of the white rat. *Journal of Comparative and Physiological Psychology, 46*, 87–89.

Hittner, J. B., & Swickert, R. (2006). Sensation seeking and alcohol use: A meta-analytic review. *Addictive Behaviors, 31,* 1383–1401.

Hobbes, T. (1640/1962). *Human nature.* Cleveland: Bell & Howell.

Hoffner, C. A., & Levine, K. J. (2005). Enjoyment of mediated fright and violence: A meta-analysis. *Media Psychology, 7,* 207–237.

Hoge, C. W., Castro, C. A., Messer, S. C., McGurk, D., Cotting, D. I., & Koffman, R. L. (2004). Combat duty in Iraq and Afghanistan, mental health problems, and barriers to care. *The New England Journal of Medicine, 351,* 13–22.

Hollenbeck, J. R., & Klein, H. J. (1987). Goal commitment and the goal-setting process: Problems, prospects, and proposals for future research. *Journal of Applied Psychology, 72,* 212–220.

Hollenbeck, J. R., Klein, H. J., O'Leary, A. M., & Wright, P. M. (1989a). Investigation of the construct validity of a self-report measure of goal commitment. *Journal of Applied Psychology, 74,* 951–956.

Hollenbeck, J. R., Williams, C. R., & Klein, H. J. (1989b). An empirical examination of the antecedents of commitment to difficult goals. *Journal of Applied Psychology, 74,* 18–23.

Holmes, T. H., & Masuda, M. (1974). Life change and illness susceptibility. In B. S. Dohrenwend & B. P. Dohrenwend (Eds.), *Stressful life events: Their nature and effects* (pp. 45–72). New York: John Wiley.

Holmes, T. H., & Rahe, R. H. (1967). The Social Readjustment Rating Scale. *Journal of Psychosomatic Research, 11,* 213–218.

Holt, K. G., Hamill, J., & Andres, R. O. (1991). Predicting the minimal energy costs of human walking. *Medicine and Science in Sports and Exercise, 23,* 491–498.

Holt, K. G., Jeng, S. F., Ratcliffe, R., & Hamill, J. (1995). Energetic costs and stability during human walking at the preferred stride frequency. *Journal of Motor Behavior, 27,* 164–178.

Holt, S., Brand, J. C., Soveny, C., & Hansky, J. (1992). Relationship of satiety to postprandial glycemic, insulin and cholecystokinin responses. *Appetite, 18,* 129–141.

Hopko, D. R., Mahadevan, R., Bare, R. L., & Hunt, M. K. (2003). The abbreviated math anxiety scale (AMAS): Construction, validity, and reliability. *Assessment, 10,* 178–182.

Hull, C. L. (1943). *Principles of behavior.* New York: Appleton-Century-Crofts.

Hull, C. L. (1951). *Essentials of behavior.* New Haven: Yale University Press.

Hull, C. L. (1952). *A behavior system.* New Haven: Yale University Press.

Hupka, R. B., Lenton, A. P., & Hutchinson, K. A. (1999). Universal development of emotion categories in natural language. *Journal of Personality and Social Psychology, 77,* 247–278.

Hur, Y-M., & Bouchard, Jr., T. J. (1997). The genetic correlation between impulsivity and sensation-seeking traits. *Behavior Genetics, 27,* 455–463.

Hursh, S. R. (1980). Economic concepts for the analysis of behavior. *Journal of the Experimental Analysis of Behavior, 34,* 219–238.

Hursh, S. R., & Bauman, R. A. (1987). The behavioral analysis of demand. In L. Green & J. H. Kagel (Eds.), *Advances in behavioral economics* (pp. 117–165). Norwood, NJ: Ablex.

Hursh, S. R., & Natelson, B. H. (1981). Electrical brain stimulation and food reinforcement dissociated by demand elasticity. *Physiology and Behavior, 26,* 509–515.

Hyland, D. A. (1973). *The origins of philosophy: Its rise in myth and the pre-Socratics.* New York: G. P. Putman's.

Imamoglu, Ç. (2000). Complexity, liking and familiarity: Architecture and non-architecture Turkish students' assessment of traditional and modern house facades. *Journal of Environmental Psychology, 20,* 5–16.

Iyengar, S. S., & Lepper, M. R. (2000). When choice is demotivating: Can one desire too much of a good thing? *Journal of Personality and Social Psychology, 79,* 995–1006.

Iyengar, S. S., Wells, R. E., & Schwartz, B. (2006). Doing better but feeling worse: Looking for the "best" job undermines satisfaction. *Psychological Science, 17,* 143–150.

Izard, C. E. (1971). *The face of emotion.* New York: Appleton-Century-Crofts.

Izard, C. E. (1992). Basic emotions, relations among emotions, and emotion-cognition relations. *Psychological Review, 99,* 561–565.

Izard, C. E. (1993). Four systems for emotion activation: Cognitive and noncognitive processes. *Psychological Review, 100,* 68–90.

Izard, C. E. (1994). Innate and universal facial expressions: Evidence from developmental and cross-cultural research. *Psychological Bulletin, 115,* 288–299.

Izard, C. E., Fantauzzo, C. A., Castle, J. M., Haynes, O. M., Rayias, M. F., & Putnam, P. H. (1995). The ontogeny and significance of infants' facial expressions in the first 9 months of life. *Developmental Psychology, 31,* 997–1013.

Izard, C. E., & Malatesta, C. Z. (1987). Perspectives on emotional development I: Differential emotions theory of early emotional development. In J. D. Osofsky (Ed.), *Handbook of infant development* (pp. 494–554). New York: John Wiley.

Jackendoff, R. (1992). Musical processing and musical affect. In M. R. Jones & S. Holleran (Eds.), *Cognitive bases of musical communication* (pp. 51–68). Washington, DC: American Psychological Association.

Jackson, J. W., & Poulsen, J. R. (2005). Contact experiences mediate the relationship between five-factor model personality traits and ethnic prejudice. *Journal of Applied Social Psychology, 35,* 667–685.

Jaffe, J. H. (1992). Opiates: Clinical aspects. In J. H. Lowinson, P. Ruiz, R. B. Millman, & J. G. Langrod (Eds.), *Substance abuse: A comprehensive textbook* (2nd ed., pp. 186–194). Baltimore: Williams & Wilkins.

Jaffe, J. H., & Anthony, J. C. (2005). Substance-related disorders. In B. J. Sadock & V. A. Sadock (Eds.), *Comprehensive textbook of psychiatry: Volume I* (8th ed., pp. 1137–1168). Philadelphia: Lippincott Williams & Wilkins.

James, W. (1884/1948). What is an emotion? *Mind, 9,* 188–204. Reprinted in W. Dennis (Ed.), *Readings in history of psychology* (pp. 290–303). New York: Appleton-Century-Crofts.

James, W. (1890/1950). *The principles of psychology.* New York: Dover Publications.

James, W. (1892). *Psychology.* New York: Henry Holt.

James, W. H. (1981). The honeymoon effect on marital coitus. *The Journal of Sex Research, 17,* 114–123.

Jankowiak, W. R., & Fischer, E. F. (1992). A cross-cultural perspective on romantic love. *Ethnology, 31,* 149–155.

Jenkins, S. R. (1994). Need for power and women's careers over 14 years: Structural power, job satisfaction, and motive change. *Journal of Personality and Social Psychology, 66,* 155–165.

Jerome, N. W. (1977). Taste experience and the development of a dietary preference for sweet in humans: Ethnic and cultural variations in early taste experience. In J. M. Weiffenbach (Ed.), *Taste and development* (pp. 235–248). Bethesda: U.S. Department of Health, Education, and Welfare.

Johansson, B. A., Berglund, M., & Lindgren, A. (2006). Efficacy of maintenance treatment with naltrexone for opioid dependence: A meta-analytical review. *Addiction, 101,* 491–503.

John, O. P. (1989). Towards a taxonomy of personality descriptors. In D. M. Buss & N. Cantor (Eds.), *Personality psychology: Recent trends and emerging directions.* New York: Springer Verlag.

John, O. P. (1990a). The "big five" taxonomy: Dimensions of personality in the natural language and in questionnaires. In L. Pervin (Ed.), *Handbook of personality theory and research.* New York: Guilford Press.

John, O. P. (1990b). The search for basic dimensions of personality: A review and critique. In P. McReynolds, J. Rosen, & G. J. Chelune (Eds.), *Advances in psychological assessment* (Vol. 7). New York: Plenum Press.

John, O. P., & Robins, R. W. (1993). Gordon Allport: Father and critic of the five-factor model. In K. H. Craik, R. Hogan, & R. N. Wolfe (Eds.), *Fifty years of personality psychology* (pp. 215–236). New York: Plenum Press.

Johnson, M. W., Bickel, W. K., & Baker, F. (2007). Moderate drug use and delay discounting: A comparison of heavy, light, and never smokers. *Experimental and Clinical Psychopharmacology, 15,* 187–194.

Johnson-Laird, P. N., & Oatley, K. (1989). The language of emotions: An analysis of a semantic field. *Cognition and Emotion, 3,* 81–123.

Jones, A. (1969). Stimulus-seeking behavior. In J. P. Zubek (Ed.), *Sensory deprivation: Fifteen years of research* (pp. 167–206). New York: Appleton-Century-Crofts.

Jones, A. C., & Gosling, S. D. (2005). Temperament and personality in dogs (*Canis familiaris*): A review and evaluation of past research. *Applied Animal Behaviour Science, 95,* 1–53.

Juliano, L. M., & Griffiths, R. R. (2004). A critical review of caffeine withdrawal: Empirical validation of symptoms and signs, incidence, severity, and associated features. *Psychopharmacology, 176,* 1–29.

Jung, C. G. (1924). *Psychological types* (H. G. Baynes, Trans.). New York: Harcourt, Brace.

Kahneman, D., Knetsch, J. L., & Thaler, R. H. (1990). Experimental tests of the endowment effect and the coase theorem. *Journal of Political Economy, 98,* 1325–1348.

Kahneman, D., & Tversky, A. (1979). Prospect theory: An analysis of decision under risk. *Econometrica, 47,* 263–291.

Kahneman, D., & Tversky, A. (1982). The psychology of preferences. *Scientific American, 246,* 160–173.

Kamman, R. (1966). Verbal complexity and preferences in poetry. *Journal of Verbal Learning and Verbal Behavior, 5,* 536–540.

Karabenick, S. A., & Youssef, Z. I. (1968). Performance as a function of achievement motive level and perceived difficulty. *Journal of Personality and Social Psychology, 10,* 414–419.

Karniol, R., & Ross, M. (1996). The motivational impact of temporal focus: Thinking about the future and the past. *Annual Review of Psychology, 47,* 593–620.

Katkin, E. S., Wiens, S., & Öhman, A. (2001). Nonconscious fear conditioning, visceral perception, and the development of gut feelings. *Psychological Science, 12,* 366–370.

Keesey, R. E. (1986). A set-point theory of obesity. In K. D. Brownell & J. P. Poreyt (Eds.), *Handbook of eating disorders.* New York: Basic Books.

Keesey, R. E., & Hirvonen, M. D. (1997). Body weight set-points: Determination and adjustment. *Journal of Nutrition, 127,* 1875–1883.

Kellaris, J. J., & Kent, R. J. (1994). An exploratory investigation of responses elicited by music varying in tempo, tonality, and texture. *Journal of Consumer Psychology, 2,* 381–401.

Kelley, A. E., & Berridge, K. C. (2002). The neuroscience of natural rewards: Relevance to addictive drugs. *The Journal of Neuroscience, 22,* 3306–3311.

Keltner, D. (1995). Signs of appeasement: Evidence for the distinct displays of embarrassment, amusement, and shame. *Journal of Personality and Social Psychology, 68,* 441–454.

Keltner, D., & Anderson, C. (2000). Saving face for Darwin: The functions and uses of embarrassment. *Current Directions in Psychological Science, 9,* 187–192.

Keltner, D., & Shiota, M. N. (2003). New displays and emotions: A commentary on Rozin and Cohen (2003). *Emotion, 3,* 86–109.

Kendler, K. S., Jacobson, K. C., Prescott, C. A., & Neale, M. C. (2003). Specificity of genetic and environmental risk factors for use and abuse/dependence of cannabis, cocaine, hallucinogens, sedatives, stimulants, and opiates in male twins. *American Journal of Psychiatry, 160,* 687–695.

Khan, L. K., & Bowman, B. A. (1999). Obesity: A major global public health problem. *Annual Review of Nutrition, 19,* xiii–xvii.

Kiecolt-Glaser, J. K., Garner, W., Speicher, C., Penn, G., Holiday, J., & Glaser, R. (1984). Pyschosocial modifiers of immunocompetence in medical students. *Psychosomatic Medicine, 46,* 7–13.

Kiecolt-Glaser, J. K., & Glaser, R. (1995). Psychoneuroimmunology and health consequences: Data and shared mechanisms. *Psychosomatic Medicine, 57,* 269–274.

Kiecolt-Glaser, J. K., McGuire, L., Robles, T. F., & Glaser, R. (2002). Psychoneuroimmunology and psychosomatic medicine: Back to the future. *Psychosomatic Medicine, 64,* 15–28.

Killeen, P. R. (2001). The four causes of behavior. *Current Directions in Psychological Science, 10,* 136–140.

Kim, S. W., Grant, J. E., Adson, D. E., & Shin, Y. C. (2001). Double-blind naltrexone and placebo comparison study in the treatment of pathological gambling. *Biological Psychiatry, 49,* 914–921.

Kimble, G. A. (1990). Mother nature's bag of tricks is small. *Psychological Science, 1,* 36–41.

Kintsch, W. (1962). Runway performance as a function of drive strength and magnitude of reinforcement. *Journal of Comparative and Physiological Psychology, 55,* 882–887.

Kirk, J. M., & de Wit, H. (2000). Individual differences in the priming effect of ethanol in social drinkers. *Journal of Studies on Alcohol, 61,* 64–71.

Kirkcaldy, B., & Furnham, A. (1991). Extraversion, neuroticism, psychoticism and recreational choice. *Personality and Individual Differences, 12,* 737–745.

Kirsner, B. R., Figueredo, A. J., & Jacobs, W. J. (2003). Self, friends, and lovers: Structural relations among Beck Depression Inventory scores and perceived mate values. *Journal of Affective Disorders, 75,* 131–148.

Klajner, F., Herman, C. P., Polivy, J., & Chabra, R. (1981). Human obesity, dieting, and anticipatory salivation to food. *Physiology and Behavior, 27,* 195–198.

Klein, H. J. (1989). An integrated control theory model of work motivation. *Academy of Management Review, 14,* 150–172.

Klein, H. J., Wesson, M. J., Hollenbeck, J. R., & Alge, B. J. (1999). Goal commitment and the goal setting process: Conceptual clarification and empirical synthesis. *Journal of Applied Psychology, 84,* 885–896.

Klein, H. J., Wesson, M. J., Hollenbeck, J. R., Wright, P. M., & DeShon, R. P. (2001). The assessment of goal commitment: A measurement model meta-analysis. *Organizational Behavior and Human Decision Processes, 85,* 32–55.

Klinger, E. (1966). Fantasy need achievement as a motivational construct. *Psychological Bulletin, 66,* 291–308.

Klinger, E. (1977). *Meaning and void: Inner experience and the incentives in people's lives.* Minneapolis: University of Minnesota Press.

Klinger, E., Barta, S. G., & Maxeiner, M. E. (1980). Motivational correlates of thought content frequency and commitment. *Journal of Personality and Social Psychology, 39,* 1222–1237.

Knetsch, J. L., & Sinden, J. A. (1984, August). Willingness to pay and compensation demanded: Experimental evidence of an unexpected disparity in measures of value. *Quarterly Journal of Economics,* pp. 507–521.

Kobasa, S. (1979). Stressful life events, personality, and health: An inquiry into hardiness. *Journal of Personality and Social Psychology, 37,* 1–11.

Kobasa, S. (1984, September). How much stress can you survive? *American Health Magazine,* pp. 64–77.

Kojima, M., & Kangawa, K. (2005). Ghrelin: Structure and function. *Physiological Reviews, 85,* 495–522.

Koob, G. F. (2002). Neurobiology of drug addiction. In D. B. Kandel (Ed.), *Stages and pathways of drug involvement: Examining the gateway hypothesis* (pp. 337–361). Cambridge: Cambridge University Press.

Koole, S. L., Greenberg, J., & Pyszczynski, T. (2006). Introducing the science to the psychology of the soul. *Current Directions in Psychological Science, 15,* 212–216.

Kraeling, D. (1961). Analysis of amount of reward as a variable in learning. *Journal of Comparative and Physiological Psychology, 54,* 560–565.

Krane, V. (1993). A practical application of the anxiety-athletic performance relationship: The zone of optimal functioning hypothesis. *The Sport Psychologist, 7,* 113–126.

Kraut, R. E. (1982). Social presence, facial feedback, and emotion. *Journal of Personality and Social Psychology, 42,* 853–863.

Kuiper, N. A., Martin, R. A., & Olinger, J. (1993). Coping humour, stress, and cognitive appraisals. *Canadian Journal of Behavioural Science, 25,* 81–96.

Kuiper, N. A., McKenzie, S. D., & Belanger, K. A. (1995). Cognitive appraisals and individual differences in sense of humor: Motivational and affective implications. *Personality and Individual Differences, 19,* 359–372.

Landers, R. N., & Lounsbury, J. W. (2006). An investigation of Big Five and narrow personality traits in relation to Internet usage. *Computers in Human Behavior, 22,* 283–293.

Landrine, H., & Klonoff, E. A. (1996). The Schedule of Racist Events: A measure of racial discrimination and a study of its negative and physical and mental health consequences. *Journal of Black Psychology, 22,* 144–168.

Lane, B., & Gullone, E. (1999). Common fears: A comparison of adolescents' self-generated and fear survey schedule generated fears. *Journal of Genetic Psychology, 160,* 194–204.

Lang, J. W. B., & Fries, S. (2006). A revised 10-item version of the achievement motive scale. *European Journal of Psychological Assessment, 22,* 216–224.

Lange, C. (1885/1968). The emotions. In W. S. Sahakian (Ed.), *History of psychology: A source book in systematic psychology* (pp. 207–211). Itasca, IL: F. E. Peacock.

Langlois, J. H., Kalakanis, L., Rubenstein, A. J., Larson, A., Hallam, M., & Smoot, M. (2000). Maxims or myths of beauty? A meta-analytic and theoretical review. *Psychological Bulletin, 126,* 390–423.

Lansing, J. B., & Heyns, R. W. (1959). Need affiliation and frequency of four types of communication. *Journal of Abnormal and Social Psychology, 58,* 365–372.

Larsen, R. J., & Ketelaar, T. (1989). Extraversion, neuroticism and susceptibility to positive and negative mood induction procedures. *Personality and Individual Differences, 10,* 1221–1228.

Larsen, R. J., & Ketelaar, T. (1991). Personality and susceptibility to positive and negative emotional states. *Journal of Personality and Social Psychology, 61,* 132–140.

Latham, G. P., & Seijts, G. H. (1999). The effects of proximal and distal goals on performance of a moderately complex task. *Journal of Organizational Behavior, 20,* 421–429.

Lay, C. (1986). At last, my research article on procrastination. *Journal of Research in Personality, 20,* 474–495.

Lazarus, R. S., & Alfert, E. (1964). Short-circuiting of threat by experimentally altering cognitive appraisal. *Journal of Abnormal and Social Psychology, 69,* 195–205.

Lazarus, R., & Cohen, J. B. (1977). Environmental stress. In I. Altman & J. F. Wohlhill (Eds.), *Human behavior and environment* (Vol. 2, pp. 89–127). New York: Academic Press.

Lazarus, R. S., & Folkman, S. (1984). *Stress, appraisal, and coping.* New York: Springer.

Lazarus, R. S., Opton, E. M., Jr., Nomikos, M. S., & Rankin, N. O. (1965). The principle of short-circuiting of threat: Further evidence. *Journal of Personality, 33,* 622–635.

Lea, S. E. G., & Roper, T. J. (1977). Demand for food on fixed-ratio schedules as a function of the quality of concurrently available reinforcement. *Journal of the Experimental Analysis of Behavior, 27,* 371–380.

Leach, J. (2004). Why people 'freeze' in an emergency: Temporal and cognitive constraints on survival responses. *Aviation, Space, and Environmental Medicine, 75,* 539–542.

Leary, M. R. (2007). Motivational and emotional aspects of the self. *Annual Review of Psychology, 58,* 317–344.

Leary, M. R., Britt, T. W., Cutlip II, W. D., & Templeton, J. L. (1992). Social blushing. *Psychological Bulletin, 112,* 446–460.

Leckart, B. T., & Bakan, P. (1965). Complexity judgments of photographs and looking time. *Perceptual and Motor Skills, 21,* 16–18.

LeDoux, J. E. (1996). *The emotional brain.* New York: Simon & Schuster.

LeDoux, J. E. (2000a). Cognitive-emotional interactions: Listening to the brain. In R. D. Lane & L. Nadel (Eds.), *Cognitive neuroscience of emotion* (pp. 129–155). New York: Oxford University Press.

LeDoux, J. E. (2000b). Emotion circuits in the brain. *Annual Review of Neuroscience, 23,* 155–184.

Lee, T. W., Locke, E. A., & Latham, G. P. (1989). Goal setting theory and job performance. In L. E. Pervin (Ed.), *Goal concepts in personality and social psychology* (pp. 291–326). Hillsdale, NJ: Lawrence Erlbaum.

Leeper, R. (1935). The role of motivation in learning: A study of the phenomenon of differential motivational control of the utilization of habits. *Journal of Genetic Psychology, 46,* 3–40.

Leeper, R. W. (1948). A motivational theory of emotion to replace "emotion as disorganized response." *Psychological Review, 55,* 5–21.

Lefcourt, H. M., & Martin, R. A. (1986). *Humor and life stress: Antidote to adversity.* New York: Springer/ Verlag.

Lefcourt, H. M., & Thomas, S. (1998). Humor and stress revisited. In W. Ruch (Ed.), *The sense of humor: Explorations of a personality characteristic* (pp. 179–202). New York: Mouton de Gruyter.

Legault, L., Green-Demers, I., & Pelletier, L. (2006). Why do high school students lack motivation in the classroom? Toward an understanding of academic motivation and the role of social support. *Journal of Educational Psychology, 98,* 567–582.

Leone, C. (1994). Opportunity for thought and differences in the need for cognition: A person by situation analysis of self-generated attitude change. *Personality and Individual Differences, 17,* 571–574.

Lepper, M. R., Greene, D., & Nisbett, R. E. (1973). Undermining children's intrinsic interest with extrinsic reward: A test of the "overjustification" hypothesis. *Journal of Personality and Social Psychology, 28,* 129–137.

Lerner, J. S., Gonzalez, R. M., Small, D. A., & Fischhoff, B. (2003). Effects of fear and anger on perceived risks of terrorism: A national field experiment. *Psychological Science, 14,* 144–150.

Lerner, J. S., & Keltner, D. (2000). Beyond valence: Toward a model of emotion-specific influences on judgment and choice. *Cognition and Emotion, 14,* 473–493.

Lerner, J. S., & Keltner, D. (2001). Fear, anger, and risk. *Journal of Personality and Social Psychology, 81,* 146–159.

Le Roy, G. (1764/1974). Letter on man. In S. Diamond (Ed.), *The roots of psychology* (pp. 564–567). New York: Basic Books.

Leshem, M., Abutbul, A., & Eilon, R. (1999). Exercise increases the preference for salt in humans. *Appetite, 32,* 251–260.

Lessov, C. N., Swan, G. E., Ring, H. Z., Khroyan, T. V., & Lerman, C. (2004). Genetics and drug use as a complex phenotype. *Substance Use and Misuse, 39,* 1515–1569.

Lester, D. (1990). Maslow's hierarchy of needs and personality. *Personality and Individual Differences, 11,* 1187–1188.

Levenson, R. W. (1992). Autonomic nervous system differences among emotions. *Psychological Science, 3,* 23–27.

Levenson, R. W. (1994). The search of autonomic specificity. In P. Ekman & R. J. Davidson (Eds.), *The nature of emotion* (pp. 252–257). New York: Oxford University Press.

Levin, R. L. (1992). The mechanisms of human female sexual arousal. *Annual Review of Sex Research, 3,* 1–48.

Levine, J. A., Eberhardt, N. L., & Jensen, M. D. (1999). Role of nonexercise activity thermogenesis in resistance to fat gain in humans. *Science, 283,* 212–214.

Lewin, K. (1933). Environmental forces in child behavior and development. In C. Murchison (Ed.), *Handbook of child psychology* (2nd ed., Chap. 14). Worcester, MA: Clark University Press.

Lewin, K. (1936). *Principles of topological psychology* (F. Heider & G. Heider, Trans.). New York: McGraw-Hill.

Lewin, K. (1938). *The conceptual representation and the measurement of psychological forces.* Durham, NC: Duke University Press.

Lewin, K., Dembo, T., Festinger, L., & Sears, P. S. (1944). Level of aspiration. In J. M. Hunt (Ed.), *Personality and the behavior disorders* (pp. 333–378). New York: Ronald Press.

Li, M. D., Cheng, R., Ma, J. Z., & Swan, G. E. (2003). A meta-analysis of estimated genetic and environmental effects on smoking behavior in male and female adult twins. *Addiction, 98,* 23–31.

Lippman, L. G. (2000). Contingent incentive value in human operant performance. *The Psychological Record, 50,* 513–528.

Lloyd, C., Alexander, A. A., Rice, D. G., & Greenfield, N. S. (1980). Life events as predictors of academic performance. *Journal of Human Stress, 6,* 15–25.

Lloyd, E. A. (2005). *The case of the female orgasm.* Cambridge: Harvard University Press.

Locke, E. A. (1991). Goal theory vs. control theory: Contrasting approaches to understanding work motivation. *Motivation and Emotion, 15,* 9–28.

Locke, E. A., Chah, D.-O., Harrison, S., & Lustgarten, N. (1989). Separating the effects of goal specificity from goal level. *Organizational Behavior and Human Decision Processes, 43,* 270–287.

Locke, E. A., & Latham, G. P. (1990). *A theory of goal setting and task performance.* Englewood Cliffs, NJ: Prentice Hall.

Locke, E. A., Latham, G. P., & Erez, M. (1988). The determinants of goal commitment. *Academy of Management Review, 13,* 23–39.

Locke, E. A., Shaw, K. N., Saari, L. M., & Lathan, G. P. (1981). Goal setting and task performance: 1969–1980. *Psychological Bulletin, 90,* 125–152.

Locke, J. (1690). *An essay concerning human understanding.* Retrieved March 10, 2008, from http://humanum.arts.cuhk.edu.hk/Philosophy/Locke/echu

Loehlin, J. C. (1992). *Genes and the environment in personality development.* Newbury Park, CA: Sage.

Loewenstein, G. (1994). The psychology of curiosity: A review and reinterpretation. *Psychological Bulletin, 116,* 75–98.

Logan, F. A. (1960). *Incentive.* New Haven: Yale University Press.

Logan, F. A., & Wagner, A. R. (1965). *Reward and punishment.* Boston: Allyn and Bacon.

Logue, A. W. (1988). Research on self-control: An integrating framework. *Behavioral and Brain Sciences, 11,* 665–709.

Logue, A. W. (1998). Laboratory research on self-control: Applications to administration. *Review of General Psychology, 2,* 221–238.

Logue, A. W., Ophir, I., & Strauss, K. E. (1981). The acquisition of taste aversions in humans. *Behavior Research and Therapy, 19,* 319–333.

Long, A. A., & Sedley, D. N. (1987). *The Hellenistic philosophers* (Vol. 1). Cambridge: Cambridge University Press.

Lorenz, K. (1971). *Studies in animal and human behaviour* (vol. II) (R. Martin, Translation). Cambridge, MA: Harvard University Press.

Lowell, E. L. (1952). The effect of need for achievement on learning and speed of performance. *Journal of Psychology, 33,* 31–40.

Lucas, R. E. (2005). Times does not heal all wounds. *Psychological Science, 16,* 945–950.

Lucas, R. E. (2007). Adaptation and the set-point model of subjective well-being. *Current Directions in Psychological Science, 16,* 75–79.

Luger, A., Deuster, P. A., Gold, P. W., Loriaux, D. L., & Chrousos, G. P. (1988). Hormonal responses to the stress of exercise. In G. P. Chrousos, D. L. Loriaux, & P. W. Gold (Eds.), *Mechanisms of physical and emotional stress* (pp. 273–280). New York: Plenum Press.

Lykken, D., & Tellegen, A. (1996). Happiness is a stochastic phenomenon. *Psychological Science, 7,* 186–189.

Lynn, R. (1966). *Attention, arousal and the orienting reaction.* Oxford: Pergamon Press.

Lyubomirsky, S., & Lepper, H. S. (1999). A measure of subjective happiness: Preliminary reliability and construct validation. *Social Indicators Research, 46,* 137–155.

Lyubomirsky, S., Sheldon, K. M., & Schkade, D. (2005). Pursuing happiness: The architecture of sustainable change. *Review of General Psychology, 9,* 111–131.

MacLean, P. D. (1986). Ictal symptoms relating to the nature of affects and their cerebral substrate. In R. Plutchik & H. Kellerman (Eds.), *Emotion: Theory, research, and experience: Vol. 3. Biological foundations of emotion* (pp. 61–90). Orlando: Academic Press.

Madden, G. J. (2000). A behavioral economics primer. In W. K. Bickel & R. E. Vuchinich (Eds.), *Reframing health behavior change with behavioral economics* (pp. 3–26). Mahwah, NJ: Lawrence Erlbaum.

Magistretti, P. J. (1999). Brain energy metabolism. In M. J. Zigmond, F. E. Bloom, S. C. Landis, J. L. Roberts, & L. R. Squire (Eds.), *Fundamental neuroscience* (pp. 389–413). San Diego: Academic Press.

Mahone, C. H. (1960). Fear of failure and unrealistic vocational aspiration. *Journal of Abnormal and Social Psychology, 60,* 253–261.

Mahut, H. (1958). Breed differences in the dog's emotional behaviour. *Canadian Journal of Psychology, 12,* 35–44.

Malinowski, B. (1941). Man's culture and man's behavior. *Sigma Xi Quarterly, 29,* 182–196.

Malmo, R. B. (1959). Activation: A neuropsychological dimension. *Psychological Review, 66,* 367–386.

Mandler, G. (1975). *Mind and emotion.* New York: John Wiley.

Mandler, G. (1984). *Mind and body: Psychology of emotion and stress.* New York: W. W. Norton.

Mandler, G. (1990). William James and the construction of emotion. *Psychological Science, 3,* 179–180.

Manstead, A. S. R., & Tetlock, P. E. (1989). Cognitive appraisal and emotional experience: Further evidence. *Cognition and Emotion, 3,* 225–239.

Marcelino, A. S., Adam, A. S., Couronne, T., Köster, E. P., & Sieffermann, J. M. (2001). Internal and external determinants of eating initiation in humans. *Appetite, 36,* 9–14.

Markman, A. B., & Brendl, C. M. (2000). The influence of goals on value and choice. In D. L. Medin (Ed.), *The psychology of learning and motivation* (Vol. 39, pp. 97–128). San Diego: Academic Press.

Marks, I. M. (1987). *Fears, phobias, and rituals.* New York: Oxford University Press.

Markus, H., & Nurius, P. (1986). Possible selves. *American Psychologist, 41,* 954–969.

Marsh, A. A., Adams, Jr., R. B., & Kleck, R. E. (2005). Why do fear and anger look the way they do? Form and social function in facial expressions. *Personality and Social Psychology Bulletin, 31,* 73–86.

Marston, A., Hart, J., Hileman, C., & Faunce, W. (1984). AJP forum: Toward the laboratory study of sadness and crying. *American Journal of Psychology, 97,* 127–131.

Martin, R., & Lefcourt, H. M. (1983). Sense of humor as a moderator of the relation between stressors and moods. *Journal of Personality and Social Psychology, 45,* 1313–1324.

Martin, R., & Lefcourt, H. M. (1984). Situational humor response questionnaire: A quantitative measure of the sense of humor. *Journal of Personality and Social Psychology, 47,* 145–155.

Martin, R. A. (2001). Humor, laughter, and physical health: Methodological issues and research findings. *Psychological Bulletin, 127,* 504–519.

Martin, R. B., & Labott, S. M. (1991). Mood following emotional crying: Effects of the situation. *Journal of Research in Personality, 25,* 218–244.

Maslow, A. H. (1970). *Motivation and personality* (2nd ed.). New York: Harper & Row.

Matsui, T., Okada, A., & Mizuguchi, R. (1981). Expectancy theory prediction of the goal theory postulate, "the harder the goals, the higher the performance." *Journal of Applied Psychology, 66,* 54–58.

Matsumoto, D., Yoo, S. H., Hirayama, S., & Petrova, G. (2005). Development and validation of a measure of display rule knowledge: The display rule assessment inventory. *Emotion, 5,* 23–40.

Mauss, I. B., Levenson, R. W., McCarter, L., Wilhelm, F. H., & Gross, J. J. (2005). The tie that binds? Coherence among emotion experience, behavior, and physiology. *Emotion, 5,* 175–190.

Mayr, E. (2001). *What evolution is.* New York: Basic Books.

Mazur, J. E. (1987). An adjusting procedure for studying delayed reinforcement. In M. L. Commons, J. E. Mazur, J. A. Nevin, & H. Rachlin (Eds.), *Quantitative analyses of behavior: Vol. 5. The effect of delay and of intervening events on reinforcement value* (pp. 55–73). Hillsdale, NJ: Lawrence Erlbaum.

McAdams, D. P. (1980). A thematic coding system for the intimacy motive. *Journal of Research in Personality, 14,* 413–432.

McAdams, D. P. (1982). Experiences of intimacy and power. Relationships between social motives and autobiographical memory. *Journal of Personality and Social Psychology, 42,* 292–302.

McAdams, D. P. (1992a). The intimacy motive. In C. P. Smith, J. W. Atkinson, D. C. McClelland, & J. Veroff (Eds.), *Motivation and personality: Handbook of thematic content analysis* (pp. 224–228). New York: Cambridge University Press.

McAdams, D. P. (1992b). The intimacy motive scoring system. In C. P. Smith, J. W. Atkinson, D. C. McClelland, & J. Veroff (Eds.), *Motivation and personality: Handbook of thematic content analysis* (pp. 229–253). New York: Cambridge University Press.

McAdams, D. P., & Constantian, C. A. (1983). Intimacy and affiliation motives in daily living: An experience sampling analysis. *Journal of Personality and Social Psychology, 45,* 851–861.

McAdams, D. P., Healy, S., & Krause, S. (1984). Social motives and patterns of friendship. *Journal of Personality and Social Psychology, 47,* 828–838.

McArdle, W. D., Katch, F. I., & Katch, V. L. (1996). *Exercise physiology: Energy, nutrition and human performance* (4th ed.). Baltimore: Williams & Wilkins.

McClelland, D. C. (1975). *Power: The inner experience.* New York: Irvington (Halsted Press, John Wiley).

McClelland, D. C. (1985). *Human motivation.* New York: Scott Foresman.

McClelland, D. C. (1987). *Human motivation.* Cambridge: Cambridge University Press.

McClelland, D. C., Atkinson, J. W., Clark, R. A., & Lowell, E. L. (1953). *The achievement motive.* New York: Appleton-Century-Crofts.

McClelland, D. C., & Boyatzis, R. E. (1982). Leadership motive pattern and long-term success in management. *Journal of Applied Psychology, 67,* 737–743.

McClelland, D. C., & Koestner, R. (1992). The achievement motive. In C. P. Smith, J. W. Atkinson, D. C. McClelland, & J. Veroff (Eds.), *Motivation and personality: Handbook of thematic content analysis* (pp. 143–152). New York: Cambridge University Press.

McClelland, D. C., & Watson, R. I. (1973). Power motivation and risk-taking behavior. *Journal of Personality, 41,* 121–139.

McCrae, R. R. (1989). Why I advocate the five-factor model: Joint factor analyses of the NEO-PI with other instruments. In D. M. Buss & N. Cantor (Eds.), *Personality psychology: Recent trends and emerging directions* (pp. 237–245). New York: Springer Verlag.

McCrae, R. R., & Costa, Jr., P. T. (1985). Updating Norman's "adequate taxonomy": Intelligence and personality dimensions in natural language and in questionnaires. *Journal of Personality and Social Psychology, 49,* 710–721.

McCrae, R. R., & Costa, Jr., P. T. (1987). Validation of the five-factor model of personality across instruments and observers. *Journal of Personality and Social Psychology, 52,* 81–90.

McDermott, J., & Hauser, M. (2005). The origins of music: Innateness, uniqueness, and evolution. *Music Perception, 23,* 29–59.

McDougall, W. (1908). *An introduction to social psychology.* London: Methuen.

McKeachie, W. J., Lin, Y. G., Milholland, J., & Isaacson, R. (1966). Students' affiliation motives, teacher warmth, and academic achievement. *Journal of Personality and Social Psychology, 4,* 457–461.

McKenzie, R. B., & Tullock, G. (1981). *The new world of economics: Explorations into the human experience* (3rd ed.). Homewood, IL: Richard D. Irwin.

McKinnon, W., Weisse, C. S., Reynolds, C. P., Bowles, C. A., & Baum, A. (1989). Chronic stress, leukocyte subpopulations, and humoral response to latent viruses. *Health Psychology, 8,* 389–402.

McNay, E. C., Canal, C. E., Sherwin, R. S., & Gold, P. E. (2006). Modulation of memory with septal injections of morphine and glucose: Effects on extracellular glucose levels in the hippocampus. *Physiology & Behavior, 87,* 298–303.

McNay, E. C., Fries, T. M., & Gold, P. E. (2000). Decreases in rat extracellular hippocampal glucose concentration associated with cognitive demand during a spatial task. *Proceedings of the National Academy of Science, 97,* 2881–2885.

McNay, E. C., & Gold, P. E. (2002). Food for thought: Fluctuations in brain extracellular glucose provide insight in the mechanisms of memory modulation. *Behavioral and Cognitive Neuroscience Reviews, 1,* 264–280.

Memmler, R. L., Cohen, B. J., & Wood, D. (1992). *Structure and function of the human body* (5th ed.). Philadelphia: J. B. Lippincott.

Mennella, J. A., & Beauchamp, G. K. (1998). Early flavor experiences: Research update. *Nutrition Reviews, 56,* 205–211.

Mennella, J. A., Jagnow, C. P., & Beauchamp, G. K. (2001). Prenatal and postnatal flavor learning by human infants. *Pediatrics, 107,* e88. Retrieved June 22, 2007, from http://www.pediatrics.org/cgi/content/full/107/6/e88

Mento, A. J., Locke, E. A., & Klein, H. J. (1992). Relationship of goal level to valence and instrumentality. *Journal of Applied Psychology, 77,* 395–405.

Messinger, D. S. (2002). Positive and negative: Infant facial expressions and emotions. *Current Directions in Psychological Science, 11,* 1–6.

Metcalfe, J., & Jacobs, W. J. (1998). Emotional memory: The effects of stress on "cool" and "hot" memory systems. In D. L. Medin (Ed.), *The psychology of learning and motivation* (Vol. 38, pp. 187–222). New York: Academic Press.

Meyerhoff, J. L., Oleshansky, M. A., & Mougey, E. H. (1988). Effects of psychological stress on pituitary hormones in man. In G. P. Chrousos, D. L. Loriaux, & P. W. Gold (Eds.), *Mechanisms of physical and emotional stress* (pp. 465–478). New York: Plenum Press.

Miller, G. A., Galanter, E., & Pribram, K. H. (1960). *Plans and the structure of behavior.* New York: Henry Holt.

Miller, N. E. (1959). Liberalization of basic S-R concepts: Extensions to conflict behavior, motivation, and social learning. In S. Koch (Ed.),

Psychology: A study of a science (Vol. 2, pp. 196–292). New York: McGraw-Hill.

Miller, R. B., & Brickman, S. J. (2004). A model of future-oriented motivation and self-regulation. *Educational Psychology Review, 16,* 9–33.

Miller, R. B., DeBacker, T. K., & Greene, B. A. (1999). Perceived instrumentality and academics: The link to task valuing. *Journal of Instructional Psychology, 26,* 250–260.

Miller, T. W. (1993). The assessment of stressful life events. In L. Goldberger & S. Breznitz (Eds.), *Handbook of stress: Theoretical and clinical aspects* (2nd ed., pp. 161–173). New York: Free Press.

Mineka, S. (1992). Evolutionary memories, emotional processing, and the emotional disorders. In D. L. Medin (Ed.), *The psychology of learning and motivation* (Vol. 28, pp. 161–206). San Diego: Academic Press.

Mineka, S., & Cook, M. (1993). Mechanisms involved in the observational conditioning of fear. *Journal of Experimental Psychology: General, 122,* 23–38.

Mittleman, M. A., Maclure, M., Sherwood, J. B., Mulry, R. P., Tofler, G. H., Jacobs, S. C., Friedman, R., Benson, H., & Muller, J. E. (1995). Triggering of acute myocardial infarction onset by episodes of anger. *Circulation, 92,* 1720–1725.

Miyaoka, Y., Sawada, M., Sakaguchi, T., & Shingai, T. (1987). Sensation of thirst in normal and laryngectomized man. *Perceptual and Motor Skills, 64,* 239–242.

Mohr, C. D., Armeli, S., Tennen, H., Carney, M. A., Affleck, G., & Hromi, A. (2001). Daily interpersonal experiences, context, and alcohol consumption: Crying in your beer and toasting good times. *Journal of Personality and Social Psychology, 80,* 489–500.

Monahan, J. L., Murphy, S. T., & Zajonc, R. B. (2000). Subliminal mere exposure: Specific, general, and diffuse effects. *Psychological Science, 11,* 462–466.

Mondin, G. W., Morgan, W. P., Piering, P. N., Stegner, A. J., Stotesbery, C. L., Trine, M. R., & Wu, M. Y. (1996). Psychological consequences of exercise deprivation in habitual exercisers. *Medicine and Science in Sports and Exercise, 29,* 1199–1203.

Monello, L. F., & Mayer, J. (1967). Hunger and satiety sensations in men, women, boys, and girls.

American Journal of Clinical Nutrition, 20, 253–261.

Monk, T., & Folkard, S. (1983). Circadian rhythms and shift work. In R. Hockey (Ed.), *Stress and fatigue in human performance* (pp. 97–121). Chichester: John Wiley.

Mook, D. G., & Votaw, M. C. (1992). How important is hedonism? Reasons given by college students for ending a meal. *Appetite, 18,* 69–75.

Morgan, W. P. (1979). Negative addiction in runners. *Physician and Sports Medicine, 7,* 57–70.

Morris, J. L. (1966). Propensity for risk taking as a determinant of vocational choice: An extension of the theory of achievement motivation. *Journal of Personality and Social Psychology, 3,* 328–335.

Morris, M., Steinberg, H., Sykes, E. A., & Salmon, P. (1990). Effects of temporary withdrawal from regular running. *Journal of Psychosomatic Research, 34,* 493–500.

Morris, W. N. (1992). A functional analysis of the role of mood in affective systems. In M. S. Clark (Ed.), *Review of personality and social psychology: Vol. 13. Emotion* (pp. 256–293). Newbury Park, CA: Sage.

Moskowitz, A. K. (2004). "Scared Stiff": Catatonia as an evolutionary-based fear response. *Psychological Review, 111,* 894–1002.

Moskowitz, H. R., Kluter, R. A., Westerling, J., & Jacobs, H. L. (1974). Sugar sweetness and pleasantness: Evidence for different psychological laws. *Science, 184,* 583–585.

Mower, G. D. (1976). Perceived intensity of peripheral thermal stimuli is independent of internal body temperature. *Journal of Comparative and Physiological Psychology, 90,* 1152–1155.

Mowrer, O. H. (1960). *Learning theory and behavior.* New York: John Wiley.

Mowrer, O. H., & Jones, H. M. (1943). Extinction and behavior variability as functions of effortfulness of task. *Journal of Experimental Psychology, 33,* 369–386.

Muraven, M., & Baumeister, R. F. (2000). Self-regulation and depletion of limited resources: Does self-control resemble a muscle? *Psychological Bulletin, 126,* 247–259.

Muraven, M., Shmueli, D., & Burkley, E. (2006). Conserving self-control strength. *Journal of Personality and Social Psychology, 91,* 524–537.

Muris, P., Merckelbach, H., & Collaris, R. (1997). Common childhood fears and their origins. *Behaviour Research and Therapy, 35,* 929–937.

Murphy, F. C., Nimmo-Smith, I., & Lawrence, A. D. (2003). Functional neuroanatomy of emotions: A meta-analysis. *Cognitive, Affective, & Behavioral Neuroscience, 3,* 207–233.

Murray, H. A. (1938). *Explorations in personality.* New York: Oxford University Press.

Muurahainen, N. E., Kissileff, H. R., Lachaussee, J., & Pi-Sunyer, F. X. (1991). Effect of a soup preload on reduction of food intake by cholecystokinin in humans. *American Journal of Physiology, 260,* R672–R680.

Myers, J. K., Lindenthal, J. J., & Pepper, M. (1974). Social class, life events, and psychiatric symptoms. In B. S. Dohrenwend & B. P. Dohrenwend (Eds.), *Stressful life events: Their nature and effects* (pp. 191–205). New York: John Wiley.

Myerson, J., & Green, L. (1995). Discounting of delayed rewards: Models of individual choice. *Journal of the Experimental Analysis of Behavior, 61,* 263–276.

Myrick, H., Anton, R. F., Li, X., Henderson, S., Drobes, D., Voronin, K., & George, M. S. (2004). Differential brain activity in alcoholics and social drinkers to alcohol cues: Relationship to craving. *Neuropsychopharmacology, 29,* 393–402.

Nakata, T., & Trehub, S. E. (2004). Infants' responsiveness to maternal speech and singing. *Infant Behavior and Development, 27,* 455–464

National Center for Health Statistics. (2006). Retrieved July 30, 2008, from http://www.cdc.gov/nchs

National Center for Posttraumatic Stress Disorder. (2008). PTSD checklist of the Department of Veterans Affairs. Retrieved February 13, 2008, from http://www.ncptsd.va.gov/ncmain/ncdocs/assmnts/ptsd_ checklist_pcl.html

Neary, R. S., & Zuckerman, M. (1976). Sensation seeking, trait and state anxiety, and the electrodermal orienting reflex. *Psychophysiology, 13,* 205–211.

Nederkoorn, C., Smulders, F. T. Y., & Jansen, A. (2000). Cephalic phase responses, craving and food intake in normal subjects. *Appetite, 35,* 45–55.

Neef, N. A., Mace, F. C., Shea, M. C., & Shade, D. (1992). Effects of reinforcer rate and reinforcer quality on time allocation: Extensions of matching theory to educational settings. *Journal of Applied Behavior Analysis, 25,* 691–699.

Neiss, R. (1988). Reconceptualizing arousal: Psychobiological states in motor performance. *Psychological Bulletin, 103,* 345–366.

Nelson, L. D., & Morrison, E. L. (2005). The symptoms of resource scarcity: Judgments of food and finances influence preference for potential partners. *Psychological Science, 16,* 167–173.

Nestler, E. J. (2005). Is there a common molecular pathway for addiction? *Nature Neuroscience, 8,* 1445–1449.

Newman, M. G., & Stone, A. A. (1996). Does humor moderate the effects of experimentally induced stress? *Annals of Behavioral Medicine, 18,* 101–109.

Nicki, R. M., & Moss, V. (1975). Preference for non-representational art as a function of various measures of complexity. *Canadian Journal of Psychology, 29,* 237–249.

Niedenthal, P. M., & Kitayama, S. (1994). *The heart's eye: Emotional influences on perception and attention.* San Diego: Academic Press.

Nieman, D. C. (1994). Exercise, upper respiratory tract infection, and the immune system. *Medicine and Science in Sports and Exercise, 26,* 128–139.

Nieuwenhuyse, B., Offenberg, L., & Frijda, N. H. (1987). Subjective emotion and reported body experience. *Motivation and Emotion, 11,* 169–182.

Nisbett, R. E., & Wilson, T. D. (1977). Telling more than we can know: Verbal reports on mental processes. *Psychological Review, 84,* 231–259.

Noftle, E. E., & Robins, R. W. (2007). Personality predictors of academic outcomes: Big five correlates of GPA and SAT scores. *Journal of Personality and Social Psychology, 93,* 116–130.

North, A. C., & Hargreaves, D. J. (1995). Subjective complexity, familiarity, and liking for popular music. *Psychomusicology, 14,* 77–93.

North, A. C., & Hargreaves, D. J. (1996). Responses to music in a dining area. *Journal of Applied Social Psychology, 26,* 491–501.

North, A. C., Hargreaves, D. J., & Hargreaves, J. J. (2004). Uses of music in everyday life. *Music Perception, 22,* 41–77.

Oatley, K., & Johnson-Laird, P. N. (1990). Semantic primitives for emotions: A reply to Ortony and Clore. *Cognition and Emotion, 4,* 129–143.

O'Brien, C. P. (2005). Anticraving medications for relapse prevention: A possible new class of psychoactive medications. *The American Journal of Psychiatry, 162,* 1423–1431.

Ogden, J., Veale, D., & Summers, Z. (1997). The development and validation of the exercise dependence questionnaire. *Addiction Research, 5,* 343–355.

Öhman, A. (1986). Face the beast and fear the face: Animal and social fears as prototypes of evolutionary analyses of emotion. *Psychophysiology, 23,* 123–145.

Öhman, A. (1993). Fear and anxiety as emotional phenomena: Clinical phenomenology, evolutionary perspectives, and information-processing mechanisms. In M. Lewis & J. M. Haviland (Eds.), *Handbook of emotions* (pp. 511–536). New York: Guilford Press.

Öhman, A., Flykt, A., & Esteves, F. (2001). Emotion drives attention: Detecting the snake in the grass. *Journal of Experimental Psychology: General, 130,* 466–478.

Öhman, A., & Mineka, S. (2001). Fears, phobias, and preparedness: Toward an evolved module of fear and learning. *Psychological Review, 108,* 483–522.

Olds, J. (1958). Self stimulation of the brain. *Science, 127,* 315–324.

Olds, J. (1977). *Drives and reinforcements: Behavioral studies of hypothalamic functions.* New York: Raven Press.

O'Malley, P. (1990). *Biting at the grave: The Irish hunger strikes and the politics of despair.* Boston: Beacon Press.

O'Malley, S. S., Krishnan-Sarin, S., Farren, C., Sinha, R., & Kreek, M. J. (2002). Naltrexone decreases craving and alcohol self-administration in alcohol-dependent subjects and activates the hypothalamo-pituitary-adrenocortical axis. *Psychopharmacology, 160,* 19–29.

Ortony, A., & Turner, T. J. (1990). What's basic about basic emotions? *Psychological Review, 97,* 315–331.

Parker, B., & Chusmir, L. H. (1991). Motivation needs and their relationship to life success. *Human Relations, 44,* 1301–1312.

Patalano, A. L., & Seifert, C. M. (1997). Opportunistic planning: Being reminded of pending goals. *Cognitive Psychology, 34,* 1–36.

Patton, J. H., Stanford, M. S., & Barratt, E. S. (1995). Factor structure of the Barratt Impulsiveness Scale. *Journal of Clinical Psychology, 51,* 768–774.

Paulhan, F. (1887/1930). *The laws of feeling* (C. K. Ogden, Trans.). London: Kegan Paul, Trench, Trubner.

Pavlov, I. P. (1927). *Conditioned reflexes*. New York: Dover.

Pavot, W., Diener, E., & Fujita, F. (1990). Extraversion and happiness. *Personality and Individual Differences, 11,* 1299–1306.

Peck, A. L. (1942). *Aristotle: Generation of animals.* Cambridge: Harvard University Press.

Pedersen, B. K., & Ullum, H. (1994). NK cell response to physical activity: Possible mechanisms of action. *Medicine and Science in Sports and Exercise, 26,* 140–146.

Peretz, I. (2006). The nature of music from a biological perspective. *Cognition, 100,* 1–32.

Perkins, C. C. (1955). The stimulus conditions which follow learned responses. *Psychological Review, 62,* 341–348.

Perkins, D. V. (1982). The assessment of stress using life event scales. *Handbook of stress: Theoretical and clinical aspects* (pp. 320–331). New York: Free Press.

Perkins, K. A., Gerlach, D., Broge, M., Grobe, J. E., & Wilson, A. (2000). Greater sensitivity to subjective effects of nicotine in nonsmokers high in sensation seeking. *Experimental and Clinical Psychopharmacology, 8,* 462–471.

Perry, A. B. (2004). Decreasing math anxiety in college students. *College Student Journal, 38,* 321–324.

Pervin, L. A. (1984). *Current controversies and issues in personality* (2nd ed.). New York: John Wiley.

Pervin, L. A. (1989). Goal concepts: Themes, issues, and questions. In L. A. Pervin (Ed.), *Goal concepts in personality and social psychology* (pp. 473–479). Hillsdale, NJ: Lawrence Erlbaum.

Peterson, P. K., Chao, C. C., Molitor, T., Murtaugh, M., Strgar, F., & Sharp, B. M. (1991). Stress and pathogenesis of infectious disease. *Reviews of Infectious Diseases, 13,* 710–720.

Petrie, M., Halliday, T., & Sanders, C. (1991). Peahens prefer peacocks with elaborate trains. *Animal Behaviour, 41,* 323–331.

Phan, K. L., Wager, T., Taylor, S. F., & Liberzon, I. (2002). Functional neuroanatomy of emotion: A meta-analysis of emotion activation studies in PET and fMRI. *NeuroImage, 16,* 331–348.

Phan, K. L., Wager, T. D., Taylor, S. F., & Liberzon, I. (2004). Functional neuroimaging studies of human emotions. *CNS Spectrums, 9,* 258–266.

Piaget, J. (1951/1976). Mastery play. In J. S. Bruner, A. Jolly, & K. Sylva (Eds.), *Play—its role in development and evolution* (pp. 166–171). New York: Basic Books.

Pick, D. F., Hurford, D. P., Bair, R. C., & Goepfert, G. L. (1990). Ice cream butterfat content by volume as a possible predictor of taste preference. *Perceptual and Motor Skills, 70,* 639–642.

Pickett, C. L., Gardner, W. I., & Knowles, M. (2004). Getting a cue: The need to belong and enhanced sensitivity to social cues. *Personality and Social Psychology Bulletin, 30,* 1095–1107.

Pieper, W. A., & Marx, M. H. (1963). Effects of within-session incentive contrast on instrumental acquisition and performance. *Journal of Experimental Psychology, 65,* 568–571.

Pignatiello, M. F., Camp, C. J., & Rasar, L. A. (1986). Musical mood induction: An alternative to the Velten technique. *Journal of Abnormal Psychology, 95,* 295–297.

Pinel, J. P. J. (1997). *Biopsychology* (3rd ed.). Boston: Allyn and Bacon.

Pinel, J. P. J., Assanand, S., & Lehman, D. R. (2000). Hunger, eating, and ill health. *American Psychologist, 55,* 1105–1116.

Piper, W. (1954/1961). *The little engine that could.* New York: Platt & Munk.

Pittman, T. S. (1998). Motivation. In D. T. Gilbert, S. T. Fiske, & G. Linzey (Eds.), *The handbook of social psychology* (Vol. 2, 4th ed., pp. 549–590). Boston: McGraw-Hill.

Pliner, P. (1982). The effects of mere exposure on liking for edible substances. *Appetite, 3,* 283–290.

Pliner, P., & Hobden, K. (1992). Development of a scale to measure the trait of food neophobia in humans. *Appetite, 19,* 105–120.

Plomin, R., DeFries, J. C., McClearn, G. E., & McGuffin, P. (2001). *Behavioral genetics* (4th ed.). New York: Worth.

Plutchik, R. (1980). *Emotion: A psychoevolutionary synthesis.* New York: Harper & Row.

Plutchik, R. (1984). Emotions: A general psychoevolutionary theory. In K. R. Scherer & P. Ekman (Eds.), *Approaches to emotion* (pp. 197–219). Hillsdale, NJ: Lawrence Erlbaum.

Polivy, J., & Herman, C. P. (1985). Dieting and bingeing: A causal analysis. *American Psychologist, 40,* 193–201.

Polivy, J., & Herman, C. P. (2002). Causes of eating disorders. *Annual Review of Psychology, 53,* 187–213.

Powers, W. T. (1973). *Behavior: The control of perception.* Chicago: Aldine.

Powley, T. L. (1977). The ventromedial hypothalamus syndrome, satiety and a cephalic phase hypothesis. *Psychological Review, 84,* 89–126.

Prentice, A. M., & Jebb, S. A. (1995). Obesity in Britain: Gluttony or sloth? *British Medical Journal, 311,* 437–439.

Pychyl, T. A., Lee, J. M., Thibodeau, R., & Blunt, A. (2000a). Five days of emotion: An experience sampling study of undergraduate student procrastination. *Journal of Social Behavior & Personality, 15,* 239–254.

Pychyl, T. A., Morin, R. W., & Salmon, B. R. (2000b). Procrastination and the planning fallacy: An examination of the study habits of university students. *Journal of Social Behavior & Personality, 15,* 135–150.

Rabkin, J. G., & Struening, E. L. (1976). Life events, stress, and illness. *Science, 194,* 1013–1020.

Rachlin, H. (1989). *Judgment, decision, and choice.* New York: W. H. Freeman.

Rachlin, H., Raineri, A., & Cross, D. (1991). Subjective probability and delay. *Journal of the Experimental Analysis of Behavior, 55,* 233–244.

Rahe, R. H., Meyer, M., Smith, M., Kjaer, G., & Holmes, T. H. (1964). Social stress and illness onset. *Journal of Psychosomatic Research, 8,* 35–44.

Rancour-Laferriere, D. (1983). Four adaptive aspects of the female orgasm. *Journal of Social and Biological Structures, 6,* 319–333.

Raskin, V. (1985). *Semantic mechanisms of humor.* Dordrecht: D. Reidel.

Ratner, S. C. (1967). Comparative aspects of hypnosis. In J. E. Gordon (Ed.), *Handbook of clinical and experimental hypnosis* (pp. 550–587). New York: The MacMillan Company.

Raudenbush, B., & Frank, R. A. (1999). Assessing food neophobia: The role of stimulus familiarity. *Appetite, 32,* 261–271.

Ravussin, E., & Danforth, Jr., E. (1999). Beyond sloth—physical activity and weight gain. *Science, 283,* 184–185.

Raynor, H. A., & Epstein, L. H. (2001). Dietary variety, energy regulation, and obesity. *Psychological Bulletin, 127,* 325–341.

Raynor, J. O. (1970/1974). Relationships between achievement-related motives, future orientation, and academic performance. *Journal of Personality and Social Psychology, 15,* 28–33. Reprinted with modifications in J. W. Atkinson & J. O.

Raynor (Eds.), *Motivation and achievement* (pp. 173–180). Washington, DC: V. H. Winston.

Rebert, W. M., Stanton, A. L., & Schwarz, R. M. (1991). Influence of personality attributes and daily moods on bulimic eating patterns. *Addictive Behaviors, 16,* 497–505.

Regan, P. C. (2000). The role of sexual desire and sexual activity in dating relationships. *Social Behavior and Personality, 28,* 51–59.

Regan, P. C., & Berscheid, E. (1999). *Lust: What we know about human sexual desire.* Thousand Oaks, CA: Sage.

Regan, P. C., Kocan, E. R., & Whitlock, T. (1998). Ain't love grand! A prototype analysis of romantic love. *Journal of Social and Personal Relationships, 15,* 411–420.

Reisenzein, R. (1983). The Schachter theory of emotion: Two decades later. *Psychological Bulletin, 94,* 239–264.

Revelle, W. (1987). Personality and motivation: Sources of inefficiency in cognitive performance. *Journal of Research in Personality, 21,* 436–452.

Rhodes, G. (2006). The evolutionary psychology of facial beauty. *Annual Review of Psychology, 57,* 199–226.

Rhodes, G., Simmons, L. W., & Peters, M. (2005). Attractiveness and sexual behavior: Does attractiveness enhance mating success? *Evolution and Human Behavior, 26,* 186–201.

Riemann, R., Angleitner, A., & Strelau, J. (1997). Genetic and environmental influences on personality: A study of twins reared together using the self- and peer report NEO-FFI scales. *Journal of Personality, 65,* 449–476.

Rinn, W. E. (1991). Neuropsychology of facial expression. In R. Feldman & B. Rime (Eds.), *Fundamentals of nonverbal behavior* (pp. 3–70). Cambridge: Cambridge University Press.

Robinson, T. E., & Berridge, K. C. (2000). The psychology and neurobiology of addiction: An incentive-sensitization view. *Addiction, 95* (supplement 2), 91–117.

Robinson, T. E., & Berridge, K. C. (2003). Addiction. *Annual Review of Psychology, 54,* 25–53.

Rogers, C. (1959). A theory of therapy, personality, and interpersonal relationships, as developed in the client-centered framework. In S. Koch (Ed.), *Psychology: A study of a science* (Vol. 3, pp. 184–256). New York: McGraw-Hill.

Rolls, B. J., Morris, E. L., & Roe, L. S. (2002). Portion size of food affects energy intake in normal-weight and overweight men and women. *American Journal of Clinical Nutrition, 76,* 1207–1213.

Rolls, B. J., Rolls, E. T., Rowe, E. A., & Sweeney, K. (1981). Sensory specific satiety in man. *Physiology and Behavior, 27,* 137–142.

Roper report. (1984). *Public Opinion, 7,* 32.

Roseman, I. J., & Smith, C. A. (2001). Appraisal theory: Overview, assumptions, varieties, controversies. In K. R. Scherer, A. Schorr, & T. Johnstone (Eds.), *Appraisal processes in emotion: Theory, methods, research* (pp. 3–19). New York: Oxford University Press.

Rosenstein, D., & Oster, H. (1988). Differential facial responses to four basic tastes in newborns. *Child Development, 59,* 1555–1568.

Rothbart, M. K. (1973). Laughter in young children. *Psychological Bulletin, 80,* 247–256.

Rothbart, M. K. (1976). Incongruity, problem solving and laughter. In A. J. Chapman & H. C. Foot (Eds.), *Humour and laughter: Theory, research, and applications* (pp. 37–54). London: Wiley.

Rothblum, E. D., Solomon, L. J., & Murakami, J. (1986). Affective, cognitive, and behavioral differences between high and low procrastinators. *Journal of Counseling Psychology, 33,* 387–394.

Rotter, J. B. (1942). Levels of aspiration as a method of studying personality. I. A critical review of methodology. *Psychological Review, 49,* 463–474.

Rozin, P. (1999). Preadaptation and the puzzles and properties of pleasure. In D. Kahneman, E. Diener, & N. Schwarz (Eds.), *Well-being: The foundations of hedonic psychology* (pp. 109–133). New York: Russell Sage Foundation.

Rozin, P., Rozin, A., Appel, B., & Wachtel, C. (2006). Documenting and explaining the common AAB pattern in music and humor: Establishing and breaking expectations. *Emotion, 4,* 349–355.

Rozin, P., & Schiller, D. (1980). The nature and acquisition of a preference for chili pepper by humans. *Motivation and Emotion, 4,* 77–101.

Ruch, W. (1988). Sensation seeking and the enjoyment of structure and content of humour: Stability of findings across four samples. *Personality and Individual Differences, 9,* 861–871.

Ruch, W. (1993). Exhilaration and humor. In M. Lewis & J. M. Haviland (Eds.), *Handbook of emotions* (pp. 605–616). New York: Guilford Press.

Ruch, W., & Ekman, P. (2001). The expressive pattern of laughter. In A. W. Kaszniak (Ed.), *Emotion, qualia, and consciousness* (pp. 426–443). Tokyo: World Scientific.

Ruch, W., & Hehl, F.-J. (1998). A two-mode model of humor appreciation: Its relation to aesthetic appreciation and simplicity-complexity of personality. In W. Ruch (Ed.), *The sense of humor: Explorations of a personality characteristic* (pp. 109–142). New York: Mouton de Gruyter.

Ruch, W., & Köhler, G. (1998). A temperament approach to humor. In W. Ruch (Ed.), *The sense of humor: Explorations of a personality characteristic* (pp. 203–228). New York: Mouton de Gruyter.

Ruderman, A. J. (1985). Dysphoric mood and overeating: A test of restraint theory's disinhibition hypothesis. *Journal of Abnormal Psychology, 94,* 78–85.

Ruderman, A. J. (1986). Dietary restraint: A theoretical and empirical review. *Psychological Bulletin, 99,* 247–262.

Rusbult, C. E. (1983). A longitudinal test of the investment model: The development (and deterioration) of satisfaction and commitment in heterosexual involvements. *Journal of Personality and Social Psychology, 45,* 101–117.

Russell, J. A. (1991). Culture and the categorization of emotions. *Psychological Bulletin, 110,* 426–450.

Rusting, C. L., & Larsen, R. J. (1997). Extraversion, neuroticism, and susceptibility to positive and negative affect: A test of two theoretical models. *Personality and Individual Differences, 22,* 607–612.

Sagi, A., & Friedland, N. (2007). The cost of richness: The effect of the size and diversity of decision sets on post-decision regret. *Journal of Personality and Social Psychology, 93,* 515–524.

Saladin, M. E., Brady, K. T., Graap, K., & Rothbaum, B. O. (2006). A preliminary report on the use of virtual reality technology to elicit craving and cue reactivity in cocaine dependent individuals. *Addictive Behaviors, 31,* 1881–1894.

Salancik, G. R. (1977). Commitment and the control of organizational behavior and belief. In B. M. Staw & G. R. Salancik (Eds.), *New directions in organization behavior* (pp. 1–54). Chicago: St. Clair Press.

Salovey, P., Rothman, A. J., Detweiler, J. B., & Steward, W. T. (2000). Emotional states and physical health. *American Psychologist, 55,* 110–121.

Sandick, B. L., Engell, D. B., & Maller, O. (1984). Perception of drinking water temperature and effects for humans after exercise. *Physiology and Behavior, 32,* 851–855.

Saucier, G. (1994). Mini-markers: A brief version of Goldberg's unipolar big-five markers. *Journal of Personality Assessment, 63,* 506–516.

Saucier, G. (2003). Mini-markers. Retrieved September 8, 2003, from http://darkwing.uoregon.edu/~gsaucier/gsau41.htm.

Savage, L. J. (1954). *The foundations of statistics.* New York: John Wiley.

Scarborough, E. (1990). Margaret Floy Washburn (1871–1939). In A. N. O'Connell & N. F. Russo (Eds.), *Women in psychology: A bio-bibliographic sourcebook* (pp. 342–349). New York: Greenwood Press.

Schachter, S., & Singer, J. E. (1962). Cognitive, social, and physiological determinants of emotional state. *Psychological Review, 69,* 379–399.

Schank, R. C., & Abelson, R. P. (1977). *Scripts, plans, goals and understanding.* Hillsdale, NJ: Lawrence Erlbaum.

Scherer, K. R. (1994). Emotion serves to decouple stimulus and response. In P. Ekman & R. J. Davidson (Eds.), *The nature of emotion: Fundamental questions* (pp. 127–130). New York: Oxford University Press.

Scherer, K. R. (1997). Profiles of emotion-antecedent appraisal: Testing theoretical predictions across cultures. *Cognition and Emotion, 11,* 113–150.

Schiffman, S. S., Graham, B. G., Sattely-Miller, E. A., & Warwick, Z. S. (1998). Orosensory perception of dietary fat. *Current Directions in Psychological Science, 7,* 137–143.

Schimmack, U., & Reisenzein, R. (2002). Experiencing activation: Energetic arousal and tense arousal are not mixtures of valence and activation. *Emotion, 2,* 412–417.

Schmid, D. A., Held, K., Ising, M., Uhr, M., Weike, J. C., & Steiger, A. (2005). Ghrelin stimulates appetite, imagination of food, GH, ACTH, and cortisol, but does not affect leptin in normal controls. *Neuropsychopharmacology, 30,* 1187–1192.

Schmitt, D. P., & 121 Members of the International Sexuality Description Project. (2004). Patterns and universals of mate poaching across 53 nations: The effects of sex, culture, and personality on romantically attracting another person's partner. *Journal of Personality and Social Psychology, 86,* 560–584.

Schopenhauer, A. (1841/1960). *Essay on the freedom of the will* (K. Kolenda, Trans.). Indianapolis: Bobbs-Merrill.

Schopenhauer, A. (1851/1970). On philosophy and the intellect. In R. J. Hollingdale (Ed.), *Essays and aphorisms* (pp. 117–132). New York: Penguin Classics.

Schuckit, M. A. (2000). *Drug and alcohol abuse: A clinical guide to diagnosis and treatment.* New York: Plenum Press.

Schuh, K. J., & Griffiths, R. R. (1997). Caffeine reinforcement: The role of withdrawal. *Psychopharmacology, 130,* 320–326.

Schulkin, J. (1991). Hedonic consequences of salt hunger. In R. C. Bolles (Ed.), *The hedonics of taste* (pp. 89–105). Hillsdale, NJ: Lawrence Erlbaum.

Schuster, M. A., Stein, B. D., Jaycox, L. H., Collins, R. L., Marshall, G. N., Elliott, M. N., Zhou, A. J., Kanhouse, D. E., Morrison, J. L., & Berry, S. H. (2001). A national survey of stress reactions after the September 11, 2001, terrorist attacks. *New England Journal of Medicine, 345,* 1507–1512.

Schwartz, B. (2004). *The paradox of choice.* New York: HarperCollins Publishers.

Schwartz, B., Ward, A., Monterosso, J., Lyubomirsky, S., White, K., & Lehman, D. R. (2002). Maximizing versus satisficing: Happiness is a matter of choice. *Journal of Personality and Social Psychology, 83,* 1178–1197.

Sechenov, I. M. (1863/1965). Reflexes of the brain. In R. J. Herrnstein & E. G. Boring (Eds.), *A source book in the history of psychology* (pp. 308–321). Cambridge: Harvard University Press.

Segal, N. L. (1999). *Entwined lives.* New York: Dutton.

Seibert, P. S., & Ellis, H. C. (1991). A convenient self-referencing mood induction procedure. *Bulletin of the Psychonomic Society, 29,* 121–124.

Seibert, S. E., & Kraimer, M. L. (2001). The five-factor model of personality and career success. *Journal of Vocational Behavior, 58,* 1–21.

Self, D. W. (2005). Neural basis of substance abuse and dependence. In B. J. Sadock & V. A. Sadock (Eds.), *Comprehensive textbook of psychiatry* (Vol. 1) (pp. 308–319). Philadelphia: Lippincott Williams & Wilkins.

Seligman, M. E. P. (1971). Phobias and preparedness. *Behavior Therapy, 2,* 307–320.

Seligman, M. E. P., & Csikszentmihalyi, M. (2000). Positive psychology. An introduction. *American Psychologist, 55,* 5–14.

Seligman, M. E. P., Maier, S. F., & Solomon, R. L. (1971). Unpredictable and uncontrollable aversive events. In F. R. Brush (Ed.), *Aversive conditioning and learning.* New York: Academic Press.

Selye, H. (1976). *The stress of life* (rev ed.). New York: McGraw-Hill.

Selye, H. (1993). History of the stress concept. In L. Goldberger & S. Breznitz (Eds.), *Handbook of stress: Theoretical and clinical aspects* (2nd ed., pp. 7–17). New York: Free Press.

Shaffer, H. J., Hall, M. N., & Vander Bilt, J. (1999). Estimating the prevalence of disordered gambling behavior in the United States and Canada: A research synthesis. *American Journal of Public Health, 89,* 1369–1374.

Shanteau, J., & Nagy, G. F. (1979). Probability of acceptance in dating choice. *Journal of Personality and Social Psychology, 37,* 522–533.

Sharpe, L. (2002). A reformulated cognitive-behavioral model of problem gambling: A biopsychosocial perspective. *Clinical Psychology Review, 22,* 1–25.

Shaver, P., Schwartz, J., Kirson, D., & O'Connor, C. (1987). Emotion knowledge: Further exploration of a prototype approach. *Journal of Personality and Social Psychology, 52,* 1061–1086.

Sheldon, K. M., Elliot, A. J., Kin, Y., & Kasser, T. (2001). What is satisfying about satisfying events? Testing 10 candidate psychological needs. *Journal of Personality and Social Psychology, 80,* 325–339.

Sheldon, K. M., & Niemiec, C. P. (2006). It's not just the amount that counts: Balanced need satisfaction also affects well-being. *Journal of Personality and Social Psychology, 91,* 331–341.

Shelley, M. K. (1994). Gain/loss asymmetry in risky intertemporal choice. *Organizational Behavior and Human Decision Processes, 59,* 124–159.

Shepperd, J. A., & McNulty, J. K. (2002). The affective consequences of expected and unexpected outcomes. *Psychological Science, 13,* 85–88.

Sherwood, J. J. (1966). Self-report and projective measures of achievement and affiliation. *Journal of Consulting Psychology, 30,* 329–337.

Shipley, Jr., T. E., & Veroff, J. (1952). A projective measure of need for affiliation. *Journal of Experimental Psychology, 43,* 349–356.

Shoemaker, P. J. H. (1982). The expected utility model: Its variants, purposes, evidence and limitations. *Journal of Economic Literature, 20,* 529–563.

Shuchter, S. R., & Zisook, S. (1993). The course of normal grief. In M. Stroebe, W. Stroebe, & R. Hansson (Eds.), *Handbook of bereavement: Theory, research, and intervention* (pp. 23–43). Cambridge: Cambridge University Press.

Siegel, S. (2005). Drug tolerance, drug addiction, and drug anticipation. *Current Directions in Psychological Science, 14,* 296–300.

Simon, H. (1955/1979). A behavioral model of rational choice. In H. Simon (Ed.), *Models of thought* (pp. 7–19). New Haven: Yale University Press.

Singer, J. E., & Davidson, L. M. (1986). Specificity and stress research. In M. H. Appley & R. Trumbull (Eds.), *Dynamics of stress* (pp. 47–61). New York: Plenum Press.

Sizer, F., & Whitney, E. (1997). *Nutrition: Concepts and controversies* (7th ed.). Belmont, CA: Wadsworth.

Skinner, B. F. (1938). *The behavior of organisms.* New York: Appleton-Century-Crofts.

Skinner, B. F. (1953). *Science and human behavior.* New York: Macmillan.

Smith, B. D., Davidson, R. A., Smith, D. L., Goldstein, H., & Perlstein, W. (1989). Sensation seeking and arousal: Effects of strong stimulation on electrodermal activation and memory task performance. *Personality and Individual Differences, 10,* 671–679.

Smith, C. A., & Lazarus, R. S. (1990). Emotion and adaptation. In L. Pervin (Ed.), *Handbook of personality theory and research* (pp. 609–637). New York: Guilford Press.

Smith, C. P. (1992). *Motivation and personality: Handbook of thematic content analysis.* New York: Cambridge University Press.

Smith, G. F., & Dorfman, D. D. (1975). The effect of stimulus uncertainty on the relationship between frequency of exposure and liking. *Journal of Personality and Social Psychology, 31,* 150–155.

Smith, S., & Myers, T. I. (1966). Stimulation seeking during sensory deprivation. *Perceptual and Motor Skills, 23,* 1151–1163.

Smith, S., Myers, T. I., & Johnson, E., III. (1967). Stimulation seeking throughout seven days of sensory deprivation. *Perceptual and Motor Skills, 25,* 261–271.

Smith, S. A., Sutherland, D., & Christopher, G. (2005). Effects of repeated doses of caffeine on mood and performance and fatigued volunteers. *Journal of Psychopharmacology, 19,* 620–626.

Smith, T. W. (1979). Happiness: Time trends, seasonal variations, intersurvey differences, and other mysteries. *Social Psychology Quarterly, 42,* 18–30.

Snyder, H. L. (1962). Saccharine concentration and deprivation as determinants of instrumental and consummatory response strengths. *Journal of Experimental Psychology, 63,* 610–615.

Snyder, M. (1983). The influence of individuals on situations: Implications for understanding the links between personality and social behavior. *Journal of Personality, 51,* 497–516.

Sokolov, Y. N. (1963). *Perception and the conditioned reflex.* New York: Macmillan.

Solomon, R. L. (1980). The opponent-process theory of acquired motivation: The costs of pleasure and the benefits of pain. *American Psychologist, 35,* 691–712.

Solomon, R. L., & Corbit, J. D. (1974). An opponent-process theory of motivation: 1. Temporal dynamics of affect. *Psychological Review, 81,* 119–145.

Solomon, S. M., & Kirby, D. F. (1990). The refeeding syndrome: A review. *Journal of Parenteral and Enteral Nutrition, 14,* 90–96.

Spangler, W. D. (1992). Validity of questionnaire and TAT measures of need for achievement: Two meta-analyses. *Psychological Bulletin, 112,* 140–154.

Sparrow, W. A., & Newell, K. M. (1998). Metabolic energy expenditure and the regulation of movement economy. *Psychonomic Bulletin and Review, 5,* 173–196.

Spatny, J., Jr. (1997). The positive effects of humor on affect and coping skills. Unpublished master's thesis, Ball State University, Muncie, Indiana.

Speisman, J. C., Lazarus, R. S., Mordkoff, A., & Davison, L. (1964). Experimental reduction of stress based on ego-defense theory. *Journal of Abnormal and Social Psychology, 68,* 367–380.

Spence, K. W., Farber, I. E., & McFann, H. H. (1956a). The relation of anxiety (drive) level to performance in competitive and non-competitive paired-associates learning. *Journal of Experimental Psychology, 52,* 296–305.

Spence, K. W., Taylor, J. A., & Ketchel, R. (1956b). Anxiety (drive) level and degree of competition in paired-associates learning. *Journal of Experimental Psychology, 52,* 303–310.

Spencer, H. (1881/1977). *The principles of psychology.* Boston: Longwood Press.

Spencer, H. (1899). *The principles of psychology* (Vol. 1). New York: D. Appleton.

Spencer, J. A. & Fremouw, W. J. (1979). Binge eating as a function of restraint and weight classification. *Journal of Abnormal Psychology, 88,* 262–267.

Spielberger, C. D. (1975). Anxiety: State-trait-process. In C. D. Spielberger & I. G. Saranson (Eds.), *Stress and anxiety: Volume 1* (pp. 115–143). New York: John Wiley & Sons.

Spinoza, B. (1677). *Ethics. Part I. Concerning God. Axiom IV.* Retrieved July 3, 2008, from http://frank.mtsu .edu/~rbombard/RB/Spinoza/ethica1.html.

Staddon, J. E. R., & Simmelhag, V. L. (1971). The "superstition" experiment: A reexamination of its implications for the principles of adaptive behavior. *Psychological Review, 78,* 3–43.

Steck, L., & Machotka, P. (1975). Preference for musical complexity: Effect of context. *Journal of Experimental Psychology, 104,* 170–174.

Steel, P. (2007). The nature of procrastination: A meta-analytic and theoretical review of quintessential self-regulatory failure. *Psychological Bulletin, 133,* 65–94.

Steel, P., & König, C. J. (2006). Integrating theories of motivation. *Academy of Management Review, 31,* 889–913.

Steiner, J. E. (1977). Facial expressions of the neonate infant indicating the hedonics of food-related chemical stimuli. In J. M. Weiffenbach (Ed.), *Taste and development* (pp. 173–189). Bethesda: U.S. Department of Health, Education, and Welfare.

Stelmack, R. M. (1990). Biological bases of extraversion: Psychophysiological evidence. *Journal of Personality, 58,* 291–311.

Stemmler, G. (1989). The autonomic differentiation of emotions revisited: Convergent and discriminant validation. *Psychophysiology, 26,* 617–632.

Stevens, S. S. (1972). *Psychophysics and scaling.* Morristown, NJ: General Learning Press.

Stewart, J., de Wit, H., & Eikelboom, R. (1984). Role of unconditioned and conditioned drug effects in the self-administration of opiates and stimulants. *Psychological Review, 91,* 251–268.

Stewart, J., & Wise, R. A. (1992). Reinstatement of heroin self-administration habits: Morphine prompts and naltrexone discourages renewed responding after extinction. *Psychopharmacology, 108*, 79–84.

Stice, E. (2001). A prospective test of the dual-pathway of bulimic pathology: Mediating effects of dieting and negative affect. *Journal of Abnormal Psychology, 110*, 124–135.

Stigler, G. J. (1950). The development of utility theory. *Journal of Political Economy, 58*(4), 307–327; (5), 373–396.

Stone, A. A., Hedges, S. M., Neale, J. M., & Satin, M. S. (1985). Prospective and cross-sectional mood reports offer no evidence of a "blue Monday" phenomenon. *Journal of Personality and Social Psychology, 49*, 129–134.

Stout, G. F. (1903). *The groundwork of psychology.* New York: Hinds & Noble.

Strain, E. C., & Griffiths, R. R. (2005). Caffeine-related disorders. In J. H. Lowinson [et al.] (Eds.), *Substance abuse: A comprehensive textbook,* (pp. 1201–1210). Philadelphia, PA.: Lippincott Williams & Wilkins.

Stratton, V. N., & Zalanowski, A. H. (1994). Affective impact of music vs. lyrics. *Empirical Studies of the Arts, 12*, 173–184.

Straub, W. F. (1982). Sensation seeking among high- and low-risk male athletes. *Journal of Sports Psychology, 4*, 246–253.

Strelau, J. (1985). Temperament and personality: Pavlov and beyond. In J. Strelau, F. H. Farley, & A. Gale (Eds.), *The biological bases of personality and behavior: Vol. 1. Theories, measurement techniques, and development* (pp. 25–43). Washington, DC: Hemisphere.

Strelau, J. (1987). The concept of temperament in personality research. *European Journal of Personality, 1*, 107–117.

Suls, J., Green, P., & Hillis, S. (1998). Emotional reactivity to everyday problems, affective inertia, and neuroticism. *Personality and Social Psychology Bulletin, 24*, 127–136.

Suls, J. M. (1983). Cognitive processes in humor appreciation. In P. E. McGhee & J. H. Goldstein (Eds.), *Handbook of humor research* (pp. 39–58). New York: Springer-Verlag.

Summers, J. J., Machin, V. J., & Sargent, G. I. (1983). Psychosocial factors related to marathon running. *Journal of Sport Psychology, 5*, 314–331.

Summers, J. J., Sargent, G. I., Levey, A. J., & Murray, K. D. (1982). Middle-aged, nonelite marathon runners: A profile. *Perceptual and Motor Skills, 54*, 963–969.

Sumner, F. C. (1924, June). The nature of emotion. *Howard Review,* pp. 181–195.

Susser, E. S., Herman, D. B., & Aaron, B. (2002). Combating the terror of terrorism. *Scientific American, 287*, 70–77.

Swift, E. M. (1998). Into the light. *Sports Illustrated, 88*, 114–118.

Symons, D. (1979). *The evolution of human sexuality.* Oxford: Oxford University Press.

Taft, C. T., Stern, A. S., King, L. A., & King, D. W. (1999). Modeling physical health and functional health status: The role of combat exposure, post-traumatic stress disorder, and personal resource attributes. *Journal of Traumatic Stress, 12*, 3–23.

Tan, S-L., Spackman, M. P., & Peasle, C. L. (2006). The effects of repeated exposure on liking and judgments of musical unity of intact and patchwork compositions. *Music Perception, 23*, 407–421.

Tang, S.-H., & Hall, V. C. (1995). The overjustification effect: A meta-analysis. *Applied Cognitive Psychology, 9*, 365–404.

Tangney, J. P., Baumeister, R. F., & Boone, A. L. (2004). High self-control predicts good adjustment, less pathology, better grades, and interpersonal success. *Journal of Personality, 72*, 271–324.

Tangney, J. P., Stuewig, J., & Mashek, D. J. (2007). Moral emotions and moral behavior. *Annual Review of Psychology, 58*, 345–372.

Tattersall, I. (1998). *Becoming human.* New York: Harcourt Brace.

Tebel, J. (1963). *From rags to riches.* New York: Macmillan.

Tellegen, A., Lykken, D. T., Bouchard, Jr., T. J., Wilcox, K. J., Segal, N. L., & Rich, S. (1988). Personality similarity in twins reared apart and together. *Journal of Personality and Social Psychology, 54*, 1031–1039.

Tesser, A. (1978). Self-generated attitude change. In L. Berkowitz (Ed.), *Advances in experimental social psychology* (Vol. 11, pp. 289–338). New York: Academic Press.

Thayer, R. E. (1967). Measurement of activation through self-report. *Psychological Reports, 20*, 663–678.

Thayer, R. E. (1978). Toward a psychological theory of multidimensional activation (arousal). *Motivation and Emotion, 2,* 1–34.

Thayer, R. E. (1989). *The biopsychology of mood and arousal.* New York: Oxford University Press.

Thayer, R. E. (2001). *Calm energy.* New York: Oxford University Press.

Thompson, J. (1941). Development of facial expression of emotion in blind and seeing children. *Archives of Psychology,* no. 264, 2–47.

Thorndike, E. L. (1898). Animal intelligence: An experimental study of the associative process in animals. *Psychological Review Monographs Supplements, 2*(8).

Thorndike, E. L. (1911). *Animal intelligence.* New York: Macmillan.

Tice, D. M., & Baumeister, R. F. (1997). Longitudinal study of procrastination, performance, stress, and health: The costs and benefits of dawdling. *Psychological Science, 8,* 454–458.

Tolman, E. C. (1932). *Purposive behavior in animals and men.* New York: Appleton-Century.

Tolman, E. C. (1955). Principles of performance. *Psychological Review, 62,* 315–326.

Tolman, E. C. (1959). The principles of purposive behavior. In S. Koch (Ed.), *Psychology: A study of a science: Vol. II. General systematic formulations, learning, and special processes* (pp. 92–157). New York: McGraw-Hill.

Tolman, E. C., & Honzik, C. H. (1930). Introduction and removal of reward, and maze performance in rats. *University of California Publications in Psychology, 4,* 257–275.

Tomkins, S. S. (1982). Affect theory. In P. Ekman (Ed.), *Emotion in the human face* (pp. 353–395). Cambridge: Cambridge University Press.

Tomkins, S. S. (1984). Affect theory. In K. R. Scherer & P. Ekman (Eds.), *Approaches to emotion* (pp. 163–195). Hillsdale, NJ: Lawrence Erlbaum.

Tooby, J., & Cosmides, L. (2005). Conceptual foundations of evolutionary psychology. In D. Buss (Ed.), *The handbook of evolutionary psychology* (pp. 5–67). Hoboken, NJ: John Wiley & Sons.

Toray, T., & Cooley, E. (1998). Coping in women college students: The influence of experience. *Journal of College Student Development, 39,* 291–295.

Tracy, J. L., & Robins, R. W. (2004). Show your pride: Evidence for a discrete emotion expression. *Psychological Science, 15,* 194–197.

Tracy, J. L., & Robins, R. W. (2007). Emerging insights into the nature and function of pride. *Current Directions in Psychological Science, 16,* 147–150.

Trainor, L. J., Tsang, C. D., & Cheung, V. H. W. (2002). Preference for sensory consonance in 2- and 4-month-old infants. *Music Perception, 20,* 187–194.

Trobst, K. K., Herbst, J. H., Masters III, H. L., & Costa, Jr., P. T. (2002). Personality pathways to unsafe sex: Personality, condom use, and HIV risk behaviors. *Journal of Research in Personality, 36,* 117–133.

Troland, L. T. (1928/1967). *The fundamentals of human motivation.* New York: Hafner.

Tubbs, M. E. (1986). Goal-setting: A meta-analytic examination of the empirical evidence. *Journal of Applied Psychology, 71,* 474–483.

Tuerlinckx, F., De Boeck, P., & Lens, W. (2002). Measuring needs with the Thematic Apperception Test: A psychometric study. *Journal of Personality and Social Psychology, 82,* 448–461.

Turkheimer, E. (2000). Three laws of behavior genetics and what they mean. *Current Directions in Psychological Science, 9,* 160–164.

Turner, T. J., & Ortony, A. (1992). Basic emotions: Can conflicting criteria converge? *Psychological Review, 99,* 566–571.

Tustin, R. D. (1994). Preference for reinforcers under varying schedule arrangements: A behavioral economic analysis. *Journal of Applied Behavior Analysis, 27,* 597–606.

Uchino, B. N., Uno, D., & Holt-Lunstad, J. (1999). Social support, physiological processes, and health. *Current Directions in Psychological Science, 8,* 145–148.

Udry, J. R. (1980). Changes in the frequency of marital intercourse from panel data. *Archives of Sexual Behavior, 9,* 319–325.

Uleman, J. S. (1987). Consciousness and control: The case of spontaneous trait inferences. *Personality and Social Psychology Bulletin, 13,* 337–354.

Utsey, S. O., & Ponterotto, J. G. (1996). Development and validation of the Index of Race-Related Stress (IRRS). *Journal of Counseling Psychology, 43,* 490–501.

Valentine, C. W. (1930). The innate bases of fear. *Journal of Genetic Psychology, 37,* 394–419.

Van Boven, L. (2005). Experientialism, materialism, and the pursuit of happiness. *Review of General Psychology, 9,* 132–142.

Van De Graaff, K. M. (1988). *Human anatomy* (2nd ed.). Dubuque, IA: Wm. C. Brown.

Van Itallie, T. B., & Kissileff, H. R. (1983). The physiological control of energy intake: An econometric perspective. *American Journal of Clinical Nutrition, 38,* 978–988.

Van Itallie, T. B., & Kissileff, H. R. (1990). Human obesity: A problem in body energy economics. In E. M. Stricker (Ed.), *Handbook of behavioral neurobiology: Vol. 10. Neurobiology of food and fluid intake* (pp. 207–240). New York: Plenum Press.

van Thriel, C., & Ruch, W. (1994). The role of surprise in humor appreciation. Unpublished manuscript, University of Düsseldorf, Düsseldorf, Germany.

Veroff, J. (1992). A scoring manual for the power motive. In C. P. Smith (Ed.), *Motivation and personality: Handbook of thematic content analysis* (pp. 286–300). New York: Cambridge University Press.

Vitz, P. C. (1966). Affect as a function of stimulus variation. *Journal of Experimental Psychology, 71,* 74–79.

Vives, L. (1538/1974). Of the soul and life. In S. Diamond (Ed.), *The roots of psychology* (pp. 521–523). New York: Basic Books.

Vlahov, D., Galea, S., Resnick, H., Ahern, J., Boscarino, J. A., Bucuvalas, M., Gold, J., & Kilpatrick, D. (2002). Increased use of cigarettes, alcohol, and marijuana among Manhattan, New York, residents after the September 11th terrorist attacks. *American Journal of Epidemiology, 155,* 988–996.

Vollmer, F. (1993). Intentional action and unconscious reason. *Journal for the Theory of Social Behaviour, 23,* 315–326.

Vrana, S. R., & Rollock, D. (1998). Physiological response to a minimal social encounter: Effects of gender, ethnicity, and social context. *Psychophysiology, 35,* 462–469.

Wager, T. D., Phan, K. L., Liberzon, I., & Taylor, S. F. (2003). Valence, gender, and lateralization of functional brain anatomy in emotion: A meta-analysis of findings from neuroimaging. *NeuroImage, 19,* 513–531.

Wagner, M. K. (2001). Behavioral characteristics related to substance abuse and risk-taking, sensation-seeking, anxiety sensitivity, and self-reinforcement. *Addictive Behaviors, 26,* 115–120.

Walster, E., Aronson, V., Abraham, D., & Rottmann, L. (1966). Importance of physical attractiveness on dating behavior. *Journal of Personality and Social Psychology, 4,* 508–516.

Wang, J., Marchant, D., & Morris, T. (2004). Coping style and susceptibility to choking. *Journal of Sport Behavior, 27,* 75–92.

Warden, C. J. (1931). The Columbia Obstruction Method. In C. J. Warden (Ed.), *Animal motivation: Experimental studies on the albino rat* (pp. 3–16). New York: Columbia University Press.

Warner, L. H. (1928/1931). A study of hunger behavior in the white rat by means of the obstruction method. Reprinted in C. J. Warden (Ed.), *Animal motivation: Experimental studies on the albino rat* (pp. 56–80). New York: Columbia University Press. (Reprinted from L. H. Warner, 1928, *Journal of Comparative Psychology, 8,* 273–299.)

Washburn, M. F. (1928). Emotion and thought: A motor theory of their relations. In M. L. Reymert (Ed.), *Feelings and emotions: The Wittenberg symposium* (pp. 104–115). Worcester, MA: Clark University Press.

Watson, D. (2000). *Mood and temperament.* New York: Guilford Press.

Watson, D., & Clark, L. A. (1994a). Emotions, moods, traits, and temperaments: Conceptual distinctions and empirical findings. In P. Ekman & R. J. Davidson (Eds.), *The nature of emotion* (pp. 89–93). New York: Oxford University Press.

Watson, D., & Clark, L. A. (1994b). *The PANAS-X: Manual for the Positive and Negative Affect Schedule—Expanded Form.* Retrieved August 28, 2003, from www.psychology.uiowa.edu/faculty/clark/PANAS-X.pdf.

Watson, D., Clark, L. A., & Tellegen, A. (1988). Development and validation of brief measures of positive and negative affect: The PANAS scales. *Journal of Personality and Social Psychology, 54,* 1063–1070.

Watson, D., Hubbard, B., & Wiese, D. (2000). General traits of personality and affectivity as predictors of satisfaction in intimate relationships: Evidence from self- and partner ratings. *Journal of Personality, 68,* 413–449.

Watson, D., & Tellegen, A. (1985). Toward a consensual structure of mood. *Psychological Bulletin, 98,* 219–235.

Watson, D., Wiese, D., Vaidya, J., & Tellegen, A. (1999). The two general activation systems of affect: Structural findings, evolutionary considerations, and psychobiological evidence. *Journal of Personality and Social Psychology, 76,* 820–838.

Watson, J. (1972/1976). Smiling, cooing and "the game." In J. S. Bruner, A. Jolley, & K. Sylva (Eds.), *Play— its role in development and evolution* (pp. 268–276). New York: Basic Books.

Watson, J. B. (1913). Psychology as the behaviorist views it. *Psychological Review, 20,* 158–177.

Watt, J. D., & Blanchard, M. J. (1994). Boredom proneness and the need for cognition. *Journal of Research in Personality, 28,* 44–51.

Weeden, J., & Sabini, J. (2005). Physical attractiveness and health in western societies: A review. *Psychological Bulletin, 131,* 635–653.

Wehr, T. A., & Rosenthal, N. E. (1989). Seasonality and affective illness. *American Journal of Psychiatry, 146,* 829–839.

Weinberg, R. S., Gould, D., & Jackson, A. (1979). Expectation and performance: An empirical test of Bandura's self-efficacy theory. *Journal of Sport Psychology, 1,* 320–331.

Weiner, B. (1972). *Theories of motivation: From mechanism to cognition.* Chicago: Rand McNally.

Weiner, B. (1985). An attributional theory of achievement motivation and emotion. *Psychological Review, 92,* 548–573.

Weiner, B., & Kukla, A. (1970). An attributional analysis of achievement motivation. *Journal of Personality and Social Psychology, 15,* 1–20.

Weisfeld, G. E. (1993). The adaptive value of humor and laughter. *Ethology and Sociobiology, 14,* 141–169.

Weiss, A., Bates, T. C., & Luciano, M. (2008). Happiness is a personal(ity) thing. *Psychological Science, 19,* 205–210.

Weiss, R. (1989). The hedonic calculus in the *Protagoras* and the *Phaedo. Journal of the History of Philosophy, 27,* 511–529.

Weldon, E., & Yun, S. (2000). The effects of proximal and distal goals on goal level, strategy development, and group performance. *Journal of Applied Behavioral Science, 36,* 336–344.

Whalen, P. J. (1998). Fear, vigilance, and ambiguity: Initial neuroimaging studies of the human amygdala. *Current Directions in Psychological Science, 7,* 177–188.

White, G. L., Fishbein, S., & Rutsein, J. (1981). Passionate love and the misattribution of arousal. *Journal of Personality and Social Psychology, 41,* 56–62.

White, R. W. (1959). Motivation reconsidered: The concept of competence. *Psychological Review, 66,* 297–333.

Wiederman, M. W., & Allgeier, E. R. (1992). Gender differences in mate selection criteria: Sociobiological or socioeconomic explanation? *Ethology and Sociobiology, 13,* 115–124.

Wiederman, M. W., & Kendall, E. (1999). Evolution, sex, and jealousy: Investigation with a sample from Sweden. *Evolution and Human Behavior, 20,* 121–128.

Wiersma, U. J. (1992). The effects of extrinsic rewards in intrinsic motivation: A meta-analysis. *Journal of Occupational and Organizational Psychology, 65,* 101–114.

Wildmann, J., Kruger, A., Schmole, M., Niemann, J., & Matthaei, H. (1986). Increase of circulating beta-endorphin-like immunoreactivity correlates with the changes in feeling of pleasantness after running. *Life Sciences, 38,* 997–1003.

Williams, A. (2006, April). Up to her eyes in gore, and loving it. *New York Times.* Retrieved July 14, 2008. From http://www.nytimes.com.

Williams, D. (1956). The structure of emotions reflected in epileptic experiences. *Brain, 79,* 29–67.

Wilson, G. T., Nathan, P. E., O'Leary, K. D., & Clark, L. A. (1996). *Abnormal psychology: Integrating perspectives.* Boston: Allyn and Bacon.

Winter, D. G. (1988). The power motive in women— and men. *Journal of Personality and Social Psychology, 54,* 510–519.

Winter, D. G. (1992). Power motivation revisited. In C. P. Smith (Ed.), *Motivation and personality: Handbook of thematic content analysis* (pp. 301–310). New York: Cambridge University Press.

Winter, D. G., John, O. P., Stewart, A. J., Klohnen, E. C., & Duncan, L. E. (1998). Traits and motives: Toward an integration of two traditions in personality research. *Psychological Review, 105,* 230–250.

Winter, D. G., Stewart, A. J., & McClelland, D. C. (1977). Husband's motives and wife's career level. *Journal of Personality and Social Psychology, 35,* 159–166.

Wise, R. A. (2004). Dopamine, learning and motivation. *Nature Reviews: Neuroscience, 5,* 1–12.

Wise, R. A., & Rompre, P. P. (1989). Brain dopamine and reward. *Annual Review of Psychology, 40,* 191–225.

Wittstein, I. S., Thiemann, D. R., Lima, J. A. C., & Baughman, K. L. et al. (2005). Neurohumoral features of myocardial stunning due to sudden emotional stress. *The New England Journal of Medicine, 352*, 539–548.

Wolf, A. V. (1958). *Thirst: Physiology of the urge to drink and problems of water lack.* Springfield, IL: Charles C. Thomas.

Wolman, B. J. (1984). *The logic of science in psychoanalysis.* New York: Columbia University Press.

Wood, W., & Eagly, A. H. (2002). A cross-cultural analysis of the behavior of women and men: Implications for the origins of sex differences. *Psychological Bulletin, 128*, 699–727.

Woods, S. C., Schwartz, M. W., Baskin, D. G., & Seeley, R. J. (2000). Food intake and the regulation of body weight. *Annual Review of Psychology, 51*, 255–277.

Woodworth, R. S. (1918). *Dynamic psychology.* New York: Columbia University Press.

Woodworth, R. S. (1958). *Dynamics of behavior.* New York: Holt.

Wren, A. M., Seal, L. J., Cohen, M. A., Brynes, A. E., Frost, G. S., Murphy, K. G., Dhillo, W. E. S., Ghatei, M. A., & Bloom, S. R. (2001). Ghrelin enhances appetite and increases food intake in humans. *The Journal of Clinical Endocrinology & Metabolism, 86*, 5992–5995.

Wright, R. A., & Dill, J. C. (1993). Blood pressure responses and incentive appraisals as a function of perceived ability and objective task demand. *Psychophysiology, 30*, 152–160.

Yeomans, M. R., Spetch, H., & Rogers, P. J. (1998). Conditioned flavour preference negatively reinforced by caffeine in human volunteers. *Psychopharmacology, 137*, 401–409.

Yerkes, R. M., & Dodson, J. D. (1908). The relation of strength of stimulus to rapidity of habit formation. *Journal of Comparative Neurology and Psychology, 18*, 459–482.

Yik, M. S. M., & Russell, J. A. (1999). Interpretation of faces: A cross-cultural study of a prediction from Fridlund's theory. *Cognition and Emotion, 13*, 93–104.

Young, P. T. (1961). *Motivation and emotion.* New York: John Wiley.

Zajonc, R. B. (1968). Attitudinal effects of mere exposure. *Journal of Personality and Social Psychology Monograph Supplement, 9*, 1–27.

Zajonc, R. B. (1980). Feeling and thinking: Preferences need no inferences. *American Psychologist, 35*, 151–175.

Zajonc, R. B. (2001). Mere exposure: A gateway to the subliminal. *Current Directions in Psychological Science, 10*, 224–228.

Zajonc, R. B., & McIntosh, D. N. (1992). Emotions research: Some promising questions and some questionable promises. *Psychological Science, 3*, 70–74.

Zautra, A. J., & Reich, J. W. (1983). Life events and perceptions of life quality: Developments in a two-factor approach. *Journal of Community Psychology, 11*, 121–132.

Zebrowitz, L. A., & Rhodes, G. (2004). Sensitivity of "bad genes" and the anomalous face overgeneralization effect: Cue validity, cue utilization, and accuracy in judging intelligence and health. *Journal of Nonverbal Behavior, 28*, 167–185.

Zeidner, M., & Matthews, G. (2005). Evaluation anxiety: Current theory and research. In A. J. Elliot & C. S. Dweck (Eds.), *Handbook of competence and motivation* (pp. 141–163). New York: The Guilford Press.

Zellner, D. A., Kern, B. B., & Parker, S. (2002). Protection for the good: Subcategorization reduces hedonic contrast. *Appetite, 38*, 175–180.

Zellner, D. A., Rohm, E. A., Bassetti, T. L., & Parker, S. (2003). Compared to what? Effects of categorization on hedonic contrast. *Psychonomic Bulletin & Review, 10*, 468–473.

Zellner, D. A., Rozin, P., Aron, M., & Kulish, C. (1983). Conditioned enhancement of human's liking for flavor by pairing with sweetness. *Learning and Motivation, 14*, 338–350.

Zentner, M. R., & Kagan, J. (1998). Infants' perception of consonance and dissonance in music. *Infant Behavior and Development, 21*, 483–492.

Zillmann, D. (1978). Attribution and misattribution of excitatory reactions. In J. H. Harvey, W. Ickes, & R. F. Kidd (Eds.), *New directions in attribution research* (pp. 335–368). Hillsdale, NJ: Lawrence Erlbaum.

Zillmann, D. (1984). *Connections between sex and aggression.* Hillsdale, NJ: Lawrence Erlbaum.

Zillmann, D. (1991). The logic of suspense and mystery. In J. Bryant & D. Zillmann (Eds.), *Responding to the screen: Reception and reaction processes* (pp. 281–303). Hillsdale, NJ: Lawrence Erlbaum Associates, Publishers.

Zubek, J. P. (1973). Behavioral and physiological effects of prolonged sensory and perceptual deprivation: A review. In J. E. Rasmussen (Ed.), *Man in isolation and confinement* (pp. 9–83). Chicago: Aldine.

Zuckerman, M. (1964). Perceptual isolation as a stress situation. A review. *Archives of General Psychiatry, 11,* 255–276.

Zuckerman, M. (1969). Theoretical formulations: I. In J. P. Zubek (Ed.), *Sensory deprivation: Fifteen years of research* (pp. 407–432). New York: Appleton-Century-Crofts.

Zuckerman, M. (1978). The search for high sensation. *Psychology Today, 11,* 38–99.

Zuckerman, M. (1979). *Sensation seeking: Beyond the optimal level of arousal.* Hillsdale, NJ: Lawrence Erlbaum.

Zuckerman, M. (1985). Biological foundations of the sensation-seeking temperament. In J. Strelau, F. H. Farley, & A. Gale (Eds.), *The biological bases of personality and behavior: Vol. 1. Theories, measurement techniques, and development* (pp. 97–113). Washington, DC: Hemisphere.

Zuckerman, M. (1990). The psychophysiology of sensation seeking. *Journal of Personality, 58,* 313–345.

Zuckerman, M. (1991). *Psychobiology of personality.* Cambridge: Cambridge University Press.

Zuckerman, M. (1994). *Behavioral expressions and biosocial bases of sensation seeking.* Cambridge: Cambridge University Press.

Zuckerman, M. (2002). Genetics of sensation seeking. In J. Benjamin, R. P. Ebstein, & R. H. Belmaker (Eds.), *Molecular genetics and the human personality* (pp. 193–210). Washington, DC: American Psychiatric Publishing.

Zuckerman, M., Ball, S., & Black, J. (1990). Influence of sensation seeking, gender, risk appraisal, and situational motivation on smoking. *Addictive Behaviors, 15,* 209–220.

Zuckerman, M., Klorman, R., Larrance, D. T., & Spiegel, N. H. (1981). Facial, autonomic, and subjective components of emotion: The facial feedback hypothesis versus the externalizer-internalizer distinction. *Journal of Personality and Social Psychology, 41,* 929–944.

Zuckerman, M., Murtaugh, T. T., & Siegel, J. (1974). Sensation seeking and cortical augmenting-reducing. *Psychophysiology, 11,* 535–542.

Zuckerman, M., Simons, R. F., & Como, P. G. (1988). Sensation seeking and stimulus intensity as modulators of cortical, cardiovascular, and electrodermal response: A cross-modality study. *Personality and Individual Differences, 9,* 361–372.

INDEX

A

Abbreviated Math Anxiety Scale, 139
achievement behaviors, goal, 283
   and goal failure, 284, 285
   and goal success, 284, 285
Achievement Goal Questionnaire, 195, 196
achievement motivation theory, 191–196
   framework, 195, 196
achievement motive, 191
Achievement Motives Scale, 193–195
achievement valence, 283, 284
action readiness, 42, 331, 355
acute stress disorder, 159
adaptation energy, 6, 167
addiction
   and cognition, 94, 95
   and drugs, 82
   and exercise, 96, 98
   and gambling, 99, 100
   negative, 96
   and personality disposition, 83
   positive, 96
affect, 319–322
   and goals, 265
affect programs, 329
affective model of negative reinforcement, 94
affective valence, 141, 142, 144
agentic theory, 11
agreeableness, 212, 225, 226
   behavioral genetics of, 217
alcohol, 78, 80, 91
Alcohol Urge Questionnaire, 89
alliesthesia, 105
amphetamines, 79
amygdala, 66
   and emotion, 344, 345
   and emotion-stimulus appraisal, 338
anorexia nervosa, 125, 126
antagonist, 88
anxiety, 139, 140
   and performance, 139, 140
   and processing efficiency, 139, 140
   state, 139
   trait, 139
appraisal, 171–173
   dimensions of, 343, 344
   of emotion stimuli, 338, 340–342
   and primary appraisal, 173
   and secondary appraisal, 173
appraisal tendency hypothesis, 357, 358
appraisal without awareness, 341, 342
Aristotle's theory, 22

arousal
   See also emotion, physiology of
   brain, 128, 129
   energetic, 129, 130
   physiological, 128
   psychological, 129
   source of, 130, 131
   and sympathetic nervous system, 128
   tense, 129, 130
arousal effects
   and affect, 142
   and inverted-U relationship, 132, 133
   and memory, 138
   and performance, 131–134
aspiration level, 265
attitude polarization, 199
attractiveness, 56, 57
automatic process, 32
automaticity, 32
auto-motive hypothesis, 205, 206

B

balance hypothesis, 203
Barratt Impulsiveness Scale, 83
beauty, 58
behavior
   choice, 13
   consummatory, 5
   instrumental, 13
   persistence, 13, 194, 195, 293, 294
behavioral ecology hypothesis, 351, 352
behavioral economizing, 307
behavioral genetics, 216–219
behaviorism, 25
Bentham, J., 23, 24, 186
binge eating, 123
biological variables, 7, 8, 18
biosocial theory, 64
body weight regulation. *See* energy regulation
boundary model, 121, 122
brain arousal, 128, 129
brain map, 44, 329
brain stimulation in rats, 85, 86
Brief Self-Control Scale, 26, 83
broaden-and-build theory, 359
buffering hypothesis, 175

C

caffeine, 78, 130
calorie, 109, 290
cannabis, 79, 80

operant thoughts, 281
operational definition, 214
opiates, 79
opioids, 99
opponent process theory, 90
opportunity costs, 289, 291
optimal level of stimulation theory, 142, 143
orgasm, 60

P
palatability, 117
PANAS-X, 333
partial reinforcement effect, 293
Perceived Stress Questionnaire, 155, 156
perception-behavior link, 283
performance goals, 195, 196
personal history, 10, 50, 51
personality, 211
  biological reality of, 213, 214
  operational definitions of, 214
personality disposition, 83
personality traits, 211
  behavioral genetics of, 216–219
  and causes of behavior, 211, 212, 220
  and happiness, 227, 228
philosophers
  ancient, 22, 23, 41, 42
  later, 23, 24, 41, 43
physical activity, 109
physical energy costs, 289, 290
physical energy resources, 6, 295
physiological arousal, 128
physiological need, 105, 185
  and goals, 266
pleasure centers, 85
pleasure principle, 25
population thinking, 28
portion size, 117, 118
positive addiction, 96
Positive and Negative Affect Schedule, 333
positive emotions, 358–363
positive psychology, 26
post-traumatic stress disorder (PTSD), 159, 162–165, 175, 179
power motive, 197
preconscious, 29, 30
preference reversal, 249–251
prejudice, 227
preparatory response hypothesis, 158
preparedness, 66–68
primary needs, 33
priming
  achievement behavior, 206
  and action, 206, 207
  and drugs, 91–93
  and gambling, 101
  and motives, 206, 207
principle of least effort, 304
  and body mass index, 306, 307

principle of utility, 24
problem focused coping, 174
processing efficiency theory, 139, 140
procrastination, 176, 177, 251, 252
projective test, 192
prospect theory, 275, 276
proximal goal, 281
psychoactive drugs, 78
psychogenic needs, 33
psychological arousal, 129
psychological distance, 37, 38
psychological energy costs, 289, 290
psychological energy resources, 6, 297
psychological force, 36–38
psychological mechanism, 52, 53
psychological needs, 33, 34, 184, 186
  and goals, 266
  and hierarchy, 187, 188
  measuring, 188–193
psychological variables, 7, 8, 19
psychoneuroimmunology, 169
psychophysiological disorders, 168
psychophysiology, 214–216
psychosomatic disorders, 168
punisher, 25, 240
push vs pull, motivation 4, 184

Q
qualia, 319

R
racism, 164, 165
readout hypothesis, 350–352
reality principle, 25
redintegration, 187
reductionism, 9
refeeding syndrome, 125
reflex reserve, 293
reflexology, 205
reinforcer, 25, 240
  and drugs, 85
  and exercise, 96, 97
  negative, 85, 94
  positive, 85, 93
  rate, 245, 246
repression, 30
research, 15–18
  correlational, 15, 16
  ethics in, 16, 17
  experimental, 15, 16
  feasibility of, 16–18
  variables, 15, 16
resources, 293–297
respondent thoughts, 281
response coherence postulate, 314, 315
response costs, 289
response resources, 293
resting metabolism, 109